AF660574

The Scourge of Unemployment in India and Psychological Health

By the same author

1. Santal Youths : An Unseen Talent. Wisdom Publication, New Delhi, 1988.
2. Social Psychology (2nd Edition). Bihar Hindi Granth Academy, Patna, Bihar, 1991.
3. Tribal Value Pattern : A Case Study of Santals. In B. Saraswati (Ed.), Tribal Thought and Culture. Concept Publishing Company, New Delhi, 1991.
4. Psycho-educative Dynamics of the Acquisition of Indian Classical Vocal Music. Bhargava Publication, Agra, 2005.

About the Author

Lal Bahadur Singh (*b.* 1949) is a professor in the Department of Psychology, T.M. Bhagalpur University, Bihar (India). He has been associated with a number of academic bodies, national and international, and is the second Asian to be recently nominated a member on an eight-member sub-committee of International Association of Applied Psychology, 'Unemployment'. He has completed a research project, "Psychological Well-being of Educated Unemployed Youth in India", sponsored by the University Grants Commission, New Delhi. Currently, he has been actively engaged in the analysis of psychological costs borne by pseudo-employed people.

He has to his credit over 70 research articles in various national and international journals of repute. Besides, he has authored three books, and is also one of the contributors to two edited books.

The Scourge of Unemployment in India and Psychological Health

Lal Bahadur Singh
Department of Psychology,
T.M. Bhagalpur University,
Bhagalpur - 812 007
Bihar (India)

CONCEPT PUBLISHING COMPANY, NEW DELHI-110059

Cataloging in Publication Data—DK
Courtesy: D.K. Agencies (P) Ltd. <docinfo@dkagencies.com>

Singh, Lal Bahadur, 1949-
The scourge of unemployment in India and psychological health / Lal Bahadur Singh.
p. ; cm.
Study conducted in undivided Bihar, India.
Includes bibliographical references (p.)
Includes index.
ISBN 8180692922

1. Unemployment—India—Bihar. 2. Unemployment—India—Jharkhand. 3. Unemployed youth—India—Bihar—Psychology. 4. Unemployed youth—India—Jharkhand—Psychology. I. Title.

DDC 331.137 954 123 22

All rights reserved. No part of this work may be reproduced, stored in a retrieval system or transmitted in any form or by any means, electronic, mechanical, photocopying, microfilming, recording or otherwise, without the prior written permission of the copyright owner and the publisher.

ISBN : 81-8069-292-2

First Published 2006

© Lal Bahadur Singh (*b.* 1949)

Published and Printed by
Ashok Kumar Mittal
Concept Publishing Company
A/15-16, Commercial Block, Mohan Garden,
New Delhi-110059 (India)

Phones : 25351460, 25351794
Fax : 091-11-25357103
Email : publishing@conceptpub.com

Foreword

Labour market problems are obviously economic and social problems but they also have without any doubt a relevant impact on the psychology of individuals. Unemployment or the exclusion from the labour market—temporarily or persistently—as psychological issues have been investigated in psychological research on the individual effects of job loss and continuing unemployment during the last 70 years. One of the most influential studies at the beginning of psychological study on unemployment was the empirical study on the coping of a small community named Marienthal in Austria close to Vienna during the Great Depression of the Thirties (Jahoda, Lazarsfeld and Zeisel, 1932/1975). We can conclude from many studies that have been conducted since then that unemployment bears a great risk of a significant deterioration of mental and physical health on the individuals affected, limits the personality development especially of young people to a great extent and is associated with a considerable risk of social exclusion besides the manifest effects of reducing the standard of living, leading into poverty and marginalization. This holds true even for those countries in which the financial situation of unemployed persons is kept from side of the society at a relatively high level compared to the former unemployment.

Many researchers since the start of the scientific investigation in the Thirties have worked on this issue—but unemployment has never become a continuous effort in psychological research. As Catalano and Dooley (2003) have found in their time-series analysis on the relationship between the unemployment rate and the publication of papers related to the issue of unemployment there was a close association between an increase of unemployment and the immediate publication of unemployment-related articles by psychologists as well as a time-lagged relationship with a lag period of 2 years. As the authors explain this can be interpreted that there are many researchers in psychology who experience something like a "sympathetic pain" with the fate of people who have been forced to leave the labour force in societies that can be defined as work-centred who respond immediately to the development or deterioration of a societal problem.

Another reaction then leads to the publication of study results that needed more time before publication what might explain the time lag period of 2 years. This refers more to empirical studies that have been planned, executed and analysed subsequent to the rise of the unemployment rate and then published in psychological journals.

What is common in both the explanations is that unemployment has always been a topic that attracted attention only when it was a crucial issue in society and therefore continuous efforts to concentrate on it, on an integrated theoretical basis were often hindered.

The second remark, I would like to make is that most of the psychological unemployment research has been done in highly developed industrialized countries where the social construction of unemployment does not allow many other ways of social integration outside employment.

Psychological research in developing countries is trying to gain more and more ground in order to make a relevant contribution to resolving relevant problems of their societies with the help of scientific investigations.

The general assumptions that have been delineated from Western unemployment research in Psychology have been taken for granted for the developing countries as well, partly because of the lack of empirical evidence from these countries and partly because of a self-centred perspective on these problems in Europe and US.

These are the two main reasons why the efforts of Lal Bahadur Singh in the last two decades to concentrate on the investigation of the psycho-social effects of unemployment in India has continuously attracted my strong interest over the years.

On the one hand he is a unique example of a psychologist who did not follow the cyclical fashions of focusing on such a topic but continuously concentrated on this area of research. On the other hand he is one of the rare researchers in a rapidly developing country like India who has broadened the debate among unemployment researchers in Europe and North America with his empirical studies.

These are some reasons why the scientific work of Lal Bahadur Singh is of extreme importance for the further development of psychological research on the effects of job loss, long-term unemployment, and the difficulties to enter the labour market in India.

Singh has continuously published in this field in international journals showing that he is quite familiar with the most advanced discussion on a scientific level and has adapted instruments and theoretical approaches from many other countries still leading in this area of research. He is known more than any other researcher in Psychology from a developing country to have made relevant contributions in a continuous way to the explanation of the individual effects of job loss.

His most recent study "The Scourge of Unemployment in India and Psychological Health" deserves special attention because it can be considered as an integration of his long-term interest in this topic unlike many other researchers who joined the field and left it when it did no longer seem to be opportunistic to focus on it.

The publication of this book can therefore be welcomed as a relevant contribution to the international debate bringing in the perspective of a developing country rapidly growing and having already become in some areas a relevant competitor for the highly-developed countries. His book may contribute, with a specific Indian perspective, to the debate on whether the conception of unemployment prevalent in Western research may be a social construction of unemployment widely neglecting experiences from the developing countries.

He is also adding more complex measures for the outcome variables like alienation, identity-crisis and life satisfaction to the sometimes rather narrow studies focusing on mental health aspects alone in many other studies.

What he specifically brings into unemployment research in Psychology is the complex understanding of the specific relationship between the individual and the social environment (feeling of indebtedness to the closer and wider social environment) and a different understanding of social duties in the Indian culture different from Western countries.

He has investigated these topics not only in unemployed people but also in employed ones thus trying to bridge the gap between coping with unemployment and the adverse effects that high unemployment may exert on those in employment. From the perspective of the Scientific committee "Unemployment and Health" of the International Commission on Occupational Health (ICOH) I can only appreciate that both aspects have been of interest to the author as he avoids the sometimes rigid distinction between the effects of unemployment and the impact of unemployment on the employed ones. Thus unemployment can be brought back to the area where it is mostly generated, the social organization of work.

The book of Lal Bahadur Singh will surely make a relevant contribution to the widening of the debate on the psycho-social effects of unemployment in a developing country like India. We can wish this publication only the wide attention that it really deserves.

Prof. Dr. Thomas Kieselbach
Chairman of the Scientific Committee Unemployment and Health of the International Commission on Occupational Health (ICOH)

Head of Institute for Psychology of Work, Unemployment and Health (IPG) University of Bremen, Germany

Preface

Unemployment has, of late, surfaced as a serious epidemiological malaise afflicting every country of the world in an alarming degree. As a recent estimate (ILO, 1996) has it, not only underdeveloped and developing countries, but even many developed ones are experiencing its stings and pangs. Nearly 1 billion people have been found to be jobless worldwide. The shocking purport of the finding is that around one third of the cumulative labour force of the world has no job. The distressing part of it is that the Third World, already poverty-ridden and hapless, shares the majority of these "pestilence-stricken multitudes". It stands self-explained that unemployment dares the entire world populace with its awesome tooth and claw. Anticipation appears fiercely assuming the garb of reality making it imminent that we are entering a 'post-job era', approaching 'the end of work' (Rifkin, 1995), or going to face 'a jobless future' (Aronowitz & DiFazio, 1994).

India is the worst victim of the problem of unemployment. It has acquired the top spot among the social problems afflicting contemporary India, eating into the vitals of her social life. In recent years, it has grown to menacing proportions, accounting for nearly 3.66 per cent of the total unemployment in the world. The government of India, of late, has proposed a number of ambitious schemes for the eradication of joblessness in the country in record time. But only the future will unfold the fate of these schemes. Currently, nothing positive can be envisaged in the field of employment. The spectre of joblessness is looming large. The future of India is virtually eclipsed by the rise of an armless and jobless militia of unemployed people. Even people possessing high academic achievements and qualifications can be seen sauntering along the road in fruitless search of jobs. This has affected them adversely and their well-being is at stake. In spite of a burgeoning interest in the study of psychophysical consequences of unemployment by our social scientists in recent days, there is still a considerable lack of systematic researches in this field. Hence, the present investigation. This study primarily aims at investigating the psychological well-being of different groups of educated unemployed young men as compared to different groups of their educated employed counterparts — mainly divided on the basis of criteria like kinds and streams of education, as well as the duration of the experiences of their particular status of employment — measured in terms of its various significant indicators like anxiety, stress, feeling of insecurity, alienation, indentity-crisis and life satisfaction in their various manifestations. In addition, the study also intends to find out the degree of their relative dependence on different strategies to cope with their situations. The investigation, thus, chiefly seeks to highlight two basic issues — the psychological well-being of, and the coping styles adopted by, different groups of the educated unemployed and employed people on an elaborate scale.

This investigation extends into ten chapters. The first chapter, Introduction and Overview, dwells upon the need of the investigation as well as extent of unemployment in India. It also describes mental health and its importance in relation to the status of employment (unemployment/employment) in the light of a good amount of relevant empirical findings carried out in this regard. Further, it records a brief account of different significant indicators of psychological well-being widely investigated to measure on them the impact of unemployment *versus* employment. The last section of this chapter attempts to present a systematic description of different select variables such as anxiety, stress, feeling of insecurity, alienation, identity-crisis and life satisfaction used as the measures of psychological health of different groups of educated unemployed *versus* employed young men in this investigation, as also of various strategies devised by them to deal with their life circumstances, by citing a large body of existing research findings obtained in India and abroad on the issue in question. The objectives, hypotheses, and the rationale behind them by employing different theoretical perspectives and empirical evidences along with observational facts emanating from culture-specific realities, typical of India, constitute the contents of the second chapter. The third chapter focuses on the strategy adopted for conducting the investigation. This chapter covers the description of the operational definition of the terms unemployment and employment, source of the sampling, control of extraneous variables, selection and distribution of sampling, the scales and measures devised for the assessment of different variables under investigation, and the procedure adopted for the collection of data.

The fourth chapter outlines the description of different techniques used for statistical analysis of the results. Chapters 5 to 8 relate to the findings obtained in this investigation and their interpretations. These chapters present a precise account of the findings of statistical comparisons among different groups of educated unemployed and employed young men, divided on the basis of forms and streams of their education, as well as the duration of the experiences of their individual status of employment, in terms of their levels on various measures of their psychological well-being, and their degrees of dependence on various strategies to deal with their situations. In addition, these chapters also attempt to acquaint with different plausible reasons being utilized to elucidate the findings furnished therein. Summary and suggestions form the content of chapter 9 which presents the quintessence of the overall effort made by the investigator. It also points out the limitations of the present investigation, and attempts to make certain useful suggestions and recommendations for further researches on the status of employment and psychological well-being as well as coping styles. In the last a systematic record of bibliography of investigations cited in connection with the main text of the present investigation.

Though no tall claims are made, the present project, to a considerable extent, provides a precise account of psychological well-being and coping styles of different groups of educated unemployed *versus* employed young men in India. All sincere efforts have been made chapterwise to present a coherent account of clearly defined areas. Addition of analytical sophistication and logical sequence to the presentation of facts has been the prime concern of the whole venture. The investigation attempts, as a whole, to offer a practical and comprehensive guide to all those who are interested in having an elaborate idea about psychological well-being and coping styles of educated unemployed and employed people in a developing country like India which has a huge unutilized manpower looking for any kind of job to lead a minimum decent life.

I have immense pleasure in introducing the work. But, I would be claiming too much if I gave all the credit to myself. The venture could not have turned into reality if I had not received help and cooperation from different sources. First, I wish to express a deep sense of gratitude to the University Grants Commission, New Delhi for providing funds that enabled me to complete this research project. I am particularly grateful to Prof. P.B. Warr, MRC/ESRC Social and

Applied Psychology Unit, Department of Psychology, University of Sheffield, Dr. N.T. Feather and Dr. G.E. O'Brien, Discipline of Psychology, The Flinders University of South Australia, Dr. A.H. Winefield, Department of Psychology, The University of Adelaide, South Australia and others for supplying me a large volume of relevant materials that helped me develop an insight into the issue in question, offering a definite framework for its conceptualization. I am greatly beholden to Dr. T. Kieselbach, Institute for Psychology of Work, Unemployment and Health (IPG), University of Bremen, Germany, in particular, who has not only kept me aware of the recent trends and developments in the field but also has been a constant source of valuable suggestions and encouragement. He is a person for whom no words can carry the depth of my gratitude. I am also deeply indebted to the late Prof. Durganand Sinha, Department of Psychology, University of Allahabad, Prof. (Retired) B.S. Gupta, Department of Psychology, Banaras Hindu University, Varanasi, and Prof. Abhay Prakash, Department of English, T.M. Bhagalpur University, who have been a constant source of valuable ideas and suggestions. My particular thanks are due to my beloved wife Meena who religiously kept up my spirit with her amiable behaviour and caressing love. In fact, she was, as she has always been, my mainstay, the living inspiration throughout this research work. My sincerest thanks are due to all of them.

September, 2005 **Lal Bahadur Singh**
Bhagalpur

Contents

List of Tables

1

Introduction and Overview

Statement of the Problem

The youth, particularly the educated ones, are the future of the nation. In other words, the fulfilment of all hopes and aspirations of the nation depends largely upon its potential youth force— the power force — which can initiate changes and usher in modernization by dint of their inherent potentialities and fervent zeal. The success of planning, to a considerable extent, lies on their shoulders as they may play an effective and dynamic role in the all round development of a developing country like India. So much so that the success and failure of all types of planning hinge upon a proper utilization of its youth force.

The need to integrate the educated youth in the mainstream of the national development programmes has been strongly stressed by the government. As a result, different plans and policies have been framed accordingly. However, the crucial question at this point is whether this type of "paper-planning" has any meaning in the face of a large-scale unemployment of the educated youth. Indeed, despite the seemingly commendable efforts made at the governmental and the non-governmental levels to remove the problems of joblessness root and branch, nothing fruitful has been achieved so far. The number of job-seekers continues to grow at a steady pace. The problem is so serious and acute that even people with high qualifications and degrees can be seen scrounging for welfare handouts. This is apparent from the fact that more than half of the job-seekers in India are matriculates and above (Ahmad, 1993; *Chronicle Yearbook*, 1999; Ray, 1995). Evidently, the problem of unemployment, largely because of the booming population explosion and lack of proper manpower planning and utilization, is rooted in the very soil of the country and continues to escalate alarmingly every year.

Such a sorry state of our youth, particularly the educated ones, has affected them adversely. Their psychophysical well-being is at stake. They are confused and often tend to lapse into a state of dejection and disappointment. Life to them appears to be dull, dreary and worthless. At the individual level, unemployment is creating different psychological dysfunctions like a feeling of loss, anxiety, stress, insecurity, reduced self-esteem, depression, alienation, hopelessness, crisis of identity, inability to adjust with the existing life-situation, etc. People encountering prolonged unemployment tend to lose hope, become resigned and apathetic, and adopt a somewhat restricted way of life. Such 'broken' individuals often try to keep their heads above frustration by becoming passive takers of whatever life offers them. Unemployment has placed a burden on a sizeable segment of our population, bringing with it both financial hardship and self-devaluation. In fact, unemployment can be as debilitating psychophysically as it is financially (Chakrapani, 1995; Feather, 1992; Fryer, 1995a; Iversen and Sabroe, 1988; Jahoda, 1982, 1988, 1995; Jin, Chandrakant and Svoboda, 1995; Kieselbach and Svensson, 1988; Rani, 1993; Singh, 1990, 1992, 1994, 2001; Singh, Kumari and Singh, 1992; Singh, Singh and Rani, 1996 a, b; Singh, Singh and Singh,1995; Warr,1985; Winefield, 1995b; Winefield and Tiggemann,1885). Needless to say, unemployment is a considerable strain on the well-being of our youth. But what is most unfortunate is that such a vital issue has not yet attracted adequate attention of our social scientists. Researches into the socio-psychological consequences of unemployment are almost non-existent, while in the west the history of research interest in the impact of unemployment goes back to the 1930s and a dramatic increase in this regard can be noted during the 1970s and the 1980s (Kieselbach, Beelmann and Stitzel, 2000; Windschuttle, 1979). Hence, the present investigation.

The Extent of Unemployment in India

Unemployment is a problem that has assumed appalling proportions, especially in the Third World countries such as India (ILO,1996). Like a monster it has sucked the vitality out of the human mind, and has reduced human existence itself to a mute, pathetic helplessness. It is already the biggest social and economic evil. There is an alarming increase in the rate of job-seekers. People all over the world have started to talk of galloping unemployment and the great army of the unemployed. The gravity of the problem can well be estimated on the basis of analysis of the recent statistics of the number of job-seekers in different states of India. Table 1.1 reports a comparative account of the ratio of unemployment in 1987 and 1990 in different states of India. Except Haryana, Manipur, Jammu and Kashmir, the Andamans and the Lakshadweep, all the states of India witnessed a rapid increase in the number of job-seekers. Further, only within three and a half

Table 1.1 : State-wise Distribution of Unemployment in India in 1987 and 1990

States	*Number of Registered Unemployed Persons (in thousand) by 31 Dec., 1987*	*Number of Registered Unemployed Persons (in thousand) by 31 May, 1990*	*Increment in percentage*
1. West Bengal	4564.7	4635.1	01.54
2. Undivided Bihar	2708.1	3162.5	16.78
3. Kerala	2990.1	3132.3	04.76
4. Undivided U.P.	2963.4	3108.1	04.88
5. Tamil Nadu	2486.2	3053.4	22.81
6. Maharashtra	2615.4	2998.3	14.64
7. Andhra	2722.0	2831.6	04.02
8. Undivided M.P.	1740.3	2033.1	16.82
9. Karnataka	1012.6	1255.1	23.94
10. Assam	0840.6	0994.5	18.31
11. Gujarat	0781.8	0941.6	20.44
12. Rajasthan	0831.7	0937.4	12.71
13. Orissa	0791.9	0868.2	09.63
14. Delhi	0706.3	0809.1	14.55
15. Punjab	0619.0	0631.1	01.95
16. Haryana	0579.8	0574.6	-00.90
17. Himachal Pradesh	0349.7	0448.8	28.34
18. Manipur	0286.8	0202.4	-29.43
19. Chandigarh	0137.2	0154.9	12.90
20. Tripura	0117.7	0151.7	28.89
21. Pondicherry	–	0113.6	–
22. Jammu & Kashmir	0127.4	0109 1	-14.36
23. Goa	0079.2	0085.1	07.45
24. Mizoram	0027.4	0042.8	56.20
25. Nagaland	0023.2	0027.4	18.10
26. Meghalaya	0019.1	0023.6	23.56
27. Andamans	1600.0	0015.6	-99.03
28. Arunachal	–	0005.1	–
29. Lakshadweep	0007.2	0005.0	-30.56
30. DNH	–	0002.2	–
Total Unemployment	31728.8	33353.3	5.12

Sources: *The Hindustan*, Patna,9th Dec.,1988, and *The Statesman,* 19th Oct., 1990.

years, the total number of job-seekers increased at the rate of about 05.12 per cent. Despite numerous steps, particularly initiated at the official level, to control the malady of unemployment, there is no respite as yet. The number of job-seekers continues to grow at a steady pace. Amazingly, it has risen to 36565.80 thousand by the end of June 1995 and has further added about 09.63 per cent new faces in the labour market just within five and a half years, indicating thereby a fast growth rate of 01.75 per cent in job-seekers (*The Times of India*, Patna, Jan.,15th, 1996). The trend is really frightening, and deserves special consideration in order to save the nation from the point of total social and economic collapse. In order to further highlight the gravity of the problem of joblessness in India, a comparative account of the ratio of educated and uneducated unemployed from 1961 onwards is furnished in Table 1.2.

From the inspection of Table 1.2 it appears that the number of job-seekers from 1961 to 1995 has multiplied about 19.95 times. There was a rapid growth in the number of educated job-seekers. As per the estimate, they constituted about 75.28 per cent of the total unemployed in India. Amazingly, however, there clearly appeared an alarming increase in the number of educated job-seekers from 1991 onwards. Thus, the educated were the worst victims of unemployment. Table 1.3 provides a detailed account of educated job-seekers of different educational grades in India.

A cursory glance at the figures of educated unemployed displayed in Table 1.3 reflects that while the number of the educated unemployed in 1961 was only 590 thousand, it rose to about 46.65 times in the year 1995. Further, recently the trend has been even more noticeable. The postgraduate degree-holders, hardly imperilled by the problem of unemployment by the end of 1971, also started to be affected gradually by the remorseless realities of life forcing them to depend upon others for their livelihood. At present, of course, the life of the highly qualified and the professional is also not free from the bane of unemployment. In order to further focus the seriousness of the problem of unemployment among the educated masses, a subject-wise distribution of unemployment is reported in Table 1.4.

A look at Table 1.4 indicates that unemployment has also effected a setback for a good number of people having degrees in different branches of knowledge. Both professionally and non-professionally educated people can be seen bewildered on account of their failure to find a job of any sort, despite possessing the required competence.

Table 1.2 : The Number of Educated and Uneducated Unemployed in India from 1961-1995 *(in thousand)*

Educational Status	*Year*									
	1961	*1971*	*1980*	*1986*	*1990*	*1991*	*1992*	*1993*	*1994*	*1995*
Educated	590	2296	8164	15088	18344.315	22434.000	27056.000	27177.000	27375.000	27525.000
Uneducated	1243	2804	8036	12724	15008.985	13865.700	9702.400	9098.500	9316.500	9040.800
Total	1833	5100	16200	27812	33353.300	36299.700	36758.400	36275.500	36691.500	36565.800

Sources :(1) P.K.Roy (1983). *Problem of Unemployment*, Delhi : Capital Publishing House;
(2) *India Economic Information Yearbook*, 1987-88, p.85;
(3) *Commerce*, 27th June, 1987;
(4) *The Statesman*, 19th Oct.,1990;
(5) *The Navbharat Times*, Patna, 27th July, 1992;
(6) *Chronicle Yearbook*, 1999, p.464; and
(7) *Rashtriya Sahara*, 1st Feb.,1997.

Table 1.3 : The Number of Educated Job-seekers Registered in Different Employment Exchanges of India (*in thousand*)

Level of Education	*Year*									
	1961	*1971*	*1980*	*1986*	*1990*	*1991*	*1992*	*1993*	*1994*	*1995*
Matric	463 (78.47%)	1297 (56.49%)	4568 (55.95%)	8683 (57.55%)	10713.080 (58.40%)	13104 (58.41%)	– –	– –	– –	15689 (57.00%)
Higher Secondary or Inter	71 (12.03%)	605 (26.35%)	2071 (25.37%)	3806 (25.23%)	4476.013 (24.40%)	5517 (24.59%)	– –	– –	– –	6881 (25.00%)
Bachelor	56 (09.49%)	394 (17.16%)	1390 (17.02%)	2306 (15.28%)	2762.654 (15.06%)	3322 (14.81%)	– –	– –	– –	4333 (15.74%)
M.A.	– –	– –	135 (01.65%)	293 (01.94%)	382.568 (02.14%)	491 (02.19%)	– –	– –	– –	622 (02.26%)
Total	590 (32.19%)	2296 (45.02%)	8164 (50.40%)	15088 (54.25%)	18344.315 (55.00%)	22434.300 (61.80%)	27056.0 (73.60%)	27177.0 (74.92%)	273375.0 (74.61%)	27525.0 (75.28%)

Sources : (1) *Commerce*, 27th June, 1987;
(2) *Chronicle Yearbook*, 1999, 464;
(3) Rani, A. (1993). *Behavioural Manifestations of Unemployed Youth,* Ph.D.Thesis,T.M.Bhagalpur University;
(4) Namasivayam, N.(2000). Educated Youth Unemployment in India. *The Indian Journal of Labour Economics*, 43(4),786-787; and
(5) Dutt, R. and Sundaram, K.P.M. (1998). *Bhartiya Arthavyavastha*, New Delhi: S.Chand & Company.

Table 1.4 : The Number of Graduates and Above Registered with Employment Exchanges during the Year 1988-91

Discipline (Graduate & above)	*Number of Unemployed (in thousand)*			
	1988	*1989*	*1990*	*1991*
1. Arts	1342.10	1466.70	1567.00	1611.80
2. Science	574.90	627.70	729.50	750.80
3. Commerce	515.50	575.70	656.60	668.60
4. Engineering	63.50	80.20	95.60	128.40
5. Medical	27.30	30.90	31.70	33.70
6. Veterinary	01.20	01.70	02.10	02.60
7. Agriculture	28.90	31.20	32.00	34.40
8. Law	12.60	14.50	14.50	14.20
9. Education	307.50	358.10	409.90	473.90
10. Others	35.60	40.70	84.00	88.80
Total	2909.10	3227.40	3622.90	3807.20

Source : Ray, P.K.(1995). *Job Market for the Educated.Employment News,* New Delhi, 15–21 April.

Indeed, the problem of unemployment has also been growing among them at a fast rate. The above statistics clearly indicate that about 318.30 thousand, 395.50 thousand and 184.30 thousand graduates and postgraduates were added to the registers of employment exchanges during the years 1989, 1990 and 1991 respectively. The addition to the registers was much larger compared to the placements offered by the employment exchanges (Ray, 1995). However, joblessness is relatively acute among people having degrees in arts and the humanities and social sciences ; among people having degrees in commerce, science and education, it is less acute, and still less among those possessing technical and professional degrees and diplomas.

Thus, the analysis of the ratio of unemployment in the educated lot from diverse angles indicates that the problem of unemployment has affected a sizeable portion of the educated people. As anticipated by 43, National Sample Survey (Dutt, 1990), the problem of unemployment would take a more serious turn in the years to come. It is expected that during the Eighth Five Year Plan the total number of job-seekers would reach about 65,000 thousand and the Ninth Five Year Plan would have to face the burden of 1,06,000 thousand unemployed in the country. With the introduction of the Eighth Five Year Plan (1992-1997), the government of India has proposed a number of schemes to wipe out the problem of unemployment by the end of 2002 AD —the target year —by which the country is expected to achieve full-employment by increasing the annual employment growth from 2 per cent in the past to 2.6 to 2.8 per cent, or generating new employment opportunities numbering about 8.5 million per year on an average over the next 10 years (Papola, 1992). In the Ninth Five Year Plan (1997-2002) too, special emphasis has been given to eradicating the deep-rooted problem of poverty and unemployment, and providing opportunity to every citizen of India to lead a minimum decent life. But only the future will unfold the fate of these wishful plannings. It is not clear from current trends if this rate of acceleration of employment opportunities can be sustained by the modest rate of macro-economic growth recorded so far, unless the growth process becomes more labour-intensive. Briefly put, currently nothing positive can be envisaged in the field of employment. Despite the well-meant intentions and sustained efforts both at the governmental and non-governmental levels to root out the problem of joblessness, nothing tangible has been achieved so far. The problem of joblessness, like Penelope's web, seems endless and tiring. Obviously, unemployment is one of the chronic problems in India. The educated, the pillar of progress and development, are the worst sufferers from the problem of unemployment. Pathetically, there is a fast growth in the number of educated unemployed. The expansion of general, technical and professional educational facilities may be considered to be one of the factors in the steady growth in the number of educated job-seekers in the country. Lack of job-oriented education along with misdirected higher education policies has also been adding fuel to the fire. Apparently, the problem of educated unemployment is a matter of grave concern. The progress of the country will certainly slow down if a suitable solution to the problem is not sought out soon.

Unemployment and Mental Health

The term mental health is extremely difficult to describe comprehensively, and as such no universally-accepted definition of the term is available. This is partly because the concept is, to a considerable degree, value-laden, being a reflection of what is considered appropriate and desirable by the members of a society. The medical profession has developed, and routinely applies, three general criteria which serve to categorize individuals as either 'mentally ill' or 'not-ill'. The first conventional criterion of ill-health is that a person feels unwell. Second, he or she has impairment in one or more functions—psychological, social, and/or physical. Third is the presence of an identifiable pattern or syndrome of symptoms, whether or not these are known to the person. But application of these three medical criteria fails to remove all conceptual or diagnostic difficulties. Mental health, as has been conceived by Nagaraja (1983), is not the mere absence of mental illness but something different. However, the three criteria are often used as the basis for medical decision-making. The view propounded by Warr (1987d) appears relevant here. He has conceived mental health as involving five main components : affective well-being, competence, autonomy, aspiration and integrated functioning, each of which itself be treated overall as a continuum.

According to Warr (1987d) affective well-being is the central component, providing a key indicator to the level of someone's mental health. In other words, the level and quality of a person's affective well-being is a primary indicator of his or her good or poor mental health. Affective well-being has been considered in terms of two separate dimensions, identified as 'pleasure' and 'arousal', with the specific quality of an affect deriving from both dimensions. Feelings may be focused upon features of the environment or upon aspects of the self. The latter are viewed within the notion of 'self-esteem'. The aforementioned two dimensions are orthogonal to each other. Any affective state may be viewed in terms of its location on the two separate dimensions, so that the specific quality of a particular affect derives from both of them. Depressed feelings, for example, are characterized by low scores on each dimension, and anxiety may be described in terms of a low score on pleasure and a high score on arousal. Affective well-being may be physiological as well as psychological. This is particularly clear in respect of low well-being, where, for example, anxiety is displayed in bodily tenseness, sweating, gastric disturbance or sleeping problems, and depressed mood is often accompanied with sleep disturbance, fatigue, and loss of appetite. According to Warr (1986, 1987d) affective well-being can be studied at two different levels : (1) context-free affective well-being, and (2) job-related affective well-being. The former covers well-being and behaviour in one's life-space generally, whereas the latter is restricted to the job environment. Job-related mental health is, for example, examined in terms of job-satisfaction, job-related anxiety or job-related depression.

The second component of mental health is referred to as competence. It includes effective coping, environmental mastery, self-efficacy, effectance motivation, and so on. It is widely held that a key feature of mental health is an ability to deal with experienced pressures, and in some ways successfully to act upon the environment (Valliant, 1977). However, it would not be wise to consider all types of low competence as evidence of poor mental health; everyone is incompetent in some respects. The key factor seems to be a link with affective well-being, in that low competence which is not associated with negative affect would usually be taken as having no bearing on mental health.

Competence may be viewed as subjective or objective. Subjective competence is experienced by the person and is described in terms of his/her beliefs about his/her ability ('self-efficacy' or 'expectations of personal mastery') to manage his/her environment. On the other hand, objective competence is evaluated by an independent observer. How successful the person is seen to be in practice can provide a measure of objective competence. Levels of subjective and objective competence are likely to be positively interrelated, but they do, of course, sometimes differ.

Autonomy is the third component of mental health. It is generally believed that mentally healthy people are able to hold out against environmental influences and determine their own opinions and actions. They feel that they are autonomous and personally responsible for what they do. However, too much autonomy as well as too little is often considered undesirable. It is thus successful interdependence, rather than extreme independence or extreme dependence, which is considered as a sign of good mental health.

Aspiration forms another component of mental health. The mentally healthy person is often viewed as someone who establishes realistic goals and makes active efforts to attain them. Such people show an interest in the environment, engage themselves in motivated activity, and attempt to extend themselves in ways that are personally significant. The converse is apathy and acceptance of the *status quo,* no matter how unsatisfactory it may appear to others. The second, third, and fourth components (competence, autonomy and aspiration) of mental health can be measured 'objectively', as would happen if assessments of a person's status on each component were rated by outside observers, or 'subjectively', as would occur if the assessments were in terms of the individual's own perceptions and evaluations.

The fifth component, integrated functioning, is qualitatively different from the others. It concerns the person as a whole and the relationship between other components. People who are mentally healthy exhibit several forms of balance, harmony and inner relatedness. The converse of this aspect of good mental health is disintegration and structural breakdown. Different investigators (Jahoda, 1958; Lazarus, 1975; Vaillant, 1977) have their own notions of integrated functioning, usually within their preferred theoretical perspective. Hence, descriptions and interpretations of this component vary quite widely (Warr, 1986, 1987d). However, it cannot be denied that this is at a more macroscopic level of mental health than the others.

Nevertheless, in order to understand the concept of mental health it is also pertinent to focus upon the features of environment that are assumed to determine one's mental health. Warr (1986, 1987 a,b,c,d) has presented an elaborate detail of such nine features of environment which have special significance for the growth or maintenance of a person's mental health. These are :

(1) Opportunity for control,
(2) Opportunity for skill use,
(3) Externally generated goals,
(4) Variety,
(5) Environmental clarity,
(6) Availability of money,
(7) Physical security,
(8) Opportunity for interpersonal contact, and
(9) Valued social position.

These environmental features, according to Warr (1986, 1987a,b,c,d,e), need to be analysed to understand the impact of unemployment on mental health. Following Jahoda (1979, 1981,1982, 1987, 1988, 1995) it may be inferred that unemployment holds one from enjoying the aforementioned opportunities and, consequently, impairs one at both physical and psychological levels. Warr (1987c,d) considers unemployment as generally inflicting negative effects on mental health. These negative effects can be related to decrements in one or more of the nine environmental features. Thus, in most cases, unemployed people have reduced opportunities for control in their lives. Their freedom to move in their own ways becomes more limited. They may see themselves as at the mercy of environmental forces and develop feelings of hopelessness, helplessness and depression. Their sense of personal worth might also suffer. The unemployed may also experience decrease in the opportunities to use the skills they already possess and to develop new skills. Their environment also presents fewer goals and task demands and less encouragement of purposeful activities. Unemployment interferes with the routine which a person followed in the past.The unemployed have a lot more time in their hands along with an absence of time-markers that help to break up the day or the week. They confront problems in structuring their time. In addition, their environment is likely to lead to a reduction in variety and their experience may become much more homogeneous than it was when they were employed. Environmental clarity is also likely to be reduced when a person becomes unemployed. It becomes more difficult to judge the consequences of behaviour and to predict the future. Life is more uncertain and anxiety-provoking, and it is relatively difficult to reach appropriate decisions and actions. Unemployment also leads to financial stringency, resulting in personal and family problems. The person may have to beg for debt and then have to repay loans, often under adverse conditions such as high interest rates. Poverty bears down on the unemployed, with all its negative psychological consequences. Social contact may be reduced because of lack of money and additional expenditure may have to be incurred due to the fact that a person is unemployed (e.g., the need to spend extra money on transport or on postage or on suitable clothing when the unemployed person attends job interviews).

Unemployment may also pose threats to physical security as when a person loses suitable accommodation because loan repayment cannot be made or when it becomes difficult for the unemployed person to pay for basic amenities of life. The unemployed person is also likely to experience reduced opportunities for interpersonal contacts. In some cases this may lead to feelings of self-isolation and loneliness, and even lack of emotional support and encouragement. Both the extent of social contact and its diversity have to be considered, as well as the types of social encounter that are affected. Thus, contact with family members and casual meetings with others may increase in frequency due to more available time, particularly in the case of young unemployed, while contact with former work colleagues and social forms of entertainment are likely to decrease. Finally, the unemployed person usually experiences a loss of valued social position. His/her claims on society rather lose legitimacy, and he/she is rendered incapable of asserting himself/herself in conflicting situations

(Kieselbach, 1987b). In most societies, being employed carries with it more status than being out of job. The loss of the socially approved role that goes with employment may cause a loss in self-esteem and a change in social identity.

Warr (1987c, d) cites evidence that supports the general prediction that transitions to lower levels for each of the nine environmental features would be expected to have adverse effects on psychological well-being. Other studies (Feather, 1990; Feather and O'Brien, 1986a,b; O'Brien, 1986; O'Brien and Feather, 1990; Rowley and Feather, 1987), especially conducted in Australia, have also supported the relevance of vitamin model proposed by Warr in describing the impact of employment status (unemployment/employment) on well-being. As indicated by Warr (1987d), the unemployed, being helpless victims of irrepressible economic circumstances, fail to enjoy a number of environmental opportunities, exposing themselves to psycho-physical ill-health. However, in order to be precise in our predictions as to the impact of unemployment on well-being, some of the important indices of mental health were sorted out and the impact of unemployment in terms of them was evaluated. In the subsequent pages a brief account of the impact of unemployment on psychological well-being measured in terms of those select indicators is presented.

Unemployment and Self-concept

Self-concept is the totality of the individual's thoughts and feelings with reference to himself/herself as an object (Rosenberg, 1979). It may be either private (the most accurate estimate of oneself as one really believes it to be; Singh, 1972) or social (the most accurate estimate of oneself as one believes other people in the group estimate one; Singh, 1972). Being one of the potent indicators of one's mental health or affective well-being (Burns, 1979; Feather, 1983b; Murgai and Sathyavathi, 1988; Warr, 1987d), it has attracted considerable attention from investigators interested in the study of unemployment and psychological well-being. Work, as Kelvin (1981) asserts, plays a central role in the development of self-concept. Obviously, occupation is an important determinant of a person's class, position and of his or her feelings of importance and self-worth (Sullivan *et al.*, 1980). Since we tend to define ourselves in terms of what we do, any change in occupational status may have far-reaching repercussions on our self-concept. Moreover, in a good number of studies carried out by Winefield and his colleagues (Tiggemann and Winefield, 1984; Winefield and Tiggemann, 1985; Winefield, Tiggemann and Goldney,1988; Winefield *et al.*, 1991), it has been recorded that securing a job, particularly a good one, has a positive impact on one's self-esteem. Hence, loss of work or unemployment is justifiably expected to lower down one's self-concept. But the findings of the studies are not conclusive in this regard. In some studies, unemployment, particularly when involuntary and prolonged, has been found to have a debilitating effect upon one's self-concept or self-esteem (Borgeon, Hates and Amundson, 1990 ; Breakwell, Harrison and Propper,1984; Donovan and Oddy, 1982; Dooley and Prause, 1995, 1997; Feather, 1985b; Feather and Barber, 1983; Fryer, 1995a; Fryer and Payne, 1986; Hagen, 1983; Jahoda, 1979; Keefe, 1984; Madonia, 1983; Patton and Noller, 1990; Perfetti and Bingham, 1983; Prause and Dooley, 1997; Rani,1993; Singh, Singh and Rani, 1996b; Singh, Singh and Singh, 1995; Sokou and Papantoniou, 2000; Tiggemann and Winefield,1984; Warr,1987c,d ; Winefield, 1995b). But in other studies a rather different picture has been presented (Cohn, 1978; Hartley, 1980; Joshi, Garon and Lechasseur, 1984; Warr, Jackson and Banks,1982). Further, some investigators have observed that the impact of unemployment on one's self-concept is considerably mediated by various personal and background characteristics of the different populations studied. Educational experience, according to Feather (1982), is one such characteristic that may mediate the impact of unemployment on self-concept. He is of the opinion that educational experiences of the successful graduates may help to immunize them against some of the initial shocks of not getting a job, and perhaps even subsequently. He has further indicated that prior to seeking employment, the successful graduates presumably develop some skills in structuring time and developing a sense of purpose and autonomy. Similar is the view expressed by Ioannidi and Mestheneos (1999). University degree, they opine, has high social value apart from its being an achievement in itself. As such university education works as a powerful deterrant and helps maintain a relatively high degree of self-esteem, without any marked deterioration, among the unemployed. The view of Feather (1982) is also consistent with the findings obtained by Shamir (1986) in an Israeli study conducted on those university degree-holders who had several years of work experience. On the basis of the analysis of data obtained from cross-sectional and longitudinal studies, Shamir (1986) has reported that global self-esteem, measured by the Rosenberg (1965) Self-Esteem Scale, is neither related to employment status (employed *versus* unemployed) nor affected by changes in employment status. However, the psychological well-being of respondents in Shamir's (1986) study was lower for unemployed subjects and was sensitive to changes in employment status. Shamir (1986) has also indicated that global self-esteem has a significant moderator effect on relations between employment status and the three indicators of psychological well-being (morale, depressive affect, and anxiety), with the high self-esteem individuals showing more resistance to the negative impact of unemployment on psychological well-being when compared with the low self-esteem individuals. Shamir (1986) justifies his results by depending upon the view delineating self-esteem as a relatively stable personality characteristic, less likely to be modified by social circumstances than by other variables. Kessler, Turner and House (1988) and Schaufeli (1992) have also found that high self-esteem acted as a resource, reducing the damage that unemployment inflicts.

Other investigators have also reported no reliable differences in the self-concept and self-esteem of well-educated professionals who are either employed or unemployed. For example, Hartley (1980) has found no significant difference in the self-esteem of employed and unemployed managers. By analysing the data from a longitudinal study, Cohn (1978) has also recorded no evidence for a significant decrease in 'satisfaction with self' as a result of job loss among highly educated white-collar workers. However, he has reported a significant decrement in self-satisfaction of blue-collar workers and less educated white-collar workers due to joblessness. Cohn (1978) has also reported that dissatisfaction with self was accentuated when there was lack of an external cause to which unemployment could be attributed. Specifically, dissatisfaction with self is significantly greater for those unemployed who belonged to areas where the local unemployment rate is low compared to those living in areas where unemployment rate is relatively high. In the opinion of Cohn (1978) the experience of status change inflicts severe effects on one's self-attitude only when an environmental indicator of external cause for employment status change is not available to the individual. The views of Cohn (1978) are fairly consistent with the discussion of attributional changes and their possible effects on the development of depressive symptoms made by Feather and his associates (Feather, 1982; Feather and Barber, 1983; Feather and Davenport, 1981). Cohn's (1978) arguments also correspond with the findings of Jackson and Warr (1987) that unemployed men in areas of England and Wales, where unemployment was chronically high, had significantly better psychological health compared to those in areas of moderate or lower unemployment. The findings obtained by Rani (1993) also support Cohn's (1978) conclusion.

In an extensive study conducted in India she has found that all the groups of unemployed and employed youth have either moderate or high level of private and social self-concepts, though the non-technically educated unemployed youth followed by the technically educated ones have the lower level of the two concepts. Like the former, she has also emphasized level of education as well as chronically higher level of unemployment in the country as responsible for such results. Similar conclusion has been drawn in two recent studies conducted by Singh, Singh and Rani (1996b) and Singh, Singh and Singh (1995) involving both technically and non-technically educated unemployed youth. However, it is remarkable to note here that Dooley, Catalano and Rook (1988) have found that the aggregate unemployment rate has an adverse effect on one's psychological well-being. The argument by Cohn (1978) is also consistent with Kelvin and Jarrett's (1985) recent account of the socio-psychological effect of unemployment on self-concept. Kelvin and Jarrett (1985) have observed that the state of unemployment provides circumstances that would heighten the tendency for people to look at themselves as unusual objects. The central cognitive processes that involve complex structures are disrupted and behaviour that has become second nature and automatic, like driving to work and arriving at one's workplace at a certain time, is no longer maintained. New adaptations have to be made and the person becomes especially responsive to information about self that comes from self-observation and from the responses of others. In regard to the former source of information, the new circumstances that confront the unemployed person, the new behaviours and adjustments that become necessary, and the extent to which the adjustments are effective in meeting situational demands and immediate goals may force changes in the unemployed person's view of self. So, too, the self-concept may be modified on the basis of how unemployed people perceive themselves to be seen by others — by family, friends, commentators in the mass media, politicians, and individuals and groups. Kelvin and Jarrett (1985) hold that unemployment may be seen as a record of the conditions and processes which undermine the functional autonomy of one's previously taken-for-granted self-concept : the unemployed individual becomes once again exceptionally dependent on how he/she is seen, and perceives himself/herself as seen, by others. Psychologically, as well as economically, unemployment is a condition of forced dependence, which makes the people deeply vulnerable to others. Following a lead from a good number of earlier studies (Bakke,1933; Beales and Lambert,1934; Jahoda, Lazarsfeld and Zeisel, 1933; Komarovsky, 1940; Marsden and Duff,1975), Kelvin and Jarrett (1985) have observed that unemployment is a kind of deprivation that involves changes in one's income, social relationship, family life, social roles, daily routine, goals and purposes, and so on.

These changes, according to them, lead to more self-observation and to increasingly negative views of self. Also, they have asserted that an emphasis within society on the work ethic affects the self-concepts of the unemployed. Whether the *Protestant ethic* is a myth or a reality, the fact that it is a part of public opinion will influence how the unemployed see themselves (Kelvin, 1980). Again, mainly on the basis of autobiographical accounts and case histories (e.g., Bakke, 1933; Beales and Lambert, 1934; Briar, 1977; Gould and Kenyon, 1972; Hill, 1978; Marsden and Duff, 1975; Zawadski and Lazarsfeld, 1935), Kelvin and Jarrett (1985) have indicated that the ascription of luck to others who are in job may help to reduce the unemployed person's feeling of personal responsibility for being unemployed; the attributed lack of understanding by others also may help unemployed people to reduce self-blame because the focus of blame is shifted outside of the self. Kelvin and Jarrett (1985) have discussed the relevance of the concept of 'stigma'and 'stigmatization'(Goffman, 1968) as influences on the self-concepts of the unemployed.

Describing the concept of stigma and stigmatization they have indicated that the unemployed may not be seen as 'scroungers' and 'dole-bludgers' when there is widespread unemployment and a number of people, including some who are personally known, are without jobs; in times of very low levels of unemployment the jobless may be seen as disadvantaged and as needing special care and help. Somewhere in the middle range of unemployment levels one might expect to find negative references to the unemployed in which the unemployed are discredited and their social identity diminishes because they are unemployed.

Kelvin and Jarrett (1985) explain these processes in relation to the principles of social comparison and reference groups —the principles enunciated by Rosenberg (1979). Thus, at some critical level of unemployment, "the unemployed" becomes a negative reference group of inadequates, the hard-core unemployed, and the unemployable and the unemployed ordinary worker feels tainted by association; he/she believes that others associate him/her with these 'inadequates', as indeed they often do. Self-concept may then be affected negatively; the unemployed person may come to internalize some of the negative views of others in perceiving and evaluating self. Thus, on the whole, from the analysis of the observation by Kelvin and Jarrett (1985) it appears that the impact of unemployment on self-concept depends on the factors related to the unemployed people themselves, existing unemployment situation and the reactions of others (family members, friends, welfare officers, employers, media, and society) towards the unemployed.

On the basis of the above discussions, it seems clear that the effects of unemployment on self-esteem considerably depend upon the nature of the population being studied, with less evidence of decrement in self-esteem following job loss among the more educated, white-collar individuals. However, it should be noted here that lower level of self-esteem may be found among the unemployed when self-esteem scores based on the negative items are uncoupled from self-esteem scores based on the positive items (Feather and Bond, 1983). Gender differences in self-esteem are also reported in the study of Feather and Bond (1983) which are further supported by his later study involving a sample of first-year psychology students (Feather, 1985b). Shamir (1986), Winefield and Tiggemann (1994), and Winefield *et al.* (1991) have also found that the self-esteem of the men was higher than that of the women. In a longitudinal study, Gurney (1980a) has found evidence indicating that self-esteem increases among female school-leavers who obtain jobs but not among male school-leavers who succeed in getting jobs. However, Wylie (1979), on the basis of a comprehensive review of the literature, has concluded that there is no firm evidence to corroborate the view that women generally have lower self-esteem than men. According to him more research is needed to ascertain the exact conditions under which gender differences in self-esteem may occur.

The age of a person also mediates the impact of unemployment on self-concept. Bachman and O'Malley (1977) have shown that self-esteem tends to increase with age. Consistent with the aforementioned findings, Rowley and Feather (1987) have found that middle-aged unemployed men are higher in global self-esteem as compared with a sample of younger unemployed males. The results of Winefield and his colleagues are also consistent with the general trend indicating global self-esteem as increasing with age (Tiggemann and Winefield,1984; Winefield and Tiggemann,1985; Winefield, Tiggemann and Goldney,1988). Thus, for whatsoever reason, global self-esteem seems to increase as young people become older; this general trend may make it difficult to identify decrement in global self-esteem as a result of negative life experience such as unemployment in longitudinal studies where age necessarily varies. Socio-economic conditions and other personal and demographic variables are also found to mediate the impact of unemployment on self-concept (Cohn, 1978; Dooley, Catalano and Rook, 1988; Jackson and Warr, 1987; Kasl and Cobb, 1982; Prause and Dooley, 1997; Schaufeli, 1988 a,b, 1992 ; Shamir, 1986).

Thus, on the basis of the analysis of a number of studies intended to see the effect of unemployment on self-concept from diverse angles, nothing conclusive can be said as to the distribution of self-concepts in the unemployed. Different variables, as mentioned above, may mediate the impact of unemployment on self-concept. Briefly put, there are conflicting results in this regard. However, in spite of the diversity of opinion existing among the findings, unemployed people, as has been observed (Jahoda, 1988; Kieselbach, 1991; Kumari, 2001; Rani, 1993; Verkleij, 1989), feel dejected and disappointed, and carry with them different negative feelings (e.g., shame, embarrassment, sense of self-defeat, frustration, etc.), liable to develop in them low and negative feelings towards them. But, there is still a considerable lack of systematic research designed to determine the impact of unemployment on self-concepts in India, suggesting the need of intensive researches in this regard.

Unemployment and Lack of Self-confidence

Self-confidence refers to one's faith in one's capability, potentiality and competence. Consistency and persistence in one's attitude and behaviour pattern usually convey an image of self-confidence. A person having high self-confidence has a unique capacity of self-determination to translate his/her desires into reality. He/she is generally rated as successful in every walk of life —interpersonal relations, problem-solving, paid employment, and so on. Apparently, he/she is a person who has adequate psychological resources to deal effectively with experienced pressures.

In a good number of investigations, self-confidence has been studied as an indicator of the mental health of an unemployed. One such study has been conducted by Feather and Davenport (1981) who have reported development of apathy, resignation, self-doubt, lack of confidence, depression, lower self-esteem, fatalistic beliefs, and so on as some of the serious consequences of unemployment. In another study, too, Feather and O'Brien (1986b) have found that unemployment, particularly prolonged, leads to diminished self-worth, decreased confidence and increased negative affect. However, on the basis of their study, O'Brien and Feather (1990) have indicated that the unemployed rate them inferior on the scale of personal competence only to those who are better employed, they show little difference from the poor employment groups in this regard. But the findings of a good number of studies have shown that the unemployed, as compared to the employed, in general, have lower self-confidence.

For example, Jackson *et al.* (1983) have recorded that unemployment has significant association with lack of concentration, lack of sleep, unhappiness, problems in decision-making, loss of confidence, strain, feelings of worthlessness, diminished confidence, and difficulties in coping. Similarly, studies by Fröhlich (1983a), Klausen and Iversen (1981), Payne, Warr and Hartley (1984) and Warr and Jackson (1984) have reported a higher degree of anxiety, worry, depression, insomnia, irritability, lack of self-confidence, listlessness, inability to concentrate and general nervousness as characterizing the psychological health of 20 to 30 per cent of unemployed men. Donovan *et al.* (1986) and Layton (1986,1987), on the basis of their longitudinal studies of male school-leavers, have arrived at a similar conclusion, indicating the unemployed as having a considerably lower level of self-confidence. Morell, Taylor and Kerr (1998) have also found a strong association between youth unemployment and loss of confidence. Tulsyan (1984) has also envisaged a substantial loss of self-confidence among the educated unemployed in India. Kieselbach and Svensson (1988) have reported that prolonged unemployment develops a feeling of demoralization (Dohrenwend *et al.*, 1980), which encompasses attitudes and behaviour showing low self-confidence, helplessness, hopelessness, undefined fear of the future, and a depressed mood. Thus, the findings of studies reviewed in this regard, with a few exceptions, have clearly indicated the undermining impact of unemployment on self-confidence. But, the aforementioned findings cannot be generalized with certainty to cover a third world country, like India, unless they are replicated systematically by taking into account the normative reality of this country.

Unemployment and Aggression

Aggression has been variously defined, but intention to harm another person or a group (the target or the surrogate of a person or group) including oneself has been widely accepted as its prime characteristic (Averiall,1982; Feshbach,1970; Secord and Backman,1974). Thus, according to Myers (1983) aggression may be conceived as physical or verbal behaviour that intends hurting someone. This, of course, excludes accidental hurts. But it does include a wide variety of actions aimed at hurting someone, no matter whether such acts succeed or not. This definition encompasses two distinct types of aggression : (1) hostile aggression, and (2) instrumental aggression. Hostile aggression is the result of anger. Its aim is to injure. Instrumental aggression is also intended to hurt, but only as a means to some other end (Buss, 1971; Feshbach, 1970). An important difference between the two kinds of aggression is that while hostile aggression is hot, the instrumental is cool. But sometimes, as stated by Bandura (1979), it is hard to distinguish between the two.

Aggression is also one of the significant indicators of well-being but has not received enough attention from the investigators interested in the study of unemployment and well-being. However, in a good number of studies (Briar,1983; Ensminger and Celentano, 1990; Singh,1990; Stokes and Cochrane, 1984) it has been found that the unemployed show a greater tendency to aggression. Similarly, Keefe (1984) has reported that the unemployed have a relatively strong feeling of anger, guilt and shame. A number of investigators (Klausen and Iversen, 1981; Ortiz, Casullo and Grillo, 1982; Payne, Warr and Hartley, 1984; Warr, 1983; Warr and Jackson, 1984) have found that the unemployed have a higher degree of anxiety, worry, depression, insomnia, irritability, lack of self-confidence, listlessness, inability to concentrate and general nervousness. Conger *et al.* (1990), Liker and Elder (1983), and McLoyd (1989) have shown that mounting economic pressure emanating from unemployment makes an individual tense, irritable and explosive.

The findings of a good number of studies (Breakwell, Harrison, and Propper,1984; Feather,1982; Oddy, Donovan and Pardoe, 1984) have indicated that the unemployed often manifest certain reactions that are fairly representative of high guilt feelings. Viney (1983) has found that the young unemployed, compared to the older ones, are significantly more anxious and helpless, and suffer more intensely from feelings of anger, guilt and shame. Recently, Singh, Kumari and Singh (1992) have reported that though both the unemployed and the employed have a moderate amount of hostility and its dimensions, the unemployed youth are relatively high on hostility and its dimensions. They have further indicated that while the job-seekers possess a high sense of guilt and low indirect aggression, the employed youth are high on irritability and, like their counterparts, low on indirect aggression. But, in another study Kumari (2001) has recorded that the educated youth unemployed for different durations, compared to the educated youth employed for different periods, have a higher amount of aggression, but the extent of aggression in them does not reach the point of vulnerability. She has further reported that the educated youth, either unemployed or employed for different durations, show a difference between them in terms of the degree and extent of aggression, and its manifestations. Thus, it appears that unemployment triggers off aggression in a significant manner. But, as is apparent, efforts to understand the degree and extent of aggression and its dimensions (viz., assault, indirect aggression, irritability, negativism, resentment, suspicion, verbal aggression and sense of guilt) in educated unemployed young men for different durations are almost non-existent. Warr (1987d) also holds a similar view that there is a need for further investigation into the impact of unemployment on the development of aggression, sense of injustice, alienation from society, anger and anti-social behaviour such as social banditry, delinquency, drug-taking, and so on.

Unemployment and Depression

Depression—one of the significant indicators of affective well-being (Warr, 1987d)—has been the subject of inquiry in many an investigation intended to study the impact of unemployment on mental health. Depression is generally an emotional state which everybody has to face in his/her day-to-day life on account of the unfulfilment or bafflement of his/her desires or after receiving some news intensely shocking to him or her. Depression of a moment is a natural phenomenon not deleterious to human health. But if a person often confronts depressive affect or if depression recurs frequently with no plausible reasons, or if it continues for a longer duration, it starts to generate various psychiatric symptoms in him/her like an extreme state of unresponsiveness to stimuli, together with self-depreciation, delusion of inadequacy, listlessness, hopelessness and different physical disturbances (Quay and LaGreca, 1986; Rosenhan and Seligman, 1984).

Unemployment has been found to result in a number of consequences. Depression is one of them (Banks and Jackson, 1982; Donovan and Oddy, 1982; Donovan *et al.*, 1986; Dooley and Catalano, 1980; Eales, 1989 ; Feather, 1982, 1989b; Feather and O'Brien, 1986a,b; Fryer, 1995a ; Jones, 1988; Morell, Taylor and Kerr, 1998 ; O'Brien and Feather, 1990; Peretti, Butcher and Cherry, 1988; Price, Van Ryn and Vinokur, 1992 ; Rife, 1990; Roy, 1978; Stokes, 1983; Sudan, 2000; Turner, Kessler and House, 1991; Warr and Parry, 1982; Winefield, 1995b; Winefield *et al.*, 1991). Warr (1984b, 1987d) has also indicated that feelings of distress, anxiety, depression, psychosomatic symptoms and family strain are some of the pronounced consequences of unemployment.

On the basis of their studies, Patton and Noller (1984, 1990) and Winefield and Tiggemann (1994) have recorded that the unemployed, compared to the employed, show increase in their scores on depression. Cochrane (1983) has also derived a similar conclusion. But there are studies wherein it has been reported that not only unemployment but also jobs of poor quality, unable to satisfy various manifest and latent needs, increase the level of depression (Brousseau, 1978; Brousseau and Prince, 1981; Mortimer and Lorence, 1979; Warr, 1983, 1987d; Winefield, Tiggemann and Goldney, 1988; Winefield, Tiggemann and Winefield, 1991). Further, Feather (1983a) and Feather and Davenport (1981) have found that depressive affect is more intense among those who see work as attractive and who have higher expectations with regard to obtaining a job, and who hanker after it. The results of the study by Feather and Barber (1983) have indicated that low expectations of finding a job in the unemployed lead to low self-esteem, perceived lack of control, helplessness, depressive affect and an inclination towards self-blame in them. This pattern of relation is consistent with the clinical literature on depressive symptoms which indicates that the more general form of depression is accompanied by feelings of helplessness, hopelessness, diminished self-esteem, faulty information processing, negative cognitive sets, and by attributional styles that are characterized by internal, stable and global attributions for negative or bad outcomes and external, unstable, and specific attributions for good events (e.g., Abramson, Seligman and Teasdale, 1978; Beck, 1967, 1976; Feather, 1983b; Feather and Barber, 1983; Feather and Tiggemann, 1984; Peterson and Seligman, 1984; Weiner, 1986).

In several studies perceived job insecurity has been identified as the most significant predictor of all stress-related variables associated with symptoms of mild depression in the general population (Dooley, Rook and Catalano, 1987). Fryer (1995a,c), Tiggemann and Winefield (1980, 1984) and Winefield (1995b) have shown that the unemployed have greater depressive affect than the employed. Further, economic depression has been found to be associated with higher level of depression (Ullah, Banks and Warr, 1985). The necessary cutbacks and losses of family responses to financial hardship tend to increase the risk of depression (Bolton and Oatley, 1987; Kessler, 1982; Kessler, Turner and House, 1988). On the basis of the abovementioned study, it may be concluded that unemployment leads to the development of depression but it can also be not denied that every kind of employment, particularly employment unrelated to the satisfaction of manifest (gaining of income) and latent (psychological) needs, does not lead to a decline in the level of depression.

Unemployment and Adjustment

Adjustment, in general, has been conceived as one's ability to cope with various situations in one's life. Inability to overcome frustrations, resolve conflicts and establish social relationship, and to bring harmony between different inner demands and those imposed upon one by the world in which one lives indicate the symptoms of poor adjustment. The latter is generally manifested in terms of physical debility and reduced psychological well-being involving higher level of anxiety, apathy, stress, hostility, unhappiness, dissatisfaction, withdrawal, incompetence, and so on.

Researches into the adjustment patterns of the unemployed people in India are scarce. However, investigations carried out abroad have indicated that the unemployed, compared to the employed, have an acute problem of adjustment in every walk of life. For example, Dumont (1977) has reported that joblessness is sensitively related to mental illness, sexual impotence, crime, alcoholism and suicide. It is said to exert a damaging influence on human health by generating coronary artery disease, hypertension, peptic ulcer and infectious diseases. Further, migration, divorce and child abuse, resulting in personal and financial pathology, are some other repercussions of unemployment. Platt (1985) and Henkel (1985, 1987) have also arrived at a similar conclusion.

However, Aho (1981) is of the view that unemployment, as such, does not directly lead to alcoholism, asociality or somatic or psychic illness. Similarly, Winefield, Tiggemann and Goldney (1988) have found no difference in the psychological adjustment of those who are dissatisfied with their jobs and those who are unemployed. Yet, the findings of a good number of studies like that of Brenner and Starrin (1988), Kieselbach and Svensson (1988), Kieselbach and Wacker (1985), O'Brien and Kabanoff (1979), Singh (1990), Tiggemann and Winefield (1984), Turner, Kessler and House (1991) and Webster (1984) have indicated that the unemployed people are relatively more vulnerable to psychological illness and are generally less well-adjusted as compared to their employed counterparts. Hagen (1983), Liem and Liem (1988), Liem and Rayman (1984), Oddy, Donovan and Pardoe (1984) and Wilson and Walker (1993) have recorded that prolonged unemployment commonly generates a serious threat to the physical and emotional well-being of those who experience it. Recently, in an Indian study conducted by Y.K.Singh (1990), the unemployed have been found to suffer more in comparison from the problems of adjustment in every walk of life (home, health, social, emotional) as well as in their totality. Singh (1994) also arrives at a similar conclusion.

However, he has indicated the employed as also carrying with them a considerable measure of problems, though moderate in nature, of adjustment in their life, especially on the social front. Studies by Donovan and Oddy (1982), Hepworth (1980), and Peterson *et al.*, (1983) have also underlined that the unemployed have poor subjective well-being and inadequate social adjustment. Roberts, Duggan and Noble (1982) have found that young unemployed people generally find themselves unable to devise their own coping strategies.

As indicated by Jackson and Warr (1984), unemployment brings a 'shock' and carries with it a 'range of stressors' (psychological, social and economic) which adversely affect our psychological well-being. Thus, it appears that unemployment is a snag in one's adjustment in different spheres of life. However, these findings, though conclusive to a certain extent, may not be so in the socio-cultural context of India, where the problem of unemployment, despite the concerted efforts of the government and the non-governmental agencies to eradicate it once and for all, has taken a serious turn. Hence, there is need for a systematic study in this regard involving various types of unemployed and employed people.

Unemployment and Time Management Behaviour

Time management generally refers to time budget or placement or structuring of time. In other words, it is a preplanning or proper distribution of time to go ahead with one's day-to-day activities. Evidently, the placement of time and time distribution are the two salient features of time management behaviour. Placement of activities and allocation of time for them depend on the relative importance attached to a particular job, and upon different immediate and anticipated socio-psychological circumstances.

It is widely accepted that time is life. Hence, in order to make one's life happy and prosperous one needs to manage one's time properly. In fact, the all-round development of an individual fully depends upon proper management and utilization of his/her time. At the psychological level, in particular, the study of time management behaviour may provide certain clues to the understanding of the degree of deterioration in one's psychological well-being or adjustment pattern as it has been asserted that the structured and purposive use of time rather than unstructured and aimless one is relatively conducive to well-being (Bond and Feather, 1988; Feather and Bond, 1983; Hepworth, 1980; Hunt, McEwen and McKenna,1985; Jahoda, 1982; Kilpatrick and Trew, 1985; Miles, Howard and Henwood, 1984; Warr, 1984c, 1987d; Warr, Banks and Ullah, 1985 ; Winefield, Tiggemann and Winefield, 1992). Hence, an analysis of the budgeting of time by an unemployed for different day-to-day activities has significance in the context of assessing his/her psychological well-being.

Investigators from the west have shown a continuing interest in how unemployed people use their time. Jahoda's view (1979,1981,

1982,1988) merits a mention here. According to her the sudden onset of unemployment destroys a person's habitual time structure for the waking day, undermines his/her sense of purpose in life, reduces his/her social contacts, results in his/her loss of status and identity, and removes the regular activities that were part of his/her daily life. Findings are, to an extent, consistent in this regard indicating that the unemployed, compared to those in job, perceive their time to be without structure or purpose. In a number of instances (Bostyn and Wight, 1987; Fagin and Little, 1984; Kilpatrick and Trew, 1982, 1985; Knulst and Schoonderwoerd, 1983; Miles, 1983; Miles, Howard and Henwood, 1984; Warr, 1984c; Warr and Payne, 1983; Winefield, Tiggemann and Winefield, 1992) it has been indicated that the unemployed men take on significantly more child care activities and meal preparation, but there is also significantly more inactivity, merely sitting around, sleeping during the day, and watching television.

Findings of these studies have confirmed that the unemployed people have difficulty in filling their days. Warr (1984c) and Warr and Payne (1983) have found the unemployed as increasingly involved in domestic activities and in the pastimes not involving any cost. Similar are the findings of Elchardus and Glorieux (1995), O'Brien and Kabanoff (1979), Swinburne (1981) and Trew and Kilpatrick (1983). They have reported that the majority of the unemployed have difficulty in organizing their time, and they structure their time by engaging themselves in domestic and leisure activities. In the study by Fröhlich (1983b) forty per cent of the unemployed men have been found to report visiting friends and neighbours more frequently, with only 6 per cent reporting a decrease. In an Indian study conducted by Sinha and Mallick (1990) it has been recorded that the educated unemployed youth spend more time on sleep, rest and leisure activities followed by job-seeking activities, play and recreation, household activities, etc. They have concluded that the unemployed people are noticeably more involved in futile and unproductive activities. In a similar quest, Rani (1993) has also shown the unemployed, whether technically or non-technically educated, as significantly more inclined towards futile and less purposive activities like sleeping and lazing, idling and gossiping, personal care and health, politicking*, hobbies and pastimes, etc.

---

* Politicking is used as a noun, especially referring to win support for yourself. This is often used for disapproving something. (see Oxford Advanced Learner's)

However, the study does not fully deny their involvement in some of the activities like self-study and academic activities, occupation-related activities, etc., assumed to be gainful in the future, and thus supportive of their well-being. Singh, Singh and Singh (1995) have also given a similar description of the time management behaviour of the unemployed. Kilpatrick and Trew (1985), on the basis of their study, have classified unemployed men into four main groups in relation to the time spent by them in various activities. Those unemployed men who spend a lot of time in active leisure and work-related activities fall into the *Active cluster;* those who spend more of their time with others than the members of any other cluster fall into the *Social cluster;* the men in the *Domestic cluster* spend a lot of their time in domestic chores; and those in the *Passive cluster* spend a large amount of their time in passive leisure and child-care activities, as compared with those lying in the other groups. The men in the latter two clusters are more home-oriented than those in the former two clusters. Kilpatrick and Trew (1985) have found that psychological well-being becomes progressively poorer as one moves from the active to the social to the domestic to the passive cluster. They have also reported other marked differences among the four groups in regard to the background characteristics and unemployment history. Furthermore, there are a number of studies wherein it has been recorded that the unemployed people are significantly less structured and purposive in the use of their time (Fryer,1995a; Hunt, McEwen and McKenna, 1985; Rowley and Feather, 1987; Sokou and Papantoniou, 2000;Warr, 1983, 1987d; Warr, Banks and Ullah, 1985; Winefield, 1995b). Feather and Bond (1983) have also found that the unemployed, as compared to the employed, show less structure and purpose in the use of their time. They have concluded that the unemployed show less engagement, less direction, less organization, and less routine in their use of time. They are of the opinion that employment imposes its own goals, structures, and routines on those who are employed, whereas the unemployed do not have these job-related requirements.

Hence, the unemployed have to fall back on their own resources and make the best they can of an uncertain world that does not include the regimen of paid employment. However, they have reported individual differences as influencing the use of time to a large extent.They have indicated that the unemployed having diminished self-esteem and higher frequency of depressive symptoms reported difficulties in the use of their time. Similarly, on the basis of their study, Rowley and Feather (1987) have demonstrated that people unemployed for a longer duration show less structure and purpose in the use of their time. They have further underlined that lack of time structure occurs among those who have lower self-esteem and higher amount of psychological distress. But they have not reported evidence of relation between lack of time structure and employment commitment. Bond and Feather (1988) have also arrived at a similar conclusion.

Feather (1989a) has found that higher levels of psychological distress are significantly associated with less time spent on each of the following activities: domestic work, entertainment through money and social contacts. He has further reported that higher levels of life satisfaction are markedly related to less time spent on domestic pastimes and with more time spent on social contacts. He has also shown that higher levels of financial stress are significantly linked with less time spent on recreations and entertainments on financial costs. However, the corresponding correlations for financial strain have been found to be negative, but not statistically significant.

Fryer and McKenna (1987,1988), on the basis of the comparison between the two middle-aged groups of workers— one,who were laid-off for a seven-week period but had a sense of purpose for the future, and another, who were made redundant— have found that the redundant men suffer greater difficulties in their use of time, and exhibit higher levels of psychological distress, as compared to the laid-off men, who cope better with their use of time. It indicates that sense of purpose is an important variable that makes a difference between the redundant and laid-off participants in terms of the use of their time. Notably, redundant participants have less sense of purpose and structure in the use of their time as compared to the laid-off ones. Warr (1987d) discusses the consequences of unemployment on a person's sense and use of time in terms of a reduction in externally generated goals, one of the environmental features in his vitamin model. Thus, according to him, in a state of unemployment fewer demands are made, objectives are reduced, and purposeful activity is less encouraged by the environment. Routines and cycles of behaviour are less often set in motion, and opportunities for traction and flow may be limited. He has further observed that an absence of demands can produce an excess of time, and remove the need to choose between activities or to allocate fixed amounts of time to individual tasks.

A general reduction in those demands that are linked to particular points (such as meal times or the start of a working day) may lead to a loss of temporal differentiation. Time-markers which, according to him, break up the day or week and indicate one's position in it are no longer as frequent or as urgent. Hence, the unemployed men may have a prolonged sense of waiting and a feeling that each day lacks structure. In terms of the vitamin model, it would be expected that these changes in purpose and structure linked to a reduction in externally generated goals and organized routines would be accompanied by impaired psychological health as evidenced by feelings of boredom, negative affective states, and so forth.

Thus, the studies on the management of time by the unemployed people for their different day-to-day activities have shown them as fairly less structured and purposive in the use of their time, though it has also been established that such activities are considerably mediated by certain psychological variables. However, in contrast with the aforementioned findings, Schaufeli (1988b) has recorded that professionally educated unemployed people have opportunities for engaging themselves in unpaid work without penalty, enabling them to use their skills and develop some purpose and meaning in their lives. But, the lone finding cannot be safely generalized, particularly in a developing country like India where people, in general, manifest certian typicality in their characteristics and behaviour patterns (Faroqi,1984; Lapierre, 1986; Pandey,1980; Singh,1990; Singh, Sinha and Kumari,1985; D.Sinha, 1988; J.B.P.Sinha, 1982a) leading them to react differently even to problems like poverty and unemployment (A.K.Singh,1975; Singh,1990, 1994; Singh, Singh and Singh, 1996; Singh, Singh and Singh, 1995) depleting the verve and vitality of the whole nation — the fact quite in correspondence with the far-reaching philosophy expressed by Oscar Lewis (1966) in his theory of *"Culture of Poverty"*. Thus, quite expectedly, the gestures like involvement in less structured and aimless activities (*viz*., gossiping, making tall talks, aram, loafing, engaging in unhealthy local and parochial politics, etc.) of the unemployed people in India are nothing but the natural manifestation of their basic personality structure.

The unemployed people in India, as can be generally seen, have lot of idle time mainly because of their prevalent non-work culture as well as general tendency to perceive the unemployed as incompetent in carrying the burden of job which requires a greater sense of responsibility, persistence and industriousness. In addition, lack of facilities for adequate recreation and of support from any corner in order to engage themselves in useful as well as purposeful activities other than gainful employment in public and private undertakings leave them unused and useless. But, the story of the employed in India is also not very impressive. On account of typical characteristics like lack of seriousness towards any assignments, easy-going temperament and ease-loving tendency along with inconducive work culture (Bajaj, 1982; Kumari, 2001; Pestonjee and Singh, 1982; Singh and Singh,1985; Singh,1994; Singh, Kumari and Singh,1992; Singh, Singh and Rani,1996a; Singh, Singh and Singh, 1995), employed people can also be seen to have a restricted scope for engaging themselves in various purposeful activities. As such, they can also be seen to be engaged in different unproductive activities like gossiping, loafing, politicking, flattering their immediate bosses or conspiring to belittle them, etc. (Kanungo, 1995 ; Sinha and Sinha, 1995). Evidently, both intra- and inter-group cultural variations, as held by Feather (1990), deserve consideration for a precise understanding of the impact of the status of employment on psychological well-being. But surprisingly, little attention has so far been paid to this subject, especially while analysing the time management behaviour of the employed as against unemployed people. This emphasises the need to further explore the issue in question by employing a positivistic as well as a culture-specific approach.

Unemployment and Locus of Control

Locus of control has been conceived as a generalized expectancy about the extent to which reinforcements are under internal or external control. Individuals may vary between two extreme orientations. On the one extreme, the internally controlled person believes that reinforcements are largely determined by personal efforts, ability and initiatives, whereas the opposite type is the externally controlled one who puts more emphasis on other people, social structures, luck or fate as the major source of reinforcement (Phares, 1987; Rotter, 1966).

Degrees of internal and external orientations have been delineated as significant predictors of psychological well-being (e.g., Archer, 1979; Lefcourt, 1982; O'Brien, 1984a,b; Spector, 1982). Thus, in order to find out the deterioration in the well-being of an unemployed person, the study into his/her control orientations deserves thorough inquiry. A good amount of evidence accumulated from research studies over the last few years tends to indicate that unemployed people are relatively more externally oriented (Feather and Barber, 1983; Feather and Davenport, 1981; Layton, 1986, 1987; O'Brien, 1984b; O'Brien and Kabanoff, 1979; Patton and Noller, 1984; Winefield, Tiggemann and Winefield, 1991; Winefield *et al.*, 1991). Other studies, particularly conducted by Feather and O'Brien, Australian psychologists, have also come out with a similar conclusion. For example, Feather and O'Brien (1986a,b), on the basis of their longitudinal studies, have revealed that the unemployed express an increased tendency to blame their unemployment on factors relating to economic recession, and a decreased tendency to blame it on the lack of motivation on their own part. In a similar vein, O'Brien and Feather (1990) have recorded that the unemployed people have higher external control, particularly in comparison to those who are suitably employed. Similar are the findings obtained by Winefield, Tiggemann and Winefield (1991) and Winefield *et al.* (1991). Rani (1993), Singh, Singh and Singh (1996) and Singh, Singh and Singh (1995), on the basis of their studies, have also reported that both groups of the technically and the non-technically educated unemployed, compared to their employed counterparts, are relatively more externally oriented. However, the employed youth have also been found to be fairly high on the external pole of locus of control, lending support to the conclusion of Faroqi (1984) indicating it as one of the typical characteristics of an Indian.

Contrary to the abovementioned findings, Dumont (1977) and Liem (1988) have found the unemployed people to be internalizing the blame for their unemployment. Tiggemann and Winefield (1984) and Winefield and Tiggemann (1985) have recorded a decrease in the externality of about the same amount for school-leavers, whether they get employed or remain unemployed. And the study by Linn, Sandifer and Stein (1985) of American middle-aged men out of work for periods less than six months has shown no longitudinal change in the locus of control scores after job loss. Likewise, Feather and O'Brien (1986a) have found no effect of unemployment on locus of control scores one year after school-leaving. However, externality becomes significantly greater one year later among those who remain without a job.

Thus, a diversity of opinion exists regarding the direction of the control mechanism of the unemployed people. However, in a majority of investigations, unemployed men have been found to be more externally oriented than their employed counterparts. The view held by O'Brien (1986) deserves mention here. He has indicated that unemployment does not ruin a person's capacity for self-reliance but, instead, delimits the number of life-situations where personal control is possible. This renders him/her necessarily externally controlled. It may, therefore, be justifiably asserted that the unemployed, compared to the employed, would be relatively more externally oriented. But, as is apparent, efforts to understand the pattern of control orientation in educated Indian unemployed young men as against their employed counterparts have been exiguous. This calls for systematic researches in this direction, particularly by taking into account the Hindu concepts of *karma* and *bhagya,* and their interdependence (Singh, Singh and Singh, 1996).

To Sum Up

From the aforementioned review of literature available on the status of employment and psychological well-being it appears that unemployment exerts various adverse effects on the psychological health of those who experience it. But the question, it seems, still remains unsettled as to which of the two, one's psychological or physical health, is more affected. An analysis of a number of studies (Breakwell *et al.*, 1984; Fryer 1995a; Fryer and Winefield, 1998; Henkel, 1987; Iversen and Sabroe, 1988; Kieselbach and Svensson, 1988; Kieselbach and Wacker, 1985; Payne, Warr and Hartley, 1984; Sabroe and Iversen, 1989; Verkleij, 1989; Warr, 1984a,b,c; Warr and Jackson, 1984; Winefield, 1995b, 1997; Winefield and Tiggemann, 1985) indicates that unemployment causes greater damage to mental or psychological health than to physical. A team of investigators (Kumari, 2001; Rani,1993; Singh,1990,1994, 2001; Singh, Kumari and Singh,1992; Singh, Singh and Rani, 1996a,b; Singh, Singh and Singh, 1995; Y.K.Singh, 1990) in India has also found that prolonged involuntary unemployment is arguably more dangerous to psychological well-being than to physical. Warr (1985) has also averred that there is no strong evidence that unemployment leads to ill-health of a primarily physical kind. Jahoda (1988), too, has concluded that unemployment results in greater psychological distress. According to her (Jahoda, 1981, 1982, 1987,1995), unemployment does not satisfy one's need for income (manifest function), nor does it support one's latent psychological functions such as time structure, wide social experience, involvement in collective purposes, identity-formation and activity, and thus ultimately renders one vulnerable to psychological uprootedness. But, contrary to the above findings, there are studies (Arnetz *et al.*, 1991; Brenner and Starrin, 1988; Cullen *et al.*, 1987; Hagen, 1983; Jin, Chandrakant and Svoboda, 1995; Liem and Rayman, 1984; Martikainen, 1990; Oddy, Donovan and Pardoe, 1984; Smith, 1987a,b; Wilson and Walker, 1993) wherein unemployment has been shown to be equally deleterious to physical and psychological health. Further, it is a fact revealed through common observation as well as empirical findings (Jahoda,1982, 1988; Vasaria, 1980) that unemployment results in an increase in poverty, leading to deficiencies in clothing, nutrition, and to some other harmful changes in life,causing reduced physical health. Thus, the findings of the studies do not clearly indicate whether unemployment debilitates psychological or physical health, necessitating further researches to resolve the tangle existing in this regard.

The Issue

The present study is aimed at assessing the psychological well-being of the technically and non-technically educated unemployed young men divided by criteria such as branch of education and duration of their status as against their employed counterparts, measured in terms of variables like anxiety, stress, feeling of insecurity, alienation, identity-crisis, and life-satisfaction— some of the significant indicators of psychological well-being. Also, the study is intended to find out the strategy generally employed by them in order to cope with their situations. The effect of the status of employment (unemployment/ employment) in relation to these variables has been analysed for the following reasons:

(1) The abovementioned select indices of psychological health are related with one or the other of the five components of mental health proposed by Warr (1987d). Hence, an analysis of the impact of the status of employment on these variables may provide a correct account of the psychological health of the educated Indian unemployed and employed young men— an important and vital segment of our society.

(2) An investigation into the psychological well-being and coping styles of the unemployed *versus* the employed would not only help to find out the causal relationship between unemployment/employment and psychological impairment, but would

also help in preparing a suitable intervention programme for promoting good mental health of those who are either unemployed or employed. Thus, the study is expected to have an implication for all concerned, especially the investigators engaged in the study of the psychological states of the unemployed and the employed young men for psychosocial interventions.

(3) Studies intended to find out the relationship of unemployment/ employment with these variables are scarce in our country.

A short description of the impact of unemployment on the aforementioned variables is as follows:

Unemployment and Anxiety

Anxiety—one of the important indicators of mental health (Spielberger, 1971)— has been variously defined. But there is a general agreement that anxiety, a transitory emotional state, is manifested in generalized feelings of fear, tension and apprehension. It is also displayed in bodily tenseness, sweating, gastric disturbance or sleeping problems, and may be described in terms of a low score on pleasure and a high score on arousal (Warr, 1987a,b,d). Goldberg and Hillier (1979) and McKenna and Payne (1984) have conceived it as a core phenomenon underlying the common syndrome of psychiatric disorder. In a good number of studies (Donovan and Oddy, 1982; Eales, 1989; Fröhlich, 1983a; Fryer, 1995a ; Klausen and Iversen, 1981; Oddy, Donovan and Pardoe, 1984; Payne, Warr and Hartley, 1984; Tiwari and Krishna, 1999; Turner, Kessler and House, 1991; Ullah, Banks and Warr, 1985; Warr, 1983, 1985; 1987a,c,d; Warr and Jackson, 1984 ; Winefield, 1995b) it has been found that the unemployed people are relatively more anxious than those who are in job. Likewise, Breakwell, Harrison and Propper (1984), Finlay-Jones and Eckhardt (1981),Gold (1978), Keefe (1984), Madonia (1983), Ortiz, Casullo and Grillo (1982), and Stokes (1983) have reported that inability in getting oneself employed results in the development of such allied symptoms of anxiety as depression, stress, worry, tension, irritability, etc., in an individual. Liem (1983a) has also indicated anxiety and despair as the reactions of job-seekers to unemployment.

In the study by Fineman (1979, 1983), too, it has been shown that unemployment raises the level of anxiety. In a similar quest, Daniel

(1974) and Estes and Wilensky (1978) have found that the unemployed have a higher level of financial anxiety. Kessler, House and Turner (1987) have also indicated job loss as causing depressed mood, anxious mood, somatization, and self-reported physical illness. In yet another study, too, Kessler, Turner and House (1988) have underscored a similar conclusion.Warr (1984a, b,1987a, c, d) has recorded feeling of distress, anxiety, depression, psychosomatic symptoms and family strain as the consequences of unemployment. In their study Warr, Banks and Ullah (1985) have found that the unemployed men experience lower level of variety which causes in them high degree of anxiety, depression and general distress. On the basis of his study, Viney (1983) has reported that the young unemployed below 20 years of age have significantly higher rates of anxiety, anger, helplessness, guilt and shame than the older ones. In another study, too, he (Viney, 1985) has indicated anxiety as one of the characteristic symptoms of the unemployed. Banks and Ullah (1986, 1987a, 1988), Masschelein and De Witte (1997), Payne and Jones (1987a) and Warr, Jackson and Banks (1988) have also shown that unemployment exacerbates distress, depression, and anxiety in those who suffer from it. Misra and Saxena (1982) have underscored that unemployed youth coming from non-family-oriented occupations express relatively higher amount of anxiety. In a similar vein, Pratap and Gupta (1985) have recorded that the professionally educated unemployed, as compared to their employed counterparts, are more anxiety-ridden, though they also have only a marginally moderate amount of the syndrome.

Thus, on the basis of the review of a host of studies on unemployment and anxiety, unemployment has been found to be one of the obvious factors leading to the development of anxiety. But there was great paucity of researches on the level of anxiety involving our unemployed young men. Hence, the present investigation involving the technically and non-technically educated unemployed young men and their different subgroups was undertaken with a view to finding out the levels of anxiety of different shades in them as against their employed counterparts.

Unemployment and Stress

The term stress refers to a state of imbalance within an individual that is elicited by an actual or perceived disparity between environmental demands and the individual capacity to cope with them. In other words, stress arises when one appraises a situation as threatening or otherwise demanding and does not have an appropriate coping response (Lazarus, 1966; Lazarus and Folkman, 1984; Lazarus and Launier, 1978; Sarafino, 1990; Singer and Davidson, 1986; Stotland, 1987; Trumbull and Appley, 1986). As noted by Sells (1970), these situations are the ones in which the person perceives that it is important to respond but an appropriate response is not immediately available. In essence, stress is a particular relationship between the person and the environment that is appraised by the person as taxing or exceeding his or her resources and endangering his or her well-being (Lazarus and Folkman, 1984). Although a single stressful event does not place great demands on the coping abilities of most people, it is when multiple problems accumulate, persisting, and straining the problem-solving capacity of the individual, that the potential for serious disorder occurs (Wills and Langner, 1980). Mechanisms linking stress to illness include serious disruptions of neuroendocrine or immune system functioning, marked changes in health-related behaviours (e.g., excessive alcohol consumption, poor diet or exercise patterns) or various failures in self-care. Characteristic symptoms of stress include physical disturbances, psychiatric morbidity, anxiety, conflict, tension, depression, etc. (Ansari *et al.,* 1979; Baum, Singer and Baum, 1981; Burke, 1986; Chatterjee, Mukherjee and Nandi, 1981; Chaturvedi, 1983; Dohrenwend and Dohrenwend, 1974; Gupta *et al.*, 1981; Liem and Liem, 1978; Nathawat and Tiwari, 1983; Prakash, Trivedi and Sethi, 1980; Schor, 1986; Selye, 1976; Singh *et al.*, 1991 ; Srivastava, 1990, 1995 ; Srivastava and Srivastava, 1991). Stress, according to Garber and Seligman (1980), is also manifested in terms of feelings of helplessness and possible loss of self-esteem. Feelings of helplessness arise owing to the perceived inability to cope with situations that demand effective response. Loss of esteem may occur to the extent that the failure to cope adequately is attributed to one's own ability or stable personality traits, as opposed to some external cause.

Stress is also one of the significant indicators of impaired psychological well-being (Chatterjee, Mukherjee and Nandi, 1981; Chaturvedi, 1983; Gupta and Srivastava, 1983; Gupta *et al.*, 1981; Nathawat and Tiwari, 1983; Prakash, Trivedi and Sethi, 1980; Srivastava, 1990, 1995 ; Srivastava and Jagdish, 1990 ; Srivastava and Singh, 1988; Srivastava and Srivastava, 1991 ; Udupa, 1980). However, it may be noted that every stroke of stress does not prove to be threatening to one's well-being. Everyone, in today's fast changing society, confronts, to some degree or the other, the pangs of stress in his/her day-to-day life, finding no immediate resort to deal with the reality. Stress of a moment or of a shorter duration is a natural phenomenon, not entirely unwholesome for human health. But if it becomes pathogenic, recurring all the time, it becomes symptomatic of poor well-being. Researches into the effects of a wide range of discrete life events tend to indicate that economic events, especially joblessness, frequently precedes the development of stress (Chakrapani, 1995, 1996; Coates, Moyer and Wellman, 1969; Kelvin and Jarrett, 1985; Keyssar, 1985; Kieselbach, 1991, 1997a, 1998a; Liem and Liem, 1978; Liem, 1987; Olafsson and Svensson, 1986 ; Shibu and Dharmangadan, 1993).

For many of those affected, unemployment appears as a stressful life event that greatly changes their everyday routine, relationships, social roles, and central aspects of perception of self and that of others (Hamilton *et al.*, 1993; Kelvin and Jarrett, 1985; Kieselbach, 1988b; Kieselbach, Lödige-Röhrs and Lünser, 1989; Kieselbach and Svensson, 1988; Kieslebach and Wacker, 1985, Kinicki and Latack, 1990; Leana and Feldman, 1988, 1992; McLoyd, 1989; Reynolds and Gilbert, 1991; Schaufeli, 1992; Schwefel, 1986; Schwefel, Svensson and Zöllner, 1987; Turner, Leana and Feldman, 1993). In most cases, unemployment generates mounting economic pressure (Elder, Jr. *et al.*, 1991; Jackson and Warr, 1984; Jahoda, 1982, 1988; Kieselbach, 1991; Payne, Warr and Hartley, 1984; Verkleij, 1989; Warr, 1987d; Warr and Jackson, 1984), liable to increasing the abrasive behaviour of men, making them more tense, distressed, irritable and explosive (Conger *et al.*, 1990; Elder, Caspi and Van Nguyen, 1986; Kessler, Turner and House, 1988; Liker and Elder, 1983; McLoyd, 1989; Pearlin *et al.*, 1981; Rodgers,1991; Ross and Huber, 1985). Further, many studies have indicated that unemployment leads to the development of different symptoms of stress in those who experience it. For example, Rayman (1981) has found that the unemployed experience a greater amount of stress in their life. He has also reported that the unemployed, as compared to the employed, have a higher level of experienced strain and negative feelings, and a lower level of happiness, life satisfaction, experience of pleasure and positive feelings.

Similarly, on the basis of his study, Stokes (1983) has maintained that the apathetic outlook of the unemployed youth is a defensive reaction to a situation that produces worry and stress. He has also indicated that the condition of unemployment eventually renders a person ineffective in his/her life and in the long run develops in him/her symptoms of psychiatric disorders. Likewise, Feather and O'Brien (1986b) and O'Brien and Feather (1990) have also found that symptoms of stress are higher among those who subsequently become unemployed. Dooley, Rook and Catalano (1987), too, have indicated perceived job insecurity as the most important predictor of all stress-related variables associated with symptoms of mild depression in general population. In the pioneering study carried out by Cobb and Kasl (1977), too, signifcantly higher physiological stress levels (of noradrenaline, uric acid and blood pressure) and altered health behaviour are observed in the phase of anticipation of job loss, which differs significantly not only from the values obtained for a control group of employed persons but also from those obtained for unemployed people (particularly in the initial phase), as also from those of others who succeed in getting themselves reemployed. This leads to the conclusion that anticipation of redundancy can produce considerable stress reactions, in severity exceeding those experienced in a later phase of unemployment. Except a few (Büssing, 1987,1990; Pelzmann, 1989), a host of investigators (Arnetz *et al.*,1987; Brenner and Levi, 1987a, b; Brenner and Starrin, 1988; Brenner *et al.*, 1989; Depolo and Sarchielli, 1985; Kieselbach, 1990b; Pelzmann, Winkler and Zewell, 1985) have also arrived at a similar conclusion. Further, Gold (1978) has reported that chronic joblessness among university graduates in the developing and developed nations is a major cause of stress in them. Madonia (1983), in his study of psychosocial reaction to chronic joblessness, has found that unemployment affects self-esteem and gives rise to frustration, tension and worry — some of the significant symptoms of stress. However, as has been suggested by Kieselbach (1991), a high level of unemployment can normalize the effects of unemployment and lead to a reduction of personally experienced stress, but it can at the same time produce an atmosphere of hopelessness. In a British study by Jackson and Warr (1987) significant differences in levels of psychiatric morbidity are found between regions of chronically high compared with regions of low unemployment. In areas with chronically high unemployment levels of psychosocial distress are found to be significantly lower, presumably because of cultural changes and community adaptation to mass unemployment. Banks and Ullah (1988) have also indicated the tendency of collective adjustment to poor employment prospects.

The findings obtained by Frese and Mohr (1987) also lend support to the abovementioned conclusion. Earlier, Kelvin and Jarrett (1985) have also reported that the unemployed are not seen as scroungers and dole-bludgers where unemployment is chronically high, and a lot of people, including some who are personally known, are without jobs. In India, describing the lesser vulnerability of the unemployed to psychological uprootedness, Singh (1994) has also adopted similar views. Leaning upon Festinger's (1957) *Cognitive-dissonance* theory, he is of the opinion that people, through identification with others having a similar history of behavioural disorder, mitigate their anxiety and tension. This phenomenon has been called by him the *identificaion effect.*

Lahelma and Kangas (1989) and Verkleij (1989) have shown that an increase in the duration of unemployment leads to increase in the level of stress. However, Brinkmann (1984), on the basis of his study of the long-term unemployed in the Federal Republic of Germany, has indicated a decrease in the level of stress with the increase in the duration of unemployment and has supported the conclusion that the process of psychological deterioration does slow down with the increase in the duration of unemployment (Harrison, 1976), especially in the male of 20-59 age group (Jackson and Warr, 1984). On the basis of a content analysis of qualitative data, Viney (1983) has found significantly higher rates for young unemployed below 20 years of age with regard to anxiousness, anger, helplessness, guilt and shame than for older ones. Earlier, Schober (1978), on the basis of a comparison of stress profile, has concluded that unemployed juveniles suffer considerably more from domestic tensions and attributions of the blame, whereas adults perceive social isolation and stigmatization induced by unemployment more intensively. Age counts a lot for variance in stress profiles. Evidently, there are certain variables which may mediate the impact of unemployment on the development of stress.

Commitment to employment is also one such variable. It should be noted that those unemployed who have a strong commitment to employment are especially exposed to strain during periods of unemployment (Jackson *et al.*, 1983). Psychological stress (Brinkmann, 1984), low levels of personal self-esteem (Feather and Bond, 1983), and depressive tendencies (Feather and Barber, 1983) are found to be of a higher degree among this group. In a longitudinal study carried out by Schultz-Gambard *et al.*, (1986), employment commitment has been shown to be the best predictor of the change in levels of self-esteem and depression. On the basis of Bakke's (1933) *Greenwich study,* Harrison (1976) has argued that prolonged unemployment would be specially stressful to those who are ambitious and have tasted success before. It has also been recorded that the unemployed having low qualifications (i.e., blue-collar workers with little or no occupational training) experience the highest level of stress (Brinkmann, 1984; Warr, 1984a, Wuggenig, 1985). Similarly, Hepworth (1980) has found that unemployed people who have problems with structuring their time before they become unemployed demonstrate higher stress levels during unemployment.

Thus, the impact of unemployment on the development of stress largely depends upon different mediating variables. But, it is a fact revealed through investigations (Campbell, 1981; Duncan, 1987) that the deterioration of one's economic status often leads to more stress than the actual hardship state itself. Unemployment, in most of the cases, leads to intense economic problems likely to develop different symptoms of psychiatric morbidity (Conger *et al.*,1990; Kessler, Turner and House,1988; Liker and Elder,1983; McLoyd,1989; Pearlin *et al.*,1981; Rodgers, 1991; Ross and Huber,1985). Thus, the consequences of unemployment are closely intertwined with the consequences of poverty (Jahoda,1982,1988). In short, unemployment can be designated as the most important predictor of all stress-related manifestations. As such, there seems to be no palpable justification for a fresh investigation into the impact of unemployment on the development of different symptoms of stress. But, strange as it may appear, efforts to understand the degree and extent of stress in educated unemployed young men in India have been virtually non-existent. Hence the present investigation.

Unemployment and Feeling of Insecurity

Security is defined, essentially, as a feeling of being liked, loved, and accepted; of belonging to and having a place in the group, of safety and of being unanxious. Insecurity, on the contrary, generally refers to the loss or absence of such feelings. It is often linked with emotional instability, feelings of rejection, inferiority, anxiety, isolation, jealousy, hostility, irritability and unhappiness. An insecure person is thus highly vulnerable to the development of neurotic or psychotic tendencies. Maslow *et al.* (1945-52) believe that security is synonymous with mental health. In the study by Helpert (1982) work has been shown to have a stabilizing influence on those who are insecure in their social contacts and who are psychologically vulnerable. Other investigators (Beale and Nethercott, 1985, 1986; Dilling, Weyerer and Castell, 1984; Dooley, Rook and Catalano, 1987; Hartley *et al.*, 1991; Ronayne, Ryan and Cullen, 1989) have also enunciated job insecurity as an important antecedent to psychological ill-health. This emphasizes that in order to have a clear account of the mental health of the unemployed, the degree and extent of the feeling of insecurity in them requires to be analyzed systematically. But surprisingly, study of the feeling of insecurity has not yet attracted a considerable attention of investigators interested in the study of mental health of the unemployed.

There has been a considerable dearth of direct studies on the relationship between unemployment and feeling of insecurity. However, in a number of studies (de Almeida Filho, 1981; Donovan and Oddy, 1982; Finlay-Jones and Eckhardt, 1981; Hepworth, 1980; Liem and Rayman, 1984; Oddy, Donovan and Pardoe, 1984; Ortiz, Casullo and Grillo, 1982; Schwefel *et al.*, 1984; Warr, 1983) unemployment has been found to precede the development of low mental health, emotional instability, irritability, worry, tension, anxiety, etc., — significant indicators of the feeling of insecurity. Fryer and Winefield (1998), Kieselbach, Beelmann and Stitzel (2000), Payne, Warr and Hartley (1984), Ståhl (1987) and Warr and Jackson (1984, 1985) have also indicated the unemployed as being confronted with the feeling of insecurity. They have reported that a majority of unemployed people are afflicted with a considerable amount of anxiety about not knowing what would happen to them in the future, whether they would become unemployable, lose their self-respect, or have insoluble money problem. Similar are the findings recorded in an American study of plant closure and employee lay-off conducted by Cobb and Kasl (1977) and Kasl (1979). They have concluded that even the anticipation of being unemployed may lead to increase in depression and feeling of insecurity. In a recent study conducted by Tiwari and Krishna (1999), too, educated unemployed youth in India have been found to run the risk of psychological insecurity. Thus, on the basis of the abovementioned findings, it appears that the unemployed, compared to the employed, suffer a greater feeling of insecurity. However, the findings of those studies need to be verified before generalizing them safely vis-à-vis an alien culture like that of India. This investigation is a step in that direction.

Unemployment and Alienation

Alienation is conceived as a psychological state in which an individual feels relatively powerless and specially isolated, and develops a sense of loss of relationship with others. In extreme forms of alienation, the individual becomes non-involved, apathetic, isolated, bewildered and without hope. A considerable lack of congruence between one's belief about how one should behave and one's actual behaviour is symptomatic of alienation. An alienated individual, according to Rotter, Chance and Phares (1972), generally fancies himself/herself as unable to control his/her own destiny. He/she lives with the thought that he/she is only a small cog in a big machine and is at the mercy of forces too strong or too vague to control. Different other investigators (Davids, 1955; Gould, 1964; Keniston, 1965, 1968; Seeman, 1959) have also identified a variety of syndromes of alienated behaviour, making the term alienation equivocal. However, some of the syndromes of alienation with one name or another have been convincingly accepted in their substance. Hence, for the adequate manoeuvring of the present investigation it was decided to measure the level of alienation in the unemployed and employed people in terms of syndromes like despair, disillusionment, unstructured universe, psychological vacuum, and narcissism, as suggested by Kureshi and Dutt (1979) on the basis of factor analysis.

Flaring-up of the feeling of alienation in its different shades has also been considered to be one of the significant reactions to unemployment. It has not yet, however, attracted much attention from investigators interested in the study of the mental health of unemployed people (Feather, 1990; Warr, 1987c, d), and hence this study. There is a considerable evidence showing that unemployed people carry with them different symptoms of alienation. For example, in a number of studies (Atkinson, Liem and Liem, 1986; Coffield, Borrill and Marshall, 1983; Fryer, 1995a; Kieselbach, 1997a, 1998a; Liem, 1983b, 1988; Liem and Rayman, 1982; Liker and Elder, 1983; Madonia, 1983; Martin and Wallace, 1985; Rantakeisu, Starrin and Hagquist, 1997; Winefield, 1995b) it has been shown that unemployed people experience a fair amount of disruption in their social relationships and contacts with relatives and friends, and develop a strong tendency to withdraw themselves from clubs and groups. Similarly, Briar (1983), Catalano *et al.* (1993), Clark and Clissold (1982) and Dumont (1977) have found that unemployment leads to the development of different syndromes of normless behaviour such as domestic violence, criminal behaviour, divorce, child abuse, suicidal ideation, etc., in those who experience it.

Kieselbach, Beelmann and Stitzel (2000) and Sudan (2000) have also indicated alienation, increased deviant and anti-social behaviour as consequences of unemployment. In a classical study conducted by Eisenberg and Lazarsfeld (1938) it has been recorded that being out of work over a long span of time is the cause of diminished motivation and a state of apathy, resignation, self-doubt, depression and fatalistic beliefs in a person. A similar picture has been presented by Fagin and Little (1984) regarding the psychological state of an unemployed. Banks and Ullah (1987b), Blanch (1990), De Witte (1992), Fryer (1995a), Jackson and Hanby (1982) and Winefield (1995b) have also reported a good deal of apathy and resignation among the unemployed. Likewise, the findings of studies (Breakwell,1986; Clark,1985; Gaskell and Smith,1985; Jackson, 1985) intended to map out the political attitude of the unemployed indicate that, amongst the unemployed, there is considerable disenchantment with or apathy towards the mainstream political system and that the young unemployed express clear verbal attitudes in favour of direct political action, lawbreaking, and violent change.

On the basis of her studies, Jahoda (1982, 1988) has concluded that unemployment undermines the sense of purpose in life, reduces social contacts, results in a loss of status and identity, removes regular activities and develops a feeling of hopelessness — some of the pronounced indicators of alienated behaviour in those who confront it. Referring to the findings of *Marienthal study,* she (Jahoda,1987) has also reported that the unemployed have a terrible feeling of apathy, despair and resignation. Similar are the findings recorded by Jahoda, Lazarsfeld and Zeisel (1971), Liem (1983a) and Powell and Driscoll (1973). Feather (1982) and Winefield *et al.* (1991) have also found that the unemployed, as compared to the employed, have more depressive symptoms, diminished self-esteem, and a higher level of anomie and apathy. In the study by Kelvin and Jarrett (1985), too, it has been shown that prolonged unemployment usually leads to resignation and apathy, but they have called for detailed studies of the process that determine change in reactions. Banks (1990) and Feather and Davenport (1981) have indicated that a prolonged period of unemployment leads to a reduction in the motivation and interest to seek employment. Mehta (1981), on the basis of his general observation, maintains that widespread unemployment, as it exists in

India, may be thought to be responsible for making our youth feel alienated. Rani (1993) and Singh, Singh and Singh (1995) have also found that the educated unemployed youth manifest different symptoms of alienation, although the employed youth, on the whole, have also been found to be moderately susceptible to alienation and its symptoms. In a similar vein, Singh, Singh and Rani (1996a) have found that the technically educated unemployed youth have greater susceptibility to alienation and its dimensions and the non-technically educated employed youth are least affected, with the non-technically educated unemployed and the technically educated employed youth being in second and third places respectively. However, all the groups have either higher or moderate amount of alienation and its dimensions. Thus, it is widely accepted that unemployed people, in general, carry certain significant symptoms of alienation with them.

However, contrary to the aforementioned findings, investigators like Fröhlich (1983a), Stokes (1983), Thomas, McCabe and Berry (1980), Warr (1984c) and Warr and Payne (1983) have reported that the unemployed do not feel themselves socially isolated and do not withdraw themselves from social contact. Nonetheless, studies (Jahoda, 1982, 1988; Singh and Sharma, 1982; Sullivan *et al.,* 1980) conducted to see the impact of economic deprivation on the development of different symptoms of alienation provide plausible reasons to believe that unemployment, being interlinked in its effects with the consequences of poverty (Jahoda, 1982, 1988; Mruck and Mey, 1992; Vasaria, 1980), generates symptoms of alienation in an individual who experiences it. Investigations (Liem, 1983a; Singh, 1994; Y.K. Singh, 1990; Ullah, Banks and Warr, 1985; Verkleij, 1989; Warr, 1985, 1987d, 1989) carried out to see the effect of unemployment on the development of anxiety and maladjustment—the symptoms of alienation (Hajda, 1961; Keniston, 1968)— also directly or indirectly provide sufficient ground for believing unemployment to be the prime cause of alienation. It may be pointed out here that unemployment, as reported by Helpert (1982), destroys an individual's foundation and throws him/her into a state where manifestations of apathy, isolation, resignation, withdrawal, hopelessness, normless behaviour, etc.,—certain significant indices of alienated behaviour (Abhimanyou, 1976; Kureshi and Dutt, 1979; Sinha and Sinha, 1974; S.N.Sinha, 1975)—are natural to prevail. Justifiably, thus, the unemployed, as compared to the employed, may be expected to feel themselves more alienated. Barring a few exceptions, however, systematic efforts to find out the degree and extent of alienation and its dimensions in educated unemployed young men vis-à-vis their employed counterparts in India and abroad, in micro perspective, are almost non-existent. This prompted the present investigation.

Unemployment and Identity-crisis

Identity-crisis or confusion refers to a person's uncertainty about his/her future role in society, as well as a sense of discontinuity between his/her personal past and his/her future (Erikson,1968). As experienced subjectively, it indicates feelings of fragmentation, indecision, and isolation and withdrawal from social and personal contacts. Sinha (1979) holds that a crisis or confusion of identity, in its intense form, manifests itself in terms of a variety of psychological reactions such as distress, anomie, desolation, isolation, loneliness, hopelessness, meaninglessness, depersonalization and a feeling of anonymity. Such an individual may also indulge in fantasy, occasional and repeated introspection, and feel too unsettled to stay in any commitment for a long time. The person may simultaneously feel like being a child and yet like an old person. Identity-confusion is also manifested in the form of excessive self-consciousness arising from an extreme self-doubt. In brief, a person encountering intense identity-crisis may be expected to have inadequate psychological well-being. Hence, in order to have an estimate of the psychological well-being of the educated unemployed young men, the study of the degree of identity-crisis in them deserves thorough consideration.

The evidence that has accumulated over the past few years in India and abroad tends to indicate unemployment as inflicting an adverse effect on the psychological well-being of those who experience it (Fryer, 1995a; Henkel, 1987; Iversen and Sabroe, 1988; Kieselbach and Svensson, 1988; Kieselbach and Wacker, 1985; Rani, 1993; Singh, 1990, 1994, 2001; Singh, Kumari and Singh, 1992; Singh and Singh, 2004; Singh, Singh and Rani, 1996a; Singh, Singh and Singh, 1995; Verkleij, 1989; Warr, 1985, 1987c,d; Winefield, 1995b; Winefield and Tiggemann, 1985). But research into the impact of unemployment on identity-crisis both in India and abroad has not received much attention. However, different dimensions of identity-crisis like anomie, distress, desolation, isolation, loneliness, indecisiveness, hopelessness, meaninglessness, withdrawal from social and personal contacts, etc., have been, to a considerable extent, systematically investigated and as such can be utilized as the basis for forming causal inferences about the impact of unemployment on identity-crisis.

On the basis of a series of investigations, Jahoda (1979, 1981, 1982, 1988, 1995) concludes that the onset of unemployment breaks down a person's habitual time-structure for the waking day, undermines his/her sense of purpose in life, reduces his/her social contacts, results in his/her loss of status and identity, and removes the regular activities that were part of his/her daily life. In addition to these, it develops in him/her a feeling of hopelessness. She has cogently argued unemployment to be leading to the disintegration of the whole life of an individual, pushing him/her into a state of indecision and stalemate. Jahoda and Rush (1980) have also indicated the unemployed as experiencing difficulty in organizing time, isolation, a sense of purposelessness, uncertainty about status and identity, and a state of inaction. In the studies by Fryer and McKenna (1987), Fryer and Payne (1986), Kieselbach (1991), Kieselbach, Beelmann and Stitzel (2000), Payne, Warr and Hartley (1984), Singh (2001), Warr and Jackson (1984, 1985) and Warr (1987d), too, the unemployed have been found to be troubled by a feeling of uncertainty about the future, making them relatively vulnerable to psychological uprootedness. Keupp (1982) has reported that unemployed people run into a deep crisis of identity, thus being exposed to the risk of employing inappropriate psychological interpretation to themselves and to their everyday problems. Similar is the finding of Keefe (1984) wherein it has been shown that the unemployed suffer from loss of identity. As indicated by Banks and Jackson (1982) and Pearlin *et al.* (1981), unemployment, being stressful, implies a threat to the identity of the unemployed people as well as to their self-esteem, social network, and financial security. However, in a lone study by Gurney (1980a, b), in contrast, it has been recorded that the unemployed do not suffer from the trauma of identity diffusion.

Unemployment, according to him, leads to stabilization of identity (Gurney, 1980a) as well as an increase in positive self-evaluation (Gurney, 1980b), particularly in those unemployed who are young. Gurney (1980a, b) is of the opinion that young people do not experience unemployment as a trauma but as a psychosocial respite with which they are able to cope constructively. Yet, there are studies wherein it has been indicated that unemployed people, compared to their employed counterparts, have a higher level of anxiety and distress (Banks and Ullah, 1987a, 1988; Fryer 1995a; Kessler, House and Turner, 1987; Kessler, Turner and House, 1988; Payne and Jones,

1987a; Viney, 1983; Warr, 1987 c,d; Winefield, 1995b), desolation (Jahoda, 1987; Liem, 1983a; Powell and Driscoll, 1973; Rani, 1993; Singh, Singh and Rani, 1996a; Singh, Singh and Singh, 1995), isolation (Atkinson, Liem and Liem, 1986; Coffield, Borrill and Marshall, 1983; Eisenberg and Lazarsfeld, 1938; Liker and Elder, 1983; Liem, 1983b, 1988; Liem and Rayman, 1982; Madonia, 1983; Martin and Wallace, 1985; Miles, Howard and Henwood, 1984; O'Brien and Kabanoff, 1979; Schober, 1978; Verhaegen, Deykin and Sand, 1994), loneliness (Martin and Wallace, 1985; Sabroe and Iversen, 1989; Tiggemann and Winefield, 1980; Verhaegen, Deykin and Sand, 1994; Verkleij, 1989; Warr, 1987c, d), anomie or normlessness (Briar, 1983; Clark and Clissold, 1982; Council of Europe,1985; Dumont, 1977; Winefield *et al.*, 1991), hopelessness (Cochrane and Billig, 1984; Fryer, 1995a; Hepworth, 1980; Harrison, 1976; Hill,1978; Kieselbach, Beelmann and Stitzel, 2000; Verkleij,1989; Winefield, 1995b; Winefield *et al.*, 1991), meaninglessness (Iversen,1989; Jahoda, 1979, 1981, 1982, 1988; Jahoda and Rush,1980; Rani, 1993), depersonalization (Dohrenwend *et al.*, 1980; Dumont, 1977; Kieselbach, 1991; Kieselbach and Svensson, 1988), social conflict (Singh, 2001; Singh, Singh and Rani, 1996b; Sudan, 2000), etc., certain significant indices of identity-crisis.

To summarize, the unemployed, compared to the employed, have been found to run the risk of a deep crisis of identity. It should be noted here that work is central to an individual's self-concept, as a source of values and of structure to life (Kelvin, 1981; Kieselbach, Beelmann and Stitzel, 2000). It helps him/her to develop a sense of personal identity (Erikson, 1968; Gurney, 1980a,b; Jahoda, 1979, 1982, 1988; Super and Hall, 1978; Warr, 1982). Jahoda (1981, 1982, 1987) and Warr (1987d) have reported that employment provides different opportunities for the betterment of one's psychological well-being. Absence of a job, on the other hand, reduces those opportunities and consequently proves detrimental to one's health. Helpert (1982) has rightly remarked that unemployment destroys an individual's foundation, leading to the development of disruption of personal and social relationships in him/her, latent conflicts and regression to sensitive dependence, normlessness, hopelessness, etc., — some of the obvious symptomatic expressions of identity-confusion. Thus, it was justifiably inferred that the unemployed, compared to the employed young men, would have a greater amount of identity-crisis. But the findings recorded from the studies carried out exclusively in European countries cannot be safely generalized in the Indian context where the problem of unemployment is chronic and where people react to it differently on account of the still-continuing, though much reduced, attachment to the extended family norms, though without much hope of getting a job. Hence, the present investigation involving different groups of both technically and non-technically unemployed and employed young men was undertaken to measure the degree and extent of identity-crisis and its dimensions in them at every possible finer level.

Unemployment and Life Satisfaction

Life satisfaction refers to retrospective evaluations of happiness of life through self-judgement. It serves as an index of one's adjustment. A person enjoying high life satisfaction has better personal and social adjustment, while the person lying on the other end has poor adjustment. Rice (1984) and Veenhoven and Jonkers (1984) have indicated it to be positively and strongly associated with absence of psychiatric symptoms. This is why in order to have a precise account of the psychological well-being of an unemployed person, the study of his/her life satisfaction merits consideration.

Life satisfaction of a person has been found to be largely dependent upon his/her economic condition (Alston and Dudley, 1973; Alvaro, 1989; Edwards and Kiemack, 1973; Sinha, 1989), indicating the affluent as enjoying greater life satisfaction and the deprived as shaken at this count. Hence, unemployment, more often a major source of economic hardship (Elder Jr. *et al.*, 1991; Jackson and Warr, 1984; Jahoda, 1982, 1988; Kieselbach, 1991; Liem, 1983a, 1988; Payne, Warr and Hartly, 1984; Verkleij, 1989; Warr,1985, 1987d; Warr and Jackson, 1984), has been expected to lessen one's satisfaction with one's life. Consistent with this expectation, a good number of investigators (Aho, 1981; Alvaro, 1989; Breakwell, Harrison and Propper, 1984; Cobb and Kasl, 1977; Cohn, 1978; Donovan and Oddy, 1982; Fryer, 1995a; Hepworth, 1980; Singh and Singh, 2004; Tiggemann and Winefield, 1980; Winefield, 1995b; Winefield *et al.*, 1991) have reported that the unemployed, compared to the employed, have a decreased life satisfaction. Based on well over a 100 studies, Fryer and Payne (1986) have also concluded that groups of the unemployed have higher mean levels of experienced strain and negative feelings, and lower mean levels of happiness, present life satisfaction, experience of pleasure and positive feelings than comparable groups of the employed. Similar are the findings recorded in the longitudinal studies carried out by Feather and O'Brien (1986a, b,1987), indicating the unemployed, compared to the employed, as reporting themselves as less competent, less pleasant, less active, less satisfied with life, and as having a fair amount of the symptoms of stress and depression. O'Brien and Feather (1990) have also found that the unemployed, compared to the employed, have higher stress, lower life satisfaction, higher depressive affect, lower perceived competence and Protestant ethic scores.

However, they have been found to differ significantly only from those on these variables who are engaged in good-quality employment. They show little difference from the poor employment groups in this regard. Justifying their findings, O'Brien and Feather (1990) have indicated that jobs providing opportunities for the maximum utilization of skills foster the psychological well-being of an individual (an employee), specially encouraging him/her to display lower depressive affect, higher life satisfaction, higher internal control and perceived competence, and to attach importance to the virtues of industriousness and individualism.

On the other hand, according to them, a job that fails to provide scopes for the utilization of skill affects a person's psychological functioning negatively, particularly developing in him/her a greater amount of depression, dissatisfaction with life, feeling of less competence and higher external control. A job of such quality also lessens his/her commitment to industriousness and challenging work. A good number of investigators (Clegg and Wall, 1990; Feather, 1985b, 1990; Fryer and Winefield, 1998; Furnham, 1985; Iversen and Sabroe, 1988; Iversen, Sabroe and Damsgaard, 1989; Kumari, 2001; O'Brien, 1984a, b, 1985b, 1986; Pareek, 1996; Payne, 1995; Rani, 1993; Singh, Kumari and Singh, 1992; Singh, Singh and Rani, 1996a; Warr, 1983, 1987b,d; Winefield, 1995a; Winefield and Tiggemann, 1990a; Winefield, Tiggemann and Goldney, 1988; Winefield, Tiggemann and Winefield, 1991; Winefield *et al.*, 1993; Winefield *et al.*, 1991) have emphasized that not only unemployment but also certain kinds of employment—mundane, routine, and tiring ones, particularly associated with low income, insecurity and poor working conditions offering little opportunity for exercising one's skills in order to experience variety or to exert influence and control over day-to-day activities at the work place—have a damaging effect on one's psychological well-being. However, it is a fact revealed through investigations (Jahoda, 1982; Warr, 1983, 1987d) that unemployed people are denied financial rewards, higher standards of living, and other positive environmental features that can come with paid employment and are deprived of an important role that is deemed to be a normal part of one's experience in a setting that offers the possibility of meeting some basic human needs. This considerably diminishes their life satisfaction. Thus, the unemployed, compared to the employed, would be expected to report diminished life satisfaction. But, it has also been found that there are individual differences in the way people react to unemployment.

Some unemployed people cope better than others and some may even discover sources of satisfaction in the alternative life-styles that they adopt (Feather, 1985a). Further, different rates of unemployment have been found to have different effects upon the psychological well-being of those who experience it (Banks and Ullah, 1988; Dooley, Catalano and Rook, 1988; Jackson and Warr, 1987; Kelvin and Jarrett, 1985; Kieselbach, 1991; Singh, 1994; Singh, Singh and Rani, 1996b). It has also been suggested that cultural variances must be taken into consideration while analysing the effect of unemployment on psychological well-being (Feather, 1990; Rani, 1993; Singh, Kumari and Singh, 1992; Warr, 1984b). Thus, on the basis of the aforementioned findings, nothing conclusive can be deduced as to the impact of unemployment on life satisfaction. It points to the need for further investigation in this regard, especially in a country like India where perhaps no serious efforts have so far been made to find out the degree of life satisfaction in the unemployed, as compared to the employed young people.

Hence, the present investigation is exclusively intended to ascertain the level of life satisfaction in the technically and non-technically educated unemployed young men as against their employed counterparts divided on different criteria. In spite of the diversity of opinion existing among the findings, unemployed people, as has been recorded (Jahoda, 1988; Kieselbach, 1991; Kieselbach, Beelmann and Stitzel, 2000; Kumari, 2001; Pratap and Gupta, 1985; Rani, 1993; Verkleij, 1989), feel dejected and disappointed, and carry with them different negative feelings (such as shame, embarrassment, sense of self-defeat, tension, frustration, etc.), liable to develop in them low satisfaction with life.

Unemployment and Coping Strategies

Coping generally refers to a typical behaviour pattern adopted by an individual to deal with the problems experienced by him. Lazarus (1987) and Lazarus and Folkman (1984) have defined coping as "... constantly changing cognitive and behavioural efforts to deal with specific external and/or internal demands that are appraised as burdensome or exceeding the resources of the person." Therefore, coping, according to them, can be conceived as a changing process that differs from automatized adaptive behaviour and is not essentially equated with adaptational success or with mastery. They consider two main forms of coping: (1) emotion-focused coping, where coping is directed towards regulating the emotional response to the problem, and (2) problem-solving coping, where coping is directed towards managing or altering the problem that is causing the distress. Thus, coping may be conceptualized as a process that helps maintain one's well-being. Factors like health and energy, positive beliefs, commitment that sustains coping, problem-solving skills, social skills, social support, and material resources serve as coping resources. Coping can also be affected by constraints (such as personal constraints, environmental constraints, and level of threat) that restrict the use of resources (Carver, Scheier and Weintraub, 1989; Cohen and Wills, 1985; Dunkel-Schetter *et al.*, 1992; Holahan and Moos, 1987; Lazarus and Folkman, 1984; McGown and Fraser, 1995; Nezu and Nezu, 1987).

People generally resort to different strategies both at cognitive and behavioural levels in order to deal with stress-inducing circumstances. However, as has been pointed out by Pareek (1982), they can be generally categorised under two basic modes of adjustment — approach and avoidance —advanced by Miller (1944, 1951, 1959). Hence, the present study has been aimed at measuring the frequency of strategies like Intrapersistive Approach Mode (IAM), Extrapersistive Approach Mode (EAM), punitive avoidance mode (PAM), and Defensive Avoidance Mode (DAM) adopted by the unemployed, as compared to the employed, in order to deal with their situation. The aforementioned coping strategies, fairly incorporating the essence disseminated in the two most distinctive strategies of approach and avoidance modes, have been recently proposed by Sinha (1989). A short description of them is as follows:

(1) Intrapersistive Approach Mode (IAM). It refers to an individual's plan to take action on his/her own to solve his/her problem. This involves active participation on the part of a person to solve the problem.

(2) Extrapersistive Approach Mode (EAM). It relates to a person's efforts at solving the problems with the help of other individuals or agencies. This involves requesting others for solution or taking help of others to find solution to the problem.
(3) Punitive Avoidance Mode (PAM). It indicates an individual's inability to solve the problem. He/she admits his/her limitations and incapability in finding a clue to his/her problems. He/she either curses his/her lot, and develops a sense of guilt (self blame) or blames the situations and outside forces for his/her failure.
(4) Defensive Avoidance Mode (DAM). A person depending on this coping strategy avoids the problem by denying it. His/her ego-defence mechanisms resort to rationalization for the problem. He/she avoids the problem on hand by ignoring the stress associated with it, and often imagines some unrealistic benefits from it.

As has been mentioned above, one of the important aims of this investigation was to find out the frequency of the different aforementioned strategies resorted to by the educated Indian unemployed and employed young men in order to cope with their various life events which is yet little understood and investigated. However, studies – though few in number – point to different coping patterns in practice among the unemployed (Iversen, 1989). Banks (1990), Kieselbach (1986) and Madonia (1983), for instance, have reported a clear tendency of withdrawal among the unemployed. Similar is the finding recorded by Ullah and Banks (1985) in their study of the unemployed confronting longer spells of unemployment. They have concluded that prolonged unemployment leads to lower expectation of getting a job and a less positive job-search attitude. Increased level of social isolation (Coffield, Borrill and Marshall, 1983; Eisenberg and Lazarsfeld, 1938; O'Brien and Kahanoff, 1979; Verhaegen, Deykin and Sand, 1994) and a fair amount of externality (Feather and Barber, 1983; Feather and O'Brien, 1986a, b; Layton, 1986, 1987; O'Brien, 1984b; O'Brien and Feather, 1990; Patton and Noller, 1984; Rani, 1993; Singh, Singh and Singh, 1996; Singh, Singh and Singh, 1995) among the unemployed, as compared to the employed, also directly and indirectly provide evidence of a clear tendency in them not to face the reality of the situation on their own, indicating them to be dependent upon the strategy of avoidance or withdrawal in order to cope with their life events. The view very much corresponds with the findings of Dunkel-Schetter *et al.* (1992) who have shown that the unemployed largely confide in the strategy of avoidance to withstand their situations. Similarly, Iversen and Klausen (1986) have indicated that an unemployed adapts to his/her plight by accepting it, though partly, as his/her fate. However, Warr (1983), by contrast, has reported that some people cope with unemployment by restructuring the values and conditions related to it. In a similar vein, Banks, Ullah and Warr (1984) have found the young unemployed for a longer duration as generally resorting to three strategies for their coping with unemployment: (a) restricting their social network to contacts with others in a similar position, (b) recognizing and building upon a common identity with the others, and (c) reducing their commitment to the labour market. On the basis of their studies of unemployed men in England, Warr and Jackson (1987) have pointed to three corresponding forms of adaptation that the unemployed resort to in order to cope with their situations:

(1) *Constructive adaptation*, where unemployed people take positive steps to develop interests and activities outside the labour market. Hobbies may be taken up, social networks expanded, and voluntary work for the community initiated and enjoyed. These positive changes can sometimes be assisted through mutual adjustment at the family level (Jackson and Walsh, 1987). Such pattern of adaptation leads to high levels of well-being and raised levels of aspiration, autonomy and sense of competence in them. But, this kind of adaptation, as indicated by Fryer and Payne (1984), is only adopted by psychologically privileged or proactive unemployed workers; it is not popular with all kinds of work-seekers. Similarly, in the study by Gurney (1980a, b) young people, unemployed for a shorter duration, cope constructively with their situation as a result of their experiencing the unemployment not as a trauma, but as a psychosocial respite.

(2) *Resigned adaptation* is a more common form of adaptation involving reduced aspirations and lower emotional investment in the environment. By adopting this form of adaptation, the unemployed people withdraw themselves from job-seeking, depend upon limited routines of behaviour, and protect

themselves from threatening events by avoiding new situations and potentially stressful or expensive activities. Although such resigned adaptation, according to Warr and Jackson (1987), may occur with a slight improvement in affective well-being, the parallel decrements that appear in aspiration, autonomy, and personal competence are usually considered to be unhealthy. By wanting less, long-term unemployed people achieve less, and become less.

(3) *Despair*, where unemployed people express a reduced level of aspiration and subsequent strong negative psychological reactions.

In addition to the aforementioned strategies adopted by unemployed people for their coping, as outlined by different investigators, Starrin and Larsson (1987), on the basis of their study for analysing the patterns of reactions among women in Sweden to unemployment in relation to wage labour and other alternative activites, have identified four different groups of unemployed people: (1) the 'give-uppers', (2) the 'clenchers', (3) 'the refocusers',and (4) the 'ambivalents', and have indicated that while the former two are particularly more vulnerable to negative consequences of unemployment and relatively passive in their activities, the latter groups have been found to enjoy their lives and to recompensate the loss of work by engaging themselves in other meaningful activities.

Thus, different strategies, as has been identified by the investigators, are adopted by unemployed people to deal with their life situation. The selection of various strategies for coping, to a great extent, has been found to depend on the nature and kinds of unemployment. Surprisingly, however, hardly any effort has been made to measure the frequency of approach and avoidance modes — the two basic modes of adjustment — among the unemployed in India in making their attempt to deal with their situations. Withdrawal and avoidance modes, rather than constructive and approach modes, are the prime coping strategies of adjustment of the unemployed people. As is evident from the review of relevant literature, this aspect of the unemployed young men in India has not received much attention of the investigators. These were the reasons for the initiation of the present investigation which aimed at defining the coping patterns of different groups of technically and non-technically educated unemployed young men as against their employed counterparts, measured in terms of the frequency of the same.

2

Objectives and Hypotheses

Objectives of the Investigation

Unemployment in India has attained alarming proportions. According to a recent estimate in 1995, the total number of the jobless had shot up to about 36,565.800 thousand. The predicament of highly educated (matriculates and above) and well-qualified people at the count of employment is fraught with all sorts of uncertainties. Astonishingly, by the end of 1995 the number of educated job-seekers in the country increased by leaps and bounds (nearly 46.65 times from 1961), constituting about 75.28 per cent (i.e., about 27,525.000 thousand) of the total unemployed (see chapter 1st, p. 5). Recently, Ray (1995) has also reported that the incidence of unemployment among the educated is much higher (12.0%) than the overall usual status unemployment of 3.77 per cent . As may be noticed, despite various concerted efforts initiated both at governmental and non-governmental levels to wipe out the malady of unemployment from the land for ever, it has become nightmarish. The vast majority of skilled and unskilled workers are hit by periods of unemployment of various durations each year. The problem of unemployment is, indeed, rooted deep in the very soil of the country and implies a major epidemiological disaster. The horrible state of our youth, particularly the educated ones, has influenced them adversely.

Unemployment has put them at particularly high risk; their psychological health is extremely palpable. A growing feeling of loss, low self-esteem, lack of self-confidence and self-control, despair, insecurity, lower level of adjustment, disillusionment, alienation, high guilt feeling, irritability, externality, psychiatric morbidity, lack of structured and purposive use of time, etc., are some of the serious psychological consequences of unemployment (Kumari, 2001; Rani, 1993; Singh, 1990, 1994, 2001; Singh, Kumari and Singh, 1992;

Singh and Singh, 2004; Singh, Singh and Rani, 1996a, b; Singh, Singh and Singh, 1996; Singh, Singh and Singh, 1995; Y. K. Singh, 1990; Sinha and Mallick, 1990). Thus, unemployment has placed a great burden on an important segment of our population which possesses great potential. What is most surprising is that such a vital issue has not yet attracted attention of our social scientists considerably. So much so that psychological research into the effects of unemployment is not of a very recent origin.

A historical account of the systematic investigation into the impact of unemployment may be found in the works of Bakke (1933, 1940 a, b), Beales and Lambert (1934), Eisenberg and Lazarsfeld (1938), Jahoda, Lazarsfeld and Zeisel (1933), Komarovsky (1940), Pilgrim Trust (1938), Zawadski and Lazarsfeld (1935), and so on. However, a spate of excellent reviews relating to this topic has appeared only in recent years (e.g., Allatt and Yeandle, 1992; Banks and Ullah, 1988; Barling, 1990; Feather, 1990; Fineman, 1987; Fryer, 1988, Fryer and Payne, 1986; Fryer and Ullah, 1987; Kieselbach, 1991; Kieselbach, Beelmann and Stitzel, 2000; Kieselbach *et al.*, 2001; Leana and Feldman, 1992; O'Brien, 1986; Schwefel, Svensson and Zöllner, 1987; Starrin, Svensson and Wintersberger, 1989; Voydanoff and Majka, 1988; Warr, 1987d; Winefield, 1995a, b, 1997; Winefield *et al.*,1993; Young and Borgen, 1990), providing a systematic account of different aspects associated with the impact of unemployment. Surprisingly, in India, too, systematic research involving variables used as the indices of psychological well-being is scant. The present investigation was thus aimed at studying the psychological well-being of the educated unemployed young men as against their employed counterparts measured in terms of anxiety, stress, feeling of insecurity, alienation, identity-crisis and life satisfaction. In addition, the study was also purported to find out the strategy generally adopted by the unemployed and employed people in order to adjust with their life events. The study of the impact of unemployment on psychological well-being and coping styles was taken into consideration on account of the following reasons :

(1) These variables, as is apparent from the inspection of the relevant literature on 'Unemployment and Mental Health' cited in the preceding section of this report, are the indicators of one's mental health.

(2) Investigations carried out to see the relationship of unemployment with the aforementioned variables are almost non-existent in our country, justifying the inclusion of these variables into the purview of the present investigation.

(3) The study is expected to provide a plausible ground to treat unemployment as one of the significant causative factors of poor psychological health.

Precisely, this study is expected to enrich our knowledge about the psychological well-being of our educated unemployed *vis-à-vis* employed young men measured in terms of the aforementioned psychological variables. Also, it is expected to add to our understanding as to the coping patterns of different groups of unemployed and employed people.This, in turn, is supposed to help educationists, planners, and social workers to chalk out plans and policies suitable for the betterment of the unemployed people. In brief, the study may help develop a holistic approach to deal with the malady of joblessness among the educated youth in India through a unified action plan.

Hypotheses

Taking into account the aims and objectives of the investigation, the following hypotheses were framed for verification :

(1) The educated unemployed young men, in general, would express poor psychological well-being as compared to their employed counterparts.

(2) The technically educated unemployed, compared to the non-technically educated unemployed, would be more vulnerable to psychological ill-health.

(3) The technically educated unemployed young men, as against their employed counterparts, would confront a higher level of morbidity in their psychological health.

(4) The non-technically educated unemployed vis-à-vis their employed counterparts would express poor psychological well-being.

(5) The technically educated employed young men, compared to the non-technically educated employed young men, would have superior psychological well-being.

(6) With an increase in the duration of their status, the unemployed, irrespective of their forms and streams of education, would show greater damage in their psychological well-being, but the reverse would be seen in the case of the educated employed.

(7) Different groups of unemployed and employed people would show marked difference in the use of different strategies resorted to cope with their life situations.

Theoretical Foundation of the Hypotheses

Different theoretical assumptions were taken into account as the logical bases of the hypotheses formulated for verification. Of them, the following were important:

The Social Exchange Theory (Blau, 1964; Burgess and Huston, 1979; Homans, 1961; Kelley, 1979; Rusbutt, 1980; Thibaut and Kelley, 1959) was, first, taken into consideration to justify the above hypotheses. According to this theory, which is in line with the *'Karma'* theory of Hindu philosophy, one receives rewards in proportion to costs and investments incurred. Any anomaly (i.e., negative outcome or even the anticipation of it) in it may compel a person to develop different reactions to distributive justice manifested in terms of different maladaptive behaviours. Education, especially the technical and professional education in India, is a relatively costly affair. Apart from making other sacrifices, one has to meet tremendous expenses to acquire knowledge and education. The technically educated young men apparently invest more towards acquiring a skill (in the form of number of years put in for mastering a skill, difficulties faced during that period, financial investment, etc.) and hence expect greater rewards as compared to their counterparts — the non-technically educated young men. But, in the face of an acute shortage of jobs, what remains for them is only unemployment. Educated young men, as indicated earlier, are also the worst victims of the problem of joblessness. They also face the grim reality that there is no way out except to surrender themselves to their fate. If there are schemes for their support and amelioration at both governmental and non-governmental levels, they are, for whatever reason, often considered by them to be of no use. Such a state of affairs makes them feel that they are being denied their due from all quarters. One cannot continue with the trauma of injustice for long; one has to succumb in the end. Hence, the technically educated unemployed young men were expected to express greater morbidity in their psychological functioning as compared to the non-technically educated unemployed young men. Investigators like Fineman (1983), Kaufman (1982), Leventhman (1981) and Singh, Singh and Rani (1996a) have also concluded that the psychological effects of unemployment are likely to be more intense as well as damaging for the highly educated and for professionals than for other job-seekers. Earlier, Brenner (1973) has also indicated that people coming from high social-class suffer more during an economic downturn. As is apparent, however, from the findings of a good number of investigations (Cohn, 1978; Hartley,1980; Rani, 1993; Shamir, 1986; Singh, 1994; Singh, Singh and Rani,1996b), it is also a fact to be noted that their educational superiority serves as a recompense, reducing the damage that unemployment inflicts.

Jahoda's Functional Approach (Jahoda, 1979, 1981, 1982, 1988, 1995; Jahoda and Rush, 1980) — a psychological deprivation model— though subjected to certain criticisms (Clegg and Wall, 1990; Feather, 1985b, 1990; Fryer, 1986; Fryer and Payne, 1986; Furnham 1985; Kessler, Turner and House, 1987; Kuhnert, 1989; O'Brien, 1985b, 1986; O'Brien and Feather, 1990; Schaufeli and Van Yperen, 1992; Swan, Dame and Carmelli, 1991 ; Winefield and Tiggemann, 1990a; Winefield, Tiggemann and Goldney, 1988; Winefield, Tiggemann and Winefield, 1991; Winefield *et al.*, 1991), was also one of the main theoretical positions available for providing plausible ground for the genuineness of the hypotheses framed for verificaton. According to Jahoda (1979, 1981, 1982, 1988, 1995), despite the dissatisfactions and frustrations accompanying their work, people are still motivated more positively towards working than not working. As she (Jahoda, 1979) puts it, "people want to work even when they hate it." She has further stated that employment serves two functions — the manifest and the latent psychological functions. The manifest function of employment is income and the latent psychological functions are time structure, enlargement of social experience, involvement in collective purposes, personal identity and activity. Jahoda (1981, 1982) has asserted that the relatively poor psychological functioning of the unemployed is due to their inability to satisfy their need for income as well as their latent psychological functions. Undeniably, failure to excercise these functions leads the unemployed to experience distress and change in self-concept, making them vulnerable to poor psychological well-being. Following Freud's (1930) views, Jahoda

(1982) has further stressed that work is man's strongest tie to reality. Unemployment, therefore, weakens a person's contact with reality and affects the person's ability to gratify certain basic human needs. To be precise, an unemployed person is deprived of many opportunities which employment offers. This exposes him/her to reduced psychological health.

Vitamin Model propounded by Warr (1987d) was also taken into account in order to rationalize the aforementioned hypotheses. In his vitamin model, Warr (1987d) has attempted to generalize that unemployment leads to a decrease in one or more of the nine environmental features—opportunity for control, use of skills, externally generated goals, variety, environmental clarity, availability of money, physical security (accommodation, food, etc.), opportunity for interpersonal contact, and valued social position. Thus, in most cases, according to him, the unemployed people have reduced opportunities for enjoying the benefits of different environmental features which are to facilitate their mental health. The model has received a considerble support and has been frequently used as the basis for the scientific explanation of the impact of the status of employment on health (Dooley, Rook and Catalano, 1987; Fryer, 1988; Fryer and McKenna, 1987; Kessler, Turner and House, 1988; Kieselbach,1991; Ronayne, Ryan and Cullen, 1989; Verkleij, 1989, Warr, 1987f, 1989). However, Warr (1987d) has not denied the toxic consequences of the vitamin—the environmental features—when taken at very high levels, leading to the conclusion that both maximal and minimal supportive environments constitute threat to one's mental health.

Erikson's Stage Theory of Psychosexual Development (Erikson, 1950, 1959, 1968, 1980, 1982) was also used to search out the basis for the tenability of the hypotheses. Based on this theory for the explanation of the relatively higher level of well-being of the employed, compared with the unemployed young men, Gurney (1980a, b) has extended a view that youth, when employed, have more opportunities to negotiate satisfactorily the stage of industry and competence. Unemployment is considered a barrier to successful transition through the industry stage and consequently leads to stagnation in psychological growth.

A Cumulative Stress Model proposed by Jackson and Warr (1984) was another theoretical formulation which was taken into consideration to find a genuine logical basis for the hypotheses formulated.

According to this model, unemployment, a kind of economic deprivation, brings a 'shock' and carries with it a 'range of stressors' (psychological, social and economic) which cumulatively reduce the well-being of an individual facing the problem of unemployment (Jackson and Warr, 1984). These may range from threats to self-esteem arising from continued failure in job-seeking to the need for greater personal and financial adjustments as time passes. On the basis of such a cumulative stress model, they have emphasized that unemployment for a longer duration would bring about a gradual deterioration in psychological health. Unemployment, evidently, removes some powerful supports to our psychological well-being. Thus, financial strain and distress emanating from joblessness (Jackson and Warr, 1984; Payne, Warr and Hartley, 1984; Warr and Jackson, 1984) can be taken to precipitate psychological uprootedness.

Thus, different theoretical bases were formulated to justify the tenability of the hypotheses framed for verification. But, it seems prudent to note here that owing to lack of opportunites and partial attachment to the extended family norms, the scene of unemployment in India is somewhat different from that which can be envisaged in the developed nations. Broadly, there are two distinct categories of unemployment —the short-term and the long-term (chronic unemployment). As may be commonly observed, on account of the underlying association with the concept of kinship with extended family norms, and the general tendency — an outcome of our typical easy-going temperament — to consider short-term unemployment as transitory and incidental, the problem of short-term unemployment is not thought of as acute and serious as the long-term one. But, the findings are rather conflicting in this regard (Bolton and Oatley, 1987; Jackson and Warr, 1984; Narayan, 1995; Warr and Jackson, 1984, 1985, 1987), as also there is lack of suitable guidelines to categorize a person either under short-term or long-term unemployed group on the basis of his/her experience of the problem of unemployment for a certain period. Wide variation follows in developed and developing or underdeveloped nations in distinguishing between the short-term and the long-term unemployed on the basis of their experience of their condition for a particular duration. This is why in order to have an objective estimate of the impact of unemployment on psychological well-being and coping styles, all those subjects were approached for this study who had been encountering the problem either for shorter or longer durations. The review of relevant literature furnished in the preceding section on the nexus between joblessness and the psychological well-being of an individual has also provided ground for justification of the different hypotheses formulated for verification in the present investigation.

Coping styles adopted by the unemployed *versus* the employed have been little investigated. As a consequence, no specific trend is available. Also, dependence on a particular coping strategy in making one's adjustment with one's environment is greatly influenced by certain socio-psychological variables (Blake and Vandiver, 1988; Carver, Scheier and Weintraub, 1989; Dunkel-Schetter *et al.*,1992; Halstead, Johnson and Cunningham, 1993; Holahan and Moos, 1985; McCrae, 1982; McGown and Fraser, 1995). These posed difficulties in the search of a reasonable ground to formulate a specific hypothesis in this connection. However, studies on the difference between the unemployed and employed people in terms of their psychological functioning (see Introduction and Overview for a detailed account) were utilized to form a logical basis in order to formulate as well as to rationalize the hypothesis of difference between the unemployed and the employed young men in terms of the degree of their reliance upon strategies devised for adjustment.

3

The Strategy of Investigation

Unemployment and Employment : An Operationalization

The present study was aimed at presenting an account of the inter- and intra-group comparisons of educated unemployed young men (experimental groups) against their employed counterparts (control groups) with regard to their psychological well-being measured in terms of variables like anxiety, stress, feeling of insecurity, alienation, identity-crisis, and life satisfaction both at macro as well as micro levels. In addition, the study was also intended to find out the degree of their dependance on different strategies resorted to effect a compromise with their lot. Status of employment (unemployment/ employment) was thus naturally treated as input (independent variables) and the psychological well-being as well as coping styles as its output (dependent variables). Unemployment has been variously defined and classified, largely depending on the socio-economic conditions of the country concerned, and the strategies and policies of the government in power there.

Different kinds of unemployment have been shown to have different implications for one's mental health (Fryer and Payne, 1984; Gniazdowski, 1987). Interestingly, for example, it has been observed that voluntary unemployment is not as debilitating psychophysically as the involuntary one (Fryer, 1995a; Fryer and Payne, 1984; Fryer and Winefield, 1998; Jahoda, 1979; 1982; Jin, Chandrakant and Svoboda, 1995; Swan, Dame and Carmelli, 1991; Warr, 1987d ; Winefield, 1995b). It is also important to note the view of L.B. Singh (1990) who feels that on account of lack of opportunities for jobs and the obsessive attachment to the extended family norms in India, the problem of short-term unemployment is not considered as acute and serious as that of the long-term (prolonged) one. But, mainly on account of the expected difficulties in managing the study as well as meeting the costs on it, it was not deemed practical to study the impact of all kinds of unemployment on psychological well-being. Hence, 'unemployment' was operationally defined at the very outset, that is, prior to the selection of sample units. Of the various definitions of unemployment available (Dholakia, 1977; Hayes and Nutman, 1981; Jahoda, 1982; Kelvin and Jarett, 1985; Mamoria and Mamoria, 1984), the one by Warr (1987d), based mainly upon the concept of "involuntary unemployment", was adopted for use. Thus, for the purpose of the present investigation, not only people out of job but also people looking for gainful employment were classified as being unemployed. Consequently, adults below the age of entering the job who do not have a job but who are not looking for one (those who are voluntarily caring for their children or otherwise not wanting employment due to some reason or the other like health problems, family responsibilities, etc.) —the non-employed (Warr, 1987d) — were excluded from the category of the unemployed. As such, it was decided to study only those technically and non-technically educated young men who, apart from being involuntarily unemployed, also had their names in different District Employment Exchanges of undivided Bihar (eastern India) for a certain period.

The group of technically educated unemployed consisted of graduates and postgraduates of engineering, medical and agriculture sciences, and the non-technically educated unemployed young men included general graduate and postgraduate degree-holders in the arts and humanities, commerce, social, and natural sciences.

Employment, on the other hand, was also variously defined and classified (Anderson, 1974; Garraty, 1978; Handy, 1984; Jahoda, 1982; Kabanoff, 1980; Parker, 1983; Warr, 1987d). It has also been recorded that different kinds of employment have different impacts on one's mental health. There is considerable evidence (Ahmad and Khanna, 1992; Bajaj, 1982; Barnes, 1992; Feather, 1985b, 1990; Furnham, 1985; O'Brien, 1985b, 1986; O'Brien and Feather, 1990; Kumari, 2001; Pestonjee and Singh, 1982; Rani, 1993; Singh, 1994, 2001; Singh, Kumari and Singh, 1992; Singh, Singh and Rani, 1996a, b; Singh, Singh and Singh, 1995) to indicate that while poor jobs (such as less paid, mundane, routine and tiring ones, particularly associated with poor working conditions offering little opportunity to exercise one's skills in order to experience variety or to exert influence and control over day-to-day activities at the workplace, etc.) are not conducive to one's health, jobs providing an opportunity for a larger economic gain (manifest functions) and the fulfilment of different latent psychological needs (such as structuring of time, enlargement of social experience, being able to be engaged in purposeful activity, acquiring status and social identity, etc.) support one's well-being. In view of this complexity, in order to maintain the precision and comprehensibility of the present investigation, the term 'employment' was also conceptualized afresh. For the present purpose, therefore, only those people were categorised as employed who were permanent employees in state enterprises and had not only been getting proportionate economic reward (salary) against the labour rendered by them (Basic salary ranging from Rs. 2200 to Rs. 3700 per month) but also enjoyed other facilities that involved their rights and responsibilities. The group of educated employed people was also divided into technically and non-technically educated employed young men, and involved individuals who had graduate and postgraduate degrees in one faculty or the other.

Thus, on the basis of the operational definitions of the terms, unemployment and employment, certain criteria—the primary criteria—were fixed for the selection of subjects, and it was decided to include only those subjects in the domain of the study who were seen as fulfilling them (see pages from 64 to 66).

The Setting

Over-population, inequality, illiteracy, inter-group conflict and disharmony, poverty and unemployment are some of the vital problems in India, posing a serious threat to its all-round development and integrity. But the problem that has implied a major epidemiological catastrophe for the country's health is unemployment. A sizeable number of our potential work force has been experiencing the trauma of worklessness in the wake of large-scale unemployment confronting the entire nation. Bihar is one of the states where the problem of unemployment has taken a serious turn. Perhaps, the state is the worst victim of the catastrophe of unemployment *vis-à-vis* other regions/ states of the country. As per a recent estimate obtained from different Employment Exchanges in undivided Bihar, about 3666.458 thousand persons were found to be registered as work-seekers at the end of Dec.,1991 (Hemant, 1994). However, there appeared a somewhat noticeable decline in the number of job-seekers in the state in 1992 and 1993 with the load of 3433.228 and 3340.041 thousand respectively. But, the trend could not continue for long. The number of the unemployed again increased to 3722.098 thousand in 1994, and 3729.527 thousand in 1995 respectively (The Office of the Central Employment Exchange, Patna, Bihar, 1995). And, if it is not tackled seriously, the number of job-seekers is expected to mushroom to about 9600.000 thousand by 2002 AD (Hemant, 1994). The situation is undeniably alarming.

The number of employment-seekers is increasing by leaps and bounds, viz., at the rate of an addition of about 800.000 thousand new faces in the labour market per year (Hemant, 1993, 1994), considerably swelling the size of the unemployed in the state. More than half of them (about 2300.000 thousand) were matriculates and above. Even people with high academic achievements and qualifications can be seen loitering about the roads in search of jobs. Also, other reports (*The Hindustan*, Patna, 1st Feb., 1993; *The Times of India*, Patna, 18th July, 1992; *The Times of India,* Patna, 30th April, 1994) on employment shrinkage in Bihar have given a sad commentary on the baffling state of employment in the state. For example, while the Bihar government (The Minister of State for Labour) itself has admitted the state as carrying the burden of altogether 5300.000 thousand unemployed persons (*The Times of India,* Patna, 18th July, 1992), the Hindustan Correspondent (*The Hindustan*, Patna, 1st Feb., 1993) holds that more than 67 per cent of Bihar's population have been experiencing the problem of unemploymemt. Admittedly, this alludes to the woeful state of employment in erstwhile Bihar, in particular, and the global context of the country, in general, mounting an excruciating pressure not only on the individuals who experience it but also on the nation as a whole. Table 3.1 focuses on the state of unemployment in the different districts of undivided Bihar at the end of 31st Dec., 1991.

An analysis of the figures reported in Table 3.1 indicates that while the district of Dhanbad, followed by Patna, confronted a greater problem of unemployment, the district of Lohardagga as well as Gumla was the least affected. However, none of the districts had zero level unemployment. All the districts were found to be facing a considerable threat by an army—the army of the unemployed. But, this alone does not provide a real picture of the state of unemployment in the different districts of undivided Bihar. Hence, in order to make the picture clearer, the escalation of the job-seekers in each of the districts was determined by taking into account their total population, as obtained from the

Table 3.1 : Distribution of Unemployment in Different Districts of Undivided Bihar by the End of 31st. Dec., 1991

	Districts	*Number of the Unemployed (in thousand)*	*Percentage Unemployment*
1.	Patna	335.829	09.16
2.	Nalanda	115.757	03.16
3.	Bhojpur	076.826	02.10
4.	Rohtas	051.121	01.39
5.	Gaya	108.155	02.95
6.	Jahanabad	029.871	00.81
7.	Nawada	043.861	01.20
8.	Aurangabad	035.973	00.98
9.	Saran	066.849	01.82
10.	Siwan	063.946	01.74
11.	Gopalganj	034.774	00.95
12.	Muzaffarpur	140.538	03.83
13.	Sitamarhi	054.283	01.48
14.	Purbi Champaran	056.334	01.54
15.	Paschimi Champaran	047.633	01.30
16.	Vaishali	053.263	01.45
17.	Darbhanga	078.329	02.14
18.	Madhubani	086.258	02.35
19.	Samastipur	115.726	03.16
20.	Begusarai	068.137	01.86
21.	Saharsa	066.432	01.81
22.	Madhepura	045.685	01.25
23.	Khagaria	105.719	02.88
24.	Purnea	076.864	02.10
25.	Katihar	038.235	01.04
26.	Bhagalpur	137.894	03.76
27.	Munger	055.923	01.53
28.	Dumka	051.261	01.40
29.	Deoghar	033.789	00.92
30.	Godda	032.304	00.88
31.	Sahebganj	040.967	01.12
32.	Dhanbad	336.640	09.18
33.	Bokaro	186.562	05.09
34.	Giridih	028.355	00.77
35.	Hazaribagh	101.406	02.77
36.	Ranchi	195.527	05.33
37.	Gumla	023.307	00.64
38.	Lohardagga	013.553	00.37
39.	Palamu	166.146	04.53
40.	Purbi Singhbhum	175.639	04.79
41.	Paschimi Singhbhum	090.787	02.48
	Grand Total	3666.458	100.00

Sources : The Office of the Central Employment Exchange, Patna, Bihar., Hemant (1994). *Bihar mein rojgar ke ghatate awasron se sthiti visphotak* (Explosive situation in Bihar due to decreasing job-opportunities). *(Hindustan,* Patna.

Table 3.2 : Distribution of Population and Proportion of Unemployment in Different Districts of Undivided Bihar

Districts	*Distribution of Population as per 1991 Census Report (in thousand)*	*Percentage Unemployment*
1. Patna	3623.225	09.27
2. Nalanda	2003.313	05.78
3. Bhojpur	3784.204	02.03
4. Rohtas	3681.875	01.39
5. Gaya	2665.217	04.06
6. Jahanabad	1173.071	02.55
7. Nawada	1358.433	03.23
8. Aurangabad	1537.946	02.34
9. Saran	2562.930	02.61
10. Siwan	2159.346	02.96
11. Gopalganj	1701.365	02.04
12. Muzaffarpur	2946.601	04.77
13. Sitamarhi	2388.822	02.27
14. Purbi Champaran	3042.303	01.85
15. Paschimi Champaran	2330.610	02.04
16. Vaishali	2144.252	02.48
17. Darbhanga	2509.083	03.12
18. Madhubani	2828.640	03.05
19. Samastipur	2715.297	04.26
20. Begusarai	1813.214	03.76
21. Saharsa	3133.556	02.12
22. Madhepura	1178.060	03.88
23. Khagaria	0986.731	10.71
24. Purnea	4474.104	01.72
25. Katihar	1821.590	02.10
26. Bhagalpur	4237.145	03.25
27. Munger	3917.724	01.43
28. Dumka	1497.266	03.42
29. Deoghar	0918.323	03.68
30. Godda	0858.678	03.76
31. Sahebganj	1297.391	03.16
32. Dhanbad	2709.170	12.43
33. Bokaro	1447.870	12.89
34. Giridih	2224.006	01.27
35. Hazaribagh	3301.508	03.07
36. Ranchi	2205.034	08.87
37. Gumla	1153.557	02.02
38. Lohardaga	0288.585	04.70
39. Palamu	3057.807	05.43
40. Purbi Singhbum	1617.170	10.86
41. Paschimi Singhbum	1789.796	05.07
Grand Total	93084.818	03.94

Source : *Manorama Yearbook 1993, 1994,* Kottayam: *Malayala Manorama.*

1991 census report. Table 3.2 presents a distribution of the population together with the proportion of the unemployed in different districts of undivided Bihar.

A look at the populationwise figure of the unemployed in different districts of undivided Bihar revealed a somewhat different trend of unemployment, Bokaro being the worst victim of the problem (12.89%), followed by Dhanbad (12.43%), Purbi Singhbhum (10.86%), Khagaria (10.71%), Patna (09.27%), Ranchi (08.87%), Palamu (05.43%), and Paschimi Singhbhum (05.07%) respectively. On the other hand, districts like Giridih (01.27%), Rohtas (01.39%), Munger (01.43%), Purnea (01.72%), Purbi Champaran (01.85%), Gumla (02.02%), and Bhojpur (02.03%) were not as hard hit by the problem of unemployment. However, South Bihar (05.76%), compared to North (03.37%), was found to be confronting more serious problem of unemployment. It was further apparent that almost every twentyfifth person in undivided Bihar was encountering the problem of joblessness. But, if we concentrate on the potential wage earner, i.e., 20 to 34 years age group constituting about 21.75 per cent of the total population of the state (*Bihar : Ek Jhalak*, 1993) in the course of analysing the escalation in the problem of unemployment in undivided Bihar, a rather lurid picture of employment may emerge. One out of every 05.52 persons representing the potential labour force can be identified to be out of job. This figure, however, too, is not realistic as a number of job-seekers, owing to some reason or the other, are often unwilling to get their names registered in the employment market. Quite a few reports appearing in the *Times of India*, Patna, March 8, 1992 also confirm this view. This clearly indicates that any data regarding joblessness in undivided Bihar are far from reality. One out of every 3 or 4 persons having all required potentialities for employment is counted as hapless in the absence of a job. Thus, the state is plagued with a relatively high level of unemployment, nearing 25 per cent or more. Virtually, the majority of people are in a state of uncertainty, moving from pillar to post even for a square meal. The catastrophe of unemployment seems to have sealed the fate of the state. This, of course, is a pathetic state, and deserves special consideration, lest the state may reach a point of no return.

In order to make further inroads into the understanding of the actual state of unemployment in undivided Bihar it was thought necessary to take into account a sex-wise distribution of job-seekers in rural and urban areas. Table 3.3 contains an overall account of sex-wise distribution of unemployment in the rural and urban areas of

Table 3.3 : Sex-wise Distribution of Unemployment in Rural and Urban Areas of Undivided Bihar by the End of 31st Dec., 1991

Sex	*Rural (in thousand)*	*Urban (in thousand)*	*Total (in thousand)*
Male	1983.619	1449.553	3433.172
Female	0132.258	0101.028	0233.286
Total	2115.877	1550.581	3666.458

Source : *The Office of the Central Employment Exchange,* Patna, Bihar.

undivided Bihar.

Persons inhabiting undivided rural Bihar constituted about 57.71 per cent of the unemployed in the state. In both rural and urban backgrounds, males were found to be affected more seriously by the problem of unemployment and overall represented 93.64 per cent of the total unemployment of the state. Ratio-wise, males, as compared to females, suffered 14.72 times more the problem of unemployment. Such a wide gap between the number of male and female unemployed people may be mainly due to the distribution of their roles prescribed in the Indian society. The society being patrilineal, females are fully dependent upon males for their maintenance; they are not expected to engage themselves in outside jobs, family chores being their sole responsibility. Apparently, the women folk do not consider themselves unemployed. They generally evaluate their status on the basis of the status of their spouse or any other prominent male member. Educational awareness in females, of late, has greatly changed their attitude towards employment, but even the educated do not like to step out of home for a job and always long to cling to their traditional roles or are made to do so by others. Though undivided rural Bihar has been witnessing a greater problem of unemployment, the evil is relatively more frightening in undivided urban Bihar which, though it forms only 13.14 per cent of the total population of the state (*Bihar: Ek Jhalak,* 1993), has been bearing the burden of more than 13.50 per cent unemployed people of its population — the ratio being more than approximately 5 times greater than the ratio of the unemployed in undivided rural Bihar, carrying a load of merely about 2.80 per cent unemployed persons of its population. This clearly indicates an awful state of employment in the urban setting of undivided Bihar. However, this also is not the whole fact. The macabre state of unemployment in undivided urban Bihar would appear more menacing if we concentrate mainly on the potential labour force (20 to 34 years age group), constituting about 29.76 per cent, i.e., 27700.000 thousand of the total population of the state Census Report, 1991), in course of the analysis of the problem of joblessness in urban setting. Further, an unemployed person in undivided urban Bihar, as can be commonly observed, is simply deprived of the opportunity of kinship support as well as integrative social network to fight with his/her lot, consequently making him/her relatively liable to impaired mental health.

The above figures, however, present only a general picture of unemployment in the state. They do not categorically narrate the predicament of the educated unemployed having degrees or diplomas in different faculties of knowledge. Table 3.4 displays the distribution of unemployment in educated persons having the degree of matriculation and above.

Table 3.4 : Distribution of Unemployment in Educated Persons (Matriculates and above) in Undivided Bihar by the End of 31st. Dec., 1991

Academic Qualifications	*Number of Unemployed (in thousand)*	*Percentage*
1. Matriculates	1584.359	66.88
2. Intermediate (I.A. + I.Sc. + I.Com)	387.661	16.37
3. Bachelor degree-holder (B.A. + B.Sc. + B.Com)	301.946	12.75
4. Master degree-holders (M.A. + M.Sc. + M.Com)	29.659	01.25
5. Engineers (B.Tech. + M.Tech)	09.497	00.40
6. Doctors (M.B.B.S. + M.S. + M.D.)	01.771	00.07
7. Veterinary degree-holders	00.012	00.00
8. Agriculture degree-holders (B.Sc.Ag. + M.Sc. Ag)	02.431	00.10
9. Degree-holder in Education (B.Ed. + M.Ed.)	14.580	00.62
10. Law degree-holders (L.L.B. + L.L.M.)	00.320	00.01
11. Diploma in Engineering	18.601	00.79
12. I.T.I.	16.777	00.71
13. Technical Apprentices	01.198	00.05
Total	2368.812	100.00

Sources : *The Office of the Central Employment Exchange*, Patna, Bihar; Rani, A.(1993). *Behavioural Manifestations of Unemployed Youth.* Ph.D. Thesis, T.M. Bhagalpur University.

Matriculates constituted the larger portion (66.88%) of the educated unemployed group followed by intermediates (16.37%) and non-professional Bachelor Degree-holders (12.75%). But, all the degree-holders were found to be facing the problem of unemployment to some extent or the other. Overall, it was found that all the groups of the educated lot, whether they were professionally or non-professionally educated, encountered the problem of unemployment and represented about 64.61 per cent of the total unemployed in the state. Further, if we consider the problem of unemployment among the educated in the context of total education in the state we will find a very dismal picture. As per a recent estimate, educated people formed about 38.48 per cent of the total population of the state (Census Report, 1991). Of them, the highly educated unemployed formed 06.61 per cent. But, if we take the total of highly educated (matric and above) in the state, and analyse the distribution of unemployment in them, a very frightening picture may emerge.

As per the 1991 Census report, the matric and above-educated groups represent about 13.50 per cent of the total educated in the state and alarmingly 89.28 per cent of them are unemployed. Not an exaggeration, there appears no hope of a halt in this connection. The problem of unemployment is apparently growing with a fast rate even in graduate and postgraduate degree-holders. As per an estimate (The Office of Central Employment Exchange, Patna, Bihar, 1995), 336.922 thousand, 565.767 thousand, 369.293 thousand, and 396.034 thousand graduate and postgraduate degree-holders in different faculties of technical and non-technical education alone were afflicted with the problem of joblessness during the year of 1992, 1993, 1994 and 1995 respectively. This shows that higher education, even the technical and the professional, has apparently no meaning for job-seekers in undivided Bihar. So much so that even the highly educated persons are facing this ordeal. Hence, it was decided to concentrate on those unemployed young men in this study who were technically and non-technically graduate and postgraduate degree-holders in different disciplines of knowledge.

An overall analysis of the problem of unemployment in undivided Bihar from diverse angles leads to the conclusion that undivided urban Bihar is facing the problem of unemployment relatively more acutely, particularly the educated unemployment. Hence, it was decided to conduct the present investigation on the educated unemployed young men inhabiting the urban areas of Patna, Gaya, Muzaffarpur, Khagaria,

Bhagalpur, Bokaro, Dhanbad, Ranchi, Purbi Singhbhum (Jamshedpur) and Paschimi Singhbhum (Chaibasa) districts of undivided Bihar. Except a few, these districts had frighteningly iniquitous concentration of the unemployed, and this was the prime reason for selecting them as venues for the present investigation.

Control of Extraneous Variables

Recent reviews (Kieselbach, 1991; Kieselbach, Beelmann and Stitzel, 2000; Warr, Jackson and Banks, 1988; Winefield, 1995b, 1997) on the impact of status of employment (unemployment/employment) have indicated that its effects on well-being are considerably mediated by a number of personal and background variables. Similarly, the strategies by which one copes with one's environment are also affected by such variables (Dunkel-Schetter *et al.*, 1992; McGown and Fraser, 1995). Age (Banks, 1990; Banks and Jackson, 1982; Banks and Ullah, 1987a, 1988; Brinkmann, 1984; Broomhall and Winefield, 1990 ; Cullen *et al.*, 1987; Daniel, 1974; Feather and O'Brien, 1986 a, b, 1987; Garcia Rodriguez, 1994 ; Hepworth, 1980; Herzog, Rodgers and Woodworth, 1982; Jackson, 1987; Jackson and Warr, 1984, 1987; Kieselbach. 1988a; McCrae, 1982; McGown and Fraser, 1995; Rowley, 1985; Rowley and Feather, 1987; Spruit and Svensson, 1987; Viney, 1983; Warr, 1987 c,d,f; Warr and Jackson, 1985; Warr, Jackson and Banks, 1988; Wets and De Witte, 1997), sex (Banks, 1990; Bolton and Oatley, 1987; Brinkmann, 1976, 1984; Daniel, 1974; Halstead, Johnson and Cunnigham, 1993; Houtman, 1990; Jick and Mitz, 1985; Kessler and McRae, 1981; Lahelma, 1992; Lahelma and Kangas, 1989; Leana and Feldman, 1991; McGown and Fraser, 1995; Muller, Hicks and Winocur, 1993; Narayan, 1995; Payne and Jones, 1987 a,b ; Raj, 1995; Warr, Banks and Ullah, 1985; Warr and Jackson, 1985; Warr, Jackson and Banks, 1982, 1988; Warr and Parry, 1982), education (Banks and Ullah, 1986; Banks, Ullah and Warr, 1984; Brinkmann, 1984; Fineman, 1983; Ioannidis and Mestheneos, 2000; Kaufman, 1982; Kieselbach, Beelmann and Stitzel, 2000 ; Leventhman, 1981; McGown and Fraser, 1995; O'Brien, 1986; Pearlin and Schooler, 1978; Schaufeli, 1988b; Shamir, 1986; Warr, 1984a, 1987d; Wuggenig, 1985), socio-economic status (Catalano and Dooley, 1983; Dunkel-Schetter *et al.*, 1992; Kaufman, 1982; Kessler, 1979; Kessler and Cleary, 1980; Kessler, Turner and House, 1987; Kouveli, Tsakiris and Sakellaropoulous, 1998; McGown and Fraser,

1995; McKenna and Payne, 1984; Menaghan, 1983; Payne and Hartley, 1987; Payne, Warr and Hartley, 1984; Rodgers, 1991; Rowley and Feather, 1987; Townsend and Davidson, 1982; Warr, Jackson and Banks, 1988; Whelan, 1992), residence (Banks, 1990; Banks and Ullah, 1986, 1988; Cohn, 1978; Dooley, Catalano and Rook, 1988; Jackson and Warr, 1987; Narayan, 1995), duration of unemployment (Banks, 1990; Bolton and Oatley, 1987; Brinkmann, 1984; Brenner and Levi, 1987 a, b; Brenner and Starrin, 1988; Feather and Davenport, 1981; Finlay-Jones and Eckhardt, 1984; Fryer and Payne, 1986; Hammarström and Olafsson, 1997; Jackson and Warr, 1984; Jones, 1992; Kumari, 2001; Narayan, 1995; Narendranathan, Nickell and Metcalf, 1982; Payne and Jones, 1987a,b; Ronayne, Ryan and Cullen, 1989; Rowley and Feather, 1987; Singh, 2001; Verkleij, 1989; Warr and Jackson, 1984, 1985, 1987; Warr, Banks and Ullah, 1985; Warr, Jackson and Banks, 1982), etc., are some of the personal and background variables found to have a moderating effect upon the impact of unemployment on well-being as well as on the preference for certain strategies for adjustment.

Hence, in order to eliminate the effects of these variables, two procedures for controlling—the matching and the addition of extraneous independent variable as a second independent variable—were taken into consideration. While following the latter procedure the duration of unemployment and employment was included in the study as a moderator independent variable, and its contribution to mediating the effect of status of employment (unemployment/employment) on psychological well-being and coping styles was analysed by comparing the psychological health of different groups of the unemployed and employed young men for different durations the former procedure, the matching, was adopted to negate the confounding effects of age, sex, education, socio-economic condition and residence from the study. For ensuring the comparability, the following criteria—the secondary one — were devised for the selection of subjects from different treatment and control groups:

(a) Age of the subjects	:	22 to 34 years
(b) Sex	:	Male
(c) Education	:	Graduate and postgraduate degree-holders
(d) Socio-economic condition	:	Middle class family; income ranging from Rs. 2,200 to Rs. 3,700 per month

(e) Residence : Urban
(f) Duration of the status of employment : 0 - 1 to 7 - above years

Thus, to have an adequate and representative sample, only those subjects were sorted out for inclusion in the list of samples who were found to be fulfilling the above criteria.

Selection of Sample and its Procedure

Relying upon the primary criteria, mainly involving the specification of the universe of the investigation adopted for the identification of the unemployed and employed young men (see from pages 64 to 66), initially 1577 technically and non-technically educated registered involuntary unemployed young men vis-à-vis their employed counterparts (N = 955) working in the state public enterprises located in different abovementioned districts chosen as venues for this study were selected as subjects to participate in this study. The method of systematic sampling was devised in order to sort out the subjects from the live registers of different Employment Exchanges as well as the attendance registers of the employees available with the concerned offices. But this was not the end of the story of selection procedure, and ensuring of equivalence among different groups of unemployed and employed young men in terms of their different personal and background characteristics mediating the impact of unemployment and employment on psychological health and coping styles. Hence, in order to ensure the comparability among different groups of subjects, secondary criteria (control mechanism) by using the procedure of frequency (average) matching was followed for the selection of subjects. It further reduced the size of the sample to 1072 unemployed and 623 employed young men respectively, and warranted simultaneously comparability and equivalence among them in terms of the secondary criteria. Thereafter, employing the procedure of systematic simple randomized sampling (sampling with replacement), 614 unemployed and 410 employed people were sampled out for the final study. In order to attain the purpose of the investigation, the two main exclusive groups were further divided into subgroups like (1) technically educated unemployed young men (N = 206), (2) non-technically educated unemployed young men (N = 408), (3) technically educated employed young men (N = 132), and (4) non-technically educated employed young men (N = 278) respectively. The former two groups served as treatment groups, and the latter ones as control groups. These four groups were again divided into different subgroups (08 in number) specially on the basis of their degrees and diplomas in the specific stream of knowledge. Further, all these groups were divided on the basis of the experience of the duration of their status of employment, and altogether 36 sets of respondents were formed. This aimed at increasing the predictability of the findings of the study at every possible level.

Comparability among the Groups

Though both the primary and secondary criteria furnished for the selection of the subjects were fully followed in selecting the subjects from different unemployed and employed groups, in order to ensure the objectivity of the comparability among the technically and non-technically educated unemployed and employed young men in terms of different aforementioned extraneous independent variables, the mean scores obtained by them in relation to their age and socio-economic conditions were compared statistically. Findings of the statistical comparison among different groups of unemployed and employed people with regard to the aforementioned two influencing independent variables are being displayed in Table 3.5.

Table 3.5 : Statistical Comparison Among Different Groups of Educated Unemployed and Employed Young Men in Terms of their Age and Socio-economic Conditions

Variables	*Technically Educated Unemployed (N = 206)*		*Non-technically Educated Unemployed (N =408)*		*Technically Educated Employed (N =132)*		*Non-technically Educated Employed (N = 278)*		
	Mean	*SD*	*Mean*	*SD*	*Mean*	*SD*	*Mean*	*SD*	*F*
Age	29.97	6.01	30.02	5.92	30,07	5.89	30.11	6.05	1.06
Economic Condition	2772.35	32.65	2772.52	31.87	2773.07	32.29	2773.02	31.92	0.94

Note : $df = 3,1020$; $p < 0.05 = 2.37$; $p < 0.01 = 3.32$.

Findings of statistical comparison among different unemployed and employed groups in terms of their age and socio-economic conditions indicated them as evenly comparable with regard to age [F (3,1020) = 1.06; $p > 0.05$] and economic condition (F= 0.94 ;

$p > 0.05$) and thus ensured their non-confounding effects on the findings expected out of the study.

However, with a view to broadening the predictability of the findings as well as for ascertaining the mediating effects of different spells of the status of employment on psychological health as well as coping styles all the eight groups of the unemployed and employed young men from different streams of education were further divided into different subgroups on the basis of the record of the duration of their experience of unemployment and employment. In all, 50 comparison groups were formed. Thus, the sample design finally emerged as follows (see Figure 3.1) :

Scales and Measures

Generally, it is easier to collect data from a sample of students rather than unemployed and employed people. The unemployed, because of their prejudices and complexes, avoid developing any contact with researchers and often become passive to any sort of enquiry. The employed, on the other hand, are mostly preoccupied with their own business, and are seldom willing to participate in an investigation demanding a long span of time. Hence, in the present study, effort was made to use verbal tests of relatively shorter length with easily comprehensible items. The selection and development of the scales and measures were based on certain scientific and practical considerations. Besides, being reliable and valid, it was also exigent that they be conveniently administered and scored. Further, the subjects participating in the investigation being graduate and postgraduate degree-holders, and belonging to a Hindi-speaking area, they were fit for self-rating verbal test materials in Hindi for eliciting information regarding the expressions of the dimensions under study. The battery of the psychological measures selected and developed for use in the study consisted of the following :

(1) A Shorter Version of Sinha's W.A.Self-analysis Form,
(2) Stress Scale,
(3) Mohsin Security-Insecurity Test,
(4) Alienation Scale,
(5) Identity-crisis Scale,
(6) Life Satisfaction Scale,
(7) Strategy of Adjustment Questionnaire, and
(8) Personal Data Sheet.

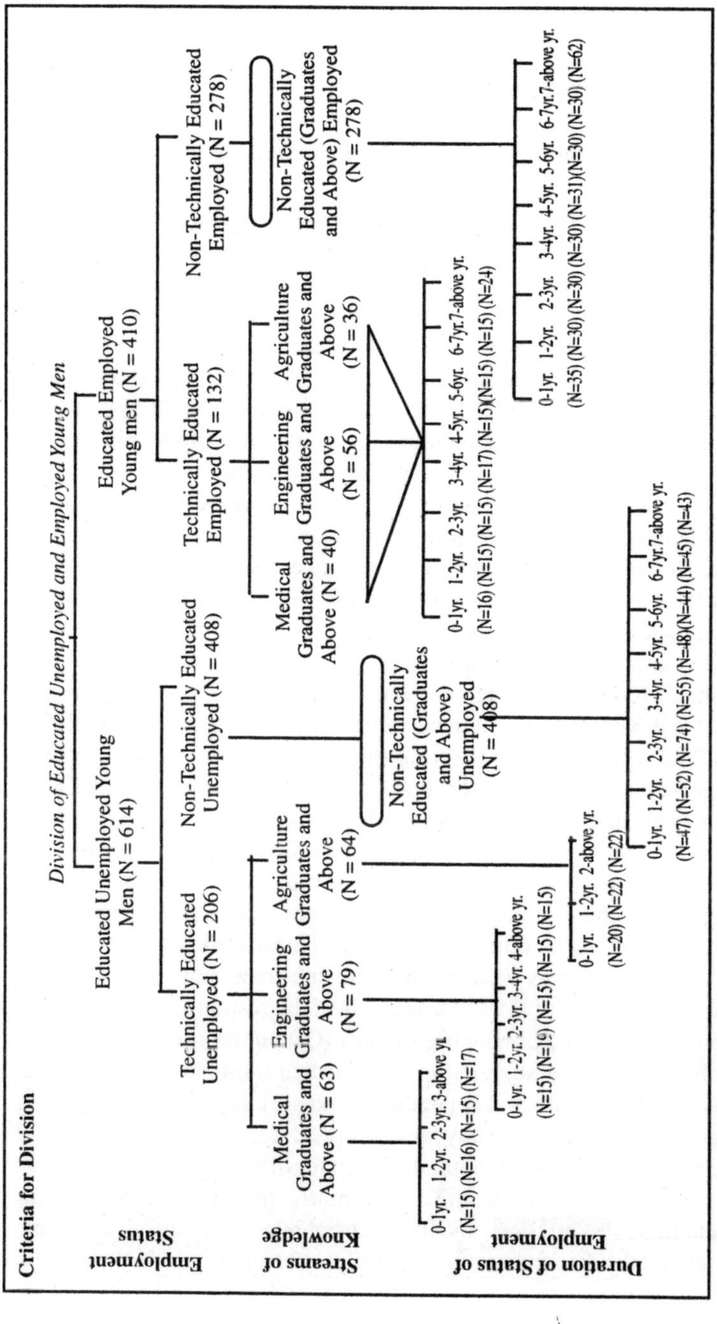

Fig. 3.1 : An Elaborate Sample Design, Number in parentheses indicates strength of the subjects in each of the groups.

A short description of development and standardization as well as the salient features of the aforementioned measures can be envisaged in the following pages:

A Shorter Version of Sinha's W.A. Self-Analysis Form

A 30-item shorter version (Khan and Hassan,1981) of Sinha's (1968) W.A. self-analysis form in Hindi with forced choice alternatives of 'yes' or 'no' was devised to find out the extent of anxiety in the subjects related to areas like general worries, somatic manifestations, psychological symptoms, and social relations. The other two areas associated with health and appearance, and guilt and shame, also measured by the original scale, were excluded. The subject's task was to read each of the statements carefully and select either of the alternatives to indicate his/her responses. Each item which was checked as 'yes' was awarded the score of one. The score of every individual would be the total number of items checked positively. Thus, the total score which one could achieve ranged between 0 and 30. Higher scores in each of the areas, as also in terms of the total scale, pointed towards pathogenic state of anxiety besetting an individual in different areas, as also at the level of his/her total anxiety. Like the original scale (Sinha, 1968), the shorter version of the anxiety scale (Khan and Hassan,1981) had also an acceptable amount of split-half reliability ($r = 0.72$) and validity, justifying the ubiquity of the scale for use in the present investigation. But before using it finally, its suitability for the present investigation was freshly determined by employing it on an incidental sample of 100 non-technically educated unemployed young men of Bhagalpur city. In addition to following different precautions, the scale was subjected to item analysis. Discriminatory Power (DP) of each of the items subsumed in the scale was determined, and only those items were retained for the scale which possessed at least the DP value of 0.50. An analysis of the responses of two sets of respondents — one having high scores (Q_3) on the anxiety scales and another having low scores (Q_1)— indicated 08 items mainly related to the areas of health and appearance, and guilt and shame as eliciting inconsistent responses. They were dropped, leaving the scale with 22 discriminatory items distributed as such for different areas of anxiety : 06 for general worries, 03 for somatic manifestations, 05 for psychological symptoms, and 08 for social relations respectively. Table 3.6 reports the discriminatory values of the retained items in the anxiety scale.

Table 3.6 : A Comparison of the Responses of High (Q_3) and Low (Q_1) Scoring Subjects in Terms of the Items Retained for W.A. Self-Analysis Form

No of Items	*Upper Quartile* X_1	*Lower Quartile* X_2	*Mean Differences* X_1-X_2
1.	0.75	0.15	0.60
2.	0.80	0.18	0.62
3.	0.90	0.09	0.81
4.	0.88	0.16	0.72
5.	0.76	0.20	0.56
6.	0.70	0.12	0.58
7.	0.80	0.08	0.72
8.	0.84	0.22	0.62
9.	0.90	0.10	0.80
10.	0.60	0.06	0.54
11.	0.70	0.09	0.61
12.	0.72	0.09	0.63
13.	0.65	0.08	0.57
14.	0.90	0.15	0.75
15.	0.92	0.30	0.62
16.	0.73	0.14	0.59
17.	0.85	0.18	0.67
18.	0.87	0.23	0.64
19.	0.77	0.14	0.63
20.	0.72	0.20	0.52
21.	0.86	0.16	0.70
22.	0.82	0.13	0.69

Thus, the items included in the modified version of the shorter form of Sinha's W.A. Self-analysis Form possessed satisfactory discriminatory power, affirming the modified version as not encouraging inconsistent responses. To ensure internal consistency of the modified version, the Cronbach Alpha coefficients and $\bar{r}_{ij}$ of various subscales, as also of the total scale, were freshly determined by concentrating on the responses of 100 non-technically educated unemployed young men. The coefficients of consistency were found to be 0.67 (0.25) for general worries, 0.61 (0.34) for somatic manifestations, 0.69 (0.31) for psychological symptoms, 0.65 (0.19) for social relations subscales, and 0. 76 (0.13) for the modified version of the total anxiety scale respectively. Thus, the scale had a sufficient measure of reliability. But, in order to ensure its applicability for other unemployed and employed groups participating in the study, its internal reliability was further determined for those groups by following the procedure adopted in the case of non-technically educated unemployed people. Table 3.7 presents an account of r_{tt} and $\bar{r}_{ij}$ for different subscales, as also for the modified version of the total scale of anxiety, for different groups : (1) the technically educated unemployed (N = 100), (2) the technically educated employed (N = 100), and (3) the non-technically educated employed young men (N = 100).

Table 3.7 : Showing r_{tt} and $\bar{r}_{ij}$ of Each of the Subscales Together with the Modified Version of the Total W.A. Self-analysis Form for Different Groups

Areas of Anxiety	*Technically Educated Unemployed*		*Technically Educated Employed*		*Non-technically Educated Employed*	
	r_{tt}	$\bar{r}_{ij}$	r_{tt}	$\bar{r}_{ij}$	r_{tt}	$\bar{r}_{ij}$
1. General Worries (N = 06)	0.65	0.24	0.63	0.22	0.66	0.25
2. Somatic Manifestations (N = 03)	0.58	0.32	0.61	0.34	0.57	0.31
3. Psychological Symptoms (N = 05)	0.64	0.26	0.67	0.29	0.65	0.27
4. Social Relations (N = 08)	0.68	0.21	0.64	0.18	0.67	0.20
Anxiety (N = 22)	0.74	0.12	0.77	0.13	0.78	0.14

Note : Figures in parentheses indicate the number of items in each of the subscales and the total scale.

Thus, the different subscales, as also the full scale, had adequate reliability, and were easy to apply and score, recommending them for suitable measure of anxiety in different areas and in totality.

Stress Scale

To measure the extent of stress and its various manifestations (e.g., suicidal tendency or ideation, emotional instability, paranoid tendency, depression, physical illness, social maladjustment, and apprehension) in different groups of educated unemployed and employed young men was another important aim of the present investigation. A number of scales (Holmes and Rahe's Schedule of Recent Experiences, 1967; Sarason, Johnson and Siegal's Life Experiences Survey, 1979; Dube, Sundaram, Mohan and Jain's Scaling of Life Events, 1980; O'Brien's Stress Symptoms Scale, 1981; Singh, Kaur and Kaur's Presumptive Stressful Events Scale, 1981, etc.) were available for use in the present study. However, the suitability of these scales is a subject of discussion as it has been frequently observed that the translated as well as the adapted versions of the tests developed in the west do not often cater to the needs of the cultural specificity of a complex culture such as that of India (Mukherjee, 1980; Sinha, 1983). With this fact in mind and subsequently in order to have a reliable and valid measure of stress and its manifestations, a 5-point Likert type stress scale was developed and standardized. A short description of the scale-development is as follows:

Framing of Items

Before framing items for the measurement of stress and its manifestations, the specific aim of the present investigation was determined. Thereafter, a perusal of authentic literature on stress (see *Stress and Anxiety* by Sagar Sharma in J. Pandey (Ed.), *Psychology in India: The State-of-the-Art* (Vol.1), 1988; *Stress and Anxiety* (Vol. 6), edited by I.G. Sarason and C.D. Spielberger, 1979) as well as rigorous consultations and discussions with the investigators involved in the study of status of employment and stress in India and abroad, as also an assessment of the observational data obtained from the behaviour pattern of the unemployed and employed people provided insight into idertifying the items potent in measuring stress and its aforementioned manifestations. Next, these items were framed in the form of statements in Hindi by fully taking into account the nature, characteristics and various behavioural indices of stress and its dimensions. Initially, altogether 52 items covering all the dimensions of stress were framed for the scale. These items along with the operational definitions of stress and its different dimensions with a short introduction of the aims of the project were given to a panel of 10 experienced judges associated with the Psychology Department of T.M. Bhagalpur University. They were requested to determine the content validity of these items, and to classify them for each of the dimensions of the proposed stress scale. On the basis of their comments, only those items were singled out for inclusion in the scale which received high consensus (at least 80%) with respect to their appropriateness in eliciting precise and objective information about stress in its totality. Eleven items not deemed representative of the universe of the content were dropped. Thus, in all, 41 items were retained for the scale. These items were further subjected to a pilot study involving 50 educated unemployed young men of Bhagalpur city to determine their applicability and expression. An analysis of their responses further led to the elimination of 07 such items as were identified as ambiguous and producing inconsistent responses. Thus, the initial form of the scale was left with 34 items, qualifying the objective in question.

Tryout and Discrimination Analysis

The preliminary form of stress scale with complete instructions was further tried out on a sample of 100 non-technically educated unemployed people selected through the incidental sampling procedure with an aim to ensure the Discriminatory Power (DP) of each of the items incorporated in the stress scale. According to Black and Champion (1976), items producing inconsistent responses do not possess adequate discriminatory power for the simple reason that if one has high scores on a scale, one would tend to respond to each of the items of that scale in such a way that one could be able to muster high scores on them and vice versa. Following the above conviction, responses elicited by each of the subjects towards each of the items of the scale were arranged systematically and their responses were analysed objectively. On the basis of the findings, two sets of respondents—one having high scores (Q_3) and another having low scores (Q_1) —were classified. Further, an attempt was made to detect those items regarding which the two groups had expressed inconsistent responses. In such cases, DP of 1.00 was accepted as a cutting point and all items (07 in number) having DP below this level were dropped, reducing the size of the scale to only 27 items. Table 3.8 gives an account of the retained items along with the values of their discriminatory power.

These items were further checked and rearranged systematically to ensure that items associated with different dimensions of stress scale were randomly distributed. This was done in order to control the chances of response biases (Hulin, 1982) in the calculation of the scale scores. But to ensure further applicability of the scale a second tryout was carried out.

Second Tryout and Final Form of the Scale

In order to determine the internal consistency (item validity) of the scale, the 27-item modified form of the stress scale was readministered

Table 3.8 : A Comparison of the Responses of the Subjects Belonging to Upper and Lower Quartiles in Terms of the Items Retained for Stress Scale

No of Items	*Upper Quartile* X_1	*Lower Quartile* X_2	*Mean Differences* $X_1 - X_2$
01	2.30	1.45	0.85
02	2.65	1.36	1.29
03	2.88	1.00	1.88
04	2.70	1.36	1.34
05	2.80	1.09	1.71
06	2.20	1.40	0.80
07	2.70	1.18	1.52
08	2.55	1.36	1.19
09	2.96	1.09	1.87
10	2.25	1.65	0.60
11	3.36	1.09	2.27
12	2.77	1.27	1.50
13	2.90	1.32	1.58
14	3.45	1.00	2.45
15	3.30	1.09	2.21
16	3.66	1.09	2.57
17	3.42	1.18	2.24
18	2.85	1.00	1.85
19	3.10	1.09	2.01
20	3.50	1.18	2.32
21	2.95	1.00	1.95
22	2.82	1.00	1.82
23	1.80	1.00	0.80
24	3.80	1.18	2.62
25	2.30	1.45	0.85
26	2.70	1.36	1.34
27	3.55	1.09	2.46
28	1.90	1.36	0.54
29	3.00	1.00	2.00
30	3.10	1.12	1.98
31	2.75	1.00	1.75
32	2.40	1.82	0.58
33	3.15	1.20	1.95
34	2.92	1.56	1.36

to the same sample of 100 subjects after an interval of one month. On the basis of their scores towards each of the items, inter-item correlation as well as item-whole correlation was computed by employing the Method of Product Moment Correlation. Table 3.9 reports the findings.

All items, except 03, of the scale were found to be interwoven positively and significantly with each other, as also with the total scale

Table 3.9 : Inter-Item and Item-Whole Correlations Computed for the Scale of Stress in the Case of Non-technically Educated Unemployed Young Men

No.of Items	*1*	*2*	*3*	*4*	*5*	*6*	*7*	*8*	*9*	*10*	*11*	*12*	*13*	*14*	*15*	*16*	*17*	*18*	*19*	*20*	*21*	*22*	*23*	*24*	*25*	*26*	*27*	*Total*
01	x	29	28	26	31	29	32	27	25	24	28	30	28	32	28	27	28	30	31	32	30	29	30	29	35	28	33	45
02		x	26	27	34	22	29	21	30	31	23	28	33	24	27	25	29	35	32	21	30	34	26	23	28	31	29	53
03			x	28	30	29	31	25	36	27	32	24	22	26	17	29	35	38	27	23	32	37	26	23	33	22	28	58
04				x	23	27	30	34	24	32	26	22	35	25	21	28	29	33	39	26	30	32	21	34	29	31	24	41
05					x	25	29	31	23	22	31	34	24	36	23	27	33	29	36	28	22	26	30	37	21	29	30	49
06						x	22	26	31	34	23	25	33	37	31	26	29	33	28	22	33	36	24	25	31	32	26	52
07							x	30	36	32	24	29	26	29	31	33	23	28	34	31	22	29	30	31	26	29	22	47
08								x	28	26	22	27	31	35	23	30	26	32	37	24	29	33	35	31	23	24	29	61
09									x	23	26	29	30	34	24	32	25	28	32	36	17	33	29	22	38	33	26	55
10										x	28	23	29	30	25	26	33	34	24	32	28	26	31	27	34	36	23	59
11											x	31	24	16	25	34	27	30	36	23	29	21	32	22	28	31	29	63
12												x	27	24	28	32	30	36	23	25	34	36	22	26	23	33	27	57
13													x	32	34	26	24	29	30	23	32	27	28	37	22	35	30	64
14														x	24	29	30	28	23	32	36	33	25	29	26	34	33	56
15															x	22	29	23	30	32	29	34	37	28	26	30	27	51
16																x	28	33	36	23	26	37	30	25	24	18	32	48
17																	x	30	34	26	29	32	28	37	28	33	31	64
18																		x	24	29	26	30	35	23	32	36	28	54
19																			x	30	24	28	33	37	26	22	34	62
20																				x	33	24	29	31	26	35	27	46
21																					x	35	25	30	27	28	36	59
22																						x	29	28	26	34	30	48
23																							x	25	30	34	26	51
24																								x	27	33	31	53
25																									x	24	30	56
26																										x	28	55
27																											x	47
Total																												x

Note : Decimals are omitted; $df = 98$; $p < 0.05 = 0.20$; $p < 0.01 = 0.25$.

scores. These three insignificantly related items were dropped in the final round, leaving the scale with 24 items distributed in the following order in different subscales: suicidal tendency (N= 01), emotional instability (N= 02), paranoid tendency (N= 03), depression (N= 09), physical illness (N = 03), social maladjustment (N = 03), and apprehensiveness (N = 03) respectively.

Instructions and Scoring Procedure

Each subject was requested to go through each of the statements carefully and indicate his responses towards them on their left side just by putting the assigned value for one of the five select response alternatives — very much (04), much (03), little (02), very little (01), and not at all (00) — fully applicable to him in his own eyes. Thus, the scale was easily scored by calculating the values specified by a subject to indicate his responses against each of the statements. The sum of scores obtained in terms of different subscales provided the measure of stress as a whole. The possible score a person could achieve on the total stress scale ranged between 0 and 96 with higher score denoting higher level of stress in him.

Estimation of Reliability

Several methods exist for determining the reliability of a measuring instrument. These methods may be divided into two broad categories: (1) external consistency procedures, and (2) internal consistency procedures. Though both the procedures have their own advantages and limitations, for convenience the latter was adopted as the measure of reliability. Notably, there were a number of formulae to compute internal consistency (r_{tt}) of a scale. But since there was a wide variation in the number of items incorporated in various subscales of stress scale and, surprisingly, the subscale measuring suicidal tendency or ideation had only one item, Hoyt's (1941) formula was used to determine r_{tt} . Table 3.10 follows r_{tt} and $\bar{r}_{ij}$ of the various subscales, as also of the total scale of stress.

Thus, the different subscales as well as full stress scale reflected evidence of a fair amount of internal consistency. Though it was also desirable to find out the temporal stability of the scale, according to Black and Champion (1976), the knowledge regarding the internal consistency of a test fairly increases the chances of the test being

Table 3.10 : Showing r_{tt} and $\bar{r}_{ij}$ of Each of the Subscales Together with Total Stress Scale for the Group of the Non-technically Educated Unemployed Young Men

Dimensions of Stress	*No. of Items*	r_{tt}	$\bar{r}_{ij}$
1. Suicidal Tendency	01	0.49	0.49
2. Emotional Instability	02	0.57	0.40
3. Paranoid Tendency	03	0.61	0.34
4. Depression	09	0.75	0.25
5. Physical Illness	03	0.68	0.41
6. Social Maladjustment	03	0.64	0.37
7. Apprehensiveness	03	0.67	0.40
Stress	24	0.81	0.15

reasonably reliable at another front, too. But, in order to ensure its applicability for other unemployed and employed groups, its internal stability was further determined for those groups by employing the procedure adopted in the case of non-technically educated unemployed people. Table 3.11 follows the results of r_{tt} and $\bar{r}_{ij}$ of each of the subscales, as also of the total scale of stress for the groups as the technically educated unemployed (N = 100), the technically educated employed (N = 100), and the non-technically educated employed (N = 100).

Table 3.11 : Showing r_{tt} and $\bar{r}_{ij}$ of Each of the Subscales Together with Total Stress Scale for Different Groups of Educated Unemployed and Employed Young Men

Dimensions of Stress	*Technically Educated Unemployed*		*Technically Educated Employed*		*Non-technically Educated Employed*	
	r_{tt}	$\bar{r}_{ij}$	r_{tt}	$\bar{r}_{ij}$	r_{tt}	$\bar{r}_{ij}$
1. Suicidal Tendency	0.47	0.47	0.44	0.44	0.46	0.46
2. Emotional Instability	0.59	0.42	0.56	0.39	0.60	0.43
3. Paranoid Tendency	0.63	0.36	0.58	0.32	0.64	0.37
4. Depression	0.68	0.19	0.71	0.21	0.67	0.18
5. Physical Illness	0.66	0.39	0.65	0.38	0.66	0.39
6. Social Maladjustment	0.69	0.43	0.62	0.35	0.67	0.40
7. Apprehensiveness	0.64	0.37	0.61	0.34	0.60	0.33
Stress	0.74	0.11	0.76	0.12	0.73	0.10

Thus, the different subscales as well as total stress scale were found to have a fair amount of internal stability, the latter substantiating them as being dependable measures of stress and its dimensions in all the groups.

Estimation of Validity

Since psychological measures are indirect, incomplete and relative (Bhushan, 1984; Marshall and Hales, 1972), determination of validity of a psychological test poses serious problems. This is the reason behind the psychologists advocating the working out of different kinds of validity of a test. In the present case, two types of validity — Content and Factorial — of stress scale were determined.

Content Validity

It may be recalled that only those items were sorted out for item analysis which were unanimously judged as representing the particular dimensions of stress scale. Those items were dropped which were either judged as related to more than one dimension or not related to any of the dimensions of stress in the opinion of the judges. This ensured the content validity of the scale of stress.

Factorial Validity

In an attempt to determine the factorial validity of the stress scale, intercorrelations between the scores obtained on different subscales of stress and also of their independent association with total scale scores were computed by employing the method of Product Moment Correlation. Table 3.12 summarizes the findings.

Table 3.12 : Inter-correlations Between Different Subscales and Total Scale Scores of Stress (Data Based on the Report of the Non-technically Educated Unemployed Young Men)

Dimensions of Stress	*1*	2	3	4	5	6	7	*Stress*
1. Suicidal Tendency	x	53	48	71	37	44	57	67
2. Emotional Instability		x	41	51	39	62	56	63
3. Paranoid Tendency			x	56	47	59	66	71
4. Depression				x	58	61	39	64
5. Physical Illness					x	37	57	59
6. Social Maladjustment						x	59	63
7. Apprehensiveness							x	68
Stress								x

Note : Decimals are omitted; $df = 98$; $p<0.05 = 0.20$; $p<0.01 = 0.25$.

Thus, the stress scale, systematically developed and standardized, exhibited a fair amount of reliability and validity. These qualities of the stress scale established its suitability for the intent in question.

Mohsin Security-Insecurity Test

A 60-item secruity-insecurity test (MSIT) developed by Mohsin (1981) in Hindi, a widely used test in psychological researches, was used to gather informations about the feeling of security-insecurity in the subjects. Like the Likert one, responses elicited by the subjects were coded 01 to 05 for each item and total score obtained by them on the test therefore ranged from 60 to 300 with higher scores denoting greater degree of insecurity. The test had reasonable odd-even (0.88) as well as test-retest (0.71) reliabilities along with an evidence of adequate validity, prompting to select it as an instrument for the measurement of the degree of security-insecurity feeling in the subject. Yet, prior to adopting it finally in order to meet the purpose of the project, its applicability as well as universality were freshly examined by fully following the precepts related with the standardization of a test. In the initial phase of the testing programme an evaluation of the appropriateness of items incorporated in MSIT was made on the basis of the report of the experts, and only those items were sorted out for pilot study which received at least 80 per cent consensus of their meaningfulness. Such items were 39 in number. But, the data obtained from a pilot study involving 50 educated unemployed of Bhagalpur city intended to test their potentiality in the elicitation of genuine responses did not approve all of them; only 26 items could register their suitability for the present purpose. These items, however, with an aim to further assess their predictability, were administered to an incidental sample of 100 non-technically educated unemployed young men of Bhagalpur city, and the responses gathered from them towards each of the items were subjected to a systematic analysis in order to ferret out their power to discriminate between the high (Q_3) and low (Q_1) scorers classified on the basis of their responses towards each of them. Like the other scales, in the present case, too, DP of 1.00 was accepted as a cutting point, and all items having DP below 1.00 were dropped, leaving the scale with only 20 items having a desired amount of discriminatory power. Table 3.13 reports the values of discriminatory power of the retained items in the modified form of the MSIT developed for the present investigation.

Table 3.13 : A Comparison of the Responses of the Subjects Belonging to Upper and Lower Quartiles in Terms of the Items Retained for Modified Version of Mohsin Security-Insecurity Test

No of Items	*Upper Quartile* X_1	*Lower Quartile* X_2	*Mean Differences* $X_1 - X_2$
1.	3.70	1.09	2.61
2.	4.40	2.45	1.95
3.	4.70	2.80	1.90
4.	4.40	1.45	2.95
5.	3.90	1.45	2.45
6.	3.70	1.90	1.80
7.	4.20	2.72	1.48
8.	4.40	1.36	3.04
9.	4.20	1.40	2.80
10.	4.50	1.45	3.05
11.	4.50	1.54	2.96
12.	4.20	1.63	2.57
13.	4.20	2.27	1.93
14.	4.30	2.45	1.85
15.	4.10	1.36	2.74
16.	4.80	1.81	2.99
17.	3.80	1.45	2.35
18.	4.40	1.54	2.86
19.	4.30	2.00	2.30
20.	3.80	1.36	2.44

Thus, the modified version of MSIT involved such items which did not promote inconsistent responses. These items were further checked and verified from different angles (e.g., structure and composition, order of presentation, etc.) in order to avoid any kind of response biases. The modified version, thereafter, was tested at the count of its reliability. The Cronbach Alpha coefficient (0.79), together with $\bar{r}_{ij}$ (0.16) of the shorter form, after being based on the responses of the same sample of 100 non-technically educated unemployed young men proved it — the MSIT — to be a dependable measure of the feeling of security-insecurity. However, in order to determine its applicability for other groups differing in their employment status, its internal consistency was also determined for them by employing the procedure adopted in the case of non-technically educated unemployed people. The Cronbach Alpha coefficients along with $\bar{r}_{ij}$ for the modified scale were 0.82 (0.19) for the technically educated unemployed (N = 100), 0.78 (0.15) for the technically educated employed (N = 100), and 0.81 (0.18) for the non-technically educated employed (N = 100) young men respectively. Thus, the modified version of MSIT had a fair amount of reliability for all the groups, and therefore was adopted for use in the present investigation.

Alienation Scale

A 21-item alienation scale developed by Kureshi and Dutt (1979) in Hindi was employed to measure the extent of alienation and its dimensions — despair (N = 09), disillusionment (N = 02), psychological vacuum (N = 02), narcissism (N = 02) and unstructured universe (N = 06)—in the subjects. Four alternative responses such as always (04), frequently (03), occasionally (02) and never (01) were given with each of the items. The subject's task was to tick one of the alternatives to indicate his/her responses. The sum of scores obtained in terms of different dimensions provided measure of the extent of total alienation expressed by the subject. The possible score one could obtain on the scale ranged from 21 to 84 with higher scores indicating greater degree of alienation. The scale had sufficient amount of reliability and validity and was clearly found to be free from response biases, ensuring its usability for this investigation. However, before trying it finally for the present investigation, the scale, like the other scales, too, was subjected to fresh scrutiny. Experts' evaluation of the suitability of the items incorporated in the original alienation scale in eliciting factual responses by a particular brand of subjects, as well as a pilot study (involving 50 non-technically educated unemployed young men of the Bhagalpur city) meant to test their behaviour in real life situation declared 06 items of the original 21-item alienation scale as not universally operative to a desired level and hence they were dropped. This set of 15-items, with an intention to further enhance their applicability in evoking authentic responses, was applied to an incidental sample of 100 non-technically educated unemployed people of Bhagalpur city, and an attempt was made to analyse their responses to each of the items in order to determine their discriminatory power. All items, except one, were found to be usable after testing them on the previously fixed criterion of a cut-off point of 1.00 deciding their discriminatory power. Of them, 08 represented despair, 02 unstructured universe, 02 psychological vacuum, 01 disillusionment, and 01 narcissism, respectively. Table 3.14 presents the values of discriminatory power obtained for the items included in the modified version of alienation scale.

Thus, the modified version of the 14-item alienation scale

Table 3.14 : A Comparison of the Responses of the Subjects Belonging to Upper and Lower Quartiles in Terms of the Items Retained for Alienation Scale

No of Items	*Upper Quartile* X_1	*Lower Quartile* X_2	*Mean Differences* $X_1 - X_2$
1.	3.45	1.88	1.57
2.	3.36	2.00	1.36
3.	3.36	2.33	1.03
4.	3.09	1.11	1.98
5.	3.37	1.44	1.93
6.	3.45	1.55	1.90
7.	3.52	2.30	1.22
8.	3.27	2.00	1.27
9.	3.48	1.88	1.60
10.	3.63	1.77	1.86
11.	3.54	1.88	1.66
12.	3.81	2.20	1:61
13.	3.10	1.00	2.10
14.	3.62	2.15	1.47

consisted of items having potentiality to discriminate between the high (Q_3) and low (Q_1) scorers on the scale. These items were further evaluated for their structural aptness, and were distributed randomly for different subscales in order to nullify sequential effect and other resultant biases in responses towards them. Internal reliabilities (r_{tt}) computed through Hoyt's (1941) formula and $\bar{r}_{ij}$ for various subscales, as also for the modified version of total alienation scale, were recorded to be 0.69 (0.22), 0.61 (0.44), 0.57 (0.40), 0.48 (0.48), 0.45 (0.45) and 0.78 (0.20) for the group of non-technically educated unemployed young men (N = 100), authenticating them as a dependable measure of alienation and its dimensions. But, as the study involved cross sections of population, its usability for them, too, was ascertained by demonstrating its reliability through the procedure adopted earlier. Table 3.15 shows r_{tt} and $\bar{r}_{ij}$ values of different subscales, as also the total alienation scale, for different groups of subjects: (1) the technically educated unemployed (N = 100), (2) the technically educated employed (N = 100), and (3) the non-technically educated employed (N = 100) young men.

Thus, the revised and modified version of various subscales including total alienation scale possessed substantial amount of reliability for all the groups of participants. Moreover, they were also easy in coding and analysis.

Table 3.15 : Showing r_{ii} and $\bar{r}_{ij}$ of Each of the Subscales Together with Total Alienation Scale (Modified Form) for Different Groups of Educated Unemployed and Employed Young Men

Dimensions of Alienation	*Technically Educated Unemployed*		*Technically Educated Employed*		*Non-technically Educated Employed*	
	r_{ii}	$\bar{r}_{ij}$	r_{ii}	$\bar{r}_{ij}$	r_{ii}	$\bar{r}_{ij}$
1. Despair	0.68	0.21	0.65	0.19	0.67	0.20
2. Unstructured Universe	0.62	0.45	0.58	0.41	0.61	0.44
3. Psychological Vacuum	0.59	0.42	0.60	0.43	0.60	0.43
4. Disillusionment	0.51	0.51	0.47	0.47	0.44	0.44
5. Narcissism	0.43	0.43	0.37	0.37	0.41	0.41
Alienation	0.76	0.18	0.74	0.17	0.77	0.19

A Scale for the Measurement of Identity-crisis

Identity-crisis or confusion is one of the most talked-about terms in the field of psychology. However, only a few psychologists in India (Das, 1982; Kakar, 1979; D. Sinha 1979) have focused their attention on this variable and its level in the unemployed as one of the potent indicators of their psychological well-being remains an unexplored area of research even to this day. One possible reason for this lack of interest may be the non-availability of such a scale to suit the requirements of a study on the problem of unemployment in the Indian context. Hence, an attempt was made to develop a scale for the measurement of identity-crisis and its dimensions by taking into account the nature of the problem in question, objectives of the investigation, as well as cultural specificity of India. The subsequent pages provide an abridged account of the development and standardization of the scale.

Framing of Items

By a thorough inspection of existing literature on the concept of identity-crisis and its manifestations in different forms (Das, 1982; Erikson, 1968; Kakar, 1979; D. Sinha, 1979), discussions with investigators, diplomat and social workers, and data gathered by observation of the behavioural manifestations of unemployed and employed people symptomatic of their identity-confusion, identity-crisis was delineated as having 12 dimensions such as depersonalization, fragmentation, uncertainty, distress, indecisiveness, social conflict, isolation, withdrawal from social and personal contact, role conflict, hopelessness, loneliness and desolation. These dimensions were further operationalized and their various behavioural manifestations were identified before the process of framing the items for the scale of identity-crisis could be started. Items for different dimensions involved in the scale were framed in the form of statements in Hindi by giving full consideration to their nature, characteristics and behavioural manifestations. Altogether 57 meaningful items were framed initially. These items together with the measured operational definitions of identity-crisis and its dimensions, as well as a brief account of the purposes of the investigation were placed before an expert body comprising 10 experienced teachers of the Dept. of Psychology, T.M. Bhagalpur University. They were requested to evaluate the authenticity (face validity) of each item carefully and to judge as to which of the dimensions the statements belonged. The items which had less than 80 per cent agreement were dropped, leaving the number of items in the preliminary form of the proposed scale to 42. These statements were further subjected to pretesting to find out their feasibility in exploring the dimensions to be measured in real life situations. The pretesting included an incidentally selected group of 50 educated unemployed young men of Bhagalpur city. On the basis of the analysis of their responses, items identified as ambiguous and inducing inconsistent responses were further dropped. Thus, altogether 30 items were retained for the identity-crisis scale.

Tryout and Discrimination Analysis

The preliminary form of the identity-crisis scale, consisting of 30 statements with clear instructions, was again administered to a group of 100 non-technically educated unemployed of Bhagalpur. The cases in the sample were drawn by incidental sampling technique. Each subject was instructed to read each of the statements included in the scale carefully and offer his responses by selecting one of the four alternative responses such as fully agree (04), agree (03), disagree (02), and fully disagree (01) as applicable to him. The purpose behind this tryout was to find out the discriminative power (DP) of each item of the scale. For the purpose of the present investigation, DP for each item was calculated as per the procedure suggested by Murphy and Likert (1938). As such, on the basis of the analysis of the summated scores obtained by the subjects' responses towards each of the items of the scale two extreme sets of respondents — high scorers (Q_3 and above) and low scorers (Q_1 and below) — were identified. Further, a computing sheet such as given by Murphy and Likert (1938) was prepared for each item and its DP was calculated by subtracting the weighted mean of the low scoring group from that of the high scoring group.

The DPs were arranged and applied as criteria of item selection. According to Goode and Hatt (1952) for item selection "as many items as possible should reach a DP of 1.00 and few, if any, should drop below 0,50". To ensure a fair discriminative capacity of the items in the present case DP of 1.00 was treated as cutting point, and items (09 in number) not touching the aforementioned mark were dropped. This further led to the reduction of the size of the scale to 21 items. Table 3.16 embodies details of DP values obtained for the items retained for the scale. These items were again verified and rearranged systematically to affirm that items related to different dimensions of identity-crisis were randomly distributed.

Table 3.16 : A Comparison of the Responses of the Subjects Belonging to Upper and Lower Quartiles in Terms of the Items Retained for Identity-crisis Scale

No. of Items	*Upper Quartile* X_1	*Lower Quartile* X_2	*Mean Differences* $X_1 - X_2$
1	3.28	1.10	2.18
2	3.36	1.45	1.91
3	3.45	1.07	2.38
4	3.05	1.32	1.73
5	3.48	1.12	2.36
6	2.80	1.25	1.55
7	3.00	1.00	2.00
8	3.08	1.26	1.82
9	3.26	1.17	2.09
10	3.30	1.30	2.00
11	2.90	1.26	1.64
12	3.40	1.46	1.94
13	2.92	1.39	1.53
14	3.38	1.06	2.32
15	2.84	1.39	1.45
16	3.12	1.08	2.04
17	2.76	1.12	1.64
18	2.87	1.05	1.82
19	3.52	1.81	1.71
20	3.10	1.15	1.95
21	3.24	1.48	1.76

Second Tryout and Final Form of the Scale

However, to ensure added authenticity, the scale was further subjected to rigorous procedures of standardization and so it was tested once again in relation to its item validity. For the purpose, the 21-item modified form of identity-crisis scale was readministered to the same group of 100 participants with non-technical degrees after a gap of one month. On the basis of their responses for each of the items, inter-item and item-whole correlations were computed with the help of Zero-order Correlation. Table 3.17 summarizes the findings.

All the items of the scale were positively and significantly interlinked with each other, as also with the total scale scores enumerated on the basis of the whole scale. The scale was thus finally left with 21 internally consistent items distributed in different subscales in the following order : depersonalization (N = 02), fragmentation (N = 02) uncertainty (N = 01), distress (N = 03), indecisiveness (N = 02), social conflict (N = 01), isolation (N = 02), withdrawal from social and personal contact (N = 01), role conflict (N = 03), hopelessness (N = 02), loneliness (N = 01) and desolation (N = 01).

Instruction and Scoring Procedure

Four alternative responses such as fully agree (04), agree (03), disagree (02), and fully disagree (01) were provided to each item of the scale. The subject was instructed to read each of the statements carefully and to express his responses towards them on the left side of the form by putting the value assigned for one of the four alternative responses applicable to him. The sum of scores obtained in terms of different subscales provided the measure of identity-crisis as a whole. Thus, the possible scores one could achieve on the identity-crisis scale ranged between 21 and 84; higher score was indicative of greater degree of identity-crisis and the lower denoted lower level.

Estimation of Reliability

There was a wide variation in the number of items incorporated in various subscales of identity-crisis. Subscales like uncertainty, social conflict, withdrawal from social and personal contact, loneliness and desolation, surprisingly, had only one item. Hence, in order to have an estimate of the reliability of the various subscales, as also of the

Table 3.17 : Inter-Item and Item-Whole Correlations Computed for the Scale of Identity-crisis in the Case of Non-technically Educated Unemployed Young Men

No. of Items	*1*	*2*	*3*	*4*	*5*	*6*	*7*	*8*	*9*	*10*	*11*	*12*	*13*	*14*	*15*	*16*	*17*	*18*	*19*	*20*	*21*	*Total*
1	x	37	26	22	41	33	29	24	27	32	35	43	28	25	39	34	31	33	44	36	40	57
2		x	35	31	39	26	32	28	23	43	29	25	33	47	24	30	21	27	34	45	26	54
3			x	28	33	25	43	23	39	37	37	29	31	36	27	44	49	31	35	24	38	49
4				x	26	32	39	41	29	25	23	28	43	24	31	33	42	27	25	38	30	58
5					x	38	31	27	32	30	34	36	21	48	33	28	32	35	29	41	28	53
6						x	34	29	35	28	40	39	36	31	38	30	34	43	41	33	39	61
7							x	30	47	34	27	24	38	39	41	45	35	42	28	31	27	48
8								x	42	23	30	35	28	37	46	29	43	32	34	39	31	51
9									x	31	36	42	25	32	37	43	28	39	51	35	49	63
10										x	44	27	35	28	25	36	23	46	22	40	38	55
11											x	29	24	43	39	27	50	48	30	28	37	57
12												x	40	36	42	32	29	27	37	39	41	62
13													x	35	38	28	31	49	42	27	36	56
14														x	33	39	42	28	30	36	34	52
15															x	41	37	26	29	25	31	47
16																x	32	36	43	28	45	59
17																	x	43	39	31	33	53
18																		x	36	30	41	55
19																			x	49	37	58
20																				x	35	50
21																					x	62
Total																						x

Note : Decimals are omitted; $df = 98$; $p < 0.05 = 0.20$; $p < 0.01 = 0.25$.

total scale of identity-crisis, Hoyt's (1941) formula was taken into consideration. Table 3.18 presents r_{tt} and r_{ij} for each of the subscales, as also of the total scale of identity-crisis.

Table 3.18 : Showing r_{tt} and $\bar{r}_{ij}$ of Each of the Subscales Together with Total Scale of Identity-crisis for the Group of the Non-technically Educated Unemployed Young Men

Dimensions of Identity-crisis	r_{tt}	$\bar{r}_{ij}$
1. Depersonalization	0.59	0.42
2. Fragmentation	0.61	0.44
3. Uncertainty	0.46	0.46
4. Distress	0.66	0.39
5. Indecisiveness	0.57	0.40
6. Social Conflict	0.42	0.42
7. Isolation	0.60	0.43
8. Withdrawal from Social and Personal Contact	0.44	0.44
9. Role Conflict	0.68	0.41
10. Hopelessness	0.58	0.41
11. Loneliness	0.51	0.51
12. Desolation	0.38	0.38
Identity-crisis	0.77	0.14

Thus, the different subscales as well as interblended form of the identity-crisis scale reflected a substantial measure of internal consistency. But, as the investigation was also intended to study the psychological states of other unemployed and employed groups, the dependability of identity-crisis scale was further ascertained for them. Table 3.19 reports the value of r_{tt} and $\bar{r}_{ij}$ obtained for different subscales, as also of the total identity-crisis scale, for the groups of the technically educated unemployed (N = 100), the technically educated employed (N = 100), and the non-technically educated employed (N = 100) people.

Thus, all the subscales including total scale of identity-crisis showed an evidence of internal consistency for all the groups of respondents involved in the investigation.

Estimation of Validity

It may be recalled that only those items were incorporated in the identity-crisis scale which had been adjudged by the panel of experts

Table 3.19 : Showing r_{ii} and $\bar{r}_{ij}$ of Each of the Subscales Together with Total Scale of Identity-crisis for Different Groups of Educated Unemployed and Employed Young Men

Dimension of Identity-crisis	*Technically Educated Unemployed*		*Technically Educated Employed*		*Non-technically Educated Employed*	
	r_{ii}	$\bar{r}_{ij}$	r_{ii}	$\bar{r}_{ij}$	r_{ii}	$\bar{r}_{ij}$
1. Depersonalization	0.61	0.44	0.58	0.41	0.60	0.43
2. Fragmentation	0.58	0.41	0.58	0.41	0.61	0.44
3. Uncertainty	0.44	0.44	0.41	0.41	0.45	0.45
4. Distress	0.64	0.37	0.62	0.35	0.65	0.38
5. Indecisiveness	0.59	0.42	0.56	0.39	0.56	0.39
6. Social Conflict	0.41	0.41	0.37	0.37	0.39	0.39
7. Isolation	0.62	0.45	0.57	0.40	0.58	0.41
8. Withdrawal from Social and Personal Contact	0.40	0.40	0.42	0.42	0.38	0.38
9. Role Conflict	0.63	0.36	0.61	0.34	0.64	0.37
10. Hopelessness	0.60	0.43	0.59	0.42	0.62	0.45
11. Loneliness	0.47	0.47	0.43	0.43	0.44	0.44
12. Desolation	0.42	0.42	0.36	0.36	0.40	0.40
Identity-crisis	0.76	0.13	0.75	0.13	0.78	0.14

as fairly appropriate in providing a true measure of a particular dimension. This showed that various subscales as well as total identity-crisis scale had a good amount of content validity. Further, inter-item and item-whole correlation (see Table 3.17) as well as positive and significant intercorrelation of one dimension with another and total scale scores (see Table 3.20) affirmed the identity-crisis scale as substantially sound in factorial validity.

Thus, the identity-crisis scale fully followed the principles of standardization in its development. This ensured its suitability as a measure of identity-crisis.

Life Satisfaction Index

Life satisfaction index developed by Neugarten, Havighurst and Tobin (1961) was devised to obtain the degree of life satisfaction in the educated unemployed and employed people participating in this investigation. The index consisted of 20 items — 12 structured with positive statements and 08 with the negative ones— with forced choice response alternatives of 'agree' or 'disagree'. The subject's task was

Table 3.20 : Inter-correlations Between Different Subscales and Total Scale Scores of Identity-crisis (Data Based on the Report of the Non-technically Educated Unemployed Young Men)

Dimensions of Identity-crisis	*1*	*2*	*3*	*4*	*5*	*6*	*7*	*8*	*9*	*10*	*11*	*12*	*IC*
01. Depersonalization	x	51	54	50	48	52	59	53	49	55	49	56	67
02. Fragmentation		x	47	52	45	51	58	57	48	61	50	54	71
03. Uncertainty			x	49	63	46	48	51	55	57	59	47	65
04. Distress				x	54	61	47	52	51	49	58	63	74
05. Indecisiveness					x	59	48	54	62	56	47	59	72
06. Social Conflict						x	54	62	63	49	64	57	68
07. Isolation							x	57	49	51	47	61	66
08. Withdrawal from Social and Personal Contact								x	61	57	52	59	65
09. Role Conflict									x	59	51	63	69
10. Hopelessness										x	64	67	73
11. Loneliness											x	65	70
12. Desolation												x	71
Identity-crisis													x

Note : Decimals are omitted; $df = 98$; $p < 0.05 = 0.20$; $p < 0.01 = 0.25$.

to tick either of the two in order to indicate his/her response to each of the statements. Response given to a positive statement in 'agree' and to a negative one in 'disagree' obtained a score of 01; response given otherwise generated no score. Total life satisfaction scores could, therefore, range from 0 to 20 with higher scores indicating greater amount of life satisfaction in the subject. Neugarten, Havighurst and Tobin (1961), Paintal (1978), Ramamurthy (1978) and Sinha (1989) reported the index as having an adequate measure of reliability and validity, ensuring its suitability as a measure of life satisfaction in the present investigation. But, as the index has been developed in an alien culture and in a foreign (English) language, its use for measuring life satisfaction, especially in Hindi-speaking people in India, is doubtful. This emphasized the need to test its ubiquity for our culture before considering it for use as a measure of life satisfaction in this investigation.

Consequently, an adapted measure of the index was required. In the preliminary round, the 20 statements contained in life satisfaction index were translated into Hindi and edited by three language experts by taking into account the meaning and spirit inherent in the original version of the index. 04 other freshly framed items were added to these 20 items in order to meet the exigency of measuring life satisfaction index in the context of cultural specificity of India. Thus, the index, at the initial stage, had 24 items. These items along with the operational definition of life satisfaction and the brief account of the aims of the investigation were given to a panel of experts constituted by 10 experienced teachers of the Psychology Department of local constituent units of T.M. Bhagalpur University. They were requested to examine their face validity in tapping one's life satisfaction. On their recommendation, 07 items which were identified as inefficacious in prompting true responses were deleted from the list of the statements included in the life satisfaction index, cutting the size of the index to 17 items. These items with clear instructions were further subjected to a pilot study to determine their clarity, perceived meaning, applicability and functioning in the actual field setting. The pilot study involved 50 non-technically educated unemployed of Bhagalpur city. An analysis of their responses further led to the dropping of those items which were found inadequate in producing genuine responses. Such items were 04 in number and thus the life satisfaction index could finally retain only 13 items. However, with an aim to further enhance the dependability of the life satisfaction index, the index was again administered to an incidental sample of 100 non-technically educated unemployed young men of Bhagalpur city by providing them certain comprehensive instructions, and a step was taken to determine the discriminatory power of each of the items incorporated in the index. To attain the purpose, first, they were divided into two extreme groups — high scorers (Q_3) and low scorers (Q_1) — on the basis of their aggregate scores on the index, and thereafter compared with regard to the mean scores obtained by them in terms of the items of the index. The findings obtained from comparison indicated 03 items as not adequate in discriminating between the high and low scorers on the index (discriminatory power of 0.50 was fixed as cutting point). Hence, they were also dropped, leaving the index ultimately with only 10 items — 06 made of positive statements and 04 of the negative ones—posessing a desired amount of discriminatory power. Table 3.21 reports the value of the discriminatory power of items retained in the final form of the life satisfaction index adapted for the present investigation.

Table 3.21 : A Comparison of the Responses of High (Q_3) and Low (Q_1) Scoring Subjects in Terms of the Items Retained for Adapted Version of the Life Satisfaction Index

No. of Items	*Upper Quartile* X_1	*Lower Quartile* X_2	*Mean Differences* $X_1 - X_2$
1.	0.76	0.25	0.51
2.	0.92	0.26	0.66
3.	0.60	0.28	0.32
4.	0.85	0.16	0.69
5.	0.80	0.05	0.75
6.	0.72	0.48	0.24
7.	0.83	0.14	0.69
8.	0.87	0.22	0.65
9.	0.88	0.15	0.73
10.	0.64	0.10	0.54
11.	0.54	0.28	0.26
12.	0.90	0.20	0.70
13.	0.66	0.13	0.53

The internal reliability (r_{tt}) of the adapted version of life satisfaction index computed by Cronbach's (1951) formula for the group of non-technically educated unemployed people was 0.67 and the consequent r_{ij} was 0.17. But, as the investigation was addressed to finding out of the amount of life satisfaction in other unemployed and employed people, too, an attempt was made to ascertain the dependability of the life satisfaction index for them also. The Cronbach

Alpha coefficients and $\bar{r}_{ij}$ drawn for different groups were as follows : 0.68 and 0.18 for the technically educated unemployed (N =100), 0.65 and 0.16 for the technically educated employed (N = 100), and 0.69 and 0.18 for the non-technically educated employed (N = 100) young men.

Thus, the adapted version of the life satisfaction index had a considerable measure of internal reliability for all groups of subjects participating in this investigation. The index was found easy in administration and interpretation. This assured the usability of the index for this investigation.

Strategy of Adjustment Questionnaire

The present study was also aimed at identifying the particular modes of strategy generally adopted by the educated unemployed and employed in order to cope with their plight. A 34-item strategy of adjustment questionnaire (Sinha, 1989) in Hindi measuring 4 kinds of strategy, i.e., Intrapersistive Approach Mode (IAM), extrapersistive approach mode (EAM), Punitive Avoidance Mode (PAM), and Defensive Avoidance Mode (DAM) resorted to by the subjects to deal with their problems, especially related with home, health, social and emotional affairs, was taken into consideration to meet the exigencies of measurement of the coping strategy devised by them. The subject was advised to concentrate first on each of the statements representing a particular problem he/she had been facing in his/her everyday life, and thereafter to indicate one of the 4 modes of strategy on which he/she most often depended to fight it out. The mode which was ticked by him/her obtained a score of one. Thus, the total score which one could achieve for a particular coping strategy ranged from 0 to 34 if one solely resorted to that particular mode of strategy for one's adjustment. Higher scores obtained in terms of a particular mode indicated greater leaning towards that strategic mode in making compromise with the situation. The questionnaire was found to demonstrate a sufficient amount ($r = 0.76$) of temporal stability (Sinha, 1989), ensuring its suitability as a tool for the measurement of coping styles of the subjects participating in this investigation. But, on account of its being developed and standardized as a measure of the coping tactics of the group of aged people, the applicability of the questionnaire deserved fresh examination before introducing it finally for use in this investigation. A two-level enquiry was made in this connection. In the first phase, the strategy of adjustment questionnaire together with the conceptual definitions of the coping and its aforementioned various modes, viz., intrapersistive approach mode, extrapersistive approach mode, punitive avoidance mode, and defensive avoidance mode, with an introductory description of the aims and objectives of the project was placed before a team of 10 experienced judges selected among the teachers of the Psychology Department of local constituent units of T.M. Bhagalpur University, Bhagalpur. They were requested to read each item as well as the 04 suggested probable responses given below each item representing four different modes of coping carefully and evaluate the degree of their potentiality to facilitate the true manifestation of the subjects with regard to their coping strategy. On the basis of their consensus, the items which failed to satisfy the aforesaid norm of item-selection were dropped. Such items were 10 in number. In addition to certain modifications in the structuring of some of the responses suggested for one or another problem statements, two statements underwent minimal modification making them representative of the universe of the content. Thus, in all, the strategy of adjustment questionnaire was left with 22 items. In the second phase of the modification, the questionnaire with certain instructions was administered to an incidental sample of 100 non-technically educated unemployed young men of Bhagalpur city with an end in view to demonstrate its suitability in a real life setting. In order to test the suitability of the questionnaire, difficulty index (validity index) of each of the items comprised in the questionnaire was determined. 07 items on being found to be relatively difficult in the eyes of the subjects were further discarded from the list of statements, leaving the modified version of the questionnaire with 15 items. Like the original one, the temporal stability of the modified version of the strategy of adjustment questionnaire was found to be 0.74 (at one month interval) for the group of non-technically educated unemployed people. Thus, the modified version of the strategy of adjustment questionnaire was fairly dependable. But, as the investigation was aimed at analysing the psychological health and coping styles of different other groups of the unemployed and employed young men, too, the temporal stability (test-retest reliability) of the modified version of the questionnaire was determined by retesting it successively for one month. Coefficients of temporal stability of the questionnaire estimated for different groups were 0.75 for the technically educated unemployed (N = 100), 0.71 for technically educated employed (N = 100), and 0.73 for the non-technically educated employed (N = 100).

Thus, the modified version of the strategy of adjustment questionnaire was found to have a satisfactory level of reliability. Hence, it was included as a tool for the measurement of coping strategies of the participants.

Personal Data Sheet (PDS)

In order to collect information regarding different personal and background variables, a Personal Data Sheet (PDS) in Hindi was prepared. All necessary precautions were taken in doing so. The sheet involved simple questions relating to age, sex, degree in or level of education, residence, caste and religion, number of members in the family, socio-economic condition of the parents, kinds and duration of unemployment/employment, means for maintenance and support system, organizational climate, etc.

Procedure

The subjects at the very outset were requested to participate sincerely and honestly in the investigation since it was expected to reveal a lot of important facts regarding their psychological well-being and coping styles. An effort was made to impress upon them that honesty and cooperation on their part were essential in making the investigation really worthwhile. Furthermore, it was emphasized that there were no good or bad answers. The answers given by them would be kept strictly confidential and that their identity would never be made public. Thus, a good rapport was established with the respondents before the administration of the measures. Thereafter, the measures were administered in the following order :

(1) A Shorter Version of Sinha's W.A. Self-analysis Form,
(2) Stress Scale,
(3) Mohsin Security-Insecurity Test,
(4) Alienation Scale,
(5) Identity-crisis Scale,
(6) Life Satisfaction Scale,
(7) Strategy of Adjustment Questionnaire, and
(8) Personal Data Sheet

Subjects were administered the scale either individually or in small group-settings. Before responding to the statements involved in the scales, the subjects were given the usual instructions, say, to read each of the statements carefully, to answer all questions and to give their true answers. They were allowed to take up the tests only when they understood the instructions completely. Though they had to complete the measures within a maximum time limit of 2 hours, in some cases (hardly 0.5%) they were given leeway in finishing the job, and to return the scales by post as per their convenience when it was found they really needed more time for it. Data-collection took a time of about one year, i.e., from July 1991 to May 1992.

Convinced of the intention of the investigation, the subjects extended their sincere participation and full cooperation. This was quite evident from their willingness to participate in the study, as well as their often searching enquiries about the findings thereof

4

Statistical Techniques Used for Analysis

The present investigation, as stated earlier, was designed to present a comparative account of inter- and intra-group differences among different groups of unemployed vis-à-vis employed young men, divided on the basis of kinds and streams of their education, as well as the duration of the status of their employment, in terms of the levels of their psychological well-being measured as it is on certain indicators such as anxiety, stress, feeling of insecurity, alienation, identity-crisis and life satisfaction in their various manifestations. Also, the study was aimed at finding out the various strategies generally used by them in order to cope with their life circumstances. To attain the above mentioned purposes, first Means, SDs, and One-Way ANOVA (One-Way Analysis of Variance) were computed. Thereafter, multiple comparisons of different pairs of Means were made by using Newman-Keuls Test. Since there was a large variation in the size of different subgroups of the educated unemployed and employed people, an attempt was made to harmonize ($\tilde{n}_h$) Mean values obtained by them in terms of various psychological reactions, as well as different coping strategies before calculating the significance of difference between the Mean scores of any two groups with regard to the aforementioned variables.

Added to the above statistical analyses, percentage and ranking were worked out on the basis of the frequency of scores obtained by each of the exclusive groups of respondents in terms of different indicators of their psychological health, as well as various strategies devised by them in order to deal with their situations.This was done simply to measure the relative vulnerability of each of them to different symptomatic reactions, as well as the degree of their relative dependence on different coping strategies.

5

Psychological Well-being and Coping Styles

The Educated Unemployed *Versus* Employed Young Men

Over the past few decades, as reported in the Introduction and Overview, a good number of investigations involving unemployed and employed people have been conducted in order to see in them the level of psychological well-being measured in terms of its various indicators. Yet, there are different important indices of psychological health like anxiety, stress, feeling of insecurity, alienation, identity-crisis and their dimensions, except life satisfaction, which have not aroused much interest in the investigators involved in the analysis of psychological well-being of unemployed people, particularly in India. It can be clearly seen that empirical evidence accumulated in this regard is still insufficient, and whatever is available does not focus the issue directly. Similarly, the coping mechanisms adopted by the unemployed and the employed have also been less systematically, as also less extensively, investigated in India and abroad. As such, following the findings of those studies it would not be wise to predict about the psychological health and coping styles of the unemployed *vis-à-vis* employed young men ; it would certainly be precipitate and, hence erroneous. This chapter dwells upon a detailed account of the findings of a statistical comparison between the two groups — one, the combined group of the educated unemployed and another, of the educated employed young men in terms of their psychological health and coping styles.

To proceed with our discussion, it is interesting to note here that except life satisfaction, variables like anxiety, stress, feeling of insecurity, alienation, identity-crisis and their dimensions used as the indicators of psychological well-being in this investigation, as it was recorded (Singh, 2001), were positively and meaningfully associated with each other, showing thus a clear tendency to form a grouping between them. Hence, for the apt and relatively comprehensive presentation of the findings, it was thought desirable to deal with the statistical differences between the unemployed and the employed people in terms of those closely interrelated indices of psychological health under one heading, and the difference between them with regard to life satisfaction under another. The record of the statistical differences in the relative dependence of the two groups on different strategies such as intrapersistive approach mode, extrapersistive approach mode, punitive avoidance mode and defensive avoidance mode, in order to effect a compromise with their situation, was sequentially posited in the end of this chapter.

The simple purpose of this comparison was to quantitatively ascertain differential level of the various aforementioned indicators of psychological health in the unemployed as against their employed counterparts. Further, it was aimed at finding out their comparative leanings towards different strategies in course of the effort made by them in order to adjust to their existing environment. These records, it was expected, found out of the statistical comparisons between the two groups — the unemployed and the employed — in terms of different variables being investigated, would serve as basis for the causal inferences about the findings likely to emerge from the intra- and inter-group comparisons among different groups of educated unemployed and employed people divided on the basis of criteria like kinds and streams of education, and the duration of the status of their employment (unemployed/employed) in terms of their psychological well-being as well as the strategies resorted to by them in order to deal with their situations at both macro and micro levels. The following pages record the findings and discussion thereof.

Level of Anxiety, Stress, Feeling of Insecurity, Alienation, Identity-Crisis and Their Dimensions: A Comparison Between Educated Unemployed and Employed Young Men

As indicated above, anxiety, stress, feeling of insecurity, alienation, identity-crisis and their dimensions have been but little investigated systematically, particularly in India, as the indicators of impaired psychological health of the unemployed *versus* employed young men. Except a few, studies carried out in this regard do not have direct as well as micro implication for the issue in question (see Introduction and Overview; pp. 35-49). Yet, the findings derived therefrom justifiably led to the assumption that the unemployed, as compared to the employed, would be more vulnerable to anxiety, stress, feeling of insecurity, alienation, identity-crisis and their dimensions. Table 5:1 consists of the summary of a statistical comparison between the unemployed and employed young men and their relative standing in terms of the abovementioned select indices of psychological health.

As expected, the unemployed, as compared to their employed counterparts, had a palpable amount (substantially moderate in extent and in some cases markedly pathological in essence) of anxiety, feeling of insecurity, alienation, identity-crisis and their dimensions (F-value ranged between 05.33 and 212.97), with the exception of stress and its dimensions (Mean scores expanded from 0.36 to 10.87) including somatic manifestation dimension (0.82) of anxiety which were not found to be symptomatic of psychological ill-health, albeit even the possession of very low scores (i.e., below the mark of 20 per cent) on stress and its dimensions, as suggested by Feather (1982), Goldberg (1972) and Warr (1984a), may indicate increased risk of becoming psychologically impaired. Thus, the unemployed were found to carry with them a substantial amount of reduced psychological well-being. However, quite interestingly, the employed young men were also found to be susceptible, to a moderate extent, in this regard, but were marginally low on nearly all the dimensions of anxiety and stress like their unemployed counterparts. Further, an analysis of the relative standing of the two groups in terms of different indices of psychological well-being revealed that while the unemployed were plagued with greater feeling of social conflict (67.25%) and less reverberating proneness to suicide (09.00%), the employed were highly troubled with the feeling of uncertainty (57.25%) and, like their counterparts, less apprehensive of suicidal tendency (02.25%). Though, on the whole, it was the job-seekers who were markedly more vulnerable to psychological ill-health, the employed young men were also found to be afflicted with psychological debilitation to a moderate extent. Thus, both the unemployed and employed people, to a considerable measure, reflected a similar pattern in their psychological reactions measured in terms of the degree and extent of different select indices of psychological health like anxiety, stress, feeling of insecurity, alienation, identity-crisis and their dimensions. Noticeably, both of them were moderately afflicted with reduced psychological health with the possession of almost a precipitating

Table 5.1 : Statistical Differences Between Educated Unemployed and Employed Young Men and Their Relative Standing in Terms of Different Indices of Their Psychological Well-being

Indices of Psychological Well-being	*Possible Score Range*	*Unemployed (N=614)*			*Employed (N=410)*			
		Mean (%)	*SD*	*Rank*	*Mean (%)*	*SD*	*Rank*	*F*
1. General Worries	0-06	3.28 (54.67)	1.64	05	2.10 (35.00)	0.87	21	132.48
2. Somatic Manifestations	0-03	0.82 (27.33)	0.39	29	0.55 (18.33)	0.32	26	27.01
3. Psychological Symptoms	0-05	2.45 (49.00)	1.34	18	1.45 (29.00)	0.71	22	134.43
4. Social Relations	0-08	3.06 (38.25)	1.59	25	1.67 (20.88)	0.83	25	132.43
5. **Anxiety**	0-22	9.61 (43.68)	3.57	23	5.77 (26.82)	2.03	23	186.28
6. Suicidal Tendency	0-04	0.36 (9.00)	0.21	33	0.09 (2.25)	0.05	33	38.64
7. Emotional Instability	0-08	3.24 (40.50)	1.87	24	2.05 (25.63)	0.89	24	89.64
8. Paranoid Tendency	0-12	2.34 (19.50)	1.31	32	1.46 (12.17)	0.68	32	43.55
9. Depression	0-36	10.87 (30.19)	4.19	26	5.40 (15.00)	2.30	29	173.78
10. Physical Illness	0-12	3.36 (28.00)	1.46	27	2.17 (18.08)	1.04	27	68.76
11. Social Maladjustment	0-12	3.25 (27.08)	1.80	30	1.59 (13.25)	0.81	31	108.45
12. Apprehensiveness	0-12	3.18 (26.50)	1.69	31	1.61 (13.42)	0.73	30	106.44
13. **Stress**	0-96	26.60 (27.71)	10.31	28	14.37 (14.97)	4.11	28	158.53
14. **Feeling of Insecurity**	20-100	53.89 (53.89)	15.14	08	41.14 (41.14)	11.49	10	206.79
15. Despair	08-32	17.35 (54.22)	4.42	07	15.06 (47.06)	3.61	06	76.21
16. Unstructured Universe	02-08	4.39 (54.88)	1.40	04	4.11 (51.38)	1.43	03	9.33
17. Psychological Vacuum	02-08	4.27 (53.38)	1.38	09	3.87 (48.38)	1.30	05	21.17
18. Disillusionment	01-04	1.87 (46.75)	0.89	21	1.48 (37.00)	0.67	19	58.25
19. Narcissism	01-04	1.80 (45.00)	0.92	22	1.63 (40.75)	0.76	12	5.33
20. **Alienation**	14-56	29.73 (53.09)	6.16	12	26.05 (46.52)	5.13	07	99.90
21. Depersonalization	02-08	3.85 (48.13)	1.59	19	2.95 (36.88)	1.21	20	93.65
22. Fragmentation	02-08	4.25 (53.13)	1.81	11	3.12 (39.00)	1.35	16	114.46

Contd.

Table 5.1 *(Contd.)*

Indices of Psychotogical Well-being	*Possible Score Range*	*Unemployed (N=614)*			*Employed (N=410)*			*F*
		Mean (%)	*SD*	*Rank*	*Mean (%)*	*SD*	*Rank*	
23. Uncertainty	01-04	2.59 (64.75)	0.98	02	2.29 (57.25)	0.92	01	24.67
24. Distress	03-12	6.21 (51.75)	2.10	15	4.87 (40.58)	1.68	13	116.74
25. Indecisiveness	02-08	4.17 (52.13)	1.62	14	3.27 (40.88)	1.24	11	91.07
26. Social Conflict	01-04	2.69 (67.25)	0.97	01	2.16 (54.00)	0.95	02	74.19
27. Isolation	02-08	3.94 (49.25)	1.59	17	3.06 (38.25)	1.18	17	91.99
28. Withdrawal from Social and Personal Contact	01-04	1.91 (47.75)	0.95	20	1.59 (39.75)	0.77	15	31.19
29. Role Conflict	03-12	6.55 (54.58)	2.11	06	4.98 (41.50)	1.79	08	152.72
30. Hopelessness	02-08	4.18 (52.25)	1.72	13	3.05 (38.13)	1.26	18	129.45
31. Loneliness	01-04	2.00 (50.00)	0.94	16	1.60 (40.00)	0.80	14	47.03
32. Desolation	01-04	2.43 (60.75)	1.27	03	1.94 (48.50)	1.03	04	13.52
33. **Identity-crisis**	21-84	44.77 (53.30)	11.42	10	34.85 (41.49)	9.20	09	212.97

Note : $df = 1,1022$; $p < 0.05 = 3.84$; $p < 0.01 = 6.64$.

amount of aforementioned different indices of well-being, except a lower, but clinically susceptible, level of the symptomatic reactions of stress and anxiety, the latter reactions were only discernible in the case of the employed young men, however.

Life Satisfaction : A Comparison Between Eduacated Unemployed and Employed Young Men

The degree of satisfaction with life in the unemployed *versus* employed has been extensively investigated, particularly by many European psychologists (vide page 49 to 51). These studies, with a few exceptions, have clearly indicated that the unemployed, as compared to the employed, have a decreased amount of satisfaction with their lives, limiting the scope of a fresh inquiry in this regard. However, the findings of those studies cannot be safely generalized in a culture like that of India which has a typical stoic worldview (Kakar, 1978; Lapierre, 1986; Paranjpe, 1984; Roy and Srivastava, 1986; Sinha, 1988) manifesting itself in the form of a distinct reaction pattern, clearly marked by indifference to the most serious problems like poverty and unemployment (Lapierre, 1986; Amar K. Singh, 1975; Singh, 1990, 1994; Singh, Kumari and Kumari, 2000; Singh, Singh and Singh, 1996 ; Singh, Singh and Singh, 1995) by fairly ascribing outside forces as responsible for their condition. They are passive, and often express a considerable lack of seriousness about any assignment, indeed (Ganesh, 1982; Kakar, 1978; Amar K.Singh,1975; Sinha, 1985; Vijaylakshmi, Shudhakar and Rao, 1985). The Indians, in general, have a peculiar and pervasive capacity to live in pain and paucity, penury and woe by enjoying every moment in their lives with fervent zeal and radiance (Lapierre, 1986; Singh, Sinha and Kumari, 1985; Sinha, 1988).They accept fortune or misfortune alike without complaint (Basham, 1971). The majority of the people, according to Kapp (1963), can be seen to be governed by *'kya farak parta hai'* (what difference does it make ?) attitude in every walk of life. More obviously, unlike in the west, they believe that every event in one's life including *harsha* (happiness) and *vishad* (despondency), *rag* (attachment) and *dves* (aversion), etc., are preordained and predetermined; only the will of the Almighty is responsible for their deeds as well as misdeeds. Worldly affluence, according to them, cannot ease a man and bring about for him happiness and satisfaction; they are inner-generated and can only be achieved through *Bhagwad kripa* (by the blessing of the Almighty) as well as through total immersion in *dharma.* A happy man, in the eyes of an Indian, is he who is able to control his desires and, more specifically, say, kill his *ahamkar* (vanity). In other words, he can enjoy real peace and happiness, if he is capable to suppress his "I". Moderation and modesty are the key to happiness (Roy and Srivastava, 1986). However, with the rapidly changing economic scenario at the global level as well as the general emphasis within contemporary society on the work ethic or the wealth ethic *(The Protestant ethic),* the Indian psyche has also been influenced considerably. An Indian, too, aspires to live a life which could provide him/her at least a minimum standard of living which can only be achieved through gainful employment. But, evidently, there is a great dearth of jobs in the country. Despite all attempts made at both governmental and non-governmental levels for quite a long time to ensure every Indian an opportunity for employment, nothing fruitful could be achieved so far in this regard. The number of job-seekers has been escalating every year in a disconcerting manner. Even a sizeable number of highly educated and well-qualified people are hard hit by the problem of unemployment

(Ahmad, 1993; Mamgain and Parashar, 2000 ; Papola, 1992; Ray, 1995). The problem of unemployment, indeed, is rooted deep in the very soil of the country. This sorry state of affairs, if we follow the findings of some of the studies (Atkinson, Liem and Liem, 1986; Conger *et al.*, 1990; Iversen, 1989; Jahoda, 1988; Kessler, Turner and House, 1988; Kieselbach, 1989, 1991; Liem and Liem, 1990; McLoyd, 1989; Warr, 1987d) wherein it has been shown that unemployment, in most of the instances, gives rise to an increased level of financial crisis, precipitating in an individual the high risk of psychological vulnerability, may be expected to minimise the level of satisfaction with life of those who are jobless. Surprisingly, no effort has been made so far to examine the ubiquity of this assumption, particularly in India. Hence, in order to verify the tenability of the abovementioned expectation, the educated unemployed and employed young men were compared statistically in terms of their life satisfaction scores. The findings obtained therefrom are reported in Table 5.2.

Table 5.2 : Statistical Differences Between Educated Unemployed and Employed Young Men and Their Relative Standing in Terms of Their Life Satisfaction

Variable	*Possible Score Range*	*Unemployed (N=614)*		*Employed (N= 410)*		
		Mean (%)	*SD*	*Mean* (%)	*SD*	*F*
Life Satisfaction	0 - 10	04.76 (47.60)	02.25	06.89 (68.90)	01.87	251.32

Note : $df = 1,1022$; $p < 0.05 = 3.84$; $p < 0.01 = 6.64$.

Consistent with the earlier findings, especially recorded in a good number of studies (Aho, 1981; Breakwell, Harrison and Propper, 1984; Donovan and Oddy, 1982; Feather and O'Brien, 1986a, b, 1987; Fryer and Payne, 1986; O'Brien and Feather, 1990) conducted in the west, educated unemployed (*Mean* = 04.76; *SD* = 02.25) vis-à-vis employed (*Mean* = 06.89; *SD* = 01.87) were found to have a relatively lower degree, though moderate in amount (47.60%), of satisfaction with their life.

To recapitulate, the summary of the results of a statistical comparison between unemployed and employed young men in terms of the degree and extent of the abovementioned different select indices (viz., anxiety, stress, feeling of insecurity, alienation, identity-crisis, life satisfaction and their dimensions) of psychological well-being, on the whole, revealed the unemployed, as compared to their employed counterparts, as substantially more afflicted with poor psychological health, particularly marked by heightened pathogenic states of social conflict (67.25%), uncertainty (64.75%) and desolation (60.75%) respectively. Further, they were also found to be precipitated with a moderate, but highly susceptible, amount of anxiety, feeling of insecurity, alienation, identity-crisis and almost all of their dimensions in addition to a moderately decreased level of satisfaction with life (47.60%; dissatisfaction scores, thus, centred around 52.40%). Notably, the employed young men, though, were also found to carry with them the risk of psychological debilitation to a moderate degree. However, both the groups were relatively less prone to stress. It was clearly evident in the case of the educated employed young men, who had also a marginally lower level of anxiety (26.82%) and its dimensions such as somatic manifestations (18.33%), psychological symptoms (29.00%) and social relations (20.88%). However, following the suggestions expressed by Feather (1982), Goldberg (1972) and Warr (1984a), they were diagnosed as having reduced psychological health even after their being least affected in terms of stress and its dimensions, as also anxiety and its manifestations, the latter was particularly discernible only in the case of the employed young men.

The reduced psychological well-being of the unemployed, as compared to that of their employed counterparts, can reasonably be described on the basis of the findings of a good number of studies (Atkinson, Lem and Liem, 1986; Elder, Jr *et al.*, 1991 ; Iversen, 1989; Jackson and Warr, 1984; Jahoda, 1982, 1988; Kelvin and Jarrett, 1985; Keyssar, 1985; Kieselbach, 1989, 1991; Verkleij, 1989; Warr, 1987d). These studies have indicated that, in the majority of cases, unemployment leads to mounting economic pressure, exposing a person particularly to the risk of psychological uprootedness, wherein a relatively high degree of symptomatic reactions like those of feelings of apathy, isolation, despair, loneliness, anxiety, insecurity, depression, meaninglessness, irritability, hostility, resignation, alienation, identity-crisis, decreased life satisfaction, maladjustment etc., of poor psychological health are most likely to manifest themselves (Banks and Ullah, 1987a; Conger *et al.*, 1990; Jahoda, 1987, Kessler, Turner and House, 1988; Liem, 1988; Liem and Liem, 1990; McLoyd, 1989; McLoyd and Flanagan, 1990; O'Brien and Feather, 1990; Rani, 1993; Singh, 1994, 2001; Singh, Kumari and Singh, 1992, Singh and Singh, 2004; Singh, Singh and Rani, 1996a; Singh, Singh and Singh, 1995). It may be noted that unemployment, for the majority of the people, represents a critical life event that greatly changes their everyday routine, income, social relationships, family life, social roles, goals and purposes, central aspects of the perception of self and others, and so on (Brenner and Starrin, 1988; Chakrapani, 1995, 1996 ; Hamilton *et al.*, 1993 ; Iversen and Sabroe, 1988; Kelvin and Jarrett, 1985; Kieselbach, 1988b; Kieselbach, Lödige-Röhrs and Lünser, 1989; Kieselbach and Svensson, 1988; Kieselbach and Wacker, 1985; Kinicki and Latack, 1990 ; Leana and Feldman, 1992 ; McLoyd, 1989; Reynolds and Gilbert, 1991; Schaufeli, 1992 ; Schwefel, Svensson and Zöllner, 1987 ; Turner, Leana and Feldman, 1993). These changes, according to Kelvin and Jarrett (1985), may lead to more self-observation and to increasingly negative views of self. The unemployed, in consequence, develop a heightened tendency to look at themselves as unusual objects. Their cognition of themselves becomes distorted to a greater or lesser degree, resulting in the development of different symptoms of psychological impairment (Higgins, 1987; Murgai and Sathyavathi, 1988). Thus, financial strain and distress emanating from joblessness (Feather, 1989a; Jahoda, 1988; Kessler, House and Turner, 1987; Kessler, Turner and House, 1988; Kieselbach, 1989; Liem and Liem, 1988) can reasonably be taken to precipitate psychological deterioration.

The proposition by Jahoda (1979) may also provide a common ground in order to deal with the findings. According to her, despite the dissatisfactions and frustrations experienced in their work, people are still motivated more positively towards working than not working. She has attempted to emphasize that people want to work even while they hate it. In her (Jahoda, 1988) eyes, work is, indeed, a primary source of positive social, psychological and material resources for the individual. Elaborating her views, she (Jahoda, 1981, 1982, 1987, 1988, 1995) has further stated that employment enables a person to earn a salary (manifest function), and at the psychological level provides him/her opportunity for time structure, enlargement of social experience, involvement in collective purpose, enhancement of social and personal identity and engagement in purposeful activity—serving as an impetus for better mental health. Joblessness keeps one from enjoying these manifest and latent benefits accompanying an employment, and thus, shatters one's psychological foundation. Taking a lead from the Freudian (Freud, 1930) assumption that the development of the ego and the control of the id require the pleasure and reality principles to work together, she has further stressed that work is man's strongest tie with reality, providing links with the environment which prevent him/her from becoming overwhelmed by fantasy and emotion.

Unemployment, therefore, weakens a person's contact with reality and affects the person's ability to gratify certain basic human needs, particularly the deeper human motivations — the psychological ones (Jahoda, 1982). Undeniably, an unemployed person is deprived of many opportunities which employment offers. This obviously affects him/her adversely, particularly on the psychological plane —proving inimical to his/her psychological balance and equipoise.Warr (1987c, d) also maintains a similar view. In his vitamin model, he (Warr, 1987d) has attempted to demonstrate that an unemployed person is deprived, to a considerable extent, of the benefits of different environmental opportunities like opportunity for control, use of skills, externally generated goals, variety, environmental clarity, availability of money, physical security, scope for interpersonal contact, and valued social position. And such privation, more often than not, precedes the development of certain symptoms of poor psychological well-being in the unemployed; manifestation of anxiety, stress, feeling of insecurity, alienation, identity-crisis in their different forms, as also a decreased life satisfaction in a substantial measure becomes particularly pronounced therein (Banks and Ullah, 1987a, 1988; Fryer and Payne, 1986 ; Keefe, 1984; Keupp, 1982; Kieselbach, 1991; Lahelma and Kangas, 1989; O'Brien and Feather, 1990 ; Singh and Singh, 2004; Singh, Singh and Rani, 1996a; Warr and Jackson, 1984, 1985; Warr, Jackson and Banks, 1988). No doubt, employment, as maintained by a good number of investigators (Arnetz *et al.*, 1987; Braunstein *et al.*,1983; Liem and Liem, 1988; Tiggemann and Winefield, 1984; Warr and Parry, 1982) is prophylactic and so, indeed, helps maintain one's psychological well-being. It should be noted here that working at a job can 'take your mind off' from problems (Warr, 1987d). Worklessness or unemployment may, thus, naturally lead to the eruption of a variety of problems in a person's life who encounters it (Kieselbach, 1989), certainly shattering his/her whole psychological balance. This, in effect, as revealed by a number of investigators (Iversen and Sabroe, 1988; Singh, 1990; Warr, 1984a, b), may produce different symptomatic reactions, particularly at the psychological level. Unemployment, invariably, throws a person into a deep crisis, exposing him/her to psychological ill-health.

In the line of the above arguments, the conclusion drawn by Fryer and Payne (1986) is relevant for the purpose of analysing the findings. On the basis of the findings of numerous studies, they have asserted that in most of the instances, the condition of unemployment, being associated with the development of the restrictive and threatening psychosocial environment, as well as the exhaustion and discouragement of trying to cope with it, comes as an assault on the personal agency. This, according to them, is psychologically terribly debilitating, producing in such a person, to a substantial measure, a sense of uprootedness from familiar surroundings, estrangement from the vital current of social, community and political life and profound uncertainty about the future. Thus, the reason behind the unemployed, as compared to the employed, as being fairly more afflicted with poor psychological health stands vindicated. It is worth noting here that people, as the agency theory (Fryer, 1986, 1988, 1995b ; Fryer and Payne, 1986; Hartley and Fryer, 1984) presumes, are agents who strive to assert themselves, and initiate and influence events. They are intrinsically motivated and live in a perceived world where every attempt depends on their view of the future as well as memories of the past. They try to make sense of what goes on and to act in accordance with these interpretations, largely governed by their values and purposes as well as their estimations of possible scenarios and outcomes. In brief, the approach conceives that people are active agents possessing sufficient potentiality to shape the content of their environments.

In other words, they are not passive objects who depend on the mercy of environmental forces in order to control and manipulate their life cycle. Rather, they actively develop ways of coping with negative events and ways of adjusting to changing circumstances even in the teeth of limits imposed by the situation. As such, they can effectively influence their environment and make it worth their lives. But, all these agentic features of people, according to the agency theory, are routinely limited, restricted, frustrated, discouraged and undercut by the socio-industrial environment, particularly by the relative or absolute poverty associated with unemployment, putting them at the risk of psychological morbidity. However, the agency theory is not a fully developed theory yet; it is a meta theory in essence. It strictly emphasizes the need to take people as active, goal-directed agents (Feather, 1990). Interestingly, the theory primarily follows a person-centred approach in describing the effects of unemployment on an individual who experiences it. It may be noted that there are other theories also vindicating the above assumptions. Nonetheless, Fryer's formulation may prove handy in formulating steps for the modification of views related to the analysis of the effects of unemployment which have ignored the importance of agentic features such as resourcefulness, planfulness, and constructive ways of coping that most of the people display in adjusting with critical life events (Feather and Volkmer, 1988; Fryer, 1988; Fryer and McKenna, 1987; Fryer and Payne, 1986; Smith and Anderson, 1986). It cannot, however, be denied that frustration of agency caused by unemployment may exert adverse effects on the psychological well-being of those who experience it.

In describing the findings, it is also pertinent to focus on the interdependence existing among family members, particularly between offspring and parents in the Indian society. Nurture and upbringing of offspring are the sole responsibility of the parents, but this is not done without expectations. Hence, as the younger members of the family — particularly the sons, who are considered to be wealth (*putra dhana*) — grow up and become able and competent after completing their education, are expected to support not only themselves but also their entire family, particularly their parents, especially in their old age. Thus, it may be noticed that parent-child relationships in India predominantly follow the principle of social exchange, though this "profit-loss business" is not wanton, as it is often thought of in the west ; it requires prudent patience and a long wait for returns on the part of the investors — the parents. In the light of this typical obligation system, obtaining employment is essential for a son in order to maintain himself and meet the consensual and normative demands of both the family and society. But, as can be envisaged, there is a huge gap between the number of jobs and the number of employment-seekers. Though the Tenth Five-Year Plan, as well as the new economic policy based on the European free-market model, too, promise to eradicate the problem of joblessness in the country to the soonest possible by increasing the annual employment potential, nothing concrete can be expected at present in the face of India's explosive population growth, compounded and complicated by its catastrophic national disharmony, particularly fomented by greater amount of poverty and economic inequality along with steep feelings of fanaticism, caste hatred, regionalism, and the increasing threat from terrorism and secessionism, as well as deepening political crises and instability. Large-scale corruptions, particularly prevalent among top politicians, policy-makers and highups have proved further deterrants to the already agonising pitiable situation. Besides, there are other criteria (e.g., back-door canvassing, bribery, nepotism, casteism, religious affiliation, regionalism, etc.) that are generally used in the selection of employees. These are undesirable bottlenecks on the way to proper appointment of deserving candidates. As a result, even people with high academic qualifications and competence are jobless. This leaves them helpless, and they find themselves unable to play their expected roles. They carry a psychological feeling with them that they are an economic liability for their family and society. Such "broken" individuals become passive recipients of whatever life offers them. Thus, the state of unemployment, particularly the prolonged type, lowers the status and prestige of those who experience it and ultimately leads to the development of self-defeat and frustration in them (Kumari, 2001). Such feelings start taking deep roots as other members of the family and society, instead of consoling them, often begin to hurl various disparaging remarks at them such as lazy, dull, indolent, inept, insincere, shirker, undeserving, etc. (Singh, 1990; Singh, Singh and Rani, 1996a). It would not be irrelevant to mention here that the work ethic in our society, as Kieselbach (1991) feels, tends to devalue the unemployed socially. This situation is usually aggravated through individualistic ideologies such as the "just world belief" that people get what they deserve (Lerner, 1980). The unemployed are generally negatively evaluated by the society which, in turn, leads to the erosion in their valued social position, make them feel deprived of their legitimate claims on society, and renders them incapable of asserting themselves in conflict situations (Kieselbach, 1987b). These changes, as may be commonly observed, do not prove wholesome for them. Rather, in most of the instances, they precipitate in them the development of increased feelings of anxiety, stress, insecurity, anomie, apathy, alienation, pessimism, identity-crisis, dissatisfaction with life, meaninglessness, etc., symptomatic of a marked deterioration in psychological health.

It also seems relevant to mention here that those who have been victims of uncontrollable life events, as can be seen, are in special need of support and reassurance from others in order to maintain their emotional harmony and well-being. If social support and assurance are not made available to them, they continue to run the risk of psychological impairment (Banks, 1990 ; Banks and Ullah, 1987a; Cohen and Syme, 1985; Finlay-Jones and Eckhardt, 1984; Kessler and McLeod, 1985; Kieselbach and Traiser, 2004; Sarason and

Sarason, 1985; Sarason *et al.*, 1987; Turner, 1983; Turner, Kessler and House, 1991; Warr and Jackson, 1985 ; Worell, 1988). As has been empirically evidenced, unemployment, for many of those affected, represents a stressful life event. And, on the other hand, it has been shown that social support enables a person to cope effectively with the stresses induced by unemployment (Benavides *et al.*, 1994; Broomhall and Winefield, 1990 ; Chakrapani, 1996 ; Clark and Clissold, 1982; Dooley, Catalano and Rook, 1988; Gore, 1978; Kessler, Turner and House, 1987, 1988 ; Kieselbach, 1997b, 1998a ; Lazarus and Folkman, 1984; Rife, 1990 ; Schaefer, Coyne and Lazarus, 1982; Vinokur and Caplan, 1987) and, thus helps promote his/her psychological well-being (Bolton and Oatley, 1987; Dooley *et al.*, 1981; Kilpatrick and Trew, 1985 ; Pearlin *et al.*, 1981; Ullah, Banks and Warr, 1985; Warr and Jackson, 1985). Interestingly, as Kieselbach (1988a) and Sachielli *et al.* (1991) maintain, the unemployed, by enjoying emotional support from the closer or wider social network, conceive of themselves as part of this frame of reference which they themselves value positively.

The feeling of being accepted as friend, child, or member of a social group and not being stigmatized as one of the unemployed enables them to reconcentrate their self-perception and, thus to counteract tendencies of social disorientation, induced by unemployment. Similarly, there is a considerable evidence to indicate that possible financial assistance extended by any source, in particular, attenuates the health-damaging effects of unemployment in a substantial measure (Finlay-Jones and Eckhardt, 1984; Ullah, Banks and Warr, 1985; Warr and Jackson, 1985).

To summarize, social support, whether it is in 'instrumental' or 'emotional form', may clearly be expected to act as a buffer against the harmful psychological effects of unemployment. Thus, in order to understand the poor psychological well-being in the educated unemployed young men in India, it seems also pertinent to acquaint oneself with the availability and functioning of the support system for them in the country. The government of India, of late, has proposed numerous schemes intended to support the Indian unemployed people. But, it is rather amazing that all the plans and policies adopted at governmental level for their amelioration as well as for rooting out the malady from the land for ever have failed pathetically. They are considered merely as political game-playing and manoeuvring; they hardly cover the end, particularly in the eyes of the unemployed.

Undeniably, for some reason or the other, getting support from governmental agencies has become a herculean task for the poor and unemployed. In recent years, voluntary organizations in India have proved to be a panacea for the welfare of the downtrodden and the needy. Nonetheless, they have not yet shown much interest in structuring suitable programmes for the welfare of the unemployed. Indeed, no sincere and amicable efforts have so far been made by them on this front. This might be mainly because of their non-participatory role in the framing of governmental policies for the welfare of the unemployed as well as their perceived inability to solve the long-continuing endemic problem of unemployment on account of the greater financial crunch emanating from lack of sufficient aids to them from the governmental and non-governmental agencies (Garain, 1994).

The role of society, in general, is also not very appreciable; it is rather distressing and disappointing. It has certainly encouraged the development of a growing sense of helplessness and despondency amongst the unemployed. As indicated above, our society, as Lerner (1980) holds, too, harbours an apathetic attitude towards the unemployed. As such, it often betrays a readiness on its part to empathise with them and act as their succour. The unemployed, particularly those belonging to poor or middle-class families, lose even familial support to maintain their well-being (Schober, 1978; Singh, 1990, 1994). Thus, the reasons behind the educated unemployed young men having reduced psychological health may be understood in the context of lack of proper and sufficient support provided by the official and other social agencies for the Indian unemployed people. This stresses the importance of social support and cooperation for the maintenance and facilitation of the psychological well-being of the unemployed. The structuring of the support system ought, however, to be based on psychological principles.

An analysis of the consequences of marked dependence of the unemployed upon others for their need-gratification may also provide another tangible ground on which to deal with the sharp deterioration in their psychological well-being. Unemployment, the worst kind of deprivation (Jahoda, 1988; Jackson and Warr, 1984; Kelvin and Jarrett, 1985; Keyssar, 1985; Liem and Liem, 1988), is a curse. Feeling economically handicapped, an unemployed feels utterly helpless, and is obliged to depend upon others (governmental agencies, voluntary social organizations, family members, relatives, friends, neighbours, etc.) in order to meet even his/her basic needs. Such dependence does not have a benign effect upon his/her well-being (Arnetz *et al.*, 1987; Frese and Mohr,1987; Kieselbach, 1990a, 1991, 1997b, 2003; Linn, Sandifer and Stein, 1985 ; World Health Organization, 1989), rather it engenders in him/her an aberrant feeling of being completely at the mercy of circumstances by forcing him/her into the role of a humble petitioner. Eating into his/her self-respect, this feeling develops in him/her a sense of worthlessness, and a feeling of inferiority (Feather and O'Brien, 1986b; Jackson *et al.*, 1983; Kieselbach, 1991; Kieselbach, Beelmann and Stitzel, 2000; Singh, 1994). The agony of all this ultimately undermines his/her psychological health.

The above discussions mainly deal with the overall deterioration in the psychological health of the unemployed. They do not specifically focus on the substantially greater amount of social conflict (67.25%) in them which also deserves to be explicated thoroughly. Reactions to economic crises may provide a means of understanding the higher level of social conflict in the educated unemployed. The whole world, especially the developing and underdeveloped nations like India, have been struggling against mounting economic pressure. Employment, a socially acceptable means of living (Chakrapani, 1996 ; Garraty, 1978), is essential for maintaining oneself, one's family, social status, self-respect and prestige. In other words, obtaining employment has become a consensual and normative demand; it has been internalized in us as a morally binding obligation (Singh, Kumari and Singh, 1992). Thus, if we fail to secure employment in spite of our best efforts, we feel as if we are violating the morally binding ethos. This often exposes us to the high risk of social conflict. However, for the sake of prediction and precision, we also need to know as to what an Indian means by employment. For an Indian, even today, employment means securing a government job, i.e., to be a *Babu* (clerk) or *Hakim* (officer) which would confer upon him/her more prestige and status. But, in the face of acute shortage of job facilities in the public and organized private sectors in India, one is often at a loss to decide what course one should opt for in relation to one's livelihood. An educcated person, normally, does not fancy a job managed by a private agency or a job related to household chores (Papola, 1992). Thus, an educated person confronting the problem of unemployment is in a fix. He/she finds himself/herself unable to decide upon his/her course of action with regard to getting a livelihood. Evidently, unemployment leads to the disintegration of the whole life of an individual, pushing him/her into a state of indecision and perplexity.

However, the educated employed young men were also found to be afflicted with reduced psychological health on a moderate level, besides being dogged by a feeling of uncertainty (57.25%). The findings can be explained in the light of poor organizational climate prevailing in almost all public enterprises of eastern India. Observational reports as well as empirical findings (Ahmad and Khanna, 1992; Bajaj, 1982; Barnes, 1992; Kanungo, 1995 ; Kumari, 2001; Pestonjee and Singh, 1982; Singh and Singh, 1985; Singh, 1994; Singh, Kumari and Singh, 1992; Singh, Singh and Rani, 1996a, b; Singh, Singh and Singh, 1995) have clearly indicated that people in jobs often have to confront a variety of problems on all fronts — financial, non-financial, and even psychological. Apart from the need for the employees to exercise their skills in order to experience variety or to exert influence and control over their working lives in many public as well as state enterprises such as education, engineering, health, corporations, etc., they even have to wait for their salaries for months on end. Additionally, the sharp deterioration in the current political scenario, mainly manifesting itself in the form of undue political interference even in the routine affairs of the local management, has led to a worsening of the situation, considerably deepening the prevailing gloom.

The majority of employees perceive the present as a more difficult time than has been seen in the history of Indian public management since independence. Anarchy and instability seem to be the order of the day. This not only resutls in strain in the individuals engaged in job, but also interferes with the effective functioning of the system at large, forcing them to accept life as it comes. In brief, the current organizational climate, particularly in this part of the country, is not fully conducive to the well-being of the employed, indirectly adding to the risk of deterioration in their health. The views of Singh, Kumari and Singh (1992) are worthwhile to mention here. They hold that employment may, over a period of time, merely slow down the intensity of one's reactivity; a bleak situation which seems likely to continue. According to them, work is only taken as a source of subsistence here; it provides only partial support to our well-being. People in jobs in this region have to compromise with various adverse situations, presumably precipitating in them the development, though in a moderate measure, of the significant symptoms of impaired psychological health; manifestation of feelings like anxiety, stress, insecurity, alienation, identity-crisis and decreased life satisfaction in their various forms becomes markedly pronounced therein.

In making a further attempt at expounding the reduced psychological health of the employed it may also be noted that social obligation system in India, despite a considerable impact of social change and modernization, is still very compact and orderly; it is, unlike the western societies, less contractual and egalitarian, and is considerably governed by certain indigenous ideologies such as an inherent desire to repay *Pitri-Rina* (debt owed to parents/ancestors), *Rishi-Rina* (debt owed to one's teachers), *Samaj-Rina* (debt owed to one's society) which one incurs in course of one's developmental stages from all these sources, still-continuing faith in the dictum of *Vasudhaiva Kutumbakam* (the whole universe is your family), pervasive desire to go with the principle of *Paropakarah Paramodharmah* (benevolence is the highest duty), faith in the cosmic reality of the self, intense emotional affinity, a strong feeling for mutual caring and dependence, etc. To summarize, discharging of one's social obligation, more or less, has taken the shape of *dharma* (duty) in India. Hence, a person is always expected to discharge his/her obligations to his/her ingroup members sincerely, particularly the family members — the most important constituents of the ingroup (S.K.Singh, 1986; Sinha and Verma, 1987)—by giving full importance to hierarchical social structures and relationships strongly embedded in Indian society and culture (Kakar, 1978; Kanungo, 1995 ; Roland, 1980; Sinha, 1990), lest he/she should be castigated and, in consequence, lose his/her social status and prestige. An employed is also not exempted from such stringent norms of social functioning (Kanungo, 1995 ; Katju, 1986; Parikh, 1979; Tripathi, 1988). In other words, an employed, too, is expected to be equally responsive simultaneously to the proper performance of the duty associated with his/her job as well as the demands, more specifically the well-being, of the ingroup members, particularly those who are totally dependent on him/her or are more near and dear to him/her. Thus, a person in job, as has been indicated by Kanungo (1995), Singh (1994) and Singh, Kumari and Singh (1992), generally has to cope at once with two sharply distinct situations — the real life situations (the family, the friends, the relatives, the neighbours, the other ingroup members, the immediate social surroundings), and the work environment (relationship with colleagues, superiors and subordinates and other physical and psychological conditions associated with work and workplace). But because of limitations of time and energy, it is difficult for the worker to honour these expectations at the same time. Further, it is also equally difficult for him/her to effect a compromise between the two strands. The failure all along in his/her attempts most likely exposes him/her to heightened tension and conflict (Kahn *et al.*, 1964) which, as has been shown in numerous studies (Brief and Aldag,1976; Caplan *et al.*, 1975; House *et al.*, 1979; Miles, 1975; Parker and DeCotiis, 1983; Pestonjee and Singh, 1982; Singh, Agarwala and Malhan, 1981; Singh, 1994; Singh, Kumari and Singh, 1992), ultimately snowball into maladaptive behaviour generally marked with the symptoms of a higher degree of anxiety, stress, feeling of insecurity, alienation, identity-crisis, dissatisfaction with life, and so on in some or the other identifiable forms. Thus, it appears that as the pressure mounts with demands from both sides, the worker is driven to a point where his/her mental balance may be lost, putting him/her at a particularly high risk of psychological ill-being.

Educated Unemployed *Versus* Employed Young Men : An Analysis of Their Dependence on Different Coping Strategies

A plethora of researches exists on strategies which people generally resort to deal with stress or negative life events faced by them (Amirkhan, 1990; Carver, Scheier and Weintraub, 1989; Cohen and Wills, 1985; Dunkel-Schetter *et al.*, 1992; Fisher and Reason, 1988; Fleishman, 1991; Goldberger and Breznitz, 1982; Halstead, Johnson and Cunningham, 1993; Holahan and Moos, 1987; Kobasa, Maddi and Kahn, 1982; Lazarus and Folkman, 1984; McGown and Fraser, 1995; Nezu and Nezu, 1987; Park, Cohen and Herb, 1990; Pearlin and Schooler, 1978; Thoits, 1983; Turner, 1983 ; Turner, Kessler and House, 1991). Unemployment, as has been indicated, represents a stressful life event, leading to the development of different symptomatic reactions in those who experience it (see page 36 to 41). But, astonishingly, the study of how the unemployed cope with their life situations has not yet received so much research attention as that of the study of their psychological well-being. Studies, as Iversen (1989) maintains, are still insufficient in this regard, making it difficult to have a systematic account of the coping patterns of the unemployed *versus* employed people. This study, thus designed, was primarily intended to focus on the relative dependence of the educated Indian unemployed *versus* employed young men on one or another strategies in order to cope with their life circumstances. The findings obtained from statistical comparison between the unemployed and employed young men and their relative dependence in terms of different strategies (viz., intrapersistive approach mode, extrapersistive approach mode, punitive avoidance mode, and defensive avoidance mode) resorted to by them in order to cope with their situations are displayed in Table 5.3.

Table 5.3 : Statistical Differences Between Educated Unemployed and Employed Young Men and Their Relative Dependence in Terms of Different Coping Strategies

		Unemployed (N=614)		*Employed (N=410)*		
Coping Strategies	*Possible Score Range*	*Mean (%)*	*SD*	*Mean (%)*	*SD*	*F*
Intrapersistive Approach Mode	0-15	9.68 (64.53)	2.80	10.28 (68.53)	2.53	12.03
Extrapersistive Approach Mode	0-15	2.03 (13.53)	1.08	1.72 (11.47)	0.79	06.34
Punitive Avoidance Mode	0-15	0.92 (06.13)	0.41	0.67 (04.47)	0.27	10.19
Defensive Avoidance Mode	0-15	2.38 (15.87)	1.35	2.33 (15.53)	1.77	0.17

Note : $df = 1,1022$; $p < 0.05 = 3.84$; $p < 0.01 = 6.64$.

Barring defensive avoidance mode ($F = 0.17$; $p > 0.05$), the unemployed and the employed young men differed between themselves significantly in terms of all the strategies adopted to cope with their life events (F-ranging from 06.34 to 12.03). Further, both the groups showed a clear tendency to depend greatly on intrapersistive approach mode in their attempt to cope with their circumstances (64.53% and 68.53% respectively); other coping strategies were little preferred by them in this regard.

Thus, the results, on the whole, indicated both the groups of educated unemployed and employed young men as relatively largely depending on intrapersistive approach mode in their attempt to grapple with the situations inimical to them. A careful analysis of the relative effectiveness of various coping strategies in managing one's life events may be helpful in finding out possible reasons as to why both the groups of unemployed and employed people, more often than not, adopt intrapersistive approach mode as their coping strategy in order to overcome their problems. As is generally accepted, all the coping strategies resorted to for adjustment are divided into two broad distinct categories : active and avoidance coping styles; and each of them involves different strategies and resources (Amirkhan, 1990; Billings and Moos, 1981; Lazarus and Folkman, 1984). Active coping refers to behaviours which confront the problem. Reliance on this coping tactics enables a person to define the problem, find solutions, weigh the alternatives and usually facilitates his/her efforts to solve the problem (Lazarus and Folkman, 1984). As suggested by Billings and Moos (1981) and Holahan and Moos (1987), this coping style may be further broken down to encompass two different strategies such as active-behavioural (attempts to deal with the problem at his/her own by an individual; the direct efforts on the part of an individual to manage the problem) and active-cognitive (efforts to manage the appraisal of the stressfulness of the event; the approach corresponding more with the tactics, 'change in environmental cognitive elements', as suggested by Festinger,1957 in order to lessen the pangs of a dissonant situation — the less direct attempts to fight with the problem). Obviously, active coping strategies, in their essence, resemble, to an extent, the approach modes of coping tactics, and so while the intrapersistive approach mode of coping may, by and large, be conceived as active-behavioural strategy where a person actively involves himself/herself in solving his/her problems, the extrapersistive one may be labelled as active-cognitive style of coping in which a person resorts to the manipulation of his/her environmental elements both at physical and psychological levels to seek out the remedy for his/her condition (such as by establishing identification with, or seeking help from, similarly-afflicted or like-minded people, by attempting to change the environmental constraints in certain special circumstances, particularly happening so on a physical level).

Avoidance coping, on the other hand, essentially calls for the avoidance or denial of the problem in order to normalize its effects (Holahan and Moos, 1987). It leads to a change in the meaning of stressful situations, and as such is conceived as a form of self-deception (Suls and Fletcher, 1985). According to Billings and Moos (1981), it serves to retain hope and optimism even in the face of hardship, to deny reality and possible consequences and to refuse to acknowledge the worst. As can be seen, punitive avoidance as well as defensive avoidance modes, analysed to define the coping patterns of the participants involved in this investigation, in their characteristic expressions, more obviously, represent two different forms of avoidance-focused coping strategies.

Studies conducted to see the relative effectiveness of active *versus* avoidance coping styles in dealing with the situational threats have indicated that there is no one perfect method of coping. Further, no single method can be uniformly applied or be effective in all stressful situations (Holahan and Moos, 1985; Ilfeld, 1980; Menaghan, 1982; Pearlin and Schooler, 1978). Yet, the superiority of active over avoidance coping tactics in mitigating threats has been widely accepted (Billings and Moos, 1981; Blake and Vandiver, 1988; Carver, Scheier and Weintraub, 1989; Holahan and Moos, 1986; Kobasa, 1982; McGown and Fraser,1995; Nakano, 1991; Suls and Fletcher, 1985). It has been shown that avoidance proves a maladaptive form of coping in most situations (Blake and Vandiver, 1988; Holahan and Moos, 1986), especially while the problem is an enduring one (Carver, Scheier and Weintraub, 1989, Kobasa, 1982). It may benefit an individual seriously afflicted with a problem only in the short run, but at the cost of making him/her relatively vulnerable to illness. If the problem is particularly serious and persistent, reliance on avoidance in order to cope with it will prove less effective, rather it will do little to change the stressor but to add to its intensity (Suls and Fletcher,1985).

To summarize, avoidance-focused coping strategies may offer only short-term relief; they seem limited in the alleviation of the serious and long-persistent situational threats. Obviously, active coping strategies may serve better in counteracting the threat. In the light of the aforementioned findings, if we take stock of the state of both unemployment and employment in India, we may find sufficient reasons to justify the substantially greater degree of dependence of both the groups of educated unemployed and employed solely on intrapersistive approach mode in their attempt to cope with their situations. As has been mentioned on more than one occasion in the preceding sections of this report, India has been facing a serious problem of unemployment, which is not expected to be eradicated in the near future with the least prudent man-made strategies— obviously an indication of their helpless surrender to fate for the solution of the malady, the most provocative of all contemporary social problems besetting Indian life and destiny. Noticeably, it has acquired menacing proportions, certainly threatening the very vigour and vitality of Indian social life. Not only the unemployed but also the entire society finds itself in a state of deep crisis, adversley affecting their health. However, the predicament of the employed is also not very encouraging. As can be envisaged, the organizational climate, particularly in most of the public enterprises of eastern India, has deteriorated sharply on account of one reason or another. Such a situation is not conducive to the health of an employee. To epitomize, both the unemployed and the employed people, to a lesser or a greater degree, suffer from problems of all kinds, which results in their reduced psychological health. An adequate social support system can protect them from total breakdown. But, this is easier said than done. In brief, support systems in our country seldon act in a well-defined manner, as a result of which people feel isolated in the midst of destitutes.

Thus, the reason behind the unemployed and employed people frequently using intrapersistive approach mode as their one and only strategy in order to fight their plight can very well be adjudged in the light of the aforementioned discussions. Indeed, both the groups confronted a large number of long-persisting problems, though considerably varying in degree and in their characteristic expressions, the greater amount of their reliance on intrapersistive approach mode — a form of active coping style — in their attempt to deal with their situations, henceforth, appears justified. Hard times, as Achyut K. Singh (1992) and I.K. Singh (1996) feel, are not always damaging; they help develop in an individual adequate potentialities and desired capabilities to face the odds. It follows the natural law of 'struggle for existence'. An individual, finding no rescue and respite, often draws up his/her own grit and gumption to protect himself/herself. In brief, misery and misfortune are not always damaging, they lead to the development of an indomitable fighting spirit sometimes. However, the way one reacts to the crises of life is important. If he/she takes them as a challenge, he/she is sure to develop certain fighting qualities that may equip him/her substantially with fortitude and aplomb. In the context of the above assertions, one may feel that our educated young men of today, whether unemployed or employed, are taking their plight as a challenge. And in order to combat it, they have developed or are in the process of developing certain desirable qualities for taking stock of the situation.

Another possible reason for describing the substantially greater reliance of the unemployed and employed people on intrapersistive approach mode for coping with their situation can be found in an analysis of the findings of a good number of studies (Billings and

Moos, 1981; Cronkite and Moos, 1984; Holahan and Moos, 1987; Pearlin and Schooler, 1978). These studies have clearly indicated that the highly educated people usually rely more on active-focused strategies in order to fight with their situations. Both the groups of participants involved in this study were either technical or non-technical graduates and postgraduates, so their larger dependence on intrapersistive approach mode in dealing with their situations does not require much justification; it is already well investigated. Level of education being the common factor in both the groups, it may obviously be the reason for it. Of course, as Sinha (1986) feels, a high level of education, especially higher education, leads to the development of inner strength and thus enables an individual to fight calamities and misfortunes. In all, education does aid an individual to gain more adaptive coping strategies in the face of stressors.

The findings obtained by Dunkell-Schetter *et al.* (1992) may also allow us to form yet another basis on which to contemplate the results of this study. In their study it has been shown that relatively highly religious people are more likely to depend on active strategies to face their negative life events. Interestingly, as may commonly be observed, despite a widespread impact of social change and modernization in every walk of life, belief in God clearly permeates the Indian psyche (Chakrapani, 1995 ; Kakar, 1978; Luthera, 1965; Amar K.Singh, 1988; I.K.Singh, 1996; Singh and Sinha, 1990). Indians conceive themselves as nothing more than a pawn in the hands of God and as such usually consider their entire life style to be solely governed by destiny (Roy and Srivastava, 1986; Singh, Singh and Singh, 1996). Thus, the reason why both the groups of the unemployed and the employed people in India more frequently use intrapersistive approach mode as their coping strategy may very well be traced to their deep-seated belief in religion. However, as D. Sinha (1988) maintains, an obsessive belief in religion, particularly in the principles of *anasakti* (non-attachment), *maya* (illusion) or in the illusory and transitory character of the world, etc., may put an individual obviously in a passive frame of mind, promoting in him/her a lack of interest in the formulation of a proper plan of action and ultimately leading to an attitude of indifference to the results of his/her action altogether. Briefly put, it may weaken his/her motivation and thus may considerably reduce his/her spirit to fight with the situation on his/her own. A greater amount of dependence in Indian character may very well exemplify it. The roots of the syndrome, according to J.B.P. Sinha (1970), do not only lie in the protective and permissive familial atmosphere but also in the religious tradition of *bhakti* (devotion) which demands nothing less than total submission on the part of the devotee to his/her *Guru* (spiritual guide) and *Govinda* (God) by fully confiding in them for emancipation from all sins and *moksha* or *nirvana* (salvation) from this worldly abode. Nonetheless, the views ought to be generalized with caution; it may be the oversimplification of the denuded truth conjoining the all-pervasive importance of religion, particualrly in the Hindu way of life. The exemplary views held by Tripathi (1988) and D.Sinha (1988), although obviously eclectic in intent, deserve mention here. By analysing a good number of cases, they have suggested not to ignore the functional value of religion in the life of an Indian. Indeed, religion, even for a modern Indian, as our general observation may clearly attest, emboldens him/her from within and thus, more or less, enables him/her to maintain spontaneous as well as unfathomable energy-current in order to meet the situational demands. Thus, there is no question of any controversy as to why both the unemployed and the employed young men in India, more often than not, depended on intrapersistive approach mode in handling their life events; it definitely befits their temperament, having a considerable amount of religiosity and attachment to the other-worldly pursuits of life. Undeniably, as has already been mentioned above, we are still very much influenced by various religious principles and dogmas spread over our different mythological writings and epics, particularly in the great *Srimad Bhagwadgita* (2.47) that tells us to value *karma* (duty) philosophy without having the expectation of *phalas* (the fruits of one's actions) in life — the *nishkam karma*. This philosophy of life definitely encourages us to face life on our own by sacrificing all our *mohas* (attachments), *bhayas* (fears) and every act proving an obstacle in the way.

In making further attempts to defend the larger dependence of the unemployed and employed young men in India on intrapersistive approach mode for their copings, the findings of Holahan and Moos (1985) may also be utilized. The findings have indicated that people with an easygoing disposition find it easy to bank on active strategies in managing their life circumstances. The ethnographical records as well as the empirical findings obtained from socio-psychological researches (see the analytical notes on Indian culture and personality as well as the values among the Indians presented in the works of Nandy and Kakar, 1980; Achyut K.Singh, 1992; Amar K.Singh, 1975;

D.Sinha, 1988; J.B.P. Sinha, 1980, 1990; Spratt, 1966; etc.) indicate that the Indians have a typical personality disposition, in general. A considerable amount of easygoing temperament may clearly be seen to dominate their behaviour pattern. What is unique about them is that they take life as it comes to them. Pain and paucity, penury and woe, fortune and misfortune, and so on are accepted by them alike without complaint (Basham, 1971; Lapierre, 1986; Singh, Sinha and Kumari, 1985). Further, '*kya farak parta hai*' (what difference does it make ?), '*jahi bidhi rakhe Ram tahi bidhi rahie*' (live as the Lord Rama wishes you to live), etc., life attitudes as well as the greater amount of tolerance, conceived as the byproduct of the impact of our culture, tradition and age-old mythological philosophy and principles, are greatly embedded in the personality disposition of the majority of the Indians and considerably guide their behaviour on most occasions. Thus, the Indian may clearly be recognized as having an easygoing temperament. The trait is not generally perceived as action-arousing; instead it acts to develop the tendency of the acceptance of one's lot. But, the acceptance of reality, as the common Indian feels, does not mean the abating of action potential in an individual; it exhorts him/her considerably for working out a strategy to stand up to the situation. If the investigators evaluate the syndrome as having a negative effect on the zeal to work, they, to an extent, misinterpret and misrepresent the basic thought associated with the phenomenon as rooted in the mind of the Indian. They have, most probably, misconstrued the inherent reality engrained in the principle of *nishkam karma* which enjoins us to accept every good or bad result alike without caring for the fulfilment of what one desires. But such an attitude which seems as leading to the development of a considerable amount of passivity in an individual does not interfere in any way with his/her potent functioning spirit and value for work orientation or action orientation.

To summarize, an easygoing personality disposition does not lessen the zeal to fight with the situation as it externally seems to be. The Indians, in general, as our above discussion related to the unique structuring of their life pattern shows, are rated high on the dimension of easygoing temperament. The over dependence of both the groups of the unemployed and employed young men in India on intrapersistive approach strategy in order to meet the situational demands, thus, stands vindicated. It is surely consistent with their unique personality disposition marked by an easygoing life style.

6

The Technically and Non-Technically Educated Unemployed and Employed Young Men : Their Psychological Well-being and Coping Styles

Level of education has been clearly shown to mediate the impact of status of employment on the psychological well-being, as well as the adoption of a particular strategy seeking adjustment (see chapter 3 for a brief account). But, quite surprisingly, despite a good amount of evidence indicating marked differences among people coming from different faculties in their characteristic psychological manifestations (Cronkite and Moos,1984; Kundu, Sanyal and Bhattacharya, 1986; McGown and Fraser, 1995; Mukerjee and Chatterji, 1986; Roy, 1995; Srivastava, 1994), the study into the differential impacts of the status of employment on the psychological health of, and the choice for a particular coping strategy by, the distinct groups of the technically and the non-technically educated people has not generated much interest among investigators in India and abroad. Researches, according to Warr, Jackson and Banks (1988), are almost insufficient in this field. And, incidentally, whatever has appeared recently in this regard is neither comprehensive nor consistent. The investigators like Kaufman (1982), Leventhman (1981), Swinburne (1981) and Warr, Jackson and Banks (1988) have reported unemployment as more harmful to the psychological well-being of those who are professionally educated. But, other investigators (e.g., Cohn, 1978; Fineman, 1983; Hartley, 1980; Little, 1976; Schaufeli, 1988b; Shamir, 1986 ; Townsend and Davidson, 1982) have not found it to be so; workers out of job with technical or professional degrees were not afflicted with a greater psychological decline. Unemployment is virtually not felt by them as quite inconducive to their psychological health. Further, Brinkmann (1984), Warr (1984a) and Wuggenig (1985) have reported that job-seekers with little or no occupational training are greatly plagued with an increased level of stress. Similar are the findings of Del Llano (1990), Hepworth (1980), Ioannidi and Mestheneos (2000), Kiesebach (2003), Rodíguez (1994) and Stokes and Cochrane (1984). They have also indicated that the semi-skilled and unskilled unemployed, as compared to those with higher occupational status, have poor psychological well-being generally manifested in terms of greater personal distress, hostility, depression, guilt, low self-esteem, lower level of life satisfaction, etc. O'Brien (1986), and Warr (1987d), on the basis of their reviews of longitudinal studies, have also concluded that unemployment has adverse effects on psychological health in adults, especially for less qualified men who have limited financial resources to draw upon. In the studies by Jackson and Warr (1984), and Warr and Jackson (1985), too, unskilled or semi-skilled unemployed men have been found to have a significantly worse psychological well-being, but they have not shown any evidence of further deterioration in their health after about 5 months. These data, precisely, suggest that psychological health declines soon after job loss but that, on an average, stabilizes at a significantly lower level after approximately 3 months. However, both of these studies do not involve the control group of skilled unemployed people, hence the findings obtained therefrom cannot be extended to a wider perspective. Besides, the abovementioned findings, McKenna and Payne (1984), Payne and Hartley (1987), and Payne, Warr and Hartley (1984) have found that there exist no significant differences between middle-class and working-class unemployed people in their psychological health. Both the groups have poor health, although working-class respondents report significantly greater financial problems and worries, and difficulties in filling their time than do their middle-class counterparts. In short, unemployment, according to them, has a *'homogenizing effect'* on psychological health of people coming from all social classes. The social class gradient in health (DHSS, 1980) does not 'inoculate' people from higher social classes against eventual morbidity.

Notably, in India, too, the investigators have not shown any noticeable interest in analysing the mediating role of different kinds of education (technical *versus* non-technical education) in relation to the impacts of status of employment on psychological health, and the preference for a particular coping strategy. There are only a few research findings so far in this regard. And, interestingly, even those, too, have been particularly obtained by Singh and his associates (Singh, 2001; Singh, Rani and Singh, 1999; Singh, Kumari and Kumari, 2000; Singh, Singh and Rani, 1996a, b; Singh and Singh, 2004; Singh, Singh and Singh, 1996; Singh, Singh and Kumari, 1998), with a clear indication of lingering inconsistencies. On the basis of the intra-group comparisons, Singh, Singh and Rani (1996a) and Singh, Singh and Singh (1996) have reported that the exclusive groups of the technically educated unemployed and employed people, as compared to the non-technically educated people with similar employment status, are more, though not significantly, prone to alienation and its symptomatic manifestations, as well as externality. These findings thus apparently suggest that the psychological effects of both unemployment and employment are more acute for the technically educated people than for the non-technically educated ones. But, other studies by them (Singh, 2001; Singh, Rani and Singh, 1999; Singh, Kumari and Kumari, 2000; Singh and Singh, 2004 ; Singh, Singh and Rani, 1996b; Singh, Singh and Kuamari, 1998) have sounded a somewhat different note.

These studies have shown that the technically educated unemployed in comparison with the non-technically educated unemployed, and the technically educated employed in comparison with the non-technically educated employed have high self-concepts, high life satisfaction, and the higher scales of development-orientation and its various dimensions. Although both the groups of technically educated people, as compared to their non-technically educated counterparts of their own specific employment status, confront a greater pang of social conflict. It may be pointed out here that technical or professional education in India is commonly seen to be associated with greater social recognition and prestige. And this may arguably be accounted for attenuating the sharp decline in the psychological health of those with degrees in such education. But, at the same time, it may also be admitted that as they (especially if they are unemployed) find that their education has no meaning in providing them with adequate livelihood in the face of a large-scale unemployment besetting the fate of the entire nation, or the reward received by them is quite disproportionate to the costs and investments incurred in the form of money and other sacrifices in acquiring their education (especially in the case of people at jobs in public enterprises), they feel themselves deeply shattered — more likely liable to precipitating in them a greater psychological risk. On the basis of an extensive analysis of the psychological health of the technically and non-technically educated unemployed and employed young men in India, Rani (1993) has also presented a mixed picture in this regard : while some symptomatic reactions have been found to be more pronounced in the case of the technically educated people, the others were conspicuous with the non-technically educated ones. The study of Pratap and Gupta (1985) also deserves to be mentioned here. They have reported that the unemployed engineers, as compared to their counterparts, are more anxiety-prone. But, their study has not included the unemployed having degrees especially in non-technical education. Further, the anxiety scores obtained by the unemployed engineers have not been found to be much aggravated but only evince a clear tendency to increase. In short, the findings by Pratap and Gupta (1985) are also not relatively broader in their prediction.

To summarize, the evidences, whether recorded in India or abroad in this connection, are rather conflicting, and even less elaborate. The picture thus remains unclear regarding the impact of status of employment on the psychological health of, and the adoption of a particular coping strategy by the people with degrees in technical and non-technical education. Hence, a systematic attempt has further been initiated to delve into the issue in question once again in an Indian context by comparing the technically and non-technically educated unemployed and employed young men with one another in terms of their psychological health, as well as the degree of their reliance on various strategies to handle their life situations. As designed, the psychological health has been measured in terms of the level of anxiety, stress, feeling of insecurity, alienation, identity-crisis and life satisfaction. On the other hand, the coping behaviour includes the strategies like intrapersistive approach mode, extrapersistive approach mode, punitive avoidance mode and defensive avoidance mode. The subsequent pages record the summary of the findings of inter- and intra-group statistical comparisons among different groups of respondents in terms of their psychological well-being and coping styles with their interpretations.

Level of Anxiety, Stress, Feeling of Insecurity, Alienation, Identity-Crisis and their Dimensions : A Comparison Among Technically and Non-technically Educated Unemployed and Employed Young Men

As already mentioned, there is a greater lack of consistency and precision in the findings accumulated so far in India and abroad on the differences among the technically and non-technically educated unemployed and employed people in their psychological health and coping styles. Also, it may be pointed out that except the studies conducted by Pratap and Gupta (1985), Rani (1993), and Singh, Singh and Rani (1996a), hardly any systematic attempt has yet been made to investigate the level of anxiety, stress, feeling of insecurity, alienation, identity-crisis, and life satisfaction in their various symptomatic manifestations, particularly among the technically and non-technically educated unemployed *vis-à-vis* employed young men in India. If there are some of the research findings, they do not have direct implications about the impact of status of employment on these select health indices for a particular brand of the educated young men. Keeping all these inadequacies and imperfections in mind, an attempt was freshly initiated to examine the issue in question. Table 6.1 involves the findings of a statistical comparison among the groups of technically and non-technically educated unemployed and employed young men in terms of their psychological health attained in terms of the degree and extent of anxiety, stress, feeling of insecurity, alienation, identity-crisis and their dimensions.

All the groups of respondents, as it appeared from an inspection of the results furnished in Table 6.1, tended to differ markedly from one another in terms of each and every indicator of psychological health (F-values ranged between 5.94 and 67.65), excepting the alienating outbreak of narcissism ($p > 0.05$). However, the findings so computed from the multiple-comparison of pairs of means, by employing Newman-Keuls Stundentized Range Test, failed to fully substantiate the findings obtained from one-way ANOVA. Notably, with the exception of significant differences between the mean scores of the technically and the non-technically educated employed only in terms of general worries (OQ = 0.46 ; CQ = 0.47), psychological symptoms (CQ = 0.39) and anxiety (OQ = 1.38;CQ = 1.27), and the technically and the non-technically educated unemployed in terms of dejection (OQ = 0.85 ; CQ = 0.71), neither the exclusive groups of

Table 6.1 : Statistical Differences Among Different Groups of Technically and Non-technically Educated Unemployed and Employed Young Men and their Relative Standing in Terms of Different Indices of their Psychological Well-being

Indices of Psychological Well-being	*Unemployed*						*Employed*						*F*
	Technically Educated (N=206)			*Non-technically Educated (N=408)*			*Technically Educated (N=132)*			*Non-technically Educated (N=278)*			
	Mean (%)	*SD*	*Rank*	*Mean (%)*	*SD*	*Rank*	*Mean (%)*	*SD*	*Rank*	*Mean (%)*	*SD*	*Rank*	
1. General Worries	3.04 (50.67)	1.67	17	3.41 (56.83)	1.62	06	1.82 (30.33)	0.97	26	2.28 (38.00)	1.23	24	50.43
2. Somatic Manifestations	0.84 (28.00)	0.44	33	0.82 (27.33)	0.43	36	0.53 (17.67)	0.29	32	0.55 (18.33)	0.30	33	9.02
3. Psychological Symptoms	2.33 (46.60)	1.35	23	2.50 (50.00)	1.34	22	1.16 (23.20)	0.62	29	1.67 (33.40)	0.86	27	51.13
4. Social Relations	3.01 (37.63)	1.57	31	3.09 (38.63)	1.58	31	1.44 (18.00)	0.79	31	1.83 (22.88)	0.94	31	45.69
5. **Anxiety**	9.23 (41.95)	4.73	29	9.82 (44.64)	4.45	29	4.96 (22.55)	2.63	30	6.34 (28.82)	3.21	29	66.72
6. Suicidal Tendency	0.32 (08.00)	0.17	39	0.38 (09.50)	0.20	39	0.08 (02.00)	0.05	39	0.08 (02.00)	0.05	39	13.28
7. Emotional Instability	3.37 (42.13)	1.76	28	3.18 (39.75)	1.64	30	1.95 (24.38)	1.01	28	2.10 (26.25)	1.08	30	30.48
8. Paranoid Tendency	2.22 (18.50)	1.14	38	2.40 (20.00)	1.26	38	1.39 (11.58)	0.74	38	1.50 (12.50)	0.79	38	14.95
9. Depression	10.59 (29.42)	5.37	32	11.02 (30.61)	5.67	32	5.23 (14.53)	2.76	34	5.49 (15.25)	2.31	35	58.09
10. Physical Illness	3.17 (26.42)	1.69	36	3.51 (29.25)	1.81	33	2.01 (16.75)	1.03	33	2.25 (18.75)	1.17	32	25.20

Contd.

Indices of Psychological Well-being	*Unemployed*						*Employed*						*F*
	Technically Educated (N=206)			*Non-technically Educated (N=408)*			*Technically Educated (N=132)*			*Non-technically Educated (N=278)*			
	Mean (%)	*SD*	*Rank*	*Mean (%)*	*SD*	*Rank*	*Mean (%)*	*SD*	*Rank*	*Mean (%)*	*SD*	*Rank*	
11. Social Maladjustment	3.14 (26.17)	1.64	37	3.32 (27.67)	1.73	35	1.54 (12.83)	0.81	37	1.62 (13.50)	0.85	37	36.46
12. Apprehensiveness	3.18 (26.50)	1.68	35	3.18 (26.50)	1.68	37	1.57 (13.08)	0.83	36	1.63 (13.58)	0.82	36	35.43
13. **Stress**	25.99 (27.07)	13.08	34	26.99 (28.11)	13.37	34	13.77 (14.34)	6.88	35	14.67 (15.28)	7.43	34	53.42
14. Lack of Self-confidence	10.91 (54.55)	4.09	07	11.64 (58.20)	3.60	05	8.28 (41.40)	2.87	10	8.94 (44.70)	3.04	09	51.21
15. Dejection	8.66 (57.73)	3.06	04	9.51 (63.40)	2.85	03	6.55 (43.67)	2.69	07	7.35 (49.00)	2.78	05	52.01
16. Pessimism	2.06 (41.20)	1.08	30	2.32 (46.40)	1.24	27	1.48 (29.60)	0.97	27	1.46 (29.20)	0.79	28	33.81
17. Emotional Responsiveness	15.95 (53.17)	5.10	10	15.98 (53.27)	4.76	15	12.23 (40.77)	4.28	12	12.66 (42.20)	4.34	15	44.95
18. Social Insecurity	12.23 (48.92)	4.68	21	12.86 (51.44)	4.18	20	9.29 (36.92)	3.68	22	9.73 (38.92)	3.51	23	46.02
19. Distrust	2.76 (55.20)	1.31	05	2.81 (56.20)	1.38	07	2.10 (42.00)	1.21	09	2.10 (42.00)	1.12	16.5	23.73
20. **Feeling of Insecurity**	52.57 (52.57)	16.44	14	55.12 (55.12)	14.40	09	39.95 (39.95)	12.89	13	42.24 (42.24)	12.77	14	67.65
21. Despair	17.36 (54.25)	4.76	08	17.37 (54.28)	4.25	11	14.70 (45.94)	3.57	06	15.26 (47.69)	3.69	07.	25.26

Contd.

Table 6.1 (*Contd.*)

Indices of Psychological Well-being	Unemployed						Employed						F
	Technically Educated (N=206)			Non-technically Educated (N=408)			Technically Educated (N=132)			Non-technically Educated (N=278)			
	Mean (%)	SD	Rank	Mean (%)	SD	Rank	Mean (%)	SD	Rank	Mean (%)	SD	Rank	
22. Unstructured Universe	4.22 (52.75)	1.58	11.5	4.48 (56.00)	1.30	08	4.28 (53.50)	1.48	02	4.02 (50.25)	1.37	03	5.94
23. Psychological Vacuum	4.15 (51.88)	1.34	16	4.33 (54.13)	1.40	12	3.93 (49.13)	1.20	04	3.88 (48.50)	1.36	06	7.00
24. Disillusionment	1.79 (44.75)	0.85	26	1.94 (48.50)	0.90	25	1.51 (37.75)	0.73	19	1.47 (36.75)	0.67	26	20.02
25. Narcissism	1.77 (44.25)	0.96	27	1.82 (45.50)	0.97	28	1.59 (39.75)	0.83	15	1.68 (42.00)	0.78	16.5	1.62
26. **Alienation**	29.29 (52.30)	6.64	15	29.95 (53.48)	5.90	14	26.02 (46.46)	4.74	05	26.31 (46.98)	5.42	08	32.73
27. Depersonalization	3.70 (46.25)	1.59	24.5	3.92 (49.00)	1.59	24	2.84 (35.50)	1.16	24	3.02 (37.75)	1.24	25	31.80
28. Fragmentation	4.33 (54.13)	1.81	09	4.21 (52.63)	1.82	17	2.89 (36.13)	1.33	23	3.24 (40.50)	1.35	20	39:53
29. Uncertainty	2.69 (67.25)	0.99	01	2.55 (63.75)	0.98	02	2.35 (58.75)	0.92	01	2.29 (57.25)	0.92	01	8.18
30. Distress	6.05 (50.42)	2.07	18	6.29 (52.42)	2.11	18	4.76 (39.67)	1.77	16	5.01 (41.75)	1.74	18	35.81
31. Indecisiveness	4.22 (52.75)	1.74	11.5	4.14 (51.75)	1.56	19	3.07 (38.38)	1.08	17	3.44 (43.00)	1.38	10	28.38
32. Social Conflict	2.66 (66.50)	1.00	02	2.71 (67.75)	0.95	01	2.08 (52.00)	0.95	03	2.26 (56.50)	0.97	02	22.29

Contd.

Indices of Psychological Well-being	Unemployed						Employed						F
	Technically Educated (N=206)			Non-technically Educated (N=408)			Technically Educated (N=132)			Non-technically Educated (N=278)			
	Mean (%)	SD	Rank	Mean (%)	SD	Rank	Mean (%)	SD	Rank	Mean (%)	SD	Rank	
33. Isolation	3.88 (48.50)	1.53	22	3.97 (49.63)	1.63	23	2.98 (37.25)	1.30	21	3.13 (39.13)	1.15	22	29.29
34. Withdrawal from Social and Personal Contact	1.85 (46.25)	0.94	24.5	1.93 (48.25)	0.96	26	1.52 (38.00)	0.79	18	1.66 (41.50)	0.78	19	9.93
35. Role Conflict	6.57 (54.75)	2.26	06	6.54 (54.50)	2.04	10	4.91 (40.92)	1.86	11	5.07 (42.25)	1.82	12.5	47.85
36. Hopelessness	4.03 (50.38)	1.74	19	4.26 (53.25)	1.71	16	2.80 (35.00)	1.04	25	3.23 (40.38)	1.42	21	42.86
37. Loneliness	1.96 (49.00)	1.02	20	2.02 (50.50)	0.98	21	1.50 (37.50)	0.78	20	1.69 (42.25)	0.84	12.5	14.59
38. Desolation	2.35 (58:75)	0.99	03	2.48 (62.00)	1.32	04	1.72 (43.00)	0.77	08	1.99 (49.75)	0.98	04	6.57
39. **Identity-crisis**	44.29 (52.73)	11.36	13	45.02 (53.60)	11.48	13	33.42 (39.79)	9.43	14	36.03 (42.89)	9.56	11	66.58

Note : $df = 3{,}1020$; $p < 0.05 = 2.60$; $p < 0.01 = 3.79$.

the unemployed nor the employed differed with each other to a substantial measure in terms of any of the symptomatic reactions. In short, if a striking difference between the mean scores of any two groups in almost all the health indices was recorded, that was only observed in the groups quite distinct in their status of employment. The findings that appeared from the comparison of the technically educated employed with both the groups of unemployed in terms of their various psychological manifestations were as follows : general worries (OQ = 1.59, 1.22; CQ = 0.47), somatic manifestations (OQ = 0.31, 0.29; CQ = 0.25) , psychological symptoms (CQ = 0.38), social relations (OQ = 1.65, 1.57; CQ = 0.55), anxiety (OQ = 4.86, 4.27; CQ = 1.27), suicidal tendency (CQ = 0.21), emotional instability (OQ = 1.42, 1.23; CQ = 0.59), paranoid tendency (OQ = 1.01, 0.83; CQ = 0.63), depression (CQ = 1.95), physical illness (CQ = 0.67), social maladjustment (OQ = 1.78,1.60; CQ = 0.75), apprehensiveness (CQ = 0.72), stress (OQ = 13.22,12.22; CQ = 4.34), lack of self-confidence (OQ = 3.36, 2.63; CQ = 1.04), dejection (CQ = 0.85), pessimism (CQ = 0.34), emotional responsiveness (OQ = 3.75,3.72; CQ = 1.39), social insecurity (OQ = 3.57,2.94; CQ = 1.24), distrust (CQ = 0.39),feeling of insecurity (OQ = 15.17,12.62; CQ = 4.26), despair (CQ = 1.24), psychological vacuum (OQ = 0.40; CQ = 0.38), disillusionment (OQ = 0.43,0.28; CQ = 0.23), alienation (OQ = 3.93,3.27; CQ = 1.73),depersonalization (CQ = 0.44), fragmentation (OQ = 1.44,1.32; CQ = 0.49), uncertainty (CQ = 0.27), distress (OQ = 1.53,1.29; CQ = 0.59), indecisiveness (OQ = 1.15, 1.07; CQ = 0.45), social conflict (CQ = 0.29), isolation (CQ = 0.43), withdrawal from social and personal contact (OQ = 0.41, 0.33; CQ = 0.27), role conflict (OQ = 1.66,1.63; CQ = 0.60), hopelessness (OQ = 1.46, 1.23; CQ = 0.47), loneliness (OQ = 0.52,0.46; CQ = 0.28), desolation (CQ = 0.59), and identity-crisis (OQ = 11.60, 10.87; CQ = 3.20). Similarly, following facts were recorded about the marked distinction of the non-technically educated employed from one or another group of the unemployed in terms of their various psychological reactions such as general worries (OQ = 1.13,0.76; CQ = 0.44), somatic manifestations (CQ = 0.23), psychological symptoms (OQ = 0.83,0.66; CQ = 0.35), social relations (CQ = 0.52), anxiety (OQ = 3.48,2.89; CQ = 1.19), suicidal tendency (OQ = 0.30,0.24; CQ = 0.20), emotional instability (CQ = 0.55), paranoid tendency (CQ = 0.59), depression (OQ = 5.53,5.10; CQ = 1.82), physical illness (CQ = 0.63), social maladjustment (OQ = 1.70,1.52; CQ = 0.70), apprehensiveness

(CQ = 0.67), stress (OQ = 12.32,11.32; CQ = 4.07), lack of self-confidence (OQ = 2.70,1.97; CQ = 0.97), dejection (OQ = 2.16, 1.31; CQ = 0.80), pessimism (OQ = 0.86,0.60; CQ = 0.36), emotional responsiveness (CQ = 1.31), social insecurity (CQ = 1.16),distrust (OQ = 0.71,0.66; CQ = 0.36), feeling of insecurity (OQ = 12.88,10.33; CQ = 3.99), despair (OQ = 2.11,2.10; CQ = 1.16), unstructured universe (OQ = 0.46; CQ = 0.42), psychological vacuum (CQ = 0.40), disillusionment (CQ = 0.24), alienation (OQ = 3.64, 2.98; CQ = 1.62), depersonalization (CQ = 0.41), fragmentation (OQ = 1.09, 0.97; CQ = 0.46), uncertainty (CQ = 0.29), distress (OQ = 1.28, 1.04; CQ = 0.55), indecisiveness (CQ = 0.42), social conflict (OQ = 0.45, 0.40; CQ = 0.27), isolation (OQ = 0.84, 0.75; CQ = 0.41), withdrawal from social and personal contact (CQ = 0.25), role conflict (CQ = 0.56), hopelessness (OQ = 1.03, 0.80; CQ = 0.44), loneliness (CQ = 0.26), desolation (OQ = 1.49; CQ = 0.56), and identity-crisis (OQ = 8.99, 8.26; CQ = 3.00). The results further revealed that the non-technically educated unemployed, followed by the technically educated ones, were apparently more vulnerable to various symptomatic reactions. The employed, particularly the technically educated ones, on the other hand, were relatively less, but altogether moderately, afflicted with different syndromes of reduced psychological health.

The symptoms which were diagnosed as being more alarming in the case of the technically educated unemployed were feeling of uncertainty (67.25%), social conflict (66.50%), desolation (58.75%), dejection (57.73%), and distrust (55.20%). Those which were more pronounced in the group of non-technically educated unemployed were social conflict (67.75%), feeling of uncertainty (63.75%), dejection (63.40%), desolation (62.00%), and lack of self-confidence (58.20%). Similarly, the more acute symptoms found in the technically educated employed involved the psychological dimensions like feeling of uncertainty (58.75%), unstructured universe (53.50%), social conflict (52.00%), psychological vacuum (49.13%), and alienation (46.46%). The symptoms which were identified as more serious in the life of the non-technically educated employed were feeling of uncertainty (57.25%), social conflict (56.50%), unstructured universe (50.25%), desolation (49.75%), and dejection (49.00%). On the other hand, the various syndromes towards which all of them were less concerned were particularly associated with the manifestations of stress; tendency to commit suicide (scores on suicidal ideation for different groups ranged between 2.00% and 9.50%) proved least scaring. Thus, on the whole, it was found that all the groups of respondents, by and large, tended to regard similar symptomatic reactions as more oppressing to them. This tendency was particularly more apparent in pointing the most pressing psychological symptom in them. Notably, all the groups of respondents, except the non-technically educated unemployed, indicated themselves extremely burdened with the sharpened feeling of uncertainty. Practically, a similar trend was exhibited by them in specifying relatively different less deeply felt psychological syndromes in them.

Life Satisfaction : A Comparison Among Technically and Non-technically and Non-technically Educated Unemployed and Employed Young Men

There exists a lot of studies, especially conducted by Feather and his associates, on the life satisfaction of unemployed vis-à-vis employed people (see chapter 1). But, surprisingly, the level of life satisfaction in technically and non-technically educated unemployed *versus* employed young men, except the one conducted by Singh and Singh (2004), has not, in all probability, so far been systematically investigated, especially in India. Although, there are studies (Cohn, 1978; Fletcher and Payne, 1980; Hepworth, 1980; Stokes and Cochrane, 1984) which may serve as a basis for causal inferences in this regard. However, the findings obtained therefrom are less elaborate, and precise (Payne, Warr and Hartley, 1984), and thus seem limited in their applicability in a wider perspective like that in India—unique in its socio-cultural fibre. Hence, this study was designed with an aim to explore possible differences among different groups of technically and non-technically educated unemployed and employed people on the scale of their life satisfaction. Table 6.2 displays the findings.

Different groups of respondents differed significantly from one another in terms of their level of life satisfaction ($F = 83.87$; $df = 3,1020$; $p < 0.01$). However, the findings yielded through multiple-comparisons indicated that only those two groups tended to differ markedly in the amount of their life satisfaction who were dissimilar in their status of employment. Seemingly, the criterion value of Q being 0.63 was clearly low as against the observed values of 2.45 and 2.18 for Q, when an attempt was made to statistically determine the difference of the non-technically educated unemployed from the

Table 6.2 : Statistical Differences Among Different Groups of Technically and Non-technically Educated Unemployed and Employed Young Men and their Relative Standing in Terms of the Degree of their Life Satisfaction

	Unemployed				*Employed*				
	Technically Educated (N=206)		*Non-technically Educated (N=408)*		*Technically Educated (N=132)*		*Non-technically Educated (N=278)*		
Variable	*Mean (%)*	*SD*	*Mean (%)*	*SD*	*Mean (%)*	*SD*	*Mean (%)*	*SD*	*F*
Life Satisfaction	5.01 (50.10)	2.33	4.60 (46.00)	2.20	7.05 (70.50)	1.71	6.78 (67.80)	1.97	83.87

Note : $df = 3,1020$; $p < 0.05 = 2.60$; $p < 0.01 = 3.79$.

discrete groups of the technically and the non-technically educated employed in terms of their mean life satisfaction scores. Similarly, the observed values of 2.04 and 1.77 for Q fairly exceeded the criterion value of Q attained to be 0.59, while the technically educated unemployed were compared separately with the groups of their employed counterparts in this regard. Further, it was revealed that while the group of technically educated employed was highly satisfied with the events taking place in their life (life satisfaction scores = 70.50%), the group of the non-technically educated unemployed was a less satisfied lot (life satisfaction scores only being 46.00%). The non-technically educated employed and the technically educated unemployed young men were ranked second and third respectively on the dimension of life satisfaction.

Technically and Non-technically Educated Unemployed and Employed Young Men : Their Dependence on Different Coping Strategies

The investigators, as it has been pointed out earlier particularly in the first chapter, remain quite indifferent so far to the study of coping patterns of the technically and the non-technically educated unemployed *versus* employed young men, especially in India. However, the study conducted by Singh, Singh and Singh (1996) on the level of externality in the technically and the non-technically educated unemployed and employed people may focus the issue to an extent. The study suggests, though indirectly, that the unemployed, in particular, are likely to confide more in the mode of avoidance in managing their existing circumstances. The study by Chakrapani (1996) and the *'identification effect'* proposed by Singh (1994) and Singh, Singh and Rani (1996b) have also indicated that the unemployed in India tend to depend on outside forces and their help and supports in making adjustment with their life situations, and thus, more or less, favour the tactics of withdrawing from, or avoidance of, the situations in doing so. But, the findings of these few indirect studies cannot be safely generalised. This prompted a detailed analysis of the dependence of the technically and the non-technically educated unemployed vis-à-vis employed people on various strategies for their adjustment. Table 6.3 records a brief account of the findings attained through a statistical comparison among them in this regard.

Table 6.3 : Statistical Differences Among Different Groups of Technically and Non-technically Educated Unemployed and Employed Young Men and their Relative Dependence in Terms of Different Coping Strategies

	Unemployed				*Employed*				
	Technically Educated (N=206)		*Non-technically Educated (N=408)*		*Technically Educated (N=132)*		*Non-technically Educated (N=278)*		
Variable	*Mean (%)*	*SD*	*Mean (%)*	*SD*	*Mean (%)*	*SD*	*Mean (%)*	*SD*	*F*
Intrapersistive Approach Mode	9.64 (64.27)	3.07	9.69 (64.60)	2.67	9.59 (63.93)	2.84	10.57 (70.47)	2.33	7.71
Extrapersistive Approach Mode	2.17 (14.47)	1.16	1.98 (13.20)	1.02	1.98 (13.20)	1.03	1.63 (10.87)	0.86	3.08
Punitive Avoidance Mode	0.92 (6.13)	0.51	0.90 (6.00)	0.43	0.94 (6.27)	0.49	0.54 (3.60)	0.32	16.62
Defensive Avoidance Mode	2.27 (15.13)	1.35	2.43 (16.20)	1.27	2.49 (16.60)	1.27	2.26 (15.07)	1.17	0.99

Note : $df = 3,1020$; $p < 0.05 = 2.60$; $p < 0.01 = 3.79$.

Groups of the technically and the non-technically educated unemployed and employed people were found to differ significantly among themselves in terms of the degree of their dependence on each of the strategies like intrapersistive approach mode ($F = 7.71$; $df = 3,1020$; $p < 0.01$), extrapersistive approach mode ($p < 0.05$), and punitive avoidance mode (F = 16.62), excepting the defensive avoidance mode (F = 0.99; $p > 0.05$) used for their adjustment. However, the findings obtained from the Newman-Keuls test did express a different note. Notably, none, but only the group of the non-technically educated employed was identified as statistically distinct in terms of their reliance on both the intrapersistive approach mode (values for CQs found to be 0.81,0.75, and 0.67 respectively) and the punitive avoidance mode (values for CQs estimated to be 0.33, 0.31 and 0.27 respectively). The group clearly had a greater leaning towards intrapersistive approach mode, and lesser towards punitive avoidance mode in handling their situation. Moreover, it was revealed that no technique other than intrapersistive approach mode (the extent of dependence on intrapersistive approach mode varied between 63.93% and 70.47%) was considered to be the lone suitable technique by all in order to deal with their situations.

To epitomize, all the aforementioned findings attained through the statistical comparisons of the technically and the non-technically educated unemployed *versus* employed young men in terms of the indicators of their psychological health, and the degree of their dependence on various coping strategies both at inter- and intra- group levels overall yielded different specific facts as follows :

(1) The non-technically educated unemployed, followed by the technically educated ones — though there being no marked differences between them in any of their symptomatic reactions, excepting the feeling of dejection —- were found to be greatly afflicted with reduced psychological health; feeling of insecurity, alienation, identity-crisis and a lower level of life satisfaction in their various characteristic manifestations were particularly more pronounced. This shows that the kinds of education — technical and non-technical — in no way mediate the impact of unemployment on psychological well-being. Apparently, unemployment is equally harmful to the psychological well-being of both the technically and non-technically educated young men who experience it. Thus, the results of this study are fairly consistent with the findings of McKenna and Payne (1984), Payne and Hartley (1987) and Payne, Warr and Hartley (1984) who have indicated that unemployment produces a *'homogenizing effect'* on psychological health of people irrespective of the social class they come from; it does not have an adverse effect only on a particular brand of educated people. Employment, as Jahoda (1988) holds, is a primary source of positive social, psychological and material expediencies for the individual. In contemporary society it serves as an important ingredient in defining a person's feeling of identity and self-worth (Erikson, 1968; Gurney, 1980a, b; Kelvin, 1981; Super and Hall, 1978), and providing a means of satisfying certain basic human needs (Jahoda, 1979, 1982; Warr, 1983). Not only does employment force us to be active, but it also propels the exercise of competence and skill (Jackson, 1987). Indeed, labour, as work ethic maintains, is good in itself. It has been accepted as indispensable for life and psychological well-being (Elchardus and Glorieux, 1995). A man or woman becomes a better person by virtue of the act of working (Terkel, 1972). Naturally, the unemployed, as it has been indicated (Jahoda, 1982; Kelvin and Jarrett, 1985; Warr, 1987c, d), are denied all these benefits. This more likely adversely affects their psychological well-being. Of course, relentless abortive attempts to secure an employment, especially under conditions where there is greater lack of some positive factors like social support to alleviate the negative effects of such attempts, leads to many negative experiences, liable for precipitating various symptoms of reduced psychological health (Banks, 1990; Feather, 1982; Fryer, 1995a; Kelvin and Jarrett, 1985; Kieselbach, Beelmann and Stitzel, 2000; Singh , 1994; Singh, Singh and Rani, 1996a; Singh, Singh and Singh, 1996; Warr, 1987c, d; Winefield, 1995b). To conclude, unemployment more likely shakes one's entire psychological foundation where symptoms like anxiety, stress, feeling of insecurity, alienation, identity-crisis, diminished life satisfaction, etc., naturally thrive on to menacing proportions. So, it, as it has been asserted (Banks, 1990; Kieselbach, 1990b; Winefield, 1995b), would not be prudent to claim that unemployment doesn't hit hard — it certainly does. Added to the abovementioned convictions, there are different other theoretical and empirical formulations as well as culture — specific realities like those of India referred to earlier in 5th chapter which may, here too, be taken into account in describing the findings showing both the groups of technically and non-technically educated unemployed as plagued more with the symptoms of psychological ill-health (see chapter 5 for a brief account).

Yet, the views held by Hill (1977, 1978) may also form a genuine ground to understand the findings. Hill maintains that the effects of unemployment are conceptually and experimentally similar to those of bereavement. According to him, jobless can be stricken by reactions similar to those that occur in bereavement. Reactions like denial, grief, and depression are more pronounced in case of bereavement. And these reactions are more or less symptomatic of anxiety, stress, feeling of insecurity, alienation, identity-crisis and diminished life satisfaction — some of the significant indicators of reduced psychological health. So, unemployment and the condition of bereavement have a greater amount of similarity in their consequences. The views propounded by Hill (1977, 1978) can thus help us understand the reasons why both the groups of technically and non-technically educated unemployed people, without any significant difference between themselves, manifest marked deterioration in their psychological health.

Another theoretical idea that also deserves consideration in describing the poor psychological well-being in the educated unemployed young men in India relates to *'Social Cognitive Theory'* propounded by Bandura (1977, 1982, 1986, 1988). The theory, in brief, enunciates that fulfilment of valued goals or standards leads to the enhancement of self-satisfaction, while frequent failures to attain these desired goals or standards produce greater dissatisfactions, more likely promoting the manifestation of different symptomatic reactions (Ahmad and Khanna, 1992; Coburn, 1978; Kanungo, 1979, 1982; Kumari, 2001; Srivastava, 1995). In the light of the above assertion, it seems reasonable to analyse one's perception of education in securing an employment in India. Not astonishingly, education — especially higher education — in the eyes of an Indian even today, is a means for securing jobs, particularly in public or governmental enterprises— the only most significant desired goal in one's life, usually grown out of the temptation to properly maintain oneslf and one's family in the face of fast deteriorating economic scenario in the country at large. But, unfortunately, despite having all capabilities, a vast majority of the educated, as mentioned earlier at different points, may commonly be seen clamouring for salaried or paid employment. Education, of course, has failed to meet their expectation of being gainfully employed. Although recent governmental schemes to provide them easy loans for self-employment have appeared as silver-linings in the all pervasive gloom of despondency. These schemes, as it has been pointed out in 5th chapter, have not borne fruitful results so far. One has really to undergo a rigors of an arduous task to reap the benefits of these schemes. In such a situation, nothing but disappointment and frustration can ensue which — if not immediately, in the long run — is most likely to lead to various psychological disturbances; a higher level of anxiety, stress, feeling of insecurity, alienation, identity-crisis, decreased amount of life satisfaction, etc., are but the natural accompaniments.

The conclusion drawn by Hamilton (1987) may also provide an arguable reason to justify the findings. The conclusion underlines that continued deterioration in the labour market may cause dire consequences for the people who fail to secure employment. It further states that unemployment is psychologically more debilitating for those who find that their academic qualifications or vocational training and proficiency are of no use for their livelihood, especially if they perceive that their failure to secure an employment is not the fault of their own but of an institutional breakdown that is beyond their control. In view of the above conclusion, if we look into the state of the labour market in India, it may apparently be found to be greatly swelled with a large number of job-seekers escalated on account of a steep and an unprecedented rise in the size of labour forces in recent years.

The greater shortage of job facilities clearly grown out of multiple factors like alarming population explosion, qualification escalation — the phenomenon referred to by Jayaram (1984), misconceived and misdirected employment policy, acute political crisis and instability, rampant internal insecurity and disharmony, etc., is generally perceived to be the sole reason behind such a boom in Indian labour market (see chapter 1st and 5th for a detailed account). Virtually, the scene of unemployment is going to be from bad to worse in future India. As per a recent projection (Singh,1998), about 47 million people are expected to be added to labour force during the period of 1996-2016. It implies that if the problem of unemployment has to be totally eradicated in the country, there is a need for creation of about 6 million jobs per annum on an average in the next two decades, if the present participation rates remain constant. But, unfortunately, nothing concrete has been done so far in this regard by the government, except making false promises, and unworthy and deceitful paper planning. It is rather pathetic to mention that the highly educated are the hardest hit by the problem of joblessness, hopelessly scrounging for even a poor job — quite incongruent to their wishes and aspirations, and above all no way prospective and supportive for them both at physical and psychological levels. Such a situation, no doubt, forces them to feel that their educational competence and proficiency have hardly any meaning for them; they are not going to meet with proper recognition with no fault of theirs. Virtually, continuing with worries and uncertainties about their future has become their '*kismet*' (lot).

And, as it has been shown (Jackson, 1988; Warr, 1985), one cannot go on with such mental agony and trauma for long; one has to ultimately lose one's psychological equipoise, and be exposed to all sorts of psychological troubles.

The findings obtained by Del Llano (1990), Del Llano *et al.*, (1996), Huppert and Garcia (1991) and Jackson (1988) may also serve as plausible basis for the explanation of the findings. These investigators have indicated that unemployment is considerably more damaging to the psychological well-being of those who come from a lower or middle-class family with the responsibility to bear the burden of people dependent on them for their subsistence and upkeep. The views held by Singh (1990) also deserve to be mentioned here. According to him, unemployment is not that psychologically harmful for the people belonging to a well-to-do family. But, if they hail from a poor or middle-class family and remain withour job, it clearly produces serious psychological consequences both for them and their family. In describing the findings in the light of the aforementioned conclusions, it is necessary to focus upon the expectations associated with a son in an Indian family. The Indian family system, as it has already been indicated earlier in the 5th chapter, is so structured and organized that a responsible and grown-up *putra* (the son) — the breadwinner — in particular, is expected to maintain not only himself but also his spouse, young children and more often his ageing parents. But, as it may commonly be seen, it is hardly possible for a jobless son coming from a poor or middle-class socio-economic background to comply even with the ordinary wishes of his family members. He may face greater financial constraints which clearly prevents him from performing his duties towards his family effectively. This puts him particularly at risk of unnecessary mental torture and humiliation, more likely abetting in him the various symptoms of psychological ill-health. The educated unemployed young men involved in this investigation apparently hailed from urban middle-class family with the income of Rs.2200 to Rs.3700 per month. Hence, it appears fairly vindicated why they suffered from greater psychological decline. Indeed, their limited financial resources to meet the expectations of their family members, as also towards themselves, may be accounted for all sorts of psychological discomforts in their life. In other words, the mounting economic pressure, particularly caused by unemployment, as it has been documented (Elder, Jr *et al.*, 1991; Iversen, 1989; Jahoda, 1988; Kieselbach, 1989, 1991, 1997a, b, 1998a; Kieselbach, Beelmann and

Stitzel, 2000;Verkleij, 1989; Warr, 1987d), is greatly damaging to the psychological health of the person concerned.

(2) Both groups of the employed, in general, were relatively less, yet more or less moderately, vulnerable to different symptomatic reactions of psychological ill-health. Thus, the findings of this study agree fairly well with the findings of a number of earlier studies (Kumari, 2001; Rani, 1993; Singh, 1990, 1994, 2001; Singh, Kumari and Singh, 1992; Singh, Singh and Rani, 1996a, b; Singh, Singh and Singh, 1996; Singh, Singh and Singh, 1995). These studies have shown that highly educated employed people in India are not entirely risk-free; they carry with them more or less a moderate amount of different psychological symptoms. In the previous chapter many reasons have been put forward to elucidate a moderate psychological deterioration in the employed in India. They are, indeed, much elaborate and comprehensive, and thus may also form an eloquent basis to justify the findings here too. In addition, there are certain other realities, typical of many of the Indian organizations, that also deserve to be analysed in order to search out further basis to explicate the findings. One such reality, as Kanungo (1995) notes, clearly relates to a greater amount of personal sense of helplessness among workers at all levels of organizations in India. In every walk of their day-to-day work and non-work business, they often manifest a passive and resigned attitude toward their environment. They feel that they can do nothing by themselves to change their environment. In other words, they believe that the external forces control them, rather than they govern their environment. The studies of Rani (1993), Singh, Singh and Singh (1996) and Singh, Singh and Singh, (1995) have also shown a marked tendency of externality among both the groups of unemployed and employed people in India. And, on the other hand, there are studies (Hacker, 1985 ; Jackson, 1983; Kanungo, 1995; Kanungo and Mendonca, 1995; Karasek, 1979; Payne, 1995; Payne and Fletcher, 1983) to record that lack of control apparently precedes the development of various symptomatic reactions like anxiety, stress, feeling of insecurity, alienation, depression, lower level of job and life satisfaction, psychosomatic symptoms, and so on.

Another important aspect of Indian organization that also deserves consideration in order to have a discreet ground to vindicate a relatively moderate amount of psychological ill-being among the educated employed in India relates to supervisory style generally practised therein. There are studies (Agarwal, 1995; Kanungo, 1995; Lal, 1983;

agriculture sciences) unemployed and employed, as compared to the non-technically educated (i.e., degree-holders in arts and humanities, social sciences, science and commerce streams) unemployed and employed, to be more vulnerable to alienation and its dimensions, especially at intra-group level. And, in another study, Singh, Singh and Singh (1996) have found no evidence of significant differences exclusively between technically and non-technically educated unemployed, and technically and non-technically educated employed, in their levels of externality.

Thus, the findings so far available on the psychological well-being of either unemployed or employed people with degrees in different specific disciplines in India are fairly inconsistent. Further, studies on psychological well-being, especially on coping styles, with an elaborate angle, are seemingly insufficient. In short, the afore-mentioned findings seem to be limited in their scope of generalization to a wider perspective. Yet, being consequent on the findings of Jackson and Warr (1987), Singh (1994), and Singh, Singh and Rani (1996b) one may lead to surmise that the technically educated unemployed, especially the degree-holders in medical sciences and agriculture who are still not much hit by the problem of joblessness, would be more vulnerable to psychological deterioration. But, this might be considered as a leap-frog, somewhat trivial in its intent. Virtually, there exists hardly any direct study so far designed with this end in view. Thus, overall, nothing tangible comes out to form a basis for drawing any definite inferences in this regard. Hence, a fresh effort has been made to inquire into the level of psychological well-being as well as coping styles of the unemployed and employed people coming from varied streams of knowledge both at inter- and intra-group levels. The following pages record the details of the findings of statistical comparisons among different groups of unemployed and employed people educated in different faculties of knowledge in terms of the level of their psychological well-being, and the degree of their reliance on different strategies resorted to in order to cope with life circumstances.

Level of Anxiety, Stress, Feeling of Insecurity, Alienation, Identity-Crisis and Their Dimensions : A Comparison Among Different Groups of Unemployed and Employed Young Men Educated in Different Specific Streams of Knowledge

As pointed out above, except for a few less detailed and less precise

Table 7.1 : Statistical Differences Among the Groups of Educated Unemployed and Employed Young Men with Degrees in Various Streams of Knowledge and their Relative Standing in Terms of Different Indices of their Psychological Well-being

Indices of Psychological Well-being	*Unemployed*											
	Technically Educated									*Non-Technically Educated (N=408)*		
	Degree-Holders in Medical Sciences (N=63)			*Degree-Holders in Eng. Sciences (N=79)*			*Degree-Holders in Agri. Sciences (N=64)*					
	Mean (%)	*SD*	*Rank*	*Mean (%)*	*SD*	*Rank*	*Mean (%)*	*SD*	*Rank*	*Mean (%)*	*SD*	*Rank*
1. General Worries	2.73 (45.50)	1.34	24	2.97 (49.50)	1.49	17	3.38 (56.33)	1.54	09	3.41 (56.83)	1.62	06
2. Somatic Manisfestations	0.87 (29.00)	0.47	32	0.78 (26.00)	0.42	33	0.79 (26.33)	0.42	37	0.82 (27.33)	0.43	36
3. Psychological Symptoms	2.17 (43.40)	1.13	26	2.42 (48.40)	1.26	20	2.39 (47.80)	1.20	25	2.50 (50.00)	1.34	22
4. Social Relations	2.86 (35.75)	1.46	31	2.96 (37.00)	1.52	31	3.34 (41.75)	1.69	30	3.09 (38.63)	1.58	31
5. **Anxiety**	8.64 (39.27)	4.29	30	9.13 (41.50)	4.62	28	9.91 (45.05)	4.41	29	9.82 (44.64)	4.45	29
6. Suicidal Tendency	0.25 (6.25)	0.13	39	0.35 (8.75)	0.19	39	0.33 (8.25)	0.18	39	0.38 (9.50)	0.20	39
7. Emotional Instability	3.16 (39.50)	1.61	29	3.25 (40.63)	1.64	29	3.72 (46.50)	1.90	27	3.18 (39.75)	1.64	30
8. Paranoid Tendency	2.11 (17.58)	1.12	38	2.06 (17.17)	1.07	38	2.52 (21.00)	1.28	38	2.40 (20.00)	1.26	38
9. Depression	9.60 (26.67)	4.85	33	9.63 (26.75)	4.84	32	12.75 (35.42)	6.43	32	11.02 (30.61)	5.67	32
10. Physical Illness	3.14 (26.17)	1.67	34	2.85 (23.75)	1.47	37	3.25 (27.08)	1.64	36	3.51 (29.25)	1.81	33

Contd.

Table 7.1 *(Contd.)*

Indices of Psychological Well-being	*Unemployed*											
	Technically Educated									*Non-Technically Educated (N=408)*		
	Degree-Holders in Medical Sciences (N=63)			*Degree-Holders in Eng. Sciences (N=79)*			*Degree-Holders in Agri. Sciences (N=64)*					
	Mean (%)	*SD*	*Rank*	*Mean (%)*	*SD*	*Rank*	*Mean (%)*	*SD*	*Rank*	*Mean (%)*	*SD*	*Rank*
11. Social Maladjustment	2.97 (24.75)	1.54	37	2.87 (23.92)	1.41	36	3.55 (29.58)	1.74	35	3.32 (27.67)	1.73	35
12. Apprehensive-ness	3.11 (25.92)	1.58	35	2.89 (24.08)	1.49	35	3.61 (30.08)	1.82	34	3.18 (26.50)	1.68	37
13. **Stress**	24.34 (25.35)	12.33	36	23.90 (24.90)	11.96	34	29.73 (30.97)	14.41	33	26.99 (28.11)	13.37	34
14. Lack of Self-confidence	10.87 (54.35)	4.75	05	11.11 (55.55)	3.50	05	10.69 (53.45)	4.11	14	11.64 (58.20)	3.60	05
15. Dejection	8.05 (53.67)	3.19	06	8.67 (57.80)	2.93	04	9.25 (61.67)	2.81	03	9.51 (63.40)	2.85	03
16. Pessimism	2.14 (42.80)	1.12	27	1.87 (37.40)	0.98	30	2.02 (40.40)	1.20	30	2.32 (46.40)	1.24	27
17. Emotional Res-ponsiveness	15.81 (52.70)	5.72	08	15.56 (51.87)	4.77	14	16.58 (55.27)	4.74	10	15.98 (53.27)	4.76	15
18. Social Insecurity	12.37 (49.48)	4.32	17	11.76 (47.04)	4.56	22	12.67 (50.68)	5.00	20	12.86 (51.44)	4.18	20
19. Disrust	2.56 (51.20)	1.34	14	2.68 (53.60)	1.28	09	3.05 (61.00)	1.24	05	2.81 (56.20)	1.38	07
20. **Feeling of Insecurity**	51.80 (51.80)	17.22	13	51.66 (51.66)	14.61	15	54.26 (54.26)	16.21	13	55.12 (55.12)	14.40	09

Contd.

Table 7.1 *(Contd.)*

Indices of Psychological Well-being	*Unemployed*											
	Technically Educated									*Non-Technically Educated (N=408)*		
	Degree-Holders in Medical Sciences (N=63)			*Degree-Holders in Eng. Sciences (N=79)*			*Degree-Holders in Agri. Sciences (N=64)*					
	Mean (%)	*SD*	*Rank*	*Mean (%)*	*SD*	*Rank*	*Mean (%)*	*SD*	*Rank*	*Mean (%)*	*SD*	*Rank*
21. Despair	17.13 (53.53)	5.20	07	16.77 (52.41)	4.39	12	18.17 (56.78)	4.70	08	17.37 (54.28)	4.25	11
22. Unstructured Universe	4.56 (57.00)	1.66	04	4.18 (52.25)	1.50	13	3.92 (49.00)	1.56	22.5	4.48 (56.00)	1.30	08
23. Psychological Vacuum	4.16 (52.00)	1.31	10.5	4.24 (53.00)	1.39	10	4.02 (50.25)	1.30	21	4.33 (54.13)	1.40	12
24. Disillusionment	1.84 (46.00)	0.87	21	1.73 (43.25)	0.84	27	1.81 (45.25)	0.85	28	1.94 (48.50)	0.90	25
25. Narcissim	1.60 (40.00)	0.79	28	1.78 (44.50)	0.94	26	1.92 (48.00)	1.10	24	1.82 (45.50)	0.97	28
26. **Alienation**	29.30 (52.32)	7.18	09	28.70 (51.25)	5.85	16	29.84 (53.29)	7.02	15	29.95 (53.48)	5.90	14
27. Depersonal-ization	3.60 (45.00)	1.74	25	3.57 (44.63)	1.65	25	3.92 (49.00)	1.34	22.5	3.92 (49.00)	1.59	24
28. Fragmentation	3.70 (46.25)	1.69	20	4.34 (54.25)	1.85	07	4.92 (61.50)	1.68	04	4.21 (52.63)	1.82	17
29. Uncertainty	2.51 (62.75)	1.12	02	2.92 (73.00)	0.84	01	2.61 (65.25)	0.99	01	2.55 (63.75)	0.98	02
30. Distress	5.92 (49.33)	2.22	18	5.92 (49.33)	1.98	18	6.30 (52.50)	2.04	16	6.29 (52.42)	2.11	18

Contd.

Table 7.1 (*Contd.*)

Indices of Psychological Well-being	*Unemployed*											
	Technically Educated									*Non-Technically Educated (N=408)*		
	Degree-Holders in Medical Sciences (N=63)			*Degree-Holders in Eng. Sciences (N=79)*			*Degree-Holders in Agri. Sciences (N=64)*					
	Mean (%)	*SD*	*Rank*	*Mean (%)*	*SD*	*Rank*	*Mean (%)*	*SD*	*Rank*	*Mean (%)*	*SD*	*Rank*
31. Indecisiveness	3.89	1.79		4.37	1.74		4.38	1.66		4.14	1.56	
	(48.63)		19	(54.63)		06	(54.75)		12	(51.75)		19
32. Social Conflict	2.75	1.02		2.65	1.01		2.59	0.99		2.71	0.95	
	(68.75)		01	(66.25)		02	(64.75)		02	(67.75)		01
33. Isolation	3.65	1.49		3.87	1.57		4.13	1.50		3.97	1.63	
	(45.63)		23	(48.38)		21	(51.63)		18	(49.63)		23
34. Withdrawal from Social and Personal contact	1.83	1.04		1.86	0.97		1.88	0.79		1.93	0.96	
	(45.75)		22	(46.50)		23	(47.00)		26	(48.25)		26
35. Role Conflict	6.22	2.43		6.46	1.91		7.03	2.42		6.54	2.04	
	(51.83)		12	(53.83)		08	(58.58)		06	(54.50)		10
36. Hopelessness	4.00	1.91		3.92	1.65		4.17	1.69		4.26	1.71	
	(50.00)		16	(49.00)		19	(52.13)		17	(53.25)		16
37. Loneliness	2.08	1.15		1.84	0.98		2.06	0.91		2.02	0.98	
	(52.00)		10.5	(46.00)		24	(51.50)		19	(50.50)		21
38. Desolation	2.35	1.03		2.38	1.00		2.31	0.96		2.48	1.32	
	(58.75)		03	(59.50)		03	(57.75)		07	(62.00)		04
39. **Identity-crisis**	42.50	13.65		44.10	10.26		46.30	9.97		45.02	11.48	
	(50.60)		15	(52.50)		11	(55.12)		11	(53.60)		13

Contd.

Table 7.1 *(Contd.)*

Indices of Psychological Well-being	*Unemployed*												
	Technically Educated									*Non-Technically Educated (N=408)*			
	Degree-Holders in Medical Sciences (N=63)			*Degree-Holders in Eng. Sciences (N=79)*			*Degree-Holders in Agri. Sciences (N=64)*						
	Mean (%)	*SD*	*Rank*	*Mean (%)*	*SD*	*Rank*	*Mean (%)*	*SD*	*Rank*	*Mean (%)*	*SD*	*Rank*	
1. General Worries	1.54 (25.67)	0.82	27	2.14 (35.67)	1.01	22	1.78 (29.67)	0.87	27	2.28 (38.00)	1.23	24	22.44
2. Somatic Manisfestations	0.58 (19.33)	0.31	30	0.42 (14.00)	0.23	33	0.61 (20.33)	0.34	32	0.55 (18.33)	0.30	33	3.93
3. Psychological Symptoms	0.82 (16.40)	0.44	32	1.21 (24.20)	0.66	29	1.44 (28.80)	0.79	28	1.67 (33.40)	0.86	27	22.07
4. Social Relations	1.50 (18.75)	0.78	31	1.31 (16.38)	0.71	31	1.52 (19.00)	0.82	33	1.83 (22.88)	0.94	31	19.90
5. **Anxiety**	4.44 (20.18)	2.31	29	5.08 (23.09)	2.63	30	5.35 (24.32)	2.77	30	6.34 (28.82)	3.21	29	28.95
6. Suicidal Tendency	0.04 (1.00)	0.02	39	0.06 (1.50)	0.04	39	0.14 (3.50)	0.08	39	0.08 (2.00)	0.05	39	5.78
7. Emotional Instability	1.63 (20.38)	0.87	28	1.98 (24.75)	1.01	28	2.24 (28.00)	1.13	29	2.10 (26.25)	1.08	30	13.48
8. Paranoid Tendency	1.22 (10.17)	0.67	38	1.47 (12.25)	0.83	36	1.48 (12.33)	0.79	38	1.50 (12.50)	0.79	38	6.66
9. Depression	5.20 (14.44)	2.69	33	5.00 (13.89)	2.61	34	5.50 (15.28)	2.73	37	5.49 (15.25)	2.31	35	26.52
10. Physical Illness	1.66 (13.83)	0.85	34	1.85 (15.42)	0.94	32	2.52 (21.00)	1.32	31	2.25 (18.75)	1.17	32	10.95

Contd.

Table 7.1 *(Contd.)*

Indices of Psychological Well-being	*Unemployed*												
	Technically Educated									*Non-Technically Educated (N=408)*			
	Degree-Holders in Medical Sciences (N=63)			*Degree-Holders in Eng. Sciences (N=79)*			*Degree-Holders in Agri. Sciences (N=64)*						
	Mean (%)	*SD*	*Rank*	*Mean (%)*	*SD*	*Rank*	*Mean (%)*	*SD*	*Rank*	*Mean (%)*	*SD*	*Rank*	
11. Social Maladjustment	1.29 (10.75)	0.71	37	1.38 (11.50)	0.80	37	1.95 (16.25)	1.03	35	1.62 (13.50)	0.85	37	16.09
12. Apprehensive-ness	1.54 (12.83)	0.81	36	1.24 (10.33)	0.65	38	1.93 (16.08)	0.97	36	1.63 (13.58)	0.82	36	15.65
13. **Stress**	12.58 (13.10)	6.39	35	12.98 (13.52)	6.23	35	15.76 (16.42)	8.01	34	14.67 (15.28)	7.43	34	23.87
14. Lack of Self-confidence	8.00 (40.00)	3.35	13	8.31 (41.55)	2.92	11	8.53 (42.65)	3.30	11	8.94 (44.70)	3.04	09	21.95
15. Dejection	6.08 (40.53)	2.82	11	6.62 (44.13)	2.72	08	6.95 (46.33)	2.67	06	7.35 (49.00)	2.78	05	23.13
16. Pessimism	1.35 (27.00)	0.84	26	1.53 (30.60)	0.83	26	1.56 (31.20)	0.87	26	1.46 (29.20)	0.79	28	14.71
17. Emotional Res-ponsiveness	11.54 (38.47)	3.62	18	12.23 (40.77)	4.28	12	12.93 (43.10)	4.47	10	12.66 (42.20)	4.34	15	19.48
18. Social Insecurity	9.03 (36.12)	3.01	21	9.29 (37.16)	3.67	20	9.56 (38.24)	3.81	20	9.73 (38.92)	3.51	23	19.94
19. Disrust	2.08 (41.60)	1.13	08	2.14 (42.80)	1.21	09	2.08 (41.60)	1.09	14	2.10 (42.00)	1.12	16.5	10.90
20. **Feeling of Insecurity**	38.08 (38.08)	11.07	19	40.12 (40.12)	12.89	13	41.61 (41.61)	13.65	13	42.24 (42.24)	12.77	14	29.12

Contd.

Table 7.1 *(Contd.)*

Indices of Psychological Well-being	*Unemployed*												
	Technically Educated									*Non-Technically Educated (N=408)*			
	Degree-Holders in Medical Sciences (N=63)			*Degree-Holders in Eng. Sciences (N=79)*			*Degree-Holders in Agri. Sciences (N=64)*						
	Mean (%)	*SD*	*Rank*	*Mean (%)*	*SD*	*Rank*	*Mean (%)*	*SD*	*Rank*	*Mean (%)*	*SD*	*Rank*	
21. Despair	14.92 (46.63)	4.01	06	14.67 (45.84)	3.57	06	14.52 (45.38)	2.73	07	15.26 (47.69)	3.69	07	11.44
22. Unstructured Universe	4.31 (53.88)	1.45	03	3.84 (48.00)	1.39	03	4.69 (58.63)	1.48	02	4.02 (50.25)	1.37	03	3.49
23. Psychological Vacuum	3.98 (49.75)	1.24	04	3.77 (47.13)	1.17	04	4.04 (50.50)	1.31	03	3.88 (48.50)	1.36	06	3.13
24. Disillusionment	1.66 (41.50)	0.92	09	1.22 (30.50)	0.65	27	1.65 (41.25)	0.69	15	1.47 (36.75)	0.67	26	8.65
25. Narcissim	1.58 (39.50)	0.79	15	1.49 (37.25)	0.75	19	1.68 (42.00)	0.88	12	1.68 (42.00)	0.78	16.5	1.03
26. **Alienation**	26.45 (47.23)	4.96	05	24.99 (44.63)	4.03	07	26.58 (47.46)	4.15	04	26.31 (46.98)	5.42	08	14.24
27. Depersonal-ization	2.75 (34.38)	1.11	24	2.77 (34.63)	1.14	25	3.00 (37.50)	1.53	21.5	3.02 (37.75)	1.24	25	13.95
28. Fragmentation	2.84 (35.50)	0.90	22.5	2.83 (35.38)	1.16	23	3.00 (37.50)	1.46	21.5	3.24 (40.50)	1.35	20	19.72
29. Uncertainty	2.38 (59.50)	0.99	1.5	2.24 (56.00)	0.92	01	2.43 (60.75)	1.05	01	2.29 (57.25)	0.92	01	4.44
30. Distress	5.02 (41.83)	1.86	07	4.44 (37.00)	1.77	21	4.82 (40.17)	1.42	17	5.01 (41.75)	1.74	18	15.54

Contd.

Table 7.1 *(Contd.)*

Indices of Psychological Well-being	*Unemployed*												
	Technically Educated									*Non-Technically Educated (N=408)*			
	Degree-Holders in Medical Sciences (N=63)			*Degree-Holders in Eng. Sciences (N=79)*			*Degree-Holders in Agri. Sciences (N=64)*						
	Mean (%)	*SD*	*Rank*	*Mean (%)*	*SD*	*Rank*	*Mean (%)*	*SD*	*Rank*	*Mean (%)*	*SD*	*Rank*	
31. Indecisiveness	3.17 (39.63)	1.12	14	2.82 (35.25)	1.02	24	3.22 (40.25)	1.22	16	3.44 (43.00)	1.38	10	12.82
32. Social Conflict	2.38 (59.50)	0.95	1.5	2.00 (50.00)	0.89	02	1.86 (46.50)	0.84	05	2.26 (56.50)	0.97	02	9.64
33. Isolation	3.04 (38.00)	1.35	20	3.12 (39.00)	1.41	16	2.78 (34.75)	1.17	23	3.13 (39.13)	1.15	22	13.03
34. Withdrawal from Social and Personal contact	1.42 (35.50)	0.70	22.5	1.54 (38.50)	0.79	17	1.60 (40.00)	0.96	19	1.66 (41.50)	0.78	19	4.25
35. Role Conflict	4.95 (41.25)	1.93	10	4.57 (38.08)	1.64	18	5.21 (43.42)	2.03	09	5.07 (42.25)	1.82	12.5	21.33
36. Hopelessness	2.62 (32.75)	1.03	25	3.13 (39.13)	1.17	15	2.65 (33.13)	0.76	24	3.23 (40.38)	1.42	21	18.44
37. Loneliness	1.54 (38.50)	0.65	16.5	1.71 (42.75)	0.92	10	1.26 (31.50)	0.52	25	1.69 (42.25)	0.84	12.5	6.70
38. Desolation	1.54 (38.50)	0.70	16.5	1.84 (46.00)	1.01	05	1.78 (44.50)	0.85	08	1.99 (49.75)	0.98	04	2.81
39. **Identity-crisis**	33.65 (40.06)	8.44	12	33.01 (39.30)	9.13	14	33.61 (40.01)	9.72	18	36.03 (42.89)	9.56	11	29.09

Note : $df = 7, 1016$; $p<0.05 = 2.02$; $p<0.01 = 2.66$.

accounts, probably nothing has so far been documented about the level of anxiety, stress, feeling of insecurity, alienation, and identity-crisis among different groups of unemployed and employed people with degrees in various specific disciplines. Hence, an attempt has been made to see through their psychological well-being measured in terms of the aforesaid variables in a broader perspective. Table 7.1 reports the summary of the findings of inter- and intra-group statistical comparisons among different groups of unemployed and employed young men educated in different streams of knowledge in terms of their degree and extent on the abovementioned indices of psychological well-being.

All the groups of unemployed and employed people from different streams of knowledge, like those of the groups of technically and non-technically educated unemployed and employed people, tended to differ markedly from one another in terms of all the health-indices (F-values extended between 2.81 and 29.12 being significant at better than the 0.01 level), excepting narcissism (F = 1.03). However, the findings of multiple-comparisons of different pairs of means indicated that there was no striking differences between any two groups, particularly at the intra-group level, in terms of the abovementioned different indicators of psychological health. Naturally, only with a few exceptions, such as a meaningful difference between the mean scores of the employed medical graduates and the non-technically educated employed in terms of psychological symptoms (OQ = 0.851; CQ = 0.78), the employed engineers and the employed degree-holders in the agriculture sciences in terms of unstructured universe (OQ = 0.85; CQ = 0.85), and the unemployed medical graduates and the agriculture graduates in terms of fragmentation (OQ = 1.22; CQ = 0.88), if there was found any marked difference between the mean scores of any two groups in terms of one or another health indices, that was mostly seen between the employed of either disciplines and the unemployed with degrees in one or another branch of knowledge.

The various indicators of psychological well-being regarding which the employed degree-holders in medical sciences showed substantial differences from different groups of unemployed were as follows : general worries (OQ = 1.87, 1.84, 1.43, 1.19; CQ = 0.96), psychological symptoms (OQ = 1.68, 1.60, 1.57, 1.35; CQ = 0.78), social relations (OQ = 1.84, 1.59, 1.46, 1.36; CQ = 1.11), anxiety (OQ = 5.47, 5.38, 4.69, 4.20; CQ = 2.60), emotional instability (OQ = 2.09, 1.62, 1.55, 1.53; CQ = 1.21), paranoid tendency (OQ = 1.30;

CQ = 1.29), depression (OQ = 7.55, 5.82, 4.43, 4.40; CQ = 3.89), physical illness (OQ = 1.85, 1.59, 1.48; CQ = 1.38), social maladjustment (OQ = 2.60, 2.03, 1.68, 1.58; CQ = 1.54), apprehensiveness (OQ = 2.07, 1.64, 1.57; CQ = 1.44), stress (OQ = 17.15, 14.41, 11.76, 11.32; CQ = 8.89), lack of self-confidence (OQ = 3.64, 3.11, 2.87, 2.69; CQ = 2.14), dejection (OQ = 3.43, 3.17, 2.59, 1.97; CQ = 1.75), pessimism (OQ = 0.97, 0.79; CQ = 0.74), emotional responsiveness (OQ = 5.04, 4.44, 4.27, 4.02; CQ = 2.86), social insecurity (OQ = 3.83, 3.64, 3.34, 2.73; CQ = 2.55), distrust (OQ = 0.97; CQ = 0.80), feeling of insecurity (OQ = 17.04, 16.18, 13.72, 13.58; CQ = 8.74), despair (OQ = 3.25, 2.45; CQ = 2.42), alienation (OQ = 3.50, 3.39; CQ = 3.40), depersonalization (OQ = 1.17, 1.17; CQ = 0.89), fragmentation (OQ = 2.08, 1.50, 1.37; CQ = 0.98), distress (OQ = 1.28, 1.27; CQ = 1.11), indecisiveness (OQ = 1.21, 1.20, 0. 97; CQ = 0.90), isolation (OQ = 1.09, 0.93; CQ = 0.87), role conflict (OQ = 2.08, 1.59, 1.51, 1.27; CQ = 1.20), hopelessness (OQ = 1.64, 1.55, 1.38, 1.30; CQ = 0.96) and identity-crisis (OQ = 12.65, 11.37, 10.45, 8.85; CQ = 6.27). Similarly, the health indices where the employed engineers exhibited a marked departure from different groups of unemployed distinct in their educational streams included the psychological dimensions like general worries (OQ = 1.27, 1.24; CQ = 0.91), psychological symptoms (OQ = 1.29, 1.21, 1.18, 0.96; CQ = 0.76), social relations (CQ = 1.13), anxiety (OQ = 4.83, 4.74, 4.05, 3.56; CQ = 2.55), emotional instability (OQ = 1.74, 1.27, 1.20, 1.18; CQ = 1.18), depression (CQ = 3.98), physical illness (CQ = 1.35), social maladjustment (CQ = 1.50), apprehensiveness (OQ = 2.37, 1.94, 1.87, 1.65; CQ = 1.47), stress (OQ = 16.75, 14.01, 11.36, 10.92; CQ = 8.70), lack of self-confidence (CQ = 2.09), dejection (OQ = 2.89, 2.63, 2.05; CQ = 1.71), pessimism (OQ = 0.79; CQ = 0.71), emotional responsiveness (OQ = 4.35, 3.75, 3.58, 3.33; CQ = 2.80), social insecurity (CQ = 2.49), distrust (OQ = 0.91; CQ = 0.73), feeling of insecurity (CQ = 8.55), despair (OQ = 3.50, 2.70; CQ = 2.48), disillusionment (OQ = 0.72, 0.62, 0.59, 0.51; CQ = 0.50), alienation (OQ = 4.96, 4.85, 4.31, 3.71; CQ = 3.56), depersonalization (CQ = 0.87), fragmentation (CQ = 1.00), uncertainty (OQ = 0.68; CQ = 0.59), distress (OQ = 1.86, 1.85, 1.48, 1.48; CQ = 1.21), indecisiveness (OQ = 1.56, 1.55, 1.32, 1.32; CQ = 0.92), social conflict (CQ = 0.58), isolation (OQ = 1.01, 0.85; CQ = 0.85), role conflict (CQ = 1.23), hopelessness (OQ = 1.13, 1.04; CQ = 0.92) and identity-crisis (OQ = 13.29, 12.01, 11.09, 9.49; CQ = 6.57). The various psychological reactions in which the employed degree-holders in agriculture sciences were found to differ significantly from different distinct groups of their unemployed counterparts consisted of reactions such as general worries (OQ = 1.63, 1.60, 1.19, 0.95; CQ = 0.95), psychological symptoms (CQ =0.74), social relations (CQ = 1.08), anxiety (OQ = 4.56, 4.47, 3.78, 3.29; CQ = 2.48), emotional instability (OQ = 1.48; CQ = 1.12), depression (CQ = 3.67), social maladjustment (CQ = 1.42), apprehensiveness (OQ = 1.68; CQ = 1.35), stress (OQ = 13.97, 11.23, 8.58; CQ = 8.20), lack of self- confidence (CQ = 2.04), dejection (OQ = 2.56, 2.30, 1.72; CQ = 1.67), pessimism (CQ = 0.69), emotional responsiveness (OQ = 3.65, 3.05, 2.88, 2.63; CQ = 2.64), social insecurity (CQ = 2.43), distrust (OQ = 0.97; CQ = 0.77), feeling of insecurity (OQ = 13.51,12.65,10.19, 10.05; CQ = 8.34), despair (OQ = 3.65, 2.85, 2.61; CQ = 2.54), alienation (OQ = 3.37; CQ = 3.28), depersonalization (OQ = 0.92, 0.92; CQ = 0.85), fragmentation (CQ = 0.96), distress (CQ = 1.18), indecisiveness (OQ = 1.16, 1.15, 0. 92; CQ = 0.88), social conflict (CQ = 0.59), isolation (CQ = 0.89), role conflict (OQ = 1.82, 1.33, 1.25; CQ = 1.13), hopelessness (OQ = 1.61, 1.52, 1.35, 1.27; CQ = 0.94), loneliness (CQ = 0.57) and identity-crisis (OQ = 12.69, 11.41, 10.49, 8.89; CQ = 6.43). Also, the different syndromes where the non-technically educated employed expressed a clear-cut difference from one or another group of the unemployed coming from varied disciplines were general worries (OQ = 1.13, 1.10; CQ = 0.88), psychological symptoms (OQ = 0.83, 0.75, 0.72; CQ = 0.72), social relations (CQ = 1.04), anxiety (OQ = 3.57, 3.48, 2.79; CQ = 2.40), emotional instability (OQ = 1.62, 1.50; CQ = 1.16), depression (CQ = 3.80), social maladjustment (CQ = 1.46), apprehensiveness (OQ = 1.98, 1.55, 1.48; CQ = 1.40), stress (OQ = 15.06, 12.32, 9.67, 9.23; CQ = 8.48), lack of self-confidence (OQ = 2.70, 2.17; CQ = 1.97), dejection (CQ = 1.61), pessimism (OQ = 0.86; CQ = 0.73), emotional responsiveness (CQ = 2.73), social insecurity (OQ = 3.13, 2.94, 2.64; CQ = 2.35), distrust (CQ = 0.75), feeling of insecurity (OQ = 12.88, 12.02, 9.56, 9.42; CQ = 8.06), despair (OQ = 2.91; CQ = 2.34), alienation (OQ = 3.64, 3.53; CQ = 3.48), depersonalization (CQ = 0.82), fragmentation (OQ = 1.68, 1.10, 0.97; CQ = 0.92), uncertainty (OQ = 0.63; CQ = 0.58), distress (CQ = 1.15), indecisiveness (OQ = 0.94, 0.93; CQ = 0.85), isolation (CQ = 0.82), role conflict (OQ = 1.96, 1.47, 1.39; CQ = 1.17), hopelessness (CQ = 0.89) and identity-crisis (OQ = 10.27, 8.99, 8.07, 6.47; CQ = 6.06). Thus, the findings of multiple-comparisons of different pairs of means, in short, indicated that each of the groups of employed, with a few variations, tended to differ significantly from each of the other groups of the educated unemployed in their different psychological reactions. The results further recorded that all the groups of the unemployed from different disciplines, particularly the degree-holders in agriculture sciences and the non-technically educated ones, altogether with no evidence of apparent difference with each other, were clearly more prone to different symptomatic reactions.

All the groups of employed, on the other hand, were fairly less psychologically disturbed, though not completely symptom-free. They, too, carried with them a moderate amount of different symptoms of psychological ill-health, excepting a less precipitating amount of anxiety and stress in their various characteristic manifestations. This was particularly marked in the case of non-technically educated employed young men, closely followed by the employed degree-holders in agriculture sciences. Besides, an attempt was also made to identify some of the pressing psychological symptoms among different groups of unemployed and employed people. The various psychological symptoms which were more precipitating for the unemployed doctors were social conflict (68.75%), feeling of uncertainty (62.75%), desolation (58.75%), unstructured universe (57.00%), and lack of self-confidence (54.35%). Those which were felt to be more acute by the unemployed engineers were feeling of uncertainty (73.00%), social conflict (66.25%), desolation (59.50%), dejection (57.80%), and lack of self-confidence (55.55%). The symptoms which were diagnosed as more pressing in the case of the unemployed degree-holders in agriculture sciences were related with the feeling of uncertainty (65.25%), social conflict (64.75%), dejection (61,67%), fragmentation (61,50%), and distrust (61.00%). The symptomatic reactions which were experienced as more frightening by the non-technically educated unemployed involved psychological dimensions like social conflict (67.75%), feeling of uncertainty (63.75%), dejection (63.40%), desolation (62.00%), and lack of self-confidence (58.20%). The symptoms which were identified as more alarming in the life of employed doctors were feeling of uncertainty (59.50%), social conflict (59.50%), unstructured universe (53.88%), psychological vacuum (49.75%), and alienation (47.23%). Those which were more pronounced in the case of the employed engineers concerned symptomatic reactions like feeling of uncertainty (56.00%), social conflict (50.00%), unstructured universe (48.00%), psychological vacuum (47.13%), and desolation (46.00%). The symptoms which appeared more afflicting for the employed degree-holders in agriculture sciences were feeling of uncertainty (60.75%), unstructured universe (58.63%), psychological vacuum (50.50%), alienation (47.46%), and social conflict (46.50%). And, those which proved more agonising for the non-technically educated employed were linked with symptoms such as feeling of uncertainty (57.25%), social conflict (56.50%), unstructured universe (50.25%), desolation (49.75%), and dejection (49.00%).

On the other hand, different symptomatic reactions which were comparatively less pressing for all the groups of respondents were, here too, mostly connected with various characteristic manifestations of stress. And, susceptibility to suicidal ideation was apparently least perceptible in them (scores on the scale of suicidal tendency for different groups of unemployed and employed people ranged between 1.00% and 9.50%), and hardly annoying. This was visible more particularly in the groups of the employed. Thus, the results, in brief, indicated a fair amount of similarity among different groups of the educated unemployed and employed people from different faculties in their different psychological reactions, particularly identified as severely experienced by them. Obviously, excepting the groups of the unemployed doctors and the non-technically educated unemployed who were deeply scourged by social conflict, all of them were highly oppressed with the feeling of uncertainty, and less with the tendency to commit suicide. However, such pattern was not consistent, especially in terms of the more severely experienced symtomatic reactions; respondents distinct in their status of employment (i.e., either employed or unemployed) tended to express dissimilarity in this connection.

Life Satisfaction : A Comparison Among Different Groups of Unemployed and Employed Young Men Educated in Different Specific Streams of Knowledge

The findings furnished in the previous chapter seem, by and large, sufficient to focus the degree of life satisfaction in different groups of unemployed and employed young men educated in different specific branches of knowledge. But, would such generalisation be appropriate in substantial measure? Interestingly, technical education generally confers degrees and diplomas in medical, engineering, agriculture sciences, etc. Similarly, non-technical education is associated with education in different disciplines like general sciences (such as physical sciences, mathematics and life sciences), commerce, social sciences, and arts and humanities. And, as it has been indicated above, education in different streams of knowledge, or in different specific subjects, requires a unique concomitance of different psychological characteristics. In other words, people from varied streams of knowledge differ considerably in their psychological characteristics. But, unfortunately, hardly any systematic attempt has so far been made, especially in India, which has given due attention to this issue while analysing the degree of life satisfaction in different groups of unemployed vis-à-vis employed people varying in their streams of education. Hence, this study was designed. Table 7.2 records the findings of a statistical comparison among different groups of educated unemployed and employed people from different specific disciplines in terms of their level of life satisfaction.

All the groups of respondents were found to differ significantly from one another in terms of the degree of their life satisfaction (F=36.77; df=7, 1016; p<0.01). The findings obtained from multiple-comparisons, however, evinced no marked difference between any two groups of the unemployed or the employed at the level of their life satisfaction. Apparently, only those two groups of respondents who were distinct in their status of employment exhibited considerable differences between themselves in their level of life satisfaction, as found with other indices of psychological health. Significantly, the observed values of Q (OQs) always outstripped the criterion values of Q (CQs) furnished in a descending order as 1.29, 1.27, 1.23, and 1.19 respectively, when the educated unemployed from each of the specific streams were separately compared with each of the groups of their employed counterparts in terms of the amount of satisfaction with their life. Further, unemployed degree-holders in all the streams of education, particularly in agriculture sciences (45.20%) and non-technical education (46.00%), were less, but moderately, satisfied in their life. All the groups of educated employed, particularly those with degrees in agriculture sciences (71.70%) and engineering (71.20%), on the other hand, felt life as relatively pleasant and charming to them.

Different Groups of Unemployed and Employed Young Men Educated in Different Specific Streams of Knowledge : Their Dependence on Different Coping Strategies

To ensure the applicability of the study relatively in a wider perspective,

Table 7.2 : Statistical Differences Among the Groups of Educated Unemployed and Employed Young Men with Degrees in Various Streams of Knowledge and their Relative Standing in Terms of the Degree of their Life Satisfaction

Variable	*Unemployed*								*Employed*								*F*
	Technically Educated						*Non-Technically Educated (N = 408)*		*Technically Educated*						*Non-Technically Educated (N = 278)*		
	Degree-Holders in Medical Sciences (N = 63)		*Degree-Holders in Eng. Sciences (N = 79)*		*Degree-Holders in Agri. Sciences (N = 64)*				*Degree-Holders in Medical Sciences (N = 40)*		*Degree-Holders in Eng. Sciences (N = 56)*		*Degree-Holders in Agri. Sciences (N = 36)*				
	Mean (%)	*SD*	*Mean (%)*	*SD*	*Mean (%)*	*SD*	*Mean (%)*	*SD*	*Mean (%)*	*SD*	*Mean (%)*	*SD*	*Mean (%)*	*SD*	*Mean (%)*	*SD*	
Life Satisfaction	5.25 (52.50)	2.08	5.23 (52.30)	2.41	4.52 (45.20)	2.38	4.60 (46.00)	2.20	6.87 (68.70)	1.81	7.12 (71.20)	1.92	7.17 (71.70)	1.49	6.78 (67.80)	1.97	36.77

Note : $df = 7, 1016$; $p < 0.05 = 2.02$; $p < 0.01 = 2.66$.

an attempt, as it was purported, was also made to find out the degrees of dependence of different groups of unemployed and employed people coming from different distinct educational streams on various strategies generally adopted to cope with their life situations. Table 7.3 displays the findings of a statistical comparison among them in this regard.

Different groups of respondents from different specific streams, like those of the technically and non-technically educated unemployed and employed people, tended to differ significantly from one another in terms of the degree of their reliance on all the strategies like intrapersistive approach mode (F=3.53; $p < 0.01$), extrapersistive approach mode (F=2.49; $p < 0.05$) and punitive avoidance mode ($p < 0.01$), except the defensive avoidance mode ($p > 0.05$), in fighting with their problems. However, the findings obtained from multiple-comparisons did not show a clear evidence of significant difference between any two groups of respondents in terms of the degree of their dependence on intrapersistive approach mode (CQ values posited in descending order as 1.65, 1.62, 1.58, 1.52, 1.46, 1.37, 1.21) and extrapersistive approach mode (CQ values obtained as such 1.17, 1.15, 1.12, 1.08, 1.03, 0.97, 0.85). The punitive avoidance mode was identified as the only strategy in terms of the degree of reliance on which some of the groups such as the unemployed degree-holders in agriculture sciences, and the employed degree-holders in agriculture sciences and non-technical education, exhibited noticeable differences particularly with those of the groups of unemployed and employed degree-holders in medical sciences and unemployed degree-holders in engineering sciences in making adjustment with their circumstances. The criterion values for Q in this connection were recorded to be 0.75, 0.73 and 0.71 which were clearly lower from the observed values obtained for Q. Further, here too, all the groups of unemployed and employed people, no matter from which streams they came, were found to trust solely in intrapersistive approach mode (the degree of their dependence ranged between 62.47% and 70.47%) and in none else in dealing with their existing circumstances.

To summarize, an analysis of the aforementioned findings related with the psychological well-being and coping styles of different groups of the unemployed and employed young men coming from different specific streams of education, on the whole, provided various significant informations such as :

1. With no clear evidence of any significant difference in their

Table 7.3 : Statistical Differences Among the Groups of Educated Unemployed and Employed Young Men with Degrees in Various Streams of Knowledge and their Relative Dependence in Terms of Different Coping Strategies

Coping Strategies	*Unemployed*								*Employed*								F
	Technically Educated								*Technically Educated*								
	Degree-Holders in Medical Sciences (N=63)		*Degree-Holders in Eng. Sciences (N=79)*		*Degree-Holders in Agri. Sciences (N=64)*		*Non-Technically Educated (N=408)*		*Degree-Holders in Medical Sciences (N=40)*		*Degree-Holders in Eng. Sciences (N=56)*		*Degree-Holders in Agri. Sciences (N=36)*		*Non-Technically Educated (N=278)*		
	Mean (%)	*SD*	*Mean (%)*	*SD*	*Mean (%)*	*SD*	*Mean (%)*	*SD*	*Mean (%)*	*SD*	*Mean (%)*	*SD*	*Mean (%)*	*SD*	*Mean (%)*	*SD*	*F*
Intrapersistive Approach Mode	9.37 (62.47)	3.17	9.94 (66.27)	2.96	9.61 (64.07)	3.10	9.69 (64.60)	2.67	9.37 (62.47)	2.65	9.81 (65.40)	3.03	9.59 (63.93)	3.23	10.57 (70.47)	2.33	3.53
Extrapersistive Approach Mode	2.17 (14.47)	1.18	1.71 (11.40)	0.91	2.63 (17.53)	1.34	1.98 (13.20)	1.02	2.06 (13.73)	1.07	1.88 (12.53)	0.98	2.04 (13.60)	1.05	1.63 (10.87)	0.86	2.49
Punitive Avoidance Mode	1.27 (8.47)	0.73	1.16 (7.73)	0.62	0.33 (2.20)	0.19	0.90 (6.00)	0.43	1.24 (8.27)	0.65	0.95 (6.33)	0.58	0.47 (3.13)	0.28	0.54 (3.60)	0.32	6.23
Defensive Avoidance Mode	2.19 (14.60)	1.14	2.19 (14.60)	1.16	2.44 (16.27)	1.26	2.43 (16.20)	1.27	2.33 (15.53)	1.23	2.36 (15.73)	1.14	2.90 (19.33)	1.52	2.26 (15.07)	1.17	0.55

Note : $df = 7, 1016$; $p < 0.05 = 2.02$; $p < 0.01 = 2.66$.

various psychological symptoms, excepting that between the unemployed degree-holders in the medical sciences and agriculture in their level of fragmentation, all the groups of unemployed from different streams of education, like those of the groups of technically and non-technically educated unemployed (see chapter six for a comprehensive account), were more vulnerable to different psychological reactions, particularly marked by increased levels of feeling of insecurity, alienation and identity-crisis in their various manifestations. This clearly implies that different streams of education do not mediate the impact of unemployment on one's psychological well-being in one way or the other. In conclusion, unemployment is equally damaging for the psychological health of all those who experience it, no matter whether they come from one or another stream of education. Thus, the results of this study agree fairly well with the findings obtained earlier in the 6th chapter that both the groups of technically and non-technically educated unemployed are equally afflicted with different symptoms of psychological ill-being. Also, the results are quite in tune with the findings of Pal (1989), Narayan (1995) and Singh, Singh and Singh (1996) who have shown that differences in the streams of education do not result in difference in the effects of unemployment on psychological well-being. In all, the conclusion by Payne, Warr and Hartley (1984), here too, has been fairly substantiated that unemployment has a *'homogenizing effect'* on psychological well-being of all the people irrespective of differences in their social background.

Many theoretical and empirical propositions as well as various idiosyncratic socio-econo-politico-cultural realities of the land have been put forward earlier in the 5th and 6th chapters to understand greater psychological deterioration, particularly marked in the form of elevated levels of anxiety, stress, feeling of insecurity, alienation, identity-crisis, and diminished life satisfaction in their different characteristic manifestations, among the groups of educated unemployed as against the groups of their employed counterparts. They are, indeed, meaningful, and may form definite logical grounds to elucidate the findings here too. Furthermore, one may also positively depend on *'Victimization Theory'* proposed by Kieselbach (1997a, b, 1998a, b) in order to search out a convincing reason to justify why all the groups of educated unemployed are more susceptible to different psychological symptoms. The theory, in brief, states that the unemployed are generally subjected to victimization mainly on three levels : (1) *primary victimization* which results in the loss of positive environmental features (viz., economic security, social integration, self-esteem, time structure, external goals, etc., cf. Jahoda,1982) associated with work ; (2) *secondary victimization* which crops up due to increasing daily hassels, financial difficulties, and experienced social stigmatization; and (3) *tertiary victimization* in which the unemployed are blamed for inadequate coping with their problem of unemployment. All these victimizations for a long period of time, as Kieselbach (1997a, b, 1998a, b) holds, more apparently shatter the psychological balance of the unemployed, exposing them to numerous psychological reactions. The findings of a number of studies (Catalano, 1991; Jin, Chandrakant and Svoboda, 1995; Kieselbach, 1988a, 1991, 1998c; Kieselbach, Beelmann and Stitzel, 2000 ; Kieselbach and Wacker, 1995; Masschelein and De Witte, 1997; Singh, Singh and Rani, 1996b, Winefield, 1995b) have also directly or indirectly lent support to the conviction that continuous and long-term victimization of the unemployed on different levels make them particularly vulnerable to psychological subversion. Hence, the reason why the unemployed from all the streams of education in India tend to manifest different symptomatic reactions appears to be fairly well investigated in the light of *victimization theory.*

However, it would not be out of place to mention here that the unemployed in India, in particular, besides their inherent acquiescence, normally fall back upon different strategies as they prefer to shift the onus on their irreversible lot, taking every event as predestined and preordained, do not show any serious concern for the consequences and react with the formal attitude of "*kya farak parta hai*" (what difference does it make !), and thus express more tolerance and equanimity in their behaviour, etc., on mental plane to lessen the agony caused by their victimization. But, all these schemes, as it may commonly be seen, fail to give them adequate psychological ease as they apprehend that they have to learn to live with the trauma of victimization only due to their being unemployed with no fault of theirs. This puts them, more often than not, under greater psychological pressure, leading to different maladaptive behaviours. Admittedly, there is a limit to withstanding the distress of victimization; one has to ultimately lose one's psychological equipoise to a substantial degree, irrespective of any socio-cultural variation. This may clearly furnish sufficient reasons to justify why the unemployed in India, despite coming from varied streams of education, like those in the west, manifest sharp decline in their psychological health; their continuous and often accelerating confrontation with victimization at various levels may apparently be accepted as liable to aggravating all sorts of psychological troubles in them.

However, the results revealed a relatively greater, though not statistically significant, vulnerability, particularly in the groups of unemployed degree-holders in agriculture sciences as well as non-technical education to different psychological symptoms. The results, thus, lend partial, though indirect, support to the conclusions of Jackson and Warr (1987), Singh (1994) and Singh, Singh and Rani (1996b) wherein it has been shown that the unemployed coming from areas with low unemployment rate, in contrast to areas with very high unemployment, are more prone to psychological uprootedness. As it may seem quite apparent from the inspection of the magnitude of educated job-seekers in India, as also in undivided Bihar, the degree-holders in the agriculture sciences are relatively less hit by the problem of unemployment. So, if the above assertions stand true, it is not quite unexpected to find them psychologically more precipitated. Virtually, they have not much opportunity for community adaptation of some kind. This in a way adversely affects their psychological well-being. But, there naturally arises a question as to why the degree-holders in medical sciences, even after their being also relatively less afflicted by the problem of unemployment, are not equally susceptible to various psychological reactions; they, however, expressed similarity in their symptomatic reactions with the degree-holders in engineering sciences who are more burdened with the problem of joblessness. The result is not surprising,though. A doctor, despite being labelled unemployed—if able and competent even to a minimal level — may commonly be seen to easily earn a substantial amount to be able to lead a minimum decent life and bear the burden of his/her dependents to a certain extent. It would not at all be unreasonable to point out here that our health consciousness, no doubt, has fairly increased in recent years on account of the education of health care and maintenance frequently disseminated through different agencies.

And, on the other hand, this is also a patent fact that there is a great lack of adequate medical facilities in India, particularly in the absence of the trained medical personnel in the country, to meet the requirements. It may, however, be another point of discussion that there is also a considerably great shortage of jobs for them in public and organized private sector enterprises. But not at all astonishing, even quacks in India earn enough as to maintain themselves and their families smoothly. Apparently, doctors in India, even after their being usually counted as unemployed for not having employment either in public or private sector organizations, have a comparatively good prospect for their livelihood. They, if willing, cannot remain idle, and may earn a substantial amount for their subsistence. This is perhaps one of the important reasons why the unemployed degree-holders in medical sciences have not exhibited as much vulnerability to different psychological reactions as the one expressed by the unemployed degree-holders in agriculture sciences. But, it is remarkable to note that a person cannot remain with the trauma of social stigma of being unemployed for long; he/she has to lose his/her psychological poise ultimately, the latter precipitating in him/her different psychological reactions. Thus, why the unemployed degree-holders in medical sciences, too, despite feeling more secure on the economic front, manifest a sharp decrease in their psychological well-being, not much lower in amount than those of the groups of unemployed degree-holders in the agriculture sciences, as also in other streams of education, may clearly be understood in the light of the above arguments. Virtually, degree-holders in medical sciences, if not employed in any of the organized sectors, though having a good earning for their maintenance through their own medical practices, are considered to be unemployed in India, and are treated by the society in the same negative way as unemployed young men with degrees in other branches of knowledge. So, unemployment is equally, though slightly less, damaging for the psychological health of the doctors faced with it as it is for the health of others.

To conclude, not the difference in educational faculties, but the prevailing negative social attitude of perceiving the unemployed as unsuccessful may be blamed for promoting all psychological afflictions in the life of jobless medical degree-holders, too. Further, the results showing a markedly greater vulnerability among the group of non-technically educated unemployed young men to different psychological reactions, despite their being comparatively much imperilled by the chronic problem of unemployment, also fail to substantiate the convictions held by Jackson and Warr (1987), Singh (1994), and Singh, Singh and Rani (1996b) that mass unemployment does not inflict much damage to psychological health. The results, however, correspond, to an extent, with the views carried by Kieselbach (1991). According to him, a high level of unemployment, no doubt, can normalize the effects of unemployment and cushion against personally experienced stress, but, at the same time, it leads to an atmosphere of hopelessness, considerably liable to encourage different symptomatic reactions, more likely to an alarming extent (Crept *et al.*, 1992; Feather, 1983a; Feather and Barber, 1983; Kieselbach, 2003; Kieselbach, Beelmann and Stitzel, 2000; Kumari, 2001; Masschelein and De Witte, 1997; Singh, 2001; Vetrone *et al.*, 1992). The reasons furnished above to explicate the marked psychological deterioration among the unemployed degree-holders in medical sciences, who experienced it somewhat less severely than the unemployed degree-holders in the agriculture sciences, may, here too, be related with the findings.

Moreover, in describing the findings, it should be pointed out that people with degrees in non-technical education — relatively less job-oriented and not up to present-day career aspirations and prospects — in India, as Singh, Kumari and Kumari (2000), and Singh, Singh and Kumari (1998) maintain, are commonly looked upon as mediocre in their calibre, and inferior to the technically educated ones on the scale of social prestige and recognition. The society, as it may commonly be observed, becomes more critical to them if they (the non-technically educated ones) are unemployed and continue with their condition for a longer spell. Thus, they gradually lose their social respect and, in consequence, sooner or later begin to consider themselves as socially excluded. This is, as it has been revealed (Kieselbach, 1990b, 1991, 2003; Kieselbach and Traiser, 2004; Kieselbach *et al.*, 2001; Singh, 1990; Warr, 1985, 1987c, d), psychologically more distressing for them, where symptoms like anxiety, stress, feeling of insecurity, alienation, identity-crisis, diminished life satisfaction, and so on are natural to exist in quite a terrifying measure. Thus, the reason why the non-technically educated unemployed show a greater drop in their psychological health may appear fairly well vindicated in the light of the above arguments.

2. All the groups of educated employed young men from different distinct streams, on the whole, were found to be considerably less psychologically afflicted. Although they, too, were not fully immune to psychological damage, and were moderately susceptible to different psychological reactions, particularly marked by feelings of insecurity, alienation and identity-crisis in their various manifestations, almost in an equal amount. Thus, the results of this study do not fairly substantiate the conclusions derived by investigators like Naik and Deshpande (1978), Sharma (1979), Sharma and Sharma (1989), Singh, Kumari and Kumari (2000), Singh, Singh and Rani (1996a), Singh, Singh and Kumari (1998), and Srivastava (1994) that the employed associated with different streams of education differ significantly from one another in the extent of their symptomatic reactions.

In the preceding chapters (see chapters 5 and 6), poor work environment, as it exists in most of the Indian organizations, both at the physical and psychological levels, in particular, has been fairly accused for moderate psychological decline among the employed in India. The very reality may, here too, be apparently connected with the findings showing all the groups of the employed, irrespective of their being associated with different distinct disciplines of education, as equally vulnerable to different psychological reactions more or less to a moderate degree. Added to above, the views held by Dayal (1988) deserve mention here to elucidate the findings. According to him, while employees in Indian organizations generally attach more importance to personalized relationships, affiliative authority and need for nurture, organizations transmit almost contrary values to the employees shaped more in the form of bureaucratization, impersonalization, emotional aloofness combined with high control of subordinates, lower autonomy, non-nurture, etc., under the colonial influence. It needs to be pointed out here that, being relatively less promised to work ethic rather than to leisure and to family ethic, Indian workers, as it has been observed (Kanungo, 1995; Sinha, 1990; Sinha and Sinha, 1995), are usually indifferent to the accomplishment of the task assigned to them or the organizational goals under contractual obligations. Thus, they generally fail to protect the interest of the organization. In all, there clearly prevails a state of conflict in most of the Indian organizations : while employees may be found to be governed by a particular class of values, organizations are governed by another. Such a state, as it has been revealed (Agarwal, 1995; Dayal, 1988; Kanungo, 1982, 1995; Kanungo and Mendonca, 1995; Lal, 1983), is not good for the health of employees. This tends to expose them to different psychological reactions, particularly followed by anxiety, stress, feeling of insecurity, alienation, identity-crisis, poor team orientation, etc., to some extent or other.

In describing the findings, it seems also reasonable to highlight that most public sector enterprises in India are today faced with the challenge of survival more likely thrown at them by the new economic policies, economic restructuring by the global economy to which they have been recently exposed. An abrupt, though not more rapid, outgrowth in the installation of multinational companies under the influence of liberal global marketing policies adopted lately by the government of India has, more probably, also put their survival at stake. Not unacceptable, our public sector organizations are still not so well equipped as to compete with techno-scientifically much modernized multinational companies in the quality of products and the skill of marketing and business. Most of them (viz., Coal India Limited, Damodar Valley Corporation, Heavy Engineering Corporation, Indian Railway Construction Company Limited, Hindustan Fertilizer Corporation, etc.) can be seen running in loss. Indeed, they are passing through a phase of acute crisis. In addition, the intended, though yet disguised, policy of the government to hand over many big public concerns such as Railway, Banking, L.I.C., Electricity, etc., to private agencies (the process of privatization or denationalization), which have their own norms of functioning, oriented more to growth and productivity and less to social justice and welfare considerations, has posed a serious threat to the existence of public sector organizations in India. Like the public sector organizations in India, the predicament of different government enterprises, especially in eastern India, is not encouraging; it is, on the contrary, quite distressing. People working there have to face all sorts of problems (see chapter 5 for a detailed account). Many of the state enterprises, particularly in this part of the country, are virtually on the verge of closure. Thus, in all, a sizeable chunk of employees in most of the public sector and state enterprises in India are, in consequence, faced with the apprehension of being laid-off or retrenched for no fault of theirs. Although on account of the strong hold of trade unionism on the functioning of organizations here, as well as a liberal and humanistic Labour Act, one is generally not anxious of being retrenched or dismissed before completing the age of retirement or the full tenure of one's service; still, due to the apathetic attitude of the government, in particular, many public sector and state enterprises, as may be commonly observed, are finding themselves unable to meet even their basic requirements in absence of adequate grants for their maintenance, and are virtually in a state of sinking. Renovation alone does not seem sufficient to save them from fall-off. They need a total restructuring with every possible techno-scientific modernization in order to make them fully viable in the perspective of global competitive market. But, this is not an easy task. Ironically, the country is still not economically self-reliant to carry the burden of heavy expenses likely to be put upon it. In such a situation, there remains no option for the government, except to leave these organizations to their own fate or shut them down without showing any positive concern for the people on jobs there. This has not only made the employees of these organizations perplexed, but has virtually forced them to run the risk of uncertainty about the future of their continuance in their jobs. In other words, there prevails a great fear of job insecurity in them. And, there are a lot of studies (Arnetz *et al.*, 1987; Arnetz *et al.*,1991; Beale and Nethercott, 1986; Brenner and Levi, 1987b; Dooley, Rook and Catalano, 1987; Fryer and McKenna, 1988; Fryer and Winefield, 1998; Hartley *et al.*, 1991; Kasl and Cobb, 1979; Ronayne, Ryan and Cullen, 1989; Schnall *et al.*, 1992) wherein it has been shown that the anticipation of involuntary job loss or fear of losing one's job may precipitate different symptoms more clearly marked by one or another manifestation of anxiety, stress, feeling of insecurity, alienation, identity-crisis, etc., to some degree or the other, particularly on a psychological level.

Extending the discussion further, it should also be pointed out that the employees anticipating lay-off or dismissal for no fault of theirs but mainly on account of the less judicious and misdirected policies of the management (the government), as Brockner (1990) holds, generally feel themselves deprived of justice, and thrown into the inferno of psychological deterioration (Catalano, 1991; Jin, Chandrakant and Svoboda, 1995; Kieselbach, 1997b; Lerner and Somers, 1992; Wiesenfeld, 1997). To summarize, an apprehension of being laid-off or of dismissal, coupled with the unjust treatment thereafter — not taking steps to care for those laid-off or dismissed following their departure from the organization i.e., not helping them to search out other gainful jobs for their livelihood, not providing them different job-related benefits or additional financial settlements — by the management, may also be taken as one of the possible reasons for producing different psychological reactions in a majority of employees working in different public sector and state enterprises of India to a considerable extent.

However, the results, on the whole, revealed the employed young men with degrees in non-technical education and agriculture sciences, like their unemployed counterparts with degrees in the same branches of knowledge, as more plagued, though not to a statistically significant account, with the bouts of different symptoms of reduced psychological health, as compared to the other groups of the educated employed. Notably, non-technical employees in India, as Singh, Kumari and Kumari (2000), Singh, Singh and Kumari (1998) and Srivastava (1994) hold, may generally be seen to be posited at the lowest rung of the organization. They have low job prestige, low income, unchallenging routine jobs to do, and have lower promotional avenues. All these conditions associated with non-technical jobs, in the light of quite a good number of research findings (Deb and Singh, 1980; Kanungo, 1995; O'Brien and Feather, 1990; Pareek, 1996; Sayeed and Rao, 1989; Sharma, 1982; Srivastava, 1994; Warr, 1987b, d; Winefield, Tiggemann and Goldney, 1988), may reasonably be held responsible for triggering a somewhat significant drop in the psychological health of the non-technically educated employed in any of the Indian organizations.

To summarize, relatively much favoured treatments to the skilled and professionally well-equipped employees in Indian organizations generally put the non-technically educated employed at back seat in all respects, more likely exposing them to different psychological reactions. Similar perspective may reasonably be adopted in dealing with a considerable psychological loss among the employed with degree in agriculture sciences. Interestingly, on account of greater reliance fairly on unusual modes for the ranking of different jobs in India in terms of their superiority, the employed degree-holders in agriculture sciences usually tend to perceive themselves superior to the non-technically educated employed in their social status and prestige, as also in immediate economic gain, but not so while comparing themselves with employed doctors and engineers in this connection, despite having a fair amount of similarity with them in the cost and investments made on the acquisition of their education. Perhaps, this is the reason why the employed with degrees in agriculture sciences are more badly off psychologically as compared to employed degree-holders in medical and engineering sciences, and less so, compared to the non-technically educated employed, though statistically only in a very small measure.

3. Except a slight variation, almost all the groups of unemployed and employed young men from different distinct streams of technical and non-technical education, like those of the composite groups of technically and non-technically educated people, expressed a clear evidence of similarity in marking out the most, and the least, pressing psychological symptoms in them. Although they differed from one another to some extent or the other in indicating the amount of their seriousness.The psychological symptoms which appeared more agonizing for all of them were related with the feelings of uncertainty, social conflict, desolation, unstructured universe and dejection; the feeling of uncertainty being the most pronounced therein, excepting those of the groups of unemployed degree-holders in medical sciences and non-technical education who were far greatly tormented by the pangs of social conflict. Similarly, here too, all the groups of respondents were relatively less susceptible mostly to different stress-related reactions; the tendency to commit suicide was posited at the lowest rung therein apparently with meagre amount, particularly so in the case of different groups of the educated employed. Different plausible reasons, especially associated with the current socio-political scenario in India, have been suggested earlier in the 6th chapter in order to vindicate a fair amount of similarity in the identification of the most, and the least, alarming symptomatic reactions among different groups of unemployed and employed people coming from different distinct disciplines. They may, here too, form definite ground to understand the findings. No doubt, all the groups of unemployed and employed in India, irrespective of the differences in their educational affiliation, have to confront more or less similar impelling socio-political reality, more likely exposing them to similar psychological reactions. Interestingly, the conclusions of Fryer and Winefield (1998) deserve mention here. According to them the psychological consequences of employment stress and unemployment distress are similar, and form part of the same continuum. Further, there are a lot of studies (Kanungo, 1995; Kanungo and Mendonca, 1995; O'Brien and Feather, 1990; Pareek, 1996; Payne, 1995; Rani, 1993; Singh, 1994, 2001; Singh, Kumâri and Singh, 1992; Singh, Singh and Rani, 1996a; Warr, 1987b,d; Winefield, 1995a; Winefield and Tiggemann, 1990a; Winefield, Tiggemann and Goldney, 1988; Winefield, Tiggemann and Winefield, 1991; Winefield *et al*., 1991) wherein it has been shown that the employed with poor quality jobs are just as badly off psychologically as the unemployed. Not irrelevantly, in an unemployment-stricken society like India's, securing a job — no matter where it congrues to the psychological frames of the aspirants or not — is usually considered to be a *vardan* (boon). To be precise, the majority of employees in India, as it may commonly be seen, are poorly employed and misplaced almost with sealed future prospects. Hence, it seems not unnatural to have a considerable similarity in the various psychological symptoms of different groups of unemployed and employed people from different distinct streams of technical and non-technical education. However, a relatively low, albeit not unruffled, escalation in the symptomatic reactions among different groups of educated employed as against the groups of their educated unemployed counterparts also seems not anomalous. The employed in India, despite faced with a variety of problems in their life both inside and outside organizations, earn, by and large, a decent level of minimum subsistence as some kind of a socially guaranteed income, more likely attenuating, though not entirely, a somewhat daunting increase in their psychological reactions supposedly to a manageable account (see chapters 6 and 8 for a comprehensive account).

4. As the trend appeared earlier, all the groups of unemployed and employed young men in India from different distinct streams of technical and non-technical education, too, heavily relied upon intrapersistive approach mode to cope with their life events; other modes did not attract them to any significant account in this regard. Various justifications have been inscribed in the 5th chapter for the greater reliance of the groups of the unemployed and the employed solely on intrapersistive approach mode in order to meet their situational demands. They should, here too, be looked upon as reliable components to expound and appraise the findings arrived at (see chapter 5 for an elaborate account).

8

Duration of Unemployment : Impact on Psychological Well-being and Coping Styles

Chapters 5th, 6th and 7th record a comparative account of the psychological well-being of, and the degree of dependence on different coping strategies by, the composite as well as the different sets of the educated unemployed and employed young men.The findings are quite encouraging and they are likely to add to our micro- prediction about the psychological well-being as well as the coping styles of the educated unemployed *vis-à-vis* employed young men in India, in particular, and at the universal scale, in general. But, such generalization does not seem prudent. Undeniably, as Feather (1990), Jahoda (1988) and Winefield (1997) caution, it would be fallacious to treat the unemployed as a homogeneous mass. As it is empirically vindicated, not only are there types and levels of education but also a number of personal and demographic variables which may considerably mediate the impact of unemployment on the psychological well-being of those who experience it (see chapter 3rd., pp. 73-74). Duration of unemployment is also one such variable (Hepworth, 1980; Jones, 1992; Kieselbach, Beelmann and Stitzel, 2000). It is generally believed that the psychological well-being of an unemployed may considerably decline with the increase in the span of his/her unemployment. However, the findings are not fairly consistent in this regard. Following a good number of research findings (e.g., Alvaro, 1989a, b; Brenner and Levi, 1987a, b; Brenner and Starrin, 1988; De Witte and Hooge, 1997; Hammarström, Janlert and Theorell, 1988; Hooge, 1995; Iversen, 1989; Iversen and Sabroe, 1987, 1988; Sarchielli *et al.*, 1991; Warr, Banks and Ullah, 1985; Warr, Jackson and Banks, 1982) it may be mentioned that there lies no 'dose-response relation' between the duration of unemployment and the severity of the psychological consequences. Interestingly, a good deal of researches, particularly conducted by the Sheffield group (Banks 1990; Banks and Ullah, 1986, 1987a, 1988; Jackson and Warr, 1984; Warr,1987c, d, e, f, 1989 ; Warr and Jackson 1985, 1987), have shown that though the long-term or continuing unemployment is obviously more psychologically debilitating, its negative effects tend to increase during the first six months and thereafter appear to stabilize on an average —*the plateau effect*—which generally occurs after about six months, indicating an adaptation or coping with the stress that unemployment produces. This pattern is particularly marked for the middle-aged people (20-59 yrs.) and not for the teenagers (16-19 yrs) and people moving towards retirement age (60-64 yrs.); the latter are relatively less palpable.

Also, it has been indicated that the long-term unemployment is considerably more health-damaging for those who put more value on paid or gainful employment (i.e., higher employment commitment) and who confront an extreme financial stress. A number of investigations (Alvaro, 1989a; Arnetz *et al.*, 1987; Baum, Fleming and Reddy, 1986; Bolton and Oatley, 1987; Brenner and Levi, 1987a, b; Brenner and Starrin, 1988; Broomhall and Winefield, 1990; De Witte, 1993; Hooge, 1995; Kieselbach, 1998c; Liem and Liem, 1988; Rowley, 1985; Rowley and Feather, 1987; Tselepi and Agrafiotis, 1997; Warr, Jackson and Banks, 1988; Wets and De Witte, 1997; Winefield, 1995b), particularly conducted in different parts of developed nations like Britain, Sweden, Germany, Greek, Australia and United States of America, by and large, also vouch for the predictability of the findings obtained by the Sheffield group across the cultures. In an earlier study, too, Harrison (1976) has found that the deterioration in the psychological health of an unemployed does slow down with the increase in the duration of his/her plight of joblessness. Yet, there is substantial evidence to show the above findings as rather limited in their ubiquity; they cannot be generalized with confidence to all societies differing markedly in their reactions to joblessness which are largely governed by a variety of factors such as national employment and welfare policies, rate of unemployment, prevalent societal strategies to deal with the life events, value for employment in one's life, existing social norms and values, typical personality dispositions, and so on. A typical example of such evidences may be found in two well-planned investigations carried out by Brinkmann (1976,1984) in order to determine the levels of stress amongst the long-term unemployed in West Germany. He has shown that the stabilization effect occurs after a year, which partially pales away again later, and which is superimposed by a large number of negative experiences such as 'daily hassles' in the familial and extra-familial lives. Finnish (Lahelma and Kangas, 1989) and Dutch (Verkleij, 1989) studies also set illustrations of this kind. Lahelma and Kangas (1989) have indicated that continuous or recurrent unemployment for a longer duration of more than one year causes a greater damage to psychological health. Similarly, in the study by Verkleij (1989) it has been discovered that some — albeit incomplete — adaptation appears after a span of three years, although even after a spell of four years a renewed escalation in stress (physical ailments, negative feelings, or depression) can be clearly noticed.

To summarize, the two studies clearly show that the psychosocial stress scores among people confronting a long-term unemployment are more likely to increase, if anything. Likewise, Hall (1985) has indicated that unemployment among the Swedish women for a long spell of two years increases in them substantially a greater risk (*i.e.*, 3.5 times) for depressive reactions as compared to the control group, though the risk may be moderated by social support. Recently, on the basis of their studies, Cortés (1997), De Witte (1994), Hammarström and Janlert (1997), Hammarström and Olofsson (1997), Kieselbach, Beelmann and Stitzel (2000) and Kieselbach *et al.*(2001) have also shown that an increasing duration of unemployment clearly leads to an increase in different health-related problems. Furthermore, even in a British study (Breakwell, Harrison and Propper, 1984) it has been found that young people experience greatest distress after an average of six weeks of joblessness, recovering somewhat after that duration. The views held by Ronayne, Ryan and Cullen (1989) deserve mention here. According to them, though average distress values may witness a clear indication of meaningful adaptation, they may skip people who are particularly susceptible. More obviously, they have endeavoured just to emphasize that a slight reduction in, or levelling off of, distress values does not really mean a positive adaptation; it may be misleading and may, therefore, dissemble the identification of those who are particularly risk-prone. Besides, it may be noted that age differences also do not act in accordance with the claim staked by the Sheffield group of investigators in moderating the impact of duration of unemployment on psychological well-being. On the basis of their studies, Cullen *et al.* (1987), Kieselbach (1988 a) and Winefield and Tiggemann (1989, 1990b) have indicated young unemployed people as markedly afflicted with a high level of psychiatric morbidity. Likewise, Viney (1983) has reported that young unemployed below 20 years of age, as compared to older ones, have significantly a greater amount of the feelings of anxiety, anger, helplessness, guilt and shame. Garcia Rodrigues (1994) has also shown that unemployed aged from 16-19 years are significantly more depressed than those who are older. The conclusion drawn by Schober (1978), on the basis of the comparison of stress profiles between the juvenile and adult unemployed, appears relevant to note here.

The conclusion explicitly indicates that both of them equally run the risk of psychological impairment; the only difference that lies between the two groups is that while the former are terribly blighted with domestic tensions and attributions of blame, the latter acutely suffer from social isolation and stigmatization caused by their plight. However, the above findings, like those of the Sheffield psychologists, too, may or may not be applicable to varying socio-cultural milieus. Nonetheless, it cannot be repudiated that the unemployed young people of today are likely to be the morbid adults of tomorrow because they, too, may resort to different maladaptive forms of coping strategies such as frequent use of alcohol and tobacco, idling and gossiping, etc., in order to relieve the tension and strain generated by their condition which may definitely prove deleterious to their long-term health (Kannas and Hietarharju, 1979). Optimistically viewed, there is no doubt that the good health of young people may help them to extenuate the distress caused by their unemployment. However, it is also a fact revealed through investigation (Olafsson and Svensson, 1986) that they may not always depend on their potentialities to fight with the malady of unemployment, they may groom in them the development of certain riskier health behaviours (with regard to eating and sleeping habits, alcohol and tobacco consumption, personal hygiene, and sporting and entertainment activities) which may agreeably precede the delayed damage to their well-being, the amount of which cannot be clearly ascertained immediately. The Sheffield psychologists' claim that a higher level of employment commitment and an extreme financial stress are two important variables which may considerably mediate the impact of duration of unemployment on psychological health has been amply substantiated (Jackson, 1988; Jackson *et al.*,1983; Rowley and Feather, 1987; Schultz-Gambard *et al.*, 1986; Warr and Jackson, 1985). However, in addition to them, there are a number of nationally as well as culturally specific moderating variables already described above, not fairly accentuated by them in their analysis of the impact of long-term unemployment on psychological health. This may clearly limit the applicability of their findings in wider perspectives.

Thus, the studies carried out to see the impact of the duration of unemployment on psychological well-being, particularly in the west, on the whole, produce conflicting and inconsistent results. Many plausible reasons have been offered for the variance in the findings (Kieselbach, 1990b, 1991; Roberts, Duggan and Noble, 1982; Warr, 1987c,d,e). But, not much importance has yet been given to the determining role of culture and specific norms and values prevalent therein in mediating the impact of the duration of unemployment on psychological well-being, though there is substantial evidence to indicate that people coming from different cultures differ significantly in their reactions to joblessness (Schaufeli,1988 b; Singh, 2001; Singh, Singh and Rani,1996 a,b; Ullah, 1988). This emphasizes the need to explore afresh the impact of the duration of unemployment on psychological well-being by fully taking into account the importance of cultural specificity of the land, as well as certain typical values prevailing therein.

It should be noted that India has a distinct socio-cultural background, making its people unique in their perception of, and reaction to, the problem of unemployment. Interestingly, in India the short-term unemployment, as it has been observed (Singh, 1990, 1994), is not perceived as psychologically precipitating as the Sheffield group of investigators, in particular, have ascribed it to be. Reasons for this may be many. Nevertheless, this may be mainly because of the following two factors: one, the still persisting underlying association with the concept of kinship with extended family norms, despite the all-pervasive impact of frequently occurring socio-technological changes and modernization on the family life of an Indian. The other is the element of stoicism ingrained in the Indian mind. This prevents an Indian from reacting sharply to any event at its initial phase. He/she is more disposed to construe it as transitory and inchoate. Such situations do come sometime or the other in the life of a person which, he/she believes, are purposely ordained by the *Parama Brahma* — the Supreme Power — to test his/her capacity to endure, as also his/her equanimity to sustain himself/herself with the changing situations. Interestingly, it fills the more orthodox even with a sense of gratitude as being one among the chosen few, in his/her estimation, to be blessed with such a favour. Stoicism is, thus, deeply embedded in fatalism, of course, in a special way. This may not appear markedly pronounced in his/her attitude in general but it is embedded in Indian psyche which he/she, consciously or unconsciously, is inclined to endorse. Added to these, the commonly observed trait of easy going temperament deeply inherent in Indian personality, in general, may, though not more imperatively, be said to be responsible for the stolid response of an Indian to short-term unemployment. People afflicted with long-term unemployment, thus, may be expected to be exposed to particularly high risk of psychological impairment. The findings of a good number of studies conducted by L.B. Singh and his associates (Singh, 1990, 1994; Singh, Kumari and Singh, 1992; Singh, Singh and Rani, 1996a,b; Singh, Singh and Singh, 1996; Singh, Singh and Singh, 1995) have also indicated so. In most of these studies it has been shown that people aged about 25 to 35 years, who have been unemployed for a long stretch, i.e., more than a span of five years, have reduced psychological well-being estimated in terms of the variables like self-concepts, social conflict, adjustment, hostility, alienation and their dimensions along with control mechanisms, various general health problems, etc. However, they, too, like their employed counterparts, have been found to be moderately palpable in most of the instances, excepting alienation and its dimensions, as well as some of the manifestations of hostility (viz., irritability, suspicion and sense of guilt) and externality.

Although, a noticeable difference always exists between them in this regard with the sharp deterioration in the health of the former. Nonetheless, it may be pointed out that these studies have not been essentially designed to focus the comparative account of the psychological well-being of the people facing different discrete durations of unemployment either being relied on cross-sectional or longitudinal research strategy. Hence, the findings accumulated therefrom clearly appear limited in their scope to make any definite predictions about the impact of different spells of unemployment on psychological well-being; the findings, at most, may simply serve as a basis for the assumption to conceive long-term unemployment as responsible for the sharp deterioration in the psychological well-being of those who experience it. Astonishingly, no systematic attempts, except a few like those carried out by Kumari (2001) and Narayan (1995), have so far been made in this regard. Kumari (2001), on the basis of an extensive analysis of the level of frustration and aggression as well as their dimensions among the educated young men afflicted with different distinct durations of unemployment, has indicated that people who have been unemployed for a long spell of 5 years and more, in particular, are very much susceptible to a symptomatic state of frustration and aggression usually manifested in different forms.

However, it must be added that people unemployed for even a short period, say, less than the span of 2 years, are also equally sensitive in this regard, though the degree of distress in them has always been found to be considerably low as compared to the former. Narayan (1995) has also reported that the longer the spell of unemployment lasts, the greater the psychological deterioration likely to precipitate in the individual concerned. These findings, nonetheless, fairly accord with those obtained by the Sheffield group of investigators. There is likely to be an interesting revelation that these findings, too, have indicated unemployment as inducing more damage to one's health, more so during the phase of the first year of its duration, though the exact time period, which may prove more threatening to the well-being, has not been clearly ascertained. Obviously, the findings, unlike the findings obtained by the Sheffield group, have, by and large, revealed that there follows a sharp increase in the severity of the effects of unemployment with the subsequent increase in its duration; no stabilization or normalizing effect occurs in this course, all nuisances related to the psychological impacts of the duration of unemployment, however, grow stridingly with the addition in the length of joblessness. However, the ubiquity of the assertion needs to be verified in larger socio-cultural perspectives by carefully using a sufficient amount of cross-cultural data accumulated discreetly both at *emic* and *etic* levels. The findings of the studies conducted by Kumari (2001) and Narayan (1995) also reveal that age may obviously mediate the impact of duration of unemployment on psychological well-being, but only the people aged nearly 30 to 35 years — the upper age limit after which one usually consumes one's hope to enter any public or organized private sector job — are likely to be particularly more vulnerable to psychological breakdown, though these studies have almost exclusively concentrated on the educated unemployed young men of about 25 to 35 years of age, and not on other age groups. It may commonly be observed that there almost lies no problem of educated juvenile job-seekers (below the age of 20 yrs.) or middle-aged unemployed (35-59 yrs.) or laid-off or redundant groups in India, particularly so in those who belong to upper middle class and affluent families.

Remarkably, the Indian social system is so peculiarly woven and latched with such idiosyncratic social norms and values that it does not allow one to see them as unemployed, in spite of their being workless. Even in exceptional situations, it is usually considered as the sole result of the sins — the *pap* — commited in one's *karma* (duty) in this life, as also in one's *purva janma* (previous births) — quite cyclic in order as Indian beliefs and ontology, in general, testify it. However, the findings obtained from only these few studies cannot be safely generalized; there is, of course, a great dearth of precise and systematic studies in India in this regard. There has probably been no systematic investigation yet in India regarding the coping tactics adopted by different groups of the educated unemployed and employed people for various distinct durations to deal with their life situations. This, of course, leaves the issue, in question, least understood and explicated. This study, therefore, primarily aims at presenting an account of the intra- and inter-group comparisons of various exclusive bands of educated unemployed and employed young men with experience of different durations of their respective status of employment in terms of their psychological well-being, as well as their relative dependence on different strategies generally used to cope with their situations at both macro and micro levels. This chapter, thus, has been divided into two sections: one comprising the findings exclusively arrived at *intra-group comparisons*, and the other deriving from the *inter-group comparisons*.

The first section of this chapter, as purported, contains the quintessence of the findings recorded from the statistical comparison made at intra-group level separately for different groups of technically and non-technically educated unemployed and employed young men; each of them was exclusively divided within themselves on the basis of the experience of the various discrete durations of their own particular status (either different forms of educated unemployment or employment) which they had been holding with them. The intra-group comparisons were primarily made with the purposes as follows:

(1) To test the applicability of the findings by the Sheffield group of investigators, in particular, and other western psychologists, in general, in relation to the impact of different distinct durations of the status of employment on psychological well-

being in a country like India which is so hard hit by the problem of joblessness.

(2) To isolate the particular time period of unemployment and employment which causes optimum damage to the psychological well-being. Also, to find out the exact time point which leads to the occurrence of *'the stabilization effect'*, particularly in the life of the unemployed in India.

(3) To identify the coping strategy largely resorted to by different groups of the unemployed and employed people in India distinct in the experience of the duration of their particular status.

The findings so obtained from within - groups comparisons made separately for different sets of participants in terms of their psychological health and coping styles are being summarized below.

Duration of Unemployment and Level of Anxiety, Stress, Feeling of Insecurity, Alienation and Identity-Crisis : The Case of the Young Unemployed Degree-holders in Medical Sciences

As proposed, in order to attain the abovementioned purposes, first, different groups of unemployed medical degree-holders for different distinct durations were statistically compared among themselves in terms of their level of anxiety, stress, feeling of insecurity, alienation and identity-crisis. Table 8.1 summarizes the findings.

The results displayed in Table 8.1 indicated that different groups of the unemployed medical degree-holders distinct in the duration of their status did not differ significantly amongst themselves in terms of the various indicators of psychological well-being, except the dimensions such as emotional responsiveness ($F = 4.27$; $df = 3,59$; $p<0.01$), narcissism ($p<0.01$), fragmentation ($F = 5.96$; $p<0.01$), role conflict ($p<0.05$) and loneliness ($F = 4.71$). The results, thus, on the whole, evinced that the different spells of unemployment did not cause any marked difference in the psychological well-being of those who had been imperilled by them. It was, however, recorded that all the groups of the unemployed with degrees in medical sciences were, by and large, relatively susceptible to psychological damage. It was further revealed that all the groups of unemployed medical degree-holders, besides the 0-1yr. group of the unemployed who showed themselves as moving in a state of uncertainty (70%), confronted an acute feeling

Table 8.1 : Statistical Differences Among the Groups of the Medical Degree-holders Unemployed for Different Discrete Durations and their Relative Standing in Terms of Different Indices of Psychological Well-being

Indices of Psychological Well-being	*Length of Unemployment (in Years)*												
	0-1(N=15)			*1-2(N=16)*			*2-3(N=15)*			*3-above (N=17)*			
	Mean	*SD*	*Rank*	*Mean*	*SD*	*Rank*	*Mean*	*SD*	*Rank*	*Mean*	*SD*	*Rank*	*F*
1. General Worries	2.80 (46.67)	1.37	25	2.69 (44.83)	1.62	13	2.40 (40.00)	1.29	27	3.04 (50.67)	1.43	21	0.35
2. Somatic Manifestations	0.80 (26.67)	0.38	33	1.13 (37.67)	0.89	26	0.47 (15.67)	0.23	38	1.06 (35.33)	0.83	31	1.61
3. Psychological Symptoms	2.53 (50.60)	1.13	19	2.06 (41.20)	1.29	24	1.93 (38.60)	1.02	29	2.28 (45.60)	1.14	27	0.48
4. Social Relations	3.13 (39.13)	1.68	29	3.50 (43.75)	1.54	18.5	2.13 (26.63)	1.51	35	2.65 (33.13)	1.55	32	1.25
5. **Anxiety**	9.27 (42.14)	3.99	26	9.38 (42.64)	4.19	20	6.93 (31.50)	2.97	30	9.05 (41.14)	3.80	29	0.87
6. Suicidal Tendency	0.27 (6.75)	0.16	39	0.04 (1.00)	0.02	39	0.47 (11.75)	0.24	39	0.29 (7.25)	0.17	39	1.41
7. Emotional Instability	3.93 (49.13)	1.31	21.5	2.06 (25.75)	1.11	33	3.80 (47.50)	1.38	21.5	2.94 (36.75)	1.58	30	2.53
8. Paranoid Tendency	1.80 (15.00)	1.11	38	1.94 (16.17)	1.08	38	2.33 (19.42)	1.23	37	2.35 (19.58)	1.42	38	0.29
9. Depression	8.73 (24.25)	3.99	37	10.38 (28.83)	3.97	31	9.40 (26.11)	3.88	36	9.82 (27.28)	3.86	34	0.11
10. Physical Illness	3.07 (25.58)	1.69	34	2.19 (18.25)	1.22	36.5	3.33 (27.75)	1.32	34	3.94 (32.83)	1.59	33	1.66
11. Social Maladjustment	3.00 (25.00)	1.24	36	2.19 (18.25)	1.37	36.5	3.67 (30.58)	1.66	32	3.06 (25.50)	1.66	36	0.73
12. Apprehensiveness	3.60 (30.00)	1.53	32	2.44 (20.33)	1.19	35	3.73 (31.08)	1.74	31	2.76 (23.00)	1.66	37	1.12
13. **Stress**	24.42 (25.44)	10.17	35	21.24 (22.13)	8.18	34	26.73 (27.84)	9.01	33	25.18 (26.23)	8.50	35	0.27

Contd.

Table 8.1 *(Contd.)*

Indices of Psychological Well-being	*Length of Unemployment (in Years)* 0-1(N=15) *Mean*	*SD*	*Rank*	1-2(N=16) *Mean*	*SD*	*Rank*	2-3(N=15) *Mean*	*SD*	*Rank*	3-above (N=17) *Mean*	*SD*	*Rank*	*F*
14. Lack of Self- confidence	12.60	4.37		8.95	3.89		11.26	4.03		10.82	3.94		1.57
	(63.00)		04	(44.75)		14	(56.30)		04	(54.10)		11	
15. Dejection	8.86	3.49		7.35	3.35		8.13	3.28		8.47	3.37		1.03
	(59.07)		08	(49.00)		07	(54.20)		07	(56.47)		08	
16. Pessimism	2.40	1.68		1.38	0.81		2.13	1.46		2.65	1.62		2.40
	(48.00)		23	(27.60)		32	(42.60)		26	(53.00)		16	
17. Emotional Responsiveness	16.33	5.64		13.38	4.07		17.46	5.93		16.17	5.09		4.27
	(54.43)		14	(44.60)		15.5	(58.20)		03	(53.90)		13	
18. Social Insecurity	12.33	4.55		11.15	3.93		12.86	4.69		13.23	4.72		1.37
	(49.32)		20	(44.60)		15.5	(51.44)		12	(52.92)		18	
19. Distrust	2.73	1.10		2.69	1.66		2.40	1.40		2.41	1.46		0.24
	(54.60)		13	(53.80)		04	(48.00)		20	(48.20)		24	
20. **Feeling of Insecurity**	55.27	16.85		44.90	17.05		54.25	18.56		53.76	19.02		1.05
	(55.27)		11	(44.90)		12	(54.25)		06	(53.76)		14	
21. Despair	16.40	4.07		16.31	4.45		17.07	5.68		18.59	6.33		0.67
	(51.25)		17	(50.97)		06	(53.34)		08	(58.09)		07	
22. Unstructured Universe	4.87	1.88		4.63	1.96		4.00	0.93		4.71	1.69		0.78
	(60.88)		06	(57.88)		03	(50.00)		16	(58.88)		05	
23. Psychological Vacuum	4.60	1.06		3.75	1.88		3.93	0.80		4.35	1.17		1.38
	(57.50)		10	(46.88)		10	(49.13)		18	(54.38)		10	
24. Disillusionment	2.20	0.94		1.44	0.63		1.87	0.74		1.88	0.99		2.15
	(55.00)		12	(36.00)		27	(46.75)		24.5	(47.00)		26	
25. Narcissism	1.40	0.51		1.25	0.45		2.13	1.06		1.65	0.79		4.19
	(35.00)		31	(31.25)		30	(53.25)		09	(41.25)		28	
26. **Alienation**	29.49	5.70		27.38	6.38		29.00	7.03		31.18	9.08		0.78
	(52.66)		16	(48.89)		08	(51.89)		11	(55.68)		09	
27. Depersonalization	3.27	1.33		3.19	1.28		3.80	1.86		4.12	2.23		1.06
	(40.88)		28	(39.88)		25	(47.50)		21.5	(51.50)		19	
28. Fragmentation	4.93	1.67		2.81	1.11		3.13	1.55		3.94	1.68		5.96
	(61.63)		05	(35.13)		28	(39.13)		28	(49.25)		22	

Contd.

Table 8.1 *(Contd.)*

Indices of Psychological Well-being	*Length of Unemployment (in Years)*												
	0-1(N=15)			*1-2(N=16)*			*2-3(N=15)*			*3-above (N=17)*			
	Mean	*SD*	*Rank*	*Mean*	*SD*	*Rank*	*Mean*	*SD*	*Rank*	*Mean*	*SD*	*Rank*	*F*
29. Uncertainty	2.80 (70.00)	1.08	01	2.06 (51.50)	1.12	05	2.80 (70.00)	1.02	02	2.41 (60.25)	1.18	03	1.61
30. Distress	5.73 (47.75)	1.98	24	5.63 (46.92)	1.93	09	6.60 (55.00)	2.82	05	5.76 (48.00)	2.17	25	0.61
31. Indecisiveness	3.93 (49.13)	1.44	21.5	3.38 (42.25)	1.96	21.5	4.20 (52.50)	1.70	10	4.06 (50.75)	2.01	20	0.63
32. Social Conflict	2.73 (68.25)	0.96	02	2.56 (64.00)	0.89	01	3.00 (75.00)	1.07	01	2.71 (67.75)	1.16	01	0.48
33. Isolation	3.33 (41.63)	1.23	27	3.38 (42.25)	0.96	21.5	4.00 (50.00)	2.00	16	3.88 (48.50)	1.62	23	0.81
34. Withdrawal from Social and Personal Contact	1.47 (36.75)	0.74	30	1.75 (43.75)	0.77	18.5	1.93 (48.25)	1.33	19	2.12 (53.00)	1.17	16	1.13
35. Role Conflict	7.00 (58.33)	2.33	09	5.06 (42.17)	2.02	23	5.67 (47.25)	2.35	23	7.12 (59.33)	2.55	04	3.02
36. Hopelessness	4.07 (50.88)	1.58	18	3.63 (45.38)	1.59	11	4.07 (50.88)	2.31	14	4.24 (53.00)	2.17	16	0.29
37. Loneliness	2.67 (66.75)	1.18	03	1.31 (32.75)	0.48	29	2.00 (50.00)	1.06	16	2.35 (58.75)	1.06	06	4.71
38. Desolation	2.40 (60.00)	0.91	07	2.50 (62.50)	1.21	02	1.87 (46.75)	0.92	24.5	2.59 (64.75)	1.00	02	1.56
39. ***Identity-crisis***	44.33 (52.77)	11.64	15	37.26 (44.36)	10.54	17	43.07 (51.27)	12.45	13	45.31 (53.94)	14.07	12	1.11

Note : $df = 3,59$; $p < 0.05 = 2.76$; $p < 0.01 = 4.13$.

of social conflict (the obtained scores ranged between 64 per cent and 75 per cent). However, all of them, without any exception, were least affected by the feeling to commit suicide, obtaining only a minimal score on the scale designed to measure the extent of the tendency (the scores lying between 1.00 per cent and 11.75 per cent). They also scored lower on all other dimensions of the stress, only with the exception of emotional instability, where they were found to be markedly afflicted to a moderate extent (the scores obtained by different groups of the unemployed varied from 25.75 to 49.13 per cent). Yet, in the light of substantial empirical evidence (e.g., Feather,1982; Goldberg, 1972; Warr,1984a), they cannot be labelled as less impervious to psychological debilitation.

Finally, the results revealed that stabilization effect as such did not appear with the unemployed medical degree-holders in India as it was recorded by the Sheffield group of investigators. However, to a certain extent, as in the case of the findings of the latter, the 0-1 yr. group of the unemployed was found to be relatively more susceptible to psychological impairment, particularly when measured in terms of the level of anxiety, stress, feeling of insecurity, alienation, identity-crisis in their various manifestations. Also, it was seen that the 1-2 yr. group of the unemployed manifested a clear tendency of decline in their psychological symptoms recorded in terms of the aforementioned indices of psychological health, except anxiety which was found to be slightly existent. But, this diminishment of psychological symptoms did not appear in the case of 2-3 yr. and 3-above yr. groups of the unemployed. Barring a fall in the level of anxiety, particularly so found in the case of 2-3 yr. group of the medical degree-holder unemployed, they showed a raised level of all the syndromes being investigated. A somewhat clear indication of the occurrence of stabilization effect in the life of the medical degree-holders in India, in all, was observed just after a span of three years of the experience of the trauma of joblessness by them. It was, however, the group of 3-above year unemployed people who, more or less, appeared to be psychologically more tormented, indicating, thus, the prolonged period of unemployment as relatively dangerous to psychological health.The results, nonetheless, failed to identify the exact period of unemployment which led to more psychological debilitation; while some dimensions of health tended to precipitate in 0-1 yr. group of the unemployed, some others in 1-2 yr. group of job-seekers and yet another dimension was found to be more susceptible either in the group of the medical degree-holders who had been unemployed for a spell of 2-3 yr . or 3-above yr. Thus, there appeared no clear-cut picture as to the exact period of unemployment which caused maximum damage to the psychological health of those facing it.

Duration of Unemployment and the Degree of Life Satisfaction : The Case of the Young Unemployment Degree-holders in Medical Sciences

Table 8.2 reports an account of the statistical comparison among different distinct groups of the medical degree-holder unemployed young men in terms of their degree of life satisfaction.

Table 8.2 : Statistical Differences Among the Groups of Medical Degree-holders Unemployed for Different Discrete Durations and their Relative Standing in Terms of the Degree of their Life Satisfaction

	Length of Unemployment (in Years)								
	0-1 (N-15)		*1-2 (N-16)*		*2-3 (N=15)*		*3-above (N=17)*		
Variable	*Mean (%)*	*SD*	*Mean (%)*	*SD*	*Mean (%)*	*SD*	*Mean (%)*	*SD*	*F*
Life Satisfaction	6.13 (61.30)	2.20	5.44 (54.40)	1.26	5.00 (50.00)	2.36	4.53 (45.30)	2.18	1.76

Note : $df = 3,59$; $p < 0.05=2.76$; $p < 0.01=4.13$.

Like the other indices of psychological health analysed in this investigation, different groups of medical degree-holders oppressed with various discrete stretches of unemployment did not show any marked difference amongst themselves in terms of the degree of satisfaction with their life (F=1.76; df=3,59; $p > 0.05$), too. However, a gradual decline in the amount of their life satisfaction was clearly noted with an increase in the duration of their status, and so the 3-above yr. group of the unemployed medical degree-holders was found to be relatively less, though not below the mark of moderate level, satisfied with their life (45.30%). Further, unlike the assertions of the Sheffield group of psychologists, the 0-1 yr. group of the unemployed did not exhibit a greater fall off in the degree of their life satisfaction, in particular, they were apparently more satisfied with their life.

Duration of Unemployment and the Degree of Dependence on Different Coping Strategies : The Case of the Young Unemployment Degree-holders in Medical Sciences

As intended, different groups of the medical degree-holders unemployed for different distinct durations were compared statistically amongst themselves in terms of their dependence on various strategies (e.g., intrapersistive approach mode, extrapersistive approach mode, punitive avoidance mode, and defensive avoidance mode) adopted by them in order to effect a compromise with their life events. Table 8.3 consists of the summary of the findings.

Table 8.3 : Statistical Differences Among the Groups of the Medical Degree-holders Unemployed for Different Discrete Durations and the Degree of their Relative Dependence in Terms of Different Coping Strategies

	Length of Unemployment (in Years)								
	0-1 (N=15)		*1-2 (N=16)*		*2-3 (N=15)*		*3-above (N=17)*		
Coping Strategies	*Mean (%)*	*SD*	*Mean (%)*	*SD*	*Mean (%)*	*SD*	*Mean (%)*	*SD*	*F*
Intrapersistive Approach Mode	10.80 (72.00)	3.41	9.63 (64.20)	1.15	8.60 (57.33)	3.96	8.53 (56.87)	3.24	1.82
Extrapersistive Approach Mode	1.33 (8.87)	0.67	1.69 (11.27)	0.93	3.53 (23.53)	1.61	2.18 (14.53)	1.38	4.43
Punitive Avoidance Mode	1.80 (12.00)	1.03	1.06 (7.07)	0.59	1.40 (9.33)	0.69	0.88 (5.87)	0.47	0.55
Defensive Avoidance Mode	1.07 (7.13)	0.56	2.63 (17.53)	1.31	1.47 (9.80)	0.74	3.41 (22.73)	1.70	6.93

Note : $df = 3,59$; $p < 0.05 = 2.76$; $p < 0.01 = 4.13$.

Different groups of the medical degree-holders unemployed for various distinct durations were found to differ significantly from one another in terms of extrapersistive approach mode ($p<0.01$) and defensive avoidance mode ($F= 6.93$; $df=3,59$; $p <0.01$), but not with regard to the rest of the other two strategies adopted for adjustment. It was, however, clearly recorded that all of them tended to resort to intrapersistive approach mode as the most favourable strategy to deal with their situations; no other strategies were found to be that convenient for them in this connection.

Duration of Unemployment and Level of Anxiety, Stress, Feeling of Insecurity, Alienation and Identity-Crisis : The Case of the Young Unemployed Degree-holders in Engineering Sciences

In verifying the predictions made about the impact of the duration of unemployment on psychological well-being, different groups of the young engineers unemployed for various distinct durations were also statistically compared amongst themselves in terms of the level of anxiety, stress, feeling of insecurity, alienation, identity-crisis and their dimensions. Table 8.4 reports the findings.

Unlike the groups of the unemployed medical degree-holders, different groups of engineers unemployed for different discrete durations showed a marked difference amongst themselves in terms of quite a good number of indicators of psychological health, except anxiety and its dimensions ($p > 0.05$). However, like the former, they were found to be susceptible to psychological ill-health in some degree or the other, though not more than to a moderate extent in most of the instances. Further, all of them, too, were greatly plagued with the trauma of either uncertainty (scores varied between 67 per cent and 85 per cent), or social conflict (scores ranged between 67 per cent and 71.75 per cent), although it did not express one-to-one similarity with the trend that was recorded in the case of different groups of the medical degree-holders who had been unemployed for various distinct spells. Similarly, they, barring the 2-3 year group of the unemployed engineers who were least affected by paranoid tendency (20 per cent), were least prone to suicidal ideation (scores varied between 1.25 per cent and 11.75 per cent). Lastly, here too, the tenability of stabilization effect could not be proved in its entirety. Notably, barring a decrease in the level of the feeling of insecurity and its dimensions like emotional responsiveness, social insecurity and distrust, particularly in the case of 1-2 year group of the unemployed engineers, the 1-2 and 2-3 year groups of the unemployed engineers witnessed an increase in the level of their other psychological symptoms. Further, it was observed that the groups of engineers unemployed for the longer durations of 3-4 and 4-above years respectively tended to express gradual decline in the level of their various psychological reactions. To summarize, the stabilization effect in the life of the unemployed engineers in India clearly appeared only after three years of continuous experience of their plight.

The findings, thus, to a certain extent, corresponded with those

Table 8.4 : Statistical Differences Among the Groups of the Engineers Unemployed for Different Discrete Durations and their Relative Standing in Terms of Different Indices of Psychological Well-being

Indices of Psychological Well-being	*Length of Unemployment (in Years)*															*F*
	0-1(N=15)			*1-2(N=19)*			*2-3(N=15)*			*3-4(N=15)*			*4-above (N=15)*			
	Mean	*SD*	*Rank*	*Mean*	*SD*	*Rank*	*Mean*	*SD*	*Rank*	*Mean*	*SD*	*Rank*	*Mean*	*SD*	*Rank*	
1. General Worries	2.80 (46.67)	1.55	16	2.84 (47.33)	1.57	14.5	3.67 (61.17)	1.76	14	2.93 (48.83)	1.69	20	2.67 (44.50)	1.38	22	0.76
2. Somatic Manifestations	0.73 (24.33)	0.37	33	0.79 (26.33)	0.40	32	1.07 (35.67)	0.56	34	0.73 (24.33)	0.37	36	0.60 (20.00)	0.32	36	0.59
3. Psychological Symptoms	2.00 (40.00)	1.00	24	2.42 (48.40)	1.17	13	2.93 (58.60)	1.10	18	2.40 (48.00)	1.10	22	2.33 (46.60)	1.18	18	0.85
4. Social Relations	2.60 (32.50)	1.40	30.5	2.37 (29.63)	1.46	31	2.93 (36.63)	1.52	33	3.47 (43.38)	1.83	27.5	3.27 (40.88)	1.59	27	0.79
5. **Anxiety**	8.13 (36.95)	4.20	27	8.42 (38.27)	3.95	28	10.61 (48.23)	4.42	28	9.53 (43.32)	4.27	29	8.87 (40.32)	4.43	28	0.75
6. Suicidal Tendency	0.07 (1.75)	0.03	39	0.05 (1.25)	0.02	39	1.07 (26.75)	0.62	38	0.47 (11.75)	0.25	39	0.20 (5.00)	0.11	39	3.75
7. Emotional Instability	2.60 (32.50)	1.36	30.5	3.26 (40.75)	1.68	24.5	3.53 (44.13)	1.82	29	3.47 (43.38)	1.86	27.5	3.40 (42.50)	1.88	26	0.45
8. Paranoid Tendency	2.07 (17.25)	1.02	37	0.89 (7.42)	0.46	38	2.40 (20.00)	1.23	39	3.27 (27.25)	1.53	34	2.00 (16.67)	1.06	37	3.79
9. Depression	6.53 (18.14)	3.05	36	8.74 (24.28)	4.32	33	13.60 (37.78)	6.60	32	10.00 (27.78)	5.88	33	9.53 (26.47)	5.10	32	2.08
10. Physical Illness	2.33 (19.42)	1.18	35	2.16 (18.00)	1.24	37	4.73 (39.42)	2.05	31	2.53 (21.08)	1.82	38	2.67 (22.25)	1.53	35	4.24
11. Social Maladjustment	1.67 (13.92)	0.90	38	2.47 (20.58)	1.41	36	4.07 (33.92)	2.29	36	3.40 (28.33)	1.82	32	2.87 (23.92)	1.90	33	1.97
12. Apprehensiveness	3.67 (30.58)	1.77	32	2.68 (22.33)	1.55	34	3.67 (30.58)	1.83	37	2.60 (21.67)	1.62	37	1.87 (15.58)	1.05	38	1.57

Contd.

Table 8.4 *(Contd.)*

Indices of Psychological Well-being	*Length of Unemployment (in Years)*															
	0-1(N=15)			*1-2(N=19)*			*2-3(N=15)*			*3-4(N=15)*			*4-above (N=15)*			
	Mean	*SD*	*Rank*	*Mean*	*SD*	*Rank*	*Mean*	*SD*	*Rank*	*Mean*	*SD*	*Rank*	*Mean*	*SD*	*Rank*	*F*
13. **Stress**	18.94	8.47		20.26	9.36		33.07	14.82		25.74	13.68		22.54	12.74		2.65
	(19.73)		34	(21.10)		35	(34.45)		35	(26.81)		35	(23.48)		34	
14. Lack of	10.13	3.97		10.37	4.08		13.47	4.37		11.87	3.87		9.94	3.56		3.57
Self- confidence	(50.65)		05	(51.85)		07	(67.35)		06	(59.35)		04	(49.70)		12	
15. Dejection	8.41	3.46		8.63	3.52		9.74	3.69		8.40	3.39		8.24	3.17		1.03
	(56.07)		02	(57.53)		03	(64.93)		08	(56.00)		10	(54.93)		07	
16. Pessimism	1.80	1.01		1.84	1.12		2.00	1.21		1.80	1.01		1.93	1.08		0.84
	(36.00)		29	(36.80)		29	(40.00)		30	(36.00)		30	(38.60)		29	
17. Emotional	14.33	5.19		13.59	4.91		18.80	6.03		16.42	5.23		15.28	4.99		5.39
Responsiveness	(47.77)		11	(45.30)		21	(62.67)		11	(54.73)		13	(50.93)		09	
18. Social Insecurity	10.27	4.38		8.95	3.72		16.40	4.85		12.81	4.47		11.14	4.03		13.29
	(41.08)		23	(35.80)		30	(65.60)		07	(51.24)		18	(44.56)		21	
19. Distrust	2.40	1.18		2.32	1.38		3.40	1.59		2.87	0.83		2.53	1.06		1.99
	(48.00)		10	(46.40)		18	(68.00)		05	(57.40)		07	(50.60)		10	
20. **Feeling of**	47.34	11.54		45.70	14.06		63.81	15.56		54.17	9.52		49.07	14.08		4.59
Insecurity	(47.34)		13	(45.70)		20	(63.81)		09	(54.17)		15	(49.07)		14	
21. Despair	16.07	3.59		16.47	3.66		20.40	5.03		15.60	4.60		15.40	3.52		3.80
	(50.22)		07	(51.47)		08	(63.75)		10	(48.75)		21	(48.13)		16	
22. Unstructured	3.73	1.58		4.05	1.54		4.00	1.46		4.60	1.59		4.53	1.30		0.92
Universe	(46.63)		17	(50.63)		09	(50.00)		26.5	(57.50)		5.5	(56.63)		06	
23. Psychological	3.33	0.82		4.26	1.59		4.40	1.40		4.53	1.60		4.67	1.05		2.32
Vacuum	(41.63)		22	(53.25)		4.5	(55.00)		23	(56.63)		09	(58.38)		03	
24. Disillusionment	1.47	0.74		1.58	0.84		2.33	1.05		1.80	0.68		1.53	0.64		2.93
	(36.75)		28	(39.50)		27	(58.25)		19.5	(45.00)		25	(38.25)		30.5	
25. Narcissism	1.67	0.82		1.84	0.96		2.00	1.20		1.87	0.99		1.53	0.74		0.55
	(41.75)		21	(46.00)		19	(50.00)		26.5	(46.75)		23.5	(38.25)		30.5	
26. **Alienation**	26.27	4.88		28.21	4.91		33.13	7.24		28.40	5.79		27.67	4.48		3.45
	(46.91)		14	(50.38)		10	(59.16)		17	(50.71)		19	(49.41)		13	

Contd.

Table 8.4 *(Contd.)*

Indices of Psychological Well-being	Length of Unemployment (in Years)															
	0-1(N=15)			1-2(N=19)			2-3(N=15)			3-4(N=15)			4-above (N=15)			
	Mean	SD	Rank	Mean	SD	Rank	Mean	SD	Rank	Mean	SD	Rank	Mean	SD	Rank	F
27. Depersonalization	3.07 (38.38)	0.96	25	3.42 (42.75)	1.64	22	4.20 (52.50)	2.37	25	3.53 (44.13)	1.25	26	3.67 (45.88)	1.72	19.5	0.94
28. Fragmentation	3.60 (45.00)	1.35	19	3.74 (46.75)	1.73	17	5.93 (74.13)	1.83	03	4.93 (61.63)	1.79	03	3.67 (45.88)	1.45	19.5	6.02
29. Uncertainty	3.00 (75.00)	0.65	01	2.68 (67.00)	0.82	1.5	3.40 (85.00)	0.74	01	2.93 (73.25)	0.59	1.5	2.53 (63.25)	1.13	02	2.61
30. Distress	5.13 (42.75)	1.68	20	5.68 (47.33)	1.73	14.5	7.40 (61.67)	2.16	13	6.20 (51.67)	1.90	16	5.27 (43.92)	1.79	23	3.69
31. Indecisiveness	4.00 (50.00)	1.73	08	4.26 (53.25)	1.82	4.5	4.87 (60.88)	1.85	15.5	4.60 (57.50)	1.92	5.5	4.13 (51.63)	1.41	08	0.61
32. Social Conflict	2.13 (53.25)	0.83	3.5	2.68 (67.00)	0.82	1.5	3.26 (81.50)	0.96	02	2.27 (56.75)	1.16	08	2.87 (71.75)	0.99	01	3.47
33. Isolation	3.87 (48.38)	1.41	09	3.21 (40.13)	1.27	26	4.87 (60.88)	2.00	15.5	4.13 (51.63)	1.19	17	3.47 (43.38)	1.55	24	2.97
34. Withdrawal from Social and Personal Contact	1.87 (46.75)	0.74	15	2.00 (50.00)	1.05	11	2.27 (56.75)	1.16	21	1.40 (35.00)	0.51	31	1.73 (43.25)	1.10	25	1.73
35. Role Conflict	6.07 (50.58)	1.33	06	6.37 (53.08)	2.11	06	6.40 (53.33)	2.38	24	6.60 (55.00)	1.45	12	6.87 (57.25)	2.13	04	0.35
36. Hopelessness	3.67 (45.88)	1.72	18	3.32 (41.50)	1.67	23	4.47 (55.88)	1.81	22	4.47 (55.88)	1.41	11	3.87 (48.38)	1.46	15	1.61
37. Lonelinness	1.53 (38.25)	0.83	26	1.63 (40.75)	0.96	24.5	2.33 (58.25)	0.82	19.5	1.87 (46.75)	1.13	23.5	1.87 (46.75)	1.06	17	1.58
38. Desolation	2.13 (53.25)	0.92	3.5	1.89 (47.25)	0.94	16	2.80 (70.00)	0.86	04	2.93 (73.25)	0.96	1.5	2.27 (56.75)	1.03	05	3.60
39. **Identity-crisis**	40.09 (47.73)	9.38	12	40.89 (48.68)	10.47	12	52.20 (62.14)	10.39	12	45.87 (54.61)	7.68	14	42.22 (50.26)	9.13	11	4.14

Note: $df = 4,74$; $p < 0.05 = 2.49$; $p < 0.01 = 3.58$.

recorded in the case of the unemployed medical degree-holders. There, too, stabilization effect did appear, though not all-discernible, after continuing with their life events completely for three years. However, 0-1 year group of the unemployed engineers was also identified as carrying considerable amount of psychological risk. This was much similar to the assumption of the Sheffield group of investigators, as was also found in the case of 0-1 year group of the unemployed medical degree-holders. Albeit, all other groups of the unemployed engineers, particularly the group faced with the problem of unemployment for 2 to 3 years, were conspicuously hard-hit at their psychological level, but only to a moderate degree in most of the instances.

Duration of Unemployment and the Degree of Life Satisfaction : The Case of the Young Unemployed Degree-holders in Engineering Sciences

Table 8.5 embodies the findings of a statistical comparison among different groups of the young unemployed engineers for different distinct spells in terms of the measure of their life satisfaction.

Different groups of the engineers unemployed for various discrete durations, like those of the groups of unemployed medical degree-holders, were not found to differ significantly from one another at the scale of their life satisfaction ($F = 0.66$; $df = 4{,}74$; $p > 0.05$). Further, it was also revealed that while the group of engineers unemployed for a spell of 0-1 year was fairly more satisfied with their life (58.70%), other groups of engineers unemployed for longer durations tended to be relatively less satisfied with their life. However, contrary to the unemployed medical degree-holders, all the groups of engineers, imperilled with longer durations of unemployment, were not equally affected in this connection; the groups of unemployed engineers for 3-4 and 4-above year durations were apparently found to be inoculated with a raised level of life satisfaction, but not competing with 0-1 year group of the unemployed engineers in this regard, albeit enjoying a moderate degree of life satisfaction like the latter. Dissatisfaction with life markedly precipitated particularly in the group of engineers who were continuously unemployed for a longer period of 2-3 years (Index of Dissatisfaction = 55.30 per cent). The subsequent groups of the unemployed engineers like those of 3-4 and 4-above year groups were found to attain a fair amount of gains in the level of their life satisfaction (Life Satisfaction scores obtained by them were 54.70

Table 8.5 : Statistical Differences Among the Groups of Engineers Unemployed for Different Discrete Durations and their Relative Standing in Terms of the Degree of their Life Satisfaction

	Length of Unemployment (in Years)										
	0-1 (N = 15)		*1-2 (N = 19)*		*2-3 (N = 15)*		*3-4 (N = 15)*		*4-above (N = 15)*		
Variable	*Mean (%)*	*SD*	*Mean (%)*	*SD*	*Mean (%)*	*SD*	*Mean (%)*	*SD*	*Mean (%)*	*SD*	*F*
Life Satisfaction	5.87 (58.70)	2.66	5.21 (52.10)	1.78	4.47 (44.70)	1.88	5.47 (54.70)	1.96	5.13 (51.30)	2.57	0.66

Note. $df = 4,74$; $p<0.05 = 2.49$; $p<0.01 = 3.58$

and 51.30 per cent respectively). Thus, the results, here too,on the whole, did not appreciably agree with the predictions made by the Sheffield group of psychologists as to the impact of durations of unemployment on one's psychological well-being .

Duration of Unemployment and the Degree of Dependence on Different Coping Strategies : The Case of the Young Unemployed Degree-holders in Engineering Sciences

Table 8.6 presents an account of the findings yielded from a statistical comparison among different discrete groups of the unemployed engineers in terms of their degree of dependence on various strategies resorted to by them in order to meet the demands of their life situations.

Besides a significant difference among different groups of the unemployed engineers for various distinct durations, like those of the groups of unemployed medical degree-holders, in terms of the use of defensive avoidance mode in handling their situations ($F = 3.54$; $df = 4{,}74$; $p < 0.05$), there existed no marked differences among them with regard to the degree of their reliance on all other techniques used for adjustment. Further, it was revealed that none of the strategies, except intrapersistive approach mode (frequency of dependence of different groups laid between 60 per cent and 74.20 per cent), as it was found in the groups of the unemployed medical degree-holders, largely suited to all of them in making their compromise with the courses of life. Noticeably, other modes for adjustment did not appear meaningful for them, though their second preference commonly went to defensive avoidance mode in this connection, but only to a minimal level.

Duration of Unemployment and the Level of Anxiety, Stress, Feeling of Insecurity, Alienation and Identify-Crisis : The Case of the Young Unemployed Degree-holders in Agriculture Sciences

Table 8.7 records the summary of the findings of a statistical comparison among different groups of agriculture degree-holders out of job for various discrete durations in terms of the level of anxiety, stress, feeling of insecurity, alienation and identify-crisis in their various manifestations.

Noticeably, similar to those of the groups of jobless medical degree-holders, there were no significant differences amongst the

Table 8.6 : Statistical Differences Among the Groups of Engineers Unemployed for Different Discrete Durations and the Degree of their Relative Dependence in Terms of Different Coping Strategies

Copying Strategies	*Length of Unemployment (in Years)*										
	0-1 (N=15)		*1-2 (N=19)*		*2-3 (N=15)*		*3-4 (N=15)*		*4-above (N=15)*		
	Mean (%)	*SD*	*Mean (%)*	*SD*	*Mean (%)*	*SD*	*Mean (%)*	*SD*	*Mean (%)*	*SD*	*F*
Intrapersistive Approach Mode	11.07 (73.80)	3.03	9.00 (60.00)	2.43	9.00 (60.00)	3.61	9.73 (64.87)	2.69	11.13 (74.20)	2.61	2.14
Extrapersistive Approach Mode	1.47 (9.80)	0.77	1.89 (12.60)	0.98	1.87 (12.47)	1.04	1.80 (12.00)	1.03	1.47 (9.80)	0.80	0.24
Punitive Avoi-dance Mode	0.67 (4.79)	0.35	1.42 (9.47)	0.75	1.80 (12.00)	0.97	0.73 (4.87)	0.39	1.13 (7.53)	0.63	1.51
Defensive Avoi-dance Mode	1.80 (12.00)	1.05	2.68 (17.87)	1.45	2.33 (15.33)	1.50	2.73 (18.20)	1.33	1.27 (8.47)	0.83	3.54

Note : $df = 4,74$; $p < 0.05 = 2.49$; $p < 0.01 = 3.58$.

Table 8.7 : Statistical Differences Among the Groups of the Agriculture Degree-holders Unemployed for Different Discrete Durations and their Relative Standing in Terms of Different Indices of Psychological Well-being

Indices of Psychological Well-being	*Length of Unemployment (in Years)*									
	0-1(N=20)			*1-2(N=22)*			*2-above (N=22)*			
	Mean (%)	*SD*	*Rank*	*Mean (%)*	*SD*	*Rank*	*Mean (%)*	*SD*	*Rank*	*F*
1. General Worries	3.70 (61.67)	1.34	06	2.56 (42.67)	1.10	27	3.95 (65.83)	1.73	02	6.55
2. Somatic Manifestations	1.00 (33.33)	0.65	33	0.58 (19.33)	0.31	38	0.82 (27.33)	0.43	35	1.94
3. Psychological Symptoms	2.40 (48.00)	1.05	24	2.41 (48.20)	1.14	22	2.36 (47.20)	1.43	27	0.02
4. Social Relations	2.80 (35.00)	1.44	31	3.23 (40.38)	1.86	30	3.86 (48.25)	2.01	24.5	1.39
5. **Anxiety**	9.90 (45.00)	3.60	25	8.82 (40.09)	3.96	31	11.00 (50.00)	5.35	23	1.36
6. Suicidal Tendency	0.35 (8.75)	0.21	39	0.27 (6.75)	0.16	39	0.36 (9.00)	0.19	39	0.11
7. Emotional Instability	3.95 (49.38)	1.85	21	3.41 (42.63)	1.66	28	3.82 (47.75)	1.87	26	0.38
8. Paranoid Tendency	1.75 (12.50)	1.03	38	3.50 (29.17)	1.67	37	2.23 (18.58)	1.14	38	2.50
9. Depression	11.80 (32.78)	4.09	34	14.09 (39.14)	5.14	32	12.27 (34.08)	5.61	32	0.39
10. Physical Illness	2.65 (22.08)	1.43	37	3.64 (30.33)	1.80	35.5	3.41 (28.42)	1.59	34	0.60
11. Social Maladjustment	4.35 (36.25)	2.29	30	3.64 (30.33)	1.83	35.5	2.73 (22.75)	1.83	37	1.64
12. Apprehensiveness	3.65 (30.42)	1.72	35	3.91 (32.58)	2.13	34	3.27 (27.25)	1.56	36	0.20

Contd.

Table 8.7 *(Contd.)*

Indices of Psychological Well-being	Length of Unemployment (in Years)									
	0-1(N=20)			1-2(N=22)			2-above (N=22)			
	Mean (%)	SD	Rank	Mean (%)	SD	Rank	Mean (%)	SD	Rank	F
13. **Stress**	28.50 (29.69)	9.82	36	32.45 (33.80)	11.06	33	28.09 (29.26)	9.06	33	0.29
14. Lack of Self-confidence	10.25 (51.25)	4.89	16.5	10.68 (53.40)	4.78	14	11.09 (55.45)	4.67	11	0.73
15. Dejection	9.40 (62.67)	3.07	05	8.23 (54.87)	2.97	10	10.13 (67.53)	3.07	01	2.52
16. Pessimism	1.70 (34.00)	0.98	32	2.06 (41.20)	1.09	29	2.27 (45.40)	1.45	29	1.21
17. Emotional Responsiveness	16.05 (53.50)	5.23	13	15.58 (51.93)	4.91	18	18.05 (60.17)	5.46	07	3.31
18. Social Insecurity	10.25 (41.00)	4.43	28	13.25 (52.92)	4.29	15	13.60 (54.40)	4.22	14	2.98
19. Distrust	3.35 (67.00)	1.00	02	3.00 (60.00)	1.20	05	3.09 (61.80)	1.51	06	2.07
20. **Feeling of Insecurity**	51.04 (51.04)	13.35	18	52.77 (52.77)	15.37	16	58.23 (58.23)	14.57	10	1.04
21. Despair	17.65 (55.16)	3.63	11	17.91 (55.97)	6.35	09	18.91 (59.03)	3.61	09	0.42
22. Unstructured Universe	4.10 (51.25)	1.59	16.5	3.64 (45.50)	1.92	25.5	4.05 (50.63)	1.09	22	0.56
23. Psychological Vacuum	4.00 (50.00)	1.26	19.5	3.91 (48.88)	1.34	21	4.14 (51.75)	1.36	19.5	0.16
24. Disillusionment	1.70 (42.50)	0.66	26.5	2.05 (51.25)	1.05	19.5	1.68 (42.00)	0.78	30	1.27

Contd.

Table 8.7 *(Contd.)*

Indices of Psychological Well-being	Length of Unemployment (in Years)									
	0-1(N=20)			1-2(N=22)			2-above (N=22)			
	Mean (%)	SD	Rank	Mean (%)	SD	Rank	Mean (%)	SD	Rank	F
25. Narcissism	1.70 (42.50)	1.03	26.5	1.91 (47.75)	1.11	23	2.14 (53.50)	1.17	15	0.82
26. **Alienation**	29.15 (52.05)	5.68	15	29.41 (52.52)	7.60	17	30.91 (55.20)	4.95	12	0.39
27. Depersonalization	3.90 (48.75)	0.79	22.5	3.73 (46.63)	1.80	24	4.14 (51.75)	1.21	19.5	0.51
28. Fragmentation	4.65 (58.13)	0.88	08	5.36 (67.00)	2.01	01	4.73 (59.13)	1.86	08	1.17
29. Uncertainty	2.75 (68.75)	0.97	01	2.59 (64.75)	1.05	2.5	2.50 (62.50)	0.96	05	0.34
30. Distress	6.00 (50.00)	1.34	19.5	6.50 (54.17)	2.87	13	6.36 (53.00)	1.59	17.5	0.32
31. Indecisiveness	4.25 (53.13)	1.32	14	5.00 (62.50)	2.14	04	3.86 (48.25)	1.17	24.5	2.82
32. Social Conflict	2.60 (65.00)	0.94	04	2.59 (64.75)	1.18	2.5	2.59 (64.75)	0.85	3.5	0.01
33. Isolation	4.35 (54.38)	1.60	12	4.36 (54.50)	1.62	11.5	3.68 (46.00)	1.21	28	1.49
34. Withdrawal from Social and Personal Contact	12.40 (60.00)	0.68	07	1.82 (45.50)	0.73	25.5	1.45 (36.25)	0.67	31	9.78
35. Role Conflict	7.95 (66.25)	2.58	03	6.86 (57.17)	2.36	07	6.36 (53.00)	2.17	17.5	2.43
36. Hopelessness	3.25 (40.63)	0.91	29	4.77 (59.63)	1.82	06	4.41 (55.13)	1.79	13	5.22

Contd.

Table 8.7 *(Contd.)*

Indices of Psychological Well-being	Length of Unemployment (in Years)									
	0-1(N=20)			1-2(N=22)			2-above (N=22)			
	Mean (%)	SD	Rank	Mean (%)	SD	Rank	Mean (%)	SD	Rank	F
37. Loneliness	1.95 (48.75)	0.76	22.5	2.18 (54.50)	1.01	11.5	2.05 (51.25)	0.95	21	0.34
38. Desolation	2.30 (57.50)	0.80	09	2.05 (51.25)	0.84	19.5	2.59 (64.75)	1.14	3.5	1.83
39. **Identity-crisis**	46.35 (55.18)	6.85	10	47.82 (56.93)	10.84	08	44.73 (53.25)	5.91	16	0.53

Note : $df = 2,61$; $p < 0.05 = 3.15$; $p < 0.01 = 4.98$.

groups of agriculture degree-holders unemployed for various distinct durations in terms of all the indices, except general worries ($F = 6.55$; $df = 2,61$; $p < 0.01$), emotional responsiveness ($p < 0.05$), withdrawal from social and personal contact ($F = 9.78$; $df = 2,61$; $p < 0.01$), and hopelessness ($p < 0.01$), of psychological well-being. Thus, here too, it was clearly apparent that different durations of joblessness did not exert differential influences on the psychological health of those who had been categorically experiencing any one of them. Further, all the groups of unemployed agriculture degree-holders, too, were found to be prone to psychological ill-health to some extent or the other, particularly to a moderate degree. Also, they tended to be least affected by the feeling of suicide (scores obtained by different groups of participants ranged between 6.75 per cent and 9.00 per cent). But, unlike their counterparts of the unemployed medical and engineering degree-holders, they were not acutely oppressed with any particular symptomatic reaction; while the 0-1 year group of the unemployed agriculture degree-holders was found to be more vulnerable to the feeling of uncertainty (68.75%), the 1-2 year group and the 2-above year group of the unemployed agriculture degree-holders were to fragmentation (67.00%) and dejection (67.53%) respectively. Finally, the phenomenon of stabilization effect was not seen to operate by any means in the case of the long-term unemployed agriculture degree-holders, too. Notably, the groups of unemployed agriculture degree-holders for longer durations (especially more than two years), instead of showing decline in their psychological symptoms, except the overall level of anxiety and its dimensions like general worries and somatic manifestations markedly present in the case of 1-2 year group of the unemployed agriculture degree-holders, tended to be more prone to psychological deterioration. In other words, possibility of losing one's psychological balance increased with the increment in the duration of one's unemployment. There was not even a bleak sign of halt in one's psychological deterioration in the mid-way. However, here too, the 0-1 year group of the unemployed agriculture degree-holders was found to be beset with psychological damage to a substantial degree, and thus the findings, to a fair extent, sustained the predictability of the assumptions proposed by the Sheffield group of psychologists.

Duration of Unemployment and the Degree of Life Satisfaction: The Case of the Young Unemployed Degree-holders in Agricultural Sciences

Table 8.8 comprises the findings of statistical comparison made among the groups of the young agriculture degree-holders quite dissimilar in the experience of the duration of their joblessness in terms of the degree of life satisfaction in them.

Table 8.8 : Statistical Differences Among the Groups of the Agriculture Degree-holders Unemployed for Different Discrete Durations and their Relative Standing in Terms of the Degree of their Life Satisfaction

	Length of Unemployement (in Years)						
	0-1 (N=20)		*1-2 (N=22)*		*2-above (N=22)*		
Variable	*Mean* (%)	*SD*	*Mean* (%)	*SD*	*Mean* (%)	*SD*	*F*
Life Satisfaction	5.20 (52.00)	2.69	4.27 (42.70)	2.58	4.09 (40.90)	1.77	1.30

Note : $df = 2,61$; $p < 0.05 = 3.15$; $p < 0.01 = 4.98$.

The trend, as it appeared with the medical and engineering degree-holders unemployed for different distinct time periods in terms of their state at the count of their life satisfaction, clearly followed in the case of the various groups of the unemployed degree-holders in agriculture sciences, too. Interestingly, the latter were also not found to differ significantly from one another in terms of the degree of their life satisfaction (F=1.30; df=2,61; p>0.05). Further, like the groups of the unemployed with degrees in other disciplines of technical education, the agriculture degree-holders, unemployed for a period of 0-1 year, expressed a greater satisfaction with their life (52%), while the other two groups of the unemployed agriculture degree-holders showed a gradual decline, though not quite perceptible, in the amount of their life satisfaction (the life satisfaction scores of the two groups were 42.70 per cent and 40.90 per cent respectively), and thus were more disappointed with the order of their life. But, while the degree of life satisfaction in the unemployed degree-holders in three independent disciplines of technical education exclusively having experience of the same duration of their plight was taken into account, the groups of the agriculture degree-holders, unemployed for different distinct durations, obviously tended to have relatively low satisfaction with their life altogether. However, the results, on the whole, here too, fairly disapprove of the authenticity of the prediction made by the Sheffield group of investigators as to the impacts of the duration of unemployment on psychological health. Nonetheless, unlike the groups of medical and engineering degree-holder unemployed young men for different distinct durations, there appeared, in the case of unemployed agriculture degree-holders, no exact time-point from where the stabilization effect started to take place in their life. It may be noted here that the absence of a sufficient number of unemployed among agriculture degree-holders, not more than three groups of them could be identified for study on the basis of the experience of the duration of their joblessness. This might be one of the prime reasons for absence of adequate marking of an exact time-point from where the stabilization effect begins to appear.

Duration of Unemployment and the Degree of Dependence on Different Coping Strategies : The Case of the Young Unemployed Degree-holders in Agricultural Sciences

Table 8.9 contains the summary of a statistical comparison made among different groups of the agriculture degree-holders out of job

Table 8.9 : Statistical Differences Among the Groups of the Agriculture Degree-holders Unemployed for Different Discrete Durations and the Degree of their Relative Dependence in Terms of Different Coping Strategies

Coping Strategies	*Length of Unemployment (in Years)*						
	0-1 (N=20)		*1-2 (N=22)*		*2-above (N=22)*		
	Mean (%)	*SD*	*Mean (%)*	*SD*	*Mean (%)*	*SD*	*F*
Intrapersistive Approach Mode	9.80 (65.33)	3.69	8.82 (58.80)	3.03	10.23 (68.20)	2.51	1.20
Extrapersistive Approach Mode	3.35 (22.33)	1.49	2.91 (19.40)	1.58	1.68 (11.20)	0.89	1.45
Punitive Avoi-dance Mode	0.10 (0.67)	0.05	0.27 (1.80)	0.17	0.59 (3.93)	0.29	2.26
Defensive Avoidance Mode	1.75 (11.67)	0.84	3.00 (20.00)	1.65	2.50 (16.67)	1.22	2.09

Note : df = 2,61; p <0.05=3.15; p<0.01=4.98.

for different time periods in terms of the degree of their dependence on various strategies in order to stand with the reality of their life.

The groups of the agriculture degree-holders jobless for different discrete durations, in contrast to the groups of the medical and engineering degree-holders unemployed with similar history of continuance with their plight, showed no marked difference among themselves in terms of the degree of their reliance on any of the strategies adopted to deal with their life events. However, all the groups of unemployed agriculture degree-holders, too, tended chiefly to fall back on intrapersistive approach mode in grappling with their situations (scores obtained by them ranged between 58.80 per cent and 68.20 per cent). Further, other modes, particularly the punitive avoidance mode, as envisaged in the case of different subgroups of unemployed medical and engineering degree-holders, could not attract them in any significant way in their effort to cope with their situation.

Duration of Unemployment and Level of Anxiety, Stress, Feeling of Insecurity, Alienation and Identity-Crisis : The Case of the Non-technically Educated Unemployed Young Men

In an attempt to investigate the impact of durations of unemployment on psychological well-being, different groups of the non-technically educated young men out of job for various distinct durations were also compared among themselves in terms of the level of the health indices like anxiety, stress, feeling of insecurity, alienation, identity-crisis, and their dimensions in them. Table 8.10 contains a brief account of the findings.

The groups of the non-technically educated unemployed young men for different durations, like those of the groups of unemployed engineers with similar experience, witnessed a significant difference amongst themselves in terms of a good number, say about 41 per cent, of the abovementioned health indices. However, except in a few such as suicidal tendency, paranoid tendency, physical illness, disillusionment, alienation, fragmentation, and desolation, they tended to evince marked differences among themselves in terms of those indicators of psychological health on which the groups of unemployed engineers were not found to differ among themselves to any substantial degree. Nonetheless, in all, like the groups of unemployed engineers, as also the ones of unemployed medical and agriculture degree-holders for different durations, the groups of non-technically educated

Table 8.10 : Statistical Differences Among the Groups of the Non-technically Educated Young Men Unemployed for Different Discrete Durations and their Relative Standing in Terms of Different Indices of Psychological Well-being

Indices of Psychological Well-being	*Length of Unemployment (in Years)* 0-1(N=47)			1-2(N=52)			2-3(N=74)			3-4 (N=55)			4-5(N=48)			5-6(N=44)			6-7(N=45)			7-above(N=43)			
	Mean (%)	*SD*	*Rank*	*Mean (%)*	*SD*	*Rank*	*Mean (%)*	*SD*	*Rank*	*Mean (%)*	*SD*	*Rank*	*Mean (%)*	*SD*	*Rank*	*Mean (%)*	*SD*	*Rank*	*Mean (%)*	*SD*	*Rank*	*Mean (%)*	*SD*	*Rank*	*F*
1. General Worries	2.74 (45.67)	1.24	23	3.06 (51.00)	1.63	17	3.27 (54.50)	1.64	08	3.38 (56.33)	1.66	05	3.75 (62.50)	1.78	04	3.64 (60.67)	1.57	04	4.07 (67.83)	1.39	02	3.51 (58.50)	1.61	08	3.19
2. Somatic Manifestations	0.60 (20.00)	0.30	37	0.81 (27.00)	0.36	34	0.72 (24.00)	0.37	37	0.76 (25.33)	0.39	35	0.85 (28.33)	0.43	36	0.80 (26.67)	0.39	36	1.40 (46.67)	0.59	31	0.74 (24.67)	0.39	38	3.46
3. Psychological Symptoms	1.91 (38.20)	1.22	29	2.50 (50.00)	1.35	21.5	2.65 (53.00)	1.37	12.5	2.24 (44.80)	1.37	24	2.58 (51.60)	1.44	24	2.59 (51.80)	1.04	17	3.20 (64.00)	0.76	05	2.33 (46.60)	1.52	28	3.80
4. Social Relations	2.40 (30.00)	1.34	31	2.85 (35.63)	1.57	30	3.19 (39.88)	2.21	30	3.11 (38.88)	2.06	31	3.00 (37.50)	1.94	31	3.34 (41.75)	1.66	30	3.93 (49.13)	1.53	29	2.88 (36.00)	1.64	31	2.35
5. **Anxiety**	7.66 (34.82)	4.21	30	9.27 (42.14)	4.42	29	9.88 (44.91)	4.67	26	9.49 (43.14)	4.81	26	10.19 (46.32)	4.82	28	10.36 (47.09)	3.41	26	12.61 (57.32)	3.41	19	9.44 (42.91)	4.62	30	4.08
6. Suicidal Tendency	0.19 (4.75)	0.09	39	0.23 (5.75)	0.14	39	0.41 (10.25)	0.24	39	0.33 (8.25)	0.19	39	0.54 (13.50)	0.27	39	0.11 (2.75)	0.06	39	0.58 (14.50)	0.28	39	0.70 (17.50)	0.37	39	2.50
7. Emotional Instability	3.38 (42.25)	1.98	26	2.56 (32.00)	1.63	31	3.09 (38.63)	1.19	31	3.20 (40.00)	1.16	29.5	3.02 (37.75)	1.28	30	2.93 (36.63)	1.44	31	3.53 (44.13)	1.26	32	3.88 (48.50)	1.24	26	1.72
8. Paranoid Tendency	2.11 (17.58)	1.17	38	1.77 (14.75)	0.89	38	2.20 (18.33)	1.18	38	2.04 (17.00)	1.38	38	3.02 (25.17)	1.91	38	2.52 (21.00)	1.34	37	2.80 (23.33)	1.00	38	3.09 (25.75)	1.66	37	2.14
9. Depression	10.21 (28.36)	5.55	32	11.12 (30.89)	6.17	32	11.15 (30.92)	5.62	32	10.45 (29.03)	4.90	33	11.56 (32.11)	6.38	33	11.11 (30.86)	6.05	32	10.38 (28.83)	5.23	37	12.23 (33.97)	6.29	32	0.46
10. Physical Illness	2.74 (22.83)	1.18	35	3.00 (25.00)	1.47	37	3.35 (27.92)	1.45	33	3.80 (31.67)	1.52	32	3.58 (29.83)	1.92	35	3.34 (27.83)	1.92	33	4.40 (36.67)	2.14	34	4.07 (33.92)	2.12	33	2.42
11. Social Maladjustment	2.51 (20.92)	1.28	36	3.54 (29.50)	1.95	33	3.18 (26.50)	1.80	35	2.95 (24.58)	1.49	36	4.19 (34.92)	2.52	32	2.39 (19.92)	1.79	38	4.58 (38.17)	2.67	33	3.35 (27.92)	1.63	36	3.51
12. Apprehensiveness	2.94 (24.50)*	1.49	34	3.12 (26.00)	1.99	36	2.91 (24.25)	1.42	36	2.71 (22.58)	1.43	37	3.10 (25.83)	1.85	37	3.27 (27.25)	1.54	34	4.16 (34.67)	2.30	35	3.56 (29.67)	1.63	35	1.41
13. **Stress**	24.09 (25.09)	13.62	33	25.42 (26.48)	13.97	35	26.32 (27.42)	14.49	34	25.49 (26.55)	13.08	34	29.02 (30.23)	16.25	34	25.68 (26.75)	12.34	35	30.42 (31.69)	13.89	36	30.89 (32.18)	15.87	34	1.09

Contd.

Table 8.10 (*Contd.*)

Indices of Psychological Well-being	Length of Unemployment (in Years)																								F
	0-1(N=47)			1-2(N=52)			2-3(N=74)			3-4 (N=55)			4-5(N=48)			5-6(N=44)			6-7(N=45)			7-above(N=43)			
	Mean (%)	SD	Rank	Mean (%)	SD	Rank	Mean (%)	SD	Rank	Mean (%)	SD	Rank	Mean (%)	SD	Rank	Mean (%)	SD	Rank	Mean (%)	SD	Rank	Mean (%)	SD	Rank	
14. Lack of Self-confidence	11.11 (55.55)	5.27	06	10.99 (54.95)	5.21	07	11.29 (56.45)	4.43	06	11.59 (57.95)	5.42	04	11.39 (56.95)	4.24	07	12.09 (60.45)	5.27	05	12.60 (63.00)	4.98	06	12.50 (62.50)	4.73	04	1.47
15. Dejection	9.10 (60.67)	4.05	03	9.08 (60.53)	3.94	04	9.66 (64.40)	3.82	03	9.45 (63.00)	4.12	02	9.91 (66.07)	3.78	02	9.48 (63.20)	4.02	03	9.71 (64.73)	3.69	04	9.68 (64.53)	3.84	02	1.36
16. Pessimism	2.13 (42.60)	1.44	25	2.31 (46.20)	1.41	26	2.19 (43.80)	1.41	28	2.05 (41.00)	1.35	27	2.56 (51.20)	1.51	26	2.25 (45.00)	1.53	29	2.51 (50.20)	1.20	28	2.67 (53.40)	1.36	19	1.23
17. Emotional Responsiveness	14.50 (48.33)	7.68	17	16.13 (53.77)	7.21	09	15.66 (52.20)	5.17	18	14.81 (49.37)	6.84	20	16.41 (54.70)	5.69	14.5	15.72 (52.40)	6.56	15	17.98 (59.93)	6.03	11	17.07 (56.90)	6.11	13	1.76
18. Social Insecurity	11.94 (47.76)	5.82	19	12.87 (50.80)	6.37	19	12.59 (50.36)	4.07	21	12.09 (48.36)	5.89	22	13.44 (53.76)	4.72	18	12.61 (50.44)	5.15	22	13.95 (55.80)	5.19	23	13.77 (55.08)	4.86	15	1.39
19. Distrust	2.28 (45.76)	1.36	22	3.08 (61.60)	1.40	03	2.86 (57.20)	1.34	05	2.80 (56.00)	1.38	06	2.67 (53.40)	1.34	19	2.75 (55.00)	1.42	08	3.02 (60.40)	1.44	09	2.98 (59.60)	1.34	06	1.64
20. **Feeling of Insecurity**	51.09 (51.09)	16.49	11	54.42 (54.42)	15.29	08	54.23 (54.23)	14.51	09	52.82 (52.82)	14.11	11	56.40 (56.40)	14.75	09	54.91 (54.91)	11.01	09	59.65 (59.65)	12.08	13	58.67 (58.67)	14.91	07	1.25
21. Despair	17.06 (53.31)	3.79	07	17.17 (53.66)	4.62	10	17.65 (55.16)	4.04	07	17.18 (53.69)	4.38	10	18.00 (56.25)	4..97	10.5	16.23 (50.72)	3.24	21	17.22 (53.81)	4.21	26	18.33 (57.28)	4.52	11	1.03
22. Unstructured Universe	4.55 (56.88)	1.50	05	4.50 (56.25)	1.36	05	4.31 (53.88)	1.17	10	4.36 (54.50)	1.25	08	4.52 (56.50)	1.34	08	4.30 (53.75)	1.09	12.5	4.78 (59.75)	1.35	12	4.60 (57.50)	1.37	10	0.79
23. Psychological Vacuum	4.00 (50.00)	1.57	13	4.15 (51.88)	1.33	15	4.19 (52.38)	1.39	17	4.09 (51.13)	1.31	15	4.21 (52.63)	1.22	21	4.52 (56.50)	1.32	06	5.02 (62.75)	1.42	07	4.65 (58.13)	1.41	09	3.00
24. Disillusionment	1.94 (48.50)	0.87	16	1.83 (45.75)	0.88	27	1.68 (42.00)	0.85	29	1.60 (40.00)	0.68	29.5	1.79 (44.75)	0.92	29	1.98 (49.50)	0.79	23.5	2.27 (56.75)	0.96	20	2.16 (54.00)	1.04	17.5	3.49
25. Narcissism	1.60 (40.00)	0.83	28	1.79 (44.75)	0.91	28	1.92 (48.00)	1.03	24	1.62 (40.50)	0.83	28	2.10 (52.50)	0.99	22	1.82 (45.50)	1.06	28	1.87 (46.75)	0.69	30	2.16 (54.00)	1.33	17.5	2.10
26. **Alienation**	29.13 (52.02)	5.47	09	29.51 (52.70)	6.61	13	29.73 (53.09)	5.49	11	28.82 (51.46)	6.00	13	30.63 (54.70)	6.94	14.5	28.84 (51.50)	4.24	18	31.19 (55.70)	4.80	24	31.94 (57.04)	6.64	12	2.05
27. Depersonalization	3.72 (46.50)	1.61	21	3.79 (47.38)	1.66	24	3.66 (45.75)	1.44	25	3.47 (43.38)	1.61	25	4.17 (52.13)	1.96	23	4.16 (52.00)	1.57	16	4.64 (58.00)	1.25	18	4.07 (50.88)	1.39	23	2.82

Contd.

Table 8.10 (*Contd.*)

Indices of Psychological Well-being	Length of Unemployment (in Years)																								
	0-1(N=47)			1-2(N=52)			2-3(N=74)			3-4 (N=55)			4-5(N=48)			5-6(N=44)			6-7(N=45)			7-above(N=43)			F
	Mean (%)	SD	Rank	Mean (%)	SD	Rank	Mean (%)	SD	Rank	Mean (%)	SD	Rank	Mean (%)	SD	Rank	Mean (%)	SD	Rank	Mean (%)	SD	Rank	Mean (%)	SD	Rank	
28. Fragmentation	3.85 (48.13)	1.73	18	4.00 (50.00)	1.97	21.5	4.05 (50.63)	1.83	20	4.00 (50.00)	1.82	17	4.50 (56.25)	1.87	10.5	3.75 (46.88)	1.60	27	5.20 (65.00)	1.55	03	4.49 (56.13)	1.80	14	8.61
29. Uncertainty	2.55 (63.75)	1.02	02	2.83 (70.75)	0.98	01	2.62 (65.50)	1.03	02	2.38 (59.50)	0.93	03	2.58 (64.50)	1.05	03	2.59 (64.75)	0.87	02	2.33 (58.25)	0.93	16	2.42 (60.50)	0.96	05	1.33
30. Distress	6.15 (51.25)	2.38	10	6.10 (50.83)	1.91	18	6.36 (53.00)	2.35	12.5	5.91 (49.25)	2.21	21	6.71 (55.92)	2.63	12	6.48 (54.00)	1.78	10.5	6.78 (56.50)	1.40	21	5.88 (49.00)	1.69	24	1.25
31. Indecisiveness	3.96 (49.50)	1.56	14.5	4.21 (52.63)	1.61	14	4.00 (50.00)	1.53	22	4.15 (51.88)	1.51	12	4.31 (53.88)	1.79	17	4.32 (54.00)	1.43	10.5	4.47 (55.88)	1.42	22	3.81 (47.63)	1.56	27	0.91
32. Social Conflict	2.64 (66.00)	0.87	01	2.77 (69.25)	1.02	02	2.65 (66.25)	1.01	01	2.75 (68.75)	0.95	01	2.81 (70.25)	0.89	01	2.61 (65.25)	1.02	01	2.73 (68.25)	0.89	01	2.72 (68.00)	0.96	01	0.27
33. Isolation	3.55 (44.38)	1.46	24	4.13 (51.63)	1.77	16	3.96 (49.50)	1.65	23	3.96 (49.50)	1.56	18.5	4.00 (50.00)	1.71	27	3.82 (47.75)	1.33	25	4.40 (55.00)	1.81	25	3.91 (48.88)	1.62	25	0.99
34. Withdrawal from Social and Personal Contact	1.68 (42.00)	0.89	27	2.02 (50.50)	0.85	20	1.77 (44.25)	0.99	27	1.96 (49.50)	0.95	18.5	2.13 (53.25)	1.02	20	2.05 (51.25)	1.01	19.5	2.09 (52.25)	0.92	27	1.84 (46.00)	1.00	29	1.45
35. Role Conflict	6.28 (52.33)	2.01	08	6.60 (55.00)	2.19	06	6.34 (52.83)	2.08	14	6.45 (53.75)	1.81	09	6.88 (57.33)	2.27	06	6.66 (55.50)	1.98	07	6.98 (58.17)	1.57	17	6.33 (52.75)	2.30	21	0.87
36. Hopelessness	3.96 (49.50)	1.63	14.5	4.23 (52.88)	1.81	12	4.20 (52.50)	1.72	16	4.02 (50.25)	1.73	16	4.35 (54.38)	1.69	16	4.30 (53.75)	1.71	12.5	4.73 (59.13)	1.48	14	4.40 (55.00)	1.87	16	0.94
37. Loneliness	1.87 (46.75)	0.95	20	1.98 (49.50)	0.92	23	2.03 (50.75)	1.03	19	1.87 (46.75)	0.90	23	2.06 (51.50)	0.91	25	1.98 (49.50)	1.09	23.5	2.40 (60.00)	0.96	10	2.05 (51.25)	1.05	22	1.50
38. Desolation	2.32 (58.00)	1.09	04	1.85 (46.25)	1.31	25	2.46 (61.50)	1.08	04	2.20 (55.00)	0.95	07	2.38 (59.50)	1.08	05	2.05 (51.25)	0.96	19.5	2.47 (61.75)	0.92	08	2.53 (63.25)	0.93	03	3.29
39. **Identity-Crisis**	52.57 (50.68)	13.31	12	44.52 (53.00)	13.03	11	44.14 (52.55)	11.23	15	43.19 (51.42)	11.31	14	46.88 (55.81)	12.98	13	44.75 (53.27)	8.70	14	49.22 (58.60)	8.50	15	44.37 (52.82)	10.90	20	1.46

Note : $df = 7{,}400$; $p < 0.05 = 2.03$; $p < 0.01 = 2.69$.

unemployed of a similar fate were found to carry with them symptoms of psychological debility to a moderate degree. But, this trend was not perceptible while an attempt was made to identify the most as well as the least affected syndromes of psychological health among the groups of non-technically educated unemployed; it just followed partly. Interestingly, as it more especially appeared with different groups of unemployed medicos, though, more or less, also appeared with the unemployed engineers and agriculture degree-holders, all the groups of non-technically educated unemployed were least oppressed with the tendency to commit suicide (the scores varied from 2.75 per cent to 17.50 per cent) and relatively more with the feeling of social conflict (the scores obtained by different groups ranged between 65.25 per cent and 70.25 per cent), save and except the group jobless for a span of 1-2 year who were deeply shattered by the feeling of uncertainty (70.75 per cent). Added to them, it was further revealed that stabilization effect, as acclaimed by the Sheffield group of investigators, did not appear in its entirety in the case of non-technically educated unemployed young men, too.

Obviously, the non-technically educated young men, jobless for longer periods of 1-2 and 2-3 years, instead of adapting themselves, showed greater risk of psychological impairment. And, there appeared an evidence of halt in the psychological deterioration of the group that had been unemployed for a longer spell of 3 to 4 years. But, the process of recovering could not be seen to operate in other groups of participants out of jobs for a period of more than 4 years, besides the group unemployed for a longer duration of more than five years who showed a slight reduction in the level of their susceptibility to different psychological reactions, except anxiety and its dimensions like psychological symptoms and social relations. Although, there emerged a pattern of ups and downs in the escalation of different syndromes, and particularly so found in the group who had been unemployed well over a prolonged period of more than seven years. Thus, in short, the assertion by Warr and his associates could not be found to record its applicability in describing the psychological health of the non-technically educated yound men in India too who had been unemployed for a prolonged period. However, like their contention, it was clearly noticed that the non-technically educated unemployed for a spell of 0-1 year, too, were found to be prone to psychological ill-health to a moderate extent. However, the groups unemployed for a longer duration, particularly for more than six years, were greatly exposed to psychological damage. The values obtained for all the health indices in the groups of non-technically educated unemployed for 6-7 and more than 7 years were found to be clearly enlarged to quite an alarming scale.

Duration of Unemployment and the Degree of Life Satisfaction : The Case of the Non-technically Educated Unemployed Young Men

Table 8.11 presents the summary of a statistical comparison among different groups of the non-technically educated unemployed for different distinct durations in terms of the degree of their satisfaction with life.

Unlike the findings recorded in the case of unemployed medical, engineering and agriculture degree-holders for various durations, the groups of the non-technically educated young men facing different bouts of joblessness overall showed significant differences among themselves in terms of the degree of their life satisfaction ($F = 4.79$; $df = 7,400$; $p < 0.01$). Although the multiple-comparisons of different pairs of means by employing Newman-Keuls Studentized Range Test did not evince so. None of the groups was found to differ markedly from another in the degree of their life satisfaction. Yet, there were a few exceptions, and so were the significant differences between the group out of work for a shorter duration of 0-1 year and the group of jobless for a prolonged period of 7-above year (OQ=1.97; CQ = 1.50), the unemployed for a shorter spell of 0-1 year and the unemployed for a longer span of 6-7 year (CQ=1.50), the unemployed for a duration of 1-2 year and the unemployed for more than 7 years (CQ=1.46), the jobless for a period of 1-2 year and the unemployed for a longer duration of 6-7 year (CQ=1.46), and the unemployed for a longer spell of 4-5 year and the unemployed over a prolonged period of more than 7 years (OQ=1.52; CQ=1.43). The results, however, further revealed that different groups of the non-technically educated unemployed for various prolonged periods, besides the group unemployed for a longer duration of 5-6 year, who expressed just slight gains in their life satisfaction, clearly exhibited a gradual decline in the level of their life satisfaction as it appeared particularly in the case of unemployed medical and agriculture degree-holders afflicted with different prolonged periods of their plight. Thus, here too, the stabilization effect as such could not be seen to occur; instead the

Table 8.11 : Statistical Differences Among the Groups of Non-technically Educated Young Men Unemployed for Different Discrete Durations and their Relative Standing in Terms of the Degree of their Life Satisfaction

	Length of Unemployment (in Years)																
	0-1 (N=47)		*1-2 (N=52)*		*2-3 (N=74)*		*3-4 (N=55)*		*4-5 (N=48)*		*5-6 (N=44)*		*6-7 (N=45)*		*7-above (N=43)*		
Variable	*Mean (%)*	*SD*	*Mean (%)*	*SD*	*Mean (%)*	*SD*	*Mean (%)*	*SD*	*Mean (%)*	*SD*	*Mean (%)*	*SD*	*Mean (%)*	*SD*	*Mean (%)*	*SD*	*F*
Life Satisfaction	5.81 (58.10)	2.12	5.37 (53.70)	2.18	4.55 (45.50)	2.25	4.56 (45.60)	2.45	4.29 (42.90)	2.37	4.64 (46.40)	1.70	3.87 (38.70)	1.79	3.84 (38.40)	1.91	4.79

Note : $df = 7{,}400$; $p<0.05=2.03$; $p<0.01=2.69$.

groups unemployed for relatively longer durations tended to be more dissatisfied with the course of their life. Further, it was also not clearly warranted that the unemployed in their initial phase tended to manifest a sharp decline in their psychological health. Interestingly, the group of the unemployed for a short run of 0-1 year, as it was revealed, enjoyed considerable life satisfaction.

Duration of Unemployment and the Degree of Dependence on Different Coping Strategies : The Case of the Non-technically Educated Unemployed Young Men

Table 8.12 records the findings of a statistical comparison among different groups of the non-technically educated unemployed for various distinct durations in terms of the degree of their reliance on different strategies in order to fight their life events.

There were no significant differences among different groups of the non-technically educated unemployed young men in terms of the use of any of the strategies in order to deal with their situations ($p > 0.05$). However, all of them, like the groups of the unemployed of different disciplines of technical education, tended to depend largely on intrapersistive approach mode in making their adjustment with the life circumstances (scores obtained by them varied between 60.87per cent and 68.33 per cent). Other modes for adjustment did not allure them by any significant way; albeit their second preference,too, commonly hinged upon defensive avoidance mode in their attempt to adapt to the situations.

Duration of Employment and Level of Anxiety, Stress, Feeling of Insecurity, Alienation and Indentity-crisis : The Case of the Technically Educated Employed Young Men

With the advent of Jahoda's (1979, 1981, 1982) highly acclaimed Functional Approach, employment, whether satisfying or dissatisfying, came to be recognized to influence our psychological well-being positively. But, the approach could not sustain its prominence for a long run; it has been challenged on various grounds. There are ample research evidences (Büssing, 1987, 1990; Clegg and Wall, 1990; Feather, 1990; Fryer and Winefield, 1998; Iversen and Sabroe,1988; Iversen, Sabroe and Damsgaard, 1989; Kumari, 2001; O'Brien, 1986; Payne, 1995; Rani, 1993; Ronayne, Ryan and Cullen 1989; Singh,

Table 8.12 : Statistical Differences Among the Groups of the Non-technically Educated Young Men Unemployed for Different Discrete Durations and the Degree of their Relative Dependence in Terms of Different Coping Strategies

Coping Strategies	Length of Unemployment (in Years)																F
	0-1 (N=47)		*1-2 (N=52)*		*2-3 (N=74)*		*3-4 (N=55)*		*4-5 (N=48)*		*5-6 (N=44)*		*6-7 (N=45)*		*7-above (N=43)*		
	Mean (%)	*SD*	*Mean (%)*	*SD*	*Mean (%)*	*SD*	*Mean (%)*	*SD*	*Mean (%)*	*SD*	*Mean (%)*	*SD*	*Mean (%)*	*SD*	*Mean (%)*	*SD*	
Intrapersistive Approach Mode	9.74 (64.93)	2.86	10.25 (68.33)	2.70	9.51 (63.40)	2.98	9.13 (60.87)	2.76	9.58 (63.87)	2.51	9.45 (63.00)	2.35	10.22 (68.13)	2.44	9.79 (65.27)	2.42	0.89
Extrapersistive Approach Mode	2.09 (13.93)	1.08	1.56 (10.40)	0.95	2.26 (15.07)	1.22	2.42 (16.13)	1.26	1.90 (12.67)	0.97	1.84 (12.27)	0.98	1.64 (10.93)	0.90	1.84 (12.27)	1.00	1.32
Punitive Avoidance Mode	1.02 (6.80)	0.56	0.87 (5.80)	0.48	0.80 (5.33)	0.43	0.95 (6.33)	0.47	0.90 (6.00)	0.44	0.98 (6.53)	0.47	1.00 (6.67)	0.51	0.79 (5.27)	0.39	0.27
Defensive Avoidance Mode	2.15 (14.33)	1.18	2.33 (15.53)	1.42	2.43 (16.20)	1.54	2.51 (16.73)	1.30	2.63 (17.53)	1.74	2.73 (18.20)	1.43	2.13 (14.20)	1.16	2.58 (17.20)	1.36	0.75

Note : $df = 7{,}400$; $p < 0.05 = 2.03$; $p < 0.01 = 2.69$.

Kumari and Singh, 1992; Singh, Singh and Rani, 1996a; Warr, 1987 c,d; Winefield, 1995a; Winefield, Tiggemann and Goldney, 1988; Winefield *et al.*, 1993) to record that not all kinds of employment are fairly conducive to the maintenance of benign psychological health. It should be noted that mundane, routine and tiresome jobs, particularly conjoined with low income, insecurity and poor working conditions providing little scope for utilizing one's skills in order to experience variety or to exert influence and control over day-to-day businesses at the work place, lead to a sharp decline in one's psychological equipoise. The findings are quite elaborate and well-nigh comprehensive. These may certainly be useful in describing the psychological well-being of an employee, particularly working in a public sector organization in eastern India where one, as it has been revealed (Ahmad and Khanna, 1992; Bajaj, 1982; Barnes, 1992; Brown, 1984; Kanungo, 1995; Kumari, 2001; Pestonjee and Singh, 1982; Singh and Singh, 1985; Singh, 1994, 2001; Singh, Kumari and Singh, 1992; Singh, Singh and Rani, 1996 a,b; Singh, Singh and Singh, 1995; P. Singh and Pant, 1982), has to live through a variety of problems both at physical and psychological levels, characterized, by and large, by poor physical working condition, inadequate and irregular payment system, restrictive and personalized senior-subordinate relationship, lower autonomy, multiplicity of masters, undue political interference even in the routine affairs of management, feeling of insecurity, etc. But, how the duration of such an employment turns in affecting one's psychological well-being, most likely, has not yet attracted a desired attention of the investigators. Although there are, of late, quite a few interesting empirical evidences which may focus the issue to a certain degree. The findings obtained by Büssing (1987,1990), for example, leads to a conclusion that prolonged precariousness of employment may attribute to the development of health risks, especially depressive disorders. Similar is the conclusion traced by Singh (1992) in his article, "Pseudo Employment : A Novel Form of Exploitation of Human Resources in Bihar"—a typical example of employment not seen in any part of the world, as also in other states of India. He holds that continuing with such kind of employment which is not offering any pecuniary gain other than a psychological satisfaction to some degree and especially so in the first few years just after the entrance in the job, may, in the long run, expose an individual to particularly high risk. Likewise, in another study by Singh *et al.* (2005), it has been found, with some departure through, that the groups of both technically and non-technically educated employed for the duration of 0-1 year and 7 and above years, in particular, are worst affected psychologically, especially marked by the acute feelings of either uncertainty or social conflict — there are, however, certain exceptions too. The adverse effect, they hold, deepens with the increase in the durations of sadly perfunctory employment. However, in contrast with the abovementioned findings, Iversen and Sabroe (1988) have reported that neither prolonged employment nor prolonged unemployment results in changes in psychological well-being, though the former — more so if it fosters the feeling of security among the workers — attenuates deterioration, especially in general health measured by GHQ (Goldberg, 1972) with the passage of time. Thus, the findings are not conclusive in this regard. However, a long persistence in a job lacking conducive physical and psychological climate may commonly be found to expose an individual at work to psychological impairment. But, the findings obtained only from a few relatively less pointed investigations as well as common observation seem not discreet to be generalized in a wider perspective; they may simply form a basis for causal inferences. Hence, the study was also designed to analyse the psychological well-being as well as coping styles of different groups separately involving the technically and non-technically educated employed for various distinct durations. Here first follows the findings (see Table 8.13) of a statistical comparison among different groups of the technically educated employed young men for various discrete durations in terms of the level of various indices of psychological health like anxiety, stress, feeling of insecurity, alienation, identity-crisis and their dimensions.

Different groups of the technically educated employed young men distinct in the experience of the duration of their status, more especially like those of the groups of unemployed medical and agriculture degree-holders, were not found to differ significantly amongst themselves at the count of any of the indices of psychological health, excepting lack of self-confidence (F=2.39; df=7,124; p<0.05), dejection (p<0.01), feeling of insecurity (F=2.31; p<0.05), fragmentation (p<0.05), indecisiveness (F =3.11; p<0.01), social conflict (F =2.60), hopelessness (p <0.01) and identity-crisis (p < 0.05). Further, all of them, too, by and large, were moderately susceptible to all the psychological reactions other than anxiety and stress as well as their various specific syndromes, though the level particularly attained in terms of anxiety and most of its dimensions by them, as per the view

Table 8.13 : Statistical Differences Among the Groups of the Technically Educated Young Men Employed for Different Discrete Durations and their Relative Standing in Terms of Different Indices of Psychological Well-being

	Length of Unemployment (in Years)																								
	0-1(N=16)			*1-2(N=15)*			*2-3(N=15)*			*3-4 (N=17)*			*4-5(N=15)*			*5-6(N=15)*			*6-7(N=15)*			*7-above(N=24)*			
Indices of Psychological Well-being	*Mean (%)*	*SD*	*Rank*	*Mean (%)*	*SD*	*Rank*	*Mean (%)*	*SD*	*Rank*	*Mean (%)*	*SD*	*Rank*	*Mean (%)*	*SD*	*Rank*	*Mean (%)*	*SD*	*Rank*	*Mean (%)*	*SD*	*Rank*	*Mean (%)*	*SD*	*Rank*	*F*
1. General Worries	2.25 (37.50)	1.19	24	1.33 (22.17)	0.73	27	2.47 (41.17)	1.35	08	1.41 (23.50)	0.77	27	1.73 (28.83)	0.89	28	1.33 (22.17)	0.72	27	2.00 (33.33)	1.07	22	1.83 (30.50)	0.94	27	1.24
2. Somatic Manifestations	0.88 (29.33)	0.52	30	0.40 (13.33)	0.23	32	.0.73 (24.33)	0.39	30	0.35 (11.67)	0.19	37	0.47 (15.67)	0.30	32	0.47 (15.67)	0.24	29	0.33 (11.00)	0.18	36	0.58 (19.33)	0.32	32	1.15
3. Psychological Symptoms	1.50 (30.00)	0.83	29	0.87 (17.40)	0.49	29	1.53 (30.60)	0.83	23	1.00 (20.00)	0.62	30	0.93 (18.60)	0.53	30	0.40 (8.00)	0.21	38	1.47 (29.40)	0.81	27	1.42 (28.40)	0.75	29	2.06
4. Social Relations	2.06 (25.75)	1.21	31	1.13 (14.13)	0.60	31	1.67 (20.88)	0.86	33	1.65 (20.63)	0.83	28	1.07 (13.38)	0.60	35	0.67 (8.38)	0.36	36	1.53 (19.13)	0.80	32	1.58 (19.75)	0.87	31	1.19
5. **Anxiety**	6.72 (30.55)	3.42	28	3.74 (17.00)	1.91	30	6.40 (29.09)	3.30	28	4.41 (20.05)	2.26	29	4.20 (19.09)	2.15	29	2.88 (13.09)	1.61	34	5.33 (24.23)	2.69	29	5.42 (24.64)	2.85	30	1.82
6. Suicidal Tendency	0.13 (3.25)	0.07	39	0.00 (0.00)	0.00	39	0.00 (0.00)	0.00	39	0.29 (7.25)	0.15	39	0.20 (5.00)	0.11	39	0.00 (0.00)	0.00	39	0.00 (0.00)	0.00	39	0.04 (1.00)	0.02	39	1.37
7. Emotional Instability	1.88 (23.50)	1.02	32	1.47 (18.38)	0.85	28	1.87 (23.38)	1.19	32	1.41 (17.63)	0.77	32	3.07 (38.38)	1.64	22	1.33 (16.63)	0.71	28	1.93 (24.13)	1.07	30	2.42 (30.25)	1.26	28	1.81
8. Paranoid Tendency	1.50 (12.50)	0.78	38	0.73 (6.08)	0.37	37.5	2.33 (19.42)	1.24	35	1.35 (11.25)	0.73	38	1.33 (11.08)	0.72	37.5	1.60 (13.33)	0.86	33	1.20 (10.00)	0.71	37	1.16 (9.67)	0.63	38	0.99
9. Depression	7.69 (21.36)	3.93	33	4.00 (11.11)	2.07	34	4.67 (12.97)	2.39	37	5.29 (14.69)	2.87	33	4.87 (13.53)	2.51	34	4.93 (13.69)	2.51	32	4.87 (13.53)	2.47	34	5.33 (14.81)	2.69	34	0.66
10. Physical Illness	1.94 (16.17)	1.04	37	1.07 (8.92)	0.63	36	2.87 (23.92)	1.52	31	2.24 (18.67)	1.16	31	2.00 (16.67)	0.93	31	1.67 (13.92)	0.85	31	2.40 (20.00)	1.30	31	1.92 (16.00)	1.04	33	1.11
11. Social Maladjustment	2.38 (19.83)	1.26	35	1.53 (12.75)	0.83	33	1.07 (8.92)	0.63	38	1.47 (12.25)	0.81	36	1.60 (13.33)	0.84	36	1.73 (14.42)	0.93	30	0.73 (6.08)	0.38	38	1.67 (13.92)	0.86	36	0.79
12. Apprehensiveness	2.50 (20.83)	1.33	34	0.73 (6.08)	0.37	37.5	2.40 (20.00)	1.35	34	1.71 (14.25)	0.95	34	1.33 (11.08)	0.74	37.5	1.00 (8.33)	0.53	37	1.73 (14.42)	0.91	33	1.25 (10.42)	0.67	37	1.55
13. **Stress**	18.02 (18.77)	9.56	36	9.93 (9.53)	4.83	35	15.21 (15.84)	7.72	36	13.76 (14.33)	7.68	35	14.40 (15.00)	8.06	33	12.26 (12.77)	6.93	35	12.86 (13.39)	7.01	35	13.79 (14.36)	8.60	35	0.62

Contd.

Table 8.13 *(Contd.)*

Indices of Psychological Well-being	Length of Unemployment (in Years): 0-1(N=16) Mean (%)	SD	Rank	1-2(N=15) Mean (%)	SD	Rank	2-3(N=15) Mean (%)	SD	Rank	3-4 (N=17) Mean (%)	SD	Rank	4-5(N=15) Mean (%)	SD	Rank	5-6(N=15) Mean (%)	SD	Rank	6-7(N=15) Mean (%)	SD	Rank	7-above(N=24) Mean (%)	SD	Rank	F
14. Lack of Self-confidence	9.82 (49.10)	2.92	05	7.27 (36.35)	2.31	15	7.73 (38.65)	2.54	09	7.46 (37.30)	2.41	13	7.61 (38.05)	2.59	24	7.59 (37.95)	2.47	15	8.93 (44.65)	2.64	10	9.25 (46.25)	2.81	06	2.39
15. Dejection	7.13 (47.53)	2.67	11	5.35 (35.67)	2.03	17	6.27 (41.80)	2.18	07	5.30 (35.33)	1.93	17	6.20 (41.33)	2.11	17	6.40 (42.67)	2.21	06	8.40 (56.00)	2.49	02	6.54 (43.60)	2.27	13	3.08
16. Pessimism	1.69 (33.80)	0.87	27	1.13 (22.60)	0.35	26	1.27 (25.40)	0.46	29	1.29 (25.80)	0.67	26	1.80 (36.00)	0.93	25	1.13 (22.60)	0.35	26	1.87 (37.40)	0.98	16	1.58 (31.60)	0.81	26	1.50
17. Emotional Responsiveness	13.69 (45.63)	4.02	13	10.40 (34.67)	3.42	19	11.27 (37.57)	3.08	13	11.41 (48.03)	3.23	11	13.61 (45.37)	3.67	07	10.93 (36.43)	3.02	18	14.01 (46.70)	4.22	08	12.47 (41.57)	3.55	18	1.32
18. Social Insecurity	10.19 (40.76)	3.22	21	7.73 (30.92)	2.51	25	7.73 (30.92)	2.39	22	8.05 (32.20)	2.56	24	10.27 (41.08)	3.34	18	10.00 (40.00)	2.74	9.5	9.87 (39.48)	2.38	14	10.08 (40.32)	3.18	19	1.59
19. Distrust	2.75 (55.00)	1.34	04	1.80 (36.00)	0.77	16	1.87 (37.40)	1.03	14	1.65 (33.00)	0.83	23	1.93 (38.60)	1.06	21	2.07 (41.40)	1.08	07	2.60 (52.00)	1.40	03	2.13 (42.60)	1.09	16	1.68
20. **Feeling of Insecurity**	45.27 (45.27)	12.75	15	33.68 (33.68)	10.72	21	36.14 (36.14)	10.97	17	35.16 (35.16)	12.42	20	41.42 (41.42)	14.27	16	38.12 (38.12)	10.42	14	45.68 (45.68)	14.85	09	42.05 (42.05)	11.07	17	2.31
21. Despair	15.31 (47.84)	3.89	08	14.60 (45.62)	3.83	04	13.53 (42.28)	1.46	06	13.00 (40.62)	4.15	09	15.47 (48.34)	3.93	06	15.73 (49.16)	3.33	04	16.00 (50.00)	3.59	5.5	14.38 (44.94)	3.33	08	1.47
22. Unstructured Universe	4.63 (57.88)	1.82	02	3.40 (42.50)	1.68	07	4.60 (57.50)	1.40	01	4.24 (53.00)	1.25	3.5	4.80 (60.00)	1.42	02	4.20 (52.50)	1.08	2.5	4.00 (50.00)	1.20	5.5	4.33 (54.13)	1.61	03	1.36
23. Psychological Vacuum	3.81 (47.63)	1.28	9.5	3.80 (47.50)	1.32	03	3.40 (42.50)	0.83	05	4.24 (53.00)	0.90	3.5	4.07 (50.88)	1.53	04	4.20 (52.50)	0.68	2.5	4.13 (51.62)	1.06	04	3.83 (47.88)	1.52	05	0.84
24. Disillusionment	1.69 (42.25)	0.79	19.5	1.67 (41.75)	0.82	08	1.53 (38.25)	0.64	11.5	1.82 (45.50)	1.03	06	1.53 (38.25)	0.74	23	1.13 (28.25)	0.35	25	1.47 (36.75)	0.52	18.5	1.29 (32.25)	0.46	25	1.64
25. Narcissism	1.56 (39.00)	0.89	22.5	1.60 (40.00)	0.74	10	1.53 (38.25)	0.64	11.5	2.00 (50.00)	1.12	05	1.67 (41.75)	0.72	14	1.27 (31.75)	0.46	21	1.60 (40.00)	0.91	13	1..50 (37.50)	0.78	24	0.99
26. **Alienation**	27.00 (48.21)	6.07	06	25.07 (44.70)	4.79	05	24.60 (43.93)	2.75	03	25.30 (45.18)	4.70	07	27.54 (49.18)	6.06	05	26.53 (47.37)	4.10	05	27.20 (48.57)	4.02	07	25.33 (45.23)	4.72	07	0.74
27. Depersonalization	3.38 (42.25)	1.82	19.5	2.73 (34.13)	0.88	20	2.60 (32.50)	0.83	21	2.82 (35.25)	1.51	18.5	2.73 (34.13)	1.16	27	2.47 (30.88)	0.64	23	2.67 (33.38)	0.82	21	3.13 (39.13)	1.03	22	0.98

Contd.

Table 8.13 (*Contd.*)

Indices of Psychological Well-being	*Length of Unemployment (in Years)* 0-1(N=16) Mean (%)	SD	Rank	1-2(N=15) Mean (%)	SD	Rank	2-3(N=15) Mean (%)	SD	Rank	3-4 (N=17) Mean (%)	SD	Rank	4-5(N=15) Mean (%)	SD	Rank	5-6(N=15) Mean (%)	SD	Rank	6-7(N=15) Mean (%)	SD	Rank	7-above(N=24) Mean (%)	SD	Rank	F
28. Fragmentation	3.63 (45.38)	1.78	14	2.67 (33.38)	0.98	22.5	2.40 (30.00)	0.63	25	2.71 (33.88)	1.57	21	3.33 (41.63)	1.59	15	2.60 (32.50)	0.91	20	2.33 (29.13)	0.72	28	3.21 (40.13)	1.44	20	2.11
29. Uncertainty	2.38 (59.50)	0.96	01	2.33 (58.25)	1.05	01	2.20 (55.00)	1.01	02	2.24 (56.00)	1.03	1.5	2.07 (51.75)	0.70	03	2.47 (61.75)	0.83	01	2.40 (60.00)	0.99	01	2.58 (64.50)	0.88	01	0.54
30. Distress	5.13 (42.75)	1.36	18	4.20 (35.00)	1.47	18	4.13 (34.42)	0.92	20	4.59 (38.25)	1.87	10	5.27 (43.92)	2.09	10	4.60 (38.33)	1.64	13	4.73 (39.42)	2.28	15	5.17 (43.08)	1.99	15	0.98
31. Indecisiveness	3.81 (47.63)	1.28	9.5	2.67 (33.38)	0.90	22.5	3.07 (38.38)	1.16	10	2.88 (36.00)	1.17	16	2.87 (35.88)	1.06	26	2.53 (31.63)	0.64	22	2.87 (35.88)	0.92	20	3.54 (44.25)	0.93	12	3.11
32. Social Conflict	2.31 (57.75)	0.87	03	1.93 (48.25)	0.96	02	1.73 (43.25)	0.80	04	2.24 (56.00)	1.09	1.5	2.47 (61.75)	0.83	01	1.60 (40.00)	0.63	9.5	1.67 (41.75)	0.90	11	2.46 (61.50)	1.02	02	2.60
33. Isolation	3.50 (43.75)	1.26	17	2.93 (36.63)	0.96	14	2.33 (29.13)	0.62	27	2.65 (33.13)	1.37	22	3.47 (43.38)	1.85	11.5	3.07 (38.38)	1.79	12	2.60 (32.50)	0.91	25	3.17 (39.63)	1.05	21	1.68
34. Withdrawal from Social and Personal Contact	1.56 (39.00)	0.81	22.5	1.47 (36.75)	0.92	12.5	1.20 (30.00)	0.41	25	1.65 (41.25)	0.86	08	1.80 (45.00)	0.94	8.5	1.60 (40.00)	0.91	9.5	1.33 (33.25)	0.49	23.5	1.54 (38.50)	0.59	23	0.85
35. Role Conflict	5.75 (47.92)	2.65	07	4.87 (40.58)	2.29	09	4.40 (36.67)	1.35	16	4.47 (37.25)	1.97	14	4.80 (40.00)	1.61	19.5	4.33 (36.08)	1.29	19	5.00 (41.67)	1.65	12	5.38 (44.83)	1.64	09	1.58
36. Hopelessness	2.94 (36.75)	1.06	25	2.60 (32.50)	0.91	24	2.40 (30.00)	0.74	25	2.41 (30.13)	0.80	25	3.47 (43.38)	1.46	11.5	2.27 (28.38)	0.70	24	2.53 (31.63)	0.74	26	3.46 (43.25)	1.02	14	4.37
37. Loneliness	1.38 (34.50)	0.81	26	1.47 (36.75)	0.83	12.5	1.40 (35.00)	0.83	18	1.41 (35.25)	0.62	18.5	1.60 (40.00)	0.91	19.5	1.47 (36.75)	0.82	16	1.33 (33.25)	0.62	23.5	1.79 (44.75)	0.72	10	0.74
38. Desolation	1.88 (47.00)	0.81	12	1.73 (43.25)	0.80	06	1.47 (36.75)	0.83	15	1.47 (36.75)	0.72	15	1.80 (45.00)	0.68	8.5	1.60 (40.00)	0.83	9.5	1.47 (36.75)	0.64	18.5	2.13 (53.25)	0.74	04	1.90
39. **Identity-crisis**	37.65 (44.82)	9.74	16	31.60 (37.62)	8.54	11	29.33 (34.92)	6.56	19	31.54 (37.55)	11.63	12	35.68 (42.48)	11.34	13	30.61 (36.44)	7.44	17	30.93 (36.82)	8.00	17	37.56 (44.71)	8.25	11	2.41

Note : $df = 7,124$; $p < 0.05 = 2.08$; $p < 0.01 = 2.79$.

held by Feather (1982), Goldberg (1972) and Warr (1984a), was also enough to mark in them the symptoms of psychological deterioration to a certain degree. In addition to the abovementioned findings, it was revealed that different groups of the technically educated employed young men were also least predisposed to suicidal ideation (scores ranged from 0.00 per cent to 7.25 per cent). They, however, exhibited a certain variation — moderate, of course —from the different groups of their technically and non-technically educated unemployed counterparts in specifying the most impetuous psychological syndrome in them. Remarkably, all the groups of technically educated employed, excepting the groups employed for spells of 2-3 year and 4-5 year who deeply suffered from the alienating fit of unstructured universe (57.50%), and the heightened feeling of social conflict (61.75%) respectively, were more obviously found to be vacillating in a state of uncertainty (scores obtained by different groups varied between 56.00 per cent and 64.50 per cent). Lastly, it was attempted to identify the group of technically educated employed for a particular period that was psychologically more harassed. The result, however, was mixed in this regard; no one group could be identified as too susceptible to all the psychological reactions: while some psychological symptoms were found to be more pronounced in one group of the technically educated employed, some others were found in the other groups. Although the group of employed for a spell of 0-1 year, in particular, was found to be more vulnerable to psychological impairment, marked by a fair amount of increment in almost all the psychological symptoms being analysed. The predicament of the groups employed for the longer duration of 6-7 and more than seven years was also not less disheartening though; their psychological health clearly tended to decline. Other groups, the group employed for a period of 1-2 year, in particular, were clearly found to enjoy better psychological health.

Duration of Employment and the Degree of Life Satisfaction : The Case of the Technically Educated Employed Young Men

Table 8.14 furnishes the details of the findings of a statistical comparison made among different groups of the technically educated employed young men for various distinct durations in terms of the degree of life satisfaction in them.

Groups of the technically educated young men in jobs for various durations, like those of the technically educated unemployed of

Table 8.14 : Statistical Differences Among the Groups of the Technically Educated Young Men Employed for Different Discrete Durations and their Relative Standing in Terms of the Degree of their Life Satisfaction

Variable	*Length of Employment (in Years)*															
	0-1 (N=16)		*1-2 (N=15)*		*2-3 (N=15)*		*3-4 (N=17)*		*4-5 (N=15)*		*5-6 (N=15)*		*6-7 (N=15)*		*7-above (N=24)*	
	Mean (%)	*SD*	*Mean (%)*	*SD*	*Mean (%)*	*SD*	*Mean (%)*	*SD*	*Mean (%)*	*SD*	*Mean (%)*	*SD*	*Mean (%)*	*SD*	*Mean (%)*	*SD*
Life Satis-faction	6.75 (67.50)	1.69	6.80 (68.00)	1.47	7.47 (74.70)	1.36	7.29 (72.09)	1.57	6.13 (61.30)	2.10	7.80 (78.00)	1.21	7.00 (70.00)	1.89	7.08 (70.80)	1.91

	F
Life Satis-faction	1.35

Note : $df = 7{,}124$; $p < 0.05 = 2.08$; $p < 0.01 = 2.79$.

different disciplines, did not show any marked difference among themselves in terms of the level of their life satisfaction (F=1.35; df=7,124; p>0.05). However, contrary to all the groups of their unemployed counterparts, different groups of the technically educated employed were apparently found to have quite a greater amount of satisfaction with their life (life satisfaction scores obtained by them ranged between 61.30 per cent and 78.00 per cent). Further, it was recorded that while the group of the technically educated people employed for a period of 5-6 year were more satisfied with their life (78.00%), the group employed for a spell of 4-5 year were less at this count (61.30%). Moreover, the results exhibited no clear-cut pattern of increase in the level of satisfaction with the addition in the duration of employment; there, of course, appeared an evidence of ups and downs in the level of life satisfaction of different groups of the technically educated employed for various distinct durations. Life satisfaction betrayed a tendency to increase consistently, though not quite perceptibly, among groups of the employed up to a period of three years of their employment, and thereafter operated in a seesaw fashion among other groups of the employed for various longer durations.

Duration of Employment and the Degree of Dependence on Different Coping Strategies : The Case of the Technically Educated Employed Young Men

Table 8.15 records a brief account of the findings of a statistical comparison among different groups of the technically educated people in jobs for various spells in terms of the degree of their dependence on various strategies in order to fight against life events encompassing.

The groups of technically educated employed young men for various distinct durations were not found to differ significantly from one another in terms of the use of intrapersistive approach mode (p>0.05) and extrapersistive approach mode (F=1.06; df=7,124; p > 0.05), but marked differences could be noticed among them in terms of the degree of their dependence on punitive avoidance mode (F=3.35; p<0.01) and defensive avoidance mode (p<0.05) in course of their attempt to manage their situation. It was further recorded that all of them, like each of the groups of their unemployed counterparts, solely devised intrapersistive approach mode in handling their situation (scores obtained by them varied between 52.87 per cent and

Table 8.15 : Statistical Differences Among the Groups of the Technically Educated Young Men Employed for Different Discrete Durations and the Degree of their Relative Dependence in Terms of Different Coping Strategies

	Length of Employment (in Years)																
	0-1 (N=16)		*1-2 (N=15)*		*2-3 (N=15)*		*3-4 (N=17)*		*4-5 (N=15)*		*5-6 (N=15)*		*6-7 (N=15)*		*7-above (N=24)*		
Coping Strategies	*Mean (%)*	*SD*	*Mean (%)*	*SD*	*Mean (%)*	*SD*	*Mean (%)*	*SD*	*Mean (%)*	*SD*	*Mean (%)*	*SD*	*Mean (%)*	*SD*	*Mean (%)*	*SD*	*F*
Intrapersistive Approach Mode	9.06 (60.40)	3.34	10.47 (69.80)	2.39	7.93 (52.87)	2.91	9.29 (61.93)	3.08	10.20 (68.00)	4.25	9.93 (66.20)	1.91	10.53 (70.20)	1.81	9.38 (62.53)	2.22	1.45
Extrape-ristive Approach Mode	2.50 (16.67)	1.32	1.87 (12.47)	0.98	2.87 (19.13)	1.45	1.94 (12.93)	1.02	2.60 (17.33)	1.35	1.33 (8.87)	0.72	1.40 (9.33)	0.76	1.50 (10.00)	0.81	1.06
Punitive Avoidance Mode	0.88 (5.87)	0.46	0.86 (5.73)	0.44	1.20 (8.00)	0.62	0.94 (6.27)	0.48	0.27 (1.80)	0.16	1.87 (12.47)	0.99	1.07 (7.13)	0.56	0.62 (4.13)	0.34	3.35
Defensive Avoidance Mode	2.56 (17.07)	1.41	1.80 (12.00)	0.85	3.00 (20.00)	1.13	2.83 (18.87)	1.51	1.93 (12.87)	1.03	1.87 (12.47)	1.06	2.00 (13.33)	1.06	3.50 (23.33)	1.82	2.62

Note : $df = 7{,}124$; $p < 0.05 = 2.08$; $p < 0.01 = 2.79$.

70.20 per cent). All other coping styles, particularly the punitive avoidance mode, hardly found favour with them in making their adjustment.

Duration of Employment and Level of Anxiety, Stress, Feeling of Insecurity, Alienation and Identity-Crisis : The Case of the Non-technically Educated Employed Young Men

Table 8.16 reports the findings derived from the statistical comparison made among different groups of the non-technically educated employed people dissimilar in their experience of the duration of their status in terms of their level of anxiety, stress, feeling of insecurity, alienation, identity-crisis and their dimensions.

Groups of the non-technically educated employed young men for different durations, similar to those of the unemployed degree-holders in engineering and non-technical education — though not clearly envisaged in one to one fashion — showed marked differences among themselves in terms of nearly half of the indices of psychological health. The indices which differentiated them from one another particularly involved psychological symptoms (F=2.44; p<0.05), emotional instability (p<0.05), paranoid tendency (F=3.37; p<0.01), depression (p<0.05), physical illness (p<0.01), social maladjustment (F=3.62), apprehensiveness (F=2.62), stress (F=2.04; p<0.05), lack of self-confidence (p<0.01), dejection (F=2.07), emotional responsiveness (F=3.38), feeling of insecurity (p<0.05), psychological vacuum (F=2.26), uncertainty (p<0.01), distress (F =2.31), social conflict ($F \doteq 2.26$), isolation (p<0.05) and identity-crisis (F=2.06). But the groups of the non-technically educated employed, like those of the groups of their technically educated employed counterparts, appeared to be less oppressed by fit of suicidal ideation (scores obtained by different groups varied between 0.75 per cent and 5.00 per cent) and perceptibly more by the feeling of uncertainty (scores of different groups ranged between 58.25 per cent and 64.25 per cent), except the groups of non-technically educated employed people for the spells of 0-1 year, 3-4 year and 4-5 year who were mostly affected by narcissism (57.25%), despair (51.78%) and social conflict (54.75%) respectively. Further, the groups of non-technically educated employed young men for various durations, too, were not found to exhibit similar patterns in their psychological reactions : while some of them were afflicted more with some

Table 8.16 : Statistical Differences Among the Groups of the Non-technically Educated Young Men Employed for Different Discrete Durations and their Relative Standing in Terms of Different Indices of Psychological Well-being

	Length of Employment (in Years)																								
	0-1(N=35)			*1-2(N=30)*			*2-3(N=30)*			*3-4 (N=30)*			*4-5(N=31)*			*5-6(N=30)*			*6-7(N=30)*			*7-above(N=62)*			
Indices of Psychological Well-being	*Mean (%)*	*SD*	*Rank*	*Mean (%)*	*SD*	*Rank*	*Mean (%)*	*SD*	*Rank*	*Mean (%)*	*SD*	*Rank*	*Mean (%)*	*SD*	*Rank*	*Mean (%)*	*SD*	*Rank*	*Mean (%)*	*SD*	*Rank*	*Mean (%)*	*SD*	*Rank*	*F*
1. General Worries	2.11 (35.17)	1.07	26	2.57 (42.83)	1.45	12	2.37 (39.50)	1.29	23	2.40 (40.00)	1.04	11.5	2.13 (35.50)	1.18	24	2.03 (33.83)	1.14	22	2.33 (38.83)	1.30	25	2.31 (38.50)	1.24	24	0.48
2. Somatic Manifestations	0.69 (23.00)	0.37	32	0.53 (17.67)	0.29	32	0.27 (9.00)	0.14	37	0.57 (19.00)	0.31	33	0.45 (15.00)	0.26	35	0.43 (14.33)	0.25	33	0.80 (26.67)	0.46	31	0.61 (20.33)	0.34	32	1.61
3. Psychological Symptoms	2.17 (43.40)	1.18	13	1.30 (26.00)	0.67	30	1.90 (38.00)	1.09	26	1.80 (36.00)	1.03	22	1.58 (31.60)	0.76	27	1.80 (36.00)	1.03	19	1.63 (32.60)	0.87	28	1.39 (27.80)	0.75	30	2.44
4. Social Relations	1.51 (18.88)	0.74	38	1.77 (22.13)	0.95	31	1.93 (24.13)	1.04	30	2.07 (25.88)	1.39	29	1.68 (21.00)	0.88	32	1.57 (19.63)	0.87	31	2.37 (29.63)	1.52	30	1.84 (23.00)	0.98	31	1.02
5. **Anxiety**	6.49 (29.50)	2.66	28	6.17 (28.05)	3.28	29	6.47 (29.41)	3.39	29	6.84 (31.09)	2.69	28	5.87 (26.68)	2.38	29	5.83 (26.50)	3.22	29	7.13 (32.41)	4.05	29	6.15 (27.95)	3.77	29	0.50
6. Suicidal Tendency	0.14 (3.50)	0.09	39	0.20 (5.00)	0.12	39	0.03 (0.75)	0.01	39	0.13 (3.25)	0.07	39	0.05 (1.25)	0.02	39	0.07 (1.75)	0.03	39	0.08 (2.00)	0.03	39	0.06 (1.50)	0.04	39	1.01
7. Emotional Instability	2.17 (27.13)	1.29	30	2.70 (33.75)	1.53	27	1.47 (18.38)	0.87	31	1.57 (19.63)	0.88	31	1.77 (22.13)	1.03	30	2.30 (28.75)	1.20	28	2.03 (25.38)	1.06	32	2.44 (30.50)	1.26	27	2.28
8. Paranoid Tendency	2.51 (20.92)	1.39	36	1.33 (11.08)	0.78	38	1.33 (11.08)	0.67	35	0.97 (8.08)	0.52	37.5	1.84 (15.33)	1.04	34	1.27 (10.58)	0.66	37.5	1.70 (14.17)	0.88	36	1.18 (9.83)	0.65	38	3.37
9. Depression	8.23 (22.86)	4.29	33	5.87 (16.31)	3.06	34	4.40 (12.22)	2.39	33	3.30 (9.17)	1.73	36	5.03 (13.97)	2.97	37	4.87 (13.53)	2.47	35	6.10 (16.94)	3.29	34	5.56 (15.44)	2.84	34	2.46
10. Physical Illness	3.37 (28.08)	1.82	29	2.00 (16.67)	1.13	33	1.80 (15.00)	0.95	32	2.33 (19.42)	1.66	32	1.97 (16.42)	1.05	33	1.83 (15.25)	1.06	32	2.63 (21.92)	1.36	33	2.06 (17.17)	1.11	33	2.83
11. Social Maladjustment	2.43 (20.25)	1.79	37	1.43 (11.92)	0.81	36	0.93 (7.75)	0.48	38	0.97 (8.08)	0.50	37.5	2.58 (21.50)	1.35	31	1.27 (10.58)	0.68	37.5	1.60 (13.33)	0.87	38	1.58 (13.17)	0.83	36	3.62
12. Apprehensiveness	2.66 (22.17)	1.67	35	1.40 (11.67)	0.77	37	1.27 (10.58)	0.68	36	1.83 (15.25)	1.04	34	1.10 (9.17)	0.61	38	1.60 (13.33)	0.83	36	1.63 (13.58)	0.89	37	1.50 (12.50)	0.76	37	2.62
13. **Stress**	21.53 (22.43)	11.52	34	14.93 (15.55)	7.31	35	11.23 (11.70)	5.71	34	11.10 (11.56)	5.63	35	14.35 (14.95)	6.56	36	13.21 (13.76)	7.01	34	15.77 (16.43)	8.24	35	14.39 (14.99)	6.75	35	2.04

Contd.

Table 8.16 *(Contd.)*

Indices of Psychological Well-being	*Length of Employment (in Years)* 0-1(N=35) Mean (%)	SD	Rank	1-2(N=30) Mean (%)	SD	Rank	2-3(N=30) Mean (%)	SD	Rank	3-4 (N=30) Mean (%)	SD	Rank	4-5(N=31) Mean (%)	SD	Rank	5-6(N=30) Mean (%)	SD	Rank	6-7(N=30) Mean (%)	SD	Rank	7-above(N=62) Mean (%)	SD	Rank	F
14. Lack of Self-confidence	9.66 (40.30)	3.17	20	9.47 (47.35)	2.96	06	9.81 (49.05)	3.24	6.5	7.67 (38.25)	2.58	16	9.16 (45.80)	2.78	05	7.93 (39.65)	2.71	14	8.20 (41.00)	2.82	21	9.02 (45.10)	2.95	11	2.79
15. Dejection	7.69 (51.27)	2.63	02	8.26 (55.07)	2.81	03	7.93 (52.87)	2.69	04	7.50 (50.00)	2.53	04	6.45 (43.00)	2.41	12	6.81 (45.40)	2.54	06	6.67 (44.47)	2.61	15	7.29 (48.60)	2.74	06	2.07
16. Pessimism	1.26 (25.20)	0.70	31	1.60 (32.00)	0.83	28	1.63 (32.60)	0.93	28	1.23 (24.60)	0.72	30	1.45 (29.00)	0.77	28	1.27 (25.40)	0.69	30	1.73 (34.60)	1.03	27	1.47 (29.40)	0.81	28	1.44
17. Emotional Responsiveness	12.45 (41.50)	3.64	18.5	13.56 (45.20)	3.49	09	14.10 (47.00)	3.66	09	10.90 (36.33)	3.06	20	11.75 (39.17)	3.17	18	10.50 (35.00)	2.97	21	12.80 (42.67)	3.25	17	13.27 (44.23)	3.42	15	3.38
18. Social Insecurity	8.79 (35.16)	3.02	27	9.87 (39.48)	3.15	19	10.87 (43.48)	3.24	17	9.07 (36.28)	2.84	21	10.16 (40.64)	3.09	16	7.97 (31.88)	2.76	27	10.04 (40.16)	2.98	22	11.08 (44.32)	3.18	14	1.72
19. Distrust	2.18 (43.60)	1.17	12	2.20 (44.00)	1.16	11	2.30 (46.00)	1.22	12	2.27 (45.40)	1.14	08	1.71 (34.20)	0.86	26	1.67 (33.40)	0.92	24	2.13 (42.60)	1.14	18	2.06 (41.20)	1.08	22	1.37
20. **Feeling of Insecurity**	42.05 (42.05)	10.52	16	44.96 (44.96)	15.05	10	46.64 (46.64)	14.33	11	38.65 (38.65)	8.40	14	40.68 (40.68)	12.12	15	36.15 (36.15)	10.63	18	41.57 (41.57)	13.64	20	44.19 (44.19)	12.62	16	2.28
21. Despair	15.06 (47.06)	4.91	08	15.67 (48.97)	4.40	04	15.57 (48.66)	3.13	08	16.57 (51.78)	3.17	01	13.94 (43.56)	2.37	09	14.33 (44.78)	2.67	08	15.00 (46.88)	4.89	07	15.63 (48.84)	3.14	05	1.61
22. Unstructured Universe	3.91 (48.88)	1.27	05	3.73 (46.63)	1.36	07	4.20 (52.50)	1.00	05	4.03 (50.38)	1.45	03	4.19 (52.38)	1.42	03	4.07 (50.88)	1.60	03	4.03 (50.38)	1.77	03	4.02 (50.25)	1.22	04	0.36
23. Psychological Vacuum	3.86 (48.25)	1.50	06	3.37 (42.13)	1.25	14	4.60 (57.50)	1.45	03	3.53 (44.13)	1.17	09	4.09 (51.13)	1.29	04	3.80 (47.50)	1.61	05	3.97 (49.63)	1.33	04	3.87 (48.38)	1.21	07	2.26
24. Disillusionment	1.57 (39.25)	0.61	23	1.50 (37.50)	0.63	22.5	1.57 (39.25)	0.77	24	1.40 (35.00)	0.50	24	1.38 (34.50)	0.71	25	1.43 (35.75)	0.68	20	1.47 (36.75)	0.78	26	1.47 (36.75)	0.67	26	0.40
25. Narcissism	2.29 (57.25)	1.25	01	1.53 (38.25)	0.86	20	1.53 (38.25)	0.57	25	1.83 (45.75)	0.99	07	1.55 (38.75)	0.93	21	1.33 (33.25)	0.76	25.5	1.60 (40.00)	0.89	23	1.68 (42.00)	0.81	20.5	1.03
26. **Alienation**	26.69 (47.66)	7.50	07	25.80 (46.07)	6.11	08	27.47 (49.05)	4.17	6.5	27.36 (48.86)	4.22	05	25.16 (44.93)	3.38	07	24.97 (44.59)	3.81	09	26.07 (46.55)	7.13	09	26.67 (47.63)	5.32	08	0.83
27. Depersonalization	3.17 (39.63)	1.22	22	2.90 (36.25)	1.32	24	3.40 (42.50)	1.40	19	2.50 (31.25)	0.51	27	3.10 (38.75)	1.30	21	2.70 (33.75)	1.15	23	3.40 (42.50)	1.45	19	3.02 (37.75)	1.21	25	2.02

Contd.

Table 8.16 *(Contd.)*

Indices of Psychological Well-being	Length of Employment (in Years) — 0-1(N=35) Mean (%)	SD	Rank	1-2(N=30) Mean (%)	SD	Rank	2-3(N=30) Mean (%)	SD	Rank	3-4 (N=30) Mean (%)	SD	Rank	4-5(N=31) Mean (%)	SD	Rank	5-6(N=30) Mean (%)	SD	Rank	6-7(N=30) Mean (%)	SD	Rank	7-above(N=62) Mean (%)	SD	Rank	F
28. Fragmentation	3.57 (44.63)	1.20	11	3.03 (37.88)	1.47	21	3.27 (40.88)	1.26	21	2.70 (33.75)	1.02	26	3.48 (43.50)	1.39	10.5	3.33 (41.63)	1.45	11	3.17 (39.63)	1.49	24	3.29 (41.13)	1.41	23	1.28
29. Uncertainty	2.03 (50.75)	0.89	03	2.37 (59.25)	0.93	01	2.57 (64.25)	0.77	01	2.03 (50.75)	0.93	02	1.83 (45.75)	0.86	06	2.33 (58.25)	1.03	01	2.40 (60.00)	0.81	01	2.56 (64.00)	0.93	1.5	3.20
30. Distress	5.43 (45.25)	1.56	09	4.97 (41.42)	1.71	15	5.27 (43.92)	1.89	14	4.47 (37.25)	1.01	18	4.39 (36.58)	1.09	23	4.50 (37.50)	1.61	15.5	5.43 (45.25)	2.05	11	5.29 (44.08)	2.04	17	2.31
31. Indecisiveness	3.46 (43.25)	1.31	14	3.23 (40.38)	1.25	17	3.50 (43.75)	1.33	15	3.20 (40.00)	1.30	11.5	3.35 (41.88)	1.25	13	2.90 (36.25)	1.27	17	3.80 (47.50)	1.65	06	3.76 (47.00)	1.46	09	1.70
32. Social Conflict	2.00 (50.00)	1.00	04	2.33 (58.25)	0.92	02	2.47 (61.75)	0.86	02	1.93 (48.25)	1.01	06	2.19 (54.75)	0.83	01	2.03 (50.75)	0.85	04	2.23 (55.75)	1.04	02	2.56 (64.00)	1.02	1.5	2.26
33. Isolation	2.94 (36.75)	0.87	25	2.80 (35.00)	0.96	26	3.20 (41.25)	1.24	20	2.73 (34.13)	1.17	25	3.10 (38.75)	0.94	21	3.00 (37.50)	1.14	15.5	3.60 (45.00)	1.38	13	3.36 (42.00)	1.20	20.5	2.28
34. Withdrawal from Social and Personal Contact	1.80 (45.00)	0.80	10	1.50 (37.50)	0.86	22.5	1.60 (40.00)	0.62	22	1.47 (36.75)	0.86	19	1.74 (43.50)	0.82	10.5	1.33 (33.25)	0.55	25.5	1.87 (46.75)	0.94	08	1.79 (44.75)	0.73	12	2.00
35. Role Conflict	5.03 (41.92)	2.11	17	4.83 (40.25)	1.76	18	5.23 (43.58)	1.85	16	4.60 (38.33)	1.25	15	4.84 (40.33)	1.46	17	5.03 (41.92)	1.94	10	5.33 (44.42)	2.19	16	5.35 (44.58)	1.84	13	0.77
36. Hopelessness	3.20 (40.00)	1.43	21	2.87 (35.88)	1.43	25	2.90 (36.25)	1.35	27	3.17 (39.63)	0.79	13	3.11 (38.88)	1.04	19	3.27 (40.88)	1.64	12	3.60 (45.00)	1.79	13	3.47 (43.38)	1.50	19	1.11
37. Loneliness	1.54 (38.50)	0.61	24	1.70 (42.50)	1.02	13	1.73 (43.25)	0.94	18	1.43 (35.75)	0.73	23	1.77 (44.25)	0.56	08	1.80 (45.00)	0.89	07	1.80 (45.00)	0.96	13	1.74 (43.50)	0.90	18	0.78
38. Desolation	1.66 (41.50)	0.84	18.5	1.90 (47.50)	0.99	05	1.87 (46.75)	0.78	10	1.67 (41.75)	0.88	10	2.17 (54.25)	1.12	02	2.06 (51.50)	0.64	02	1.93 (48.25)	0.94	05	2.08 (52.00)	0.98	03	1.46
39. **Identity-crisis**	35.83 (42.65)	9.08	15	34.43 (40.99)	9.25	16	37.11 (44.18)	8.58	13	31.90 (37.98)	6.69	17	35.07 (41.75)	6.71	14	34.28 (40.81)	10.37	13	38.57 (45.92)	12.53	10	38.27 (45.56)	10.16	10	2.06

Note : $df = 7{,}270$; $p < 0.05 = 2.04$; $p < 0.01 = 2.71$.

psychological subversions, others suffered from different symptoms. Moreover, the groups of non-technically educated people having the experience of their jobs for shorter (i.e., 0-1 year) and longer spells of 6-7 and above 7 years were also more psychologically vulnerable. In addition, the groups of non-technically educated employed, too, were, by and large, found to be moderately afflicted, but not to the extent of the different groups of their unemployed counterparts, at their psychological level.

Duration of Employment and the Degree of Life Satisfaction : The Case of the Non-technically Educated Employed Young Men

Table 8.17 involves an account of the findings obtained from a statistical comparison made of different groups of the non-technically educated employed people for various distinct durations in terms of the degree of their life satisfaction.

The groups of non-technically educated employed people for different discrete durations, too, did not show any marked differences among themselves in terms of the degree of their life satisfaction (F=1.56; df=7, 270; p>0.05). Further, all of them, like those of the groups of their technically educated employed counterparts, were found to be greatly contented with the order of their life (the obtained life satisfaction scores by different groups of the non-technically educated employed ranged between 60.30 per cent and 74.80 per cent). And, in the case of non-technically educated employed, too, there appeared an evidence of ups and downs in the amount of life satisfaction, though not statistically quite perceptible, across different groups of the employed, distinct in the experience of the duration of their jobs. Nonetheless, dissimilar to the technically educated employed people, the non-technically educated people at jobs for the period of 0-1 year (obtained life satisfaction score = 72.00) and 4-5 year (obtained life satisfaction score = 74.80) were found to be far more satisfied with their life.

Duration of Employment and the Degree of Dependence on Different Coping Strategies : The Case of the Non-technically Educated Employed Young Men

Table 8.18 reports the findings of a statistical comparison among the groups of non-technically educated employed people with the continuous experience of the distinct durations of their obtained status

Table 8.17 : Statistical Differences Among the Groups of the Non-technically Educated Young Men Employed for Different Discrete Durations and their Relative Standing in Terms of the Degree of their Life Satisfaction

	Length of Employment (in Years)																
	0-1 (N=35)		*1-2 (N=30)*		*2-3 (N=30)*		*3-4 (N=30)*		*4-5 (N=31)*		*5-6 (N=30)*		*6-7 (N=30)*		*7-above (N=62)*		
Variable	*Mean* (%)	*SD*	*Mean* (%)	*SD*	*Mean* (%)	*SD*	*Mean* (%)	*SD*	*Mean* (%)	*SD*	*Mean* (%)	*SD*	*Mean* (%)	*SD*	*Mean* (%)	*SD*	*F*
Life Satisfaction	7.20 (72.00)	1.73	6.53 (65.30)	1.72	6.03 (60.30)	2.27	6.87 (68.70)	1.59	7.48 (74.80)	1.39	6.57 (65.70)	2.30	6.77 (67.70)	1.94	6.76 (67.60)	2.23	1.56

Note. $df = 7{,}270$; $p < 0.05 = 2.04$; $p < 0.01 = 2.71$.

Table 8.18 : Statistical Differences Among the Groups of the Non-technically Educated Young Men Employed for Different Discrete Durations and the Degree of their Relative Dependence in Terms of Different Coping Strategies

	Length of Employment (in Years)																
	0-1 (N=35)		*1-2 (N=30)*		*2-3 (N=30)*		*3-4 (N=30)*		*4-5 (N=31)*		*5-6 (N=30)*		*6-7 (N=30)*		*7-above (N=62)*		
Coping Strategies	*Mean* (%)	*SD*	*Mean* (%)	*SD*	*Mean* (%)	*SD*	*Mean* (%)	*SD*	*Mean* (%)	*SD*	*Mean* (%)	*SD*	*Mean* (%)	*SD*	*Mean* (%)	*SD*	*F*
Intrapersistive Approach Mode	10.23 (68.20)	2.43	10.07 (67.13)	2.39	10.77 (71.80)	2.64	11.70 (78.00)	1.34	10.52 (70.13)	1.95	11.07 (73.80)	2.65	10.57 (70.47)	2.05	10.15 (67.67)	2.49	1.87
Extraperistive Approach Mode	1.83 (12.20)	1.02	1.87 (12.47)	1.01	1.53 (10.20)	0.90	1.17 (7.80)	0.69	1.77 (11.80)	1.02	1.27 (8.47)	0.74	1.80 (12.00)	1.07	1.71 (11.40)	0.97	1.61
Punitive Avoidance Mode	0.49 (3.27)	0.25	0.60 (4.00)	0.32	0.57 (3.80)	0.30	0.43 (2.87)	0.27	0.84 (5.60)	0.40	0.50 (3.33)	0.28	0.40 (2.67)	0.21	0.52 (3.47)	0.31	0.66
Defensive Avoidance Mode	2.45 (16.33)	1.12	2.46 (16.40)	1.53	2.13 (14.20)	1.26	1.70 (11.33)	0.95	1.87 (12.47)	1.06	2.16 (14.40)	1.15	2.23 (14.87)	1.25	2.62 (17.47)	1.47	1.19

Note. $df = 7{,}270$; $p < 0.05 = 2.04$; $p < 0.01 = 2.71$.

in terms of the degree of their reliance on different strategies in order to meet the existing situational demands.

Unlike the groups of technically educated employed people, but not quite exclusively, different groups of non-technically educated employed for various durations were not found to differ significantly from one another in terms of their dependence on any of the coping strategies. However, like all their unemployed and employed counterparts, they, more often than not, resorted to intrapersistive approach mode in fighting their problems (scores obtained by them extended between 67.13 per cent and 78 per cent). Further, they, too, depended least on other modes in coping with their situations, and particularly so on the punitive avoidance mode (scores of different groups ranged from 2.67 per cent to 5.60 per cent).

To sum up, all the abovementioned findings, *inter alia,* obtained from the statistical comparisons of different exclusive groups of the educated unemployed and employed young men over various distinct periods in terms of their psychological well-being and coping styles at intra-group level led to the following interesting facts :

1. There was no clear evidence of stabilization effect or adaptation in any of the exclusive groups of the technically and non-technically educated unemployed young men for different distinct durations in India. A pattern of ups and downs in the escalation of psychological symptoms was noticed in all the groups. In other words, halt in psychological decline in one group of the unemployed for a particular period was not found to overspread to other subsequent groups of the unemployed for various discrete durations or spill over from the unemployed for one duration to another; there obviously emerged a nonlinear pattern in this connection. Thus, the results, like those of the findings of Brinkmann (1976, 1984), Lahelma and Kangas (1989) and Verkleij (1989), clearly showed that the stabilization effect, as proposed by the Sheffield group of psychologists, does not operate in its entirety in the life of the long-term unemployed in India. The typical worldview of India embedded in deep-seated religious beliefs and values may provide a working ground on which to deal with the findings. The whole material world, as the Indian in general conceives, is a *maya* — an illusion (Kapp, 1963; Pande and Naidu, 1986; Singh, 1982); nothing is eternal in itself here. Everything happening at the cognitive or affective or conative level is *Bhagwad leela* — quite an inexplicable and unpredictable play of God (Thapar, 1982). So, every event in one's life, including *sukha* (happiness) and *dukha* (sorrow), *anand* (pleasure) and *kashta* (pain), *rag* (affinity) and *dvesha* (malice), etc., — conceived as seemingly predestined, and also as the direct outcome of the sum total of one's *karma* (deeds), good or bad, done in this life as well as in the *purva janma* (previous births) — are not to last for one's life time. They are obviously passing phases, and are very much cyclical in order and behaviour (Lapierre, 1986). This leads to a natural conclusion that the Indians usually vacillate between positive and negative currents of life with the hope that one has to replace the other in due course evidently in a circulatory fashion; none of them is everlasting or permanent. And, this is exactly so in the case of the unemployed and the impoverished in India, too. Hence, it seems not unnatural to have an inconsistent pattern of stabilization effect among different exclusive groups of the long-term educated unemployed young men in India. Maybe, as the expectation for good predominates their psyche, they tend to recover from their distress and vice versa.

The results may further be expounded on the basis of the typical personality dispositions of the Indians in general. Added to the possession of numerous undesirable traits (see Kakar, 1978; Kanungo, 1995; Sinha, 1988; Sinha, 1990), they are also rated considerably high on the dimensions of ambiguity and instability (Lannoy, 1983; Sinha, 1979; Thapar, 1982; Vatsyayan, 1982) making it difficult for one to predict accurately their reaction pattern in a given situation. Virtually, mystery all over shrouds Indian culture and personality. So, it is not surprising in any way if an unemployed in India for a longer spell manifests a discordant pattern of stability effect; it, however, congrues with his basic personality dispositions. To sum up, it is being suggested that the peculiarity ingrained in a culture and the personality dispositions of its people ought to be taken into account while describing the appearance of stability effect across cultures or nations.

Moreover, in depicting the inconsistent pattern of stabilization effect among the long-term educated unemployed, the findings of Branthwaite and Garcia (1985), Buss and Redburn (1983), and Stafford (1982) may also be taken into account. These findings confirm that the absence of sufficient help and support to the long-term unemployed (Buss and Redburn, 1983; Stafford, 1982), as well as worsening of the labour market (Branthwaite and Garcia, 1985) may lead to the disappearance of stabilization effect. As it has already been detailed in the 5th chapter, any scheme and/or intervention programmes undertaken both officially and voluntarily for the amelioration of the unemployed have appeared fruitless. They are considered to be just a political gimmick; they hardly serve the purpose, particularly in the eyes of the unemployed. Indeed, securing any assistance from any agency is both tiresome and vexatious for the unemployed, forcing them to move and float in uncertainty. Further, an alarming spate, particularly in the number of educated labour force in the face of apparently dwindling job opportunities — the employment shrinkage — has, of late, greatly perverted the composition and behaviour of the labour market in India (Mamgain and Parashar, 2000; Maurya, 2004; Ray, 1995; Singh, 1998; Sinha, 1996). It has driven the labour market to function in a more domineering fashion where occurrence of various malpractices in the selection and placement of personnel is the natural outcome. However, the advent of multinationals in the Indian market, as well as liberalization and globalization of economic policy have considerably raised the hopes of the job-seekers to get themselves both suitably and gainfully employed in the near future, as these developments in the Indian economic scenario, on account of their being well-planned and relatively futuristic in orientation, are perceived as associated with the acceleration of job opportunities both in the national and the international labour market (Dev, 2000). But, nothing positive has yet appeared on the front of employment. The horizon of hope is slowly but surely turning into a mirage of despair for the job-seekers. Remarkably, a downward trend has recently been noted in the growth rate during the period of 1991-97 vis-á-vis the period of 1980-90 (Verma, 1997).

To summarize, there are various schemes and programmes for the help and support of the unemployed in India. But, all of them, due to some reasons or the other, are, more or less, mismanaged, relatively nonfunctional and really of little use. Similarly, the labour market, on account of the greater supply of the labour force mushrooming due to lack of systematic programmes for human resources management, has virtually lost its credibility in the eyes of the competent and well-qualified job-seekers. Different states, except a very few, can be seen to be bearing the major brunt of employment-shrinkage (Ramesh, 1994). The market providing salaried employment, as it has been indicated by Sinha (1996), appears to be virtually exhausted — there is almost a glut in that market. But, hopes for a better tomorrow, though a faint one, seems still alive among the unemployed in India simply because of different reformative as well as challenging steps initiated, of late, by the government on the front of employment generation. In compendium, such a diverse perception of intervention programmes, as well as employment market may naturally lead to mixed psychological reactions among the unemployed. In other words, while the hopes for being gainfully employed would predominate their psyche, they may show a decline, though not more, in their symptoms. On the other hand, the reverse would follow in the case of the dwindling of such hopes in them. It should be noted here that hopes, according to Erikson (1963), refer to the psychological strength which is gained from successful resolution of the *trust-versus-mistrust conflict.* Thus, why an inconsistent pattern of stabilization effect appears among the long-term educated unemployed in India may well be comprehended in the light of the aforementioned discussion. Indeed, a long-term unemployed in India may clearly be found hanging between hope and hopelessness on account of the conflicting situation arising from the confusing and relatively less prudent employment policy, as well as intervention programmes. Thus, in the light of the convictions of Kieselbach (1990b), it is being suggested that the social context of unemployment ought to be taken into account while analysing the development of adaptation and stabilization of the psychological well-being among the long-term unemployed; it may change their course to a substantial degree. Adaptaion or stabilization is not a general rule. As may commonly be seen, there are considerable differences in the availability of welfare benefits among various countries, and that may account much for producing different patterns of adaptation and stabilization among the people continuously unemployed over a long period of time.

2. There could not be identified a group of technically or non-technically educated unemployed young men for a specific period as psychologically more vulnerable : while some health indices were found to be abnormally high in the case of 0-1 year group of the unemployed, some others were found in the case of 1-2 year group of the unemployed, and yet others in the rest of the groups out of jobs for various distinct spells. However, each of the exclusive groups of the technically and non-technically educated unemployed, particularly for shorter (i.e., 0-1 year) and longer durations, excepting the group of unemployed engineers in which 2-3 year group was found to be more prone to psychological ill-health, and the unemployed for longer durations such as 3-4 and more than 4 years were seen as showing gradual fall in their psychological risk, were altogether greatly susceptible to psychological impairment. Although the satisfaction with life in any of the groups of the unemployed over a period not exceeding one year did not come down sharply; it was appreciably high in all of them, but was altogether seen to decrease gradually with the addition in the duration of joblessness of various distinct groups of the educated young men of every discipline. Notwithstanding, all the groups of educated young men, barring a few exceptions, out of job for one or another duration, on the whole, were highly oppressed with reduced psychological health without, however, transcending the moderate level. In other words, duration of unemployment, by and large, appeared to have a homogenizing effect, with similarly poor psychological health in each of the groups confronting one or another distinct duration of unemployment.

The greater decline in psychological health among all the exclusive groups of the educated young men jobless for a period of 0-1 year, relying upon the widely-held assertions of Warr (1987 c, d, e), may reasonably be attributed to rapid decrements in most of the environmental opportunities such as availability of money (feature number 6), physical security (feature number 7), control over one's activities and events (feature number 1), use of skills (feature number 2), ability to predict and plan (feature number 5 — the environmental clarity), social contact (feature number 8) and valued social position (feature number 9) during the initial days of joblessness. Such decrements, according to Warr (1987c,d,e), precede the development of a variety of problems at all fronts of life, more likely resulting in sharp deterioration in the psychological well-being of those who have been faced with it. The views certainly hold their applicability across cultures. A good number of investigators (Feather, 1990; Kieselbach, 1991; O'Brien and Feather, 1990; Singh, 1994, 2001; Singh, Singh and Rani, 1996 a, b) have used them as bases particularly for the psychological explanation of the impact of the status of employment on well-being. But, it appears pertinent to note here that what yields more adverse effects on the psychological well-being is perhaps the greater uncertainty accompanied by the initial period of unemployment all around in the life of a person endangered with it. Noticeably, with the sudden onset of joblessness, a person afflicted with it, as warranted by Warr (1987 c,d,e,f), as well as common observation, has to strive to deal with the complexities of official procedures, learn about job-seeking practices, take up new patterns of interaction with family members, evaluate him/her or himself/herself in relation to personal values, and experience unusual pressures from outside people. In brief, an unemployed is required to develop a new pattern of adaptation. But, this is not an easy task, especially with the possibility of immediate gains in the attainment. He or she may confront a lot of conflict and tension in this course (Hertz, 1988; Hooge, 1995; Kieselbach, 1987b; Stokes, 1983; Verkleij, 1989), most possibly, as it has been reported (Singh, 1997; Sinha, 1990; Srivastava, 1990, 1995), exposing him or her to particularly high psychological risk.

Perceived value of education in the life of the Indian also deserves special attention in order to elucidate the findings. As may be commonly observed, despite constant and well-intended efforts, particularly initiated after independence, to make the Indian education system scientifically as well as realistically more relevant to the wishes and aspirations of the masses, no significant gains could be achieved so far. It may seem to be inherent with numerous drawbacks, particularly in its being not basically job-oriented. Even the higher and the technical education can be found to be deficient in many ways which defeats their real objectives. In consequence, the charm for such education, as it may be commonly observed, has decreased to a considerable degree in recent years. Yet, in the eyes of the majority of the people, the higher, especially the technical or professional, education is, by and large, conceived as promoting desired skills and competence for securing a livlihood and employment. So, if an Indian, in spite of all flaws of the current educational system, enters the higher, mainly the technical or professional, education, he/she joins it with certain hopes and aspirations of being gainfully employed after the completion of his or her education. But, as he/she suddenly finds that his or her educational qualification and competence are not going to do any immediate good to him or her in the face of a large-scale unemployment besetting the fate of the entire nation, his or her dreams are shattered. This, more likely, puts him/her in danger of psychological imbalance; manifestation of reactions like anxiety, stress, feeling of insecurity, alienation, identity-crisis, dissatisfaction with life, etc., in some form or the other becomes quite pronounced.

The findings, indicating the long-term educated unemployed people, in general, as plagued with greater psychological damage, show certain departure from the conclusion drawn by the Sheffield group of psychologists in this connection. As it may be envisaged, besides a few exceptions, no positive adaptation could be marked among any of the exclusive groups of the technically and the non-technically educated young men in India out of job for quite a long duration. Reasons for the findings are not far to seek; they may be searched out in various prevailing theoretical and empirical facts as well as existing socio-cultural realities of India. One such plausible ground may be found in the work of Dohrenwend *et al.* (1980). According to them, despite all possible sources available for the maintenance of psychological harmony, people facing prolonged unemployment often feel themselves demoralized. This results in lack of self-confidence, helplessness, hopelessness, inefficiency, fatalism, undefined fear of the future, depressed mood, etc. These are some of the significant symptomatic reactions which may very well give an account of poor psychological well-being (Abramson, Seligman and Teasdale,1978; Quay and LaGreca, 1986; Rani, 1993; Rosenhan and Seligman, 1984; Seligman, 1975; Warr, 1987d). It would not be imprudent to note here that our society, as held by Kieselbach (1990 b), usually reacts to the unemployed with a *'victim-blaming attitude.'* As such, those remaining unemployed for longer periods are perceived as personally responsible for their lot, despite the mass unemployment being a hard social reality almost on a universal scale. In other words, they are socially devalued by the society (Fryer and Winefield, 1998 ; Kieselbach, 1991; Kieselbach, Beelmann and Stitzel, 2000; Warr, 1985). Such a negative attitude towards the unemployed most likely makes them feel utterly demoralized. In consequence, they may lose their hope for any kind of positive change in their life, albeit only to accuse themselves for their fate to continue with this stigmatized social position all along the life for no fault of theirs.

Thus, they develop defeatism, frustration, and carry with them a considerable lack of the feeling of self-respect and strength as well. All these unwholesome changes ultimately lead to a considerable damage to their psychological well-being. In the light of the above discussion, if we contemplate the psychological well-being of the long-term educated unemployed in India, a somewhat different picture could come out. Interestingly, unlike the west, the unemployed in India have various ways to relieve their tension and conflict aggravated by their condition of worklessness. Singh (1994), Singh, Singh and Rani (1996 b) have recently referred to one such strategy, called as *'identification effect'* which may enable the unemployed to allay their anxiety and tension by associating with those who have a similar history.

Another commonly practised approach relates to their *chalega* attitude (compromising attitude) which, according to Kanungo (1995), may urge them to accept, and to remain content with the *status quo* and mediocrity. A greater amount of *putra* or *santan moha* (an obsessed attachment to son or children) in Indian parents and elders, in particular, may also serve as a succour to the unemployed by instilling in them the feeling of being loved, liked and accepted to a considerable degree in their family and society. This, in turn, helps them to attenuate their stress and strain arising out of the long spell of their joblessness, and thus enabling them to fight the psychological nuisance and unstability. Added to them are loafing, gossiping, politicking, etc., some of the societal strategies which are generally devised by the long-term unemployed in order to release their tension and distress. But, it seems not imprudent to note here that the Indian mind and life philosophy have changed considerably with the fast changing socio-politico-economic scenario in the country in recent years.

As may commonly be observed, different socially esteemed qualities like *sneh* (affection), *shradha* (reverence), sacrifice, sensitivity for others, penance, philanthropism, etc., have considerably lost their significance in the life of the Indian, and hankering after economic affluence, on the other hand, has gained higher value. Familial and social ties, and kinship bonds have markedly weakened gradually, more so in the urban setting. It would be not an exaggeration to mention here that nobody likes to extend help without any expectation of return. Indeed, *svartha* (personal interest), of late, relatively comes in a big way in governing one's action and behaviour in any particular situation (Chakraborty, 1995; Dayal, 1988; Singh, 1997; D. Sinha, 1988; J.B.P. Sinha, 1982a). In such situations, can an unemployed, particularly a long-term one, hope for an adequate help and support from his/her family and society ? Not surprisingly, he/she, instead of being helped and solaced, falls prey to various depreciating remarks of even his/her near and dear ones, and, in effect, completely runs under constant pressures of agony and disappointment with no hope for tangible change. This situation becomes relatively distressing as well as aggravating if he/she hails from a poor or middle-class family with no or a very few supportive hands (Singh, 1990; 1994; Singh, Singh and Rani, 1996 a; see chapter 5th for details). Such a state of affairs may not only distort his/her perception of himself/herself, but also of the society as well. He/she may conceive himself/herself as an economic liability for his/her family and society, depending always on the mercy of outside forces for his/her maintenance. This, in turn, more likely encourages in him/her the development of a greater feeling of demoralization. And a continuous and prolonged demoralization, as it has been shown (Council of Europe, 1985; Dohrenwend *et al.*, 1980; Feather, 1990; Liem, 1988), may lead to the exacerbation of various psychological reactions such as lack of self-confidence, helplessness, hopelessness, undefined fear of the future, depression, etc; symptomatic of anxiety, stress, feeling of insecurity, alienation, decreased life satisfaction and identity-crisis (Khan and Hassan, 1983; Kumari, Sinha and Singh, 1996; Kureshi and Dutt, 1979; Rani, 1993; Rosenhan and Seligman, 1984; Sarafino, 1990; Singh, Singh and Sinha, 1996; Sinha, 1979; Uniyal and Joshi, 1978).

Thus, in India, too, what accounts more for deterioration in the psychological well-being of the educated young people unemployed for longer durations fairly appears to be associated with their greater feeling of demoralization caused by the frequent failures in securing a job, despite their awareness of being well-qualified and competent—a factor, according to Jackson (1988), propping among the victim the feeling of abrupt denial of their skills and experience, and thus promoting in them a reduced feeling of personal efficacy.

A Cumulative Stress Model presented by Jackson and Warr (1984) may also be taken into account to justify the findings. The model, more specifically, enunciates that in addition to the shock of becoming jobless, remaining without a job leads to the breaking out of a range of stressors (viz., psychological, social and economic) which cumulatively impair the well-being of those who have been afflicted with it. These may range from threats to self-esteem arising from frequent failures to secure a job to the need for greater personal and financial adjustments as time passes. On the basis of such a cumulative stress model, Jackson and Warr (1984) have attempted to generalize that a prolonged period of unemployment would increase considerable psychological risk. Feather (1982) and Stafford, Jackson and Banks (1980) have also indicated that involuntary and prolonged loss of work is substantially associated with various symptoms of psychological ill-health. On the basis of their studies, Lahelma and Kangas (1989) and Verkleij (1989) have also reported that people out of job for longer durations more likely show an increment in their psychological stress scores, if any thing. Thus, the reason why the educated unemployed young men faced with long-term unemployment report more deterioration in their psychological health appears to be fairly well investigated. It may commonly be observed that with the increase in the duration of joblessness, there increases the probability of the worsening of the psycho-social situation. Unemployment, according to Chakrapani (1995, 1996), more precisely, in the Indian context, represents a unique stress situation because, while in other kinds of stress an individual may cope with the stress (demand) by making appropriate efforts or adjustments to acquire the needed response potentials, in unemployment no such actions enable him/her to get rid of the problem or restore balance and equipoise. The individual's demand on the environment persists, and remains unmet or unsatisfied as long as job opportunities fail to open up. Unemployment is, indeed, a generalised objective structural feature over which the individual has almost no control.

And stress, as Dodge and Martin (1970) assert, is a product of specific socially structured situations inherent in the organization of modern technological societies. It should be noted that a continuous and prolonged unemployment is more likely to produce a greater amount of stress which, more often than not, manifests in terms of anxiety, emotionality, depression, maladjustment, hostility, psychiatric morbidity, psychological disability, etc. (Chakrapani, 1995, 1996) — certain symptomatic reactions of reduced psychological health. Unemployment, undeniably, is as debilitating physio-psychologically as it is financially (Aggarwal and Goyal, 2000; Nelson, 1974). It, according to Kieselbach (1989), always leads to a multiple affliction with psychological, social, familial, financial and health problems. And, an increse in its duration is likely to make its effects more complicated.

Harrison's (1976) discussion, mostly based upon the conclusion of Eisenberg and Lazarsfeld (1938), may also provide a plausible basis in order to rationalize the findings picturing the long-term unemployed as beset with poor psychological well-being. According to Harrison (1976), prolonged unemployment, in most of the people, usually props the development of acute personal dilemmas and fundamental questions about their identity and value to society. Following a lead from Bakke's (1933) *Greenwich study,* Harrison has further underscored that long-term unemployment is especially stressful for those who are ambitious and previously successful. In the light of the above assertions, if we desire to analyse the state of the long-term educated unemployed in India, it would be right to mull over the problems associated with the acquisition of higher education, particularly the technical and professional ones. As per the strict statutory provision existing in India, a person can enter higher, more especially the technical or professional, education only after being declared successful in different competitive examinations organized to select suitable candidates. An individual's dreams and wishes are fulfilled only after being suitably and gainfully employed. It should be noted here that all such education in India is a relatively costly affair. Apart from other ordeals, one has to meet with a great amount of expenditure to acquire knonwledge and education, particularly the professional acumen and proficiency. But in the face of an acute shortage of jobs in the country, what remains for that person is unemployment. Highly educated and well-qualified persons are the worst victims of the problem of unemployment, constituting about 75.28 per cent of the total unemployed force in the country by the end of 1995 (*Chronicle Year Book,* 1999; p.464). Evidently, they find that there is no way out but to surrender themselves to their fate. As has been indicated earlier, even if there are schemes for their support at both governmental and non-governmental levels, for whatever reason they are often considered by them to be of no use. This sorry state of affairs impels them to feel that they are being denied their due from all quarters. It is remarkable that one cannot continue with the trauma of injustice for long; one has to succumb in the end.

Obviously, such a situation more likely shatters the whole psychological foundation of the unemployed : vulnerability to different symptomatic reactions such as anxiety, stress, feeling of insecurity, alienation, dissatisfaction with life and identity-crisis in their various manifestations — some of the significant indicators of psychological impairment — often then becomes considerably pronounced. Thus, repeated failures of our highly educated and well-qualified young men to earn a livelihood may be accounted for as one of the significant causative forces underlying the greater deterioration in the psychological health of the long-term educated unemployed young men in India. Ironically, education — once considered to be a sure way of getting a satisfactory employment— has pathetically failed in linking one to gainful employment in the present context. In other words, education in India is not job-oriented; it apparently lacks pragmatism, especially in terms of the acquisition of economic independence and prosperity.

In making further attempt to deal with the findings we may also depend on the views of a good number of investigators (Feather and Davenport, 1981; Feather and O'Brien, 1986b; Liem, 1988). These investigators have clearly indicated that the prolonged period of unemployment results in qualitative changes in causal attributions for being unemployed, and that usually shift from external to internal, despite a considerable evidence that many of the causes of unemployment are external and socio-economic. This shifting becomes more evident, especially when the persons concerned fail to obtain employment, despite their relentless efforts, and find that others — similar to them in many respects — finally succeed in securing a job (Feather and O'Brien, 1986 b). This, more often than not, compels them to see themselves as deficient in their ability and competence, predisposing in them, as it has been reported (Feather and Barber, 1983), the development of low self-esteem, higher level of depression, and feeling of hopelessness and helplessness — by and large strongly associated with many a symptom like anxiety, stress, feeling of insecurity, alienation, identity-crisis, etc., to some extent or other, of poor psychological well-being (Singh, 2001).

The theory of Social Exchange, as dealt with in chapter 2, also enunciates that such situations may lead to a series of reactions to distributive justice symptomatic of psychological impairment. The study by P. Singh (1985) has also demonstrated that an inequitable distribution of reward makes an individual feel himself/herself distressed and dissatisfied, and also leads him/her to express various negative reactions towards role allocator. Studies like those conducted by Frese (1985), Gurney (1981), Janoff-Bulman (1979), Kessler, House and Turner (1987), Kieselbach and Svensson (1988), Liem (1988) and Schore (1984) have also indicated that recurrent self-blaming for unemployment is threatening to one's emotional equipoise and psychological well-being. It may cause a number of symptomatic reactions like loss of self-respect, self-efficacy, self-confidence, anxiety, worry, apathy, irritation, sense of guilt, helplessness, etc. More obviously, it, as Schore (1984), in particular, holds, may often lead to many destructive consequences both for the workers and their families.Thus, the reason why the people afflicted with long-term unemployment manifests a sharp deterioration in their psychological health appears to be fairly vindicated in the light of the abovementioned discussions.The arguments may definitely be found to be accredited with a fair amount of reality and precision. Nonetheless, there still exists a wrangle whether the imputing of self or outside forces for being unemployed is dangerous to psychological health. The findings are rather conflicting in this regard. Notably, contrary to the aforementioned convictions, there are studies (Lefcourt, 1982; O'Brien, 1984 a,b, 1986; Spector, 1982) which record that a recurrent mode of accusing the outside forces for governing one's plight also does not always help one maintain a benign psychological health. Further, it seems also reasonable to look at the findings of Feather (1990) and Kelley (1967).

These findings have indicated that people tend to blame themselves rather than the perceptible situational constraints during the periods of low rather than high unemployment. The views held by Langer (1983) also seem relevant to mention here. According to him, people tend to attribute their negative states more to causal features in the environment than to aspects of themselves, and that positive states are more likely to be thought of as being due to their own characteristics than to the environment. Thus, in the light of these findings, it might be thought that in a country like India, where the problem of unemployment — a major negative life event — has become quite alarming, the unemployed are not likely to accuse themselves for their state, but the outside forces, possibly one of the significant causative factors responsible for the decline in their psychological health. Seemingly, this is because a recently conducted study by Singh, Singh and Singh (1996) has clearly shown a pervasive tendency among the educated unemployed in India to lay blame on the constraints in the environment for their unemployment. Thus, it appears somewhat imprudent to elucidate the deterioration in the psychological health among the long-term educated unemployed solely in the light of the studies showing in them a marked tendency to blame themselves for their plight. Yet, the feasibility of the approach to deal with the psychological ill-health among the long-term unemployed on the basis of their self-blaming tendency cannot be challenged outright; the approach blends with a certain amount of reality. The realization that one's joblessness is self-inflicted is an exacerbating condition of the health effect of unemployment. Undeniably, unemployment, being stressful (Chakrapani, 1995,1996; Kessler, House and Turner, 1987), causes a considerable deterioration in the health of the people by arousing a persistent tendency in them to accuse themselves for their joblessness. Kelvin and Jarrett (1985) have also focused that the shifting of onus from the self to extraneous forces helps the unemployed to inure themselves to their plight by reducing the damage caused by the acceptance of personal responsibility for their predicament. Thus, in all, an attempt to judge the reduced psychological well-being among the long-term educated unemployed in the light of their self-blaming tendency may be subjected to questions, yet its genuinity as one of the convincing and provident tools for explanation can in no way be altogether ignored. It may commonly be observed, as the hopes for finding a job wear off, that the unemployed usually begin to accuse themselves for their failure, making their cognition of themselves, as Kelvin and Jarrett (1985) hold, more or less, distorted. Dejection and disappointment escalate all along in their life (Higgins,1987), and the manifestation of different negative feelings (such as shame, embarrassment, sense of self-defeat, frustration, etc.) becomes markedly frequent in their behaviour (Kieselbach, 1991; Kieselbach, Beelmann and Stitzel, 2000; Kumari, 2001; Rani, 1993; Verkleij, 1989).

And, all these changes may clearly witness the deterioration in their psychological health. Virtually, it might be another facet of discussion that the unemployed often tend to ascribe their failure in securing an employment to various outside factors, particularly their fate. Although fate, too, is generally conceived to be one's own inner property which is, even in the eyes of a modern and progressive Indian, by and large, shaped with the very inception of the embryo, that only the will of the Almighty — the *Parama Brahma* — can effect a change in it. So, it would not be wrong to conclude that if an individual blames his/her fate for his/her joblessness, he/she is actually accusing himself/herself for the same — certainly one of his/her innate inner resources. It is, therefore, suggested that one ought to be moderate in one's views while familiarizing with various important indigenous concepts such as fate, conceived to be the determiner of every good and bad event in one's life, with a view to employing it as one of the devices for the explanation of the psychological consequences of prolonged unemployment. Not irrelevantly, the meaning and importance of such a concept largely depends on the culture-specific value attached to it.

The findings obtained in quite a good number of studies (Broomhall and Winefield, 1990; Hepworth, 1980; Jackson, 1988; Jackson and Warr, 1984; Kieselbach, Beelmann and Stitzel, 2000; Kilpatrick and True, 1985; Rowely and Feather, 1987; Smith, 1991; Tselepi and Agrafiotis, 1997; Warr, 1987d; Warr and Jackson, 1985, 1987; Warr, Jackson and Banks, 1982; Winefield, 1995b) may also form yet another plausible ground to further explicate the findings. These studies have clearly indicated that the middle-aged people (20–59 years), as compared to the teenagers (16–19 years) and the older people closer to retirement (60–64 years), are particularly vulnerable to reduced psychological health. In the light of the aforementioned findings, if we look into the basic qualifications required for employment in public and private sector organizations in India, a clear picture about the psychclogical state of the long-term educated unemployed may very well emerge. It should be mentioned that in addition to various other qualifications, a person usually becomes employable only after crossing the age of about 20 years, and remains so by the age of about 30 years. However, this limit may slightly vary from one state to another, largely depending on the state employment policy aimed at achieving the objective of 'full employment', the nature of the jobs and the immediate situations calling for a fresh recruitment. It may also ease for the scheduled castes and the tribes, as well as the backward class people under the clauses of job reservation policy proposed to provide them more opportunities to enter the jobs, and thus to attain a relatively healthy and socially acceptable life.

Thus, unlike in the west, the juveniles or the teenagers almost below the age of 21 years looking for employment are not considered as unemployed in India. However, like other under-developed and developing nations, India, too, is greatly hit by the problem of child and juvenile labour — one of the important indicators of a backward economy — involved in one or another petty job hardly conforming to the prescribed norms of the Indian Labour Penal Code (Jain, 1996). But, a child or a teenage employed in various clandestine jobs, in the eyes of an Indian, is not usually considered employed. It is not a service in the true sense of the term; it is just a means to earn something to secure a square meal in the absence of an adequate human resource development programme even after more than half a century of independence, despite big promises at official level, which are far from being congruent to the ambitions of the poor and the downtrodden. A job or service — a contractual relationship in essence, and distinct from work, a duty performed for the sake of one's family (Sinha and Sinha,1988; Tripathi,1995) —is one which is normally achieved either in public or private sector enterprises after fulfilling the prerequisites associated with the acquisition of that job. To summarize, all who are hankering after jobs are not officially designated as unemployed in India; only those are labelled as jobless who have been workless even after approaching the age of 21 year, besides fulfilling other conditions for the jobs which they aspire to find.

It may be recalled, all the groups of participants involved in this investigation were aged between 22 and 34 years with the mean age of about 30 years — the employable population in undivided Bihar, fairly representing the middle-aged group. It seems relevant to mention here that this is the age around which the Indians, particularly the males, in general, get married, have children, and bear the burden of their nurture and upbringing. Added to them, they are expected to maintain not only themselves, but also their parents and other dependents, especially if they continue to be part of an extended family — one of the significant characteristics of the Indian society and culture, despite a good amount of changes manifested in the Indian social life in recent years.

To summarize, in India, too, this is not an age of loitering and merry-making, but an age of shouldering various social responsibilities and obligations which cannot be carried on with an empty pocket. Indeed, early middle-aged men, as Estes and Wilensky (1978) maintain, are particularly prone to a family *"life-cycle squeeze"*. In other words, their family responsibilities are much greater, and so are their financial commitments. This focuses the importance of paid or gainful employment for them. Thus, why the educated young men out of job for a longer spell tend to manifest various problems in their psychological functioning stands fairly vindicated in the light of the above arguments; their inability to carry out their responsibilities to their family effectively in absence of gainful employment may clearly be thought of as being responsible for all sorts of psychological nuisances in their life (Jackson, 1988). Obviously, the young adult people, as Levinson *et al.* (1978) hold, have usually two broad life tasks to accomplish at this age —one, to achieve economic independence, and another, to take on family responsibility. And, unemployment, more often than not, acts as a barrier to the successful accomplishment of both of them which may ultimately lead to many a symptomatic reaction in those who have been afflicted with it. The condition of unemployment, undeniably, puts an individual into a state of crisis and confusion where the problem of psychological imbalance is only natural. In short, that unemployment, as Smith (1991) holds, is a killer — particularly of the middle-aged people — has now become irrefutable.

3. Both the groups of the technically and the non-technically educated young men employed for one or another duration, like all the groups of their unemployed counterparts, were, by and large, moderately susceptible to reduced psychological health, but not so seriously as it was noticed in the case of the latter. The groups of the employed that were indentified as more oppressed with various syndromes of psychological impairment were clearly associated with the shorter and the longer durations. However, the employed for all the durations were obviously well satisfied with the order of their life. Thus, the results, on the whole, formed a U-shaped pattern in relation to the impact of the duration of employment on psychological health, if measured in terms of the degree and extent of anxiety, stress, feeling of insecurity, alienation, identity-crisis and their dimensions, excepting the index of life satisfaction.

An inconducive job environment, especially prevailing all over the state public enterprises in eastern India, as well as the inability of an employee to stand satisfactorily by various cross demands simultaneously arisen out of the real life situations and the work environment may, here too, be taken into consideration in order to understand the overall moderate deterioration in the psychological state of the educated young men in jobs for various distinct durations. See chapter 5, where the two provocative situations have been extensively addressed. Undeniably, working in such situations for an employed in India more likely develops in him/her a tendency to compromise reluctantly at every front of his/her life which is not always supportive to his/her psychological health, though only prompting a moderate risk.

But, quite surprisingly, people in jobs both for shorter and longer durations in India have been found to be psychologically more vulnerable, and that deserves serious concern. First, we may take into account the psychological state of the educated young men employed for just a short span. Keeping in view the worst ever employment scenario in the country, it may clearly be thought that securing a job, for a person, in India in the face of a large-scale unemployment, would definitely appear as a relief. Further, a little fear of abrupt termination or retrenchment among the workers in Indian organizations before completing the age of retirement, mainly because of the liberal and humanistic Labour Act, as well as a strong hold of trade unionism on the functioning of an organization, may also make finding a job amply satisfying. Nonetheless, finding a job, as it may be commonly observed, as also it has been revealed (Kieselbach, 1990b), clearly accompanies new experiences for the entrants — experiences with which they are not generally accustomed. Noticeably, they are not only required to forget the behaviours associated with the unemployed role, but also to acquire an adequate ability and competence to equip themselves to the demands enjoined with the employed role. They also need to adopt new routines and often fit themselves even with worse job characteristics. Added to them, they are expected to develop a new interaction pattern with quite alien people like superiors, subordinates and co-workers. In summary, they have to learn a lot to adapt to entirely novel life situations, by and large, less clear and less well-defined in most of the Indian organizations (Kanungo,1995). And, as it may commonly be observed, this is not quite easy for the novices and the inexperienced people to imbibe all these qualities necessary to their effective adaptation to the organization in a short time. In consequence, the newcomers may confront numerous problems at every level of their functioning at the initial period of their employment. This most likely exposes them to negative life experiences which may ultimately increase different symptomatic reactions frequently marked by a greater amount of anxiety, stress, feeling of insecurity, alienation, identity-crisis, dissatisfaction, and so on. Studies on entrance in new, especially 'bad'jobs, job-transitions and work-role ambiguity (Billings and Moos,1982; Burke, 1986; Dijkhuizen, 1980; Firth,1985; Fryer and Winefield, 1998; Kanungo,1995; Kieselbach, 1990 b; Latack, 1984; Payne, 1995; Srivastava, 1995; Werbel, 1983; Winefield, 1995a; Winefield *et al.*, 1993) may reasonably vindicate the ubiquity of the aforementioned arguments. These studies, in essence, may clearly provide reason to believe that the initial phase of employment, on account of its largely being associated with lack of clarity everywhere, is not conducive to psychological health. Virtually, there are no clear job expectations regarding what the employees are supposed to do on the job. Further, it is also not clearly known to them whether they can get what they value most through their job behaviour for the satisfaction of their important needs. This situation of uncertainty is extremely exasperating, considerably jeopardizing their psychological balance.

The assertions made in a good number of investigations (Gardell, 1971; Hartley *et al.*, 1991; Iversen and Sabroe,1988; Iversen, Sabroe and Damsgaard,1989; Kanungo, 1995; Singh, Kumari and Singh,1992; Singh *et al.*, 2005; Singh, Singh and Rani,1996a, b; Warr,1987c, d; Winefield, 1995a; Winefield, Tiggemann and Goldney, 1988) may reasonably be taken into account in order to form a possible basis on which to rationalize the greatly reduced psychological health among the educated young men in jobs in India for quite a long period. These investigations have clearly shown that low or inadequate salary and irregularity in its payment more often prove deterimental to psychological well-being in particular, considerably arousing a variety of erratic and maladaptive behaviours in an individual.

The aforementioned assertions, if reasonably apt in their predictability and generality, the relation existing between the expectations towards an employed in an Indian family and the greater inadequacy and irregularity prevalent in the salary and other pecuniary benefits paid to him/her deserves thorough inquiry in order to explore the clues underlying the psychological affliction of the educated employed in India for longer durations. Not impertinently, an empolyed in India, particularly if he/she belongs to a lower or middle-class family, and incidentally is the only earning member therein, is generally expected to bear every responsibility of the family. Bringing about all-round pride and prosperity to his/her family is, indeed, his/her sole responsibility — the basic *dharma* (the prime duty). Precisely, all hopes and desires of the family apparently stick to him/her. Further, it should also be noted here that the concern for the welfare of the family, frequently shaped in the form of *moha* (an obsessed attachment), especially towards the spouse, the children, and the ageing parents, gradually increases with the increase in age, and this greatly involves the earning member who always hankers after getting everything well-settled during the tenure of his/her service. Virtually, an employed in India is usually believed to be the *ox* — the humble being who bears any load without complaint — of a bullock-cart on whose shoulders largely depend all the responsibility to drive the whole family to affluence and distinction — the high socially valued destination. In other words, he/she is expected not only to comply with the consensual and normative demands of the family but also to push the family to the peak of glory and opulence in return for the obligation of the family on him/her in the form of various sacrifices, particularly the economic one, during the period of his/her career-building. Failing to discharge it properly is likely to tarnish his/her image and prestige not only in the family but also in the society at large. But, as has already been pointed out earlier in the 5th chapter, there are many governmental concerns, especially in the eastern Indian states, where an employee has even to remain without salary for months together — not to talk of other facilities available to him/her as per the provisions made in the Indian service code. Noticeably, payment of salary in various governmental enterprises is so irregular and inadequate that it is hardly possible for him/her to keep all the promises to his/her family. He/she, of course, often runs into hardship; even to meet the basic requirements of the family in the face of an unprecedented price-rise in the country sometimes becomes problematic for him/her. This state of affairs is likely to develop in him/her an increased amount of tension and conflict, most probably liable for all sorts of psychological nuisances in his/her life.

Yet, another prospective reason to further justify a greater amount of psychological decline among the groups of the technically and the non-technically educated people employed for long may be searched out by the analysis of the conclusion drawn by Büssing (1987, 1990). The conclusion — almost congruent to the preceding one in its spirit of generality and prediction — clearly affirms that the prolonged or continued experience of a precarious job by an employed may adversely affect his/her psychological well-being, more often precipitating in him/her various apparent symptoms of depressive disorders. In the light of the aforementioned assertion, if we look at the organizational climate as it especially exists in most of the public concerns in India, workers at every level, as it has been indicated in the 5th chapter, would be found to be imperilled by a certain amount of uncertainty and precariousness as well as all kinds of insecurity prevailing therein. It has clearly become difficult for them to cope with excessive political pressures frequently appearing even in their daily routines (Singh, Singh and Rani, 1996 b; Tripathi, 1995). Personal initiative, originality and independence in thinking and decision-making in any of the affairs related to working life meet with social disapproval. They have to follow the tactics of blind conformity and compliance if they wish to sail better in their organizations (Kanungo,1995). In short, the organizational climate in India is in no way ideally conducive, and thus working therein for a long period, if the above assertion holds true in its intent, is likely to result in greater psychological harm. A good number of investigators (Arnetz *et el*, 1987; Beale and Nethercott,1986; Brenner and Levi, 1987b; Dooley, Rook and Catalano, 1987; Fryer and Winefield, 1998; Iversen and Sabroe, 1988; Payne, 1995; Ronayne, Ryan and Cullen, 1989; Winefield, 1995a) have also unanimously shown that such organizational environments lead to an eruption of various psychological problems in the life of an employed. Thus, why the people in jobs even for quite a long period in India have a poor psychological well-being may be understood in the light of the abovementioned discussion. Chronically precarious and altogether an unhealthy organizational climate in India may, indeed, be said to be responsible for all kinds of psychological inflictions in the life of an employee.

4. All the groups of the educated unemployed and employed young men for one or another duration, barring a few exceptions, were found to be greatly oppressed with an acute feeling of either uncertainty or social conflict, but very little with suicidal tendency. The findings have been well taken in the 5th and the 6th chapters. So, there is no need for their further justification. One may readily find a rationale from them to comprehend them. Yet, an attempt has been made to elucidate why a greater feeling of uncertainty overshadows the life of all the groups of the unemployed and employed people in India. As may commonly be observed, nothing is clearly defined in an Indian setting; everything, as it has been reported by Kanungo (1995) and J.B.P. Sinha (1982b), would appear delusive and ambiguous. Noticeably, mystery largely pervades Indian culture and personality (Chakraborty, 1991; Kapp, 1963; Sinha, 1988). In such a situation, it is not unlikely for all the groups of the educated unemployed and employed people to run a greater risk of uncertainty in their life. Virtually, to live in uncertainty, as it has been pointed out (Kanungo, 1995; J.B.P. Sinha, 1982b), has clearly taken the shape of a life-course for an Indian.

Suicidal tendency, conspicuous by its presence only in negligible amount, in all the groups of unemployed and employed people in India highlights their limitless *moha* (an obsessed fondness) for life generally conceived to be the most precious possession in the eyes of the majority of Indians. Interestingly, despite a good degree of scientific awareness and modernization, the precepts expressed in *Garuda Puranas* (chapter16; Hymn : 13 and 14) and *Ramcharita Manas* (1/8/1) still have a considerable influence on the mind of Indians in that one cannot attain human life unless and until one completes the life cycle of the entire 8.4 million species (*yonis*) supposed to be created by the *Parama Brahma* —the Supreme Power — in the universe by successfully performing the *dharma* (duty or moral conduct) and *karma* (moral practices) enjoined with each of the cycles. Even a minor fault on one's part in this long sojourn is not, in any way, condonable. One has to meet with a tough and stringent sanction — one has to freshly start one's journey and to successfully move across all the cycles unless the 'ultimate end' — *the attainment of human life* —is really achieved. In other words, one has to undergo an ordeal of the highest level of endless penance with *purna shardha* (complete reverence), *bhakti* (devotion), and, above all,with *purna atmasamarpan bhava* (sense of complete submission) for an undefined period, extending through successive births, in order to be able to alight in a human body (*manava tana*). Virtually, Indian psyche may yet be clearly found to be invigorated with the axiom depicted in the *Ramcharita Manas* (7/43/4 ; 7/121/5) that acquisition of human life is the singular bliss endowed by the Almighty. All the mobile and immboile beings (*char* and *achar jeevas*), as also the Supreme Being, aspire to enter the mortal coil of man. The human body is acceptedly the only sacred and sure means leading its captive soul to heaven and hell as well as *purna moksha* (the ultimate salvation) along with the acquisition of *parmanand gyana* (knowledge of the highest bliss), *bhakti* (devotion), and *vairagya* (detachment). It should also be mentioned that Indians, as Kakar (1978) feels, generally subscribe to the view that the world is a benign place and someone will always come to help, should an exigency arise.

Added to the above convictions, Indians are still thoroughly imbued with an expressive life philosophy as illustrated in various mythological literatures, especially in *Ishavasyopanishad* (Hymn : 3) that an attempt to commit suicide is the greatest vice. There is no excuse for it in the court of the Almighty; one would not only be denied salvation but would be condemned to live in hell eternally to suffer the 'stings and arrows' and the bitterest tortures. To summarize, the human life and the world, in the eyes of Indians, are all-adorable and beautiful, and an attempt to commit suicide is, in all ways, a challenge against, and definace of, the dictates of the Almighty. As such, Indians are seldom incited by an impulse to terminate their life despite sharp pricks from thorns of life and endless bleeding. The sufferings are, quite often, palliated as they are presumed to be the outcome of various external sources, especially the *prarabdha* (predestination), solely governed by the Almighty (Lapierre, 1986; Singh, Singh and Singh,1996). Although the incidence of suicide in India, as per a report compiled by the *National Crime Records Bureau 1998 (2000),* has increased at an alarming rate in recent years. As it is evident, the rate of suicides (the number of suicides per lakh of popuation) which has been recorded to be 8.1 in 1988 rose to 10.8 in 1998, registering an increase of 62.9 per cent during the decade. It is relatively high among the males (male-females fatality ratio = 59 : 41), among mega city (23 in all) dwellers (9.4%), and among those in the group of 15-29 years (37.6%) and 30-44 years (35.6%). The report has also indicated the factors leading to suicidal deaths. Of these, unemployment has been found to account for only 1.67 per cent of the total number of suicides, though it greatly implicates the males who stand at 86.42 per cent. However, in all, the incidence of suicides in India is still relatively low as compared to that in different affluent western and non-western countries where suicide has come out as one of major causes of death (Centres for Disease Control and Prevention, 1995; Neeleman, Wessly and Wadsworth, 1998; Schmidtke *et al.*, 1996). Further, an attempt to commit suicide or even to contemplate it in India, as it has been indicated above, is not, in any way, considered to be a socially approved behaviour. It is thought to be the most sinful act and is condemned on all hands. Thus, why all the exclusive groups of educated unemployed and employed people for various durations are apparently least prone even to suicidal ideation fairly stands vindicated in the light of the above arguments.

5. Irrespective of the experiences of different distinct durations of their exclusive status of unemployment and employment, all the groups of respondents tended to solely depend on intrapersistive approach mode in dealing with their environments. The findings are encouraging and really worthwhile. The 5th chapter records various plausible reasons which have been put forward to justify the greater leaning of the exclusively combined groups of the educated unemployed and employed young men towards intrapersistive approach mode to withstand the various events of life. The reasons are quite exclusive, and all-encompassing, and, thus, may, here too, be applicable in dealing with the findings (see chapter 5 for detail).

The second and last section of this chapter contains the quintessence of the results exclusively obtained from inter-group comparisons made among the various groups of the educated unemployed and employed young men for different specific durations, broadly ranging from 0-1 year to 7-above year, in terms of the level of anxiety, stress, feeling of insecurity, alienation, identity-crisis and life satisfaction — some of the potent indices of psychological well-being — at both macro and micro levels. Also, it subsumes the details of various strategies resorted to by them in order to meet the immediate demands of their environment. The subsequent pages record the findings and discussion thereof.

Level of Anxiety, Stress, Feeling of Insecurity, Alienation, Identity-Crisis and Their Dimensions : A Comparison Among Different Groups of Educated Unemployed and Employed Young Men for a Duration of 0-1 Year

Table 8.19 reports the findings of a statistical comparison among different groups of the educated unemployed and employed people for the shortest stint of 0-1 year in terms of their level of anxiety, stress, feeling of insecurity, alienation, identity-crisis and their various characteristic manifestations.

All the groups of educated unemployed and employed people for a period of 0-1 year were found to differ significantly from one another in terms of a good number of the abovementioned health indices, mostly associated with the dimensions of feeling of insecurity (F-values ranging from 2.37 to 3.55) and identity-crisis (F-values varied between 2.28 and 5.19). However, the findings obtained from the multiple-comparison between different pairs of means did not indicate so in most of the instances, the difference of one group from another was not found to be real. Most of them rather tended to manifest a greater similarity in their symptomatic reactions. Nevertheless, if there were recorded any meaningful differences between any two groups in their psychological reactions, they were, more often than not, between the groups quite distinct in their status of employment. Some of the prominent health indices, towards which the technically educated employed showed marked differences from one or the other exclusive group of the unemployed, involved the psychological dimensions like emotional instability (OQ = 2.08, 2.06; CQ = 1.93), emotional responsiveness (OQ = 2.64, 2.36; CQ = 1.28), withdrawal from social and personal contact (OQ = 0.84; CQ = 0.82), role conflict (OQ = 2.20; CQ = 2.21) and loneliness (OQ = 1.29;CQ = 0.90). The various striking psychological symptoms where the non-technically educated employed tended to differ significantly from one or the other group of the unemployed were general worries (OQ = 1.59; CQ = 1.36), emotional responsiveness (CQ = 1.33), isolation (OQ = 1.41; CQ = 1.39), role conflict (OQ = 2.92; CQ = 2.29), and loneliness (OQ = 1.12; CQ = 0.83). The results further revealed that the unemployed, particularly the degree-holders in the agriculture and the medical sciences, were greatly plagued with reduced psychological health.The employed, however, on the whole, were also not quite

Table 8.19 : Statistical Differences Among Different Groups of Educated Unemployed and Employed Young Men for a Duration of 0 -1 Year and their Relative Standing in Terms of Different Indices of Psychological Well-being

Indices of Psychological Well-being	*Unemployed*												*Employed*						
	Technically Educated									*Non-technically Educated (N=47)*			*Technically Educated (N=16)*			*Non-technically Educated (N=35)*			
	Degree-holders in Medical Sciences (N=15)			*Degree-holders in Engineering Sciences (N=15)*			*Degree-holders in Agriculture Sciences (N=20)*												
	Mean (%)	*SD*	*Rank*	*Mean (%)*	*SD*	*Rank*	*Mean (%)*	*SD*	*Rank*	*Mean (%)*	*SD*	*Rank*	*Mean (%)*	*SD*	*Rank*	*Mean (%)*	*SD*	*Rank*	*F*
1. General Worries	2.80 (46.67)	1.37	25	2.80 (46.67)	1.55	16	3.70 (61.67)	1.34	06	2.74 (45.67)	1.24	23	2.25 (37.50)	1.19	24	2.11 (35.17)	1.07	26	4.27
2. Somatic Manifestations	0.80 (26.67)	0.38	33	0.73 (24.33)	0.37	33	1.00 (33.33)	0.65	33	0.60 (20.00)	0.30	37	0.88 (29.33)	0.52	30	0.69 (23.00)	0.37	32	0.90
3. Psychological Symptoms	2.53 (50.60)	1.13	19	2.00 (40.00)	1.00	24	2.40 (48.00)	1.05	24	1.91 (38.20)	1.22	29	1.50 (30.00)	0.83	29	2.17 (43.40)	1.18	13	1.64
4. Social Relations	3.13 (39.13)	1.68	29	2.60 (32.50)	1.40	30.5	2.80 (35.00)	1.44	31	2.40 (30.00)	1.34	31	2.06 (25.75)	1.21	31	1.51 (18.88)	0.74	38	2.77
5. **Anxiety**	9.27 (42.14)	3.99	26	8.13 (36.95)	4.20	27	9.90 (45.00)	3.60	25	7.66 (34.82)	4.21	30	6.72 (30.55)	3.42	28	6.49 (29.50)	2.66	28	2.75
6. Suicidal Tendency	0.27 (6.75)	0.16	39	0.07 (1.75)	0.03	39	0.35 (8.75)	0.21	39	0.19 (4.75)	0.09	39	0.13 (3.25)	0.07	39	0.14 (3.50)	0.09	39	0.60
7. Emotional Instability	3.93 (49.13)	1.31	21.5	2.60 (32.50)	1.36	30.5	3.95 (49.38)	1.85	21	3.38 (42.25)	1.96	26	1.88 (23.50)	1.02	32	2.17 (27.13)	1.29	30	5.06
8. Paranoid Tendency	1.80 (15.00)	1.11	38	2.07 (17.25)	1.02	37	1.75 (12.50)	1.03	38	2.11 (17.58)	1.17	38	1.50 (12.50)	0.78	38	2.51 (20.92)	1.39	36	0.72
9. Depression	8.73 (24.25)	3.99	37	6.53 (18.14)	3.05	36	11.80 (32.78)	4.09	34	10.21 (28.36)	5.55	32	7.69 (21.36)	3.93	33	8.23 (22.86)	4.29	33	1.71

Contd.

Table 8.19 *(Contd.)*

Indices of Psychological Well-being	*Unemployed*												*Employed*						
	Technically Educated									*Non-technically Educated (N=47)*			*Technically Educated (N=16)*			*Non-technically Educated (N=35)*			
	Degree-holders in Medical Sciences (N=15)			*Degree-holders in Engineering Sciences (N=15)*			*Degree-holders in Agriculture Sciences (N=20)*												
	Mean (%)	*SD*	*Rank*	*Mean (%)*	*SD*	*Rank*	*Mean (%)*	*SD*	*Rank*	*Mean (%)*	*SD*	*Rank*	*Mean (%)*	*SD*	*Rank*	*Mean (%)*	*SD*	*Rank*	*F*
10. Physical Illness	3.07 (25.58)	1.69	34	2.33 (19.42)	1.18	35	2.65 (22.08)	1.43	37	2.74 (22.83)	1.18	35	1.94 (16.17)	1.04	37	3.37 (28.08)	1.82	29	1.14
11. Social Maladjustment	3.00 (25.00)	1.24	36	1.67 (13.92)	0.90	38	4.35 (36.25)	2.29	30	2.51 (20.92)	1.28	36	2.38 (19.83)	1.26	35	2.43 (20.25)	1.79	37	2.91
12. Apprehensive-ness	3.60 (30.00)	1.53	32	3.67 (30.58)	1.77	32	3.65 (30.42)	1.72	35	2.94 (24.50)	1.49	34	2.50 (20.83)	1.33	34	2.66 (22.17)	1.67	35	0.94
13. **Stress**	24.42 (25.44)	10.17	35	18.94 (19.73)	8.47	34	28.50 (29.69)	9.82	36	24.09 (25.09)	13.62	33	18.02 (18.77)	9.56	36	21.53 (22.43)	11.52	34	1.21
14. Lack of Self-confidence	12.60 (63.00)	4.37	04	10.13 (50.65)	3.97	05	10.25 (51.25)	4.89	16.5	11.11 (55.55)	5.27	06	9.82 (49.10)	2.92	05	9.66 (40.30)	3.17	20	2.18
15. Dejection	8.86 (59.07)	3.49	08	8.41 (56.07)	3.46	02	9.40 (62.67)	3.07	05	9.10 (60.67)	4.05	03	7.13 (47.53)	2.67	11	7.69 (51.27)	2.63	02	2.61
16. Pessimism	2.40 (48.00)	1.68	23	1.80 (36.00)	1.01	29	1.70 (34.00)	0.98	32	2.13 (42.60)	1.44	25	1.69 (33.80)	0.87	27	1.26 (25.20)	0.70	31	3.07
17. Emotional Responsiveness	16.33 (54.43)	5.64	14	14.33 (47.77)	5.19	11	16.05 (53.50)	5.23	13	14.50 (48.33)	7.68	17	13.69 (45.63)	4.02	13	12.45 (41.50)	3.64	18.5	3.55
18. Social Insecurity	12.33 (49.32)	4.55	20	10.27 (41.08)	4.38	23	10.25 (41.00)	4.43	28	11.94 (47.76)	5.82	19	10.19 (40.76)	3.22	21	8.79 (35.16)	3.02	27	2.37
19. Distrust	2.73 (54.60)	1.10	13	2.40 (48.00)	1.18	10	3.35 (67.00)	1.00	02	2.28 (45.76)	1.36	22	2.75 (55.00)	1.34	04	2.18 (43.60)	1.17	12	1.88

Contd.

Table 8.19 *(Contd.)*

Indices of Psychological Well-being	*Unemployed*												*Employed*						
	Technically Educated									*Non-technically Educated (N=47)*			*Technically Educated (N=16)*			*Non-technically Educated (N=35)*			
	Degree-holders in Medical Sciences (N=15)			*Degree-holders in Engineering Sciences (N=15)*			*Degree-holders in Agriculture Sciences (N=20)*												
	Mean (%)	*SD*	*Rank*	*Mean (%)*	*SD*	*Rank*	*Mean (%)*	*SD*	*Rank*	*Mean (%)*	*SD*	*Rank*	*Mean (%)*	*SD*	*Rank*	*Mean (%)*	*SD*	*Rank*	*F*
20. **Feeling of Insecurity**	55.27 (55.27)	16.85	11	47.34 (47.34)	11.54	13	51.04 (51.04)	13.35	18	51.09 (51.09)	16.49	11	45.27 (45.27)	12.75	15	42.05 (42.05)	10.52	16	2.84
21. Despair	16.40 (51.25)	4.07	17	16.07 (50.22)	3.59	07	17.65 (55.16)	3.63	11	17.06 (53.31)	3.79	07	15.31 (47.84)	3.89	08	15.06 (47.06)	4.91	08	1.61
22. Unstructured Universe	4.87 (60.88)	1.88	06	3.73 (46.63)	1.58	17	4.10 (51.25)	1.59	16.5	4.55 (56.88)	1.50	05	4.63 (57.88)	1.82	02	3.91 (48.88)	1.27	05	1.70
23. Psychological Vacuum	4.60 (57.50)	1.06	10	3.33 (41.63)	0.82	22	4.00 (50.00)	1.26	19.5	4.00 (50.00)	1.57	13	3.81 (47.63)	1.28	9.5	3.86 (48.25)	1.50	06	1.35
24. Disillusionment	2.20 (55.00)	0.94	12	1.47 (36.75)	0.74	28	1.70 (42.50)	0.66	26.5	1.94 (48.50)	0.87	16	1.69 (42.25)	0.79	19.5	1.57 (39.25)	0.61	23	2.35
25. Narcissism	1.40 (35.00)	0.51	31	1.67 (41.75)	0.82	21	1.70 (42.50)	1.03	26.5	1.60 (40.00)	0.83	28	1.56 (39.00)	0.89	22.5	2.29 (57.25)	1.25	01	0.61
26. **Alienation**	29.49 (52.66)	5.70	16	26.27 (46.91)	4.88	14	29.15 (52.05)	5.68	15	29.13 (52.02)	5.47	09	27.00 (48.21)	6.07	06	26.69 (47.66)	7.50	07	1.91
27. Depersonalization	3.27 (40.88)	1.33	28	3.07 (38.38)	0.96	25	3.90 (48.75)	0.79	22.5	3.72 (46.50)	1.61	21	3.38 (42.25)	1.82	19.5	3.17 (39.63)	1.22	22	1.37
28. Fragmentation	4.93 (61.63)	1.67	05	3.60 (45.00)	1.35	19	4.65 (58.13)	0.88	08	3.85 (48.13)	1.73	18	3.63 (45.38)	1.78	14	3.57 (44.63)	1.20	11	3.02
29. Uncertainty	2.80 (70.00)	1.08	01	3.00 (75.00)	0.65	01	2.75 (68.75)	0.97	01	2.55 (63.75)	1.02	02	2.38 (59.50)	0.96	01	2.03 (50.75)	0.89	03	3.21

Contd.

Table 8.19 *(Contd.)*

Indicès of Psychological Well-being	*Unemployed*												*Employed*						
	Technically Educated									*Non-technically Educated (N=47)*			*Technically Educated (N=16)*			*Non-technically Educated (N=35)*			
	Degree-holders in Medical Sciences (N=15)			*Degree-holders in Engineering Sciences (N=15)*			*Degree-holders in Agriculture Sciences (N=20)*												
	Mean (%)	*SD*	*Rank*	*Mean (%)*	*SD*	*Rank*	*Mean (%)*	*SD*	*Rank*	*Mean (%)*	*SD*	*Rank*	*Mean (%)*	*SD*	*Rank*	*Mean (%)*	*SD*	*Rank*	*F*
30. Distress	5.73 (47.75)	1.98	24	5.13 (42.75)	1.68	20	6.00 (50.00)	1.34	19.5	6.15 (51.25)	2.38	10	5.13 (42.75)	1.36	18	5.43 (45.25)	1.56	09	1.36
31. Indecisiveness	3.93 (49.13)	1.44	21.5	4.00 (50.00)	1.73	08	4.25 (53.13)	1.32	14	3.96 (49.50)	1.56	14.5	3.81 (47.63)	1.28	9.5	3.46 (43.25)	1.31	14	0.95
32. Social Conflict	2.73 (68.25)	0.96	02	2.13 (53.25)	0.83	3.5	2.60 (65.00)	0.94	04	2.64 (66.00)	0.87	01	2.31 (57.75)	0.87	03	2.00 (50.00)	1.00	04	2.83
33. Isolation	3.33 (41.63)	1.23	27	3.87 (48.38)	1.41	09	4.35 (54.38)	1.60	12	3.55 (44.38)	1.46	24	3.50 (43.75)	1.26	17	2.94 (36.75)	0.87	25	3.22
34. Withdrawal from Social and Personal Contact	1.47 (36.75)	0.74	30	1.87 (46.75)	0.74	15	2.40 (60.00)	0.68	07	1.68 (42.00)	0.89	27	1.56 (39.00)	0.81	22.5	1.80 (45.00)	0.80	10	3.24
35. Role Conflict	7.00 (58.33)	2.33	09	6.07 (50.58)	1.33	06	7.95 (66.25)	2.58	03	6.28 (52.33)	2.01	08	5.75 (47.92)	2.65	07	5.03 (41.92)	2.11	17	5.19
36. Hopelessness	4.07 (50.88)	1.58	18	3.67 (45.88)	1.72	18	3.25 (40.63)	0.91	29	3.96 (49.50)	1.63	14.5	2.94 (36.75)	1.06	25	3.20 (40.00)	1.43	21	2.28
37. Lonelinness	2.67 (66.75)	1.18	03	1.53 (38.25)	0.83	26	1.95 (48.75)	0.76	22.5	1.87 (46.75)	0.95	20	1.38 (34.50)	0.81	26	1.54 (38.50)	0.61	24	4.90
38. Desolation	2.40 (60.00)	0.91	07	2.13 (53.25)	0.92	3.5	2.30 (57.50)	0.80	09	2.32 (58.00)	1.09	04	1.88 (47.00)	0.81	12	1.66 (41.50)	0.84	18.5	2.78
39. **Identity-crisis**	44.33 (52.77)	11.64	15	40.09 (47.73)	9.38	12	46.35 (55.18)	6.85	10	42.57 (50.68)	13.31	12	37.65 (44.82)	9.74	16	35.83 (42.65)	9.08	15	3.46

Note : $df = 5,142$; $p < 0.05 = 2.27$; $p < 0.01 = 3.14$.

symptom-free. They, too, were, more or less, moderately afflicted with psychological ill-health. Moreover, it was found that besides the respective groups of non-technically educated unemployed and employed people, who felt the stress and distress of social conflict (66.00%) and narcissism (57.25%), all the groups of technically educated unemployed and employed young men were extremely troubled with the feeling of uncertainty (scores obtained by them ranged between 59.50 per cent and 75.00%). Nevertheless, there was no variation among the groups while an attempt was made to identify in them the least agonizing symptomatic reaction : perceptibly all of them were found to be least inclined towards suicidal tendency (their scores for suicidal tendency varied between 1.75 per cent and 8.75 per cent).

Life Satisfaction : A Comparison Among Different Groups of Educated Unemployed and Employed Young Men for a Duration of 0-1 Year

Table 8.20 contains the summary of a statistical comparison among different groups of educated unemployed and employed people in terms of the level of their life satisfaction.

Different groups of educated unemployed and employed young men for a short spell of 0-1 year showed a marked difference among themselves in the degree of their life satisfaction ($F = 2.80$; $df = 5,142$; $p<0.05$). But, the findings obtained from Newman-Keuls test showed that there were no clear-cut differences between any two groups in terms of the level of their life satisfaction, though the difference between the mean satisfaction scores of the unemployed degree-holders in the agriculture sciences (*Mean* = 5.20; *SD* = 2.69) and the non-technically educated employed people (*Mean* = 7.20; *SD* = 1.73) quite apparently approached the level of significance (the observed value of Q being 2.00 as against the criterion value of Q at 2.33). Further, it was recorded that except the group of unemployed degree-holders in agriculture sciences (52.00%), all the groups of participants, particularly the groups of technically (67.50%) and non-technically (72.00%) educated employed were highly contented with the goings of their life.

Table 8.20 : Statistical Differences Among Different Groups of Educated Unemployed and Employed Young Men for a Duration of 0-1 year and their Relative Standing in Terms of the Degree of their Life Satisfaction

	Unemployed								*Employed*				
	Technically Educated						*Non-technically Educated (N=47)*		*Technically Educated (N=16)*		*Non-technically Educated (N=35)*		
Variable	*Degree-holders in Medical Sciences (N=15)*		*Degree-holders in Engineering Sciences (N=15)*		*Degree-holders in Agriculture Sciences (N=20)*								
	Mean (%)	*SD*	*Mean (%)*	*SD*	*Mean (%)*	*SD*	*Mean (%)*	*SD*	*Mean (%)*	*SD*	*Mean (%)*	*SD*	*F*
Life satisfaction	6.13 (61.30)	2.20	5.87 (58.70)	2.66	5.20 (52.00)	2.69	5.81 (58.10)	2.12	6.75 (67.50)	1.69	7.20 (72.00)	1.73	2.80

Note : $df = 5,142$; $p<0.05 = 2.27$; $p<0.01 = 3.14$.

Educated Unemployed and Employed Young Men for a Duration of 0-1 Year: Their Dependence on Different Strategies Devised for their Adjustment

Table 8.21 displays the summary of the findings of a statistical comparison of different groups of educated unemployed and employed young men for the duration of 0-1 year in terms of their reliance upon various strategies in order to withstand the demands of their existing environment.

Different groups of educated unemployed and employed people with a short-term exposure to the status of their employment evinced a significant difference among themselves in terms of use of punitive avoidance mode ($F = 2.67$; $p < 0.05$) and defensive avoidance mode ($p < 0.05$) for adjusting with their situations. But, no substantial difference was noticed among them in terms of employing the coping strategies like intrapersistive ($p > 0.05$) and extrapersistive approach ($F = 2.04$; $df = 5,142$; $p > 0.05$) modes. Lastly, the results showed that all of them hardly confided in others but the intrapersistive approach mode (the extent of dependence of different groups varied between 60.40 per cent and 73.80 per cent) in dealing with their life events.

Level of Anxiety, Stress, Feeling of Insecurity, Alienation, Identity-Crisis and their Dimensions : A Comparison Among Different Groups of Educated Unemployed and Employed Young Men for a Duration of 1-2 Year

Table 8.22 records the findings of a statistical comparison among different groups of educated unemployed and employed young men for a period of 1-2 year in terms of the degree and extent of anxiety, stress, feeling of insecurity, alienation and identity-crisis in their various manifestations.

All the groups of educated unemployed and employed people for a duration of 1-2 year had a considerable difference among themselves in terms of quite a large number of the abovementioned health indices, except alienation in all its dimensions, barring only the unstructured universe ($F = 2.49$; $df = 5,148$; $p < 0.05$). But, a comparison of each mean score with each of the remaining mean scores by employing Newman-Keuls Test evinced a fair amount of similarity between different pairs of means obtained by the groups of educated unemployed and employed people, particularly marked at the intra-

Table 8.21 : Statistical Differences Among Different Groups of Educated Unemployed and Employed Young Men for a Duration of 0-1 year and the Degree of their Relative Dependence in Terms of Different Coping Strategies

Coping Strategies	*Unemployed*								*Employed*				
	Technically Educated						*Non-technically Educated (N=47)*		*Technically Educated (N=16)*		*Non-technically Educated (N=35)*		
	Degree-holders in Medical Sciences (N=15)		*Degree-holders in Engineering Sciences (N=15)*		*Degree-holders in Agriculture Sciences (N=20)*								
	Mean (%)	*SD*	*Mean (%)*	*SD*	*Mean (%)*	*SD*	*Mean (%)*	*SD*	*Mean (%)*	*SD*	*Mean (%)*	*SD*	*F*
Intrapersistive Approach Mode	10.80 (72.00)	3.41	11.07 (73.80)	3.03	9.80 (65.33)	3.69	9.74 (64.93)	2.86	9.06 (60.40)	3.34	10.23 (68.20)	2.43	1.01
Extrapersistive Approach Mode	1.33 (8.87)	0.67	1.47 (9.80)	0.77	3.35 (22.33)	1.49	2.09 (13.93)	1.08	2.50 (16.67)	1.32	1.83 (12.20)	1.00	2.04
Punitive Avoidance Mode	1.80 (12.00)	1.03	0.67 (4.79)	0.35	0.10 (0.66)	0.05	1.02 (6.80)	0.56	0.88 (5.87)	0.46	0.49 (3.27)	0.25	2.67
Defensive Avoidance Mode	1.07 (7.13)	0.56	1.80 (12.00)	1.05	1.75 (11.67)	0.84	2.15 (14.33)	1.18	2.56 (17.07)	1.41	2.45 (16.33)	1.12	2.77

Note : $df = 5{,}142$; $p<0.05 = 2.27$; $p = 3.14$.

group level. Notably, if there was a significant difference between the mean scores of any two groups, that was invariably between the employed, particularly the technically educated ones, and the unemployed people of one or another discipline. Some of the prominent indicators of psychological health regarding which the technically educated employed, who were found to be psychologically the least vulnerable, showed a marked difference from one or the other group of the educated unemployed people in their mean scores were as follows: general worries (OQ = 1.73; CQ = 1.57), psychological symptoms (OQ = 1.63, 1.55, 1.54; CQ = 1.28), social relations (OQ = 2.37, 2.09; CQ = 1.92), anxiety (OQ = 5.51, 5.40, 4.95, 4.55; CQ = 4.49), paranoid tendency (OQ = 2.77; CQ = 2.15), depression (OQ = 10.09; CQ = 7.28), physical illness (OQ = 2.57; CQ = 2.47), apprehensiveness (OQ = 5.73; CQ = 2.83), stress (OQ = 22.92; CQ = 16.80), dejection (OQ = 3.73, 3.28, 2.91, 2.88; CQ = 1.38), emotional responsiveness (OQ = 5.73, 5.18, 3.19, 3.16, 2.98; CQ = 1.23), social insecurity (OQ = 5.50, 5.14, 3.42, 2.14; CQ = 1.33), feeling of insecurity (OQ = 20.46, 18.77, 18.77; CQ = 15.98), fragmentation (OQ = 2.70;CQ = 1.76), distress (OQ = 2.30; CQ = 2.04), indecisiveness (OQ = 2.33; CQ = 1.70), isolation (OQ = 1.43; CQ = 1.41), hopelessness (OQ = 2.17; CQ = 1.68), and identity-crisis (OQ = 16.29, 12.58; CQ = 12.07). In addition, it was clearly recorded that all the groups of the unemployed, on the whole, were greatly vulnerable to various psychological reactions. The technically educated employed, followed by the non-technically educated ones, on the other hand, were fairly less psychologically unsettled, though not entirely risk-free. They, too, were found to be suffering from various symptoms of psychological affliction to quite a moderate extent, excepting a decreased amount of anxiety and stress in their various manifestations. This was found more particularly in the technically educated employed people. Futhermore, all the groups of unemployed and employed people for a spell of 1-2 year, too, were least prone to suicidal ideation (scores of different groups in this regard ranged between 0.00 per cent and 6.75 per cent). But, they were found to vary among themselves in pointing out the most acute psychological symptom in them. Although all of them, excepting the respective groups of the unemployed degree-holders in medical and agriculture sciences who suffered from a keen sense of social conflict (64.00%) and fragmentation (67.00%), reported themselves as moving in a heightened state of uncertainty (scores obtained by them on the scale of uncertainty varied between 58.25 per cent and 70.75 per cent).

Table 8.22 : Statistical Differences Among Different Groups of Educated Unemployed and Employed Young Men for a Duration of 1-2 Year and their Relative Standing in Terms of Different Indices of Psychological Well-being

Indices of Psychological Well-being	*Unemployed*												*Employed*						
	Technically Educated									*Non-technically Educated (N=52)*			*Technically Educated (N=15)*			*Non-technically Educated (N=30)*			
	Degree-holders in Medical Sciences (N=16)			*Degree-holders in Engineering Sciences (N=19)*			*Degree-holders in Agriculture Sciences (N=22)*												
	Mean (%)	*SD*	*Rank*	*Mean (%)*	*SD*	*Rank*	*Mean (%)*	*SD*	*Rank*	*Mean (%)*	*SD*	*Rank*	*Mean (%)*	*SD*	*Rank*	*Mean (%)*	*SD*	*Rank*	*F*
1. General Worries	2.69 (44.83)	1.62	13	2.84 (47.33)	1.57	14.5	2.56 (42.67)	1.10	27	3.06 (51.00)	1.63	17	1.33 (22.17)	0.73	27	2.57 (42.83)	1.45	12	2.96
2. Somatic Manifestations	1.13 (37.67)	0.89	26	0.79 (26.33)	0.40	32	0.58 (19.33)	0.31	38	0.81 (27.00)	0.36	34	0.40 (13.33)	0.23	32	0.53 (17.67)	0.29	32	1.68
3. Psychological Symptoms	2.06 (41.20)	1.29	24	2.42 (48.40)	1.17	13	2.41 (48.20)	1.14	22	2.50 (50.00)	1.35	21.5	0.87 (17.40)	0.49	29	1.30 (26.00)	0.67	30	6.93
4. Social Relations	3.50 (43.75)	1.54	18.5	2.37 (29.63)	1.46	31	3.23 (40.38)	1.86	30	2.85 (35.63)	1.57	30	1.13 (14.13)	0.60	31	1.77 (22.13)	0.95	31	4.50
5. **Anxiety**	9.38 (42.64)	4.19	20	8.42 (38.27)	3.95	28	8.82 (40.09)	3.96	31	9.27 (42.14)	4.42	29	3.74 (17.00)	1.91	30	6.17 (28.05)	3.28	29	5.13
6. Suicidal Tendency	0.04 (1.00)	0.02	39	0.05 (1.25)	0.02	39	0.27 (6.75)	0.16	39	0.23 (5.75)	0.14	39	0.00 (0.00)	0.00	39	0.20 (5.00)	0.12	39	1.27
7. Emotional Instability	2.06 (25.75)	1.11	33	3.26 (40.75)	1.68	24.5	3.41 (42.63)	1.66	28	2.56 (32.00)	1.63	31	1.47 (18.38)	0.85	28	2.70 (33.75)	1.53	27	2.28
8. Paranoid Tendency	1.94 (16.17)	1.08	38	0.89 (7.42)	0.46	38	3.50 (29.17)	1.67	37	1.77 (14.75)	0.89	38	0.73 (6.08)	0.37	37.5	1.33 (11.08)	0.78	38	4.71
9. Depression	10.38 (28..83)	3.97	31	8.74 (24.28)	4.32	33	14.09 (39.14)	5.14	32	11.12 (30.89)	6.17	32	4.00 (11.11)	2.07	34	5.87 (16.31)	3.06	34	5.87

Contd.

Table 8.22 *(Contd.)*

Indices of Psychological Well-being	Unemployed: Technically Educated: Degree-holders in Medical Sciences (N=16) Mean (%)	SD	Rank	Degree-holders in Engineering Sciences (N=19) Mean (%)	SD	Rank	Degree-holders in Agriculture Sciences (N=22) Mean (%)	SD	Rank	Non-technically Educated (N=52) Mean (%)	SD	Rank	Employed: Technically Educated (N=15) Mean (%)	SD	Rank	Non-technically Educated (N=30) Mean (%)	SD	Rank	F
10. Physical Illness	2.19 (18.25)	1.22	36.5	2.16 (18.00)	1.24	37	3.64 (30.33)	1.80	35.5	3.00 (25.00)	1.47	37	1.07 (8.92)	0.63	36	2.00 (16.67)	1.13	33	2.88
11. Social Mal-adjustment	2.19 (18.25)	1.37	36.5	2.47 (20.58)	1.41	36	3.64 (30.33)	1.83	35.5	3.54 (29.50)	1.95	33	1.53 (12.75)	0.83	33	1.43 (11.92)	0.81	36	3.16
12. Apprehe-nsiveness	2.44 (20.33)	1.19	35	2.68 (22.33)	1.55	34	3.91 (32.58)	2.13	34	3.12 (26.00)	1.99	36	0.73 (6.08)	0.37	37.5	1.40 (11.67)	0.77	37	3.87
13. **Stress**	21.24 (22.13)	8.18	34	20.26 (21.10)	9.36	35	32.45 (33.80)	11.06	33	25.42 (26.48)	13.97	35	9.53 (9.93)	4.83	35	14.93 (15.55)	7.31	35	5.20
14. Lack of Self-confidence	8.95 (44.75)	3.89	14	10.37 (51.85)	4.08	07	10.68 (53.40)	4.78	14	10.99 (54.95)	5.21	07	7.27 (36.35)	2.31	15	9.47 (47.35)	2.96	06	2.19
15. Dejection	7.35 (49.00)	3.35	07	8.63 (57.53)	3.52	03	8.23 (54.87)	2.97	10	9.08 (60.53)	3.94	04	5.35 (35.67)	2.03	17	8.26 (55.07)	2.81	03	4.97
16. Pessimism	1.38 (27.60)	0.81	32	1.84 (36.80)	1.12	29	2.06 (41.20)	1.09	29	2.31 (46.20)	1.41	26	1.13 (22.60)	0.35	26	1.60 (32.00)	0.83	28	2.87
17. Emotional Responsiveness	13.38 (44.60)	4.07	15.5	13.59 (45.30)	4.91	21	15.58 (51.93)	4.91	18	16.13 (53.77)	7.21	09	10.40 (34.67)	3.42	19	13.56 (45.20)	3.49	09	4.82
18. Social Insecurity	11.15 (44.60)	3.93	15.5	8.95 (35.80)	3.72	30	13.23 (52.92)	4.29	15	12.87 (50.80)	6.37	19	7.73 (30.92)	2.51	25	9.87 (39.48)	3.15	19	3.54
19. Distrust	2.69 (53.80)	1.66	04	2.32 (46.40)	1.38	18	3.00 (60.00)	1.20	05	3.08 (61.60)	1.40	03	1.80 (36.00)	0.77	16	2.20 (44.00)	1.16	11	3.66

Contd.

Table 8.22 *(Contd.)*

Indices of Psychological Well-being	*Unemployed*												*Employed*						
	Technically Educated									*Non-technically Educated (N=52)*			*Technically Educated (N=15)*			*Non-technically Educated (N=30)*			
	Degree-holders in Medical Sciences (N=16)			*Degree-holders in Engineering Sciences (N=19)*			*Degree-holders in Agriculture Sciences (N=22)*												
	Mean (%)	*SD*	*Rank*	*Mean (%)*	*SD*	*Rank*	*Mean (%)*	*SD*	*Rank*	*Mean (%)*	*SD*	*Rank*	*Mean (%)*	*SD*	*Rank*	*Mean (%)*	*SD*	*Rank*	*F*
20. **Feeling of Insecurity**	44.90 (44.90)	17.05	12	45.70 (45.70)	14.06	20	52.77 (52.77)	15.37	16	54.42 (54.42)	15.29	08	33.68 (33.68)	10.72	21	44.96 (44.96)	15.05	10	5.11
21. Despair	16.31 (50.97)	4.45	06	16.47 (51.47)	3.66	08	17.91 (55.97)	6.35	09	17.17 (53.66)	4.62	10	14.60 (45.62)	3.83	04	15.67 (48.97)	4.40	04	1.30
22. Unstructured Universe	4.63 (57.88)	1.96	03	4.05 (50.63)	1.54	09	3.64 (45.50)	1.92	25.5	4.50 (56.25)	1.36	05	3.40 (42.50)	1.68	07	3.73 (46.63)	1.36	07	2.49
23. Psychological Vacuum	3.75 (46.88)	1.88	10	4.26 (53.25)	1.59	4.5	3.91 (48.88)	1.34	21	4.15 (51.88)	1.33	15	3.80 (47.50)	1.32	03	3.37 (42.13)	1.25	14	1.49
24. Disillusionment	1.44 (36.00)	0.63	27	1.58 (39.50)	0.84	27	2.05 (51.25)	1.05	19.5	1,83 (45.75)	0.88	27	1.67 (41.75)	0.82	08	1.50 (37.50)	0.63	22.5	1.75
25. Narcissism	1.25 (31.25)	0.45	30	1.84 (46.00)	0.96	19	1.91 (47.75)	1.11	23	1.79 (44.75)	0.91	28	1.60 (40.00)	0.74	10	1.53 (38.25)	0.86	20	1.51
26. **Alienation**	27.38 (48.89)	6.38	08	28.21 (50.38)	4.91	10	29.41 (52.52)	7.60	17	29.51 (52.70)	6.61	13	25.07 (44.77)	4.79	05	25.80 (46.07)	6.11	08	2.11
27. Depersonalization	3.19 (39.88)	1.28	25	3.42 (42.75)	1.64	22	3.73 (46.63)	1.80	24	3.79 (47.38)	1.66	24	2.73 (34.73)	0.88	20	2.90 (36.25)	1.32	24	2.16
28. Fragmentation	2.81 (35.13)	1.11	28	3.74 (46.75)	1.73	17	5.36 (67.00)	2.01	01	4.00 (50.00)	1.97	21.5	2.67 (33.38)	0.98	22.5	3.03 (37.88)	1.47	21	7.37
29. Uncertainty	2.06 (51.50)	1.12	05	2.68 (67.00)	0.82	1.5	2.59 (64.75)	1.05	2.5	2.83 (70.75)	0.98	01	2.33 (58.25)	1.05	01	2.37 (59.25)	0.93	01	2.03

Contd.

Table 8.22 (*Contd.*)

Indices of Psychological Well-being	*Unemployed*												*Employed*						
	Technically Educated									*Non-technically Educated (N=52)*			*Technically Educated (N=15)*			*Non-technically Educated (N=30)*			
	Degree-holders in Medical Sciences (N=16)			*Degree-holders in Engineering Sciences (N=19)*			*Degree-holders in Agriculture Sciences (N=22)*												
	Mean (%)	*SD*	*Rank*	*Mean (%)*	*SD*	*Rank*	*Mean (%)*	*SD*	*Rank*	*Mean (%)*	*SD*	*Rank*	*Mean (%)*	*SD*	*Rank*	*Mean (%)*	*SD*	*Rank*	*F*
30. Distress	5.63 (46.92)	1.93	09	5.68 (47.33)	1.73	14.5	6.50 (54.17)	2.87	13	6.10 (50.83)	1.91	18	4.20 (35.00)	1.47	18	4.97 (41.42)	1.71	15	3.63
31. Indecisiveness	3.38 (42.25)	1.96	21.5	4.26 (53.25)	1.82	4.5	5.00 (62.50)	2.14	04	4.21 (52.63)	1.61	14	2.67 (33.38)	0.90	22.5	3.23 (40.38)	1.25	17	5.49
32. Social Conflict	2.56 (64.00)	0.89	01	2.68 (67.00)	0.82	1.5	2.59 (64.75)	1.18	2.5	2.77 (69.25)	1.02	02	1.93 (48.25)	0.96	02	2.33 (58.25)	0.92	02	2.05
33. Isolation	3.38 (42.25)	0.96	21.5	3.21 (40.13)	1.27	26	4.36 (54.50)	1.62	11.5	4.13 (51.63)	1.77	16	2.93 (36.63)	0.96	14	2.80 (35.00)	0.96	26	5.69
34. Withdrawal from Social and Personal Contact	1.75 (43.75)	0.77	18.5	2.00 (50.00)	1.05	11	1.82 (45.50)	0.73	25.5	2.02 (50.50)	0.85	20	1.47 (36.75)	0.92	12.5	1.50 (37.50)	0.86	22.5	2.05
35. Role Conflict	5.06 (42.17)	2.02	23	6.37 (53.08)	2.11	06	6.86 (57.17)	2.36	07	6.60 (55.00)	2.19	06	4.87 (40.58)	2.29	09	4.83 (40.25)	1.76	18	4.93
36. Hopelessness	3.63 (45.38)	1.59	11	3.32 (41.50)	1.67	23	4.77 (59.63)	1.82	06	4.23 (52.88)	1.81	12	2.60 (32.50)	0.91	24	2.87 (35.88)	1.43	25	6.12
37. Lonelinness	1.31 (32.75)	0.48	29	1.63 (40.75)	0.96	24.5	2.18 (54.50)	1.01	11.5	1.98 (49.50)	0.92	23	1.47 (36.75)	0.83	12.5	1.70 (42.50)	1.02	13	2.67
38. Desolation	2.50 (62.50)	1.21	02	1.89 (47.25)	0.94	16	2.05 (51.25)	0.84	19.5	1.85 (46.25)	1.31	25	1.73 (43.25)	0.80	06	1.90 (47.50)	0.99	05	0.76
39. **Identity-crisis**	37.26 (44.36)	10.54	17	40.89 (48.68)	10.47	12	47.82 (56.93)	10.84	08	44.52 (53.00)	13.03	11	31.60 (37.62)	8.54	11	34.43 (40.99)	9.25	16	6.47

Note : $df = 5{,}148$; $p < 0.05 = 2.27$; $p < 0.01 = 3.14$.

Life Satisfaction : A Comparison Among Different Groups of Educated Unemployed and Employed Young Men for a Duration of 1-2 Year

Table 8.23 presents a comparative account of the degree of life satisfaction found in different groups of educated unemployed and employed people for a spell of 1-2 year.

A cursory look at Table 8.23 showed a significant difference among different groups of the technically and non-technically educated unemployed and employed people in terms of their level of life satisfaction (F = 4.73; df = 5,148; p<0.01). However, the findings obtained from a multiple-comparison of different pairs of means with each other did not confirm this. Evidently, none but only the group of the unemployed degree-holders in the agriculure sciences (Mean = 4.27; SD = 2.58) was found to be markedly distinct, particularly so from those of the groups of the technically (*Mean* = 6.80; *SD* = 1.47) and the non-technically (*Mean* = 6.53; *SD* = 1.72) educated employed young men in the degree of satisfaction with their life (OQ = 2.53, 2.26; CQ = 1.99). Moreover, it was noted that barring the group of the unemployed degree-holders in the agriculture sciences who expressed a greater amount of dissatisfaction with their life (Index of dissatisfaction = 57.30 per cent; i.e., the satisfaction level was only 42.70 per cent), both the groups of technically (68.00%) and non-technicallly (65.30%) educated employed were well contented with the order of their life.

Educated Unemployed and Employed Young Men for a Duration of 1-2 year : Their Dependence on Different Strategies Devised for their Adjustment

Table 8.24 summarizes the findings of a statistical comparison of different groups of educated unemployed and employed young men for a span of 1-2 year in terms of the degree of their dependence on strategy like intrapersistive approach mode, extrapersistive approach mode, punitive avoidance mode and defensive avoidance mode in order to deal with the situation.

Like those of the groups of educated unemployed and employed young men for a short spell of 0-1 year, the unemployed and employed people for a period of 1-2 year did not show any marked difference among themselves in terms of the degree of their reliance upon

Table 8.23 : Statistical Differences Among Different Groups of Educated Unemployed and Employed Young Men for a Duration of 1 - 2 year and their Relative Standing in Terms of the Degree of their Life Satisfaction

Variable	*Unemployed*								*Employed*				
	Technically Educated						*Non-technically Educated (N=52)*		*Technically Educated (N=15)*		*Non-technically Educated (N=30)*		
	Degree-holders in Medical Sciences (N=16)		*Degree-holders in Engineering Sciences (N=19)*		*Degree-holders in Agriculture Sciences (N=22)*								
	Mean (%)	*SD*	*Mean (%)*	*SD*	*Mean (%)*	*SD*	*Mean (%)*	*SD*	*Mean (%)*	*SD*	*Mean (%)*	*SD*	*F*
Life Satisfaction	5.44 (54.40)	1.26	5.21 (52.10)	1.78	4.27 (42.70)	2.58	5.37 (53.70)	2.18	6.80 (68.00)	1.47	6.53 (65.30)	1.72	4.73

Note : $df = 5,148$; $p < 0.05 = 2.27$; $p < 0.01 = 3.14$.

Table 8.24 : Statistical Differences Among Different Groups of Educated Unemployed and Employed Young Men for a Duration of 1 - 2 year and the Degree of their Relative Dependence in Terms of Different Coping Strategies

Coping Strategies	*Unemployed*								*Employed*				
	Technically Educated						*Non-technically Educated (N=52)*		*Technically Educated (N=15)*		*Non-technically Educated (N=30)*		
	Degree-holders in Medical Sciences (N=16)		*Degree-holders in Engineering Sciences (N=19)*		*Degree-holders in Agriculture Sciences (N=22)*								
	Mean (%)	*SD*	*Mean (%)*	*SD*	*Mean (%)*	*SD*	*Mean (%)*	*SD*	*Mean (%)*	*SD*	*Mean (%)*	*SD*	*F*
Intrapersistive Approach Mode	9.63 (64.20)	1.15	9.00 (60.00)	2.43	8.82 (58.80)	3.03	10.25 (68.33)	2.70	10.47 (69.80)	2.39	10.07 (67.13)	2.39	1.68
Extrapersistive Approach Mode	1.69 (11.27)	0.93	1.89 (12.60)	0.98	2.91 (19.40)	1.58	1.56 (10.40)	0.95	1.87 (12.47)	0.98	1.87 (12.47)	1.01	1.40
Punitive Avoidance Mode	1.06 (7.07)	0.59	1.42 (9.47)	0.75	0.27 (1.80)	0.17	0.87 (5.80)	0.48	0.86 (5.73)	0.44	0.60 (4.00)	0.32	3.09
Defensive Avoidance Mode	2.63 (17.53)	1.31	2.68 (17.87)	1.45	3.00 (20.00)	1.65	2.33 (15.53)	1.42	1.80 (12.00)	0.85	2.46 (16.40)	1.53	1.30

Note : $df = 5,148$; $p<0.05 = 2.27$; $p<0.01 = 3.14$.

different strategies devised to cope with their situation, with the exception of their dependence on punitive avoidance mode (F = 3.09; df = 5,148; p<0.05). Further, the latter groups, too, resorted only to intrapersistive approach mode (the extent of reliance of different groups ranged between 58.80 per cent and 69.80 per cent) in order to cope with the existing circumstances.

Level of Anxiety, Stress, Feeling of Insecurity, Alienation, Identity-Crisis and Their Dimensions : A Comparison Among Different Groups of Educated Unemployed and Employed Young Men for a Duration of 2-3 Year

Table 8.25 reports the findings of a statistical comparison of different groups of educated unemployed and employed people for a moderately prolonged period of 2-3 year in terms of their level of anxiety, stress, feeling of insecurity, alienation, identity-crisis and their symptomatic reactions.

Each of the groups of respondents tended to differ significantly from one another in terms of their level in all the indicators of psychological health (F-values varied between 2.50 and 9.98), except most of the dimensions of alienation together with paranoid tendency, pessimism and loneliness. But, the multiple- comparison of pairs of means showed that there was no meaningful difference between any two groups, especially at intra-group level, in terms of the various health indicators which, as F-ratios warranted, were found to be palpable in differentiating one group of respondents from another to a significant extent (see Table 8.25). So, with a few exceptions such as a noticeable difference between the mean scores of the technically and the non-technically educated employed in terms of lack of self-confidence (OQ = 2.08; CQ = 1.47), the unemployed degree-holders in the agriculture and the engineering sciences in terms of lack of self-confidence (OQ = 2.38; CQ = 1.36), the unemployed degree-holders in the medical and the engineering sciences in terms of lack of self-confidence (OQ = 2.21;CQ = 1.26), the non-technically educated unemployed and the unemployed degree-holders in the engineering sciences in terms of lack of self-confidence (OQ = 2.18;CQ = 1.13), the technically and the non-technically educated employed in terms of dejection (OQ = 1.66;CQ = 1.43), the unemployed degree-holders in the medical and the engineering sciences in terms of dejection (OQ = 1.53; CQ = 1.32), the unemployed

Table 8.25 : Statistical Differences Among Different Groups of Educated Unemployed and Employed Young Men for a Duration of 2-3 year and their Relative Standing in Terms of Different Indices of Psychological Well-being

Indices of Psychological Well-being	*Unemployed*												*Employed*						
	Technically Educated									*Non-technically Educated (N=74)*			*Technically Educated (N=15)*			*Non-technically Educated (N=30)*			
	Degree-holders in Medical Sciences (N=15)			*Degree-holders in Engineering Sciences (N=15)*			*Degree-holders in Agriculture Sciences (N=22)*												
	Mean (%)	*SD*	*Rank*	*Mean (%)*	*SD*	*Rank*	*Mean (%)*	*SD*	*Rank*	*Mean (%)*	*SD*	*Rank*	*Mean (%)*	*SD*	*Rank*	*Mean (%)*	*SD*	*Rank*	*F*
1. General Worries	2.40 (40.00)	1.29	27	3.67 (61.17)	1.76	14	3.95 (65.83)	1.73	02	3.27 (54.50)	1.64	08	2.47 (41.17)	1.35	08	2.37 (39.50)	1.29	23	3.62
2. Somatic Mani-festations	0.47 (15.67)	0.23	38	1.07 (35.67)	0.56	34	0.82 (27.33)	0.43	35	0.72 (24.00)	0.37	37	0.73 (24.33)	0.39	30	0.27 (9.00)	0.14	37	2.83
3. Psychological Symptoms	1.93 (38.60)	1.02	29	2.93 (58.60)	1.10	18	2.36 (47.20)	1.43	27	2.65 (53.00)	1.37	12.5	1.53 (30.60)	0.83	23	1.90 (38.00)	1.09	26	3.71
4. Social Relations	2.13 (26.63)	1.51	35	2.93 (36.63)	1.52	33	3.86 (48.25)	2.01	24.5	3.19 (39.88)	2.21	30	1.67 (20.88)	0.86	33	1.93 (24.13)	1.04	30	3.77
5. **Anxiety**	6.93 (31.50)	2.97	30	10.61 (48.23)	4.42	28	11.00 (50.00)	5.35	23	9.88 (44.91)	4.67	26	6.40 (29.09)	3.30	28	6.47 (29.41)	3.39	29	5.21
6. Suicidal Tendency	0.47 (11.75)	0.24	39	1.07 (26.75)	0.62	38	0.36 (9.00)	0.19	39	0.41 (10.25)	0.24	39	0.00 (0.00)	0.00	39	0.03 (0.75)	0.01	39	3.38
7. Emotional Instability	3.80 (47.50)	1.38	21.5	3.53 (44.13)	1.82	29	3.82 (47.75)	1.87	26	3.09 (38.63)	1.19	31	1.87 (23.38)	1.19	32	1.47 (18.38)	0.87	31	6.48
8. Paranoid Tendency	2.33 (19.42)	1.23	37	2.40 (20.00)	1.23	39	2.23 (18.58)	1.14	38	2.20 (18.33)	1.18	38	2.33 (19.42)	1.24	35	1.33 (11.08)	0.67	35	1.03
9. Depression	9.40 (26.11)	3.88	36	13.60 (37.78)	6.60	32	12.27 (34.08)	5.61	32	11.15 (30.92)	5.62	32	4.67 (12.97)	2.39	37	4.40 (12.22)	2.39	33	7.37

Contd.

Table 8.25 (*Contd.*)

Indices of Psychological Well-being	*Unemployed*												*Employed*						
	Technically Educated									*Non-technically Educated (N=74)*			*Technically Educated (N=15)*			*Non-technically Educated (N=30)*			
	Degree-holders in Medical Sciences (N=15)			*Degree-holders in Engineering Sciences (N=15)*			*Degree-holders in Agriculture Sciences (N=22)*												
	Mean (%)	*SD*	*Rank*	*Mean (%)*	*SD*	*Rank*	*Mean (%)*	*SD*	*Rank*	*Mean (%)*	*SD*	*Rank*	*Mean (%)*	*SD*	*Rank*	*Mean (%)*	*SD*	*Rank*	*F*
10. Physical Illness	3.33 (27.75)	1.32	34	4.73 (39.42)	2.05	31	3.41 (28.42)	1.59	34	3.35 (27.92)	1.45	33	2.87 (23.92)	1.52	31	1.80 (15.00)	0.95	32	3.74
11. Social Mal-adjustment	3.67 (30.58)	1.66	32	4.07 (33.92)	2.29	36	2.73 (22.75)	1.83	37	3.18 (26.50)	1.80	35	1.07 (8.92)	0.63	38	0.93 (7.75)	0.48	38	5.65
12. Apprehensive-ness	3.73 (31.08)	1.74	31	3.67 (30.58)	1.83	37	3.27 (27.25)	1.56	36	2.91 (24.25)	1.42	36	2.40 (20.00)	1.35	34	1.27 (10.58)	0.68	36	3.47
13. **Stress**	26.73 (27.84)	9.01	33	33.07 (34.45)	14.82	35	28.09 (29.26)	9.06	33	26.32 (27.42)	14.49	34	15.21 (15.84)	7.72	36	11.23 (11.70)	5.71	34	5.24
14. Lack of Self-confidence	11.26 (56.30)	4.03	04	13.47 (67.35)	4.37	06	11.09 (55.45)	4.67	11	11.29 (56.45)	4.43	06	7.73 (38.65)	2.54	09	9.81 (49.05)	3.24	6.5	6.16
15. Dejection	8.13 (54.20)	3.28	07	9.74 (64.93)	3.69	08	10.13 (67.53)	3.07	01	9.66 (64.40)	3.82	03	6.27 (41.80)	2.18	07	7.93 (52.87)	2.69	04	5.71
16. Pessimism	2.13 (42.60)	1.46	26	2.00 (40.00)	1.21	30	2.27 (45.40)	1.45	29	2.19 (43.80)	1.41	28	1.27 (25.40)	0.46	29	1.63 (32.60)	0.93	28	1.97
17. Emotional Responsiveness	17.46 (58.20)	5.93	03	18.80 (62.67)	6.03	11	18.05 (60.17)	5.46	07	15.66 (52.20)	5.17	18	11.27 (37.57)	3.08	13	14.10 (47.00)	3.66	09	6.57
18. Social Insecurity	12.86 (51.44)	4.69	12	16.40 (65.60)	4.85	07	13.60 (54.40)	4.22	14	12.59 (50.36)	4.07	21	7.73 (30.92)	2.39	22	10.87 (43.48)	3.24	17	7.12
19. Distrust	2.40 (48.00)	1.40	20	3.40 (68.00)	1.59	05	3.09 (61.80)	1.51	06	2.86 (57.20)	1.34	05	1.87 (37.40)	1.03	14	2.30 (46.00)	1.22	12	3.08

Contd.

Table 8.25 *(Contd.)*

Indices of Psychological Well-being	*Unemployed*												*Employed*						
	Technically Educated									*Non-technically Educated (N=74)*			*Technically Educated (N=15)*			*Non-technically Educated (N=30)*			
	Degree-holders in Medical Sciences (N=15)			*Degree-holders in Engineering Sciences (N=15)*			*Degree-holders in Agriculture Sciences (N=22)*												
	Mean (%)	*SD*	*Rank*	*Mean (%)*	*SD*	*Rank*	*Mean (%)*	*SD*	*Rank*	*Mean (%)*	*SD*	*Rank*	*Mean (%)*	*SD*	*Rank*	*Mean (%)*	*SD*	*Rank*	*F*
20. **Feeling of Insecurity**	54.25 (54.25)	18.56	06	63.81 (63.81)	15.56	09	58.23 (58.23)	14.57	10	54.23 (54.23)	14.51	09	36.14 (36.14)	10.97	17	46.64 (46.64)	14.33	11	7.07
21. Despair	17.07 (53.34)	5.68	08	20.40 (63.75)	5.03	10	18.91 (59.03)	3.61	09	17.65 (55.16)	4.04	07	13.53 (42.28)	1.46	06	15.57 (48.66)	3.13	08	6.57
22. Unstructured Universe	4.00 (50.00)	0.93	16	4.00 (50.00)	1.46	26.5	4.05 (50.63)	1.09	22	4.31 (53.88)	1.17	10	4.60 (57.50)	1.40	01	4.20 (52.50)	1.00	05	0.84
23. Psychological Vacuum	3.93 (49.13)	0.80	18	4.40 (55.00)	1.40	23	4.14 (51.75)	1.36	19.5	4.19 (52.38)	1.39	17	3.40 (42.50)	0.83	05	4.60 (57.50)	1.45	03	1.85
24. Disillusionment	1.87 (46.75)	0.74	24.5	2.33 (58.25)	1.05	19.5	1.68 (42.00)	0.78	30	1.68 (42.00)	0.85	29	1.53 (38.25)	0.64	11.5	1.57 (39.25)	0.77	24	2.19
25. Narcissism	2.13 (53.25)	1.06	09	2.00 (50.00)	1.20	26.5	2.14 (53.50)	1.17	15	1.92 (48.00)	1.03	24	1.53 (38.25)	0.64	11.5	1.53 (38.25)	0.57	25	1.71
26. **Alienation**	29.00 (51.89)	7.03	11	33.13 (59.16)	7.24	17	30.91 (55.20)	4.95	12	29.73 (53.09)	5.49	11	24.60 (43.93)	2.75	03	27.47 (49.05)	4.17	6.5	5.08
27. Depersonalization	3.80 (47.50)	1.86	21.5	4.20 (52.50)	2.37	25	4.14 (51.75)	1.21	19.5	3.66 (45.75)	1.44	25	2.60 (32.50)	0.83	21	3.40 (42.50)	1.40	19	2.50
28. Fragmentation	3.13 (39.13)	1.55	28	5.93 (74.13)	1.83	03	4.73 (59.13)	1.86	08	4.05 (50.63)	1.83	20	2.40 (30.00)	0.63	25	3.27 (40.88)	1.26	21	9.76
29. Uncertainty	2.80 (70.00)	1.02	02	3.40 (85.00)	0.74	01	2.50 (62.50)	0.96	05	2.62 (65.50)	1.03	02	2.20 (55.00)	1.01	02	2.57 (64.25)	0.77	01	2.75

Contd.

Table 8.25 *(Contd.)*

Indices of Psychological Well-being	*Unemployed*												*Employed*						
	Technically Educated									*Non-technically Educated (N=74)*			*Technically Educated (N=15)*			*Non-technically Educated (N=30)*			
	Degree-holders in Medical Sciences (N=15)			*Degree-holders in Engineering Sciences (N=15)*			*Degree-holders in Agriculture Sciences (N=22)*												
	Mean (%)	*SD*	*Rank*	*Mean (%)*	*SD*	*Rank*	*Mean (%)*	*SD*	*Rank*	*Mean (%)*	*SD*	*Rank*	*Mean (%)*	*SD*	*Rank*	*Mean (%)*	*SD*	*Rank*	*F*
30. Distress	6.60 (55.00)	2.82	05	7.40 (61.67)	2.16	13	6.36 (53.00)	1.59	17.5	6.36 (53.00)	2.35	12.5	4.13 (34.42)	0.92	20	5.27 (43.92)	1.89	14	5.05
31. Indecisivness	4.20 (52.50)	1.70	10	4.87 (60.88)	1.85	15.5	3.86 (48.25)	1.17	24.5	4.00 (50.00)	1.53	22	3.07 (38.38)	1.16	10	3.50 (43.75)	1.33	15	2.88
32. Social Conflict	3.00 (75.00)	1.07	01	3.26 (81.50)	0.96	02	2.59 (64.75)	0.85	3.5	2.65 (66.25)	1.01	01	1.73 (43.25)	0.80	04	2.47 (61.75)	0.86	02	4.64
33. Isolation	4.00 (50.00)	2.00	16	4.87 (60.88)	2.00	15.5	3.68 (46.00)	1.21	28	3.96 (49.50)	1.65	23	2.33 (29.13)	0.62	27	3.30 (41.25)	1.24	20	4.99
34. Withdrawal from Social and Personal Contact	1.93 (48.25)	1.33	19	2.27 (56.75)	1.16	21	1.45 (36.25)	0.67	31	1.77 (44.25)	0.99	27	1.20 (30.00)	0.41	25	1.60 (40.00)	0.62	22	2.72
35. Role Conflict	5.67 (47.25)	2.35	23	6.40 (53.33)	2.38	24	6.36 (53.00)	2.17	17.5	6.34 (52.83)	2.08	14	4.40 (36.67)	1.35	16	5.23 (43.58)	1.85	16	3.82
36. Hopelessness	4.07 (50.88)	2.31	14	4.47 (55.88)	1.81	22	4.41 (55.13)	1.79	13	4.20 (52.50)	1.72	16	2.40 (30.00)	0.74	25	2.90 (36.25)	1.35	27	5.76
37. Lonelinness	2.00 (50.00)	1.06	16	2.33 (58.25)	0.82	19.5	2.05 (51.25)	0.95	21	2.03 (50.75)	1.03	19	1.40 (35.00)	0.83	18	1.73 (43.25)	0.94	18	1.74
38. Desolation	1.87 (46.75)	0.92	24.5	2.80 (70.00)	0.86	04	2.59 (64.75)	1.14	3.5	2.46 (61.50)	1.08	04	1.47 (36.75)	0.83	15	1.87 (46.75)	0.78	10	5.35
39. **Identity-crisis**	43.07 (51.27)	12.45	13	52.20 (62.14)	10.39	12	44.73 (53.25)	5.91	16	44.14 (52.55)	11.23	15	29.33 (34.92)	6.56	19	37.11 (44.18)	8.58	13	9.98

Note : $df = 5{,}165$; $p < 0.05 = 2.27$; $p < 0.01 = 3.13$.

medical graduates and the non-technically educated unemployed in terms of dejection (OQ = 1.61; CQ = 1.32), the unemployed degree-holders in the medical and the agriculture sciences in terms of dejection (OQ = 2.00; CQ = 1.32), the non-technically educated unemployed and the unemployed degree-holders in the engineering sciences in terms of emotional responsiveness (OQ = 3.14; CQ = 3.12), the technically and the non-technically educated employed in terms of social insecurity (OQ = 3.14; CQ = 1.28), the non-technically educated unemployed and the unemployed degree-holders in the engineering sciences in terms of social insecurity (OQ = 3.81; CQ = 1.18), the unemployed degree-holders in the medical and engineering sciences in terms of social insecurity (OQ = 3.54; CQ = 1.11), the unemployed degree-holders in the agriculture and the engineering sciences in terms of social insecurity (OQ = 2.80; CQ = 0.98), the unemployed degree-holders in the medical and the engineering sciences in terms of fragmentation (OQ = 2.80; CQ = 1.68) and the non-technically educated unemployed and the unemployed degree-holders in engineering sciences in terms of fragmentation (OQ = 1.88; CQ = 1.50), if there was any substantial difference between the mean scores of any two groups, that was consistently recorded between the employed, especially the technically educated ones, and the unemployed degree-holders in one or another branch of knowledge. The health indices where the technically educated employed people, who were identified as psychologically more poised, tended to differ significantly from one or another distinct group of the educated unemployed, involved the psychological dimensions like psychological symptoms (OQ = 1.40; CQ = 1.34), social relations (OQ = 2.20; CQ = 2.23), suicidal tendency (OQ = 1.07; CQ = 0.92), emotional instability (OQ = 1.95, 1.93; CQ = 1.93), depression (OQ = 8.93, 7.61; CQ = 7.00), social maladjustment (OQ = 3.00; CQ = 2.65), stress (OQ = 17.86; CQ = 14.83), lack of self-confidence (OQ = 5.74, 3.56, 3.53, 3.36, 2.08; CQ = 1.47), dejection (OQ = 3.86, 3.47, 3.39, 1.86, 1.66; CQ = 1.43), emotional responsiveness (OQ = 7.53, 6.78, 6.19, 4.39; CQ = 3.38), social insecurity (OQ = 8.67, 5.87, 5.13, 4.86, 3.14; CQ = 1.28), distrust (OQ = 1.53; CQ = 1.42), feeling of insecurity (OQ = 27.67, 22.09, 18.11, 18.09; CQ = 15.67), despair (OQ = 6.87, 5.38, 4.12; CQ = 4.16), alienation (OQ = 8.53, 6.31; CQ = 5.64), depersonalization (OQ = 1.60; CQ = 1.57), fragmentation (OQ = 3.53, 2.33; CQ = 1.74), uncertainty (OQ = 1.20; CQ = 0.99), distress (OQ = 3.27, 2.47, 2.23, 2.23; CQ = 2.24), indecisiveness (OQ = 1.80; CQ =

1.52), social conflict (OQ = 1.53,1.27; CQ = 1.00), isolation (OQ = 2.54, 1.67, 1.63; CQ = 1.62), withdrawal from social and personal contact (OQ = 1.07; CQ = 0.95), role conflict (OQ = 2.00, 1.96, 1.94; CQ = 1.47), hopelessness (OQ = 2.07, 2.01, 1.80; CQ = 1.76), desolation (OQ = 1.33, 1.12; CQ = 1.05) and identity-crisis (OQ = 22.87, 15.40, 14.81, 13.74; CQ = 10.88).

The non-technically educated employed, like their technically educated counterparts, registered a substantial difference from one or another group of the unemployed in terms of the psychological reactions spotted as inducing a meaningful difference among different groups of respondents (see Table 8.25), but only on the half of them. The various indicators of psychological health on which the non-technically educated employed, as the multiple-comparison of pairs of means showed, expressed a marked difference from different distinct groups of the unemployed were somatic manifestations (OQ = 0.80; CQ = 0.81), suicidal tendency (OQ = 1.03; CQ = 0.89), emotional instability (OQ = 2.35, 2.33, 2.07; CQ = 2.00), depression (OQ = 9.20, 7.87; CQ = 7.24), physical illness (OQ = 2.93; CQ = 2.41), social maladjustment (OQ = 3.13, 2.73; CQ = 2.74), stress (OQ = 21.84, 16.86, 15.50; CQ = 15.35), lack of self-confidence (OQ = 3.66, 1.48, 1.45; CQ = 1.42), dejection (OQ = 2.20, 1.81, 1.73; CQ = 1.38), emotional responsiveness (OQ = 3.70; CQ = 3.27), social insecurity (OQ = 5.53, 2.73, 1.99, 1.72; CQ = 1.24), feeling of insecurity (OQ = 17.17; CQ = 15.15), despair (OQ = 4.83; CQ = 4.02), alienation (OQ = 5.66; CQ = 5.45), fragmentation (OQ = 2.80; CQ = 1.68), isolation (OQ = 1.57; CQ = 1.56) and identity-crisis (OQ = 15.09; CQ = 10.51) respectively. Further,it appeared that all the groups of unemployed, particularly the engineers, were generally more susceptible to reduced psychological health, and the employed, especially the technically educated ones, were comparatively less, but moderately, prone in this regard. Moreover, it was found that all the groups of unemployed and employed people for a duration of 2-3 year, excepting the group of unemployed degree-holders in engineering sciences who were least oppressed with the bouts of paranoid thoughts, were least incited by suicidal ideation. But, a variation was noticed while an effort was made to find out the most aggravated symptom in them. The groups of unemployed degree-holders in medical sciences and non-technically educated unemployed were seriously entrapped in the whirl of social conflict (liability of the respective groups to social conflict stood 75.00 per cent and 66.25 per cent), while the groups of unemployed degree-holders in engineering sciences and the non-technically educated employed in the whirl of uncertainty (scores of the two groups on the scale of uncertainty were 85.00 per cent and 64.25 per cent). Further, while the unemployed degree-holders in agriculture sciences felt themselves highly dejected (67.53%), the technically educated employed were greatly distressed with alienating reaction like unstructured universe (57.50%).

Life Satisfaction : A Comparison Among Different Groups of Educated Unemployed and Employed Young Men for a Duration of 2-3 Year

Table 8.26 offers the summary of the findings of a statistical comparison among different groups of educated unemployed and employed people for a spell of 2-3 year at the scale of their life satisfaction.

There appeared a significant difference among all the groups of educated unemployed and employed people in their level of life satisfaction ($F = 7.18$; $df = 5,165$; $p<0.01$). But, as it was apparent from the multiple-comparison of pairs of means, there was no meaningful difference between any two groups of the unemployed and employed people in this regard. Although there were exceptions and those were the perceptible differences between unemployed degree-holders in agriculture sciences and technically educated employed (OQ = 3.38; CQ = 2.22), unemployed degree-holders in engineering sciences and technically educated employed (OQ = 3.00; CQ = 2.15), non-technically educated unemployed and technically educated employed (OQ = 2.92; CQ = 2.05), and unemployed degree-holders in medical sciences and technically educated employed (OQ = 2.47; CQ = 1.92). The results further indicated that all the groups of unemployed, particularly the degree-holders in agriculture sciences (Index of life satisfaction = 40.90 per cent), were noticeably less satisfied with their life in comparison to those of the technically (Degree of life satisfaction = 74.70 per cent) and the non-technically (Level of life satisfaction = 60.30 per cent) educated employed people.

Educated Unemployed and Employed Young Men for a Duration of 2-3 Year: Their Dependence on Different Strategies Devised for their Adjustment

Table 8.27 presents a comparative description about the degree of

Table 8.26 : Statistical Differences Among Different Groups of Educated Unemployed and Employed Young Men for a Duration of 2-3 year and their Relative Standing in Terms of the Degree of their Life Satisfaction

Variable	*Unemployed*								*Employed*				
	Technically Educated						*Non-technically Educated (N=74)*		*Technically Educated (N=15)*		*Non-technically Educated (N=30)*		
	Degree-holders in Medical Sciences (N=15)		*Degree-holders in Engineering Sciences (N=15)*		*Degree-holders in Agriculture Sciences (N=22)*								
	Mean (%)	*SD*	*Mean (%)*	*SD*	*Mean (%)*	*SD*	*Mean (%)*	*SD*	*Mean (%)*	*SD*	*Mean (%)*	*SD*	*F*
Life Satisfaction	5.00 (50.00)	2.36	4.47 (44.70)	1.88	4.09 (40.90)	1.77	4.55 (45.50)	2.25	7.47 (74.70)	1.36	6.03 (60.30)	2.27	7.18

Note. $df = 5,165$; $p<0.05 = 2.27$; $p<0.01=3.13$.

Table 8.27 : Statistical Differences Among Different Groups of Educated Unemployed and Employed Young Men for a Duration of 2 - 3 Year and the Degree of their Relative Dependence in Terms of Different Coping Strategies

Coping Strategies	*Unemployed*								*Employed*				*F*
	Technically Educated						*Non-technically Educated (N=74)*		*Technically Educated (N=15)*		*Non-technically Educated (N=30)*		
	Degree-holders in Medical Sciences (N=15)		*Degree-holders in Engineering Sciences (N=15)*		*Degree-holders in Agriculture Sciences (N=22)*								
	Mean (%)	*SD*	*Mean (%)*	*SD*	*Mean (%)*	*SD*	*Mean (%)*	*SD*	*Mean (%)*	*SD*	*Mean (%)*	*SD*	
Intrapersistive Approach Mode	8.60 (57.33)	3.96	9.00 (60.00)	3.61	10.25 (68.20)	2.51	9.51 (63.40)	2.98	7.93 (52.87)	2.91	10.77 (71.80)	2.64	2.46
Extrapersistive Approach Mode	3.53 (23.53)	1.61	1.87 (12.47)	1.04	1.68 (11.20)	0.89	2.26 (15.07)	1.22	2.87 (19.13)	1.45	1.53 (10.20)	0.90	2.70
Punitive Avoidance Mode	1.40 (9.33)	0.69	1.80 (12.00)	0.97	0.59 (3.93)	0.29	0.80 (5.33)	0.43	1.20 (8.00)	0.62	0.57 (3.80)	0.30	2.68
Defensive Avoidance Mode	1.47 (9.80)	0.74	2.33 (15.53)	1.50	2.50 (16.67)	1.22	2.43 (16.20)	1.54	3.00 (20.00)	1.13	2.13 (14.20)	1.26	1.42

Note : $df = 5,165$; $p < 0.05 = 2.27$; $p < 0.01 = 3.13$

dependence of different groups of unemployed and employed people for a span of 2-3 year on various strategies generally employed by them for their adjustment.

All the groups of unemployed and employed people differed significantly among themselves in terms of the use of each of the strategies resorted to for their adjustment, except the defensive avoidance mode (see Table 8.27). But, quite similar to the trend, as it appeared earlier, all of them largely fell back upon intrapersistive approach mode (their extent of dependence laid between 52.87 per cent and 71.80 per cent) and hardly others in fighting their life situations.

Level of Anxiety, Stress, Feeling of Insecurity, Alienation, Identity-Crisis and Their Dimensions : A Comparison Among Different Groups of Educated Unemployed and Employed Young Men for a Duration of 3 - 4 Year

Table 8.28 comprises the findings of a statistical comparison among different groups of educated unemployed and employed young men for a longer span of 3-4 year in terms of their level of anxiety, stress, feeling of insecurity, alienation, identity-crisis and their different characteristic manifestations.

As the trend appeared earlier, there existed a considerable difference among different groups of respondents in terms of their level on most of the indicators of their psychological health, except a few indicators like somatic manifestations, suicidal tendency, physical illness, apprehensiveness, unstructured universe, psychological vacuum, disillusionment, narcissism, alienation and uncertainty (see Table 8.28). However, the statistical differences yielded through one-way ANOVA among various groups were not fully acceptable. The findings of the multiple-comparison of different pairs of means indicated no evidence of significant difference between the mean scores of any two groups with an exclusive record of either unemployment or employment. Thus, if there was a substantial difference between the mean scores of any two groups, it was always between the mean scores of two groups from two distinct status of employment. The health indices towards which the technically educated employed showed a marked difference from one or another group of the educated unemployed people were as follows: general worries (OQ = 1.97, 1.63; CQ = 1.63), anxiety (OQ = 5.12, 5.08,

Table 8.28 : Statistical Differences Among Different Groups of Educated Unemployed and Employed Young Men for a Duration of 3-4 Year and their Relative Standing in Terms of Different Indices of Psychological Well-being

Indices of Psychological Well-being	Unemployed									Employed						
	Technically Educated						Non-technically Educated (N=55)			Technically Educated (N=17)			Non-technically Educated (N=30)			
	Degree-holders in Medical Sciences (N=17)			Degree-holders in Engineering Sciences (N=15)												
	Mean (%)	SD	Rank	Mean (%)	SD	Rank	Mean (%)	SD	Rank	Mean (%)	SD	Rank	Mean (%)	SD	Rank	F
1. General Worries	3.04 (50.67)	1.43	21	2.93 (48.83)	1.69	20	3.38 (56.33)	1.66	05	1.41 (23.50)	0.77	27	2.40 (40.00)	1.04	11.5	5.37
2. Somatic Manifestations	1.06 (35.33)	0.83	31	0.73 (24.33)	0.37	36	0.76 (25.33)	0.39	35	0.35 (11.67)	0.19	37	0.57 (19.00)	0.31	33	1.95
3. Psychological symptoms	2.28 (45.60)	1.14	27	2.40 (48.00)	1.10	22	2.24 (44.80)	1.37	24	1.00 (20.00)	0.62	30	1.80 (36.00)	1.03	22	2.84
4. Social Relations	2.65 (33.13)	1.55	32	3.47 (43.38)	1.83	27.5	3.11 (38.88)	2.06	31	1.65 (20.63)	0.83	28	2.07 (25.88)	1.39	29	2.95
5. **Anxiety**	9.05 (41.14)	3.80	29	9.53 (43.32)	4.27	29	9.49 (43.14)	4.81	26	4.41 (20.05)	2.26	29	6.84 (31.09)	2.69	28	4.97
6. Suicidal Tendency	0.29 (7.25)	0.17	39	0.47 (11.75)	0.25	39	0.33 (8.25)	0.19	39	0.29 (7.25)	0.15	39	0.13 (3.25)	0.07	39	0.60
7. Emotional Instability	2.94 (36.75)	1.58	30	3.47 (43.38)	1.86	27.5	3.20 (40.00)	1.16	29.5	1.41 (17.63)	0.77	32	1.57 (19.63)	0.88	31	5.43
8. Paranoid Tendency	2.35 (19.58)	1.42	38	3.27 (27.25)	1.53	34	2.04 (17.00)	1.38	38	1.35 (11.25)	0.73	38	0.97 (8.08)	0.52	37.5	3.79
9. Depression	9.82 (27.28)	3.86	34	10.00 (27.78)	5.88	33	10.45 (29.03)	4.90	33	5.29 (14.69)	2.87	33	3.30 (9.17)	1.73	36	7.55

Contd.

Table 8.28 *(Contd.)*

Indices of Psychological Well-being	*Unemployed*									*Employed*						
	Technically Educated						*Non-technically Educated (N=55)*			*Technically Educated (N=17)*			*Non-technically Educated (N=30)*			
	Degree-holders in Medical Sciences (N=17)			*Degree-holders in Engineering Sciences (N=15)*												
	Mean (%)	*SD*	*Rank*	*Mean (%)*	*SD*	*Rank*	*Mean (%)*	*SD*	*Rank*	*Mean (%)*	*SD*	*Rank*	*Mean (%)*	*SD*	*Rank*	*F*
10. Physical Illness	3.94 (32.83)	1.59	33	2.53 (21.08)	1.82	38	3.80 (31.67)	1.52	32	2.24 (18.67)	1.16	31	2.33 (19.42)	1.66	32	2.38
11. Social Maladjustment	3.06 (25.50)	1.66	36	3.40 (28.33)	1.82	32	2.95 (24.58)	1.49	36	1.47 (12.25)	0.81	36	0.97 (8.08)	0.50	37.5	5.90
12. Apprehensiveness	2.76 (23.00)	1.66	37	2.60 (21.67)	1.62	37	2.71 (22.58)	1.43	37	1.71 (14.25)	0.95	34	1.83 (15.25)	1.04	34	1.38
13. **Stress**	25.18 (26.23)	8.50	35	25.74 (26.81)	13.68	35	25.49 (26.55)	13.08	34	13.76 (14.33)	7.68	35	11.10 (11.56)	5.63	35	5.07
14. Lack of Self-confidence	10.82 (54.10)	3.94	11	11.87 (59.35)	3.87	04	11.59 (57.95)	5.42	04	7.46 (37.30)	2.41	13	7.67 (38.25)	2.58	16	4.69
15. Dejection	8.47 (56.47)	3.37	08	8.40 (56.00)	3.39	10	9.45 (63.00)	4.12	02	5.30 (35.33)	1.93	17	7.50 (50.00)	2.53	04	4.72
16. Pessimism	2.65 (53.00)	1.62	16	1.80 (36.00)	1.01	30	2.05 (41.00)	1.35	27	1.29 (25.80)	0.67	26	1.23 (24.60)	0.72	30	5.26
17. Emotional Responsiveness	16.17 (53.90)	5.09	13	16.42 (54.73)	5.23	13	14.81 (49.37)	6.84	20	11.41 (38.03)	3.23	11	10.90 (36.33)	3.06	20	4.20
18. Social Insecurity	13.23 (52.92)	4.72	18	12.81 (51.24)	4.47	18	12.09 (48.36)	5.89	22	8.05 (32.20)	2.56	24	9.07 (36.28)	2.84	21	3.46
19. Distrust	2.41 (48.20)	1.46	24	2.87 (57.40)	0.83	07	2.80 (56.00)	1.38	06	1.65 (33.00)	0.83	23	2.27 (45.40)	1.14	08	3.33

Contd.

Table 8.28 (*Contd.*)

Indices of Psychological Well-being	*Unemployed*									*Employed*						
	Technically Educated						*Non-technically Educated (N=55)*			*Technically Educated (N=17)*			*Non-technically Educated (N=30)*			
	Degree-holders in Medical Sciences (N=17)			*Degree-holders in Engineering Sciences (N=15)*												
	Mean (%)	*SD*	*Rank*	*Mean (%)*	*SD*	*Rank*	*Mean (%)*	*SD*	*Rank*	*Mean (%)*	*SD*	*Rank*	*Mean (%)*	*SD*	*Rank*	*F*
20. **Feeling of Insecurity**	·53.76 (53.76)	19.02	14	54.17 (54.17)	9.52	15	52.82 (52.82)	14.11	11	35.16 (35.16)	12.42	20	38.65 (38.65)	8.40	14	10.59
21. Despair	18.59 (58.09)	6.33	07	15.60 (48.75)	4.60	21	17.18 (53.69)	4.38	10	13.00 (40.62)	4.15	09	16.57 (51.78)	3.17	01	4.07
22. Unstructured universe	4.71 (58.88)	1.69	05	4.60 (57.50)	1.59	5.5	4.36 (54.50)	1.25	08	4.24 (53.00)	1.25	3.5	4.03 (50.38)	1.45	03	0.81
23. Psychological Vacuum	4.35 (54.38)	1.17	10	4.53 (56.63)	1.60	09	4.09 (51.13)	1.31	15	4.24 (53.00)	0.90	3.5	3.53 (44.13)	1.17	09	2.18
24. Disillusionment	1.88 (47.00)	0.99	26	1.80 (45.00)	0.68	25	1.60 (40.00)	0.68	29.5	1.82 (45.50)	1.03	06	1.40 (35.00)	0.50	24	1.62
25. Narcissism	1.65 (41.25)	0.79	28	1.87 (46.75)	0.99	23.5	1.62 (40.50)	0.83	28	2.00 (50.00)	1.12	05	1.83 (45.75)	0.99	07	0.75
26. **Alienation**	31.18 (55.68)	9.08	09	28.40 (50.71)	5.79	19	28.82 (51.46)	6.00	13	25.30 (45.18)	4.70	07	27.36 (48.86)	4.22	05	1.96
27. Depersonalization	4.12 (51.50)	2.23	19	3.53 (44.13)	1.25	26	3.47 (43.38)	1.61	25	2.82 (35.25)	1.51	18.5	2.50 (31.25)	0.51	27	4.15
28. Fragmentation	3.94 (49.25)	1.68	22	4.93 (61.63)	1.79	03	4.00 (50.00)	1.82	17	2.71 (33.88)	1.57	21	2.70 (33.75)	1.02	26	7.17
29. Uncertainty	2.41 (60.25)	1.18	03	2.93 (73.25)	0.59	·1.5	2.38 (59.50)	0.93	03	2.24 (56.00)	1.03	1.5	2.03 (50.75)	0.93	02	2.35

Contd.

Table 8.28 *(Contd.)*

Indices of Psychological Well-being	*Unemployed*									*Employed*						
	Technically Educated						*Non-technically Educated (N=55)*			*Technically Educated (N=17)*			*Non-technically Educated (N=30)*			
	Degree-holders in Medical Sciences (N=17)			*Degree-holders in Engineering Sciences (N=15)*												
	Mean (%)	*SD*	*Rank*	*Mean (%)*	*SD*	*Rank*	*Mean (%)*	*SD*	*Rank*	*Mean (%)*	*SD*	*Rank*	*Mean (%)*	*SD*	*Rank*	*F*
30. Distress	5.76 (48.00)	2.17	25	6.20 (51.67)	1.90	16	5.91 (49.25)	2.21	21	4.59 (38.25)	1.87	10	4.47 (37.25)	1.01	18	4.29
31. Indecisiveness	4.06 (50.75)	2.01	20	4.60 (57.50)	1.92	5.5	4.15 (51.88)	1.51	12	2.88 (36.00)	1.17	16	3.20 (40.00)	1.30	11.5	4.41
32. Social Conflict	2.71 (67.75)	1.16	01	2.27 (56.75)	1.16	08	2.75 (68.75)	0.95	01	2.24 (56.00)	1.09	1.5	1.93 (48.25)	1.01	06	3.56
33. Isolation	3.88 (48.50)	1.62	23	4.13 (51.63)	1.19	17	3.96 (49.50)	1.56	18.5	2.65 (33.13)	1.37	22	2.73 (34.13)	1.17	25	6.15
34. Withdrawal from Social and Personal Contact	2.12 (53.00)	1.17	16	1.40 (35.00)	0.51	31	1.98 (49.50)	0.95	18.5	1.65 (41.25)	0.86	08	1.47 (36.75)	0.86	19	2.72
35. Role Conflict	7.12 (59.33)	2.55	04	6.60 (55.00)	1.45	12	6.45 (53.75)	1.81	09	4.47 (37.25)	1.97	14	4.60 (38.33)	1.25	15	10.40
36. Hopelessness	4.24 (53.00)	2.17	16	4.47 (55.88)	1.41	11	4.02 (50.25)	1.73	16	2.41 (30.13)	0.80	25	3.17 (39.63)	0.79	13	6.18
37. Lonelinness	2.35 (58.75)	1.06	06	1.87 (46.75)	1.13	23.5	1.87 (46.75)	0.90	23	1.41 (35.25)	0.62	18.5	1.43 (35.75)	0.73	23	3.85
38. Desolation	2.59 (64.75)	1.00	02	2.93 (73.25)	0.96	1.5	2.20 (55.00)	0.95	07	1.47 (36.75)	0.72	15	1.67 (41.75)	0.88	10	8.29
39. **Identity-crisis**	45.31 (53.94)	14.07	12	45.87 (54.61)	7.68	14	43.19 (51.42)	11.31	14	31.54 (37.55)	11.63	12	31.90 (37.98)	6.69	17	10.24

Note : $df = 4{,}129$; $p < 0.05 = 2.44$; $p < 0.01 = 3.47$.

4.65; CQ = 4.65), emotional instability (OQ = 2.06; CQ = 2.02), stress (OQ = 14.64, 14.39, 14.08; CQ = 13.94), lack of self-confidence (OQ = 4.41, 4.13, 3.36; CQ = 1.33), dejection (OQ = 4.15, 3.17, 3.10; CQ = 1.29), pessimism (OQ = 1.36; CQ = 1.36), emotional responsiveness (OQ = 5.01, 4.76, 3.40; CQ = 1.18), social insecurity (OQ = 5.18, 4.76, 4.04; CQ = 1.28), feeling of insecurity (OQ = 19.01, 18.60, 17.66; CQ = 13.54), despair (OQ = 5.59; CQ = 4.32), fragmentation (OQ = 2.23; CQ = 1.55), indecisiveness (OQ = 1.72; CQ = 1.55), isolation (OQ = 1.49; CQ = 1.43), role conflict (OQ = 2.65, 2.13, 1.98; CQ = 1.80), hopelessness (OQ = 2.06, 1.82, 1.61; CQ = 1.50), loneliness (OQ = 0.94; CQ = 0.88), desolation (OQ = 1.46, 1.11; CQ = 0.93) and identity-crisis (OQ = 14.33, 13.47, 11.65, CQ = 10.69). The indicators of psychological well-being on which the group of the non-technically educated employed registered a clear tendency of difference from the various groups of the unemployed consisted of the dimensions like paranoid tendency (OQ = 2.30; CQ = 2.05), depression (OQ = 7.16, 6.70, 6.52; CQ = 6.39), social maladjustment (OQ = 2.43; CQ = 2.21), lack of self-confidence (OQ = 4.20, 3.92, 3.15; CQ = 1.29), pessimism (OQ = 1.41; CQ = 1.19), emotional responsiveness (OQ = 5.52, 5.27, 3.91; CQ = 1.24), social insecurity (OQ = 4.16, 3.74, 3.02; CQ = 1.23), feeling of insecurity (OQ = 15.52, 15.11, 14.27; CQ = 12.95), depersonalization (OQ = 1.62; CQ = 1.49), fragmentation (OQ = 2.23; CQ = 1.62), isolation (OQ = 1.40, CQ = 1.36), role conflict (OQ = 2.52, 2.00, 1.85; CQ = 1.72), loneliness (OQ = 0.92; CQ = 0.85), desolation (OQ = 1.26, 0.92; CQ = 0.89) and identity-crisis (OQ = 13.97, 13.41, 11.29; CQ = 10.23). Added to the above comparative account, it was further recorded that all the groups of job-seekers, particularly the engineers, apparently carried with them a greater amount of different symptoms of psychological ill-being. The groups of the educated employed, especially the technically educated ones, on the other hand, were psychologically least precipitated, but were, by and large, moderately susceptible to various psychological reactions. Lastly, here too, all the groups of respondents were seen to be clearly least prone to the tendency to commit suicide (scores of different groups on the scale of suicidal tendency ranged between 3.25 per cent and 11.75 per cent). But, here too, as the trend appeared earlier, no congruence was envisaged in the response of different groups of the unemployed and employed people in indicating the most agonizing psychological syndrome in them. However, all of them, excepting the group of non-technically educated employed who felt more despair (51.78%), were also afflicted greatly with the feeling of either uncertainty or social conflict (see Table 8.28).

Life Satisfaction : A Comparison Among Different Groups of Educated Unemployed and Employed Young Men for a Duration of 3-4 Year

Table 8.29 embodies the findings of a statistical comparison among different groups of educated unemployed and employed people for a longer span of 3-4 year in terms of the degree of their life satisfaction.

Table 8.29 : Statistical Differences Among Different Groups of Educated Unemployed and Employed Young Men for a Duration of 3-4 Year and their Relative Standing in Terms of the Degree of their Life Satisfaction

Variable	*Unemployed*						*Employed*				
	Technically Educated				*Non-technically Educated (N=55)*		*Technically Educated (N=17)*		*Non-technically Educated (N=30)*		
	Degree-holders in Medical Sciences (N=17)		*Degree-holders in Engineering Sciences (N=15)*								
	Mean (%)	*SD*	*Mean (%)*	*SD*	*Mean (%)*	*SD*	*Mean (%)*	*SD*	*Mean (%)*	*SD*	*F*
Life Satisfaction	4.53 (45.30)	2.18	5.47 (54.70)	1.96	4.56 (45.60)	2.45	7.29 (72.29)	1.57	6.87 (68.70)	1.59	9.96

Note : df = 4,129; p<0.05 = 2.44; p<0.01 = 3.47.

All of them tended to differ significantly from one another in terms of the degree of their life satisfaction (F = 9.96; df = 4,129; p<0.01). But, the multiple-comparison of different pairs of means indicated that only those two groups of respondents tended to differ markedly in their level of life satisfaction who were distinct in their status of employment. So, what appeared more frequently was the clear evidence of substantial differences between unemployed degree-holders in medical sciences and technically educated employed (OQ = 2.77; CQ = 2.09), unemployed degree-holders in medical sciences and non-technically educated employed (OQ = 2.34; CQ = 2.09), non-technically educated unemployed and technically educated employed (OQ = 2.73; CQ = 2.00), and non-techincally educated unemployed and non-technically educated employed (OQ = 2.30; CQ = 2.00). The results also showed that each and every group of the job-seekers, particularly the unemployed degree-holders in medical sciences (Index of Life satifaction = 45.30 per cent), were apparently less content with the goings-on in their life as compared to those of the groups of technically (life satisfaction scores = 72.29 per cent) and non-technically (amount of life satisfaction = 68.70 per cent) educated employed young men.

Educated Unemployed and Employed Young Men for a Duration of 3-4 Year: Their Dependence on Different Strategies Devised for their Adjustment

Table 8.30 details an account of the degree of dependence of different groups of educated unemployed and employed young men for a longer spell of 3-4 year on the coping strategies like intrapersistive approach mode, extrapersistive approach mode, punitive avoidance mode and defensive avoidance mode.

There were marked differences among different groups of unemployed and employed people in terms of the quantum of their reliance on all the strategies, except the defensive avoidance mode, in order to cope with their situations (see Table 8.30). However, no two groups, as it was apparent from the findings obtained from Newman-Keuls test, showed any substantial differences between themselves in this regard. Although there were exceptions, and that appeared in the form of noticeable differences between unemployed degree-holders in the medical sciences and non-technically educated employed (OQ = 3.17; CQ = 2.61), non-technically educated unemployed and employed (OQ = 2.57; CQ = 2.50), technically educated employed and non-technically educated employed (OQ = 2.41; CQ = 2.34), and unemployed engineers and non-technically educated employed (OQ = 1.97; CQ = 2.01) mainly in terms of the degree of their dependence on intrapersistive approach mode for adjustment. Lastly, here too, each of the groups of respondents were found to rely largely upon intrapersistive approach mode in dealing with their environment (level of dependence of different groups on intrapersistive approach mode varied between 56.87 per cent and 78.00 per cent).

Table 8.30 : Statistical Differences Among Different Groups of Educated Unemployed and Employed Young Men for a Duration of 3 - 4 Year and the Degree of their Relative Dependence in Terms of Different Coping Strategies

	Unemployed						*Employed*				
	Technically Educated				*Non-technically Educated (N=55)*		*Technically Educated (N=17)*		*Non-technically Educated (N=30)*		
Coping Strategies	*Degree-holders in Medical Sciences (N=17)*		*Degree-holders in Engineering Sciences (N=15)*								
	Mean (%)	*SD*	*Mean (%)*	*SD*	*Mean (%)*	*SD*	*Mean (%)*	*SD*	*Mean (%)*	*SD*	*F*
Intrapersistive Approach Mode	8.53 (56.87)	3.24	9.73 (64.87)	2.69	9.13 (60.87)	2.76	9.29 (61.93)	3.08	11.70 (78.00)	1.34	5.99
Extrapersistive Approach Mode	2.18 (14.53)	1.38	1.80 (12.00)	1.03	2.42 (16.13)	1.26	1.94 (12.93)	1.04	1.17 (7.80)	0.69	2.73
Punitive Avoidance Mode	0.88 (5.87)	0.47	0.73 (4.87)	0.39	0.95 (6.33)	0.47	0.94 (6.27)	0.48	0.43 (2.87)	0.27	0.90
Defensive Avoidance Mode	3.41 (22.73)	1.70	2.73 (18.20)	1.33	2.51 (16.73)	1.30	2.83 (18.87)	1.51	1.70 (11.33)	0.95	2.63

Note : $df = 4{,}129$; $p<0.05 = 2.44$; $p<0.01 = 3.47$.

Level of Anxiety, Stress, Feeling of Insecurity, Alienation, Identity-Crisis and their Dimensions : A Comparison Among Different Groups of Educated Unemployed and Employed Young Men for a Duration of 4-5 year

Table 8.31 displays the findings of a statistical comparison among different groups of educated unemployed and employed young men for a longer spell of 4-5 year in terms of the degree and extent of their psychological well-being manifested in the form of various symptomatic reactions of anxiety, stress, feeling of insecurity, alienation and identity-crisis.

All the groups of respondents were found to differ significantly from one another in their level of all the aforementioned psychological dimensions (F-values ranged between 2.83 and 12.76), except a few

Table 8.31 : Statistical Differences Among Different Groups of Educated Unemployed and Employed Young Men for a Duration of 4-5 year and their Relative Standing in Terms of Different Indices of Psychological Well-being

Indices of Psychological Well-being	*Unemployed*						*Employed*						
	Technically Educated Degree-holders in Engineering Sciences (N=15)			*Non-technically Educated (N=48)*			*Technically Educated (N=15)*			*Non-technically Educated (N=31)*			
	Mean (%)	*SD*	*Rank*	*Mean (%)*	*SD*	*Rank*	*Mean (%)*	*SD*	*Rank*	*Mean (%)*	*SD*	*Rank*	*F*
1. General Worries	2.67 (44.50)	1.38	22	3.75 (62.50)	1.78	04	1.73 (28.83)	0.89	28	2.13 (35.50)	1.18	24	9.96
2. Somatic Manifestations	0.60 (20.00)	0.32	36	0.85 (28.33)	0.43	36	0.47 (15.67)	0.30	32	0.45 (15.00)	0.26	35	1.63
3. Psychological Symptoms	2.33 (46.60)	1.18	18	2.58 (51.60)	1.44	24	0.93 (18.60)	0.53	30	1.58 (31.60)	0.76	27	8.86
4. Social Relations	3.27 (40.88)	1.59	27	3.00 (37.50)	1.94	31	1.07 (13.38)	0.60	35	1.68 (21.00)	0.88	32	8.10
5. **Anxiety**	8.87 (40.32)	4.43	28	10.19 (46.32)	4.82	28	4.20 (19.09)	2.15	29	5.87 (26.68)	2.38	29	12.30
6. Suicidal Tendency	0.20 (5.00)	0.11	39	0.54 (13.50)	0.27	39	0.20 (5.00)	0.11	39	0.05 (1.25)	0.02	39	2.91
7. Emotional Instability	3.40 (42.50)	1.88	26	3.02 (37.75)	1.28	30	3.07 (38.38)	1.64	22	1.77 (22.13)	1.03	30	3.49
8. Paranoid Tendency	2.00 (16.67)	1.06	37	3.02 (25.17)	1.91	38	1.33 (11.08)	0.72	37.5	1.84 (15.33)	1.04	34	2.83
9. Depression	9.53 (26.47)	5.10	32	11.56 (32.11)	6.38	33	4.87 (13.53)	2.51	34	5.03 (13.97)	2.97	37	7.00

Contd.

Table 8.31 *(Contd.)*

Indices of Psychological Well-being	*Unemployed*						*Employed*						*F*
	Technically Educated *Degree-holders in Engineering Sciences (N=15)*			*Non-technically Educated (N=48)*			*Technically Educated (N=15)*			*Non-technically Educated (N=31)*			
	Mean (%)	*SD*	*Rank*	*Mean (%)*	*SD*	*Rank*	*Mean (%)*	*SD*	*Rank*	*Mean (%)*	*SD*	*Rank*	
10. Physical Ilness	2.67 (22.25)	1.53	35	3.58 (29.83)	1.92	35	2.00 (16.67)	0.93	31	1.97 (16.42)	1.05	33	3.81
11. Social Maladjustment	2.87 (23.92)	1.90	33	4.19 (34.92)	2.52	32	1.60 (13.33)	0.84	36	2.58 (21.50)	1.35	31	4.07
12. Apprehensiveness	1.87 (15.58)	1.05	38	3.10 (25.83)	1.85	37.	1.33 (11.08)	0.74	37.5	1.10 (9.17)	0.61	38	6.22
13. **Stress**	22.54 (23.48)	12.74	34	29.02 (30.23)	16.25	34	14.40 (15.00)	8.06	33	14.35 (14.95)	6.56	36	6.21
14. Lack of Self-confidence	9.94 (49.70)	3.56	12	11.39 (56.95)	4.24	07	7.61 (38.05)	2.59	24	9.16 (45.80)	2.78	05	3.09
15. Dejection	8.24 (54.93)	3.17	07	9.91 (66.07)	3.78	02	6.20 (41.33)	2.11	17	6.45 (43.00)	2.41	12	7.90
16. Pessimism	1.93 (38.60)	1.08	29	2.56 (51.20)	1.51	26	1.80 (36.00)	0.93	25	1.45 (29.00)	0.77	28	5.15
17. Emotional Responsiveness	15.28 (50.93)	4.99	09	16.41 (54.70)	5.69	14.5	13.61 (45.37)	3.67	07	11.75 (39.17)	3.17	18	3.16
18. Social Insecurity	11.14 (44.56)	4.03	21	13.44 (53.76)	4.72	18	10.27 (41.08)	3.34	18	10.16 (40.64)	3.09	16	3.31
19. Distrust	2.53 (50.60)	1.06	10	2.67 (53.40)	1.34	19	1.93 (38.60)	1.06	21	1.71 (34.20)	0.86	26	4.94

Contd.

Table 8.31 *(Contd.)*

Indices of Psychological Well-being	*Unemployed*						*Employed*						
	Technically Educated *Degree-holders in Engineering Sciences (N=15)*			*Non-technically Educated (N=48)*			*Technically Educated (N=15)*			*Non-technically Educated (N=31)*			
	Mean (%)	*SD*	*Rank*	*Mean (%)*	*SD*	*Rank*	*Mean (%)*	*SD*	*Rank*	*Mean (%)*	*SD*	*Rank*	*F*
20. **Feeling of Insecurity**	49.07 (49.07)	14.08	14	56.40 (56.40)	14.75	09	41.42 (41.42)	14.27	16	40.68 (40.68)	12.12	15	10.61
21. Despair	15.40 (48.13)	3.52	16	18.00 (56.25)	4.97	10.5	15.47 (48.34)	3.93	06	13.94 (43.56)	2.37	09	6.76
22. Unstructured Universe	4.53 (56.63)	1.30	06	4.52 (56.50)	1.34	08	4.80 (60.00)	1.42	02	4.19 (52.38)	1.42	03	0.74
23. Psychological Vacuum	4.67 (58.38)	1.05	03	4.21 (52.63)	1.22	21	4.07 (50.88)	1.53	04	4.09 (51.13)	1.29	04	0.85
24. Disillusionment	1.53 (38.25)	0.64	30.5	1.79 (44.75)	0.92	29	1.53 (38.25)	0.74	23	1.38 (34.50)	0.71	25	1.92
25. Narcissism	1.53 (38.25)	0.74	30.5	2.10 (52.50)	0.99	22	1.67 (41.75)	0.72	14	1.55 (38.75)	0.93	21	3.10
26. **Alienation**	27.67 (49.41)	4.48	13	30.63 (54.70)	6.94	14.5	27.54 (49.18)	6.06	05	25.16 (44.93)	3.38	07	5.96
27. Depersonalization	3.67 (45.88)	1.72	19.5	4.17 (52.13)	1.96	23	2.73 (34.13)	1.16	27	3.10 (38.75)	1.30	21	4.15
28. Fragmentation	3.67 (45.88)	1.45	19.5	4.50 (56.25)	1.87	10.5	3.33 (41.63)	1.59	15	3.48 (43.50)	1.39	10.5	3.44
29. Uncertainty	2.53 (63.25)	1.13	02	2.58 (64.50)	1.05	03	2.07 (51.75)	0.70	03	1.83 (45.75)	0.86	06	4.29

Contd.

Table 8.31 *(Contd.)*

Indices of Psychological Well-being	*Unemployed*						*Employed*						
	Technically Educated Degree-holders in Engineering Sciences (N=15)			*Non-technically Educated (N=48)*			*Technically Educated (N=15)*			*Non-technically Educated (N=31)*			
	Mean (%)	*SD*	*Rank*	*Mean (%)*	*SD*	*Rank*	*Mean (%)*	*SD*	*Rank*	*Mean (%)*	*SD*	*Rank*	*F*
30. Distress	5.27 (43.92)	1.79	23	6.71 (55.92)	2.63	12	5.27 (43.92)	2.09	10	4.39 (36.58)	1.09	23	8.10
31. Indecisiveness	4.13 (51.63)	1.41	08	4.31 (53.88)	1.79	17	2.87 (35.88)	1.06	26	3.35 (41.88)	1.25	13	4.86
32. Social Conflict	2.87 (71.75)	0.99	01	2.81 (70.25)	0.89	01	2.47 (61.75)	0.83	01	2.19 (54.75)	0.83	01	3.70
33. Isolation	3.47 (43.38)	1.55	24	4.00 (50.00)	1.71	27	3.47 (43.38)	1.85	11.5	3.10 (38.75)	0.94	21	2.28
34. Withdrawal from Social and Personal Contact	1.73 (43.25)	1.10	25	2.13 (53.25)	1.02	20	1.80 (45.00)	0.94	8.5	1.74 (43.50)	0.82	10.5	1.33
35. Role Conflict	6.87 (57.25)	2.13	04	6.88 (57.33)	2.27	06	4.80 (40.00)	1.61	19.5	4.84 (40.33)	1.86	17	12.76
36. Hopelessness	3.87 (48.38)	1.46	15	4.35 (54.38)	1.69	16	3.47 (43.38)	1.46	11.5	3.11 (38.88)	1.04	19	4.90
37. Lonelinness	1.87 (46.75)	1.06	17	2.06 (51.50)	0.91	25	1.60 (40.00)	0.91	19.5	1.77 (44.25)	0.56	08	1.44
38. Desolation	2.27 (56.75)	1.03	05	2.38 (59.50)	1.08	05	1.80 (45.00)	0.68	8.5	2.17 (54.25)	1.12	02	0.58
39. **Identity-crisis**	42.22 (50.26)	9.13	11	46.88 (55.81)	12.98	13	35.68 (42.48)	11.34	13	35.07 (41.75)	6.71	14	9.12

Note : $df = 3{,}105$; $p < 0.05 = 2.70$; $p < 0.01 = 3.98$.

particularly associated with some of the alienating outbursts. However, here too, the findings attained through Newman-Keuls Test indicated that no one group of respondents tended to differ markedly from the other in their psychological reactions, especially if he two had a similar status of employment. Noticeably, in all the instances, except a few such as a perceptible difference between the mean scores of the technically and the non-technically educated employed in terms of lack of self-confidence (OQ = 1.55; CQ = 1.26), the unemployed degree-holders in engineering sciences and the non-technically educated unemployed in terms of lack of self-confidence (OQ = 1.45; CQ = 1.04), the unemployed degree-holders in the engineering sciences and the non-technically educated unemployed in terms of dejection (OQ = 1.67; CQ = 1.04), the non-technically and the technically educated employed in terms of emotional reponsiveness (OQ = 1.86; CQ = 1.22), the unemployed degree-holders in the engineering sciences and the non-technically educated unemployed in terms of emotional responsiveness (OQ = 1.13; CQ = 1.00), and the unemployed degree-holders in engineering sciences and the non-technically educated unemployed in terms of social insecurity (OQ = 2.30; CQ = 0.96), only those two groups of respondents showed a considerable difference between themselves in their standing on various health indices who were apparently dissimilar in their status of employment. The various psychological symptoms in which the technically educated employed registered a clear-cut difference from the unemployed degree-holders in engineering sciences or the non-technically educated unemployed were as follows : general worries (OQ = 2.02; CQ = 1.54), psychological symptoms (OQ = 1.65, 1.40; CQ = 1.20), social relations (OQ = 2.20, 1.93; CQ = 1.67), anxiety (OQ = 5.99, 4.67; CQ = 3.93), lack of self-confidence (OQ = 3.78, 2.33; CQ = 1.26), dejection (OQ = 3.71, 2.04; CQ = 1.26), emotional responsiveness (OQ = 2.80, 1.67; CQ = 1.13), social insecurity (OQ = 3.17; CQ = 1.09), feeling of insecurity (OQ = 14.98; CQ = 12.13), indecisiveness (OQ = 1.45; CQ = 1.48), role conflict (OQ = 2.08, 2.07; CQ = 1.67), and identity-crisis (OQ = 11.20; CQ = 9.83). The indicators of psychological health where the non-technically educated employed tended to differ markedly from the groups of unemployed included dimensions like general worries (OQ = 1.62; CQ = 1.44), social relation (OQ = 1.59; CQ = 1.56), anxiety (OQ = 4.32; CQ = 3.67), depression (OQ = 6.53; CQ = 6.40), lack of self-confidence (OQ = 2.23; CQ = 1.18), dejection (OQ = 3.46, 1.79; CQ = 1.18), emotional responsiveness (OQ = 4.66, 3.53; CQ = 1.22), social insecurity (OQ = 3.28; CQ = 1.17), feeling of insecurity (OQ = 15.72; CQ = 13.01), despair (OQ = 4.07; CQ = 3.95), distress (OQ = 2.32; CQ = 2.06), role conflict (OQ = 2.04, 2.03; CQ = 1.55), and identity-crisis (OQ = 11.81; CQ = 10.54). Further, it was also noticed that the unemployed, particularly the non-technically educated ones, on the whole, were greatly afflicted with various symptoms of psychological impairment. On the contrary, the employed, in general, possessed a benign psychological health to a considerable degree. Nonetheless, they, too, were moderately exposed to psychological risk. Lastly, quite in contrast to the trends appearing earlier, all the groups of respondents rated themselves highly tense with the feeling of social conflict (scores obtained by different groups on social conflict scale varied between 54.75 per cent and 71.75 per cent) and least with suicidal ideation (scores for different groups on the scale of suicidal tendency ranged between 1.25 per cent and 13.50 per cent).

Life Satisfaction : A Comparisn Among Different Groups of Educated Unemployed Young Men for a Duration of 4-5 Year

Table 8.32 depicts a comparative account of the degree of life satisfaction enjoyed by different groups of unemployed and employed young men for a longer span of 4-5 year.

A significant difference was noticed among all the groups of participants in their level of life satisfaction ($F = 13.20$; $df = 3,105$;

Table 8.32 : Statistical Differences Among Different Groups of Educated Unemployed and Employed Young Men for a Duration of 4-5 year and their Relative Standing in Terms of the Degree of their Life Satisfaction

	Unemployed				*Employed*				
	Technically Educated		*Non-technically Educated*		*Technically Educated*		*Non-technically Educated*		
Variable	*Degree-holders in Engineering Sciences (N=15)*		*(N=48)*		*(N=15)*		*(N=31)*		
	Mean (%)	*SD*	*Mean (%)*	*SD*	*Mean (%)*	*SD*	*Mean (%)*	*SD*	*F*
Life Satisfaction	5.13 (51.30)	2.57	4.29 (42.90)	2.37	6.13 (61.30)	2.10	7.48 (74.80)	1.39	13.20

Note : $df = 3,105$; $p<0.05 = 2.70$; $p<0.01 = 3.98$.

$p<0.01$). However, as it appeared from the statistical comparison of different pairs of means, no two groups of respondents differed markedly between themselves, if they were exclusively labelled as either unemployed or employed. Thus, if meaningful differences were recorded in the mean life satisfaction scores between any two groups, they were between the non-technically educated unemployed and the employed (OQ = 3.19; CQ = 2.19), the unemployed engineers and the non-technically educated employed (OQ = 2.35; CQ = 2.05). The groups of unemployed were not found greatly distinct from that of the technically educated employed in their level of life satisfaction. Also, it was clearly seen that while both the groups of unemployed were less satisfied with the order of their life, the employed, particularly the non-technically educated ones (74.80 per cent), were more satisfied.

Educated Unemployed and Employed Young Men for a Duration of 4-5 year : their Dependence on Different Strategies Devised for their Adjustment

Table 8.33 : Statistical Differences Among Different Groups of Educated Unemployed and Employed Young Men for a Duration of 4-5 Year and the Degree of their Relative Dependence in Terms of Different Coping Strategies

Coping Strategies	*Unemployed*				*Employed*				
	Technically Educated — *Degree-holders in Engineering Sciences (N=15)*		*Non-technically Educated (N=48)*		*Technically Educated (N=15)*		*Non-technically Educated (N=31)*		
	Mean (%)	*SD*	*Mean (%)*	*SD*	*Mean (%)*	*SD*	*Mean (%)*	*SD*	*F*
Intrapersistive Approach Mode	11.13 (74.20)	2.61	9.58 (63.87)	2.51	10.20 (68.00)	4.25	10.52 (70.13)	1.95	1.58
Extrapersistive Approach Mode	1.47 (9.80)	0.80	1.90 (12.67)	0.97	2.60 (17.33)	1.35	1.77 (11.80)	1.02	0.62
Punitive Avoidance Mode	1.13 (7.53)	0.63	0.90 (6.00)	0.44	0.27 (1.80)	0.16	0.84 (5.60)	0.40	1.72
Defensive Avoidance Mode	1.27 (8.47)	0.83	2.63 (17.53)	1.74	1.93 (12.87)	1.03	1.87 (12.47)	1.06	3.15

Note. df = 3,105; $p<0.05$ = 2.70; $p<0.01$ = 3.98.

Table 8.33 presents a short description of the degree of dependence of different groups of unemployed and employed people for a longer period of 4-5 year on various coping strategies.

No group of respondents tended to differ from another to a substantial measure in terms of the use of any of the strategies adopted to fight his life events, excepting that of the defensive avoidance mode ($F = 3.15$; $df = 3,105$; $p<0.05$). Further, here too, all the groups of unemployed and employed young men greatly confided in intrapersistive approach mode in effecting compromise with their existing situations (the degree of reliance of different groups on intrapersistive approach mode was between 63.87 per cent and 74.20 per cent). Clearly, other modes of adjustment failed to attract them in any fair amount in this connection.

Level of Anxiety, Stress, Feeling of Insecurity, Alienation, Identity-Crisis and their Dimensions : A Comparison Among Different Groups of Educated Unemployed and Employed Young Men for a Duration of 5-6 year

Table 8.34 describes the summary of a statistical comparison among different groups of educated unemployed and employed people for a prolonged period of 5-6 year in terms of the degree and extent of various manifestations of anxiety, stress, feeling of insecurity, alienation and identity-crisis in them.

All the groups of respondents, here too, showed a considerable difference among themselves in terms of their level on each of the aforementioned symptomatic reactions (F-values ranged between 3.42 and 37.08), barring somatic manifestations, suicidal tendency, unstructured universe, psychological vacuum, uncertainty, loneliness and desolation. However, the statistical comparisons of different pairs of means, particularly at intra-group level, did not exhibit so in all. Notably, with the exception of significant differences between the technically and the non-technically educated employed in terms of psychological symptoms (OQ = 1.40; CQ = 0.86), and the technically and the non-technically educated employed in terms of anxiety (OQ = 2.95; CQ = 2.73) exclusively at intra-group level, there recorded substantial differences only between those two groups of respondents in their level of various symptomatic reactions who held two distinct status of employment. The prominent health indices where the technically educated employed tended to differ from their unemployed

Table 8.34 : Statistical Differences Among Different Groups of Educated Unemployed and Employed Young Men for a Duration of 5-6 Year and their Relative Standing in Terms of Different Indices of Psychological Well-being

	Unemployed			*Employed*						
	Non-technically Educated (N=44)			*Technically Educated (N=15)*			*Non-technically Educated (N=30)*			
Indices of Psychological Well-being	*Mean (%)*	*SD*	*Rank*	*Mean (%)*	*SD*	*Rank*	*Mean (%)*	*SD*	*Rank*	*F*
1. Ceneral Worries	3.64 (60.67)	1.57	04	1.33 (22.17)	0.72	27	2.03 (33.83)	1.14	22	18.63
2. Somatic Manifestations	0.80 (26.67)	0.39	36	0.47 (15.67)	0.24	29	0.43 (14.33)	0.25	33	2.45
3. Psychological Symptoms	2.59 (51.80)	1.04	17	0.40 (8.00)	0.21	38	1.80 (36.00)	1.03	19	27.07
4. Social Relations	3.34 (41.75)	1.66	30	0.67 (8.38)	0.36	36	1.57 (19.63)	0.87	31	26.48
5. **Anxiety**	10.36 (47.09)	3.41	26	2.88 (13.09)	1.61	34	5.83 (26.50)	3.22	29	37.08
6. Suicidal Tendency	0.11 (2.75)	0.06	39	0.00 (0.00)	0.00	39	0.07 (1.75)	0.03	39	2.79
7. Emotional Instability	2.93 (36.63)	1.44	31	1.33 (16.63)	0.71	28	2.30 (28.75)	1.20	28	4.00
8. Paranoid Tendency	2.52 (21.00)	1.34	37	1.60 (13.33)	0.86	33	1.27 (10.58)	0.66	37.5	4.33
9. Depression	11.11 (30.86)	6.05	32	4.93 (13.69)	2.51	32	4.87 (13.53)	2.47	35	13.05
10. Physical Ilness	3.34 (27.83)	1.92	33	1.67 (13.92)	0.85	31	1.83 (15.25)	1.06	32	6.72
11. Social Maladjustment	2.39 (19.92)	1.79	38	1.73 (14.42)	0.93	30	1.27 (10.58)	0.68	37.5	3.42
12. Apprehensive-ness	3.27 (27.25)	1.54	34	1.00 (8.33)	0.53	37	1.60 (13.33)	0.83	36	9.14
13. **Stress**	25.68 (26.75)	12.34	35	12.26 (12.77)	6.93	35	13.21 (13.76)	7.01	34	13.22
14. Lack of Self-confidence	12.09 (60.45)	5.27	05	7.59 (37.95)	2.47	15	7.93 (39.65)	2.71	14	7.21
15. Dejection	9.48 (63.20)	4.02	03	6.40 (42.67)	2.21	06	6.81 (45.40)	2.54	06	6.15
16. Pessimism	2.25 (45.00)	1.53	29	1.13 (22.60)	0.35	26	1.27 (25.40)	0.69	30	8.79
17. Emotional Responsiveness	15.72 (52.40)	6.56	15	10.93 (36.43)	3.02	18	10.50 (35.00)	2.97	21	6.83
18. Social Insecurity	12.61 (50.44)	5.15	22	10.00 (40.00)	2.74	9.5	7.97 (31.88)	2.76	27	7.72
19. Distrust	2.75 (55.00)	1.42	08	2.07 (41.40)	1.08	07	1.67 (33.40)	0.92	24	6.67
20. **Feeling of Insecurity**	54.91 (54.91)	11.01	09	38.12 (38.12)	10.42	14	36.15 (36.15)	10.63	18	29.77

Contd.

Table 8.34 *(Contd.)*

Indices of Psychological Well-being	*Unemployed*			*Employed*						
	Non-technically Educated (N=44)			*Technically Educated (N=15)*			*Non-technically Educated (N=30)*			
	Mean	*SD (%)*	*Rank*	*Mean*	*SD (%)*	*Rank*	*Mean*	*SD (%)*	*Rank*	*F*
21. Despair	16.23 (50.72)	3.24	21	15.73 (49.16)	3.33	04	14.33 (44.78)	2.67	08	3.43
22. Unstructured Universe	4.30 (53.75)	1.09	12.5	4.20 (52.50)	1.08	2.5	4.07 (50.88)	1.60	03	0.28
23. Psychological Vacuum	4.52 (56.50)	1.32	06	4.20 (52.50)	0.68	2.5	3.80 (47.50)	1.61	05	2.57
24. Disillusionment	1.98 (49.50)	0.79	23.5	1.13 (28.25)	0.35	25	1.43 (35.75)	0.68	20	10.35
25. Narcissism	1.82 (45.50)	1.06	28	1.27 (31.75)	0.46	21	1.33 (33.25)	0.76	25.5	3.99
26. **Alienation**	28.84 (51.50)	4.24	18	26.53 (47.37)	4.10	05	24.97 (44.59)	3.81	09	8.25
27. Depersonalization	4.16 (52.00)	1.57	16	2.47 (30.88)	0.64	23	2.70 (33.75)	1.15	23	15.23
28. Fragmentation	3.75 (46.88)	1.60	27	2.60 (32.50)	0.91	20	3.33 (41.63)	1.45	11	3.56
29. Uncertainty	2.59 (64.75)	0.87	02	2.47 (61.75)	0.83	01	2.33 (58.25)	1.03	01	0.70
30. Distress	6.48 (54.00)	1.78	10.5	4.60 (38.33)	1.64	13	4.50 (37.50)	1.61	15.5	14.47
31. Indecisiveness	4.32 (54.00)	1.43	10.5	2.53 (31.63)	0.64	22	2.90 (36.25)	1.27	17	16.63
32. Social Conflict	2.61 (65.25)	1.02	01	1.60 (40.00)	0.63	9.5	2.03 (50.75)	0.85	04	8.21
33. Isolation	3.82 (47.75)	1.33	25	3.07 (38.38)	1.79	12	3.00 (37.50)	1.14	15.5	3.81
34. Withdrawal from Social and Personal Contact	2.05 (51.25)	1.01	19.5	1.60 (40.00)	0.91	9.5	1.33 (33.25)	0.55	25.5	6.27
35. Role Conflict	6.66 (55.50)	1.98	07	4.33 (36.08)	1.29	19	5.03 (41.92)	1.94	10	11.72
36. Hopelessness	4.30 (53.75)	1.71	12.5	2.27 (28.38)	0.70	24	3.27 (40.88)	1.64	12	10.50
37. Lonelinness	1.98 (49.50)	1.09	23.5	1.47 (36.75)	0.82	16	1.80 (45.00)	0.89	07	1.49
38. Desolation	2.05 (51.25)	0.96	19.5	1.60 (40.00)	0.83	9.5	2.06 (51.50)	0.64	02	1.62
39. **Identity-Crisis**	44.75 (53.27)	8.70	14	30.61 (36.44)	7.44	17	34.28 (40.81)	10.37	13	19.14

Note : $df = 2{,}86$; $p < 0.05 = 3.10$; $p < 0.01 = 4.85$.

counterparts were general worries (OQ = 2.30; CQ = 1.26), psychological symptoms (OQ = 2.19; CQ = 0.86), social relations (OQ = 2.67; CQ = 1.20), anxiety (OQ = 7.88;CQ = 2.73), depression (OQ = 6.18;

CQ = 4.34), apprehensiveness (OQ = 2.27; CQ = 1.81), stress (OQ = 13.42; CQ = 9.96), lack of self-confidence (OQ = 4.50; CQ = 2.34), dejection (OQ = 3.08; CQ = 0.98), pessimism (OQ = 1.12; CQ = 1.00), emotional responsiveness (OQ = 4.79; CQ = 2.24), social insecurity (OQ = 2.61; CQ = 1.94), feeling of insecurity (OQ = 16.79; CQ = 8.40), disillusionment (OQ = 0.84; CQ = 0.60), depersonalization (OQ = 1.69; CQ = 1.13), distress (OQ = 1.88; CQ = 1.29), indecisiveness (OQ = 1.79; CQ = 1.10), social conflict (OQ = 1.01; CQ = 0.78), role conflict (OQ = 2.33; CQ = 1.60),hopelessness (OQ = 2.03; CQ = 1.34), and identity-crisis (OQ = 14.14; CQ = 7.83). With a few exceptions, the group of non-technically educated employed also expressed apparent differences from that of their unemployed counterparts mostly in terms of the abovementioned health indices. The observed values of Q as against the criterion values of Q noted for the differences between the non-technically educated employed and the unemployed people in terms of their various symptomatic reactions were as follows : general worries (OQ = 1.60; CQ = 1.11), psychological symptoms (OQ = 0.79 CQ = 0.76), social relations (OQ = 1.77; CQ = 1.06),anxiety (OQ = 4.53; CQ = 2.40), depression (OQ = 6.25; CQ = 4.94), physical illness (OQ = 1.51; CQ = 1.52), apprehensiveness (OQ = 1.67; CQ = 1.60), stress (OQ = 12.47; CQ = 8.76), lack of self-confidence (OQ = 4.16; CQ = 2.05), dejection (OQ = 2.67; CQ = 0.86), pessimism (OQ = 0.98; CQ = 0.88), emotional responsiveness (OQ = 5.22; CQ = 2.55), social insecurity (OQ = 4.64; CQ = 2.21), distrust (OQ = 1.08; CQ = 1.09), feeling of insecurity (OQ = 18.86; CQ = 9.56), disillusionment (OQ = 0.54; CQ = 0.53), alienation (OQ = 3.87; CQ = 3.50), depersonalization (OQ = 1.46; CQ = 1.00), distress (OQ = 1.98; CQ = 1.46), indecisiveness (OQ = 1.42; CQ = 0.96), withdrawal from social and personal contact (OQ = 0.72; CQ = 0.74), role conflict (OQ = 1.63; CQ = 1.41), and identity-crisis (OQ = 10.47; CQ = 6.89). In addition, while the group of unemployed young men, here too, was found to be psychologically more vulnerable, both the groups of the technically and non-technically educated employed were less, though moderately, susceptible to psychological ill-being. Furthermore, like the trend as it appeared throughout the investigation, all the groups of respondents were least exposed to the tendency to commit suicide. However, they did not express such unanimity in indicating the most tormenting psychological symptom in them. Noticeably, the unemployed were plagued with a greater amount of social conflict (65.25 per cent), whereas the groups of employed were greatly scared with an intense feeling of uncertainty (levels of uncertainty in the two groups of employed were found to be 61.75 per cent and 58.25 per cent).

Life Satisfaction : A Comparison Among Different Groups of Educated Unemployed and Employed Young Men for a Duration of 5-6 Year

Table 8.35 narrates the level of life satisfaction among the groups of educated unemployed and employed people for a longer duration of 5 - 6 year.

Overall, there were highly significant differences among different

Table 8.35 : Statistical Differences Among Different Groups of Educated Unemployed and Employed Young Men for a Duration of 5-6 year and their Relative Standing in Terms of the Degree of their Life Satisfaction

	Unemployed		*Employed*				
	Non-technically Educated (N=44)		*Technically Educated(N=15)*		*Non-technically Educated (N=30)*		
Variable	*Mean (%)*	*SD*	*Mean (%)*	*SD*	*Mean (%)*	*SD*	*F*
Life Satisfaction	4.64 (46.40)	1.70	7.80 (78.00)	1.21	6.57 (65.70)	2.30	19.80

Note : $df = 2,86$; $p < 0.05 = 3.10$; $p < 0.01 = 4.85$.

groups of the unemployed and employed people in their level of life satisfaction ($F = 19.80$; $df = 2,86$; $p<0.01$). However, as it was quite apparent from the multiple-comparison of means, only the group of unemployed was markedly distinct in this regard (OQ = 3.16,1.93; CQ = 1.60); there was a greater congruence in the mean life satisfaction scores between the technically and the non-technically educated employed young men (CQ = 1.41). Further, here too, while both the groups of technically (Index of life satisfaction = 78.00%) and non-technically educated employed (Index of life satisfaction = 65.70%) perceived life as highly delightful, the group of the umemployed indicated it to be less, but moderately, satisfactory (Index of life satisfaction = 46.40%).

Educated Unemployed and Employed Young Men for a Duration of 5-6 Year: their Dependence on Different Strategies Devised for their Adjustment

Table 8.36 involves a comparative account of the degree of dependence of different groups of educated unemployed and employed people for a prolonged period of 5-6 year on different tactics devised to effect a compromise with their life circumstances.

Table 8.36 : Statistical Differences Among Different Groups of Educated Unemployed and Employed Young Men for a Duration of 5-6 year and the Degree of their Relative Dependence in Terms of Different Coping Strategies

	Unemployed		*Employed*				
	Non-technically Educated (N=44)		*Technically Educated(N=15)*		*Non-technically Educated (N=30)*		
Coping Strategies	*Mean (%)*	*SD*	*Mean (%)*	*SD*	*Mean (%)*	*SD*	*F*
Intrapersistive Approach Mode	9.45 (63.00)	2.35	9.93 (66.20)	1.91	11.07 (73.80)	2.65	4.09
Extrapersistive Approach Mode	1.84 (12.27)	0.98	1.33 (8.87)	0.72	1.27 (8.47)	0.74	1.97
Punitive Avoidance Mode	0.98 (6.53)	0.47	1.87 (12.47)	0.99	0.50 (3.33)	0.28	7.43
Defensive Avoidance Mode	2.73 (18.20)	1.43	1.87 (12.47)	1.06	2.16 (14.40)	1.15	1.79

Note : $df = 2{,}86$; $p<0.05 = 3.10$; $p<0.01 = 4.85$.

The statistical comparison of different groups of unemployed and employed people in terms of the amount of their reliance on various coping strategies yielded mixed results. No marked differences were found among them in terms of the degree of their dependence on extrapersistive apporoach mode and defensive avoidance mode. But, they showed considerable differences in the amount of embracing intrapersistive approach mode ($p<0.05$) and punitive avoidance mode ($F = 7.43$; $p<0.01$) as their coping strategies. Although the differences of one group of respondents from another in their level of dependence on these two coping strategies also did not appear fully perceptible. No one group of respondents was found to differ significantly from another in the amount of the use of intrapersistive approach mode for their adjustment, particularly at 0.01 level. Similarly, the non-technically educated unemployed and employed groups did not exhibit any marked differences between themselves in their level of reliance upon punitive avoidance mode; both of them were only found to be distinct from that of the technically educated employed people to a substantial measure in this regard (CQ = 0.96 and 0.85). However, all the groups of respondents, here too, solely relied on intrapersistive approach mode in fitting themselves with their situations (their degree of dependence arounded between 63.00 per cent and 73.80 per cent).

Level of Anxiety, Stress, Feeling of Insecurity, Alienation, Identity-Crisis and their Dimensions : A Comparison Among Different Groups of Educated Unemployed and Employed Young Men for a Duration of 6-7 year

Table 8.37 yields the findings of a statistical comparison among different groups of unemployed and employed people for a longer spell of 6-7 year in terms of their level on various measures such as anxiety, stress, feeling of insecurity, alienation and identity-crisis of psychological well-being.

Similar to the trend as it was recorded earlier, all the groups of respondents, overall, tended to differ markedly from one another in terms of all the abovementioned measures of psychological health (F-values varied between 3.85 and 31.29), barring a few alienating reactions such as despair, unstructured universe and narcissism in particular. However, here too, the findings obtained from multiple-comparison clearly indicated that there always existed significant differences only between those two groups of respondents in their psychological reactions who did not hail from a similar status of employment. Clearly, the unemployed were found to be fairly distinct from those of the exclusive groups of technically and non-technically educated employed people in their various psychological reactions. The different indicators of psychological health in which the technically educated employed showed noticeable differences from that of their unemployed counterparts were general worries (OQ = 2.07; CQ = 1.22), somatic manifestations (OQ = 1.07; CQ = 0.78), psychological symptoms (CQ = 0.92), social relations (CQ = 1.40), anxiety (OQ = 7.28;CQ = 3.34), depression (OQ = 5.51; CQ = 5.28), physical illness (CQ = 1.74), social maladjustment (OQ = 3.85; CQ =

Table 8.37 : Statistical Differences Among Different Groups of Educated Unemployed and Employed Young Men for a Duration of 6-7 year and their Relative Standing in Terms of Different Indices of Psychological Well-being

Indices of Psychological Well-being	*Unemployed*			*Employed*						
	Non-technically Educated (N=45)			*Technically Educated (N=15)*			*Non-technically Educated (N=30)*			
	Mean (%)	*SD*	*Rank*	*Mean (%)*	*SD*	*Rank*	*Mean (%)*	*SD*	*Rank*	*F*
1. General Worries	4.07 (67.83)	1.39	02	2.00 (33.33)	1.07	22	2.33 (38.83)	1.30	25	19.03
2. Somatic Manifestations	1.40 (46.67)	0.59	31	0.33 (11.00)	0.18	36	0.80 (26.67)	0.46	31	8.96
3. Psychological Symptoms	3.20 (64.00)	0.76	05	1.47 (29.40)	0.81	27	1.63 (32.60)	0.87	28	25.90
4. Social Relations	3.93 (49.13)	1.53	29	1.53 (19.13)	0.80	32	2.37 (29.63)	1.52	30	15.55
5. **Anxiety**	12.61 (57.32)	3.41	19	5.33 (24.23)	2.69	29	7.13 (32.41)	4.05	29	25.69
6. Suicidal Tendency	0.58 (14.50)	0.28	39	0.00 (0.00)	0.00	39	0.08 (2.00)	0.03	39	4.46
7. Emotional Instability	3.53 (44.13)	1.26	32	1.93 (24.13)	1.07	30	2.03 (25.38)	1.06	32	6.96
8. Paranoid Tendency	2.80 (23.33)	1.00	38	1.20 (10.00)	0.71	37	1.70 (14.17)	0.88	36	4.67
9. Depression	10.38 (28.83)	5.23	37	4.87 (13.53)	2.47	34	6.10 (16.94)	3.29	34	6.70
10. Physical Ilness	4.40 (36.67)	2.14	34	2.40 (20.00)	1.30	31	2.63 (21.92)	1.36	33	9.38
11. Social Maladjustment	4.58 (38.17)	2.67	33	0.73 (6.08)	0.38	38	1.60 (13.33)	0.87	38	19.69
12. Apprehensiveness	4.16 (34.67)	2.30	35	1.73 (14.42)	0.91	33	1.63 (13.58)	0.89	37	9.70
13. **Stress**	30.42 (31.69)	13.89	36	12.86 (13.39)	7.01	35	15.71 (16.43)	8.24	35	14.07
14. Lack of Self-confidence	12.60 (63.00)	4.98	06	8.93 (44.65)	2.64	10	8.20 (41.00)	2.82	21	10.95
15. Dejection	9.71 (64.73)	3.69	04	8.40 (56.00)	2.49	02	6.67 (44.47)	2.61	15	6.00
16. Pessimism	2.51 (50.20)	1.20	28	1.87 (37.40)	0.98	16	1.73 (34.60)	1.03	27	3.85
17. Emotional Responsiveness	17.98 (59.93)	6.03	11	14.01 (46.70)	4.22	08	12.80 (42.67)	3.25	17	5.64
18. Social Insecurity	13.95 (55.80)	5.19	23	9.87 (39.48)	2.38	14	10.04 (40.16)	2.98	22	5.30
19. Distrust	3.02 (60.40)	1.44	09	2.60 (52.00)	1.40	03	2.13 (42.60)	1.14	18	3.98
20. **Feeling of Insecurity**	59.65 (59.65)	12.08	13	45.68 (45.68)	14.85	09	41.57 (41.57)	13.64	20	17.38

Contd.

Table 8.37 *(Contd.)*

Indices of Psychological Well-being	*Unemployed*			*Employed*						
	Non-technically Educated (N=45)			*Technically Educated (N=15)*			*Non-technically Educated (N=30)*			
	Mean (%)	*SD*	*Rank*	*Mean (%)*	*SD*	*Rank*	*Mean (%)*	*SD*	*Rank*	*F*
21. Despair	17.22 (53.81)	4.21	26	16.00 (50.00)	3.59	5.5	15.00 (46.88)	4.89	07	2.37
22. Unstructured Universe	4.78 (59.75)	1.35	12	4.00 (50.00)	1.20	5.5	4.03 (50.38)	1.77	03	1.57
23. Psychological Vacuum	5.02 (62.75)	1.42	07	4.13 (51.62)	1.06	04	3.97 (49.63)	1.33	04	6.36
24. Disillusionment	2.27 (56.75)	0.96	20	1.47 (36.75)	0.52	18.5	1.47 (36.75)	0.78	26	10.10
25. Narcissism	1.87 (46.75)	0.69	30	1.60 (40.00)	0.91	13	1.60 (40.00)	0.89	23	1.24
26. **Alienation**	31.19 (55.70)	4.80	24	27.20 (48.57)	4.02	07	26.07 (46.55)	7.13	09	9.95
27. Depersonalization	4.64 (58.00)	1.25	18	2.67 (33.38)	0.82	21	3.40 (42.50)	1.45	19	17.31
28. Fragmentation	5.20 (65.00)	1.55	03	2.33 (29.13)	0.72	28	3.17 (39.63)	1.49	24	31.29
29. Uncertainty	2.33 (58.25)	0.93	16	2.40 (60.00)	0.99	01	2.40 (60.00)	0.81	01	0.06
30. Distress	6.78 (56.50)	1.40	21	4.73 (39.42)	2.28	15	5.43 (45.25)	2.05	11	9.46
31. Indecisiveness	4.47 (55.88)	1.42	22	2.87 (35.88)	0.92	20	3.80 (47.50)	1.65	06	7.31
32. Social Conflict	2.73 (68.25)	0.89	01	1.67 (41.75)	0.90	11	2.23 (55.75)	1.04	02	7.80
33. Isolation	4.40 (55.00)	1.81	25	2.60 (32.50)	0.91	25	3.60 (45.00)	1.38	13	8.00
34. Withdrawal from Social and Personal Contact	2.09 (52.25)	0.92	27	1.33 (33.25)	0.49	23.5	1.87 (46.75)	0.94	08	4.22
35. Role Conflict	6.98 (58..17)	1.57	17	5.00 (41.67)	1.65	12	5.33 (44.42)	2.19	16	10.73
36. Hopelessness	4.73 (59.13)	1.48	14	2.53 (31.63)	0.74	26	3.60 (45.00)	1.79	13	13.48
37. Lonelinness	2.40 (60.00)	0.96	10	1.33 (33.25)	0.62	23.5	1.80 (45.00)	0.96	13	8.96
38. Desolation	2.47 (61.75)	0.92	08	1.47 (36.75)	0.64	18.5	1.93 (48.25)	0.94	05	8.13
39. **Identity-Crisis**	49.22 (58.60)	8.50	15	30.93 (36.82)	8.00	17	38.57 (45.92)	12.53	11	21.92

Note : $df = 2,87$; $p < 0.05 = 3.10$; $p < 0.01 = 4.85$.

2.15), apprehensiveness (CQ = 2.02), stress (OQ = 17.56; CQ = 12.04), lack of self-confidence (CQ = 0.92), dejection (OQ = 1.31; CQ = 0.99), emotional responsiveness (CQ = 0.94), social insecurity (CQ =

1.07), feeling of insecurity (OQ = 13.97; CQ = 10.13), disillusionment (CQ = 0.72), depersonalization (OQ = 1.97; CQ = 1.08), fragmentation (CQ = 1.22), distress (CQ = 1.54), indecisiveness (OQ = 1.60; CQ = 1.23), social conflict (CQ = 0.81), isolation (CQ = 1.34), role conflict (OQ = 1.98; CQ = 1.55), hopelessness (OQ = 2.20; CQ = 1.29), loneliness (CQ = 0.78), desolation (CQ = 0.76), and identity-crisis (OQ = 18.29; CQ = 8.53). Interestingly, save and except a few variations, the non-technically educated employed, too, were found to be fairly distinct from that of the group of educated unemployed people in terms of the same symptomatic reactions. The obtained values for significance of difference between the two groups in terms of the various symptoms were as follows: general worries (OQ = 1.74; CQ = 1.08), psychological symptoms (CQ = 0.81), social relations (CQ = 1.23), anxiety (OQ = 5.48; CQ = 2.94), emotional instability (CQ = 1.47), physical illness (CQ = 1.53), social maladjustment (OQ = 2.98; CQ = 1.89), apprehensiveness (OQ = 2.53; CQ = 2.30), stress (OQ = 14.71; CQ = 10.59), lack of self-confidence (CQ = 1.04), dejection (OQ = 3.04; CQ = 1.13), emotional responsiveness (CQ = 1.07), social insecurity (CQ = 0.94), feeling of insecurity (OQ = 18.08; CQ = 11.52), disillusionment (CQ = 0.64), alienation (OQ = 5.12; CQ = 4.79), depersonalization (OQ = 1.24; CQ = 0.95), fragmentation (CQ = 1.07), distress (CQ = 1.35), role conflict (OQ = 1.65; CQ = 1.37), hopelessness (CQ = 1.14), and identity-crisis (OQ = 10.65; CQ = 7.50). Further, the results, similar to that of the prevailing trends, indicated the unemployed as greatly liable to psychological deterioration, while the groups of employed, particularly the technically educated ones, on the whole, were less, but moderately, prone to various symptomatic reactions. Moreover, all the groups of respondents, here too, were least susceptible to suicidal ideation (scores on the scale of suicidal tendency ranged between 0.00 per cent and 14.50 per cent), and more to the feeling of either social conflict (68.25 per cent), as it was particularly seen in the case of the unemployed people, or uncertainty—especially found with the technically (60.00 per cent) and the non-technically (60.00 per cent) educated employed people.

Life Satisfaction : A Comparison Among Different Groups of Educated Unemployed and Employed Young Men for a Duration of 6-7 Year

Table 8.38 focuses a comparative amount of life satisfaction among different groups of unemployed and employed people for an extended span of 6-7 year.

Table 8.38 : Statistical Differences Among Different Groups of Educated Unemployed and Employed Young Men for a Duration of 6-7 year and their Relative Standing in Terms of the Degree of their Life Satisfaction

	Unemployed		*Employed*				
	Non-technically Educated (N=45)		*Technically Educated (N=15)*		*Non-technically Educated (N=30)*		
Variable	*Mean (%)*	*SD*	*Mean (%)*	*SD*	*Mean (%)*	*SD*	*F*
Life Satisfaction	3.87 (38.70)	1.79	7.00 (70.00)	1.89	6.77 (67.70)	1.94	28.95

Note : $df = 2{,}87$; $p < 0.05 = 3.10$; $p < 0.01 = 4.85$.

The results, here too, maintained the earlier trends with noticeable differences among different groups of respondents in terms of the level of their life satisfaction ($F = 28.95$; $df = 2{,}87$; $p<0.01$). However, in actuality, both groups of the employed had a greater amount of similarity between themselves in their mean life satisfaction scores (OQ = 0.23; CQ = 1.40). Each of them showed apparent differences only from that of their unemployed counterparts in this regard (CQ = 1.59). It was further envisaged that the technically (Index of life satisfaction = 70.00 per cent) followed by the non-technically (Index of life satisfaction = 67.70 per cent) educated employed were greatly pleased with the order of their life. On the other hand, the group of unemployed felt life as comparatively more deserted and barren (Index of life satisfaction = 38.70 per cent).

Educated Unemployed and Employed Young Men for a Duration of 6-7 Year: Their Dependence on Different Strategies Devised for their Adjustment

Table 8.39 provides a comparative picture of the degree of dependence of different groups of educated unemployed and employed people for a prolonged period of 6-7 year on different strategies in order to face their life events.

Table 8.39 : Statistical Differences Among Different Groups of Educated Unemployed and Employed Young Men for a Duration of 6-7 year and the Degree of their Relative Dependence in Terms of Different Coping Strategies

Coping Strategies	*Unemployed*		*Employed*				
	Non-technically Educated (N=45)		*Technically Educated (N=15)*		*Non-technically Educated (N=30)*		
	Mean (%)	*SD*	*Mean (%)*	*SD*	*Mean (%)*	*SD*	*F*
Intrapersistive Approach Mode	10.22 (68.13)	2.44	10.53 (70.20)	1.81	10.57 (70.47)	2.05	0.25
Extrapersistive Approach Mode	1.64 (10.93)	0.90	1.40 (9.33)	0.76	1.80 (12.00)	1.07	0.32
Punitive Avoidance Mode	1.00 (6.67)	0.51	1.07 (7.13)	0.56	0.40 (2.67)	0.21	3.08
Defensive Avoidance Mode	2.13 (14.20)	1.16	2.00 (13.33)	1.06	2.23 (14.87)	1.25	0.14

Note : $df = 2,87$; $p < 0.05 = 3.10$; $p < 0.01 = 4.85$.

In contrast with the trends obtained above, non-significant differences were found among different groups of respondents in terms of the degree of their dependence on various coping strategies. However, they, like those of the groups of unemployed and employed people for different distinct durations, relied largely on intrapersistive approach mode in their effort to facilitate their existing environments; their degree of dependence on this strategy was exceedingly high and it lay between 68.13 per cent and 70.47 per cent.

Level of Anxiety, Stress, Feeling of Insecurity, Alienation, Identity-Crisis and Their Dimensions : A Comparison Among Different Groups of Educated Unemployed and Employed Young Men for a Duration of 7-Above Year

Table 8.40 shows the findings from a statistical comparison among different groups of unemployed and employed people over a prolonged period of more than 7 years in terms of their level of various symptomatic manifestations associated with anxiety, stress, feeling of insecurity, alienation and identity-crisis.

Table 8.40 : Statistical Differences Among Different Groups of Educated Unemployed and Employed Young Men for a Duration of 7- Above Year and their Relative Standing in Terms of Different Indices of Psychological Well-being

Indices of Psychological Well-being	*Unemployed*			*Employed*						
	Non-technically Educated (N=43)			*Technically Educated (N=24)*			*Non-technically Educated (N=62)*			
	Mean (%)	*SD*	*Rank*	*Mean (%)*	*SD*	*Rank*	*Mean (%)*	*SD*	*Rank*	*F*
1. General Worries	3.51 (58.50)	1.61	08	1.83 (30.50)	0.94	27	2.31 (38.50)	1.24	24	11.30
2. Somatic Manifestations	0.74 (24.67)	0.39	38	0.58 (19.33)	0.32	32	0.61 (20.33)	0.34	32	0.51
3. Psychological Symptoms	2.33 (46.60)	1.52	28	1.42 (28.40)	0.75	29	1.39 (27.80)	0.75	30	7.82
4. Social Relations	2.88 (36.00)	1.64	31	1.58 (19.75)	0.87	31	1.84 (23.00)	0.98	31	5.60
5. **Anxiety**	9.44 (42.91)	4.62	30	5.42 (24.64)	2.85	30	6.15 (27.95)	3.77	29	9.72
6. Suicidal Tendency	0.70 (17.50)	0.37	39	0.04 (1.00)	0.02	39	0.06 (1.50)	0.04	39	11.97
7. Emotional Instability	3.88 (48.50)	1.24	26	2.42 (30.25)	1.26	28	2.44 (30.50)	1.26	27	7.46
8. Paranoid Tendency	3.09 (25.75)	1.66	37	1.16 (9.67)	0.63	38	1.18 (9.83)	0.65	38	14.71
9. Depression	12.23 (33.97)	6.29	32	5.33 (14.81)	2.69	34	5.56 (15.44)	2.84	34	22.27
10. Physical Ilness	4.07 (33.92)	2.12	33	1.92 (16.00)	1.04	33	2.06 (17.17)	1.11	33	16.34
11. Social Maladjustment	3.35 (27.92)	1.63	36	1.67 (13.92)	0.86	36	1.58 (13.17)	0.83	36	9.72
12. Apprehensive-ness	3.56 (29.67)	1.63	35	1.25 (10.42)	0.67	37	1.50 (12.50)	0.76	37	16.02
13. **Stress**	30.89 (32.18)	15.87	34	13.79 (14.36)	8.60	35	14.39 (14.99)	6.75	35	26.58
14. Lack of Self-confidence	12.50 (62.50)	4.73	04	9.25 (46.25)	2.81	06	9.02 (45.10)	2.95	11	9.76
15. Dejection	9.68 (64.53)	3.84	02	6.54 (43.60)	2.27	13	7.29 (48.60)	2.74	06	7.13
16. Pessimism	2.67 (53.40)	1.36	19	1.58 (31.60)	0.81	26	1.47 (29.40)	0.81	28	16.85
17. Emotional Responsiveness	17.07 (56.90)	6.11	13	12.47 (41.57)	3.55	18	13.27 (44.23)	3.42	15	14.69
18. Social Insecurity	13.77 (55.08)	4.86	15	10.08 (40.32)	3.18	19	11.08 (44.32)	3.18	14	1.21
19. Distrust	2.98 (59.60)	1.34	06	2.13 (42.60)	1.09	16	2.06 (41.20)	1.08	22	7.83
20. **Feeling of Insecurity**	58.67 (58.67)	14.91	07	42.05 (42.05)	11.07	17	44.19 (44.19)	12.62	16	22.30

Contd.

Table 8.40 *(Contd.)*

Indices of Psychological Well-being	*Unemployed*			*Employed*						
	Non-technically Educated (N=43)			*Technically Educated (N=24)*			*Non-technically Educated (N=62)*			
	Mean (%)	*SD*	*Rank*	*Mean (%)*	*SD*	*Rank*	*Mean (%)*	*SD*	*Rank*	*F*
21. Despair	18.33 (57.28)	4.52	11	14.38 (44.94)	3.33	08	15.63 (48.84)	3.14	05	10.76
22. Unstructured Universe	4.60 (57.50)	1.37	10	4.33 (54.13)	1.61	03	4.02 (50.25)	1.22	04	2.45
23. Psychological Vacuum	4.65 (58.13)	1.41	09	3.83 (47.88)	1.52	05	3.87 (48.38)	1.21	07	5.00
24. Disillusionment	2.16 (54.00)	1.04	17.5	1.29 (32.25)	0.46	25	1.47 (36.75)	0.67	26	13.21
25. Narcissism	2.16 (54.00)	1.33	17.5	1.50 (37.50)	0.78	24	1.68 (42.00)	0.81	20.5	4.32
26. **Alienation**	31.94 (57.04)	6.64	12	25.33 (45.23)	4.72	07	26.67 (47.63)	5.32	08	15.75
27. Depersonalization	4.07 (50.88)	1.39	23	3.13 (39.13)	1.03	22	3.02 (37.75)	1.21	25	9.98
28. Fragmentation	4.49 (56.13)	1.80	14	3.21 (40.13)	1.44	20	3.29 (41.13)	1.41	23	8.84
29. Uncertainty	2.42 (60.50)	0.96	05	2.58 (64.50)	0.88	01	2.56 (64.00)	0.93	1.5	0.38
30. Distress	5.88 (49.00)	1.69	24	5.17 (43.08)	1.99	15	5.29 (44.08)	2.04	17	1.56
31. Indecisiveness	3.81 (47.63)	1.56	27	3.54 (44.25)	0.93	12	3.76 (47.00)	1.46	09	0.30
32. Social Conflict	2.72 (68.00)	0.96	01	2.46 (61.50)	1.02	02	2.56 (64.00)	1.02	1.5	0.59
33. Isolation	3.91 (48.88)	1.62	25	3.17 (39.63)	1.05	21	3.36 (42.00)	1.20	20.5	3.13
34. Withdrawal from Social and Personal Contact	1.84 (46.00)	1.00	29	1.54 (38.50)	0.59	23	1.79 (44.75)	0.73	12	1.12
35. Role Conflict	6.33 (52.75)	2.30	21	5.38 (44.83)	1.64	09	5.35 (44.58)	1.84	13	3.44
36. Hopelessness	4.40 (55.00)	1.87	16	3.46 (43.25)	1.02	14	3.47 (43.38)	1.50	19	5.08
37. Lonelinness	2.05 (51.25)	1.05	22	1.79 (44.75)	0.72	10	1.74 (43.50)	0.90	18	1.44
38. Desolation	2.53 (63.25)	0.93	03	2.13 (53.25)	0.74	04	2.08 (52.00)	0.98	03	3.29
39. **Identity-crisis**	44.37 (52.82)	10.90	20	37.56 (44.71)	8.25	11	38.27 (45.56)	10.16	10	5.54

Note : $df = 2,126$; $p < 0.05 = 3.07$; $p < 0.01 = 4.78$.

The results, here too, indicated that all the groups of respondents overall differed significantly from one another in the level of most of their psychological symptoms, excepting a few, particularly associated with some of the dimensions of identity-crisis (See Table 8.40). However, the findings attained through the multiple-comparison, here too, exhibited that it was the group of unemployed who were fairly distinct in their level of different symptoms of psychological impairment, the groups of employed expressing a greater amount of similarity between themselves in this conection. The various indicators of psychological well-being where the group of technically educated employed differed markedly from that of their unemployed counterparts were general worries (OQ = 1.68; CQ = 1.06), psychological symptoms (CQ = 0.75), social relations (CQ = 1.23), anxiety (OQ = 4.02; CQ = 2.92), suicidal tendency (CQ = 0.47), emotional instability (CQ = 1.36), paranoid tendency (CQ = 1.28), depression (OQ = 6.90; CQ = 3.66), physical illness (CQ = 1.30), social maladjustment (CQ = 1.27), apprehensiveness (CQ = 1.37), stress (OQ = 17.10; CQ = 8.06), lack of self-confidence (OQ = 3.25; CQ = 0.71), dejection (CQ = 0.91), pessimism (CQ = 0.65), emotional responsiveness (CQ = 1.05), distrust (CQ = 0.73), feeling of insecurity (OQ = 16.62; CQ = 8.92), despair (CQ = 2.50), disillusionment (CQ = 0.53), alienation (OQ = 6.61; CQ = 3.86), depersonalization (CQ = 0.75), fragmentation (CQ = 1.05), and identity-crisis (OQ = 6.81; CQ = 6.84). Not unusual, the non-technically educated employed, too, tended to differ substantially from that of the group of unemployed in terms of almost all the aforesaid reactions. The specific findings obtained in this regard were as follows : general worries (OQ = 1.20; CQ = 0.93), psychological symptoms (CQ = 0.85), anxiety (OQ = 3.29; CQ = 2.58), suicidal tendency (CQ = 0.42), emotional instability (CQ = 1.21), paranoid tendency (OQ = 1.91; CQ = 1.13), depression (CQ = 3.23), physical illness (OQ = 2.01; CQ = 1.15), social maladjustment (CQ = 1.44), apprehensiveness (CQ = 1.21), stress (OQ = 16.50; CQ = 7.12), lack of self-confidence (CQ = 0.80), dejection (CQ = 0.80), pessimism (OQ = 1.20; CQ = 0.74), emotional responsiveness (CQ = 0.93), distrust (CQ = 0.82), feeling of insecurity (OQ = 14.48; CQ = 7.88), despair (CQ = 2.21), disillusionment (CQ = 0.47), alienation (OQ = 5.27; CQ = 3.41), depersonalization (CQ = 0.84), fragmentation (CQ = 0.93), hopelessness (OQ = 0.93; CQ = 0.93), and identity-crisis (OQ = 6.10; CQ = 6.04). Moreover, the results, in tune with the general trends, showed that the unemployed, as compared to their employed counterparts, carried with them a higher degree of different psychological symptoms, though the groups of the latter, too, were, more or less, moderately aroused to various psychological syndromes. Also, all the groups of respondents, here too, were more oppressed with the thought of either uncertainty or social conflict (their scores on these two dimensions ranging between 64.00 per cent and 68.00 per cent), and least with the thought to commit suicide (their extent of proneness to suicidal tendency varied from 1.00 per cent to 17.50 per cent — quite negligible in effect).

Life Satisfaction : A Comparison Among Different Groups of Educated Unemployed and Employed Young Men for a Duration of 7-Above Year

Table 8.41 demonstrates the level of life satisfaction among the groups of unemployed and employed people for a longer duration of more than seven years.

Table 8.41 : Statistical Differences Among Different Groups of Educated Unemployed and Employed Young Men for a Duration of 7 - Above Year and their Relative Standing in Terms of the Degree of their Life Satisfaction

Variable	*Unemployed*		*Employed*				
	Non-technically Educated (N=43)		*Technically Educated (N=24)*		*Non-technically Educated (N=62)*		
	Mean (%)	*SD*	*Mean (%)*	*SD*	*Mean (%)*	*SD*	*F*
Life Satisfaction	3.84 (38.40)	1.90	7.08 (70.80)	1.91	6.76 (67.60)	2.23	30.49

Note : $df = 2,126$; $p<0.05 = 3.07$; $p<0.01=4.78$.

The overall difference among different groups of respondents from one another in their level of life satisfaction (F = 30.49), here too, was found to be statistically significant at higher than a level 0.01. However, as the findings obtained from multiple-comparison indicated, there was no marked difference between the technically and the non-technically educated employed people in their level of life satisfaction (OQ = 0.32; CQ = 1.24). It was the group of the unemployed that manifested a clear tendency to be distinct in this regard (CQ = 1.40). Further, here too, while both the groups of technically (Index of life satisfaction = 70.80 per cent) and non-technically (Index of life satisfaction = 67.60 per cent) employed expressed a greater degree of contentment in their life, the unemployed the least (Index of life satisfaction = 38.40 per cent).

Educated Unemployed and Employed Young Men for a Duration of 7- Above Year : Their Dependence on Different Strategies Devised for Their Adjustment

Table 8.42 furnishes the detalis of the degree of reliance of different groups of unemployed and employed people for a longer spell of more than 7-years upon various coping strategies like intrapersistive approach mode, extrapersistive approach mode, punitive avoidance mode and defensive avoidance mode.

Table 8.42 : Statistical Differences Among Different Groups of Educated Unemployed and Employed Young Men for a Duration of 7- Above Year and the Degree of their Relative Dependence in Terms of Different Coping Strategies

Coping Strategies	*Unemployed*		*Employed*				
	Non-technically Educated (N=43)		*Technically Educated(N=24)*		*Non-technically Educated (N=62)*		
	Mean (%)	*SD*	*Mean (%)*	*SD*	*Mean (%)*	*SD*	*F*
Intrapersistive Approach Mode	9.79 (65.27)	2.42	9.38 (62.53)	2.22	10.15 (67.67)	2.49	0.92
Extrapersistive Approach Mode	1.84 (12.27)	1.00	1.50 (10.00)	0.81	1.71 (11.40)	0.97	0.53
Punitive Avoidance Mode	0.79 (5.27)	0.39	0.62 (4.13)	0.34	0.52 (3.47)	0.31	1.00
Defensive Avoidance Mode	2.58 (17.20)	1.36	3.50 (23.33)	1.82	2.62 (17.47)	1.47	1.89

Note : $df = 2,126$; $p < 0.05 = 3.07$; $< 0.01 = 4.78$.

No group of respondents with an experience of its status of employment for a longer duration of more than 7 years, particularly like those of the groups of unemployed and employed people for a prolonged period of 6-7 year, showed any marked differences from another in terms of its dependence on any of the above coping strategies. However, here too, each of the groups of respondents manifested a clear tendency to resort only to intrapersistive approach mode, and to none other, in order to meet its situational demands. Their extent of dependence on this coping style was apparently found to be lying between 62.53 per cent and 67.67 per cent.

Taken together all the abovementioned findings obtained from statistical comparions at the inter-group level in terms of various indices of psychological health as well as coping styles yielded significant facts enumerated, in brief, below:

1. All the groups of the educated unemployed people for each and every specific duration were found to be apparently more precipitated with various symptoms of psychological ill-health, particularly marked out in terms of the degree and extent of anxiety, stress, feeling of insecurity, alienation, life satisfaction, identity-crisis and their various pronounced manifestations. This clearly shows that unemployment is always more dangerous to psychological health in particular. The findings are quite in line with the findings of a good number of investigations carried out in India (Kumari, 2001; Rani, 1993; Singh, 1990, 1994, 2001; Singh, Kumari and Singh, 1992; Singh and Singh, 2004; Singh, Singh and Rani,1996a; Singh, Singh and Singh, 1995) and abroad (Banks and Jackson, 1982; Fryer, 1995a; Iversen and Sabroe, 1988; Jackson, 1985; Jackson and Warr, 1984; Jahoda, 1988,1995; Kieselbach, 2003; Masschelein and De Witte, 1997; Sabroe and Iversen, 1989; Warr, 1984b,1985,1987 c,d; Winefield, 1995b). These investigations have also indicated that unemployment, in most of the instances, causes a sharp deterioration in psychological health. Unemployment, as it has been indicated earlier especially in chapter 1 and 5, is, obviously, a critical life event associated with a summation of 'daily hassles', certainly leading to the development of all sorts of psychological subversions in those who have been oppressed with it (Damstrup, 1987; De Witte, 1994; Kanner *et al.*, 1981; Kieselbach, 1991; Kieselbach and Svensson, 1988; Kieselbach and Wacker, 1985, Masschelein and De Witte, 1997; Singh, Singh and Singh, 1995; Verkleij, 1989; Westcott, Svensson and Zöllner, 1985).

Furthermore, it should also be pointed out that unemployment, no matter whatsoever be its duration, apparently causes a marked erosion in social status and prestige of those who experience it (Fryer and Winefield,1998; Iversen and Sabroe, 1988; Kieselbach, 1989, 1991, 1996, 1997a; Singh, 2001; Sokou and Papantoniou, 2000;

Sudan, 2000; Warr, 1985, 1987d). Evidently, the unemployed are generally perceived as *'second-class citizens'* (Warr, 1985), always looking for welfare handouts even to meet their basic needs (Feather, 1990; Kelvin and Jarrett, 1985). However, of late, the unemployed in India, in particular, as it may commonly be seen, usually depend on numerous clandestine and unscrupulous strategies in order to maintain their social status and prestige. These may range from the soft ones such as licking one's lips, involving oneself in petty local and parochial politics, frequent exhibitions of one's links with the influential personalities, especially the political bigwigs and their aides, sycophancy, etc., to the more harsh ones like involvement in *dadagiri or mawaligiri* acts (rowdyism or hooliganism), crime, terrorism, political extremism, etc. These, no doubt, help them attain pseudo-prestige, and thus, more or less, serve as source of vicarious satisfaction for them. But, all their elation disappears as soon as they find themselves subjected to outside attacks even with tightened lips. This, in turn, as it has been shown by Breakwell *et al.* (1984) and Singh, Singh and Rani (1996b), more often than not, develops in them a negative view towards themselves, which ultimately leads to the eruption of various psychological reactions; higher level of anxiety, stress, feeling of insecurity, alienation, identity-crisis, and lower level of life satisfaction, etc., naturally manifest therein (Burns, 1979; Feather, 1983b; Feather and Bond, 1983; Feather and O'Brien, 1986a; Man and Devisse, 1987; McLennan, 1987; Murgai and Sathyavathi,1988; Rani, 1993).

Yet, different plausible reasons which have been emphasized, especially in chapter 5, to justify the poor psychological well-being amongst the unemployed as against the employed may very well be relevant, here too, in describing the findings. They are, indeed, fairly elaborate and precise in their predictability. But, just in order to make the presentation free from monotony, it was thought advisable not to depict them here at all. Someone who is curious may very well evaluate their applicability in the 5th chapter, and reasonably relate them with the findings obtained here. Thus, the reasons why the educated unemployed people manifest various symptoms of reduced psychological health appear to be fairly well investigated in the light of the aforementioned arguments. Moreover, *the Stage Theory of Psychosexual Development* propounded by Erikson (1950, 1959, 1968, 1980, 1982), not employed elsewhere before to substantiate the diminished psychological well-being among the unemployed vis-à-vis the employed in the present investigation, was taken into consideration to see the findings in a somewhat new perspective. Relying upon the proposition enumerated in *the Stage Theory of Psychosexual Development,* Gurney (1980a, b) has attempted to highlight that the employed have more opportunities to negotiate satisfactorily the stage of industry and competence. On the other hand, unemployment, according to him, proves a barrier to successful transition through the industry stage and consequently leads to stagnation in psychological growth which, in turn, leads to different maladaptive behaviours indicative of psychological ill-health. De Witte (1989) and Kieselbach (1989) have also arrived at a similar conclusion, indicating unemployment as impeding psychosocial development, and hence promoting numerous unwholesome psychic reactions.

2. The groups of the employed, on the whole, had better psychological health. Although they, too, were not entirely risk-free, and were, more or less, moderately afflicted with various symptoms of psychological impairment. Numerous arguments have already been proposed in the 5th, 6th, 7th and 8th chapters in order to justify the overall moderate psychological decline among the educated employed people. These arguments obviously put special emphasis on the poor organizational climate as especially persisting in the state public concerns in eastern India, as also on the incompetence of an employee to meet two incompatible demands—one imposed by the work environment, and the other by the family members and the society at large — in the same breath. These may apparently be conjoined with the findings obtained here. Undeniably, frequent encounters with such circumstances, as it is quite well established (Burke, 1986; Dayal. 1988; Kanungo, 1995; Kanungo and Mendonca, 1995; Payne and Fletcher, 1983; Rohmert, 1986; Singh, 1994; Singh, Kumari and Singh, 1992; Sinha, 1985), are particularly not conducive to psychological health, leading to the exposition of different symptomatic reactions; a greater degree of anxiety, stress, feeling of insecurity, alienation, helplessness, hopelessness, low life satisfaction, low self-reliance, etc., is commonly noticed therein. Thus, in all, Jahoda (1979, 1982, 1987, 1988, 1995) may be accused of being unnecessarily a little too optimistic in her prediction; her views cannot be universally generalized. But, the positive impact of employment in one's life, as it has been asserted by Jahoda in her widely recognized Functional Approach —especially in a country like India which is faced with the baffling problem of mass unemployment—can in no way be thoroughly abrogated; it has definitely a fair amount of reality. No doubt, even the poor employment, as Jahoda (1982) has cogently emphasized, is always preferable to no employment, and so it may also serve as something of a prophylactic against an abrupt psychological decay. This, as she asserts, may openly be attributed to its inherent potentiality to satisfy various needs both at physical and psychological levels, though not to a very clear account (Feather and O'Brien, 1990). Thus, it may appear clearly vindicated why the employed in India, despite their persistent confrontations with various challenges in all walks of life, usually manifest just a marginally moderate amount of deterioration in their psychological well-being. Indeed, their employment, especially in the face of a harsh reality of a large-scale unemployment besetting the fate of the entire nation, more likely provides them an upper hand in the society, and as such invests them with a certain amount of social status and prestige. Interestingly, it is not unreasonable to mention here that whatsoever the pain and pity pervading their life, they, if at jobs in public sector organizations or government offices in particular, are generally perceived as having something 'unique' and 'extra' in them, fairly assuring their social acceptability to a greater degree. And, all these positive developments in their life are likely to attenuate their psychological deterioration, and consequently considerably help them maintain a good psychological health all the time, as compared to their unemployed counterparts.

To summarize, social acceptibility as reassurance may be credited with minimizing the tension and conflict more likely caused by their inability to come up to various normative and permissible expectations at a time, and thus for their satisfactory psychological well-being.

3. Like that of the general trend indicated earlier, either the feeling of uncertainty or social conflict, barring a few exceptions, was marked as the most precipitating symptomatic reaction among all the groups of educated unemployed and employed people in India. On the other hand, all of them, hardly with any deviation among themselves, were least, almost negligibly, aroused by the tendency to commit suicide. Both the facts have been carefully dealt with in the 5th and subsequent chapters on being consequent upon different possible reasons. For a detailed account, see the aforementioned chapters.

4. Here too, all the groups of respondents, whether unemployed or employed for one or another duration, solely relied on intrapersistive approach mode in making adjustment with their existing situations.

Such a pervasive tendency among the unemployed and employed people in India at large has been properly rationalized in the light of various assumptions, especially associated with the typicality very much embedded in their life pattern, depicted in chapter five. For a complete understanding of every detail, one may go through the descriptions furnished at the end of that chapter.

9

Epilogue

Investigators, on account of an alarming increase in the number of job-seekers worldwide in recent years, have shown enormous interest in the study of the effects of unemployment on psychological well-being. There appeared a series of researches in this regard from 1980 onward. Notably, besides a number of books on the psychology of work and unemployment published by Allatt and Yeandle (1992), Alvaro (1989), Banks and Ullah (1988), Barling (1990), Elchardus and Glorieux (1995), Feather (1990), Hammarström (1996), Leana and Feldman (1992), O'Brien (1986), Warr (1987), A.H.Winefield *et al.* (1993), and others, as well as several edited volumes and four journals such as *Social Science and Medicine* in 1987, the *Journal of Social Issues* in 1988, the *Journal of Occupational and Organisational Psychology* in 1992, the *Journal of Adolescence* in 1997 and *Social Justice Research* in 1997 have devoted whole issues to the topic. But, all the publications mainly focus on the situation prevailing in most of the European countries (see chapters 1st and 2nd for a detailed account), leaving the picture of several developing and underdeveloped nations at this count almost in gloom where the problem of unemployment has undoubtedly acquired a monstrous shape, inflicting many harmful effects on one's life.

India is one of the developing nations which has also been facing a high level of unemployment — the ugliest ever in its history, proving a stumbling-block to its progress and prosperity to a substantial degree. Quite distressingly, the highly educated and well-qualified are hardest hit by unemployment. They find themselves in a state of pathetic helplessness to secure a livelihood even to lead a minimum decent life, imposing serious threats to their physio-psychological well-being. But, astonishingly, such a vital issue has not yet attracted the attention of our investigators in any substantial measure. It is less analysed and little understood. And, if some evidences are available, they are not all-inclusive; they are sparse and not systematic, indeed. Further, it is a reality to be admitted that the findings of the studies conducted abroad cannot be safely generalized in a country like India which has a strikingly distinct socio-cultural background characterised by specific indigenous social norms and values, making its people unique in their reaction pattern even to such serious problems as poverty and unemployment. In short, there is needed an elaborate inquiry hinged with native approach in this regard in order to be precise in our prediction as to the psychological state of the unemployed *versus* employed people in India. Hence, this study was primarily designed to find out the level of psychological well-being among different groups of educated unemployed and employed young men measured in terms of its indicators like anxiety, stress, feeling of insecurity, alienation, identity-crisis and life satisfaction in their various manifestations. Also, the study aimed at ascertaining the degree of their relative dependence on different strategies employed to cope with their life circumstances.

Taking into account the aforementioned objectives of the investigation, the following research questions were put for verification :

(1) The educated unemployed young men, in general, would manifest poor psychological well-being as compared to their employed counterparts.

(2) The technically educated unemployed young men, compared to the non-technically educated unemployed young men, would be more vulnerable to psychological ill-health.

(3) The technically educated unemployed young men as against their employed counterparts would show greater impairment in their psychological health.

(4) The non-technically educated unemployed young men *vis-à-vis* their employed counterparts would have reduced psychological well-being.

(5) The technically educated employed young men, compared to the non-technically educated employed ones, would enjoy superior psychological health.

(6) With the increase in the duration of their status the unemployed, irrespective of their forms and streams of education, would show greater damage in their psychological well-being, but the reverse would be seen in the case of the educated employed people.

(7) Different groups of educated unemployed and employed young men would register marked difference in the degree of their relative dependence on different strategies resorted to cope with their situations.

Different theoretical assumptions such as social exchange theory (Blau, 1964; Burgess and Huston, 1979; Homans, 1961; Kelley, 1979; Rusbutt, 1980; Thibaut and Kelley, 1959), functional approach (Jahoda, 1979, 1981, 1982, 1988, 1995; Jahoda and Rush, 1980), vitamin model (Warr,1987d), stage theory (Erickson, 1950, 1959, 1968, 1980, 1982), and cumulative stress model (Jackson and Warr, 1984) were relied upon to form discreet bases for the hypotheses formulated for verification. Besides, a good amount of relevant empirical evidences on the effects of unemployment *versus* employment on psychological well-being, as well as the socio-cultural realities typical of India largely governing one's reaction pattern to various life events, were also taken into consideration in order to rationalize the aforementioned hypotheses being subjected to verification.

In order to examine the objectivity of the aforementioned hypotheses the study was conducted on a sample of 1024 educated young men — 614 unemployed and 410 employed. To proceed with the aims of the investigation, the two main exclusive groups were further divided into 4 sub-groups : (1) technically educated unemployed (N = 206), (2) non-technically educated unemployed (N = 408), (3) technically educated employed (N = 132), and (4) non-technically educated employed (N = 278). These subgroups, on the basis of their degrees and diplomas in various streams of knowledge, were again split into 8 independent sets of respondents. And, each of them was later separated on the basis of the experience of the duration of its particular status into 36 sets of respondents. The group of technically educated young men consisted of graduates and postgraduates of engineering, medical and agriculture sciences, and the non-technically educated people included general graduate and postgraduate degree-holders in the arts and humanities, commerce, social, and natural sciences. Two criteria — *primary and secondary* — were strictly followed in the selection of the subjects for this study. Consequent upon primary criterion, only those technically and non-technically educated young men from different disciplines of education were approached to participate in the study who, apart from being involuntarily unemployed as the definition given by Warr (1987d), had their names in different District Employment Exchanges of undivided Bihar (the eastern India) for various durations. On the other hand, only those educated persons were categorised as employed who were permanent employees in different state enterprises, and had not only been getting proportionate economic reward (salary) against the labour rendered by them (Basic salary ranging from Rs. 2200 to Rs. 3700 per month) but also enjoyed other facilities that involved their rights and responsibilities. Further, relying upon secondary criterion — *the control mechanism* — different groups of technically and non-technically educated unemployed and employed young men were made comparable in terms of different personal and background variables such as age (22 to 34 yrs.), sex (male), education (graduate and postgraduate degree-holders), socio-economic condition (income ranging from Rs.2200 to Rs.3700 per month) and residence (urban). Also, an attempt was made to control the impacts of the experience of the duration of one's status of employment on one's psychological well-being. And in doing so, the duration of the status of employment (0-1 yr. to 7-above yrs) was included in the study as a moderator independent variable, and its contribution to mediating the impact of status of employment (unemployment/employment) on psychological well-being, and preference for a particular coping strategy was separately analysed by comparing the psychological health, and coping styles of different groups of the educated unemployed and employed young men for different durations. The procedure of systematic simple randomized sampling involving the technique of sampling with replacement was employed in order to select the subjects for different groups of the technically and non-technically educated unemployed and employed people.

Scales and measures like the shorter version (Khan and Hassan, 1981) of Sinha's (1968) W.A. self-analysis form, stress scale, security-insecurity test (Mohsin, 1981), alienation scale (Kureshi and Dutt, 1979), identity-crisis scale, life satisfaction index (Neugarten, Havighurst and Tobin, 1961), strategy of adjustment questionnaire (Sinha, 1989), and personal data sheet were administered in order to have a reliable and valid estimate of different variables subjected to investigation, as well as to collect informations regarding personal and background characteristics of the subjects, etc. Of the aforementioned scales and measures, the scales of stress and identity-crisis were developed and standardized by meticulously following the principles for the development of scales. The other scales adopted for use in the present investigation, though having a fair amount of reliability and validity, underwent rigorous verification before their final application. They were carefully modified by fully keeping in view the requirements of the investigation. All the scales were found to be fairly reliable and valid, and appeared good enough for eliciting genuine informations for the dimensions which they measured.

All these scales and measures were administered to the subjects either individually or in small group settings from July 1991 to May 1992. But, with each subject selected for the study, the investigator first established rapport to elicit sincere and candid responses. The subjects were allowed to take up the tests only when they appeared to be conversant with each and every item involved in different scales, as well as the usual instructions furnished therein. Although they had to complete all the measures within a maximum time limit of 2 hours, very few of them were given leeway in completing them, and returning them by post as per their convenience when it was found that they really needed more time for it.

In order to make the findings more precise and objective, the data obtained from different scales and measures underwent various statistical treatments. The computation of *Means, SDs, One-Way Analysis of Variance, Newman-Keuls Test, Percentage and Ranking* was mainly given importance to meet the purposes in this connection.

The summary of the results of a statistical comparison between the combined groups of the educated unemployed (N = 614) and the employed (N = 410) young men in terms of their degree and extent of anxiety, stress, feeling of insecurity, alienation, identity-crisis, life satisfaction and their dimensions — the indicators of psychological well-being — indicated the former, as compared to the latter, to be greatly afflicted with reduced psychological health with increased levels of anxiety, feeling of insecurity, alienation, identity-crisis and the decreased level of life satisfaction in their various manifestations. The symptoms like feeling of social conflict (67.25%), uncertainty (64.75%) and desolation (60.75%) were found to be more pressing for them. But, the employed were also not completely immune to psychological ill-health; they, too, were moderately susceptible to different psychological reactions, particularly experiencing exacerbated feelings of uncertainty (57.25%), social conflict (54.00%) and unstructured universe (51.38%) almost like their unemployed counterparts but, apparently, not to their scale. Both the groups also showed similarity in pointing less agonizing symptoms experienced by them, and, seemingly, various stress-related reactions, particularly the tendency to commit suicide, were relatively less annoying to them, though the levels that these reactions got in touch with, if the convictions of Feather (1982), Goldberg (1972) and Warr (1984a) are well-founded, were also, more or less, symptomatic of psychological deterioration. In sequence, the comparison between the two groups in terms of the degree of their dependence on different coping strategies such as intrapersistive approach mode, extrapersistive approach mode, punitive avoidance mode and defensive avoidance mode indicated that they differed significantly between themselves in terms of the degree of their reliance on all the strategies, excepting defensive avoidance mode, in order to fight their life circumstances. But, they, it was quite apparent, exhibited a clear tendency to confide largely in intrapersistive approach mode and none other in effecting compromise with their situations.

The findings of a statistical comparison *(One-Way ANOVA)* among the groups of technically educated unemployed (N= 206), non-technically educated unemployed (N = 408), technically educated employed (N = 132), and non-technically educated employed (N = 278) young men in terms of the abovementioned different indicators of psychological well-being revealed that they differed significantly from one another in their levels on each and every measure of psychological health, excepting the alienating outbreak of narcissism. However, the finding so computed from the multiple-comparison of pairs of means failed to fully substantiate the findings obtained from *One-Way ANOVA*. Notably, with the exception of significant differences between the mean scores of the technically and the non-technically educated employed only in terms of general worries, psychological symptoms and anxiety, and the technically and the non-technically educated unemployed in terms of dejection, neither the groups afflicted with the problem of unemployment, nor the groups having employment did register significant difference in terms of any of the symptomatic reactions at intra-group level. In other words, if a striking difference between the mean scores of any two groups in terms of almost each and every health indices was recorded, that was mainly observed between the groups quite distinct in their status of employment. It was further revealed that the non-technically educated unemployed, followed by the technically educated ones, were apparently more vulnerable to various psychological reactions expressed in the form of higher levels of anxiety, feeling of insecurity, alienation, identity-crisis, and the lower level of life satisfaction in their varied manifestations. The employed, particularly the technically educated ones, on the other hand, was relatively less, though altogether moderately, afflicted in this connection. Remarkably, here too, all the groups of respondents, whether unemployed or employed, were, more or less, oppressed with feelings of uncertainty, social conflict, desolation and dejection; the feeling of uncertainty being extremely poignant though, but it was not so only for the group of the non-technically educated unemployed people who found themselves deeply wrenched with social conflict as with others. Similarly, here too, different stress-related reactions, particularly the tendency to commit suicide, were relatively less pressing for all of them. Lastly, the results, like the trend in the case of the composite groups of the educated unemployed and employed people, indicated that though different groups of technically and non-technically educated unemployed and employed young men differed significantly both at inter- and intra-group levels in the degree of their dependence specially on the coping strategies like intrapersisitive approach mode and punitive avoidance mode, they clearly tended to mainly trust in intrapersistive approach mode in dealing with their life events.

Further comparisons made among different groups of unemployed and employed young men from different streams of technical and non-technical education in terms of their psychological well-being by employing *One-Way ANOVA* also showed all of them, like those of the composite groups of the technically and non-technically educated unemployed and employed people, as differing significantly from one another in terms of their levels on all the indicators of psychological well-being, excepting narcissism. However, here too, an analysis of the findings obtained from multiple-comparisons of different pairs of means indicated that barring a few exceptions such as meaningful differences between the mean scores of the employed degree-holders in medical sciences and the employed degree-holders in non-technical education in terms of psychological symptoms, the employed engineers and the employed degree-holders in agriculture sciences in terms of unstructured universe, and the unemployed degree-holders in medical sciences and the unemployed degree-holders in agriculture sciences in terms of fragmentation, neither the groups of unemployed nor the groups of employed from different distinct streams of education tended to express any marked difference at intra-group level in this regard. It was further recorded that all the groups of educated unemployed, particularly the degree-holders in agriculture sciences and non-technical education, like those of the combined groups of the technically and non-technically educated unemployed young men, were relatively highly pressed with different symptoms of reduced psychological health. All the groups of educated employed, on the other hand, were considerably less badly off psychologically. However, they, particularly the employed degree-holders in non-technical education and agriculture sciences, too, were not completely symptom-free, and were altogether moderately prone to different psychological reactions, excepting a few, mostly associated with different symptomatic reactions of stress. Notably, here too, all the groups of educated unemployed and employed people, only with a slight variation from the trend as it appeared earlier, indicated the feelings of uncertainty, social conflict, desolation, unstructured universe and dejection as most agonizing for them; the feeling of uncertainty being the most pronounced therein, save and except the groups of unemployed degree-holders in medical sciences and non-technical education, who were far deeply afflicted with the feeling of social conflict. Similarly, here too, different stress-related reactions, particularly the tendency to commit suicide, were found to be relatively less inflicting for all of them. An analysis of the coping patterns adopted by different groups of unemployed and employed young men from different distinct streams of education showed all of them as largely relying upon intrapersistive approach mode in meeting their situational demands, irrespective of a clear evidence of significant differences especially at inter-group level in terms of the degree of their dependence on all the coping strategies, excepting defensive avoidance mode.

Added to the above, with an aim to further add to the predictability of the findings, an attempt was also made to find out whether different distinct groups of technically and non-technically educated unemployed and employed for different distinct durations differ significantly in their psychological well-being as well as in their degree of dependence on various coping strategies both at inter- and intra-groups levels or not. The salient findings obtained from intra-group comparisons were as follows :

(a) A clear evidence of stabilization effect or adaptation as such did not appear in any of the exclusive groups of the technically and non-technically educated unemployed young men for different distinct durations in India. A pattern of ups and downs was altogether recorded in the increment of different symptomatic reactions in all the groups.

(b) No such group of technically and non-technically educated unemployed for a specific period could be identified who were psychologically more afflicted. Notably, while the levels of some health indices were more alarming in the group of unemployed for one specific duration, the levels of others were more frightening in the group of unemployed for other specific duration, and so on. However, each of the separate groups of the educated unemployed, particularly for shorter (i.e., 0-1 year) and longer spells, excepting the group of unemployed engineers, were altogether greatly vulnerable to different symptomatic reactions. Although all the groups of unemployed for a span of one year, in particular, did not show an alarming decline in the level of satisfaction with their life, this was observed only with them and not with others. However, with a few exceptions, all the groups of educated unemployed for one or another duraton, on the whole, were more, though moderately, vulnerable to psychological ill-health.

(c) Both the groups of the technically and the non-technically educated young men in jobs for different distinct durations were, by and large, just as badly off psychologically as their unemployed counterparts, but not so seriously as it appeared with the latter. Further, the groups of the employed for shorter and longer durations were more susceptible to poor psychological well-being. Although the group of employed for each and every duration had fairly greater life satisfaction.

(d) Besides having a good amount of similarity, here too, in different more agonizing and less agonizing symptomatic reactions, all the groups of educated unemployed and employed people for one or another duration, barring a few exceptions, were found to be relatively greatly oppressed with the feeling of either uncertainty or social conflict, and very little with suicidal tendency.

(e) Irrespective of the differences in the duration of the status of employment, each of the distinct groups of the unemployed and employed people, here too, expressed a clear tendency to depend solely on intrapersistive approach mode in effecting a compromise with their life events.

In sequence, the findings of inter-group comparisons separately made among different groups of educated unemployed and employed people for different specific durations in terms of their levels on various indicators of psychological well-being, too, indicated that all the groups of unemployed for each of the specific durations suffered greater damage at the count of their psychological health. The groups of employed, on the other hand, had altogether better psychological health. However, they, too, were not fully unaffected, and were, more or less, moderately exposed to different symptomatic reactions. Further, here too, all the groups of unemployed and employed for each of the particular durations showed a marked similarity among themselves in the identification of different more seriously as well as less seriously experienced symptomatic reactions by them. Significantly, all of them, with a few exceptions, were far greatly burdened with the feeling of either uncertainty or social conflict, and, on the other hand, much less, almost negligible in amount, with suicidal ideation. Lastly, here too, intrapersistive approach mode came out as the only most popular strategy generally resorted to by different groups of the educated unemployed and employed people in order to deal with their situation; other coping strategies failed to record any of their obvious significance in this connection.

Thus, in all, there was recorded the summary of the findings of inter- and intra-group statistical comparisons of different groups of unemployed and employed young men, chiefly divided on the basis of criteria like types and streams of education, as well as the duration of their status of employment, in terms of their levels on different indicators of psychological health, and the degree of their relative dependence on various coping strategies. An analysis of all those findings, on the whole, led to the establishment of the following significant trends :

(1) All the groups of unemployed, irrespective of differences in the type and stream of their education, as well as the duration of their status of employment, were particularly at greater risk of psychological ill-health with marked elevation in the amount of all the symptomatic reactions, excepting a few,

but the amount of that, too, was enough to label them as psychologically vulnerable.

(2) The groups of employed were relatively less psychologically afflicted. But, they, too, were not fully immune to psychological impairment, and were, by and large, moderately susceptible to different symptomatic reactions, excepting a few, particularly associated with the manifestations of stress and anxiety.

(3) All the groups of educated unemployed and employed young men, with hardly any variation, were far greatly oppressed with an acute feeling of either uncertainty or social conflict, and, on the other hand, relatively quite less with the feeling to commit suicide.

(4) Each and every group of the unemployed and the employed people tended to depend solely on intrapersistive approach mode in dealing with their life circumstances; other modes of adjustment hardly attracted any of them to a significant count.

Thus, the findings of this study, in brief, may help develop a precise and comprehensive idea about the psychological well-being and coping styles of different groups of unemployed and employed young men in India varying in the disciplines of their education, as well as the duration of the status of their employment. The findings, of course, lend themselves to a range of theoretical interpretations. However, it needs to be emphasized that the findings of this study may apply only to educated unemployed and employed young men for different durations, and not to population at large. Notably, as it has been maintained (Feather, 1990; Jahoda, 1988; Winefield, 1997), it would be fallacious to treat different kinds of unemployed and employed people as homogeneous masses. They may vary considerably in their needs, interests, abilities, values and life-circumstances, and in the importance which they may attach to employment. In short, there may be seen a wide variation in their reaction pattern. Further, there are different personal and personality factors which also play a significant role in influencing the impact of status of employment on psychological well-being (see Winefield, 1995b). In addition, one cannot deny the role of cultural variations in mediating the effect of status of employment on health. People from developed, developing and underdeveloped nations, probably because of differences in welfare benefits, cultural norms and values, traditional levels of unemployment, social support networks, and so on, may clearly be seen to differ among themselves markedly in their reactions to, and their strategy to deal with, various life events. To be precise, it would not be judicious to transfer the results found in one group to another without any reasonable precept. There may be found a clear evidence of variation on different points among different kinds of unemployed, as also employed people. Thus, for a wider applicability, the coverage of the study should be extended to a wide range of samples divided on the basis of different criteria like cultural specificity, economic condition, caste affiliation particularly in the context of reservation policy, ethnicity, types of unemployment and employment, availability of support system, personal and personality factors, and so forth.

With a considerable change in the attitudes and lifestyles of women in India, in the wake of fast-growing economic pressure, frequent social changes and modernisation, giving rise to an acute awareness in them of an altogether new role, as distinctly different from the traditional ones, there has been a keenness as never before for education among the females with particular emphasis on employment — a recent but important consideration for the marriage and for better prospects of a secured future even in marital life. Their options are as wide and open as those of their male counterparts, and hardly any field of activity has thus been left as man's sole domain. Their education, however, appears not to be appropriately worthwhile in providing them sufficient opportunity for gainful employment. Though women, known for their complex psychic structure, as also for their uniquely interblended temperaments of compassion, endurance and sacrifice, are far less imperilled in India by the problem of unemployment in comparison with their male counterparts, many well-qualified and competent women, especially coming from middle-class families, can be seen standing hopelessly in a long queue of job-seekers. Incidentally, this field of study still remains a virgin-land untouched and unpursued, as no sincere effort has, it seems, been initiated to analyse the psychic state of such women in comparison to their male counterparts, calling for a more detailed inquiry in this regard. This, it is hoped, would throw open vast vistas of meaningful informations with regard to female psyche, which would go a long way in effecting a social transformation so urgently needed in the country.

In order to broaden the scope of a study, it is also suggested to concentrate on a wider set of those variables on which unemployment may exert its effects. Besides the variables studied, there are a lot of other dependent variables that require more specific attention. Namely, the condition under which unemployment is followed by a sense of injustice, apathy towards society, lack of interest in work, anger and aggression, antisocial behaviour such as crime and delinquency, cheating and blackmailing, smoking, drug-taking, and so forth. The study of some of these variables would shift the attention from concern with the impact of unemployment on the individual to concern with the impact thereof on the masses. In the light of the views held by Feather (1990) and Singh, Singh and Singh (1996), it also seems reasonable to mention that the meaning and significance of a variable may vary across cultures. For example, both the unemployed and employed people in India, in general, as it has been demonstrated (Singh, Singh and Singh, 1996), rely both upon internal and external forces simultaneously to a considerable extent in ascribing their lot. This is akin to the typical worldview in India emphasising the need to take every event as consequent upon both inside and outside forces, the *karma* and *bhagya* philosophy. To be precise, in a culture, particularly like that of India, the two dimensions of control — internal and external — are generally considered as independent of each other. Hence, in order to have a precise account of the characteristic manifestation of a variable, it would be fairly judicious to determine its culture-specific meaning and significance before including it finally in a scientific inquiry.

The findings of this study, on account of its being based on a cross-sectional design solely employing self-report measures and scales which have numerous limitations, cannot be interpreted causally. Hence, in order to have definite conclusions about casue-effect relations between status of employment (unemployment/employment) and one's psychological state, there is a clear need for longitudinal studies involving multi-method approach such as projective tests, case study, intensive interview, etc., constructed with acceptable psychometric properties, with satisfactory levels of reliability and a fair amount of validity. Perhaps, no such kind of study has yet been conducted in India. This also calls for well-planned longitudinal studies on the impact of status of employment on psychological well-being, as also on preference for different coping strategies.

By way of suggesting a new dimension to scientific inquiry, it is also stressed that one should be impressionable to climatic constraints in the organization in India, especially while analysing the psychological well-being and coping styles of the persons in jobs. More especially, undue political interference in the normal business of the organization and with the employees working there, perception of political instability and anarchism in the country, downsizing decisions of the government — the management — etc., are variables that require considerable attention in future researches oriented to present an account of the levels of psychological well-being of the employees, and their degrees of dependence on various coping strategies. In addition, job insecurity, increased job pressures, and reduced promotional opportunities more likely resulting from government moves to reduce unemployment are also some of the phenomena that need due consideration in future studies designed to compare unemployed and employed groups in terms of their psychological well-being and coping patterns. There are studies (Fryer and Winefield, 1998; O'Brien and Feather, 1990; Payne, 1995; Prause and Dooley, 1997; Singh *et al.,* 2005; Winefield, 1995a; Winefield, Tiggemann and Goldney, 1988; Winefield, Tiggemann and Winefield, 1991b; Winefield *et al.*, 1993) in which it has been shown that the psychological distress resulting from unsatisfactory employment is similar to that associated with unemployment. Virtually, the quality of employment, as Winefield (1995b) maintains, needs to be taken into account while focusing on the psychological well-being of the unemployed as against the employed.

In the face of recent government moves to shut down or privatize different public sector organizations, especially those which are ailing due to some reason or the other, the study of the psychological distress caused by the anticipation of being laid-off or redundant among employees working there also deserves close attention. Seemingly, the phenomenon of lay-off or redundancy is fairly distinct from unemployment in its spirit, and has not yet generated any marked interest in our investigators to delve into its psychological impact. An unemployed is generally conceived as one who, despite having every potentiality to enter the job, fails to secure a gainful employment in any public undertaking; such a person has virtually no taste of employment. The incidence of lay-off or redundancy, on the other hand, occurs only after job loss. The decision of such dismissal or retrenchment is usually forcibly imposed by the management. In short, employment is the prerequisite for the incidence of lay-off or redundancy in the labour market. There are studies (Catalano, 1991;

Jin, Chandrakant and Svoboda, 1995; Kieselbach, 1991, 1997a, 1998a,b,c; Kieselbach and Wacker, 1995) where it has been shown that job loss in a labour society has many harmful effects on one's psychological well-being. So, the incidence of lay-off or redundancy or even the anticipation of it, as it has been documented (Arnetz *et al.*, 1991; Burchell, 1992; Fryer and McKenna, 1987, 1988; Kieselbach, 1997a, 1998a, b, c, 2003; Schnall *et al.*, 1992), is as dangerous for one's psychological health as is unemployment. The issue, however, has not been addressed in unemployment researches in India so far. This, particularly in the changing scenario of government moves to restructure different public sector enterprises in the light of increasing globalisation, flexibilisation, and world-wide economic competition, underlines the need to design a scientific inquiry into the psychological impact of being laid-off or made redundant or the fear of being so, as against being differently unemployed or employed. In addition, the psychological damage produced by the phenomenon of pseudo-employment (Singh, 1992)— a unique form of employment without any concomitant economic gain, not seen in any part of the world and even in India, except in Bihar — has also been little investigated, and thus invites a much well-designed intensive probe in this regard. This may help to broaden the scope of predictability as to the psychological costs of pseudo-employment, as also of unemployment.

Yet another important dimension that deserves to be taken into account in future researches relates to social justice. Unfortunately, despite a lot of emphasis presently on social justice on a universal scale, neither the researches on the impact of unemployment have addressed unemployment from the viewpoint of social justice nor have researches on social justice have dwelt incisively upon job loss and unemployment as social problems, notwithstanding a few exceptions in this regard (Dalbert, 1996, 1997; Henry, 1994; Kieselbach, 1997a,b,1998b; Lerner and Somers, 1992; Montada, 1994). As a matter of fact, more well-conceived researches are needed in India and abroad to enrich knowledge in this novel field of unemployment research. This kind of research is expected to lead to the development of a judicious, humanitarian approach towards the jobless and the unemployed all the world over, and specially in the third world countries like India, which have a larger labour force, and which, in order to get rid of their economic ills, have started thinking in terms of taking recourse to the *not-so-humane method* of downsizing in their enterprises.

Finally, to mitigate the misery caused by unemployment as well as bad employment, sufficient attention needs to be focused on this human malaise on a global level. Many intervention programmes have, of late, been suggested for the help of the unemployed as well as the people engaged in unsatisfactory jobs. But, this cannot be expected to be a one-man endeavour. Thus, in the light of the views held by Feather (1990) and Fryer (1992), it may be proposed that not only the psychologists, but all the social scientists ought to make concerted efforts to suggest steps to deal with the predicament caused by unemployment, as also by poor employment.

Thus, a range of important questions that deserve attention has been put forth in order to have a precise and comprehensive account of the impact of status of employment on psychological well-being, and the preference for strategies adopted to cope with that. However, despite all limitations and shortcomings, the findings synthesized on the basis of this study are pregnant with many valuable ideas which, it is hoped, would add to our knowledge regarding the impact of status of employment on psychological well-being, as also the preference for different coping strategies, particularly in a third world country like India, which has huge unutilized man power. The findings of this study, in fine, would provide new directions to our knowledge in this regard, and certainly prove to be of both theoretical and pragmatic importance.

Bibliography

Abhimanyou, T. (1976). *A study of some psychological dimensions of political efficacy and cynicism.* Ph.D. Thesis, University of Udaipur, Udaipur.

Abramson, L.Y., Seligman, M.E.P., and Teasdale, J.D. (1978). Learned helplessness in humans : Critique and reformulation. *Journal of Abnormal Psychology, 87,* 49-74.

Agarwal, M. (1995). Psycho-social determinants of 'egoistical' relative deprivation in organisations. *Management and Labour Studies, 20,* 15-31.

Aggarwal, S.C., and Goyal, J.K.(2000). Trends in youth unemployment in India. *The Indian Journal of Labour Economics, 43,* 641-655.

Ahmad, D.K. (July 31, 1993). Doing your own thing to beat unemployment. *The Times of India* (Career and Competition Times), Patna.

Ahmad, S., and Khanna, P. (1992). Job stress and job satisfaction of middle level hotel employees. *Journal of Personality and Clinical Studies, 8,* 51-56.

Aho, S. (1981). Life situation of unemployed youth in the light of research. *Psykologia, 16,* 275-283.

Allatt, P., and Yeandle, S. (1992). *Youth unemployment and the family: Voices of disordered times.* London: Routledge.

Alston, J.P., and Dudley, C.J. (1973). Age, occupation and life satisfaction. *Gerontologist, 13,* 58-61.

Alvaro, J.L. (1989a). Desempleo juvenil y salud mental. In J.R. Torregrosa, J. Bergere, and J.L. Alvaro (Eds.), *Juventud, trabajo y desempleo: Un análisis psicosociológico.* (Youth Unemployment and Mental Health., *pp. 305-319).* Madrid: Ministerio de Trabajo y Seguridad Social.

Alvaro, J.L. (1989b). *Desempleo y bienestar psicológico.* (Unemployment and psycological well-being). Madrid : Universidad Complutense de Madrid.

Aminabhavi, V., and Dharanendriah, A.S. (1994). A study of vocational interest of doctors, engineers and men-in-general. *Social Science International, 10,* 17-27.

Amirkhan, J. (1990). A factor-analytically derived measure of coping : The coping strategy indicator. *Journal of Personality and Social Psychology, 59,* 1066-1074.

Anderson, N. (1974). *Man's work and leisure,* Leiden : E.J.Brill.

Ansari, A.A., Sampurna, T.V., Udupa, K.N., and Agarwal, P. (1979). Trait of anxiety in relation to achievement motive in certain stress disorders. *Indian Journal of Clinical Psychology, 6,* 185-189.

Archer, R.P. (1979). Relationship between locus of control and anxiety. *Journal of Personality Assessment, 43,* 617–626.

Arnetz, B.B., Brenner, S.-O., Levi, L., Hjelm, R., *et al.* (1991). Neuroendocrine and immunologic effects of unemployment and job insecurity. *Psychotherapy and Psychosomatics, 55,* 76-80.

Arnetz, B.B., Wasserman, J., Petrini, B., Brenner, S-O., Levi, L., Eneroth, P., Salovaara, H., Hjelm, R., Salovaara, L., Theorell, T., and Petterson, I.L. (1987). Immune function in unemployed women. *Psychosomatic Medicine, 49,* 3-12.

Aronowitz, S., and DiFazio, W. (1994). *The jobless future : Sci-tech and the dogma of work.* Minneapolis : Univeristy of Minneapolis Press.

Ashforth, B.E. (1986). *The experience of powerlessness in the operating core of the machine bureaucracy.* Unpublished doctoral dissertation, University of Toronto.

Atkinson, T., Liem, T., and Liem, J.(1986). The social costs of unemployment : Implications for social support. *Journal of Health and Social Behaviour, 27,* 317-331.

Averiall, J.R. (1982). *Anger and Aggression : An essay on emotion.* New York : Springer–Verlag.

Bachman, J.G., and O'Malley, P.M. (1977). Self-esteem in young men : A longitudinal analysis of the impact of educational and occupational attainment. *Journal of Personality and Social Psychology, 35,* 365-380.

Bajaj, P. (1982). Alienation as related to perception of organizational climate. *Indian Journal of Industrial Relations, 17,* 563-572.

Bakke, E.W. (1933). *The unemployed man.* London : Nisbet.

Bakke, E.W. (1940a). *Citizens without work.* New Haven : Yale University Press.

Bakke, E.W. (1940b). *The Unemployed Worker.* New Haven : Yale University Press.

Bandura, A. (1977). Self-efficacy : Toward a unifying theory of behavioural change. *Psychological Review, 84,* 191-215.

Bandura, A. (1979). The social learning perspective : Mechanisms of aggression. In H.Toch (Ed.), *Psychology of crime and criminal justice.* New York : Holt, Rinehart and Winston.

Bandura, A. (1982). Self-efficacy mechanism in human agency. *American Psychologist, 37,* 122-147.

Bandura, A. (1986). *Social foundations of thought and action : A social cognitive theroy.* Englewood Cliffs, NJ : Prentice-Hall.

Bandura, A. (1988). Self-regulation of motivation and action through goal systems. In V. Hamilton, G.H.Bower, and N.H. Frijda (Eds), *Cognitive perspectives on emotion and motivation (pp. 37-61).* Dordrecht : Kluwer Academic Publishers.

Banks, M.H. (1990). The psychological consequences of youth unemployment. In R.A.Roe, and R.Burckhardt (Eds.), *Professional psychology: Developments and benefits (pp.1-12).* Lisse, The Netherland : Swets and Zeitlinger B.V.

Banks, M.H., and Jackson, P.R. (1982). Unemployment and risk of minor psychiatric disorder in young people : Cross-sectional and longitudinal evidence. *Psychological Medicine, 12,* 789-798.

Banks, M.H., and Ullah, P. (1986). Unemployment and less qualified urban youth. *Employment Gazette, 94,* 205-210.

Banks, M.H., and Ullah, P. (1987a). *Youth unemployment : Social and psychological perspectives* (Department of Employment Research Paper No. 61). London : HMSO.

Banks, M.H., and Ullah, P. (1987b). Political attitudes and voting among unemployed and employed youth. *Journal of Adolescence, 10,* 201-206.

Banks, M.H., and Ullah, P. (1988). *Youth unemployment in the 1980s : Its psychological effects.* London : Croom Helm.

Banks, M.H., Ullah, P., and Warr, P.B. (1984). Unemployment and less qualified urban young people. *Employment Gazette, 92,* 343-346.

Barling, J. (1990). *Employment, stress and family functioning.* Chichester, U.K. : Wiley.

Barness, B.L. (1992). Stress adjustments of railway personnel. *Journal of Personality and Clinical Studies, 8,* 57-61.

Basham, A.L. (1971). *The wonder that was India.* Calcutta : Rupa and Co.

Baum, A., Fleming, R., and Reddy, D.M. (1986). Unemployment

stress : Loss of control, reactance and learned helplessness. *Social Science and Medicine, 22,* 509-516.

Baum, A., Singer, J.E., and Baum, C.S. (1981). Stress and the environment. *Journal of Social Issues, 37,* 4-35.

Beale, N., and Nethercott, S. (1985). Job loss and family morbidity : A study of a factory closure. *Journal of the Royal College of General Practitioners, 35,* 510-514.

Beale, N., and Nethercott, S.(1986). Job loss and health : The influence of age and previous morbidity. *Journal of the Royal College of General Practitioners, 36,* 261-264.

Beales, H.L., and Lambert, R.S. (1934). *Memoirs of the unemployed.* London : Gollanz.

Beck, A.T. (1967). *Depression : Clinical, experimental and theoretical aspects.* New York : Harper.

Beck, A.T. (1976). *Cognitive therapy and the emotional disorders.* New York : International Universities Press.

Benavides, F.G., García, A.M., Sáez-Lloret, I., and Librero, J. (1994). Unemployment and health in Spain : The influence of socio-economic environment. *European Journal of Public Health, 4*, 103-107.

Berman, J.J., Murphy-Berman, M.V., and Singh, P. (1985). Cross-cultural similarities and differences in perceptions of fairness. *Journal of Cross-Cultural Psychology, 16,* 55-67.

Bhushan, L.I. (1984). *Problems of determining validity of attitude and value tests.* Paper presented at the meeting of the National Test Library, NCERT, New Delhi.

Billings, A.G., and Moos, R.H. (1981). The role of coping responses and social resources in attenuating the stress of life events. *Journal of Behavioural Medicine, 4,* 157-189.

Billings, A.G., and Moos, R.H. (1982). Work stress and stress-buffering roles of work and family resources. *Journal of Occupational Behaviour, 3,* 215-232.

Black, J.A., and Champion, D.J. (1976). *Methods and issues in social research.* New York : John Wiley and Sons.

Blake, R., and Vandiver, T. (1988). The association of health with stressful life changes, social support and coping. *Family Practice Research Journal, 7,* 205-218.

Blanch, J.M. (1990). *Del viejo al nuevo paro : Un análisis psicológico y social.* [From the old to the new unemployment : A psychological and social analysis]. Barcelona: Promociones y Publicaciones Universitarias.

Blau, P.M. (1964). *Exchange and power in social life.* New York : John Wiley.

Bolton, W., and Oatley, K. (1987). A longitudinal study of social support and depression in unemployed men. *Psychological Medicine, 17,* 453-460.

Bond, M.J., and Feather, N.T. (1988). Some correlates of structure and purpose in the use of time. *Journal of Personality and Social Psychology, 55,* 321-329.

Borgeon, W.A., Hates, W.E., and Amundson, N.E. (1990). The experience of unemployment for university graduates : The exploratory study. *Journal of Employment Counselling, 27,* 104-112.

Bostyn, A.M., and Wight, D. (1987). Inside a community : Value associated with money and time. In S.Fineman (Ed.), *Unemployment : Personal and social consequences (pp.138-154).* London : Tavistock.

Branthwaite, A., and Garcia, S. (1985). Depression in the young unemployed and those on Youth Opportunities Schemes. *British Journal of Medical Psychology, 58,* 67-74.

Braunstein, W.B., Powell, B.J., Mc Gowan, J.E., and Thoreson, R.W.(1983). Employment factors in outpatient recovery of alcoholics : A multivariate study. *Addictive Behaviours, 8,* 345-351.

Breakwell, G.M. (1986). Political and attributional responses of the young short-term unemployed. *Political Psychology, 7,* 265-278.

Breakwell, G.M., Collie, A., Harrison, B., and Propper, C. (1984). Attitudes towards the unemployed: Effects of threatened identity. *British Journal of Social Psychology, 7,* 265-278.

Breakwell, G.M., Harrison, B., and Propper, C. (1984). Explaining the psychological effects of unemployment for young people : The importance of specific situational factors. *British Journal of Guidance and Counselling, 12,* 132-140.

Brenner, M.H. (1973). *Mental illness and the economy.* Cambridge, MA : Harward University Press.

Brenner, S.-O., and Levi, L. (1987a). Long-term unemployment among Swedish women. *Social Science and Medicine, 25,* 153-161.

Brenner, S.-O., and Levi, L. (1987b). Vulnerability among long-term unemployed: A longitudinal study of mental and physical health among Swedish women at different phases of unemployment—Some preliminary results. In D. Schwefel, P.-G. Svensson, and

H.F.K. Zöllner (Eds), *Unemployment, social vulnerability, and health in Europe (pp. 239-256).* New York: Springer-Verlag.

Brenner, S.-O., Petterson, I-L., Arnetz, B., and Levi, L. (1989). Stress reactions to unemployment among Swedish blue-coller workers. In B. Starrin, P.-G. Svensson, and H. Wintersberger (Eds.), *Unemployment, poverty and quality of working life: Some European experiences (pp. 101-114).* Berlin: Edition Sigma.

Brenner, S.-O., and Starrin, B. (1988). Unemployment and health in Sweden : Public issues and private troubles. *Journal of Social Issues, 44,* 125-140.

Briar, K.H. (1977). The effect of long-term unemployment on workers and their families. *Dissertation Abstracts International, 37,*6062.

Briar, K.H. (1983). Unemployment : Toward a social work agenda. *Social Work, 28,* 211-216.

Brief, A.P., and Aldag, R.J. (1976). Correlates of role indices. *Journal of Applied Psychology, 61,* 468-472.

Brinkmann, C. (1976). Finanzielle und psychosoziale Belastungen während der Arbeitslosigkeit. *Mitteilungen aus der Arbeitsmarkt- und Berufsforschung, 9, 397-413.*

Brinkmann, C. (1984). Die individuellen Folgen längerfristiger Arbeitslosigkeit. *Mitteilungen aus der Arbeitsmarkt-und Beruforschung, 17,* 454-473.

Brockner, J. (1990). Scope of justice in the workplace : How supervisors react to co-workers' lay-offs. *Journal of Social Issues, 46,* 95-106.

Broomhall, H.S., and Winefield, A.H. (1990). A comparison of the affective well-being of young and middle aged unemployed men matched for length of unemployment. *British Journal of Medical Psychology, 63,* 43-52.

Brousseau, K.R. (1978). Personality and job experience. *Organizational Behaviour and Human Performance, 22,* 235-252.

Brousseau, K.R., and Prince, J.B. (1981). Job-person dynamics : An extension of longitudinal research. *Journal of Applied Psychology, 66,* 59-62.

Brown, L.D. (1984). Effective change strategies for public enterprises : Lessons from turnaround cases. *Vikalpa, 9,* 97-112.

Burchell, B. (1992). Towards a social psychology of the labour market : Or why we need to understand the labour market before we can understand unemployment. *Journal of Occupational and Organisational Psychology, 65, 345-354.*

Burgess, R.L., and Huston, T.L. (Eds.), (1979). *Social exchange in developing relationships.* New York : Academic Press.

Burke, R.J. (1986). Occupational and life stress and the family : Conceptual frameworks and research findings. *International Review of Applied Psychology, 35,* 347-369.

Burns, R.B. (1979). *The self-concept : Theroy, measurement, development and behaviour.* London : Longman.

Buss, A.H. (1971). Aggression pays. In J.L. Singer (Ed.), *The control of aggression and violence : Cognitive and physiological factors.* New York: Academic Press.

Buss, T.F., and Redburn, F.S. (1983). *Mass unemployment : Plant closings and community mental health.* Beverly Hills : Sage.

Büssing, A. (1987). Arbeitsplatzunsicherheit und Antizipation von Arbeitslosigkeit als Stadien des Arbeitslosigkeitsprozesses. *Soziale Welt, 38,* 310-329.

Büssing, A. (1990). Differentielle Arbeitslosigkeitsforschung am Beispiel moderierender Effekte der psychischen und psychosomatischen Auswirkungen von Arbeitsplatzunsicherheit. In T. Kieselbach (Ed.), *Arbeitslosigkeit und Gesundheit—Ergebnisse der europäischen Arbeitslosenforschung* (Series 'Psychology of Social Inequality', *Vol. 3).* Weinheim : Deutscher Studien Verlag.

Campbell, A. (1981). *The sense of well-being in America : Recent patterns and trends.* New York : McGraw-Hill.

Caplan, R.D., Cobb, S., French, J.R.P., Van Harrison, R., and Pinneau, S.R. (1975). *Job demands and worker health.* Washington : US Department of Health, Education and Welfare.

Carver, C., Scheier, M., and Weintraub, J. (1989). Assessing coping strategies : A theoretically based approach. *Journal of Personality and Social Psychology, 56,* 276-283.

Catalano, R.A. (1991). Health effects of economic insecurity. *American Journal of Public Health, 81,* 1148-1152.

Catalano, R.A., and Dooley, D. (1983)..Health effects of economic instability : A test of economic stress hypothesis. *Journal of Health and Social Behaviour, 24,* 46-60.

Catalano, R.A., Dooley, D., Novaco, R.W., Wilson, G., and Hough, R. (1993). Using ECA survey data to examine the effects of job layoffs on violent behaviour. *Hospital and Community Psychiatry, 44,* 874-879.

Centres for Disease Control and Prevention (1995). Suicide among children, adolescents, and young adults—United States, 1980-1992. *Journal of American Medical Association, 274,* 451-452.

Chadha, V., and Chadha, N. (1995). Generation and employment of scientific and technical manpower in India. *Management and Labour Studies, 20* 135-150.

Chakraborty, S.K. (1991). *Management by values.* Oxford : Oxford Publishing Compnay.

Chakraborty, S.K.(1995). *Ethics in management : Vedantic perspective.* New Delhi : Oxford University Press.

Chakrapani, C. (1995). *Unemployment stress : A study of educated unemployed.* New Delhi : Vikas Publishing House.

Chakrapani, C. (1996). Unemployment as a stressor : Role of socio-psychological factors. *Indian Journal of Social Work, 57,* 578-590.

Chatterjee, R.N., Mukherjee, M., and Nandi, D.N. (1981). Life events and depression. *Indian Journal of Psychiatry, 23,* 333-337.

Chaturvedi, M.K. (1983). *Human stress and stressors : A sociological study.* New Delhi : Cosmo Publications.

Chronicle Yearbook (1999). *Educated unemployed in India.* New Delhi : Chronicle Publisher.

Clark, A.W. (1985). The effects of unemployment on political attitude. *Australian and New Zealand Journal of Sociology, 21,* 100-108.

Clark, A.W., and Clissold, M.P. (1982). Correlates of adaptation among unemployed and employed young men. *Psychological Reports, 50,* 887-893.

Clegg, C., and Wall, T. (1990). The relationship between simplified jobs and mental health : A replication study. *Journal of Occupational Psyhology, 63,* 289-296.

Coates, D., Moyer, S., Wellman, B. (1969). Yorklea study : Symptoms, problems, and life events. *Canadian Journal of Public Health, 60,* 471-481.

Cobb, S., and Kasl, S.V. (1977). *Termination : The consequences of job loss.* Cincinatti : U.S.Department of Health, Education and Welfare.

Coburn, D. (1978). Work and general psychological and physical well-being. *International Journal of Health Services, 8,* 415-435.

Cochrane, C.M. (1983). *Unemployment : Its relationship to self-esteem and depression in applicants for general enlistment in the*

Australian army. Unpublished Master's thesis, The Flinders Univeristy of South Australia, Bedford Park, South Australia.

Cochrane, R., and Billig, M. (1984). "I am not National Front myself, but ... ." *New Society, 68* (No. 1121), 255-258.

Coffield, F., Borrill, C., and Marshall, S. (1983). How young people try to survive being unemployed. *New Society, 64* (No. 1072), 332-334.

Cohen, S., and Syme, S.L.(Eds.), (1985). *Social support and health.* New York : Academic Press.

Cohen, S., and Wills, T.A. (1985). Stress, social support, and the buffering hypothesis. *Psychological Bulletin, 98,* 310-357.

Cohn, R.M. (1978). The effect of employment status change on self-attitudes. *Social Psychology, 41,* 81-93.

Conger, R.D., Elder, G.H., Frederick, O., Lorenz, K.J., Conger, R.L., Simons, L.B., Whitbeck, S.H., and Melby, J.N. (1990). Linking economic hardship to marital quality and instablity. *Journal of Marriage and Family, 52,* 643-656.

Cortés, I. (1997). *Relació entre l' atur i la salut mental d' una mostra de la població activa catalana entrevistada en l' Enquesta de Salut de Catalunya 1994.* (Relationship between unemployment and mental health in a sample of the active population interviewed in the 1994 Catalan Health Survey). Barcelona: Institut Municipal de la Salut.

Council of Europe (1895). *The effects of long-term unemployment on health* (Report of a study group for the 18th meeting of the European Health Committee). Strasbourg [CDSP (85) 26].

Crept, P., Vetrone, G., Piazzi, A., Costa, M., and Lombardi, V. (1992). Aspetti psicologici della disoccupazione giovanile nella città di Foggia: Studio trasversale. (Psychological aspects of youth unemployment in the town of Foggia: Transversal study). *Difesa Sociale, 2,* 39-54.

Cronbach, L.J. (1951). Coefficient alpha and the internal structure of test. *Psychometrika, 16,* 297-334.

Cronkite, R., and Moos, R. (1984). The role of predisposing and moderating factors in the stress-illness relationship. *Journal of Health and Social Behaviour, 25,* 372-393.

Cullen, J.H., Ryan, G.M., Cullen, K.M., Ronayne, T., and Wynne, R.F. (1987). Unemployed youth and health : Findings from the pilot phase of a longitudinal study. In L.Levi (Ed.), *Unemployment and health (Special Issue). Social Science and Medicine, 25,* 133-146.

Dalbert, C. (1996). *Ulper den umgang mit Ungerechtigkett : Eine Psychologische Analyse.* (Dealing with injustice : A psychological analysis). Berlin: Huber.

Dalbert, C. (1997). Coping with an unjust fate : The case of structural unemployment. *Social Justice Research, 10,* 175-189.

Damstrup, V.L. (1987). The effects of youth unemployment : A review of the literature. In D.Schwefel, P.-G. Svensson, and H.F.K. Zöllner (Eds.), *Unemployment, social vulnerability, and health in Europe (pp. 167-183).* New York : Springer-Verlag.

Daniel, W.W. (1974). *A national survey of the unemployed.* London : Political and Economic Planning Institute.

Das, V. (1982). Reflections on the social construction of adulthood. In S.Kakar (Ed.), *Identity and adulthood (pp. 89-104).* Delhi : Oxford University Press.

Davids, A. (1955). Alienation, social apperception and ego-structure. *Journal of Consulting Psychology, 19,* 21-27.

Dayal, I. (1988). Managing high technology strategic organizations. In P.N.Khandwalla (Ed.), *Social development.* New Delhi : Sage Publications.

de Almeida Filho, N. (1981). Unemployment, underemployment and mental health in a low income neighbourhood in Salvador Bahia, Brazil. *Journal Brasileiro de Psiquiatria, 30,* 463-470.

Deb, P. C., and Singh, H. (1980). A study of university teachers : Their achievement and job satisfaction. *Indian Psychological Review, 19,* 7-19.

Del Llano, J. (1990). *Desempleo y salud: Relación existente entre la situación de desempleo y el estado de salud en población en edad de trabajar del municipio de Madrid.* (Unemployment and health: Relationship between unemployment and health among working age people from Madrid). Madrid: Universidad Complutense de Madrid.

Del Llano, J., Aracil, E., Del Llano, M., González, J.L., Fernández, F., Román, B., and Esquivias, M. (1996). Una enfermedad llamada paro: La trastienda del desempleo de larga duración. (An illness called unemployment: The background of long-term unemploment). *Gaceta Sanitaria, 10,* 73-80.

Depolo, M., and Sarchielli, G. (1985). *Job insecurity, psychological well-being and social representation : A case of cost sharing in industrial relations.* Paper presented at the North- West European Conference on the Psychology of Work and Organization, Aachen, 1-3 April.

Dev, M.S. (2000). Economic liberalisation and employment in South Asia. *Economic and Political Weekly,* Jan. 8 and Jan.15.

De Witte, H. (1989). Liever moe dan lui: Werkloosheid en tewerkstelling van jongeren in Vlaanderen. (Rather tired than idle: Employment and unemployment of youngsters in Flanders). *Tijdschrift voor Sociologie, 10,* 509-545.

De Witte, H. (1992). Unemployment, political attitudes and voting behaviour. *Politics and the Individual, 2,* 29-41.

De Witte, H. (1993). Gevolgen van langdurige werkloosheid voor het psychisch welzijn: Overzicht van de onderzoeksliteratuur. (Consequences of long-term unemployment on the psychological well-being: Overview of the research literature). *Psychologica Belgica, 33,* 1-35.

De Witte, H. (1994). ('t Is geen) leven zonder werk: Een overzicht van recente literatuur over de psychische gevolgen van werkloosheid. [(No) life without a job: An overview of the recent literature on the psychological consequences of unemployment]. *Welzijnsgids-Noden, werken, 12,* 1-23.

De Witte, H., and Hooge, J. (1997). Aanpassing aan werkloosheid? Een cross-sectionele vergelijking van kort- en langdurig werklozen. (Adaptation to unemployment? A cross-sectional comparison of short- and long-term unemployed persons). *Gedrag and Gezondheid, 25,* 145-155.

Dharanendriah, A.S., and Havalappanavar, N.B. (1986). Personal needs of medical students. *Psychological Studies, 31,* 125-126.

Dholakia, J. (1977). *Unemployment and employment policy in India.* New Delhi : Sterling Publication.

D.H.S.S. (1980). *Inequalities in health.* Report of a Research Working Group (Black). London : DHSS.

Dijkhuizen, N. Van (1980). *From stressors to strains.* Lisse : Swets and Zeitlinger.

Dilling, H., Weyerer, S., and Castell, R. (1984). *Psychische erkrankungen in der bevölkerung.* Stuttgart: Enke.

Dodge,D., and Martin, W. (1970). *Social stress and chronic illness.* Notredame : Ind University of Notredame Press.

Dohrenwend, B.P., Shrout, P.E., Egri, C., and Mendelsohn, F.S. (1980). Nonspecific psychological distress and other dimensions of psychopathology : Measures for use in the general population. *Archives of General Psychiatry , 37,* 1229-1238.

Dohrenwend, B.S., and Dohrenwend, B.P. (1974). *Stressful life events : Their nature and effects.* New York: John Wiley.

Donovan, A., and Oddy, M. (1982). Psychological aspects of unemployment : An investigation into the emotional and social adjustment of school-leavers. *Journal of Adolescence, 5,* 15-30.

Donovan, A., Oddy, M., Pardoe, R., and Ades, A. (1986). Employment status and psychological well-being : A longitudinal study of 16-year-old school-leavers. *Journal of Child Psychology and Psychiatry, 27,* 65-76.

Dooley, D., and Catalano, R.A. (1980). Economic change as a cause of behavioural disorder. *Psychological Bulletin, 87,* 450-468.

Dooley, D., Catalano, R.A., Jackson, R., and Brownell, A. (1981). Economic life, and symptom changes in non-metropolitan community. *Journal of Health and Social Behaviour, 22,* 144-154.

Dooley, D., Catalano, R.A., and Rook, K.S. (1988). Personal and aggregate unemployment and psychological symptoms. *Journal of Social Issues, 44,* 107-123.

Dooley, D., and Prause, J. (1995). Effect of unemployment on school-leavers' self-esteem. *Journal of Occupational and Organizational Psychology, 68,* 177-192.

Dooley, D., and Prause, J. (1997). Effect of students' self-esteem on later employment status : Interactions of self-esteem with gender and race. *Applied Psychology : An International Review, 46,* 175-198.

Dooley, D., Rook, K.S., and Catalano, R.A. (1987). Job and non-job stressors and their moderators. *Journal of Occupational Psychology, 60,* 115-132.

Dube, S., Sundaram, K.R., Mohan, D., and Jain, P. (1980). *Scaling of life events : A cross-cultural study in the community setting of Delhi.* Paper presented at the Vth International Conference of Cross-Cultural Psychology, Bhubaneshwar.

Dumont, P. (1977). Is mental health possible under our economic system? No! *Psychiatric Opinion, 14,* 9-11, 32-33, 44-45.

Duncan, G.J. (1987). The volatility of family income over the life course. In P.B. Baltes, D.L. Featherman, and R.M. Lerner (Eds.), *Life-span development and behaviour (Vol. 7).* Hillsdale NJ : Erlbaum.

Dunkel-Schetter, C., Feingstein, L., Taylor, S., and Falke, R. (1992). Patterns of coping with cancer. *Health Psychology, 11,* 79-87.

Dutt, R. (1990). Desh mein berojgar ki bhayanak sthiti (Horrible state of unemployment in the country). *Arthashastri,* November Issue (No-221), 39-45.

Eales, M.J. (1989). Shame among unemployed men. *Social Science and Medicine, 28.* 783-789.

Edwards, J.N., and Klemack, D.L. (1973). Correlates of life satisfaction. *Journal of Gerontology, 28,* 497-502.

Eisenberg, P., and Lazarsfeld, P.F. (1938). The psychological effects of unemployment. *Psychological Bulletin, 35,* 358-390.

Elchardus, M., and Glorieux, I. (1995). *Niet aan de arbeid voorbij: De werkloosheidservaring als reflectie over arbeid, solidariteit en sociale cohesie.* (Not beyond work: The experience of unemployment as a reflection on labour, solidarity and social cohesion). Brussel: VUBPRESS.

Elder, G.H., Jr., Caspi, A., and Van Nguyen, T. (1986). Resourceful and vulnerable children : Family influences in hard times. In R.K. Silbereisen, H. Eyferth, and G. Rudinger (Eds.), *Development as action in context : Problem behaviour and normal youth development (pp. 167-186).* New York : Springer.

Elder, G.H.Jr., Conger, R.D., Foster, E.M., and Ardelt, M. (1991). Families under economic pressure. *Journal of Family Issues.*

Ensminger, M.E., and Celentano, D.D.(1990). Gender differences in the effect of unemployment on psychological distress. *Social Science and Medicine, 30,* 469-477.

Erikson, E.H. (1950). *Childhood and society.* New York : Norton.

Erikson, E.H. (1959). Identity and the life cycle. *Psychological Issues, 1,* 50-100.

Erikson, E.H. (1963). *Childhood and society (2nd ed.).* New York : Norton.

Erikson, E.H. (1968). *Identity : Youth and crisis.* New York : Norton.

Erikson, E.H. (1980). *Identity and the life cycle.* New York : Norton.

Erikson, E.H. (1982). *The life cycle completed.* New York : Norton.

Estes, R.J., and Wilensky, H.L. (1978). Life cycle squeeze and the normal curve. *Social Problems, 25,* 277-292.

Fagin, L., and Little, M. (1984). *The forsaken families : The effects of unemployment on family life.* Harmondsworth : Penguin.

Faroqi, M.A. (1984). Are Indians external ? *Psychological Studies, 29,* 101-106.

Feather, N.T. (1982). Unemployment and its psychological correlates : A study of depressive symptoms, self-esteem, Protestant ethic values, attributional style and apathy. *Australian Journal of Psychology, 34,* 309-323.

Feather, N.T. (1983a). Causal attributions and beliefs about work and unemployment among adolescents in State and independent secondary schools. *Australian Journal of Psychology, 35,* 211-232.

Feather, N.T. (1983b). Some correlates of attributional style : Depressive symptoms, self-esteem and Protestant ethic values. *Personality and Social Psychology Bulletin, 9,* 125-135.

Feather, N.T. (1985a). Masculinity, femininity, self-esteem and subclinical depression. *Sex Roles, 12,* 491-500.

Feather, N.T. (1985b). The psychological impact of unemployment : Empirical findings and theoretical approaches. In N.T. Feather (Ed.), *Australian psychology : Review of research (pp.265-295).* Sydney : Allen and Unwin.

Feather, N.T. (1989a). Reported changes in behaviour after job loss in a sample of older unemployed men. *Australian Journal of Psychology, 41,* 175-185.

Feather, N.T. (1989b). The effects of unemployment on work values and motivation. In U.W. Kleinbeck, H.H. Quast, H. Thierry, and H.Hacker (Eds.), *Work motivation (pp. 201-229).* Hillsdale, NJ : Erlbaum.

Feather, N.T. (1990). *The psychological impact of unemployment.* New York : Springer-Verlag.

Feather, N.T. (1992). Expectancy value theory and unemployment effects. *Journal of Occupational and Organizational Psychology, 65,* 315-330.

Feather, N.T., and Barber, J.G. (1983). Depressive reactions and unemployment. *Journal of Abnormal Psychology, 92,* 185-195.

Feather, N.T., and Bond, M.J. (1983). Time structure and purposeful activity among employed and unemployed university graduates. *Journal of Occupational Psychology, 56,* 241-254.

Feather, N.T., and Davenport, P.R. (1981). Unemployment and depressive affect : A motivational and attributional analysis. *Journal of Personality and Social Psychology, 41,* 422-436.

Feather, N.T., and O'Brien, G.E. (1986a). A longitudinal study of the effects of employment and unemployment on school-leavers. *Journal of Occupational Psychology, 59,* 121-144.

Feather, N.T., and O'Brien, G.E. (1986b). A longitudinal analysis of the effects of different patterns of employment and unemployment on school-leavers. *British Journal of Psychology, 77,* 459-479.

Feather, N.T., and O'Brien, G.E. (1987). Looking for employment : An expectancy-valence analysis of job-seeking behaviour among young people. *British Journal of Psychology, 78,* 251-272.

Feather, N.T., and Tiggemann, M. (1984). A balanced measure of attributional style. *Australian Journal of Psychology, 36,* 267-283.

Feather, N.T., and Volkmer, R.E.(1988). Preference for situations involving effort, time pressure, and feedback in relation to Type A behaviour, locus of control, and test anxiety. *Journal of Personality and Social Psychology, 55,* 266-271.

Feshbach, S. (1970). Aggression. In P.H. Mussen (Ed.), *Carmichael's manual of child psychology (Vol. 3).* New York : Wiley.

Festinger, L. (1957). *A theroy of cognitive dissonance.* Standford : California, Standford University Press.

Fineman, S. (1979). A psychological model of stress and its application to managerial unemployment. *Human Relations, 32,* 323-345.

Fineman, S. (1983). *White collor unemployment : Impact and stress.* Chichester, UK : Wiley.

Fineman, S. (1987). *Unemployment : Personal and social consequences.* London : Tavistock.

Finlay-Jones, R.A., and Eckhardt, B. (1981). Psychiatric disorder among the young unemployed. *Australian and New Zealand Journal of Psychiatry, 15,* 265-270.

Finlay-Jones, R.A., and Eckhardt, B. (1984). A social and psychiatric survey of unemployment among young people. *Australian and New Zealand Journal of Psychiatry, 18,* 135-143.

Firth, J. (1985). Personal meanings of occupational stress. *Journal of Occupational Psychology, 58,* 139-148.

Fisher, S., and Reason, J. (Eds.), (1988). *Handbook of life stress, cognition and health.* Chichester : Wiley.

Fleishman, R. (1991). Styles of information seeking under threat : Personal and situational aspects of monitoring and blunting. *Personality and Individual Differences, 12,* 141-149.

Fletcher, B., and Payne, R.L. (1980). Stress and work : A review and theoretical framework (Part I). *Personnel Review, 9,* 19-29.

French, J.R.P., Caplan, R.D., and Van Harrison, R. (1982). *The mechanisms of job strain.* New York : Wiley.

Frese, M. (1985). Zur Verlaufsstruktur der psychischen Auswirkungen von Arbeitslosigkeit (The process structure of the psychological consequences of unemployment). In T. Kieselbach, and A. Wacker

(Eds.), *Individuelle und gesellschaftliche Kostem der Massenarbeitslosigkeit, Psychologische Theorie und Praxis* (Individual and societal costs of unemployment., *pp.224-241).* Beltz, Weinheim.

Frese, M., and Mohr, G. (1987). Prolonged unemployment and depression in older workers : A longitudinal study of intervening variables. *Social Science and Medicine, 25,* 173-178.

Freud, S. (1930). *Civilization and discontents.* London : Hogarth.

Fröhlich, D. (1983a). Economic deprivation, work orientation and health : Conceptual ideas and some empirical findings. In J.John, D.Schwefel, and H.F.K.Zöllner (Eds.), *Influences of economic instablity on health.* Berlin : Springer.

Fröhlich, D. (1983b) *The use of time during unemployment.* Assen : Van Gorcum.

Fryer, D. (1986). Employment deprivation and personal agency during unemployment : A critical discussion of Jahoda's explanation of the psychological effects of unemployment. *Social Behaviour, 1,* 3-23.

Fryer, D. (1988). The experience of unemployment in social context. In S. Fisher, and J. Reason (Eds.), *Handbook of life stress, cognition and health (pp. 211-238).* Chichester : Wiley.

Fryer, D. (1992). Editorial : Introduction to Marienthal and Beyond. *Journal of Occupational and Organizational Psychology, 65,* 257-268.

Fryer, D. (1995a). Benefit agency ? Labour market disadvantage, deprivation and mental health. *The Psychologist, 8,* 265-272.

Fryer, D. (1995b). Agency restriction theory. In Nicholson (Ed.), *Encyclopedic dictionary of organizational behaviour (p. 112).* Oxford : Blackwell.

Fryer, D.(1995c). Social and psychological consequences of unemployment : From interviewing to intervening. In R. Hicks, P. Creed, W. Patton, and J. Tomlinson (Eds.), *Unemployment : Developments and transitions.* Brisbane : Australian Academic Press.

Fryer, D., and McKenna, S.P. (1987). The laying off of hands—Unemployment and the experience of time. In S.Fineman (Ed.), *Unemployment : Personal and social consequences (pp. 47-73).* London : Tavistock.

Fryer, D., and McKenna, S.P. (1988). Redundant skills : Temporary unemployment and mental health. In M. Patrickson (Ed.),

Readings in organizational behaviour (pp.44-70). Sydney : Harper and Row.

Fryer, D., and Payne, R.L. (1984). Pro-active behaviour in unemployment : Findings and implications. *Leisure Studies, 3,* 273-295.

Fryer, D., and Payne, R.L. (1986). Being unemployed : A review of the literature on the psychological experience of unemployment. In C.L.Cooper, and I. Robertson (Eds.), *International review of industrial and organizational psychology (pp. 235-278).* Chichester : Wiley.

Fryer, D., and Ullah, P. (Eds.), (1987). *Unemployed people : Social and psychological perspectives.* Milton Keynes : Open University Press.

Fryer, D., and Winefield, A.H. (1998). Employment stress and unemployment distress as two varieties of labour market induced psychological strain : An explanatory framework. *The Australian Journal of Social Research, 5,* 3-18.

Furnham, A. (1985). Youth unemployment : A review of literature. *Journal of Adolescence, 8,* 109-124.

Ganesh, S.R. (1982). *Quality of life in Indian organizations : An irreverent view.* Indian Institute of Management, Ahmedabad, W.P. No. 407.

Garain, S. (1994). Government-NGO interface in India : An overview. *Indian Journal of Social Work, 55,* 337-346.

Garber, J., and Seligman, M.E.P. (1980). *Human helplessness : Theory and applications.* New York : Academic Press.

Garcia Rodriguez, Y. (1994). *Psycho-social effects of unemployment on Spanish youth.* Unpublished Manuscript.

Gardell, B. (1971). Alienation and mental health in the modern industrial environment. In L.Levi (Ed.), *Society, stress and disease (Vol. I).* Oxford : Oxford University Press.

Garraty, J.A. (1978). *Unemployment in history.* New York : Harper and Row.

Gaskell, G., and Smith, P. (1985). An investigation of youth's attributions for unemployment and their political attitudes. *Journal of Economic Psychology, 6,* 65-80.

Gniazdowski, A. (1987). *Full-employment policy in Poland and some of its effects related to workers' health.* Paper presented to the WHO workshop "Unemployment, Poverty, and Quality of Working Life—Innovative Interventions to Counteract Damaging Health Effects," Vienna, 12-13 May.

Goffman, E. (1968). *Stigma : Notes on the management of spoiled identity.* Harmonds-worth : Penguin.

Gold, J.H. (1978). University students, mental health and development. *Canadian Psychiatric Association Journal, 23,* 303-308.

Goldberg, D.P. (1972). *The detection of psychiatric illness by questionnaire.* London : Oxford University Press.

Goldberg, D.P., and Hillier, V.F. (1979). A scaled version of the general health questionnaire. *Psychological Medicine, 9,* 139-145.

Goldberger, L., and Breznitz, S. (Eds.), (1982). *Handbook of stress : Theoretical and clinical aspects.* New York : Free Press.

Goode, W.J., and Hatt, D.K. (1952). *Methods in social research.* New York : MC Graw-Hill.

Gore, S. (1978). The effect of social support in moderating the health consequences of unemployment. *Journal of Health and Social Behaviour, 19,* 157-165.

Gould, L.J. (1964). *The alienation syndrome : Psychological correlates and behavioural consequences.* Doctoral dissertation, Michigan : University of Michigan, Ann Arbor, University Microfilms, No 66848.

Gould, T., and Kenyon, J. (1972). *Stories from the dole queue.* London : Temple Smith.

Gupta, L.N., Bhatia, B.L., Godra, R.C., Vyas, J.N., and Singhal, S. (1981). Life events, physical illness, and psychiatric morbidity. *Indian Journal of Psychiatry, 23,* 338-342.

Gupta, L.N., and Srivastava, D. (1983). Life events and course of a physical illness. *Indian Journal of Psychiatry, 25,* 317-321.

Gupta, M.S. (1984). *Psychology of engineering creativity.* New Delhi : Cosmo Publications.

Gurney, R.M. (1980a). Does unemployment affect the self-esteem of school-leavers. *Australian Journal of Psychology, 32,* 175-182.

Gurney, R.M. (1980b). The effects of unemployment on the psychosocial development of school-leavers. *Journal of Occupational Psychology, 53,* 205-213.

Gurney, R.M. (1981). Leaving school, facing unemployment, and making attributions about the cause of unemployment. *Journal of Vocational Behaviour, 18,* 79-91.

Hacker, W. (1985). Activity : A fruitful concept in industrial psychology. In M. Frese, and J. Sabini (Eds.), *Goal-directed behaviour : The concept of action in psychology.* Hillsdale : Erlbaum.

Hagen, D.Q. (1983). The relationship between job loss and physical and mental illness. *Hospital and Community Psychiatry, 34,* 438-441.

Hajda, J. (1961). Alienation and integration of student intellectuals. *American Sociological Review, 26,* 758-777.

Hall, E.M. (1985). *Depression in unemployed Swedish women.* Reports from the Department of Stress Research, Karolinska Institute, 181.

Halstead, N., Johnson, S., and Cunningham, W. (1993). Measuring coping in adolescents : An application of the Ways of Coping Checklist. *Journal of Clinical Child Psychology, 22,* 337-344.

Hamilton, S.F. (1987). Adolescent problem behaviour in the United States and the Federal Republic of Germany : Implications for prevention. In K. Hurrelmann, F.X.Kaufmann, and F. Lösel (Eds.), *Social intervention : Potential and constraints (pp.185-204).* Berlin : Walter de Gruyter.

Hamilton, V.L., Hoffman, W.S., Broman, C.L., and Rauma, D. (1993). Unemployment, distress and coping : A panel study of autoworkers. *Journal of Personality and Social Psychology, 65,* 234-247.

Hammarström, A. (1996). *Arbetslöshet och ohälsa — Om ungodmars livsvillkor.* (Unemployment and ill-health — On vital conditions of youth). Lund: Studentlitteratur.

Hammarström, A., and Janlert, U. (1997). Nervous and depressive symptoms in a longitudinal study of youth unemployment — Selection or exposure. *Journal of Adolescence, 20,* 293-305.

Hammarström, A., Janlert, U., and Theorell, T. (1988). Youth unemployment and ill-health : Results from a 2-year follow-up study. *Social Science and Medicine, 26,* 1025-1033.

Hammarström, A., and Olofsson, B.-L. (1997). Hälsa och missbruk - Samband med arbetslöshet och marginalisering. [Health and substance abuse—Relationship between unemployment and marginalisation]. In J. Carle, and I. Julkunen (Eds.), *Arbetslöshetens villkor—Om ungdom, arbetslöshet och marginalisering i 90-talets Norden* (Unemployment conditions—On young persons, umployment and marginalisation in the Nordic countries in the 1990s]. Köpenhamn.

Handy, C. (1984). *The future of work.* Oxford : Blackwell.

Harrison, R. (1976). The demoralizing experience of prolonged unemployment. *Department of Education Gazette, 84,* 339-348.

Hartley, J. F. (1980). The impact of unemployment on the self-esteem of managers. *Journal of Occupational Psychology, 53,*147-155.

Hartley, J.F., and Fryer, D.M.(1984). The psychology of unemployment : A critical appraisal. In E.M.Stephenson, and J.H.Davis (Eds.), *Progress in applied social psychology (Vol. 2., pp. 3-30).* Chichester : Wiley.

Hartley, J.F., Jacobson, D., Klandermans, B. van Vuuren, T., Greenhalgh, L., and Sutton, R. (1991). *Unemployed people as involuntary, poorly paid, low status, insecure, public service workers.* London : Sage.

Hayes, J., and Nutman, P. (1981). *Understanding the unemployed* London : Tavistock.

Helpert, H.R. (1982). Psychic and psychosomatic disorders of the unemployed. *Paraxis der Psychotherapie und Psychosomatik, 27,* 151-160.

Hemant (August 30, 1993). Bihar mein 35 lakh berojgaro ke sath 21vi sadi ka swagat hoga (Bihar will welcome 21st century with 35 lakh unemployed). *Hindustan,* Patna.

Hemant (January, 3, 1994). Bihar mein rojgar ke ghatate awasron se sthiti visphotak (Explosive situation in Bihar due to decreasing job-opportunities). *Hindustan,* Patna.

Henkel, D. (1985). Arbeitslosigkeit als Risikofaktor für Alkoholgefährdung und Hindernis für Rehabilitationsprozesse. In T.Kieselbach, and A.Wacker (Eds.), *Individuelle und gesellschaftliche Kosten der Massenarbeitslosigkeit—Psychologische Theorie und Praxis (pp. 66-83).* Weinheim : Beltz.

Henkel, D. (1987). Arbeitslosigkeit und Alkoholismus. *Drogalkohol* (ISPA - Press), *II,* 79-106.

Henry, S. (1994). Employee dismissal : Justice at work. *Annual Report of American Academy of Political and Social Sciences* (Special Issue), 536.

Hepworth, S.J. (1980). Moderating effects of the psychological impact of unemployment. *Journal of Occupational Psychology, 53,* 139-145.

Hertz, D. (1988). Identity—lost and found : Patterns of migration and psychological and psychosocial adjustment of migrants. *Acta Psychiatrica Scandinavica, 78,* 159-165.

Herzog, A.R., Rodgers, W.L., and Woodworth, J. (1982). *Subjective well-being among different age groups.* Ann Arbor, Michigan : Institute for Social Research.

Higgins, E.T. (1987). Self-discrepancy : A theory relating self and affect. *Psychological Review, 94,* 319-340.

Hill, J.M.M. (1977). *The social and psychological impact of unemployment.* London : Tavistock.

Hill, J.M.M. (1978). The psychologcial impact of unemployment. *New Society, Jan.* 118-120.

Holahan, C.J., and Moos, R.H. (1985). Life stress and health : Personality, coping and family support in stress resistance. *Journal of Personality and Social Psychology, 49,* 739-747.

Holahan, C.J., and Moos, R.H. (1986). Personality, coping and family resources in stress resistance : A longitudinal analysis. *Journal of Personality and Social Psychology, 51,* 389-395.

Holahan, C., and Moos, R. (1987). Personal and contextual determinants of coping strategies. *Journal of Personality and Social Psychology, 52,* 946-955.

Holland, J.L. (1973). *Making vocational choices : A theory of careers.* Englewood Cliffs, NJ : Prentice-Hall.

Holmes, T.S., and Rahe, R.H. (1967). The social readjustment rating scale. *Journal of Psychosomatic Research, II,* 213-218.

Homans, G.C. (1961). *Social behaviour : Its elementary forms.* New York : Harcourt, Brace and World.

House, J.S., McMichael, A.J., Wells, A.J., Kaplan, B.H., and Landerman, L.R. (1979). Occupational stress and health among factory workers. *Journal of Health and Social Behaviour, 20,* 139-160.

Houtman, I. (1990). Personal coping resources and sex differences. *Personality and Individual Differences, II,* 53-63.

Hoyt, C. (1941). Test reliability estimated by analysis of variance. *Psychometrika, 6,* 153-160.

Hooge, J. (1995). *Wie neemt deel aan het Individueel Begeleidings-plan? Psycho-sociaal profiel en opvolging van de deelnemers.* (Who participates in the individual counselling plan? Psychosocial profile and follow-up of the participants). Leuven: Katholieke Universiteit Leuven, Hoger Instituut voor de Arbeid.

Hulin, C.L. (1982) Some reflections on general performance dimensions and halo rating error. *Journal of Applied Psychology, 67,* 165-170.

Hunt, S.M., McEwen, J., and McKenna, S.P. (1985). Measuring health status : A new tool for clinicians and epidemiologists. *Journal of the Royal College of General Practioners, 35,* 185-188.

Huppert, F.A., and Garcia, A.W. (1991). Qualitative differences in psychiatric symptoms between high risk groups on a screening test (GHQ-30). *Social Psychiatry and Psychiatric Epidemiology, 26,* 252-258.

Ilfeld, F.W. (1980). Coping styles of Chicago adults : Description. *Journal of Human Stress, 6,* 2-10.

ILO (International Labour Organization) (1996). *World employment report.* Geneva : ILO.

Ioannidi, E., and Mestheneos, E. (1999). *Cocooned or trapped? Greek National Report.* SOSTRIS Working Paper 5, Social Strategies in Risk Societies. University of East London: Department of Sociology.

Ioannidi, E., and Mestheneos, E. (2000). *Unqualified unemployed youth : Greek National Report.* SOSTRIS Working Paper 7, Social Strategies in Risk Societies. University of East London: Department of Sociology.

Iversen, L. (1989). Unemployment and mortality. *Stress Medicine, 5,* 85-92.

Iversen, L., and Klausen, H. (1986). Alcohol consumption among laid-off workers before and after closure of a Danish Shipyard : A 2-year follow-up study. *Social Science and Medicine, 22,* 107-109.

Iversen, L., and Sabroe, S. (1987). Plant closure, unemployment and health experiences from the declining ship buiding industry. In D. Schwefel, P.-G. Svensson, and H.F.K. Zöllner (Eds.), *Unemployment, social vulnerability and health in Europe (pp. 31-47).* Berlin : Sprigner-Verlag.

Iversen, L., and Sabroe, S. (1988). Psychological well-being among unemployed and employed people after a company closedown : A longitudinal study. *Journal of Social Issues, 44,* 141-152.

Iversen, L., Sabroe, S., and Damsgaard, M. T. (1989). Hospital admission before and after shipyard closure. *British Medical Journal, 299,* 1073-1076.

Jackson, M.P. (1985). *Youth unemployment.* London : Croom Helm.

Jackson, M.P., and Hanby, V. (1982). *The British work creation programme.* Aldershot : Gower.

Jackson, P.R. (1987). *The social construction of unemployment. SAPU Memo 881.*

Jackson, P.R. (1988). Life course position as a mediator of the impact of unemployment on psychological health. *SAPU Memo 746.*

Jackson, P.R., Stafford, E.M., Banks, M.H., and Warr, P.B. (1983). Unemployment and psychological distress in young people : The moderating role of employment commitment. *Journal of Applied Psychology, 68,* 525-535.

Jackson, P.R., and Walsh, S. (1987). Unemployment and the family. In D. Fryer, and P. Ullah (Eds.), *Unemployed people : Social and psychological perspectives (pp.194-216).* Milton Keynes : Open University Press.

Jackson, P.R., and Warr, P.B. (1984). Unemployment and psychological ill-health : The moderating role of duration and age. *Psychological Medicine, 14,* 605-614.

Jackson, P.R., and Warr, P.B. (1987). Mental health of unemployed men in different parts of England and Wales. *British Medical Journal, 295,* 525.

Jackson, S.E. (1983). Participation in decision making as a strategy for reducing job-related strain. *Journal of Applied Psychology, 68,* 3-19.

Jahoda, M. (1958). *Current concepts of positive mental health.* New York : Basic Books.

Jahoda, M. (1979). The impact of unemployment in the 1930s and 1970s. *Bulletin of the British Psychological Society, 32,* 309-314.

Jahoda, M. (1981). Work, employment and unemployment : Values, theories and approaches in social research. *American Psychologist, 36,* 184-191.

Jahoda, M. (1982). *Employment and unemployment : A social-psychological analysis.* Cambridge : Cambridge University Press.

Jahoda, M. (1987). Unemployed men at work. In D. Fryer, and P. Ullah (Eds.), *Unemployed people : Social and psychological perspectives (pp. 1-73).* Milton Keynes : Open University Press.

Jahoda, M. (1988). Economic recession and mental health : Some conceptual issues. *Journal of Social Issues, 44,* 13-23.

Jahoda, M. (1995). Manifest and latent functions. In Nicholson (Ed.), *Encyclopedic dictionary of organizational behaviour (pp. 317 318).* Oxford : Blackwell.

Jahoda, M., Lazarsfeld, P.F. and Zeisel, H. (1933). *Marienthal : The sociography of an unemployed community* (English translation, 1971) Chicago : Aldine.

Jahoda, M., and Rush, J. (1980). *Work, employment and unemployment.* Occasional Paper Series *(No. 12),* Science Policy Research Unit, Sussex University.

Jain, M. (1996). Child labour : A growing phenomenon in India. *The Social Engineer, 5,* 58-69.

Janoff-Bulman, R. (1979). Characterological *versus* behavioural self-blame : Inquiries into depression and rape. *Journal of Personality and Social Psychology, 37,* 1798-1809.

Jayaram, N. (December, 1994). Urbanization and educational growth. *Bulletin of Madras Development Seminar Series, 14 (No. 12).*

Jick, T.D., and Mitz, L.F. (1985). Sex differences in work stress. *Academy of Managament Review, 10,* 408-420.

Jin, R.L., Chandrakant, P.S., and Svoboda, T.J. (1995). The impact of unemployment on health : A review of the evidence. *Journal of Canadian Medical Association, 153,* 529-540.

Jones, G. (1971). *The role of science and technology in developing countries.* London : OUP.

Jones, L. (1988). Unemployment and social integration : A review. *Journal of Sociology and Social Welfare, 15,* 161-176.

Jones, L. (1992). Specifying the temporal relationship between job loss and consequences : Implications for service delivery. *Journal of Applied Social Sciences, 16,* 37-62.

Joshi, P., Garon, L., and Lechasseur, S. (1984). Self-esteem and loneliness among unemployed women. *Psychological Reports, 54,* 903-906.

Kabanoff, B. (1980). Work and non-work : A review of models, methods and findings. *Psychological Bulletin, 88,* 60-77.

Kahn, R.L., Wolfe, D.M., Quinn, R.P., and Snoek, J.D. (1964) *Organizational stress : Studies in role conflict and ambiguity.* New York : Wiley.

Kakar, S. (1978). *The inner experience.* Delhi : Oxford Univeristy Press.

Kakar, S. (Ed.), (1979). *Identity and adulthood.* Delhi : Oxford Univeristy Press.

Kannas, L., and Hietarharju, M. (1979). Työttömista nourista sairaita keski-ikaisiä. *Sosiaa-linen Aikakauskirja, 1,* 37-45 (quoted from U. Janlert, 1985).

Kanner, A.D., Coyne, J.C., Schaefer, C., and Lazarus, R.S. (1981). Comparison of two modes of stress measurement : Daily hassles and uplifts *versus* major life events. *Journal of Behavioural Medicine, 4,* 1-39.

Kanungo, R.N. (1979). The concepts of alienation and involvement revisited. *Psychological Bulletin, 86,* 119-138.

Kanungo, R.N. (1982). *Work alienation.* New York : Praeger.

Kanungo, R.N. (1995). Culture and work alienation : Western models and eastern realities. In H.S.R. Kao, D. Sinha, and Ng, Sek-Hong (Eds.), *Effective organizations and social values (pp. 233-250).* New Delhi : Sage Publications.

Kanungo, R.N., and Mendonca, M. (1995). Employee alienation, empowerment and work design. *The Social Engineer, 4,* 38-51.

Kapp, W.K. (1963). *Hindu culture, economic development and economic planning in India.* Bombay : Asia Publishing House.

Karasek, R.A. (1979). Job demands, job decision latitude, and mental strain : Implications for job redesign. *Administrative Science Quarterly, 24,* 285-308.

Kasl, S.V. (1979). Changes in mental health status associated with job loss and retirement. In M.E. Barrett, R.M. Rose, and G.L.Klerman (Eds.), *Stress and mental disorder (pp. 179-200).* New York : Raven Press.

Kasl, S.V., and Cobb, S. (1979). Some mental health consequences of plant closing and job loss. In L.A. Ferman, and J.P. Gordus (Eds.), *Mental health and the economy (pp. 255-300).* Upjohn : Kalamazoo.

Kasl, S.V., and Cobb, S. (1982). Validity of stress effects among men experiencing job loss. In L. Goldberger, and S. Breznitz (Eds.), *Handbook of stress : Theoretical and clinical aspects (pp. 445-465).* New York : Free Press.

Katju, P. (1986). *Certain factors related to member integration in a multi-national organization.* Unpublished doctoral dissertation, University of Allahabad.

Kaufman, H.G. (1982). *Professionals in search of work : Coping with the stress of job loss and underemployment.* New York : Wiley.

Keefe, T. (1984). The stress of unemployment. *Social Work, 29,* 264-268.

Kelley, H.H.(1967). Attribution theory in social psychology. In D.Levine (Ed.), *Nebraska symposium on motivation (Vol. 15., pp. 192-238).* Lincoln : University of Nebraska Press.

Kelley, H.H.(1979). *Personal relationships : Their structures and processes.* Hillsdale, N.J. : Lawrence Erlbaum.

Kelvin, P. (1980). Social psychology 2001 : The social-psychological bases and implications of structural unemployment. In R. Gilmour, and S. Duck (Eds.), *The development of social psychology (pp. 293-316).* New York : Academic Press.

Kelvin, P. (1981). Work as a source of identity : The implication of unemployment. *British Journal of Guidance and Counselling, 9,* 2-4.

Kelvin, P., and Jarrett, J.E. (1985). *Unemployment : Its social - psychological effects.* Cambridge : Cambridge Univeristy Press.

Keniston, K. (1965). *The uncommitted.* New York : Harcourt Brace Jovanovich, Inc.

Keniston, K. (1968). *Young radicals—Notes on committed youth.* New York : Harcourt, Brace and World.

Kessler, R.C. (1979). Stress, social status and psychological distress. *Journal of Health and Social Behaviour, 20,* 259-272.

Kessler, R.C. (1982). A disaggregation of the relationship between socio-economic status and psychological distress. *American Sociological Review, 47,* 752-764.

Kessler, R.C., and Cleary, P.D. (1980). Social class and psychological distress. *American Sociological Review, 45,* 463-478.

Kessler, R.C., House, J.S., and Turner, J.B. (1987). Unemployment and health in a community sample. *Journal of Health and Social Behaviour, 28,* 51-59.

Kessler, R.C., and McLeod, J.D. (1985). Social support and mental health in community samples. In S. Cohen, and S.L. Syme (Eds.), *Social support and health (pp. 219-240).* New York : Academic Press.

Kessler, R.C., and McRae, J.A. (1981). Trends in the relationship between sex and psychological distress : 1957-1976. *American Sociological Review, 46,* 443-452.

Kessler, R.C., Turner, J.B., and House, J.S. (1987). Intervening processes in the relationship between unemployment and health. *Psychological Medicine, 17,* 949-961.

Kessler, R.C., Turner, J.B., and House, J.S. (1988). Effects of unemployment on health in a community survery : Main, modifying, and mediating effects. *Journal of Social Issues, 44,* 69-85.

Keupp, H. (1982). Soziale Kontrolle : Psychiatrisierung, Psychologisierung, Medikalisierung, Therapeutisierung. In H. Keupp, and D. Rerrich (Eds.), *Psychosoziale Praxis (pp. 189-198).* Munchen : Urban and Schwarzenberg.

Keyssar, A. (1985). *Out of work.* Cambridge, M.A. : Harvard University Press.

Khan, S.R., and Hassan. Q. (1981). A shorter version of Sinha's W.A. self-analysis form. *Psychological Studies, 26,* 8-9.

Khan, S.R., and Hassan, Q. (1983). Tension as a factor in evaluation of past, present and future. *Indian Journal of Clinical Psychology, 10,* 257-262.

Kieselbach, T. (1986). *Zielsetzung und Konzeption der Regionalen Arbeitsgemeinschaft "Arbeitslosigkeit und Gesundheit" Bremen.* (Conception and goals of the regional working group "Unemployment and Health" Bremen). Unpublished Manuscript.

Kieselbach, T. (1987a). Self-disclosure and help-seeking as determinants of vulnerability : Case studies of unemployed from social-psychiatric services and demands for health and social policy. In D. Schwefel, P.-G. Svensson, and H.F.K. Zöllner (Eds.), *Unemployment, social vulnerability and health in Europe (pp. 281-303).* New York : Springer-Verlag.

Kieselbach, T. (1987 b). Gesellschaftliche und individuelle Bewältigung von Arbeitslosigkeit. In H. Moser (Ed.), *Bedrohung und Beschwichtigung. Die politische und die seelische Gestalt technischer, wirtschaftlicher und gesundheitlicher Gefährdungen (Fortschritte der Politischen Psychologie, Sonderband 1., pp. 28-55).* Weinheim : Deutscher Studien Verlag.

Kieselbach, T. (1988a). Youth unemployment and health effects. *The International Journal of Social Psychiatry, 34,* 83-96.

Kieselbach, T. (1988 b). Familie unter dem Druckder Arbeitslosgkeit : "Opfer - durch - Nähe" und Quelle sozialer Unterstützung. In K. Menne, and K. Alter (Eds.), *Gesellschaft im Umbruch—Antworten der Erziehungsberater (pp. 47-76).* München : Juventa.

Kieselbach, T. (1989). A multisectoral approach for the improvement of the psychosocial situation of the unemployed. In B. Starrin, P.-G. Svensson, and H. Wintersberger (Eds.), *Unemployment, poverty and quality of working life (pp. 295-334).* Berlin : Edition Sigma.

Kieselbach, T. (1990 a). Help-Seeking and coping with unemployment. In R.A. Young, and W.A. Borgen (Eds.), *Methodological approaches to the study of career (pp. 163-184).* New York : Praeger Publishers.

Kieselbach, T. (1990 b). *Health impact of long-term unemployment, re-employment and precarious work.* Paper presented in the 3rd International Conference on Social Stress, London, Regents College, 18-20 June.

Kieselbach, T. (1991). Unemployment. In R.M. Lerner, A.C. Petersen, and J. Brooks - Gunn (Eds.), *Encyclopedia of adolescence (pp. 1187-1201).* New York and London : Garland Publishing, Inc.

Kieselbach, T. (1996). Arbeitslosigkeit und Entfremdung : Zur psychosozialen Bedeutung von Arbeitslosenarbeit als Aufbrechen von Entfremdungsphänomenen (Unemployment and alienation. On the psychosocial meaning of interventions with the unemployed as a means to counteract phenomenon of alienation) : In F. Wolski-Prenger (Ed.), *Arbeitslosenarbeit—Erfahrungen, Konzepte, Ziele (Working with the unemployed —experiences, concepts and goals; pp 187-210).* Opladen : Leske and Budrich.

Kieselbach, T. (1997a). Job loss, unemployment, and social injustices : An introduction. *Social Justice Research, 10,* 111-125.

Kieselbach, T. (1997b). Unemployment, victimization, and perceived injustices : Future perspectives for coping with occupational transitions. *Social Justice Research, 10,* 127-151.

Kieselbach, T. (1998a). *Unemployment and health : A future scenario for coping with occupational transitions.* Paper presented at the International Symposium on "Restructuring Work and the Life Course", Univeristy of Toronto, 7-9 May.

Kieselbach, T. (1998 b). Unemployment and experienced injustices : The social responsibility of the organization for cushioning the process of downsizing. In H.Lange, A.Löhr, and H. Steinmann (Eds.), *Working across cultures : Ethical perspectives for intercultural management* (Issues in Business Ethics, *Vol. 9., pp. 191-210).* Dordrecht/Boston/London : Kluwer Publishers.

Kieselbach,T. (1998c). Arbeitslosigkeit (Unemployment). In Statistisches Bundesamt (Ed.), *Gesundheitsbericht für Deutschland (Health report for Germany., pp. 116-121).* Stuttgart : Metzler-Poeschl.

Kieselbach,T. (2003). Youth unemployment and the risk of social exclusion: Comparative analysis of qualitative data. In A.L. Blasco, W. Mc Neish, and A. Walther (Eds.), *Young people and contradictions of inclusion: Towards integrated transition policies in Europe (pp. 43-64).* Great Britain: The Policy Press.

Kieselbach, T., Beelmann, G., and Stitzel, A. (2000). Youth unemployment and health : Comparative report. In T. Kieselbach (Ed.), *Youth unemployment and health : A comparison of six Europeon countries (pp. 15-34).* Opladen : Leske + Budrich.

Kieselbach,T., Beelmann, G., Stitzel, A., and Traiser, U. (2001). Empirical analysis of the risk of social exclusion of long-term unemployed young people in six countries of the EU. In T. Kieselbach, K. Van Heeringen, M. La Rosa, L. Lemkow, K. Soku, and B. Starrin (Eds.), *Living on the edge — An empirical analysis on long-term youth unemployment and some exclusion in Europe.* Oploden: Lesket Budrich.

Kieselbach, T., Lödige-Röhrs, L., and Lünser, A. (1989). *Die Kinder von Arbeitslosen— "Opfer-durch-Nähe". Ergebnisse der psychologischen Arbeitslosenforschung Zu den Auswirkungen von Arbeitslosigkeit auf die Familie. Theoretisches Hintergrundpapier zum Forum der Sozialdemokratischen Partei Deutschlands (SPD) "Gestohlene Kindheit —Verborgene Folgelasten der Langzeitarbeitslosigkeit,"* Bonn, 16th November 1989. Bonn : Author.

Kieselbach, T., and Svensson, P.-G. (1988). Health and social policy responses to unemployment in Europe. *Journal of Social Issues, 44,* 173-191.

Kieselbach,T., and Traiser, U. (2004). Long-term unemployment and the risk of social exclusion among young people: Recommendation for activation policies. In A.S. Pascual (Ed.), *Are activation policies converging in Europe? The European Employment strategy for young people (pp. 415-449).* Brussels: ETUI.

Kieselbach, T., Van Heeringen, K., La Rosa, M., Lemkow, L., Sokou, K., and Starrin, B. (Eds.), (2001). *Living on the edge — An empirical analysis on long-term youth unemployment and social exclusion on Europe.* Opladen: Lesket Budrich.

Kieselbach, T., and Wacker, A. (Eds.), (1985). *Individuelle und gesellschaftliche Kosten der Massenarbeitslosigkeit—Psychologische Theorie und Praxis.* Weinheim, Basel : Beltz.

Kieselbach, T., and Wacker, A. (Eds.), (1995). *Bewältigung von Arbeitslosigkeit im sozialen Kontext—Programme, Initiativen, Evaluationen* (Coping with unemployment in a social context—Programs, initiatives, evaluations., 2nd ed.). Weinheim : Deutscher Studien Verlag.

Kilpatrick, R., and Trew, K. (1982). What unemployed men do : A Belfast sample. Paper presented to *Understanding Unemployment Conference,* Belfast.

Kilpatrick, R., and Trew, K. (1985). Life-styles and psychological well-being among unemployed men in Northern Ireland. *Journal of Occupational Psychology, 58,* 207-216.

Kinicki, A.J., and Latack, J.C. (1990). Explication of the construct of coping with involuntary job loss. *Journal of Vocational Behaviour, 36,* 339-360.

Kipnis, D. (1976). *The powerholders.* Chicago, IL : University of Chicago Press.

Klausen, H., and Iversen, I. (1981). *The closing of Nordhavan shipyard.* Copenhagen : Institute for Social Medicine.

Knulst, W., and Schoonderwoerd, L. (1983). *Waar blijft de Tijd.* Rijswijk : Sociaal en Cultureel Planbureau.

Kobasa, S. (1982). Commitment and coping in stress resistence among lawyers. *Journal of Personality and Social Psychology, 42,* 707-717.

Kobasa, S., Maddi, S., and Kahn, S. (1982). Hardiness and health : A prospective study. *Journal of Personality and Social Psychology, 42,* 168-172.

Komarovsky, M. (1940). *The unemployed man and his family : The effect of unemployment upon the status of the man in 59 families.* New York : Macmillan.

Kouveli, A., Tsakiris, E., and Sakellaropoulous, K. (1998). *Consumption behaviour, consumption models and way of living in the Greek Rural Regions.* National Centre of Social Studies: EKKE.

Kroes, W. (1981). Psychological job stress and worker health : A programmatic effort. In L. Levi (Ed.), *Society, stress and disease (Vol. 4).* Oxford : Oxford University Press.

Kuhnert, K.W. (1989). The lalent and manifest consequences of work. *Journal of Psychology, 123,* 417-427.

Kumari, R. (2001). *Educated job-seekers : Frustration and aggression.* New Delhi : Commonwealth Publishers.

Kumari, R., Sinha, B.N., and Singh, L.B. (1996). Development of stress scale. *Indian Journal of Psychological Issues, 4,* 18-24.

Kundu, R., Sanyal, N., and Bhattacharya, A. (1986). Personality pattern of art students. *Indian Journal of Community Guidance Service, 3,* 41-47.

Kureshi, A., and Dutt, M. (1979). Dimensions of alienation—A factor-analytic study. *Psychologia, 22,* 99-105.

Lahelma, E. (1992). Unemployment and mental well-being : Elaboration of the relationship. *International Journal of Health Sciences, 22,* 261-274.

Lahelma, E., and Kangas, R. (1989). Unemployment, re-employment, and psychic well-being in Finland. In B. Starrin, P.-G. Svensson, and H. Wintersberger (Eds.), *Unemployment, poverty, and quality of working life : Some European experiences (pp.135-164).* Berlin : Edition Sigma.

Lal, J. (1983). Decision making style and situational variables : A study of managers in large enterprises. *Decision, 10,* 269-281.

Langer, E.J. (1983). *The psychology of control.* Beverly Hills : Sage.

Lannoy, R. (1983). *The speaking tree : A study of Indian culture and society.* New York : Oxford University Press.

Lapierre, D. (1986). *The city of joy.* London : Arrow Books Ltd.

La Rocco, J.M., House, J.S., and French, J.R.P. (1980). Social support, occupational stress, and health. *Journal of Health and Social Behaviour, 21,* 202-218.

Latack, J.C. (1984). Career transitions within organizations : An exploratory study of work, nonwork, and coping strategies. *Organizational Behaviour and Human Performance, 34,* 296-322.

Layton, C. (1986). Employment, unemployment and response to the General Health Questionnaire. *Psychological Reports, 58,* 807-810.

Layton, C. (1987). Externality and unemployment : Change score analyses on Rotter's locus of control scale for male school-leavers and men facing redundancy. *Personality and Individual Differences, 8,* 149-152.

Lazarus, R.S. (1966). *Psychological stress and the coping process.* New York : McGraw-Hill.

Lazarus, R.S. (1975). The healthy personality : A review of conceptualizations and research. In L.Levi (Ed.), *Society, stress and disease (Vol. 2).* Oxford : Oxford University Press.

Lazarus, R.S. (1987). Coping. In R.J. Corsini (Ed.), *Concise encylopedia of psychology.* New York : John Wiley and Sons.

Lazarus, R.S., and Folkman, S. (1984). *Stress, appraisal, and coping.* New York : Springer-Verlag.

Lazarus, R.S., and Launier, R. (1978). Stress-related transactions between persons and environment. In L.A. Pervin, and M.Lewis (Eds.), *Perspectives in interactional psychology (pp.287-327).* New York : Plenum.

Leana, C.R., and Feldman, D.C. (1988). Individual responses to job loss : Perceptions, reactions, and coping behaviour. *Journal of Management, 14,* 375-389.

Leana, C.R., and Feldman, D.C. (1991). Gender differences in responses to unemployment. *Journal of Vocational Behaviour, 38,* 65-77.

Leana, C.R., and Feldman, D.C. (1992). *Coping with job loss : How individuals, organizations, and communities respond to layoffs.* Lexington, MA: Lexington Books.

Lefcourt, H.M. (1982). *Locus of control : Current trends in theory and research.* Hillsdale : Erlbaum.

Lerner, M.J. (1980). *The belief in a just world : A fundamental delusion.* New York : Plenum Press.

Lerner, M.J., and Somers, D. (1992). Employees' reactions to an anticipated plant closure : The influence of positive illusions. In L. Montada, S.H. Filipp, and M.J. Lerner, (Eds.), *Life crises and the experience of loss in adulthood (pp. 229-254).* NJ : Erlbaum, Hillsdale.

Leventhman, P.G. (1981). *Professionals out of work.* New York : Free Press.

Levinson, D.J., Darrow, C.N., Klein, E.B., Levinson, M.H., and McKee, B. (1978). *The seasons of man's life.* New York: Knopf.

Lewis, O. (1966). The culture of poverty. *Scientific American, 215,* 19-25.

Liem, J.H., and Liem, R. (1990). Understanding the individual and family effects of unemployment. In J. Eckenrode, and S. Gore (Eds.), *Stress between work and family.* New York : Plenum Press.

Liem, R. (1983a). *Reconsidering the concept of social victim : The case of unemployment.* Paper presented at the Annual Meeting of the American Psychological Association, Anaheim, C.A.

Liem, R. (1983b). *Unemployment : Personal and family effects.* Paper presented at the Conference on Unemployment during Economic Recession, Bunker Hill Community College and the Massachusetts Department of Manpower Development.

Liem, R. (1987). The psychological costs of unemployment : A comparison of findings and definitions. *Social Research, 54,* 319-353.

Liem, R. (1988). Unemployed workers and their families : Social victims or social critics ? In P.Voydanoff, and L.J.Majka (Eds.), *Families and economic distress : Coping strategies and social policy (pp.135-151).* Beverly Hills, CA : Sage.

Liem, R., and Liem, J.H. (1978). Social class and mental illness reconsidered : The role of economic stress and social support. *Journal of Health and Social Behaviour, 19,* 139-156.

Liem, R., and Liem, J.H. (1988). Psychological effects of unemployment on workers and their families. *Journal of Social Issues, 44,* 87-105.

Liem, R., and Rayman, P. (1982). Health and social costs of unemployment : Research and policy consideration. *American Psychologist, 37,* 1116-1123.

Liem, R., and Rayman, P. (1984). Perspectives on unemployment, mental health and social policy. *International Journal of Mental Health, 13,* 3-17.

Liker, J.K., and Elder, G.H. (1983). Economic hardship and marital relations in the 1930s. *American Sociological Review, 48,* 343-359.

Linn, N.W., Sandifer, R., and Stein, S. (1985). Effects of unemployment on mental and physical health. *American Journal of Public Health, 75,* 502-506.

Little, C.B. (1976). Technical-professional unemployment : Middle-class adaptability to personal crises. *Sociological Quarterly, 18,* 262-274.

Luthera, V.P. (1965). Religious impartiality. *Seminar, 67,* 19-22.

Madonia, J.F. (1983). The trauma of unemployment and its consequences. *Social Casework, 64,* 482-488.

Mamgain, R.P., and Parashar, V. (2000). Enhancing employment ability of youth through education and training. *The Indian Journal of Labour Economics, 43,* 757-780.

Mamoria, C.B., and Mamoria, S. (1984). *Industrial labour, social security and industrial peace in India.* Allahabad : Kitab Mahal.

Man, A., and Devisse, T. (1987). Locus of control, mental ability, self-esteem and alienation. *Social Behaviour and Personality, 15,* 233-236.

Marsden, D., and Duff, E. (1975). *Workless : Some unemployed men and their families.* Harmondsworth : Penguin.

Marshall, J.C., and Hales, L.W.(1972).*Essentials of testing.* Reading, Mass : Addition-Wesley.

Masschelein, R., and De Witte, H. (1997). Preventieve gezondheidszorg in de arbeidssfeer. (Preventive health care for the labour market). In *Vlaams Preventiecongres 1997 (pp. 585-603).* Diegem: Kluwer Editorial.

Martikainen, P.T. (1990). Unemployment and mortality among Finnish men, 1981-1985. *British Medical Journal, 301,* 407-411.

Martin, R., and Wallace, J. (1985). Women and unemployment : Activities and social contact. In B.Roberts, R. Finnegan, and D.Gallie (Eds.), *New approaches to economic life (pp. 417-430).* Manchester : Manchester University Press.

Maslow, A.H., *et al.* (1945-1952). *Security-insecurity inventory.* Palo, Alto, California : Consulting Psychologists Press.

Maurya, O.P. (July 24-30, 2004) Employment cenario in India at a glance. *Employment News, 29, 1-2.*

McCrae, R. (1982). Age differences in the use of coping mechanisms. *Journal of Gerontology, 37,* 454-460.

McGown, A., and Fraser, G. (1995). The effect of sociodemographic variables on the use of active and avoidance coping strategies. *Psychological Studies, 40,* 157-169.

McKenna, S.P., and Payne, R.L. (1984). A comparison of the General Health Questionnaire and the Nottingham Health Profile in a study of unemployed and re-employed men. *SAPU Memo 696.*

McLennan, J.P. (1987). Irrational beliefs in relation to self-esteem and depression. *Journal of Clinical Psychology, 43*, 89-91.

McLoyd, V.C. (1989). Socialization and development in a changing economy : The effects of paternal job and income loss on children. *American Psychologist, 44*, 293-302.

McLoyd, V.C., and Flanagan, C.A. (Eds.), (1990). *Economic stress : Effects on family life and child development.* New Direction for Child Development, No. 46, Jossey-Bass, Inc.

Mehta, P. (1976). Work satisfaction and democratic outlook : The role of worker participation. *NLI Bulletin, 2,* 302-308.

Mehta, P. (1981). Political processes and behaviour. In U.Pareek (Ed.), *A survey of research in psychology, 1971-1976 (Part 2; pp. 579-615).* Bombay : Popular Prakashan.

Menaghan, E. (1982). Measuring coping effectiveness : A panel analysis of marital problems and coping efforts. *Journal of Health and Social Behaviour, 23,* 220-234.

Menaghan, E. (1983). Individual coping efforts : Moderators of the relationship between life stress and mental health outcomes. In H. Kaplin (Ed.), *Psychological stress : Trends in theory and research (pp. 157-191).* New York : Academic Press.

Miles, I. (1983). *Adaptation to unemployment?* University of Sussex : Science Policy Reseach Unit Report.

Miles, I., Howard, J., and Henwood, F. (1984). *Dependence, interdependence and changing work roles.* University of Sussex : Science Policy Reseach Unit Report.

Miles, R.H. (1975). An empirical test of causal inference between role perceptions of conflict and ambiguity and various personal outcomes. *Journal of Applied Psychology, 60,* 334-339.

Miller, N.E. (1944). Experimental studies of conflict. In J. Mc V. Hunt (Ed.), *Personality and the behaviour disorders (Vol.1., pp.431-465).* New York : Ronald Press.

Miller, N.E. (1951). Comments on theoretical models : Illustrated by the development of a theory of conflict behaviour. *Journal of Personality, 20,* 82-100.

Miller, N.E. (1959). Liberalization of basic S-R concepts : Extension to conflict behaviour, motivation and social learning. In S.Koch (Ed.), *Psychology : A study of a sciecne (Vol.2).* New York : McGraw-Hill.

Misra, A.M., and Saxena, N.K. (1982). A study of manifest anxiety among unemployed youth of family and non-family oriented occupational groups. *Indian Journal of Applied Psychology, 19,* 7-10.

Mohsin, S.M. (1981). *Manual of directions and norms for Mohsin security-insecurity test.* Varanasi : Rupa Psychological Centre.

Montada, L. (1994). Arbeitslosigkeit—ein Gerechtigkeit - sproblem? (Unemployment—a social justice problem ?). In L.Montada (Ed.), *Arbeitslosigkeit und soziale Gerechtigkeit., pp. 53-86* (Unemployment and social justice). Frankfurt/M : Campus.

Morell, S.L., Taylor, R.J., and Kerr, C.B. (1998). Job loss, unemployment and young people's health. *Medical Journal of Australia, 168,* 236-240.

Mortimer, J.T., and Lorence, J. (1979). Occupational experience and the self-concept : A longitudinal study. *Social Psychology Quarterly, 42,* 307-323.

Mruck, K., and Mey, G. (1992). *Jugendarbeitslosigkeit und lokale Identität : Ergebnisse einer Befragung Jugendlicher und junger Erwachsener aus den Berliner Bezirken Kreuzberg und Tiergarten.* (Young Persons' Unemployment and Local Identity : Results of a Survey of Adolescents and Young Adults from the Districts Kreuzberg and Tiergarten in Berlin). Berlin: Technische Universität Berlin.

Mukerjee, M., and Chatterji, S. (1986). Effect of group variation on the factor structure of the 16 PF. *Psychological Studies, 31,* 136-140.

Mukherjee, B.N. (1980). Psychological theory and reaserch methods. In U. Pareek (Ed.), *A survey of research in psychology, 1971-76 (Part 1; pp. 3-135).* Bombay : Popular Prakashan.

Muller, J., Hicks, R., and Winocur, S. (1993). The effects of employment and unemployment on psychological well-being in Australian clerical worker : Gender differences. *Australian Journal of Psychology, 45,* 103-108.

Murgai, N., and Sathyavathi, K. (1988). Personality and depressive congnitons. *Indian Journal of Clinical Psychology, 15,* 19-23.

Murphy-Berman, M.V., Berman, J.J., Singh, P., Pachauri, A., and Kumar, P. (1984). Factors affecting allocation to needy and meritorious recipients : A cross-cultural comparison. *Journal of Personality and Social Psychology, 46,* 1267-1272.

Murphy, G., and Likert, R. (1938). *Public opinion and the individual : A psychological study of student attitudes on public questions, with a retest five years later.* New York : Harper.

Myers, D.G. (1983). *Social psychology.* Japan : McGraw-Hill Book Company.

Nagaraja, J. (1983). Mental health limits, priorities and psychoethics. *Indian Journal of Psychiatry, 25,* 3-6.

Naik, N., and Deshpande, M.V. (1978). Study of alienation amongst bank employees : An exploration. *National Labour Institute Bulletin, 4,* 273-278.

Nakano, K. (1991). Coping strategies and psychological symptoms in a Japanese samples. *Journal of Clinical Psychology, 47,* 346-350.

Namasivayam, N. (2000). Educated youth unemployment in India. *The Indian Journal of Labour Economics, 43,* 786-787.

Nandy, A., and Kakar, S. (1980). Culture and personality. In U. Pareek (Ed.), *A survey of research in psychology, 1971-76 (Part I; pp. 136-167).* Bombay : Popular Prakashan.

Narayan, S. (1995). *Subjective well-being among unemployed.* Proceedings of the 82nd. Session of the Indian Science Congress, Calcutta.

Narendranathan, W., Nickell, S., and Metcalf, D. (1982). *An investigation into the incidence and dynamic structure of sickness and unemployment in Britain, 1965-1975.* London : Centre for Labour Economics.

Nathawat, S.S., and Tiwari, K. (1983). *Psychological determinants of stress disorders.* Paper presented at the seminar on Stress, Anxiety and Mental Health, University of Allahabad, Allahabad.

National Crime Records Bureau (1995). *Accidental deaths and suicides in India.* Faridabad : Government of India Press.

Neeleman, J., Wessely, S., and Wadsworth, M. (1998). Predictors of suicide, accidental death, and premature natural death in a general-population birth cohort. *Lancet, 351,* 93-97.

Nelson, H. (1974). How to be successfully fired. *Behaviour Today, 5,* 118-119.

Neugarten, B.L., Havighurst, R.T., and Tobin, S.S. (1961). Measurement of life satisfaction. *Journal of Gerontology, 16,* 134-143.

Nezu, A., and Nezu, C. (1987). Psychological distress, problem solving and coping reactions : Sex role differences. *Sex Roles, 16,* 205-214.

O'Brien, G.E. (1981). Locus of control, previous occupation and satisfaction with retirement. *Australian Journal of Psychology, 33,* 305-318.

O'Brien, G.E. (1984a). Reciprocal effects between locus of control and job attributes. *Australian Journal of Psychology, 36,* 57-74.

O'Brien, G.E. (1984b). Locus of control, work and retirement. In H.M. Lefcourt (Ed.), *Research with the locus of control construct (Vol. 3; pp.7-72).* New York : Academic Press.

O'Brien, G.E. (1985a). Distortion in unemployment research : The early studies of Bakke and their implications for current research on employment and unemployment. *Human Relations, 38,* 877-894.

O'Brien, G.E. (1985b). The effect of employment on behaviour : Recent development in Australian organizational psychology. In N.T.Feather (Ed.), *Australian psychology : Review of research.* Sydney : Allen and Unwin.

O'Brien, G.E. (1986). *Psychology of work and unemployment.* Chichester : John Wiley.

O'Brien, G.E., and Feather, N.T. (1990). The relative effects of unemployment and quality of employment on the affect, work values and personal control of adolescents. *Journal of Occupational Psychology, 63,*151-165.

O'Brien, G.E., and Kabanoff, B. (1979). Comparison of unemployed and employed workers on work values, locus of control and health variables. *Australian Psychologist, 14,* 143-154.

Oddy, M., Donovan, A., and Pardoe, R. (1984). Do Government training schemes for unemployed school-leavers achieve their objectives? A psychological perspective. *Journal of Adolescence, 7*, 377-385.

Olafsson, O., and Svensson, P. (1986). Unemployment related lifestyle changes and health disturbances in adolescents and children in the Western countries. *Social Science and Medicine, 22*, 1105-1113.

Ortiz, O., Casullo, M.M., and Grillo, O. (1982). Descriptive epidemiology of psychiatric disorder in the city of Taleve (Argentina). *Acta Psiquiotrica of Psicologica de America Latina, 28*, 281-292.

Paintal, H.K. (1978). A correlational study of three tools for measuring successful ageing. *Indian Journal of Clinical Psychology, 5*, 69-76.

Pal, G.C. (1989). *Some socio-psychological correlates of employment potential : A comparative study of medical and engineering graduates.* Unpublished M.Phil Dissertation, JNU, New Delhi.

Pal, S.K. (1968a). Personality needs of engineering, law, medical and teacher-training students in an Indian university. *Journal of Social Psychology, 74*, 135.

Pal, S.K. (1968b). Personality patterns of engineering, law, medical and teacher-training students : A comparative study. *Journal of Social Psychology, 74*, 287-288.

Pal, S.K. (1968c). Personality adjustment of engineering and medical students. *Indian Journal of Applied Psychology, 5*, 82-84.

Pal, S.K. (1969). *Personality study of engineering, law, medical and teacher-training students.* Allahabad : United Publishers.

Pande, N., and Naidu, R.K. (1986). Effort and outcome orientations as moderators of stress-strain relationship. *Psychological Studies, 32*, 207-214.

Pandey, J. (1980). *Social-psychological study of ingratiation* (ICSSR Report). New Delhi : ICSSR.

Pandey, J. (1986). Sociocultural perspectives on ingratiation. In B. Maher, and W. Maher (Eds.), *Progress in experimental personality research (Vol. 14; pp. 205-229).* New York : Academic Press.

Papola, T.S. (15-21 August, 1992). Employment generation in the eight plan. *Employment News, 17*, 3-8.

Paranjpe, A.C. (1984). *Theoretical psychology : The meeting of East and West.* New York : Plenum Press.

Pareek, U. (1982). *Organizational role pics : Booklet, score sheet and manual.* Ahmedabad : Navin Publications.

Pareek, U. (1996). Executive group and burnout. *The Social Engineer, 5,* 23-29.

Parikh, I.J. (1979). *Role orientation and role perfomance of Indian managers (Working Paper No. 300).* Ahmedabad : Indian Institute of Management.

Park, C., Cohen, L., and Herb, L. (1990). Intrinsic religiousness and religious coping as life stress moderators for Catholics *versus* Protestants. *Journal of Personality and Social Psychology, 59,* 562-574.

Parker, D.F., and DeCotiis, T.A. (1983). Organizational determinants of job stress. *Organizational Behaviour and Human Performance, 32,* 160-177.

Parker, S. (1983). *Leisure and work.* London : Allen and Unwin.

Patton, W., and Noller, P. (1984). Unemployment and youth : A longitudinal study. *Australian Journal of Psychology, 36,* 399-413.

Patton, W., and Noller, P. (1990). Adolescent self-concept : Effects of being employed, unemployed or returning to school. *Australian Journal of Psychology, 42,* 247-259.

Payne, R.L. (1995). Stress. In Nicholson (Ed.), *Encyclopedic dictionary of organizational behaviour (pp. 539-542).* Oxford : Blackwell.

Payne, R.L., and Fletcher, B.C. (1983). Job demands, supports and constraints as predictors of psychological strain among school teachers. *Journal of Vocational Behaviour, 22,*136-147.

Payne, R.L., and Hartley, J. (1987). A test of a model for explaining the affective experience of unemployed men. *Journal of Occupational Psychology, 60,* 31-47.

Payne, R.L., and Jones, J.G. (1987a). Social class and re-employment : Changes in health and perceived financial circumstances. *Journal of Occupational Behaviour, 8,* 175-184.

Payne, R.L., and Jones, J.G. (1987b). The effects of long-term unemployment on attitudes to employment. *Journal of Occupational Behaviour, 8,* 351-358.

Payne, R.L., Warr, P.B., and Hartley, J. (1984). Social class and psychological ill-health during unemployment. *Sociology of Health and Illness, 1,* 152-174.

Pearlin, L.I., Lieberman, M.A., Menaghan, E.S., and Mullen, J.T. (1981). *The stress process. Journal of Health and Social Behaviour, 22,* 337-356.

Pearlin, L.I., and Schooler, C. (1978). The structure of coping. *Journal of Health and Social Behaviour, 19,* 2-21.

Pelzmann, L. (1989). Adaptational responses to economic stressors. In B.Starrin, P.-G. Svensson, and H.Wintersberger (Eds.), *Unemployment, poverty, and quality of working life : Some European experiences (pp. 275-284).* Berlin : Edition Sigma.

Pelzmann, L., Winkler, N., and Zewell, E. (1985). Antizipation von Arbeitslosigkeit. In T. Kieselbach, and A. Wacker (Eds.), *Individuelle und gesellschaftliche Kosten der Massenarbeitslosigkeit : Psychologische Theorie und Praxis (pp. 256-268).* Weinheim : Beltz-Verlag.

Peretti, P.O., Butcher, C.A., and Cherry, I.C. (1988). Influence of chronic unemployment on self perceived psychological effects of males. *Journal of the Indian Academy of Applied Psychology, 14,* 3-6.

Perfetti, L.J., and Bingham, W.C. (1983). Unemployment and self-esteem in metal refinery workers. *Vocational Guidance Quarterly, 31,* 195-202.

Pestonjee, D.M., and Singh, U.B. (1982). *Job satisfaction as a function of role stress, locus of control, participation and organizational climate in an electric supply company.* Ahmedabad : Indian Institute of Management.

Peterson, C., and Seligman, M.E.P. (1984). Causal explanation as risk factor in depression : Theory and evidence. *Psychological Review, 91,* 347-374.

Peterson,E., *et al.* (1983). Work and unemployment during the crisis. *Psykologisk Skriftserie Aarhus, 8,* 216.

Phares, E.J. (1987). Locus of control. In R.J. Corsini (Ed.), *Concise Encyclopedia of psychology.* New York : Wiley.

Pilgrim Trust. (1938). *Men without work.* Cambridge : Cambridge University Press.

Platt, S. (1985). Suicidal behaviour and unemployment : A literature review. In G. Westcott, P.-G. Svensson, and H.F.K. Zöllner (Eds.), *Health policy implications of unemployment (pp. 87-132).* Copenhagen : World Health Organization.

Powell, D.H., and Driscoll, S.P.F. (1973). Middle-class professionals face unemployment. *Society, 10,* 18-26.

Prakash, R., Trivedi, J.K., and Sethi, B.B. (1980). Life events in depression. *Indian Journal of Psychiatry, 22,*56.

Pratap, M. (1994). *Personality characteristics of arts, medical and engineering students.* Unpublished Ph.D. thesis, Magadh University, Bodh Gaya.

Pratap, S., and Gupta, N.K. (1985). Unemployment and psychological well-being in professional graduates. *Journal of Higher Education, 10,* 271-272.

Prause, J., and Dooley, D. (1997). Effects of underemployment on school-leavers' self-esteem. *Journal of Adolescence, 20,* 243-260.

Price, R.H., Van Ryn, M., and Vinokur, A.D. (1992). Impact of a preventive job search intervention on the likelihood of depression among the unemployed. *Journal of Health and Social Behaviour, 33,* 158-161.

Quay, H.C., and LaGreca, A.M. (1986). Disorders of anxiety, withdrawal and dysphoria. In H.C.Quay, and J.S. Werry (Eds.), *Psychopathological disorder of childhood.* New York : Wiley.

Raj, S.J.M. (1995). *A comparative study of unemployed women and men on general health.* Proceedings of the 82nd Session of the Indian Science Congress, Calcutta.

Ramamurthy, P.V. (1978). *The sixth decade and after.* Tirupati : S.V.University Press.

Ramesh, J. (April 30, 1994). Need to creat jobs stressed. *The Times of India,* Patna.

Rani, A. (1993). *Behavioural manifestations of unemployed youth.* Unpublished Ph.D. thesis, T.M. Bhagalpur University, Bhagalpur.

Rantakeisu, U., Starrin, B., and Hagquist, C. (1997). Unemployment, shame and ill-health — An exploratory study. *Scandinavian Journal of Social Welfare, 6,* 13-23.

Ray, P.K. (15-21 April, 1995). Job market for the educated. *Employment News, 20,* 1-3.

Rayman, P. (1981). *Department of Sociology,* Brandeis University, Waltham, Mass Personal Communication.

Reynolds, S., and Gilbert, P. (1991). Psychological impact of unemployment : Interactive effects of vulnerability and protective factors on depression. *Journal of Counselling Psychology, 38,* 76-84.

Rice, R.W. (1984). Organizational work and the overall quality of life. In S. Oskamp (Ed.), *Applied social psychology annual (Vol. 5).* Beverly Hills : Sage.

Rife, J.C.(1990). Social support and depression among older unemployed workers. *Clinical Gerontologist, 10,* 42-45.

Rifkin, J. (1995). *The end of work : The decline of the global labour force and the dawn of the post-market era.* New York : Putnam.

Roberts, K., Duggan, J., and Noble, M. (1982). Out-of-school youth in high unemployment areas : An empirical investigation. *British Journal of Guidance and Counselling, 10,* 1-11.

Rodgers, B. (1991). Socio-economic status, employment and neurosis. *Social Psychiatry and Psychiatric Epidemiology, 26,* 104-114.

Rodriguez, E. (1994). Health consequences of unemployment in Barcelona. *European Journal of Public Health, 4,* 245-251.

Rohmert, W. (1986). Ergonomics : Conceprt of work, stress and strain. *International Review of Applied Psychology, 35,* 159-181.

Roland, A. (1980). *Towards a psychoanalytic psychology of hierarchical relationships in Hindu India.* Paper presented to the Indian Psychoanalytic Societies, Bombay.

Ronayne, T., Ryan, G.M., and Cullen, J.H. (1989). Health effects of work and exclusion from work : Approaches to understanding, monitoring, and intervening. In B.Starrin, P.-G. Svensson, and H. Wintersberger (Eds.), *Unemployment, poverty, and quality of working life : Some European experiences (pp. 197-234).* Berlin : Edition Sigma.

Rosenberg, M. (1965). *Society and the adolescent self-image.* Princeton, NJ : Princeton University Press.

Rosenberg, M. (1979). *Conceiving the self.* New York : Basic Books.

Rosenhan, D.L., and Seligman, M.E.P. (1984). *Abnormal psychology.* New York : Norton.

Ross, C.E., and Huber, J. (1985). Hardship and depression. *Journal of Health and Social Behaviour, 26,* 312-327.

Rotter, J.B. (1966). Generalized expectancies for internal *versus* external control of reinforcement. *Psychological Monographs, 80,* 1-28.

Rotter, J.B., Chance, J.E., and Phares, E.J. (1972). *Application of social learning theory of personality.* New York : Holt Rinehart and Winston.

Rowley, K.M. (1985). *Age by duration comparisons for un/underemployed Australian males.* Unpublished B.A.Honours thesis, The Flinders University of South Australia, Bedford Park, South Australia.

Rowley, K.M., and Feather, N.T. (1987). The impact of unemployment in relation to age and length of unemployment. *Journal of Occupational Psychology, 60,* 323-332.

Roy, A. (1978). Vulnerability factors and depression in women. *British Journal of Psychiatry, 133,* 106-110.

Roy D.D. (1995). Differences in personality factors of experienced teachers, physicians, bank managers and fine artists. *Psychological Studies, 40,* 51-56.

Roy, R., and Srivastava, R.K. (1986). *Dialogues on development.* New Delhi : Sage Publications.

Rusbutt, C.E.(1980). Commitment and satisfaction in romantic associations : A test of investment model. *Journal of Experimental Social Psychology, 16,* 172-186.

Sabroe, S., and Iversen, L. (1989). Unemployment, social support, psychological well-being and psychosomatic symptoms. In B. Starrin, P.-G. Svensson, and H. Wintersberger (Eds.), *Unemployment, poverty and quality of working life : Some European experiences (pp. 63-78).* Berlin : Edition Sigma.

Sarafino, E.P. (1990). *Health psychology : Bio-psycho-social interactions.* New York : John Wiley and Sons.

Sarason, B.R., Shearin, E.N., Pierce, G.R., and Sarason, I.G. (1987). Interrelations of social support measures : Theoretical and practical implications. *Journal of Personality and Social Psychology, 52,* 813-832.

Sarason, I.G., Johnson, J.H., and Siegel, J.M.(1979). Assessing the impact of life changes: Development of the life experiences survey. In I.G. Sarason, and C.D.Spielberger (Eds.), *Stress and anxiety (Vol. 6; pp. 131-149).* New York : John Wiley and Sons.

Sarason, I.G., and Spielberger, C.D. (Eds.), (1979). *Stress and anxiety.* New York : John Wiley and Sons.

Sarason, I.G., and Sarason, B.R. (Eds.), (1985). *Social Support : Theory, research and applications.* Boston : Martinus Nijhoff.

Sarchielli, G., Depolo, M., Fraccaroli, F., and Colasanto, M. (1991). *Senza lavoro : Vincoli, strategie e risorse per la costruzione sociale della occupabilità.* (Without work: Ties, strategies and resources for the social building of employment). Bologna: II Mulino.

Sayeed, D.B., and Rao, M.L. (1989). Managerial response to organizational systems' barriers : An assessment. *Indian Journal of Industrial Relations, 24,* 357-370.

Schaefer, C., Coyne, J.C., and Lazarus, R.S.(1982). The health-related functions of social support. *Journal of Behavioural Medicine, 4,* 381-406.

Schaufeli, W.B. (1988a). Perceiving the causes of unemployment : An evaluation of the causal dimensions scale in a real-life situation. *Journal of Personality and Social Psychology, 54,* 347-356.

Schaufeli, W.B. (1988b). *Unemployment and psychological health : An investigation among Dutch professionals.* Unpublished Doctoral Dissertation, Ryksuniversiteit Groningen.

Schaufeli, W.B. (1992). Unemployment and mental health in well- and poorly-educated school-leavers. In C.H.A. Verhaar, L.G.Jansma *et al.* (Eds.), *On the mysteries of unemployment (pp. 253-271).* The Netherlands : Kluwer.

Schaufeli, W.B., and Van Yperen, N.W. (1992). Unemployment and psychological distress among graduates : A longitudinal study. *Journal of Occupational and Organizational Psychology, 65,* 291-305.

Schmidtke, A., Bille-Brahe, U., DeLeo, D., *et al.* (1996). Attempted suicide in Europe : Rates, trends and sociodemographic characteristics of suicide attempters during the period 1989-1992. Results from the WHO/EURO study on parasuicide. *Acta Psychiatrica Scandinavica, 93,* 327-338.

Schnall, P.L., Landsbergis, P.A., Pieper, C.F., Schwartz, J., Dietz, D., Gerin, W., Schlussel, Y., Warren, K., and Pickering, T.G. (1992). The impact of anticipation of job loss on psychological distress and worksite blood pressure. *American Journal of Industrial Medicine, 21,* 417-432.

Schober, K. (1978). Arbeitslose Jugendliche : Belastungen und Reaktionen der Betroffenen. *Mitteilungen aus der Arbeitsmarkt- und Berufsforschung, 11,* 198-215.

Schor, E.L. (1986). Use of health care services by children and diagnoses received during presumably stressful life transitions. *Pediatrics, 77,* 834-841.

Schore, L. (1984). The Fremont experience : A counselling program for dislocated workers. *International Journal of Mental Health, 13,* 154-168.

Schultz-Gambard, J., Balz, H.J., Drewski, R., and Mowka, K. (1986). *Weitere Ergebnisse der Bielefelder Längsschnittstudie zu Auswirkungen von Arbeitslosigkeit.* Unpublished manuscript, University of Bielefeld.

Schwefel, D. (1986). Unemployment, health and health services in German-speaking countries. *Social Science and Medicine, 22,* 409-430.

Schwefel, D., John, J., Potthof, P., and Hechler, A. (1984). Unemployment and mental health : Perspectives from the Federal Republic of Germany. *International Journal of Mental Health, 13,* 35-50.

Schwefel, D., Svensson, P.-G., and Zöllner, H.F.K.(Eds.), (1987). *Unemployment, social vulnerability and health in Europe.* New York : Springer.

Secord, P.F., and Backman, C.W. (1974). *Social psychology.* Tokyo : McGraw-Hill Kogakusha.

Seeman, M. (1959). On the meaning of alienation. *American Sociological Review, 24,* 783-791.

Seligman, M.E.P. (1975). *Helplessness : On depression, development and death.* San Farncisco, CA : Freeman.

Sells, S.B. (1970). On the nature of stress. In J.E. McGrath (Ed.), *Social and psychological factors in stress (pp. 134-139).* New York : Holt, Rinehart and Winston.

Selye, H. (1976). *Stress in health and disease.* Woburn Mass : Butterworth.

Shamir, B. (1986). Self-esteem and the psychological impact of unemployment. *Social Psychology Quarterly, 49,* 61-72.

Sharma, I. (1982). Job satisfaction among public sector managers. *Lok Udyog, 16,* 15-21.

Sharma, S. (1979). A comparative study of general anxiety among engineers and white collor workers as function of certain demographic variables. *Indian Psychological Review, 17,* 1-5.

Sharma , S. (1988). Stress and anxiety. In J. Pandey (Ed.), *Psychology in India : The state-of-the-art (Vol.1; pp. 191-248).* New Delhi : Sage Publications.

Sharma, V., and Sharma, S. (1989). Organizational role stress and anxiety : A comparative study of bureaucrats and technocrats. *Indian Journal of Industrial Relations, 24,* 281-288.

Shibu, D., and Dharmangadan, B. (1993). Unemployment and social stress. *The Creative Psychologist, 5,* 65-70.

Singer, J.E., and Davidson, L.M. (1986). Specificity and stress research. In M.H. Appley, and R. Trumbull (Eds.), *Dynamics of stress : Physiological, psychological, and social perspectives.* New York : Plenum.

Singh, Achyut K. (1992). *Education and national character.* New Delhi : Ashis Publication.

Singh, Amar. K. (1975). Hindu culture and economic development in India. *Indian Social and Psychological Studies Publication, 1,* 89-108.

Singh, Amar K. (1988). Intergroup relations and social tensions. In J. Pandey (Ed.), *Psychology in India : The state-of-the-art (Vol. 2., pp. 159-223).* New Delhi : Sage Publications.

Singh, A.K.,and Sharma, V.K. (1982). Prolonged deprivation and alienation in Indian youth. *Research in Psychology, 1,* 37-45.

Singh, Anup K., Jayaratne, S., Siefert, K., and Chess, W.A. (1991). Supportive and conflicting social networks and stress-strain relationship—Moderating effects. *Management and Labour Studies, 16,* 88-95.

Singh, Arbind K., Rani, A., and Singh, L.B. (1999). Level of development-orientation among the educated unemployed and educated employed youth. *Journal of Community Guidance and Research, 16,* 21-32.

Singh, B., Agarwala, U.N., and Malhan, N.K. (1981). The nature of managerial role conflict. *Indian Journal of Industrial Relations, 17,* 1-26.

Singh, C.B.P. (1997). The Hindu mental health : Conceptual inquiry. *Abhigyan, 15,* 65-72.

Singh, C.B.P., and Singh, R.B.P. (1985). The excercises of power. *Managerial Psychology, 6,* 59-70.

Singh, G., Kaur, D., and Kaur, H. (1981). Presumptive stressful events scale (PSE scale). *Indian Journal of Clinical Psychology, 8,* 173.

Singh, I.K. (1996). *Some socio-psychological dynamics of Indian classical vocal music.* Ph.D. thesis, T.M. Bhagalpur University, Bhagalpur.

Singh, K.K., (1982). Culture and personality. *Seminar, 276,* 24-29.

Singh, L.B. (1990). General health problems of the educated unemployed youths. *Indian Journal of Social Work, 51,* 605-614.

Singh, L.B. (1992). Pseudo-employment : A novel form of exploitation of human resources in Bihar. *The Indian Journal of Labour Economics, 35,* 04-06.

Singh, L.B. (1994). Unemployed educated young men in India : Their problems of adjustment. *Indian Journal of Social Work, 55,* 357-367.

Singh, L.B. (2001). *Psychological well-being of educated unemployed youths.* Report of the U.G.C. Research Project, University Department of Psychology, T.M. Bhagalpur University, Bhagalpur.

Singh L.B., Kumari, R., and Kumari, M. (2000). Level of development-orientation in educated unemployed young men : The reality. *Indian Journal of Social Work, 61,* 384-393.

Singh, L.B.,Kumari, R., and Singh, I. K. (1992). Extent of hostility in educated Indian unemployed youth : A micro analysis. *International Journal of Psychology, 27,* 89-97.

Singh L.B., and Singh A.K. (2004). Educated Unemployed and employed youth in India : Their level of life satisfaction. *Indian Journal of Industrial Relations, 39,* 505-516.

Singh, L.B., Singh, A.K., Kumari, S., and Jha B. (2005). Technically and non-technically and non-technically educated employed young men in India : A analysis of their psychological costs. *Indian Journal of Industrial Relations, 40,* 500-528.

Singh, L.B., Singh, A.K., and Rani, A. (1996 a). Alienation : A symptomatic reaction of educated unemployed youth in India. *International Journal of Psychology, 31,* 101-110.

Singh, L.B., Singh, A.K., and Rani, A. (1996 b). Level of self-concepts in educated unemployed young men in India : An empirical analysis. *Journal of Economic Psychology,17,* 629-643.

Singh, L.B., Singh, A.K., and Singh, Arbind K. (1996). Are educated unemployed youth in India externally oriented ? *Indian Journal of Social Work, 57,* 563-577.

Singh, L.B., Singh, Arun K., and Singh, S.K. (1995). Educated unemployed youth : Their psychological health. *Journal of Community Guidance and Research, 12,* 43-54.

Singh, L.B., Singh, Arbind K., and Sinha, B.N. (1996). Construction of an identity-crisis scale. *Journal of Psychometry, 9,* 6-12.

Singh, L.B., Singh, P.P., and Kumari, M.(1998). Educated unemployed young men in India : An analysis of their level of development-orientation. *Applied Psychology : An International Review, 47,* 571-574.

Singh, L.B., and Sinha, B.N.(1990). Tribal value pattern: A case study of the Santals. In B. Saraswati (Ed.), *Tribal thought and culture (pp. 183-192).* New Delhi: Concept Publishing Company.

Singh, L.B., Sinha, B.N.,and Kumari, R.(1985). Authoritarianism and intolerance of ambiguity in Santals : An appraisal. *Man in India, 65,* 234-245.

Singh, L.P.(August 15-21, 1998). Population growth vis-à-vis human resource development in India. *Employment News, 23,* 3 and 13.

Singh, P. (1979). *Occupational values and styles of Indian managers.* New Delhi : Wiley Eastern.

Singh, P. (1985). *Perceptions and consequences of equity in social and organizational contexts.* Unpublished doctoral dissertation, University of Allahabad, Allahabad.

Singh, P., and Das, G.S. (1977). Managerial style of Indian managers. *ASCI Journal of Management, 7,* 1-11.

Singh, P., and Pant, K. (1982). Public enterprises in India : A case of managerial helplessness. *Indian Journal of Industrial Relations, 18,* 175-193.

Singh, R. (1985). A test of the relative-ratio model of reward division with students and managers in India. *Genetic, Social and General Psychology Monographs,113,* 365-384.

Singh, R.D., and Verma, S.C.(1992). Mathematics as a function of intelligence, sex and age : A study of attitudes of high school students. *Indian Educational Review, 27,* 47-55.

Singh, S.K. (1986). *Social groups within a work organisation* . Doctoral dissertation,Patna University.

Singh, U.P. (1972). *Personality of criminals.* Agra : Ram Mehra and Company.

Singh, Y.K. (1990). *Reactions to joblessness.* Unpublished Ph.D. thesis, T.M. Bhagalpur University, Bhagalpur.

Sinha, A. (October 13, 1996). Educated, therefore unemployed ? *The Sunday Times of India,* Patna.

Sinha, B.N., and Mallik, M.K. (1990). The educated unemployed youth : How do they spend their time. *Man in Asia, 3,* 17-22.

Sinha, D. (1968). *Manual for Sinha W.A. self-analysis form.* Varanasi : Rupa Psychological Corporation.

Sinha, D. (1979). The young and the old : Ambiguity of role models and values among Indian youth. In S.Kakar (Ed.), *Identity and adulthood (pp. 56-64).* Delhi : Oxford University Press.

Sinha, D. (1983). Human assessment in Indian context. In S.H. Irvine, and J.W. Berry (Eds.), *Human assessment and cultural factors (pp.17-34).* New York : Plenum Press.

Sinha, D. (1986). Bring radical change in education. *Yojana, 30,* 26-30.

Sinha, D. (1988). Basic Indian values and behaviour dispositions in the context of national development : An appraisal. In D.Sinha, and S.H.R. Kao (Eds.), *Social values and development : Asian perspectives (pp. 31-55).* New Delhi : Sage Publications.

Sinha, J.B.P. (1970). *Development through behaviour modification.* Bombay : Allied Publishers.

Sinha, J.B.P. (1980). *The nurturant task leader.* New Delhi : Concept Publishing Company.

Sinha, J.B.P. (1982a). The Hindu (Indian) identity. *Dynamic Psychiatry, 15,* 148-160.

Sinha, J.B.P. (1982b). The spirit and the frame. *Seminar, 276,* 14-17.

Sinha, J.B.P. (1985). *Cultural influence on appraisal system in Indian work organizations.* Paper presented at the International Seminar on 'Selection and Appraisal Systems,' New Delhi.

Sinha, J.B.P. (1990). *Work culture in the Indian context.* New Delhi : Sage Publications.

Sinha, J.B.P., and Sinha D. (1988). *Role of social values in Indian organizations.* Paper presented at the Symposium on 'Social Values and Effective Organizations : Indigenous Management in Developing and Newly Industrialized Countries,' National Central University, Taipei.

Sinha, J.B.P., and Sinha, D. (1995). Role of social values in Indian organizations. In H.S.R. Kao, D.Sinha, and Ng Sek-Hong (Eds.), *Effective organizations and social values (pp. 164-173).* New Delhi : Sage Publications.

Sinha, J.B.P., and Verma, J. (1987). Structure of collectivism. In C.Kagitcibasi (Ed.), *Growth and progress in cross-cultural psychology (pp.123-129).* Lisse, The Netherlands : Swets and Zetlinger.

Sinha, J.N.P. (1989). *Problems of ageing.* New Delhi : Classical Publishing Company.

Sinha, S.N. (1975). Violence and disruption on campus. In A.K.P. Sinha, and S. Das (Eds.), *Violence behaviour : A symposium.* Delhi : S.Chand and Co.

Sinha, S.R., and Sinha, J.B.P. (1974). Campus activism as a function of alienation among college students. *Journal of Social and Economic Studies, 2,* 75-87.

Smith, R. (1987a). More evidence on unemployment and health. *British Medical Journal, 294,* 1047-1048.

Smith, R. (1987b). *Unemployment and health : A disaster and a challenge.* Oxford : Oxford University Press.

Smith, R. (1991). Unemployment : Here we go again. *British Medical Journal, 302,* 606-607.

Smith, T.W., and Anderson, N.B. (1986). Models of personality and disease : An interactional approach to Type A behaviour and cardiovascular risk. *Journal of Personality and Social Psychology, 50,* 1166-1173.

Sokou, K. (1987). Unemployment in a developing country: The case of Greece. In D. Schwefel, P. -G. Svensson, and H. F. K. Zöllner (Eds.), *Unemployment, social vulnerability and health (pp. 118-128).* Springer-Verlag.

Sokou, K., and Papantoniou, V. (2000). Youth unemployment and health in Greece. In T. Kieselbach, G. Beelmann, and A.Stitzel, (Eds.), *Youth unemployment and health: A comparison of six European countries (pp. 137-152).* Opladen:Leske+Budrich.

Spector, P.F. (1982). Behaviour in organizations as a function of employee's locus of control. *Psychological Bulletin, 91,* 482-497.

Spielberger, D. (1971). *Anxiety : Current trends in theory and research.* New York and London : Academic Press.

Spratt, P. (1966). *Hindu culture and personality.* Bombay : Manaktalas.

Spruit, I.P., and Svensson, P.-G. (1987). Young and unemployed : Special problems ? In D. Schwefel, P.-G. Svensson, and H.F.K. Zöllner (Eds.), *Unemployment, social vulnerability, and health in Europe (pp. 196-208).* New York : Springer-Verlag.

Srivastava, A.K. (1990). *Occupational stress, job involvement, and mental health of employees in public and private sector organization : A comparative study.* Report on I.C.S.S.R. Research Project.

Srivastava, A.K. (1995). Role stress and mental health of the male partners in dual-career couples. *Psychological Studies, 40,* 11-17.

Srivastava, A.K., and Jagdish, K. (1990). Moderating effect of job attitudes on occupation stress-mental health relationship. *Indian Journal of Applied Psychology, 27,* 98-102.

Srivastava, A.K., and Singh, H.S. (1988). Modifying effects of coping strategies on the relation of organizational role stress and mental health. *Psychological Reports, 62,* 1097-1109.

Srivastava, A.K., and Srivastava, P. (1991). Person-environment fit and mental health of employees. *Industrial Psychiatry Journal, 4,* 79-84.

Srivastava, N.C. (1993). Verbal test of intelligence as a predictor of success in science and mathematics. *Psycho-Lingua, 23,* 65-70.

Srivastava, S.K. (1994). Anxiety and adjustment among industrial workers. *Management and Labour Studies, 19,* 99-103.

Srivastava, S.S. (1988). *Academic group differences in the level of mental health of postgraduate students.* Proceedings of the Seventy Fifth Session of the Indian Science Congress, Pune.

Stafford, E.M. (1982). The impact of the Youth Opportunities Programme on young people's employment prospects and psychological well-being. *British Journal of Guidance and Counselling, 10, 12-21.*

Stafford, E.M., Jackson, P.R., and Banks, M.H. (1980). Employment, work involvement and mental health in less qualified young people. *Journal of Occupational Psychology, 53,* 291-304.

Ståhl, R.(1987). *Att vara rustad och att bli drabbad.* (Being armed and being defeated). Örebro: Högskolan i Örebro.

Starrin, B., and Larsson, G. (1987). Coping with unemployment—A contribution to the understanding of women's unemployment. *Social Science and Medicine, 25,* 163-171.

Starrin, B., Svensson, P.-G., and Wintersberger, H. (Eds.), (1989). *Unemployment, poverty and quality of working life : Some European experiences.* Berlin : Edition Sigma.

Stokes, G. (1983). Work, unemployment and leisure. *Leisure Studies,* 2, 269-286.

Stokes, G., and Cochrane, R. (1984). A study of the psychological effects of redundancy and unemployment. *Journal of Occupational Psychology, 57,* 309-322.

Stotland, E. (1987). Stress. In R. Corsini (Ed.), *Concise encyclopedia of psychology.* New York: John Wiley and Sons.

Sudan, F.K. (2000). Causes and consequences of unemployment among youth : Some exploratory notes. *The Indian Journal of Labour Economics, 43,* 781.

Sullivan, T.J., Thompson, K., Wright, R., Gross, G., and Spady, D. (1980). *Social problems: Divergent perspectives.* New York : John Wiley and Sons.

Suls, J., and Fletcher, B. (1985). The relative efficacy of avoidant and nonavoidant coping strategies : A meta-analysis. *Health Psychology, 4,* 249-288.

Super, D.E., and Hall, D.T. (1978). Career development : Exploration and planning. *Annual Review of Psychology, 29,* 333-372.

Swan, G.E., Dame, A., and Carmelli, D. (1991). Involuntary retirement, Type A behaviour, and current functioning in elderly men : 27-year follow-up of the Western Collaborative Group Study. *Psychology and Aging, 6,* 384-391.

Swinburne, P. (1981). The psychological impact of unemployment on managers and professional staff. *Journal of Occupational Psychology, 54,* 47-64.

Terkel, S. (1972). *Working : People talk about what they feel about what they do.* New York : Pantheon Books.

Thapar, R. (1982). The contradictions. *Seminar, 276,* 20-23.

Thibaut, J.W., and Kelley, H.H. (1959). *The social psychology of groups.* New York : John Wiley.

Thoits, P. (1983). Dimensions of life events that influence psychological distress : An evaluation and synthesis of the literature. In H.B. Kaplan (Ed.), *Psychosocial stress : Trends in theory and research (pp. 33-103).* New York : Academic Press.

Thomas, L.E., McCabe, E., and Berry, J.E. (1980). Unemployment and family stress : A reassessment. *Family Relations, 29,* 517-524.

Tiggemann, M., and Winefield, A.H.(1980). Some psychological effects of unemployment in school-leavers. *Australian Journal of Social Issues, 15,* 269-276.

Tiggemann, M., and Winefield, A.H. (1984). The effects of unemployment on the mood, self-esteem, locus of control and depressive affect of school-leavers. *Journal of Occupational Psychology, 57,* 33-42.

Tiwari, M.K., and Krishna, K.P. (1999). Personality characteristics of the educated unemployed. *Behaviorometric, 16,* 24-29.

Townsend, P., and Davidson, N. (1982). *Inequalities in health.* Harmondsworth : Pelican Books.

Trew, W., and Kilpatrick, R. (1983). *The daily life of the unemployed.* Department of Psychology, Queen's University of Belfast.

Tripathi, R.C. (1988). Aligning development to values in India. In D.Sinha, and H.S.R. Kao (Eds.), *Social values and development : Asian Perspectives (pp.315-333),* New Delhi : Sage Publications.

Tripathi, R.C. (1995). Interplay of values in the functioning of Indian organizations. In H.S.R.Kao, D.Sinha, and Ng Sek-Hong (Eds.), *Effective organizations and social values (pp. 174-192).* New Delhi : Sage Publications.

Trumbull, R., and Appley, M.H. (1986). A conceptual model for examination of stress dynamics. In M.H. Appley, and R. Trumbull (Eds.), *Dynamics of stress : Physiological, psychological, and social perspectives.* New York : Plenum.

Tselepis, C., and Agrafiotis, D. (1997). Sexoualikotita ke kinonikes anaparastasis : H periptosi ton neon anergon. (Sexuality and social representations : The case of young unemployed). *Arheia Aids, 5,* 61-65.

Tulsyan, S.L. (July 1, 1984). Econonics of educated unemployment and capital formation in India. *University News,* 5-6.

Turner, J.B., Kessler, R.C., and House, J.S. (1991). Factors facilitating adjustment to unemployment.: Implications for intervention. *American Journal of Community Psychology, 19,* 521-542.

Turner, J.B., Leana, C.R., and Feldman, D.C. (1993). Coping with job loss : How individuals, organizations and communities respond to layoffs. *Personnel Psychology, 46,* 212-215.

Turner, R.L. (1983). Direct, indirect, and moderating effects of support on psychological distress and associated conditions. In H.B.Kaplan(Ed.), *Psychosocial stress : Trends in theory and research (pp. 105-155).* New York : Academic Press.

Udupa, K.N. (1980). Role of stress in cancer. *Indian Journal of Cancer, 17,* 7-10.

Ullah, P. (1988). *Cross-cultural differences between English and Australian youths in the psychological experience of unemployment.* Paper presented at 24th International Congress of Psychology, Sydney, Australia.

Ullah, P., and Banks, M.H. (1985). Youth unemployment and labour market withdrawal. *Journal of Economic Psychology, 6,* 51-64.

Ullah, P., Banks, M.H., and Warr, P.B. (1985). Social support, social pressures and psychological distress during unemployment. *Psychological Medicine, 15,* 283-295.

Uniyal, M.P., and Joshi, D. (1978). A study of dependent proneness, insecurity and inferiority in relation to socio-economic status. *ISPT Journal of Research, 2,* 126-131.

Vaillant, G.E. (1977). *Adaptation to life.* Boston : Little, Brown.

Vasaria, P. (1980). Poverty and unemployment in India. *Indian Journal of Agricultural Economics, 35,* 1-19.

Vatsyayan, K. (1982). Individually and collectively. *Seminar, 276,* 18-19.

Veenhoven, R., and Jonkers, T. (1984). *Data-book of happiness.* Dordrecht : Reidel.

Verhaegen. L., Deykin, E., and Sand, E. (1994). Depressive symptoms and employment status among Belgian adolescents. *Revue Epidémiologique et Santé Publique, 42,* 119-127.

Verkleij, H. (1989). Vulnerabilities of very long-term unemployed in the Netherlands : Results of a longitudinal study. In B. Starrin, P.-G. Svensson, and H. Wintersberger (Eds.), *Unemployment, poverty and quality of working life : Some European experiences (pp. 79-100).* Berlin : Edition Sigma.

Verma, K. (October 3, 1997). Rethink the reform strategy. *Business Standard, Calcutta, 23,* 11.

Verma, R.P., and Sinha, R.P. (1983). A study of job satisfaction among employees of private and public sector. *Indian Journal of Labour Economics, 25,* 112-120.

Vetrone, G., Crepet, P., Costa, M., Piazzi, A., Di Tommaso, L., Ferrara, R., Petrangeli, L., and Frighi, L. (1992). Aspetti psicologici della disoccupazione giovanile nella provincia di Siena : Studio trasversale. (Psychological aspects of youth unemployment in the province of Siena : A transversal study). *Difesa Sociale, 5,* 71-82.

Vijaylakshmi, S., Shudhakar, U.V., and Rao, V.K. (1985). *Role of counselling in the Indian context : A reevaluation.* U.G.C. National Seminar, Department of Psychology, Utkal University, Bhubaneshwar.

Viney, L. L. (1983). Psychological reactions of young people to unemployment. *Youth and Society, 14,* 457-474.

Viney, L.L. (1985). They call you a dole bludger : Some experiences of unemployment. *Journal of Community Psychology, 13,* 31-45.

Vinokur, A., and Caplan, R.D. (1987). Attitudes and social support : Determinants of job-seeking behaviour and well-being among the unemployed. *Journal of Applied Social Psychology, 17,* 1007-1024.

Vinokur, A., and Selzer, M.L. (1975). Desirable *versus* undesirable life events : Their relationship to stress and mental distress. *Journal of Personality and Social Psychology, 32,* 329-337.

Voydanoff, P., and Majka, L.J. (Eds.), (1988). *Families and economic distress : Coping strategies and social policy.* Beverly Hills : Sage.

Warr, P.B. (1982). Psychological aspects of employment and unemployment. *Psychological Medicine, 12,* 7-11.

Warr, P.B. (1983). Work, jobs and unemployment. *Bulletin of the British Psychological Society, 36,* 305-311.

Warr, P.B.(1984a). Job loss, unemployment, and psychological well-being. In V. Allen, and E.Van de Vliert (Eds.), *Role transitions (pp. 263-285)*. New York : Plenum Press.

Warr, P.B. (1984b). Economic recession and mental health : A review of research. *Tijdschrift Voor Sociale Gezondheidszorg, 62,* 298-308.

Warr, P.B.(1984c). Reported behaviour changes after job loss. *British Journal of Social Psychology, 23,* 271-275.

Warr, P.B. (1985). Twelve questions about unemployment and health. In B. Roberts, R. Finnegan, and D. Gallie (Eds.), *New approaches to economic life (pp. 302-318)*. Manchester : Manchester University Press.

Warr, P.B. (1986). A vitamin model of jobs and mental health. In G. Debus, and H.W. Schroiff (Eds.), *The psychology of work and organization (pp. 157-164)*. North Holland : Elsevier Science Publishers.

Warr, P.B. (1987a). *Psychology at work.* Harmondsworth : Penguin.

Warr, P.B. (1987b). Job characteristics and mental health. In P.B. Warr (Ed.), *Psychology at work (pp. 247-269)*. Harmondsworth : Penguin.

Warr, P.B. (1987c). Workers without a job. In P.B. Warr (Ed.), *Psychology at work (pp. 335-356)*. Harmondsworth : Penguin.

Warr, P.B. (1987d). *Work, unemployment, and mental health.* Oxford : Clarendon Press.

Warr, P.B. (1987e). The psychological impact of continuing unemployment : Some longitudinal data and a general model. In D. Schwefel, P.-G. Svensson, and H.F.K. Zöllner (Eds.), *Unemployment, social vulnerability and health in Europe (pp. 267-280)*. New York : Springer-Verlag.

Warr, P.B. (1987f). This unhappy bread. *New Society, 81,* 16-18.

Warr, P.B. (1989). Individual and community adaptation to unemployment. In B. Starrin, P.-G. Svensson, and H. Wintersberger (Eds.), *Unemployment, poverty and quality of working life : Some European experiences (pp. 27-44)*. Berlin : Edition Sigma.

Warr, P.B., Banks, M.H., and Ullah, P. (1985). The experience of unemployment among black and white urban teenagers. *British Journal of Psychology, 76,* 75-87.

Warr, P.B., and Jackson, P.R. (1984). Men without jobs : Some correlates of age and length of unemployment. *Journal of Occupational Psychology, 57,* 77-85.

Warr, P.B., and Jackson, P.R. (1985). Factors influencing the psychological impact of prolonged unemployment and of re-employment. *Psychological Medicine, 15,* 795-807.

Warr, P.B., and Jackson, P.R. (1987). Adapting to the unemployed role : A longitudinal investigation. *Social Science and Medicine, 25,* 1219-1224.

Warr, P.B., Jackson, P.R., and Banks, M.H. (1982). Duration of unemployment and psychological well-being in young men and women. *Current Psychological Research, 2,* 207-214.

Warr, P.B., Jackson, P.R., and Banks, M.H. (1988). Unemployment and mental health : Some British studies. *Journal of Social Issues, 44,* 47-68.

Warr, P.B., and Parry, G. (1982). Paid employment and women's psychological well-being. *Psychological Bulletin, 91,* 498-516.

Warr, P.B., and Payne, R.L. (1983). Social class and reported changes in behaviour after job loss. *Journal of Applied Social Psychology, 13,* 206-222.

Webster, I. (1984). Health costs of unemployment. *Mental Health in Australia, 12*, 17-23.

Weiner, B. (1986). *An attributional theory of motivation and emotion.* New York : Springer-Verlag.

Werbel, J.D. (1983). Job change : A study of an acute job stressor. *Journal of Vocational Behaviour, 23,* 242-250.

Westcott, G., Svensson, P.-G., and H.F.K. Zöllner (Eds.), (1985). *Health policy implications of unemployment.* Copenhagen : World Health Organization.

Wets, J., and De Witte, H. (1997). *Van onsuccesvolle zoeker naar succesvolle vinder ? Een onderzoek naar het psycho-sociaal profiel van de werklozen in de Duitstalige Gemeenschap.* (From unsuccessful searcher to successful finder? A research on the psycho-social profile of unemploed persons in the German-speaking community). Leuven : Katholieke Universiteit Leuven, Hoger Instituut voor de Arbeid.

Whelan, C.T. (1992). The role of income, life-style deprivation and financial strain in mediating the impact of unemployment on psychological distress : Evidence from the Republic of Ireland. *Journal of Occupational and Organizational Psychology, 65,* 321-344.

Wills, T.A., and Langner, T.S. (1980). Socio-economic status and stress. In I.L. Kutash, and L.B. Schlesinger (Eds.), *Handbook on stress and anxiety (pp. 159-173).* San Francisco : Jossey-Bass.

Wilson, S.H., and Walker, G.M. (1993). Unemployment and health : A review. *Public Health, 107,* 153-162.

Windschuttle, K. (1979). *Unemployment : A social and political analysis of the economic crisis in Australia.* Melbourne : Penguin.

Wiesenfeld, B.M. (1997). Procedural unfairness and managers surviving layoffs : Self-threat and coping in the context of organizations. *Social Justice Research, 10,* 225-239.

Winefield, A.H. (1995a). Unemployment, occupational stress and psychological distress. In R. Hicks, P. Creed, W. Patton, and J.Tomlinson (Eds.), *Unemployment : Development and transitions.* Brisbane : Australian Academic Press.

Winefield, A.H. (1995b). Unemployment : Its psychological costs. In C.L.Cooper, and I. Robertson (Eds.), *International review of industrial and organizational psychology (Vol.10; Chapter 5; pp. 169-212).* London : Wiley.

Winefield, A.H. (1997). Introduction to the psychological effects of youth unemployment : International perspectives. *Journal of Adolescence, 20,* 237-241.

Winefield, A.H., and Tiggemann, M. (1985). Psychological correlates of employment and unemployment : Effects, predisposing factors and sex differences. *Journal of Occupational Psychology, 58,* 229-242.

Winefield, A.H., and Tiggemann, M. (1989). Unemployment duration and affective well-being in the young. *Journal of Occupational Psychology, 62,* 327-336.

Winefield, A.H., and Tiggemann, M. (1990a). Employment status and psychological well-being : A longitudinal study. *Journal of Applied Psychology, 75,* 455-459.

Winefield, A. H., and Tiggemann, M. (1990b). Length of unemployment and psychological distress : Longitudinal and cross-sectional data. *Social Science and Medicine, 31,* 461-465.

Winefield, A.H., and Tiggemann, M. (1994). Affective reactions to employment and unemployment as a function of prior expectations and motivation. *Psychological Reports, 75,* 243-247.

Winefield, A. H., Tiggemann, M., and Goldney, R. D. (1988). Psychological concomitants of satisfactory employment and unemployment in young people. *Social Psychiatry and Psychiatric Epidemiology, 23, 149-157.*

Winefield, A. H., Tiggemann, M., and Winefield, H.R. (1991). The psychological impact of unemployment and unsatisfactory employment in young men and women : Longitudinal and cross-sectional data. *British Journal of Psychology, 82,* 473-486.

Winefield, A. H., Tiggemann, M., and Winefield, H.R. (1992). Spare time use and psychological well-being in employed and unemployed young people. *Journal of Occupational and Organizational Psychology, 65,* 307-313.

Winefield, A. H., Tiggemann, M., Winefield, H.R., and Goldney, R.D. (1993). *Growing up with unemployment : A longitudinal study of its psychological impact.* London : Routledge.

Winefield, A. H., Winefield, H.R., Tiggemann, M., and Goldney, R.D. (1991). A longitudinal study of the psychological effects of unemployment and unsatisfactory employment on young adults. *Journal of Applied Psychology 76,* 424-431.

World Health Organization (1989). *Unemployment and methodology and theory for research : International comparisons.* Report on a study group, WHO, Regional office for Europe (EUR/ICP/HSR 822), Copenhagen.

Worell, J. (1988). Women's satisfaction in close relationships. *Clinical Psychological Review, 8,* 477-498.

Wuggenig, U. (1985). Sozialer Rang und Arbeitslosigkeit—Gemeinsamkeiten und Unterschiede der Arbeitslosigkeitserfahrung bei Arbeitern und Akademikern. In T. Kieselbach, and A.Wacker (Eds.), *Individuelle und gesellschaftliche Kosten der Massenarbeitslosigkeit—Psychologische Theorie und Praxis (pp. 207-223).* Weinheim, Basel : Beltz.

Wylie, R. (1979). *The self-concept.* London : University of Nebraska Press.

Young, R.A., and Borgen, W.A. (Eds.), (1990). *Methodological approaches to the study of career.* New York : Praeger.

Zawadski, B., and Lazarsfeld, P.F. (1935). The psychological consequences of unemployment. *Journal of Social Psychology, 6,* 224-251.

INDEX